C000194030

RAOUL FIEBIG · FRANK HEINE · FRANK LOSE

THE GREAT PASSENGER SHIPS OF THE WORLD

FOUNDED BY ARNOLD KLUDAS

COSTA LUMINOSA in Norway (photo: Mike Louagie)

RAOUL FIEBIG · FRANK HEINE · FRANK LOSE

FOUNDED BY ARNOLD KLUDAS

THE GREAT PASSENGER SHIPS OF THE WORLD

DIE GROSSEN PASSAGIERSCHIFFE DER WELT

Illustrated register of all 858 passenger ships worldwide
exceeding 10 000 GRT/GT

Koehlers Verlagsgesellschaft · Hamburg

References

Båtologen, Viken
Cruise & Ferry Info, Halmstad
Cruising Monthly, Gloucester
Designs, Halmstad
Faergefarten, Kopenhagen
Ferries, Havetoftloit
Ferry & Cruise Review, Douglas
Guide, Halmstad
Lloyd's List, London
Marine News, Kendal
Market, Halmstad
Sea Lines, Windsor
Ships monthly, Burton-on-Trent
Steamboat Bill, East Providence
www.maritimematters.com
Yahoo! Internet E-Groups:
        Ferries of Northern Europe
        Ferries of Southern Europe
        Ferries Outside Europe
        LinersList

Book jacket photos

Cover   CELEBRITY CONSTELLATION (left), CELEBRITY ECLIPSE (middle) and
        KRONPRINS FREDERIK (right) entering the German port of Warnemünde.
        (photo: Hans-Joachim Hellmann)
Back   INDEPENDENCE OF THE SEAS and MSC DIVINA in Philipsburg, St. Maarten.
        (photo: Andy Hernandez)

We will gladly send a complete list of available titles.
Please send an e-mail with your address to: vertrieb@koehler-books.de
Visit us on the internet: www.koehler-books.de

Bibliographical information of the German National Library
The German National Library registers this publication in the German
National Bibliography; detailed bibliographical data can be called up on
the internet: http://dnb.d-nb.de.

ISBN 978–3-7822–1245–8
Koehlers Verlagsgesellschaft, Hamburg
© 8. new edition 2015 by Koehlers,
in Maximilian Verlag GmbH & Co. KG

All rights reserved.

Authors: Raoul Fiebig | Frank Heine | Frank Lose
Assistance with translation: Christopher Watson
Production: Inge Mellenthin
Printing: DZS Grafik, Slovenia

Content

VOYAGER in Norway (photo: Mike Louagie)

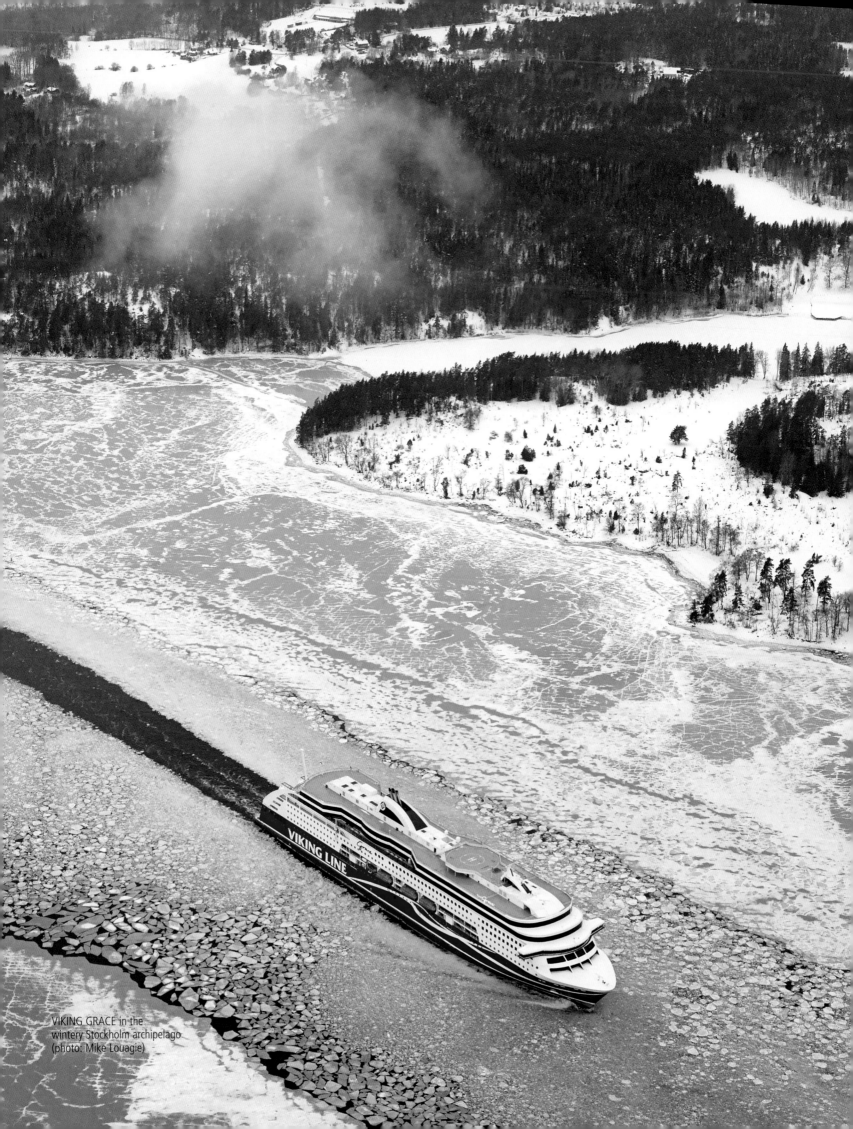

VIKING GRACE in the
wintery Stockholm archipelago
(photo: Mike Louagie)

Vorwort

Sechs Jahre nach dem letztmaligen Erscheinen der „Große Passagierschiffe der Welt" liegt die nunmehr achte, überarbeitete Ausgabe vor. Wie in allen Ausgaben zuvor, wurden die Lebensläufe aller zu diesem Zeitpunkt existierenden Passagierschiffe und Fähren über 10.000 BRT/BRZ auf den neuesten Stand gebracht und mit einem möglichst aktuellen Foto versehen. Aber auch diesmal hat es wieder einige Änderungen gegeben. Die augenfälligste dürfte sein, dass diese Ausgabe erstmals ausschließlich in englischer Sprache erscheint, um nach all den Jahren auch den zahlreichen Anfragen von nicht deutschsprachigen Lesern gerecht zu werden. Die gleichzeitige, parallele Herausgabe einer deutschen Ausgabe verbietet sich leider aufgrund der derzeitigen Lage auf dem Büchermarkt. Die Lebensläufe der einzelnen Schiffe wurden aber so weit wie möglich vereinheitlicht, sodass sich diese mit Hilfe einer Stichwortübersetzung jedem interessierten Leser auch ohne tiefergehende Englischkenntnisse erschließen sollten.

Als weiteren Mitautor haben wir Raoul Fiebig, der uns auch schon bei den letzten Ausgaben mit Rat und Tat zur Seite stand, in unser Autorenteam aufgenommen, um seine anerkannte Fachexpertise im immer weiter wachsenden Bereich der Kreuzfahrtschiffe für unsere Leser nutzbar zu machen – was der Begründer dieses Werkes, Arnold Kludas, übrigens außerordentlich befürwortet hat.

Wie die Aufstockung des Autorenteams zeigt, setzt sich der Trend zu immer mehr Kreuzfahrtschiffen also unverändert fort, während die Anzahl von Fährschiffen weiter abnimmt. Gerade in Nordeuropa kommen immer weniger neue Fährschiffe zur Ablieferung und so können einige Vertreter der Gattung in diesem Bereich eine mittlerweile mehr als 20-jährige Einsatzzeit vorweisen (besonders zu erwähnen ist hier die 1983 gebaute STENA DANICA, die seit Anbeginn auf ein und derselben Route im Einsatz ist – eine Zeitspanne, die vor Jahrzehnten noch undenkbar war). Im Mittelmeer, wo die Reedereien zum Großteil auf Gebrauchttonnage setzen, sind in den letzten Jahren viele alte Fähren den geänderten SOLAS-Vorschriften zum Opfer gefallen. Da im Gegensatz zu Nordeuropa der Neubauboom in Japan aber ungebrochen ist, hat das zur Folge, dass der prozentuale Anteil von Second-Hand-Fährschiffsankäufen aus Japan im Mittelmeer immer weiter zunimmt. Während die Fährschifffahrt in China mit zahlreichen Neubauten weiterhin immense Entwicklungsfortschritte zeigt, setzt man in Indonesien und auf den Philippinen nach wie vor fast ausschließlich auf japanische Gebrauchttonnage. Gerade in den letztgenannten Bereichen gestaltete sich übrigens die Suche nach brauchbarem Fotomaterial für uns ziemlich schwierig, womit dort auch die eine oder andere Lücke in unserer Fotodokumentation zu begründen ist.

Im Vorwort der letzten Ausgabe war bezweifelt worden, dass die Größe der Kreuzfahrtschiffe nach der kurz zuvor in Dienst gestellten OASIS OF THE SEAS noch weiter steigen würde, was sich insoweit bisher bewahrheitet hat. Zwar wird die OASIS OF THE SEAS insgesamt drei Schwesterschiffe erhalten, noch größere Neubauten sind allerdings bisher nicht in Planung. Der Trend zu immer mehr 100 000-Tonnern ist hingegen ungebrochen, von denen inzwischen 62 über die Weltmeere kreuzen und sich weitere 31 in Planung befinden. Auch wenn wir vor

Preface

Six years have passed since the last appearance of "The Great Passenger Ships of the World", and we are now delighted to present our revised eighth edition. As with previous editions, the lives of all the passenger ships and ferries over 10,000 GRT/GT in existence at the time of publication have been brought up to date and illustrated with the most recent photographs available. As is customary with a new edition, there have also been some changes. Most notably, this edition is being printed exclusively in English for the very first time. This allows us, after all these years, to answer the numerous queries we have received from our non-German readership. Unfortunately, the current state of the publishing market has not permitted the release of a parallel German edition. Nevertheless, the lives of the individual ships have been standardized to the greatest possible extent, allowing all interested German-speaking readers who do not possess a deep knowledge of English to access the information with the help of our translated key.

We are pleased to announce that Raoul Fiebig, who gave a great deal of support with previous editions, has joined our team as an additional co-author this time around. This will allow our readers to benefit from his renowned expertise on the constantly expanding cruise ship sector. His appointment received the wholehearted support of Arnold Kludas, the founder of this publication.

As reflected in our expanded team of authors, the trend for ever-increasing numbers of cruise ships remains unchanged. At the same time, however, the number of ferries in the world continues to decline. Fewer and fewer ferries are being delivered to northern Europe, with the consequence that some vessels of this type have now been in operation for more than 20 years (particularly worthy of note is the STENA DANICA, which has been deployed on the same route since it was built in 1983 – a service life that would have been unimaginable several decades ago). In the Mediterranean, where shipping companies largely rely on second-hand tonnage, many old ferries have fallen victim to changing SOLAS regulations in recent years. In contrast to northern Europe, however, the construction boom in Japan remains undiminished. As a result, an ever-growing percentage of second-hand ferries bought in from Japan is currently operating in the Mediterranean. And although ferry shipping is still going from strength to strength in China, which can boast large numbers of newly constructed vessels, the markets in Indonesia and the Philippines continue to rely almost exclusively on second-hand Japanese tonnage. It has proved difficult to acquire usable photographic material for these latter regions, which explains the very occasional gap in our pictorial documentation.

In our preface to the previous edition, we expressed doubt as to whether the size of cruise ships would continue to increase after the OASIS OF THE SEAS, which entered service shortly before publication. So far, this forecast has proven accurate. Although the OASIS OF THE SEAS will have three sister ships in total, no larger vessels have yet been planned. Nevertheless, the trend for more and more ships over 100,000 GT continues uninterrupted: 62 are currently cruising the world's oceans, and a further 31 are in the planning stage. Six years ago, we assumed

sechs Jahren davon ausgingen, dass der Markt irgendwann einmal gesättigt wäre, sind die Auftragsbücher der Werften nun wieder gut gefüllt – auch weil die Reedereien zunehmend China als bedeutenden Kreuzfahrtmarkt entdecken. Aber im Grunde bauen heute lediglich drei große Werften (Fincantieri, Meyer/Meyer Turku und STX France) über 70 % der Kreuzfahrtschiffe für vier große Reedereikonzerne (Carnival, Royal Caribbean, NCL und MSC). Viele der neueren, großen Kreuzfahrtschiffe gehören zu zahlenmäßig großen Einheitsbauten, bei denen es reedereiabhängig nur einige mehr oder weniger markante Unterschiede gibt. Der „Rest" der Kreuzfahrer läuft mehr oder weniger unter fernerliefen, ist aber mitnichten weniger interessant, sondern bietet wesentlich abwechslungsreichere Erscheinungsformen, wie die Fotos im Hauptteil dieses Buches zeigen. Von den im Hauptteil der fünfbändigen Erstausgabe, deren letzter Band im Sommer 1974 erschien, vorgestellten Passagierschiffen sind im Übrigen heute noch dreizehn aktiv und somit im Hauptteil dieser nunmehr achten Auflage enthalten. Weitere finden sich in den Anhängen.

Bedanken möchten wir uns daher bei den vielen Fotografen, die uns wieder einmal ihre besten Aufnahmen zur Verfügung gestellt haben. Die Namen werden jeweils bei den Fotos genannt.
Ein Besonderer Dank gebührt Tsuyoshi Ishiyama, der uns erneut mit Daten und vor allen Dingen Fotos aus Japan unterstützt hat. Bei Marko Stampehl und Uwe Jakob bedanken wir uns für das Durchsehen der Daten und Lebensläufe, was viele Fehler aus dem Manuskript eliminiert hat. Besonders danken möchten wir auch Richard Seville für zusätzliche Hilfestellung bei der Übersetzung.

Abschließend möchten wir noch auf das Magazin FERRIES hinweisen, welches Sie bis zum Erscheinen der nächsten Ausgabe der „Großen Passagierschiffe der Welt" über die Veränderungen in der Kreuz- und Fährschifffahrt auf dem Laufenden halten kann.
Zu beziehen ist FERRIES mit vier Ausgaben pro Jahr über Frank Heine, Schmiedestrasse 28, 24986 Mittelangeln, www.ferries-online.de.

Paderborn, Dammholm und Bünde, im Januar 2016
Raoul Fiebig | Frank Heine | Frank Lose

that the market would become saturated at some point. Nevertheless, the order books of shipyards are being filled once more, partly thanks to shipping companies' increasing discovery of China as an important cruise market. Fundamentally, however, over 70% of all cruise ships built today are constructed by just three big shipyards (Fincantieri, Meyer/Meyer Turku and STX France) for four major shipping groups (Carnival, Royal Caribbean, NCL and MSC). Many of the newer, larger cruise ships belong to the sizeable number of standardized vessels that only differ in a handful of (more or less notable) ways to suit the company that commissioned them. Although the "rest" of the cruise ships might be considered "outsiders", they are no less interesting for it – as can be seen from the photos in this book, they display a far greater variety of design. Incidentally, of the passenger ships that appeared in the main part of this work's five-volume first edition – the last volume of which was released in the summer of 1974 – thirteen are still in service today and are included in the main section of this eighth edition. Others are mentioned in the appendices.

We would like to thank the many photographers who have again contributed to this book by providing us with their very best photos. Their names appear next to their respective works.
Our special thanks go to Tsuyoshi Ishiyama, who has once again aided us with data and – above all –photos from Japan. We would also like to thank Marko Stampehl and Uwe Jakob for checking the data and the lives of the ships, eliminating many errors from the manuscript in the process. Our particular thanks also go to Richard Seville for his additional help with the translation.

Last but not least, we would like to bring your attention to FERRIES, a magazine that will keep you up to date with the developments in the world of cruise and ferry shipping until we compile the next edition of "The Great Passenger Ships of the World." Released in German four times a year, FERRIES can be ordered via Frank Heine, Schmiedestrasse 28, 24986 Mittelangeln, www.ferries-online.de.

Paderborn, Dammholm and Bünde, January 2016
Raoul Fiebig | Frank Heine | Frank Lose

Important notes for this new edition

I. General comments

This book presents a chronological list of all of the 841 passenger ships over 10,000 GRT/GT in existence in the world today, including newbuilds. The entries are arranged according to the date of delivery by the builders, except in the case of sister ships, which are always listed immediately after the lead vessel. Appendices 1–4 provide simplified lists of passenger vessels that only see limited service or are no longer in service.

II. Historical data

All facts and figures presented in this book have been researched carefully. Nevertheless, we would like to apologize for any errors that may have crept in. The copy deadline was December 2015, which means that the technical data of ships delivered after this time – and that of vessels delivered shortly before – may be provisional. Ships' technical and historical information is always given in the following sequence:

1) Type
The individual types of propulsion are given before each ship's name as follows:
ms = motor ship;
ts = turbine ship

2) Ship's name
Each ship's name is spelled in Latin letters, as seen on the hull. New ways of spelling names are increasingly encountered, e.g. "AIDAprima" instead of "AIDA Prima", or "SuperStar" instead of "Super Star". Even shipping companies are occasionally inconsistent with names, which can lead to confusion. This problem also occurs with the transliteration of ship's names that are not written in Latin script. As accents or phonetic symbols are almost never given to the capital letters on the hull, they have also been omitted here.

3) IMO No.
In 1987, the International Maritime Organisation (IMO) introduced a unique designation for each ship in the form of an IMO number. This originally goes back to the register numbers issued in Lloyd's Register of Shipping. Each ship is allocated a unique IMO No., which does not change over the course of the vessel's life and is never issued twice. Some vessels in this book do not have an IMO number, as these were formerly warships (troop carriers), for which no number is issued. The IMO number of a few vessels could no longer be determined or, in the case of newbuilds, was not yet known.

4) Shipping company and home port
Where possible, reference is made here to the shipping company colours worn by the vessel. Additional notes are only given in exceptional cases. Legal addenda (e.g. AG or Ltd.) after company names are nearly always omitted. The company name may also be given in a distinct, abbreviated form. The home port indicated for each ship is not necessarily the location of the shipping company itself, but always refers to the national flag carried by the vessel.

5) Shipyard, place of construction; Yard No.
Such legal addenda as Pty. or GmbH do not appear alongside the company names here, either. In addition, company names are occasionally written in abbreviated form. The place of construction and – without exception – the shipyard's Yard No. are given after the shipyard's name.

6) Gross measurement
In 1994, all of the measurement systems that had hitherto been used were officially rendered invalid. These systems had made it possible to omit enormous capacities from ships' measurements. For example, the large vehicle decks of RoRo ferries were hardly ever included in the old calculations. Under the new rules, however, these ships saw their quoted gross tonnage increase by up to 50 %! The difference can also be considerable for other passenger vessels. One example of this is the TROPICALE. Commissioned in 1981 with 22,919 GRT, she was defined as being 35,190 GT in 1994, without a conversion having taken place. For vessels commissioned with a GRT measurement, the GT measurement is indicated at the appropriate moment in the ship's life when the new value was first included in Lloyd's Register.

7) Deadweight
Deadweight is given as tdw (t = 1,000 kg, occasionally also 1,016 kg). In contrast to other technical data, the change in deadweight is mentioned only in the case of major conversions. This serves as an additional indication of ship type in this book. A low tdw in relation to GT/GRT indicates a pure passenger ship or ferry, while a high tdw in relation to GT/GRT indicates a passenger/cargo ship or a cargo ferry.

8) Ship length
The overall length – the length of the hull at its longest point – is always given.

9) Beam
The moulded beam of the hull is indicated. Wherever the largest beam exceeds this measurement by more than 10 cm, this value is also given (in brackets).

10) Propulsion systems
The number and type of propulsion systems are indicated using clear abbreviations. The manufacturer comes after the semicolon. If the unit was not built in the manufacturer's main plant, the manufacturing company is given after the hyphen. Some ships incorporate combined propulsion systems, comprising e.g. diesel engines and gas turbines or various other turbines. These include e.g. COGES (Combined Gas Turbine and Steam Turbine Electric Drive system) or Integrated Electric Propulsion (IEP).

11) Engine output
The propulsive power of the engines in vessels commissioned before 1977 is given in bhp for motor ships or in shp for turbine ships. The international system for designating physical units became binding in 1977. According to this system, the output should be given in kilowatts (kW). These units are used in this book for all engines built from

9

1977 (1 kW = 1.36 hp; 1 hp = 0.735 kW). As well as producing the energy needed to propel the ship, the generators driven by the main engines in diesel and turbo-electric craft are also used to generate the considerable quantity of electricity required throughout the vessel. As a result, the performance of these main engines is significantly higher than is necessary for propulsion. In such cases, the propulsive power of the electric drive motors is indicated in addition to the main engines' overall performance.

12) Means of propulsion
Number of propellers or other means of propulsion, e.g. water jets or pod drives, including Azipod pods from ABB, Mermaid and Aquamaster units from Rolls-Royce, SSP from Siemens/Schottel and pod drives from STN Atlas/Wärtsilä (designated as Dolphin).

13) Speed
The service speed is given in knots, one knot being defined as one nautical mile (1.852 km) per hour. Top speeds are given afterwards in brackets (if known).

14) Passenger capacity
This is such a complex field that the creation of a useful, standardized system does not seem possible. The basic rule on cruise ships today is that two-bed cabins are the norm. In some cases, sofa or wall beds make additional occupancy possible (e.g. for children). This is given in brackets. The situation is more complicated regarding ferries. On short trips, no cabins or beds are necessary – only deck passengers are present. For longer night passages, cabins with different standards of comfort are offered alongside dormitories and/or Pullman seats. We have attempted to give as many details as possible in each case. Figures in brackets are maximum figures. In this book, the term "Pullman" covers not only airplane-style seats, but also the sleeping berths screened off by curtains on ferries.

15) Car, truck, trailer or rail wagon capacity
The car capacity shown is the total capacity on the special, low car decks. Because of the vehicles' different sizes – and because truck lanes and rail decks can also be occupied by cars when necessary – this number should be seen as an approximate value. In addition, trucks, trailers and rail wagons come in various different lengths. By preference, the overall length of suitable queuing lanes with an adequate deck height is given for these vehicles. For trucks, this refers to lane metres of 3 m in width. The track length – i.e. the total usable length of track on board – is given for rail wagons.

16) Crew size
Unfortunately, crew size could not be determined for every ship. The relationship of this figure to the number of passengers provides a basis for assessing the standard of service on offer.

III. Historical data of ships

1) Lives of the ships
All key facts and figures relating to the life of each ship are given in the chronological accounts. These include renamings, changes of shipping company (cf. point II. 4, however), major conversion work, accidents with serious consequences and, of course, the final fate of the vessel.

2) Routes
This book often only includes general route details for cruise ships, as these differ from season to season and even from trip to trip. Detailed information is given on the routes of ferries, although the occasional short charter or route change cannot be indicated. A diagonal slash separating two or more ports indicates that the service runs to or from either of these ports.

3) Other events worth mentioning
Increasing numbers of larger and larger ships with ever more complex technology result in more and more "standard problems". These include, for example, "teething troubles" with the introduction of such new technologies as pod drives; the infection of large numbers of passengers on board (e.g. food poisoning from salmonella); and slight collisions, groundings or similar mishaps. Although all of these can cause losses running into the millions due to repair costs and cancelled trips, only special cases are reported here.

As the authors and publisher decided to publish this edition in English, here is a glossary of the most important terms in German and English for the benefit of our German readers who are unfamiliar with English:

Da sich Autoren und Verlag entschieden haben, diese Ausgabe in englischer Sprache herauszubringen, sind nachstehend die wichtigsten Begriffe in deutscher und englischer Sprache zusammengestellt:

Technische Daten		Lebenslauf	
IMO No.	IMO-Nr.	launched	Stapellauf
Yard No.:	Baunr.:	floated out	aufgeschwommen
GRT	BRT	christened	Taufe
GT	BRZ	delivered	abgeliefert
length oa	Länge ü.a.	first voyage	erste Reise
beam	Breite	first cruise	erste Kreuzfahrt
bhp	PSe	maiden cruise	Jungfernkreuzfahrt
shp	PSw	maiden voyage	Jungfernreise
screws	Schrauben	in service	im Fährdienst
cabins	Kabinen	in liner service	im Liniendienst
pass. unberthed	Deckspassagiere	last voyage	letzte Reise
cars	PKW	renamed	umbenannt
trucks	LKW	home port	Heimathafen
lane metres	Spurmeter	laid up	aufgelegt
track length	Gleislänge	until	bis
crew	Besatzung	then	anschl.
		charter	Charter

The ships in chronological sequence

AZORES ex STOCKHOLM (photo: Michael Segeth)

ms STOCKHOLM

IMO No. 5383304
Svenska Amerika Linien, Gothenburg
Götaverken, Gothenburg; Yard No.: 611

11700 GRT / 5550 tdw / 160.08 m length oa /
21.04 m beam / two 8-cyl. diesels; Götaverken /
12000 bhp / 2 screws / 18 (20) kn / pass. 113 1st,
282 tourist class / crew 200

9.9.1946 launched / 10.1947 first sea trials / 7.2.1948
delivered / 21.2.1948 maiden voyage in service
Gothenburg—New York. Occasional cruises / 1953
after conversion at AG Weser in Bremen 12644 GRT,
pass. 86 1st, 584 tourist class / 1956 installation of
stabilisers. 1st cl. reduced to 24 pass. / 25.7.1956
collision in thick fog 100 nm off New York with the
Italian liner ANDREA DORIA, which sank hours later
with 47 dead. The severely damaged STOCKHOLM,
on which five persons were victim of the collision,
reached New York under her own power. Repaired
until 5.11.1956 at Bethlehem Steel / 3.1.1960
VÖLKERFREUNDSCHAFT, Freier Deutscher Gewerkschaftsbund, managed by VEB Deutsche Seereederei,
Rostock. 568 pass. in 215 outside cabins / 24.2.1960
first Black Sea cruise / 19.11.1963 to VEB Deutsche
Seereederei, Rostock / 1972 12068 GRT / 1974 to
VEB Deutfracht Seereederei, Rostock. 11970 GRT /
4.1985 VOLKER, Neptunus Rex Enterprises, Panama /
8.1985 laid up in Oslo Fjord / 11.12.1985 laid up in
Southampton / 20.12.1986 towed to Oslo as FRIDTJOF
NANSEN, accommodation ship for refugees / 5.1989
to StarLauro, Genoa. Towed to Genoa, then start of
conversion at Varco Chiapella Shipyard, Genoa / 1993
ITALIA I, Nina S.p.A., Naples / 10.1994 delivered as
ITALIA PRIMA. 15614 GT, 2153 tdw, two 16-cyl.
diesels geared to 2 screws; Wärtsilä, 11000 kW,
14 kn, 500 (566) pass. in 250 cabins / 31.10.1994 first
Mediterranean cruise / 22.12.1995 five-year charter by
Neckermann Seereisen, in each case 254 days per year,

45 days for Nina / 12.1995 first Caribbean cruise /
1997 16144 GT / 6.1.1998 Neckermann charter
prematurely terminated; laid up in Genoa / 1998 for
five months used as accommodation ship at Expo 98
in Lisbon / 9.1998 five-year charter by Air Maritim
Seereisen (Valtur Tourist). Renamed VALTUR PRIMA.
Caribbean cruises from Cuba / 2001 laid up in Havana
following bankruptcy of Valtur / 7.2002 CARIBE,
three-year charter by Festival Cruises for Caribbean
and Mexico cruises / 2.2004 laid up in Havana /
10.2004 laid up in Lisbon / 7.1.2005 ATHENA, Classic
International Cruises, Madeira. Cruises for Vivamare
Urlaubsreisen, amongst others / 4.2006 five-year full
charter by Travelscope / 3.2007 charter cancelled by
Travelscope, cruises for Classic International Cruises /
2008 Mediterranean cruises under charter by Vision
Cruceros / 1.2009 deployment for Classic International
Cruises / 6.6.–12.11.2009 cruises under charter by
Phoenix Reisen / 15.9.2012 arrested in Marseilles /
2.2013 to Portuscale Cruises, then laid up / 7.2013
renamed AZORES / 10.3.–5.9.2014 cruises under
charter by Ambiente Kreuzfahrten / 12.1.2015 first
cruise under bareboat charter by Cruise & Maritime
Voyages (Global Maritime Group) / 5.–10.2016
planned cruises in the French market, sub-charter by
Rivages du Monde as ASTORIA /

ts FUNCHAL

IMO No. 5124162
Empresa Insulana de Navegação, Lisbon
Helsingør Skibsv. og Maskinbyg., Helsingør;
Yard No.: 353

10031 GRT / 2975 tdw / 152.65 m length oa /
19.05 m beam / two sets of geared turbines /
13800 shp / 2 screws / 20 (22.5) kn / pass. 80 1st,
320 tourist class, 100 pass. unberthed / crew 208

10.2.1961 launched / 10.10.1961 sea trials,
9824 GRT / 4.11.1961 maiden voyage in service
Lisbon—Madeira—Azores, also deployed for cruises /
11.1972–4.1973 at Nederlandse Dok en Scheepsbouw,
Amsterdam for conversion into motor ship: two 9-cyl.
diesels; Stork-Werkspoor, 10000 bhp, 17 kn, 442 (548)
pass. in 204 cabins, crew 155. Only cruises / 1974 to
Cia. Portuguesa des Transportes Maritimos, Lisbon /
1985 to Arcalia Shipping Co., Panama, 9470 GRT /
1997 9563 GT / 2001 cruises for Classic International
Cruises or various charterers / 7.9.2001 home port
Madeira / 9.2010 laid up in Lisbon, conversion work
according to SOLAS 2010 / 2.2013 to Portuscale
Cruises / 15.8.2013 first sea trials after conversion /
2.9.2013 first cruise under charter by Latitude Travel /
2.1.2015 laid up in Lisbon /

FUNCHAL (photo: Uwe Jakob)

ms ALEKSANDR PUSHKIN
IMO No. 6417097
Baltic Shipping Co., Leningrad
Mathias-Thesen-Werft, Wismar; Yard No.: 126

19 860 GRT / 5180 tdw / 176.28 m length oa /
23.55 m beam / two 7-cyl. diesels; Sulzer-Cegielski /
21 000 bhp / 2 screws / 20.5 kn / pass. 130 1st,
620 tourist class / crew 220

26.4.1964 launched / 14.8.1965 completion, then
international cruises / 13.4.1966 entered service Leningrad—Montreal with various ports of call, from 1967
also via Bremerhaven. Outside summer season cruises /
1973 only one passenger class. Cruises worldwide excl.
USA / 1979–1984 under full charter by Transocean
Tours / 1985 to Far Eastern Shipping Co., Vladivostok.
Cruises from Sydney for CTC Cruises / 6.2.1990 laid
up in Singapore / 1991 **MARCO POLO**, Orient Lines,
Nassau / 6.1991 transferred to Greece, conversion at
Neorion Shipyard, Syros: 20 502 GRT, 850 pass. in 425
cabins / 11.1993 first Mediterranean cruise / 1995
22 080 GT / 22.3.2008 to Global Maritime Group
under charter by Transocean Tours / 31.12.2009 after
bankruptcy of Transocean Tours premature termination
of charter / 2.1.2010 under full charter by Cruise &
Maritime Voyages /

MARCO POLO ex ALEKSANDR PUSHKIN (photo: Alexander Brede)

OCEAN MAJESTY ex JUAN MARCH (photo: Frank Heine)

ms JUAN MARCH
IMO No. 6602898
Cia. Trasmediterranea, Valencia
Union Naval de Levante, Valencia; Yard No.: 93

9977 GRT / 1700 tdw / 130.64 m length oa /
19.21 m beam / two 7-cyl. diesels; B&W-MTM /
16 000 bhp / 2 screws / 21 kn / pass. 124 1st,
376 tourist class, 250 Pullman, 325 pass. unberthed /
100 cars /

4.12.1965 launched / 21.7.1966 delivered / 16.8.1966
maiden voyage in service Valencia—Balearics,
later also Barcelona—Canaries / 31.1.1985 **SOL
CHRISTIANA**, Sol Lines, Limassol, service Piraeus—
Rhodes—Limassol—Alexandria / 4.1986 **KYPROS
STAR**, Opale Lines, Limassol, service Limassol—
Egypt / 1989 service Brindisi—Patras under charter

by Adriatica / 1989 **OCEAN MAJESTY**, Majestic International Cruises, Piraeus. Up to 1994 conversion into
cruise ship in Perama: 10 417 GT, 1031 tdw, two 16-cyl.
diesels; Wärtsilä, 12 000 kW, 20 kn, 544 (613) pass. in
272 cabins / 22.4.1994 first cruise as **OLYMPIC** under
charter by Epirotiki / 1995 renamed **OCEAN MAJESTY** /
1995 renamed **HOMERIC**, under charter by Epirotiki /
1995 again **OCEAN MAJESTY**, under charter by e.g.
Page & Moy Cruises from Harwich / 1996 under charter
by Nouvelles Frontieres / 12.1997–4.1998 charter
voyages from Puerto Vallarta for Apple Vacations, also
1998–99 / 11.2000–2001 cruises under charter by
Indian Ocean Cruise Line, which was however prematurely terminated; then cruises under charter by Page
& Moy Cruises / 2003 home port Madeira / 1.9.2009
after end of charter laid up in Greece / 2010–2012
Mediterranean cruises for various charterers / 5.2013

first cruise under summer charter by Hansa Touristik
for several years /

ms PATRICIA
IMO No. 6620773
Svenska Lloyd, Gothenburg
Lindholmens Varv, Gothenburg; Yard No.: 1095

8897 GRT / 2591 tdw / 140.80 m length oa /
20.73 (20.96) m beam / four 6-cyl. diesels geared
to 2 screws; Pielstick-Lindholmen / 10 080 bhp /
18 kn / 748 pass. in cabins / 200 cars /

29.9.1966 launched / 15.3.1967 completed / 5.4.1967
maiden voyage in service Southampton—Bilbao /
1.9.1977 laid up in Gothenburg / 1.9.1978 **STENA
OCEANICA**, Stena Line, Gothenburg / 31.10.1978–
2.1979 heightened by one deck at Smith's Docks,
Middlesbrough; 10 034 GRT, 141.20m length oa,
22.61 m beam, 17.5 kn, 930 pass. in cabins, 370
pass. unberthed, 275 cars / 4.1979 renamed **STENA
SAGA** / 28.5.1979 entered service Frederikshavn—
Oslo / 5.1988 **LION QUEEN**, Lion Ferry, Gothenburg /
18.5.–6.1988 conversion at Nobiskrug, Rendsburg /
9.6.1988 entered service Grenaa—Halmstad, later
also Grenaa—Helsingborg / 23.11.1989–3.1990
conversion at HDW Nobiskrug, Rendsburg / 14.3.1990
renamed **CROWN PRINCESS VICTORIA** / 19.4.1990
to BC Stena Line, Victoria / 5.5.–17.10.1990 service
Victoria—Seattle / 11.1990 **CROWN PRINCESS**,
Stena Crown Princess, Nassau / 12.1990 renamed
PACIFIC STAR / 23.12.1990 day cruises San Diego—
Ensenada under charter by Starlite Cruises / 6.1993
renamed **SUN FIESTA**, day cruises Fort Lauderdale—Freeport under charter by Sun Fiesta Cruises /
10.3.1994 **LION QUEEN**, Lion Ferry, Gothenburg.
14 139 GT / 1.4.1994 again service Grenaa—Halmstad / 19.5.1995 entered service Karlskrona—Gdynia,
home port Gdynia / 1996 12 764 GT / 18.6.1997
last voyage in service Karlskrona—Gdynia, home
port Nassau / 8.1997 to New Century Cruise Lines,
Nassau / 9.1997 for conversion to Singapore, then
short cruises from Singapore; discontinued after

AMUSEMENT WORLD ex PATRICIA (photo: Jonathan Boonzaier)

17 380 bhp / 2 screws / 21 kn / 540 pass. in cabins / 220 cars / crew 225

27.4.1968 stern section launched / 21.6.1968 floated out / 29.11.1968 delivered / 21.12.1968 first cruise from Miami / 9.–10.1976 converted in Jacksonville, 114 new cabins instead of car deck. Now 736 pass. in cabins / 1985 converted in Jacksonville: 928 pass. in 378 cabins. Ducktail fitted / 1988 to Kloster Cruise, Nassau / 1994 15 781 GT / 7.1995 **BOLERO**, Festival Cruises, Panama, conversion in Piraeus: crew 350 / 22.12.1995 first cruise from Genoa / 1999–2000 under charter by First Choice Cruises / 3.2001 under three-year charter by Spanish Cruise Line / 27.1.2004 laid up in Gibraltar after bankruptcy of owner / 11.2004 **ORIENT QUEEN**, Abou Merhi Cruises, Panama / 2005 Mediterranean cruises / 8.2006 to Louis Cruises / 4.9.2006 first cruise from Piraeus to Istanbul / 18.12.2006 world cruise under charter by Delphin Kreuzfahrten / 7.2007 home port Piraeus / 4.2009 home port Majuro / 29.11.2009–11.3.2010 South America cruises under charter by CVC / 3.2011 home port Valletta / 6.9.2013 renamed **LOUIS AURA**, cruises for Louis Cruises and various charterers / 6.11.2015 laid up in Piraeus /

14 days / 1997 **PUTRI BINTANG**, deployed as casino ship from Kukup / 2.1998 renamed **AMUSEMENT WORLD**, short cruises from Kukup, later from Pasir Gudang, Singapore and Penang for New Century Cruise Lines / 2005 to Universal Ship Management, Funafuti, two daily casino voyages from Penang, Malaysia / 2010 conversion of car deck into casino / 14.9.2012 home port Malakal Harbor /

ms BOHEME
IMO No. 6810811
Wallenius Bremen, Bremen
Wärtsilä, Turku; Yard No.: 1161

9866 GRT / 7500 tdw / 134.32 m length oa / 19.91 (21.04) m beam / two 8-cyl. diesels; Sulzer-Wärtsilä / 14 000 bhp / 2 screws / 21 kn / 460 pass. in cabins / crew 198

12.2.1968 launched / 12.11.1968 delivered / 7.12.1968 maiden cruise Miami—Charlotte Amalie under charter by Commodore Cruise Line / 1970 conversion at Blohm+Voss, Hamburg: 10 328 GRT, 540 pass. in 234 cabins / 3.1981 to Hanseatic Caribbean, Panama / 1984 7056 GRT / 9.1986 **FREEWINDS**, International Association of Scientologists, registered for San Donato Properties Corp., Panama. Seven-day cruises from Willemstad for Majestic Cruise Lines / 1996 9780 GT / 4.2008 while under conversion in Willemstad large quantities of asbestos found on board and work discontinued. The ship was taken to Cartagena for decontamination where the interior was completely renewed / 2009 again in service /

ms STARWARD
IMO No. 6821080
Klosters Rederi, Oslo
AG Weser, Werk Seebeck, Bremerhaven;
Yard No.: 935

12 949 GRT / 3241 tdw / 160.13 m length oa / 22.81 m beam / two 16-cyl. diesels; MAN /

FREEWINDS ex BOHEME (photo: Cees Bustraan)

LOUIS AURA ex STARWARD (photo: Ulrich Streich)

LEISURE WORLD ex SKYWARD (photo: Jonathan Boonzaier)

ms SKYWARD

IMO No. 6921828
Klosters Rederi, Oslo
AG Weser, Werk Seebeck, Bremerhaven;
Yard No.: 942

16 254 GRT / 2110 tdw / 160.13 m length oa /
22.80 m beam / two 16-cyl. diesels; MAN /
17 380 bhp / 2 screws / 21 kn / 750 pass. in cabins /
crew 250

27.4.1969 stern section launched / 28.6.1969
floated out / 10.12.1969 delivered / 3.1.1970 first
Caribbean cruise Miami / 1988 to Kloster Cruise,
Nassau / 9.9.1979 at the end of a seven-day cruise 30
nm off Miami an auxiliary engine caught fire, leading
to breakdown of the main engines. The passengers
were taken over by sister ship STARWARD / 1990
920 pass. in 364 cabins / 1991 **SHANGRILA WORLD**,
Sembawang Johnson Shipmanagement, Nassau.
Cruises from Singapore / 1992 renamed **ASEAN
WORLD** / 1992 renamed **FANTASY WORLD** / 1993
renamed **CONTINENTAL WORLD** / 1993 renamed
LEISURE WORLD / 1994 15 653 GT / 2000 managed
by New Century Cruise Lines, Nassau / 4.2006 home

PRINCESS OF ACADIA (photo: Shipfax/Mac Mackay)

port Funafuti / 6.9.2012 home port Malakal Harbor,
casino cruises in the Strait of Malacca /

ROYAL IRIS ex EAGLE (photo: Frank Heine)

ms PRINCESS OF ACADIA

IMO No. 7039567
Canadian Pacific, Saint John
Saint John Shipbuilding & Drydock Co., Saint John;
Yard No.: 1098

10 109 GRT / 2447 tdw / 146.31 m length oa /
20.12 (20.53) m beam / four 16-cyl. diesels
geared to 2 screws; General Motors / 11 500 bhp /
18.75 kn / 9 pass. in 7 cabins, 641 pass.
unberthed / 159 cars, 480 lane metres / crew 42

1971 launched as **PRINCESS OF NOVA** / 15.5.1971
delivered as **PRINCESS OF ACADIA** / 27.5.1971 maiden
voyage in service Saint John—Digby / 24.12.1974 to
Transport Canada, then under charter by CP Ships /
1979 registered for CN Marine / 1984 10051 GRT /
1987 registered for Marine Atlantic / 1.4.1997 Bay
Ferries charter, again service Saint John—Digby /
27.7.2015 last voyage in service Digby—Saint John,
then laid up in Saint John / 11.9.2015 laid up in
Halifax / 3.11.2015 laid up in Sydney, Nova Scotia /

ms EAGLE

IMO No. 7032997
General Steam Nav. Co., London
Dubigeon Normandie, Nantes; Yard No.: 123

METROPOLIS ex SHIRETOKU MARU (photo: Gerolf Drebes)

11609 GRT / 2085 tdw / 142.12 m length oa / 21.90 (22.64) m beam / two 12-cyl. diesels geared to 2 screws; Pielstick-Atlantique / 21800 bhp / 23 kn / 740 pass. in cabins / 200 cars / crew 138

16.10.1970 launched / 16.5.1971 delivered / 18.5.1971 maiden voyage in service Southampton—Lisbon—Tangier / 21.11.1974–3.1975 laid up in Falmouth / 22.3.1975 entered service Southampton—Lisbon—Tangier—Algeciras / 19.12.1975 AZUR, Nouvelle Compagnie de Paquebots, Marseilles / 21.3.1976 Mediterranean cruises / 11.1981–4.1982 conversion into cruise ship: 10718 GRT, 1039 pass. in 344 cabins / 1982 Mediterranean cruises from Toulon / 1983 13965 GRT / 1985 cruises in Canada and the Caribbean / 7.1986 laid up in Lisbon / 26.1.1987 THE AZUR, Chandris Cruises, Panama. 8936 GRT, 680 pass. / 11.4.1987 first cruise from Genoa / 5.1994 to Festival Cruises, Mediterranean cruises / 1995 9159 GT / 1999 1334 pass. in 360 cabins / 2.2004 arrested in Gibraltar after bankruptcy of Festival Cruises / 24.6.2004 ELOISE, Cruise Eloise, Panama / 23.7.2004 ROYAL IRIS, Mano Maritime, Panama, conversion in Perama / 19.5.2005 first cruise from Haifa to Alanya / 11.2014 laid up in Chalkis /

ms SHIRETOKU MARU
IMO No. 7215161
Nihon Enkai Ferry, Tokyo
Kanasashi Shipbuilding, Shimizu; Yard No.: 1008

7875 GRT / 3144 tdw / 153.55 m length oa / 22.84 (22.89) m beam / two 18-cyl. diesels; MAN-Kawasaki / 20000 bhp / 2 screws / 20.3 (22.78) kn / 761 pass. unberthed / 112 trucks + 114 cars / crew 52

20.4.1972 delivered / 27.4.1972 entered service Tokyo—Kushiro / 4.1974 service Tokyo—Tomakomai / 1987 to Minoan Lines, Heraklion / 1989 renamed N. KAZANTZAKIS, after conversion in Perama: 7883 GRT, 1040 pass. in 334 cabins, 760 pass. unberthed, 300 cars, 18.75 kn / 5.1990 service Piraeus—Heraklion / 1994 11174 GT / 1997 12500 GT / 12.2000 end of deployment for Minoan Lines / 4.2001 MING FAI PRINCESS, Pacific Cruises, Panama, after conversion casino cruises between Hainan and Vietnam, also from Hong Kong / 2002 17261 GT / 2.2007 METROPOLIS, Metropolis Cruise, Panama. Casino cruises from Hong Kong / 4.2009 home port Tarawa / 4.2013 home port Montego Bay /

ms ERIMO MARU
IMO No. 7214521
Nihon Enkai Ferry, Tokyo
Kanasashi Shipbuilding, Shimizu; Yard No.: 1015

7845 GRT / 3097 tdw / 154.33 m length oa / 22.81 m beam / two 18-cyl. diesels; MAN-Kawasaki / 20000 bhp / 2 screws / 20.25 (22.35) kn / 140 pass. in cabins, 621 pass. unberthed / 114 trucks + 115 cars /

31.7.1972 delivered / 3.8.1972 entered service Tokyo—Tomakomai / 30.6.1987 to Minoan Lines, Heraklion, later for conversion work to Perama / 1988 renamed KING MINOS / 8.1988 delivered after conversion: 9651 GRT, 848 pass. in 250 cabins, 652 deck pass. / 8.1988 service Patras—Igoumenitsa—Corfu—Ancona / 1992 service Piraeus—Heraklion / 1997 10164 GRT / 6.2001–23.9.2001 service Igoumenitsa—Corfu—Brindisi / 10.5.2002 to Maritime Way, Limassol, then seasonal ferry service Patras—Igoumenitsa—Corfu—Brindisi, laid up in winter / 23.6.–9.2004 service Genoa—Tangier under charter by Comanav / 12.2004 MAWADDAH, Namma Lines, Panama / 2005 service Safaga/Suez—Jeddah / 2010 home port Jeddah /

MAWADDAH ex ERIMO MARU (photo: Richard Seville)

ms ROYAL VIKING STAR

IMO No. 7108930
Royal Viking Line, Oslo
Wärtsilä, Helsinki; Yard No.: 395

21847 GRT / 3595 tdw / 177.7 m length oa /
25.19 m beam / four 9-cyl. diesels geared to
2 screws; Sulzer-Wärtsilä / 10000 bhp / 21 kn /
539 pass. in cabins / crew 326

12.5.1971 launched / 26.6.1972 delivered, then
cruises / 30.8.–22.11.1981 lengthening at Seebeckwerft, Bremerhaven: 28221 GRT, 5656 tdw, 205.47 m
length oa, 758 pass. / 1984 829 pass. in 401 cabins /
1988 to Kloster Cruise, Nassau / 1990 28492 GRT /
4.1991 renamed **WESTWARD** / 5.1994 **STAR ODYS-
SEY**, Royal Cruise Line, Nassau. 28668 GT, 690 pass.,
then Mediterranean cruises / 10.1996 **BLACK WATCH**,
Fred. Olsen Cruise Lines, Nassau / 15.11.1996 first
cruise for Fred. Olsen / 1997 home port Hvitsten /
1998 28670 GT / 2000 902 pass. in 435 cabins /
2001 home port Valletta / 2002 home port Nassau /
21.4.–19.6.2005 conversion at Blohm+Voss, Hamburg:
four 7-cyl. diesels geared to 2 screws; MAN B&W,
14000 kW / 2009 28613 GT /

ms ROYAL VIKING SKY

IMO No. 7218395
Royal Viking Line, Oslo
Wärtsilä, Helsinki; Yard No.: 396

21891 GRT / 3595 tdw / 177.7 m length oa /
25.19 m beam / four 9-cyl. diesels geared to
2 screws; Sulzer-Wärtsilä / 10000 bhp / 21 kn /
536 pass. in cabins / crew 324

25.5.1972 launched / 5.6.1973 delivered, then cruises /
10.9.–27.11.1982 lengthening at Seebeckwerft,
Bremerhaven: 28078 GRT, 5660 tdw, 205.47 m length
oa, 710 (812) pass. in 399 cabins / 1987 to Kloster
Cruise, Nassau / 1991 renamed **SUNWARD** / 1992
BIRKA QUEEN, Birka Line, Nassau. Cruises from Stockholm to St. Petersburg and Riga / 10.1992–5.1993
chartered back to Kloster as **SUNWARD** / 6.1993
GOLDEN PRINCESS, bareboat charter by Princess

BLACK WATCH ex ROYAL VIKING STAR (photo: Alexander Brede)

BOUDICCA ex ROYAL VIKING SKY (photo: Luis Miguel Correia)

Cruises. 804 pass. in 402 cabins / 13.6.1993 first
Alaska cruise from San Francisco / 1996 28388 GT /
7.7.1996 after engine room fire in Strait of Juan de
Fuca breakdown of propulsion plant, ship towed to
Victoria / 13.7.1996 transferred to San Francisco for
repairs / 1997 **SUPERSTAR CAPRICORN**, Star Cruises,
Singapore. After conversion 1022 pass. in 402 cabins,
crew 600 / 3.1998 short casino cruises from New York,
discontinued in early May because of high losses /
9.1998 **HYUNDAI KUMGANG**, four-year charter by
Hyundai Merchant Marine, Panama / 18.11.1998
first cruise from South Korea / 27.6.2001 last voyage
for Hyundai / 12.2001 renamed **SUPERSTAR CAPRI-
CORN** / 2002 cruises from Laem Chabang / 17.1.2004
GRAND LATINO, Viajes Iberojet, Panama / 21.6.2004
first Western Mediterranean cruise from Barcelona /
10.2005 **BOUDICCA**, Fred. Olsen Cruise Lines,
Nassau / 5.12.2005 start of conversion at Blohm+Voss,
Hamburg: four 7-cyl. diesels geared to 2 screws; MAN
B&W, 14000 kW / 25.2.2006 first cruise from Dover
to the Canaries / 2012 28551 GT / 25.1.2015 engine
room fire off the Moroccan coast, the cruise was
discontinued two days later in Santa Cruz de Tenerife /
7.2.2015 back in service after completion of repairs /

ALBATROS ex ROYAL VIKING SEA (photo: Hans-Joachim Hellmann)

ms ROYAL VIKING SEA

IMO No. 7304314
Royal Viking Line, Oslo
Wärtsilä, Helsinki; Yard No.: 397

21848 GRT / 3594 tdw / 177.7 m length oa /
25.20 m beam / four 9-cyl. diesels geared to
2 screws; Sulzer-Wärtsilä / 10000 bhp / 2 screws /
21 kn / 536 pass. in cabins / crew 324

19.1.1973 launched / 16.11.1973 delivered / 25.11.1973 maiden voyage (charter) in service Bergen—Newcastle / 17.12.1973 first cruise / 11.3.–5.6.1983 lengthening at Seebeckwerft, Bremerhaven: 28 018 GRT, 5660 tdw, 205.46 m length oa, 812 pass. in 399 cabins / 29.11.1983 151 survivors of the sunken Indonesian ferry DOJO rescued off Celebes / 1987 to Kloster Cruise, Nassau / 1991 ROYAL ODYSSEY, Royal Cruise Line management until 1995 / 1995 28 518 GT / 1997 NORWEGIAN STAR, 5-year charter by Norwegian Capricorn Line (Norwegian Cruise Line); cruises from Australia. 28 018 GT, 1200 pass. / 11.2001 renamed NORWEGIAN STAR 1 / 7.6.2002 CROWN, casino cruises between Shanghai and Cheju Island under charter by Crown Investments / 11.2002 laid up in Shanghai / 9.6.2003 first Mediterranean cruise under charter by Halkion Viajes, marketing name "Mare Nostrum" / 17.11.2003 laid up in Genoa / 2.2004 ALBATROS, Club Cruise, Nassau, charter with purchase option. 28 518 GT / 25.4.2004 first cruise from Monte Carlo under charter by Phoenix Reisen / 27.9.–12.2005 conversion at Blohm+Voss, Hamburg: four 6-cyl. diesels geared to 2 screws; Wärtsilä, 15 840 kW, 22 kn / 27.11.2008 arrested in Vigo as a result of financial problems of Club Cruise, a day later continuation of voyage, later laid up in Bremerhaven / 20.12.2008 under management of V.Ships Leisure again in service for Phoenix Reisen /

ms CASSIOPEIA
IMO No. 7210305
Ocean Ferry, Tokushima
Hashihama Zosensho, Imabari; Yard No.: 310

7462 GRT / 2815 tdw / 137.85 m length oa / 23.42 m beam / two 18-cyl. diesels geared to 2 screws; Pielstick / 19 080 bhp / / 21.75 (23) kn / 790 pass. / 102 trucks + 104 cars / crew 70

16.2.1972 launched / 29.6.1972 delivered, then service Tokushima—Chiba / 1.1976 IZU NO. 3, Ocean Tokyu Ferry, Kitakyushu, 7454 GRT, then service Tokyo—Tokushima—Kokura / 1991 IONIAN EXPRESS, Strintzis Lines, Piraeus; after conversion in Perama 8797 GRT, 188 pass. in 94 cabins, 2512 pass. unberthed

of which 350 Pullman, 400 cars / 1991 renamed SUPERFERRY / 4.1992 service Rafina—Cyclades / 5.1992 service Patras—Igoumenitsa—Ancona / 1993 429 pass. in 179 cabins, 971 pass. unberthed / 1994 14 797 GT / 5.3.1994 entered service Swansea—Cork for Swansea-Cork Ferries (Strintzis Lines) / 15.3.1999–10.2000 Swansea-Cork Ferries charter after Strintzis Lines sold the subsidiary / 2000 home port Valletta / 2001 renamed BLUE AEGEAN, service Piraeus—Paros—Naxos—Santorini for Blue Ferries (Strintzis Lines) / 8.4.2002 renamed SUPERFERRY, Swansea-Cork Ferries, Kingstown / 8.4.2002 again service Swansea—Cork / 2003 15 127 GT / 8.2006 to Namma International Trading / 7.10.2006 last voyage Swansea—Cork / 11.2006 MAHABBAH, Namma Lines, Kingstown / 11.12.2006 entered service Suez—Jeddah, later also Safaga—Duba and Jeddah—Port Sudan / 3.2007 home port Jeddah /

ms SPIRIT OF LONDON
IMO No. 7211517
P&O Lines, London
Cant. Nav. dell Tirreno e Riuniti, Riva Trigoso; Yard No.: 290

17 370 GRT / 2352 tdw / 163.30 m length oa / 22.80 (24.82) m beam / four 10-cyl. diesels geared to 2 screws; Fiat / 18 000 bhp / 20.5 kn / 736 pass. in 364 cabins / crew 322

Keel-laying as SEAWARD for Klosters Rederi / 30.3.1971 contract to P&O / 29.4.1972 christened SPIRIT OF LONDON / 11.5.1972 launched / 11.10.1972 delivered / 11.11.1972 maiden voyage Southampton—San Juan / 17.1.1973 first cruise on U.S. West Coast / 9.10.1974 SUN PRINCESS, Princess Cruises / 2.1989 STARSHIP MAJESTIC,

OCEAN DREAM ex SPIRIT OF LONDON as FLAMENCO I (photo: Marko Stampehl)

MAHABBAH ex CASSIOPEIA (photo: Tony Davis)

Premier Cruise Line, Nassau, then general overhaul at Lloyd Werft, Bremerhaven / 5.1989 after conversion 17 503 GRT / 1994 17 042 GT / 5.3.1995 renamed SOUTHERN CROSS, under bareboat charter by CTC Cruises / 8.3.1995 first cruise from Tilbury / 10.1997 FLAMENCO, Festival Cruises, Nassau / 3.12.1997 first cruise / 2003 marketed by Spanish organiser Travel Plan (Globalia). 7-day cruises from Barcelona / 27.1.2004 arrested in Gibraltar after bankruptcy of the owner / 3.2004 ELYSIAN FLAMENCO, Elysian Cruise Lines, Nassau / 4.2004 renamed NEW FLAMENCO, home port Panama. First 7-day cruise Valencia—Canaries for Spanish tour operator Globalia / 12.2006 chartered for 45 days as hotel ship during Asia Games in Doha / 1.–2.2007 chartered as hotel ship to Abu Dhabi Tourism Development & Investment / 3.11.2007 to Club Cruise, Panama / 1.2008–25.6.2008 used as accommodation ship in Prony, New Caledonia under charter by mining company Goro Nickel / 7.7.2008 renamed FLAMENCO I / 7.2008 arrested in Singapore / 13.3.2009 auctioned off to Singapore Star Shipping, later laid up off Port Klang / 8.2011 OCEAN DREAM, Runfeng Ocean Deluxe Cruises, Freetown, conversion in Shanghai / 1.2012 short cruises from Haikou to Vietnam, discontinued after a short time / 2012 laid up in Sattahip, later off Laem Chabang / 3.2014 to Shanghai Estime Ship Management, Lome, again laid up /

ms VISBY
IMO No. 7205910
Rederi AB Gotland, Visby
Brodogradiliste "Jozo Lozovina"-Mozor, Trogir;
Yard No.: 161

6665 GRT / 1552 tdw / 123.86 m length oa / 20.48 (20.86) m beam / six 16-cyl. diesels geared to 2 screws; Nohab / 14 400 bhp / 18.5 kn / 379 pass. in cabins, 1292 pass. unberthed / 300 cars /

12.2.1972 launched / 29.10.1972 delivered / 12.1972 service Nynäshamn/Oskarshamn—Visby / 9.1980 renamed **DROTTEN**, also service Västervik—Visby / 24.5.–31.8.1982 service Naantali—Mariehamn—Kapellskär under charter by Viking Line (SF Line) with marketing name "Aurella" / 4.1983–27.12.1984 service Genoa—Barcelona under charter by Miura Line / 2.10.1985 to Corsica Ferries, Panama / 2.10.1985 renamed **CORSICA VIVA II**, home port Panama, then entered service Savona/Livorno—Corsica / 10.1988–4.1989 lengthening at Industri Navali Meccaniche Affini, La Spezia: 12 120 GT, 146.6 m length oa, 844 pass. in 223 cabins, 1016 pass. unberthed, 460 cars, 670 lane metres / 4.1989 renamed **CORSICA REGINA** / 1996 12 988 GT / 8.1994 13 004 GT, 1472 tdw / 1996 renamed **SARDINIA REGINA**, home port Olbia, service Livorno—Golfo Aranci for Sardinia Ferries / 1999 various services from France and Italy to Corsica and Sardinia / 2000 1040 pass. in 222 cabins, 1017 pass. unberthed / 2005 home port Genoa /

ms GOTLAND
IMO No. 7305253
Rederi AB Gotland, Visby
Brodogradiliste "Jozo Lozovina"-Mozor, Trogir;
Yard No.: 164

6643 GRT / 1472 tdw / 123.90 m length oa / 20.50 (20.86) m beam / six 16-cyl. diesels geared to 2 screws; Nohab / 14 400 bhp / 2 screws / 19.5 kn / 379 pass. in 222 cabins, 1368 pass. unberthed / 300 cars /

12.2.1973 launched / 26.11.1973 delivered, then remaining work in Oskarshamn / 11.3.–24.5.1974 service Travemünde—Trelleborg under charter by TT-Linie / 4.6.–9.1974 service Helsinki—Nynäshamn—Gdansk under charter by Polferries / 9.1974 service Visby—Oskarshamn and Visby—Nynäshamn for Rederi AB Gotland / 1987 service Visby—Oskarshamn/Västervik / 9.1.–30.1.1988 service Ebeltoft—Sjællands Odden under charter by Mols-Linien / 31.1.–10.2.1988 service Grenaa—Hundested under charter by Grenaa-Hundested Linien / 2.1988–26.2.1988 service Belfast—Liverpool under charter by Belfast Car Ferries / 19.5.–11.9.1988 service Caen—Portsmouth under charter by Brittany Ferries / 9.1988 further short-term charters in service Dieppe—Newhaven under charter by Dieppe Ferries as well as Liverpool—Belfast and Rosslare—Cherbourg/Le Havre under charter by Irish Continental Line / 3.2.1989 **CORSICA VICTORIA**, Corsica Ferries, Panama, then entered service Savona—Bastia—Livorno / 1990 lengthening at I.N.M.A., La Spezia: 13 085 GT, 146.55 m length oa, 844 pass. in 223 cabins, 1016 pass. unberthed, 460 cars, 670 lane metres / 1990 service Livorno/Genoa—Bastia / winter 1996–97 service Fort de France—Pointe-a-Pitre under charter by Caribia Ferries / from 2.1.1998 various services from France and Italy to Corsica and Sardinia / 2000 13 005 GT, 1040 pass. in 222 cabins, 760 pass. unberthed, home port Genoa /

SARDINIA REGINA ex VISBY (photo: Frank Heine)

CORSICA VICTORIA ex GOTLAND (photo: Frank Heine)

ms SUN VIKING
IMO No. 7125861
Royal Caribbean Cruise Line, Oslo
Wärtsilä, Helsinki; Yard No.: 394

18 559 GRT / 3202 tdw / 171.69 m length oa / 23.98 m beam / four 9-cyl. diesels geared to 2 screws; Sulzer-Wärtsilä / 18 000 bhp / 21 kn / 882 pass. in 381 cabins / crew 320

27.11.1971 launched / 10.11.1972 delivered / 12.1972 maiden cruise from Miami / 1994 18 455 GT / 1.1998 **SUPERSTAR SAGITTARIUS**, Star Cruises, Panama. Cruises from Port Klang / 9.1998 **HYUNDAI PONGNAE**, Hyundai Merchant Marine, Panama / 11.1998 first cruise with South Korean tourists to Kumgangsan Mountain in North Korea / 2001 laid up for sale / 2002 short cruises from Xiamen under charter by Hainan Tropical View Investments / 8.2002 casino cruises from Haikou to Halong Bay / 9.2002 **PONGNAE**, Actinor Shipping, laid up in Busan / 4.2003 **OMAR III**, Kong Way Shipping. Casino cruises from Hong Kong / 10.2005 Casino cruises from Singapore / 6.2007 **LONG JIE**, Asian Cruise / 3.2011 **ORIENTAL DRAGON**, Capital Dragon Global Holding, short cruises from Chinese ports / 2013 deployed as casino ship in Hong Kong for Metropolis Cruise Group /

ORIENTAL DRAGON ex SUN VIKING (photo: Gerolf Drebes)

ms VEGA
IMO No. 7332672
Higashi Nippon Ferry, Tomakomai
Naikai SB. & Eng. Co., Setoda; Yard No.: 379

6702 GRT / 2323 tdw / 136.71 m length oa /
22.41 m beam / two 16-cyl. diesels geared to
2 screws; Pielstick-Nippon / 18900 bhp /
21.5 (23.77) kn / 283 pass. in cabins, 564 pass.
unberthed / 75 trucks + 60 cars / crew 40

31.8.1973 launched / 1.12.1973 delivered, then
service Tomakomai—Sendai / 1984 to Shin Higashi
Nippon Ferry, Tomakomai / 1991 **MYTILENE**, Maritime
Co. of Lesvos, Chios. Conversion in Perama: 565 pass.
in cabins, 1235 pass. unberthed, service Piraeus—
Chios—Mytilene—Thessaloniki / 1997 10737 GT, 540
pass. in 250 cabins, 1195 pass. unberthed / 5.2.2015
laid up with engine damage in Karlovasi (Samos) /

MYTILENE ex VEGA (photo: Frank Heine)

AF CLAUDIA PRIMA ex ORION (photo: Frank Lose)

ms ORION
IMO No. 7302342
Taiyo Ferry, Kanda
Hayashikane SB. & Eng., Shimonoseki;
Yard No.: 1167

7276 GRT / 2923 tdw / 140.87 m length oa /
22.41 (22.43) m beam / two 18-cyl. diesels;
MAN-Mitsubishi / 20000 bhp / 2 screws /
21.5 (24.3) kn / 794 pass. unberthed / 94 trucks
+ 72 cars / crew 56

1972 launched / 28.2.1973 delivered, then service
Osaka—Kanda / 1978 service Tokyo—Matsusaka in
Fuji Ferry charter, 7268 GRT / 1979 to Kyushu Kyuko
Ferry K.K., Tokyo / 11.1980 renamed **FERRY NISHIKI
MARU**, 7537 GRT, 94 trucks + 42 cars / 3.12.1980
entered service Osaka—Kobe—Beppu under char-
ter by Kansai Kisen / 1983 conversion at Kurushi-
ma Dockyard / 1984 after end of charter renamed
ORION, 7324 GRT, 788 pass. unberthed, 110 trucks
+ 50 cars, service Osaka—Shin Moji / 1989 **VIEW
OF NAGASAKI**, Glory Shipping, Honduras / 3.1989
DAEDALUS, Minoan Lines, Heraklion / 1989–1991
conversion in Perama: 10417 GRT, 2903 tdw, 802
pass. in 254 cabins, 612 pass. unberthed, then service

RIGEL I ex BORE I (photo: Frank Heine)

Patras—Igoumenitsa—Corfu—Ancona / 1995 service Venice—Igoumenitsa—Corfu—Ancona, 15 039 GT / 2002 service Thessaloniki—Cyclades—Heraklion / 24.10.2005 **RIVIERA ADRIATICA**, Adria Ferries, Panama / 15.12.2005 entered service Durres—Ancona / 6.2006 in summer service Marseilles/Alicante—Algeria in Algerie Ferries charter, laid up in winter / 12.2008 again service Durres—Bari for Adria Ferries, later also to Ancona and Trieste / 4.2010 home port Limassol / 16.2.2012 renamed **AF CLAUDIA PRIMA**, home port Naples /

ms BORE I

IMO No. 7224459
Ångfartygs Ab Bore, Turku
Wärtsilä, Turku; Yard No.: 1199

8528 GRT / 2100 tdw / 128.02 m length oa / 22.05 m beam / four 9-cyl. diesels geared to 2 screws; Sulzer-Wärtsilä / 18 000 bhp / 22 kn / 432 pass. in 169 cabins, 823 pass. unberthed / 344 cars, 585 lane metres / crew 140

11.7.1972 launched / 15.3.1973 delivered / 17.3.1973 maiden voyage in service Stockholm—Mariehamn—Turku for Silja Line / 11.7.1980 to Finska Ångfartygs Ab / 1.9.1980 renamed **SKANDIA** / 18.11.1982 laid up in Turku / 11.5.1983 entered service Larvik—Frederikshavn under charter by Larvik-Frederikshavn-ferjen / 7.6.–2.8.1983 service Turku—Stockholm, then laid up in Turku / 16.9.–1.10.1983 service Stockholm—Mariehamn—Turku / 5.10.1983 **STENA BALTICA**, Stena Line, Nassau / 19.10.1983 **ILICH**, Baltic Shipping Co., Leningrad, after conversion in Gothenburg: 12 281 GT, 1775 tdw / 30.5.1984 entered service Leningrad—Stockholm / 6.9.1991 home port St. Petersburg / 27.3.1995 entered service Nynäshamn—Riga—St. Petersburg for Baltic Line / 7.12.1995 arrested in Stockholm / 28.8.1996 auctioned off to ScanSov Transport / 10.1996 renamed **ANASTASIA V**,

home port Limassol / 2.1997 arrested in Turku / 5.1997 **WINDWARD PRIDE**, Windward Venture, Kingstown / 5.7.–12.8.1997 service St. Lucia—Barbados—St. Vincent—Trinidad—Venezuela / 10.1997 **BALTIC KRISTINA**, Estonian Shipping Co., Tallinn / 30.10.1997 first voyage in freight service Tallinn—Stockholm for Estline, 34 pass. / 1998 licensed to carry 360 pass. / 26.12.2000–30.9.2002 service Kapellskär—Paldiski under charter by Tallink / 17.10.2002 to JSC Riga Sea Line, Riga / 20.12.2002 entered service Riga—Stockholm / 15.10.2005 laid up in Riga after bankruptcy of owner / 21.12.2005 auctioned off to Riga Free Port / 3.2007 **ATLAS 1**, Euro 7 Fernseh & Marketing, Panama, service Brindisi—Cesme planned but not realised / 4.2007 renamed **BADIS** / 7.7.2007 entered service Al Hoceima—Almeria under charter by Lineas Maritimas Europeas (Comarit), then service Algeciras—Tangier / 7.9.2007 laid up in Algeciras, later in Istanbul / 11.2007 **RIGEL**, Ventouris Ferries,

Panama / 12.12.2007 entered service Bari—Durres / 4.2011 numerous evacuation voyages to Libya / 4.2013 renamed **RIGEL I**, home port Limassol /

ms FERRY HAKOZAKI

IMO No. 7314371
Meimon Car Ferry, Kitakyushu
Onomichi Zosen, Onomichi; Yard No.: 240

7309 GRT / 2919 tdw / 138.61 m length oa / 22.15 m beam / two 14-cyl. diesels; MAN-Mitsubishi / 15 200 bhp / 2 screws / 19.1 (22.9) kn / 900 pass. unberthed / 370 cars or 100 trucks + 90 cars / crew 52

28.5.1973 delivered, then service Osaka—Shin Moji / 1982 to Keihan Rentan Kogyo, Kitakyushu / 1986 to Meimon Taiyo Ferry, Kitakyushu / 3.1992 **FERRY COSMO**, Onomichi Zosen, Kobe / 8.–12.1992 service

ST. JOAN OF ARC ex FERRY HAKOZAKI (photo: Irvine Kinea)

Osaka—Beppu under charter by Kansai Kisen / 1994 **ABOITIZ SUPERFERRY V**, Aboitiz Shipping Corp., Panama. 7237 GRT, then service between the islands of the Philippines / 1995 to William Lines, Cebu City, 11 638 GT / 1996 **SUPERFERRY 5**, WG&A Jebsens, Cebu City / 2004 to Aboitiz Transport Systems, Manila / 1.2011 to Negros Navigation Co., Cebu / 6.2012 **ST. JOAN OF ARC**, 2Go Travel, Cebu /

ms AURELLA
IMO No. 7310260
SF Line, Mariehamn
J.J. Sietas, Hamburg; Yard No.: 702

7210 GRT / 1325 tdw / 125.63 m length oa / 21.40 (21.65) m beam / two 16-cyl. diesels; Stork-Werkspoor / 18 900 bhp / 2 screws / 21 kn / 330 pass. in cabins, 1270 pass. unberthed / 420 cars /

17.3.1973 launched / 30.6.1973 delivered / 3.7.1973 maiden voyage in service Kapellskär—Mariehamn—Naantali for Viking Line / 21.9.1973 ran aground in the Åland archipelago, refloated after two and a half weeks, then repair in Stockholm / 3.11.1973 back in service / 9.1981 laid up in Mariehamn / 20.1.1982 **SAINT PATRICK II**, Irish Continental Line, Dublin, then conversion at Amsterdamsche D.D.: 7985 GRT, 780 pass. in cabins, 300 cars / 2.6.1982 alternating service Rosslare/Cork—Cherbourg/Le Havre, interrupted by numerous charter deployments (as follows) / 24.11.1982–1.4.1983 service Rotterdam—Hull under charter by North Sea Ferries / 21.4.–22.6.1983 and from 15.12.1983–4.1.1984 service Belfast—Liverpool under charter by Belfast Car Ferries / 2.1984 service Dublin—Liverpool and Dublin—Holyhead under charter by B+I Line / 19.10.–3.11.1984 service Rosslare—Pembroke under charter by B+I Line / 12.1984 service Belfast—Liverpool under charter by Belfast Car Ferries / 3.1985 and 9.1985 service Cuxhaven/Hamburg—Harwich under charter by DFDS / 16.10.1985–23.5.1986 service Gothenburg—Frederikshavn—Moss under charter by Stena Line / 9.–10.1986 service Belfast—Liverpool under charter by Belfast Car Ferries / 1.10.1987–3.1988 service Belfast—Liverpool under charter by Belfast Car Ferries / 3.10.1988–5.4.1989 service Rosslare—Pembroke under charter by B+I Line / 15.9.–30.9.1989 service Portsmouth—Cherbourg—Channel Islands, then until 11.3.1990 service Dover—Calais, both under charter by Sealink / 22.9.1990–4.1991 service Dover—Zeebrugge under charter by P&O European Ferries / 13.2.–4.3.1992 service Rosslare—Pembroke under charter by B+I Line / 12.1992–4.1993 and from 9.1993–3.1994 service Tallinn—Helsinki under charter by Tallink, home port Tallinn / 1994 11 481 GT, only service for Irish Ferries, initially in the Irish Sea, from 31.5.1996 only between Ireland and France / 7.9.1996 laid up in Le Havre / 5.1998 renamed **EGNATIA II**, home port Valletta, under charter by Hellenic Mediterranean Lines / 24.6.1998 entered service Patras—Igoumenitsa—Brindisi for HML / 5.2000 renamed **VILLE DE SETE**, home port Madeira, 792 pass. in 175 cabins, 708 deck pass. / 13.5.–15.9.2000 service Sète—Palma de Mallorca under charter by Balear Express / 12.3.2001 renamed **CITY OF CORK**, home port Valletta / 15.3.–12.2001 service Swansea—Cork under charter by Swansea-Cork Ferries / 22.5.2002 **C.T.M.A. VACANCIER**, Cooperative de Transport Maritime et Aerien, Cap-aux-Meules / 4.6.2002 entered service Montreal—Cap-aux-Meules / 2014 service Montreal—Chandler—Cap-aux-Meules—Chandler—Quebec—Montreal /

C.T.M.A. VACANCIER ex AURELLA (photo: Marc Piché)

MARKO POLO ex PETER WESSEL (photo: Frank Heine)

ms PETER WESSEL
IMO No. 7230599
Larvik-Frederikshavnferjen, Larvik
A. et C. du Havre, Le Havre; Yard No.: 212

6801 GRT / 1200 tdw / 128.12 m length oa / 19.61 (19.99) m beam / four 8-cyl. diesels geared to 2 screws; Werkspoor-Dujardin / 20 400 bhp / 21.5 kn / 492 pass. in 137 cabins, 1008 pass. unberthed / 270 cars, 468 lane metres /

23.10.1972 launched / 20.7.1973 delivered / 19.8.1973 maiden voyage in service Larvik—Frederikshavn / 30.3.1984 **ZEELAND**, registered for Admiral Shipping, Nassau / 2.4.1984–25.3.1986 service Hoek van Holland—Harwich under charter by S.M. Zeeland / 2.4.1986 **STENA NORDICA**, Stena Line, Gothenburg / 4.5.1986 entered service Gothenburg—Frederikshavn—Moss / 23.11.1988 **MARKO POLO**, Jadrolinija, Rijeka. Service along Yugoslavian coast as well as to Ancona, Venice, Corfu and Patras / 14.10.1989–1990 accommodation ship for ethnic refugees in Hamburg, Croatian flag / 10.1.–23.10.1992 service Rostock—Trelleborg/Rønne under charter by TR-Line / 11.1992–1993 laid up in Hamburg during repairs / 5.1993–1.1994 service Patras—Igoumenitsa—Bari under charter by New Olympic Ferries / 5.–9.1994 service Sète—Nador under charter by Comanav / 1995 to Jadrolinija Cruises, Rijeka. Service Split—Ancona and liner services on the coast of Croatia. 10 154 GT / 2000 675 pass. in 137 cabins, 825 pass. unberthed / 24.10.2009 grounded on a voyage from Rijeka to Split at Sit as a result of faulty navigation / 20.11.2009 refloated, then repairs in Mali Losinj, where sponsons fitted at stern / 24.5.2010 again in service for Jadrolinija /

AEGEAN ODYSSEY ex NARCIS (photo: Frank Heine)

1972 launched / 8.1973 delivered as cargo ferry, then service in the Mediterranean / 1985 **ALKYON**, Dolphin Hellas Shipping, Piraeus / 1986 start of conversion into cruise ship in Chalkis; renamed **AEGEAN DOLPHIN** / 1988 delivered after conversion: 11563 GT, 140.50 m length oa, 20.80 m beam, 720 pass. in 288 cabins; then cruises from Venice / 1989 **DOLPHIN**, cruises from Australia for South Pacific Cruise Services / 9.1989 charter terminated because of inadequate speed / 1990 renamed **AEGEAN DOLPHIN** / 1991-spring 1992 cruises under charter by Epirotiki / 31.10.1994 laid up in Piraeus / 1996 renamed **AEGEAN I**, Mediterranean cruises for Discovery Cruises / 5.1996 under charter by Renaissance Cruises / 1998 to Golden Sun Cruises (later operating as Golden Star Cruises), Piraeus / 2003 650 pass. in 288 cabins / 6.2005 75% of shares in ship acquired by Louis Hellenic Cruises / 5.2008 to Voyages to Antiquity / 2009 conversion in Keratsini: 12094 GT, 378 pass. in 198 cabins / 4.2010 renamed **AEGEAN ODYSSEY**, home port Valletta / 4.5.2010 first cruise Piraeus—Aegean and Turkey /

ms NARCIS

IMO No. 7225910
Zim Israel Navigation Co., Haifa
Santierul Naval Galatz, Galatz; Yard No.: 617

8224 GRT / 4174 tdw / 128.33 m length oa / 20.50 m beam / two 14-cyl. diesels; Pielstick-Crossley / 10300 kW / 2 screws / 17 kn / 12 pass. in cabins / 880 lane metres /

ms FERRY TENRYU

IMO No. 7326609
Tokyu Ferry, Tokyo
Koyo Dockyard, Mihara; Yard No.: 651

8224 GRT / 3508 tdw / 162.06 m length oa / 21.59 m beam / two 18-cyl. diesels geared to 2 screws; Pielstick-Ishikawajima / 18000 bhp / 21 (22.5) kn / 596 pass. unberthed / 970 lane metres, 114 trucks and 92 cars /

10.8.1973 delivered, then service Tokyo—Kokura / 1974 service Niigata—Otaru under charter by Shin Nihonkai Ferry / 1978 **FERRY SUZURAN**, Shin Nihonkai Ferry Co., Otaru. 8847 GRT / 1984 laid up / 1995 **UTOPIA 3**, Nishinippon Kisen, Panama. 15771 GT, 72 pass. in 12 cabins, 574 pass. unberthed, service Shimonoseki—Tsingtao / 2003 **MANILA BAY 1**, Gothong Lines, Cebu; service between the islands of the Philippines, later laid up in Cebu /

MANILA BAY 1 ex FERRY TENRYU (photo: Irvine Kinea)

EUROPEAN EXPRESS ex TAKACHIO MARU (photo: Frank Heine)

ms TAKACHIHO MARU

IMO No. 7355272
Nippon Car Ferry, Tokyo
Nippon Kokan, Shizuoka; Yard No.: 322

9536 GRT / 2598 tdw / 159.52 m length oa / 21.54 m beam / two 18-cyl. diesels geared to 2 screws; MAN-Mitsubishi / 36000 bhp / 25.6 (27.4) kn / 1016 pass. / 150 cars, 62 trucks / crew 59

15.2.1974 delivered, then service Kawasaki—Hyuga / 1990 to Seacon Ferry, Tokyo continued service Kawasaki—Hyuga / 1992 to Marine Express, Tokyo / 1993 service Osaka—Miyazaki / 1996 service Kobe—Hyuga / 1998 service discontinued, then laid up / 11.9.1999 **HO MARU**, Access Ferries, Limassol / 1999 renamed **MILLENNIUM EXPRESS**, 15074 GT / 2.5.2000 entered service Piraeus—Limassol—Haifa for Access Ferries / 6.2000 service Tunis—Genoa/Marseilles under charter by Cotunav / 9.2000 again service Piraeus—Limassol—Haifa for Access Ferries / 3.2003 service Santo Domingo—Mayaguez under charter by Ferries del Caribe / 4.–6.2003 service San Juan—Santo Domingo under charter by Ferries del Caribe / 7.2003 service Brindisi—Cesme for Access Ferries / 1.2004 service Algiers—Palma de Mallorca/Barcelona/Sète/Marseilles under charter by CNAN Maghreb Line / 24.9.2006 arrival in Hamburg for engine overhaul / 5.2007 renamed **EUROPEAN EXPRESS** / 7.6.2007 return after conversion, then summer ferry service Marseilles—Algiers/Oran under charter by Algerie Ferries / 6.–9.2008 service Sète—Nador under charter by Comanav, later laid up / 15.7.2010 entered service Piraeus—Mytilene—Chios under charter by NEL Lines, home port Panama 2012 to NEL Lines / 1.7.–3.9.2013 service Igoumenitsa—Corfu—Bari in joint service Ventouris Ferries-NEL Lines, occasionally also to Kefalonia and Zante / 14.9.2013 service Piraeus—Chios—Mytilene—Limnos—Thessaloniki, also Kavala—Limnos—Mytilene—Chios—Karlovasi / 1.2.–30.9.2014 service Piraeus—Syros—Fourni—Ikaria, then laid up in Keratsini after bankruptcy of shipping company /

ms COLUMBIA
IMO No. 7320095
Alaska Marine Highways Systems, Juneau
Lockheed Shipbuilding, Seattle; Yard No.: 142

3946 GRT / 2508 tdw / 127.41 m length oa / 25.91 m beam / two 16-cyl. diesels geared to 2 screws; Enterprise / 18 400 bhp / 21 kn / 324 pass. in cabins, 676 pass. unberthed / 140 cars, 844 lane metres /

3.5.1973 launched / 6.1974 delivered / 20.6.1974 maiden cruise Seattle—Juneau—Seattle / 5.7.1974 entered service Seattle—Alaska / 15.10.1974 hit a rock near Sitka, then repairs in Seattle / 6.10.1989 entered service Bellingham—Alaska / 1999 13 009 GT / 6.6.2000 fire in engine room, passengers evacuated, towed to Juneau for repairs / 2010 home port Ketchikan /

COLUMBIA (photo: Tony Davis)

ms SAPPORO MARU
IMO No. 7377567
Nihon Enkai Ferry, Tokyo
Hayashikane SB. & Eng., Shimonoseki; Yard No.:1177

11 097 GRT / 4213 tdw / 163.99 m length oa / 24.01 m beam / two 14-cyl. diesels geared to 2 screws; MAN / 28 000 bhp / 22.25 (25.7) kn / 404 pass. in 88 cabins, 400 pass. unberthed / 55 cars, 1207 lane metres / crew 68

9.4.1974 launched / 25.7.1974 delivered / 2.8.1974 maiden voyage in service Tokyo—Tomakomai / 1985 service Oarai—Tomakomai / 1987 again service Tokyo—Tomakomai / 1.11.1990 to Blue Highway Line, Tokyo / 1991 renamed **SUN FLOWER SAPPORO** / 6.1998 **IONIAN VICTORY**, Strintzis Lines, Piraeus, then conversion in Perama: 11 089 GT, 339 pass. in 108 cabins, 148 cars, 55 trucks, 1207 lane metres / 30.6.1998 entered service Patras—Igoumenitsa—Corfu—Ancona/Venice / 2000 **BLUE SKY**, Blue Ferries (Strintzis Lines), Piraeus / 2001

19 539 GT / 20.2.2004 **IONIAN SKY**, Agoudimos Lines, Piraeus / 23.6.2004 entered service Igoumenitsa—Corfu—Brindisi / 2008 service Patras—Igoumenitsa—Bari / 2009 service Igoumenitsa—Corfu—Brindisi, home port Limassol / 2.7.–4.9.2011 service Bari—Durres / 20.7.–10.9.2012 service Igoumenitsa—Corfu—Bari / 6.2013 to NEL Lines, Limassol / 7.7.2013 entered service Thessaloniki/Kavala to Lemnos, Mytilene, Chios, Samos and Ikaria / 13.9.2013 laid up in Ambelaki with engine damage /

IONIAN SKY ex SAPPORO MARU (photo: Frank Lose)

ms STENA NAUTICA

IMO No. 7349039
Stena Line, Gothenburg
Rickmers Werft, Bremerhaven; Yard No.: 379

5443 GRT / 2840 tdw / 120.78 m length oa /
19.00 (19.51) m beam / two 12-cyl. diesels; MaK /
14 080 bhp / 2 screws / 20.25 kn / 116 pass. in
cabins, 1084 pass. unberthed / 420 cars, 792 lane
metres /

3.2.1974 launched / 1.10.1974 delivered / 10.1974
renamed **MARINE NAUTICA**, service North Sydney—
Port-aux-Basques under charter by CN Marine / 1981
home port Ottawa / 1983 home port Nassau / 1.1986
charter assumed by Marine Atlantic / 25.6.1986
CORSICA MARINA II, Corsica Ferries, Panama, then
service Livorno—Bastia. 112 pass. in 28 cabins, 1348
pass. unberthed, 479 cars / 1994 12 120 GT; 21.6 m
beam / 1999 renamed **CORSICA MARINA SECONDA**,
home port Genoa / 2000 12 035 GT /

ms STENA NORMANDICA

IMO No. 7360605
Stena Line, Gothenburg
Rickmers Werft, Bremerhaven; Yard No.: 380

5443 GRT / 2541 tdw / 120.78 m length oa /
19.00 (19.51) m beam / two 12-cyl. diesels; MaK /
14 080 bhp / 2 screws / 20.25 kn / 116 pass.
in cabins, 1084 pass. unberthed / 420 cars,
792 lane metres /

11.5.1974 launched / 11.12.1974 delivered / 12.1974–
1.1975 service Marseilles/Alicante—Algiers under
charter by CNAN / 22.4.1975 entered service Gothenburg—Kiel for Stena Line / 6.1975 also service Gothenburg—Frederikshavn / 1.1976 cargo ferry service
USA—Persian Gulf / 4.1976 service Gothenburg—
Frederikshavn for Stena Line / 22.6.–24.12.1976
service Gedser—Travemünde under charter by Gedser-
Travemünde Ruten / 2.1977 service Gothenburg—
Frederikshavn for Stena Line / 1.3.–11.3.1977 service
Rotterdam—Hull under charter by North Sea Ferries /
11.3.1977–21.1.1978 cargo ferry service Rotter-
dam—Ipswich under charter by North Sea Ferries /
13.2.–26.4.1978 service Southampton—Le Havre
under charter by Normandy Ferries / 4.1978 service
Gothenburg—Frederikshavn, later also cargo service
Gothenburg—Kiel / 7.–12.1978 service Marseilles—
Algeria under charter by CNAN / 3.4.1979 entered
service Fishguard—Rosslare under charter by Sealink
British Rail; 21.50 m beam / 2.1984 home port
Nassau / 15.4.1985 **ST. BRENDAN**, Sealink UK, Nassau,
continued service Fishguard—Rosslare / 10.1989 to
Nav.Ar.Ma. Lines, Naples, chartered back by Sealink /
12.3.1990 **MOBY VINCENT**, Moby Lines, Naples,
5607 GRT / 5.1990 service Livorno/Genoa—Bastia /
1.6.–2.10.1993 service Umeå—Vaasa under charter

CORSICA MARINA SECONDA ex STENA NAUTICA (photo: Frank Heine)

MOBY VINCENT ex STENA NORMANDICA (photo: Frank Lose)

DELPHIN ex BELORUSSIYA (photo: Cees Bustraan)

SARDINIA VERA ex MARINE ATLANTICA (photo: Nikolaos Saratzis)

entered service Piraeus—Naxos—Samos—Ikaria under charter by Kallisti Ferries, laid up during winter in Piraeus / 6.2009 services discontinued, later laid up in Vado Ligure / 25.6.2010 service Nice/Savona—Ile Rousse/Calvi and Livorno—Golfo Aranci for Corsica Sardinia Ferries /

ms BELORUSSIYA
IMO No. 7347536
Black Sea Shipping Co., Odessa
Wärtsilä, Turku; Yard No.: 1212

16 631 GRT / 2251 tdw / 156.27 m length oa / 21.80 (22.05) m beam / two 18-cyl. diesels geared to 2 screws; Pielstick-Wärtsilä / 18 000 bhp / 21.3 kn / 504 pass. in cabins, 505 pass. unberthed; on cruises 350 pass. / 256 cars, 23 trucks / crew 191

6.3.1974 launched / 15.1.1975 delivered, then cruises in European waters / 1980 13 251 GRT. Under charter by CTC Cruises, deployed e.g. in Australia / 1986 installation of cabins into car deck at Lloyd Werft, Bremerhaven: 650 pass. in 232 cabins / 1991 Ukraine flag; now transliterated as BYELORUSSIYA / 25.10.1992 capsized during a dry-dock accident in Singapore, under water partially up to boat deck / 1.1993 righted by Smit-Tak / 17.5.1993 arrival for repairs at Lloyd Werft, Bremerhaven: 16 214 GT, 590 pass. in 244 cabins, crew 210 in 97 cabins / 9.12.1993 returned as KAZAKHSTAN II, under charter by Delphin Seereisen / 22.12.1993 first voyage from Genoa around Africa / 6.1995 to Lady Lou Shipping Co., Limassol. Then deployed by Delphin Seereisen / 19.5.1996 DELPHIN, Sea Delphin Shipping, Valletta, then under charter by Delphin Seereisen. 554 pass. in 235 cabins / 14.12.1998 registered for Dolphin Maritime / 22.7.2003 end of charter / 8.2003 short cruises from Haifa for Diesenhaus, Israel / 10.2003 arrested in Haifa, later laid up in Marseilles / 12.2003 laid up in Hamburg / 2.2004 in five-year charter to Hansa Kreuzfahrten / 10.5.2004 first cruise from Bremerhaven /

by Silja Line under marketing name "Wasa Sun" / 1994 service Livorno/Genoa—Bastia / 1996 12 108 GT / 5.1997–7.1997 service Tangier—Algeciras under charter by Comanav / 1998 home port Madeira / 1999 home port Naples / 1.6.2000 entered service Civitavecchia—Olbia / 2001 service Livorno—Bastia /

ms MARINE ATLANTICA
IMO No. 7360617
Stena Line, Gothenburg
Rickmers Werft, Bremerhaven; Yard No.: 381

5441 GRT / 2840 tdw / 120.00 m length oa / 19.00 (19.51) m beam / two 12-cyl. diesels; MaK / 14 080 bhp / 2 screws / 20.25 kn / 116 pass. in cabins, 1084 pass. unberthed / 420 cars, 792 lane metres /

4.5.1974 keel-laying as STENA ATLANTICA / 18.12.1974 launched as MARINE ATLANTICA / 30.5.1975 delivered / 6.1975 service North Sydney—Port-aux-Basques/Argentia under charter by CN Marine / 10.1979 home port Ottawa / 1983 home port Nassau / 1.1986 charter assumed by Marine Atlantic / 6.1986 to Tourship, Nassau / 9.1986 end of services for Marine Atlantic / 1987 CORSICA VERA, Corsica Ferries, Nassau / 1987 renamed SARDINIA VERA, home port Olbia, service Livorno—Olbia / 1994 11 637 GT / 1996 service Civitavecchia—Golfo Aranci / 1998 12 107 GT, 112 pass. in 28 cabins, 1129 pass. unberthed, 479 cars; 21.60 m beam / 4.3.2001 laid up in Dieppe / 11.4.2001–30.3.2006 service Dieppe—Newhaven under charter by Transmanche Ferries / 27.5.2006 again service Civitavecchia—Golfo Aranci for Sardinia Ferries / 13.11.2007 laid up in Piraeus / 25.6.2008

25

12.2006 home port Nassau / 16.10.2010 arrested in Venice after bankruptcy of owner / 2011 to Vishal Cruises PVT / 10.12.2011 renovation work started at Viktor Lenac Shipyard, Rijeka / 3.4.2012 first cruise Venice—Istanbul under charter by Passat Kreuzfahrten / 2.9.2014 end of charter, laid up initially in Bremerhaven, later in Rijeka / 1.2015 accommodation ship in Rijeka under charter by U.S. Navy /

ms GRUZIYA
IMO No. 7359400
Black Sea Shipping Co., Odessa
Wärtsilä, Turku; Yard No.: 1213

16 331 GRT / 3004 tdw / 156.27 m length oa / 21.80 (22.05) m beam / two 18-cyl. diesels geared to 2 screws; Pielstick-Wärtsilä / 18 000 bhp / 21 kn / 504 pass. in cabins, 505 pass. unberthed; on cruises 350 pass. / 256 cars, 23 trucks / crew 191

18.10.1974 launched / 30.6.1975 delivered, then deployed mainly for cruises, incl. for TUI / 1980 13 251 GRT / 1984 650 pass. in 276 cabins, 110 pass. unberthed / 1994 15 402 GT / 23.5.–15.6.1994 refugee accommodation ship in Kingston under charter by U.S. Military Sealift Command / 1995 ODESSA SKY, Blasco UK, Monrovia / 26.8.1995 arrested in Montreal / 8.1996 home port Odessa / 11.9.1996 arrived for general overhaul at Turbo Technik, Wilhelmshaven, there again arrested / 5.8.1998 sold by auction to Eltec Europe Shipping, Kingstown / 8.1998 conversion at Bredo, Bremerhaven / 27.3.1999 delivered as CLUB I to Club Cruise, Kingstown. 15 402 GT, then cruises in Europe / 12.5.2000 renamed VAN GOGH, cruises from Cuba under charter by Nouvelles Frontieres / 4.2002 under long-term full charter to Travelscope / 1.2008 after Travelscope bankruptcy realisation of planned world cruise by owner Club Cruise, home port Majuro / 6.–10.2008 cruises under charter by Metropolis Tur, then laid up in Bay of Eleusis / 1.8.2009 SALAMIS FILOXENIA, Salamis Tours, Limassol, conversion in Keratsini / 2010 short cruises from Limassol for Salamis Cruise Lines /

ms AZERBAYDZHAN
IMO No. 7359474
Black Sea Shipping Co., Odessa
Wärtsilä, Turku; Yard No.: 1221

16 631 GRT / 2251 tdw / 156.24 m length oa / 21.80 (22.05) m beam / two 18-cyl. diesels geared to 2 screws; Pielstick-Wärtsilä / 18 000 bhp / 21.5 kn / 505 pass. in cabins, 505 pass. unberthed; on cruises 350 pass. / 256 cars, 23 trucks / crew 191

14.4.1975 launched / 18.12.1975 delivered, then deployed mainly for cruises under charter by CTC Cruises / 1978 13 251 GRT / 1984 conversion at Lloyd Werft, Bremerhaven: 13 252 GRT. 650 pass. in 230 cabins. Then cruises under charter by Seetours / 1991 Ukraine flag / 1995 15 410 GT / 1996 ARKADIYA, Blasco UK, Monrovia. Under charter by Royal Venture Cruise / 7.1996 to Ocean Agencies, Odessa / 1.6.1998 ISLAND HOLIDAY, Norsong Shipping Co., Nassau. Short cruises for SeaEscape from Florida / 1.11.1998 ENCHANTED CAPRI, short cruises from New Orleans under charter by Commodore Cruise Line / 12.2000 after bankruptcy of owner arrested in New Orleans / 2003 laid up in Coatzacoalcos / 21.10.2003 to International Shipping Partners, Nassau / 7.7.2004

SALAMIS FILOXENIA ex GRUZIYA (photo: Frank Heine)

ENCHANTED CAPRI ex AZERBAYDZHAN (photo: Andy Hernandez)

accommodation ship off Ciudad del Carmen under charter by Demar / 1.11.2007 to Demar, Nassau / 10.2008 home port Ciudad del Carmen /

ms KARELIYA
IMO No. 7359498
Black Sea Shipping Co., Odessa
Wärtsilä, Turku; Yard No.: 1223

16 631 GRT / 2402 tdw / 156.27 m length oa / 21.80 (22.05) m beam / two 18-cyl. diesels geared to 2 screws; Pielstick-Wärtsilä / 18 000 bhp / 21 kn / 504 pass. in cabins, 505 pass. unberthed; on cruises 350 pass. / 256 cars, 23 trucks / crew 91

14.4.1976 launched / 12.1976 delivered, then deployed mainly for cruises, initially in the Black Sea, incl. under charter by CTC Cruises / 1980 13 251 GRT / 1.6.1981 grounded off Arrecife, pass. evacuated / 30.7.1981 arrival at Tyne for repairs and conversion; superstructure enlarged. 650 pass. in 237 cabins / 12.1982 renamed LEONID BREZHNEV / 1984 13 252 GRT / 1989 renamed KARELIYA / 1992 15 065 GRT / 1995 to Maddock Trading, Monrovia, 15 791 GT/ 1996 home port Odessa / 17.3.–7.1997 arrested in Noumea, then until 1.1997 in Odessa / 1.4.1998 OLVIA, managed by Kaalbye Shipping International / 2000 under three-year charter by Peace Boat / 17.9.2001 to K & O Shipping, Odessa. Cruises under charter by Metropolis Tur / 20.12.2004 CT NEPTUNE, Wide Asia, Panama. As casino ship to Hong Kong / 14.4.2005 to Walden Maritime / 2.2006 renamed NEPTUNE / 7.2011 STARRY METROPOLIS, Metropolis Cruise Group, Tarawa, then again casino ship in Hong Kong / 4.2013 home port Montego Bay /

STARRY METROPOLIS ex KARELIYA (photo: Gerolf Drebes)

ms METTE MOLS
IMO No. 7358755
Mols-Linien, Ebeltoft
Helsingør Værft, Helsingør; Yard No.: 405

4948 GRT / 1560 tdw / 115.35 m length oa /
20.50 (20.60) m beam / four 6-cyl. diesels geared
to 2 screws; B&W Helsingør / 16 400 bhp / 19 kn /
68 pass. in 20 cabins, 1500 pass. unberthed /
420 cars, 504 lane metres /

26.7.1974 launched / 26.2.1975 delivered / 18.3.1975
entered service Ebeltoft—Odden Færgehavn / 7.1975
grounding off Ebeltoft, then repair in Aarhus /
23.1.1979 collision with breakwater in Ebeltoft /
2.1985 5170 GRT / 1996 11 668 GT / 26.3.1996
renamed METTE MO / 7.1996 laid up in Grenaa /
12.11.1996 BANASSA, Comarit, Tangier, 47 pass. in
22 cabins. 1453 pass. unberthed / 1996 registered as
BANASA, service Tangier—Algeciras / 10.11.2003–
1.4.2004 installation of new engines in Frederikshavn: four 8-cyl. diesels; MAN B&W, 10 880 kW /
2.4.2004–11.5.2005 assembly of sponsons at stern at
Blohm+Voss, Hamburg; 11 907 GT, 118.0 m length oa,
then again service Tangier—Algeciras / 15.3.2012 after
bankruptcy of shipping company laid up at Algeciras /
8.2015 home port Lome / 20.8.2015 arrival in Aliaga
for scrapping, there beached, a little later towed
off / 10.2015 to European Seaways, then repairs in
Perama, renamed GALAXY / 2015 MOBY KISS, Moby
Lines, Italy / 2016 service Livorno—Bastia planned /

ms NILS HOLGERSSON
IMO No. 7362108
Travemünde-Trelleborg Linie, Lübeck
Werft Nobiskrug, Rendsburg; Yard No.: 682

12 515 GRT / 2700 tdw / 148.88 m length oa /
23.50 (23.98) m beam / two 16-cyl. diesels geared
to 2 screws; Pielstick B&V / 20 800 bhp / 22 kn /
712 pass. in 280 cabins, 888 pass. unberthed /
440 cars, 810 lane metres / crew 125

26.10.1974 launched / 8.4.1975 delivered, then
maiden cruise Travemünde—Gothenburg—Oslo /

MOBY KISS ex METTE MOLS as BANASA (photo: Selim San)

THEOFILOS ex NILS HOLGERSSON (photo: Frank Lose)

20.4.1975 entered service Travemünde—Trelleborg, until 1981 in winter Mediterranean and Caribbean cruises / 1.1981 to TT-Saga-Line, Lübeck / 18.9.1984 last voyage in service Trelleborg—Travemünde / 20.9.1984 to TT-Line (Transport Tasmania), Devonport / 3.10.1984 arrival for conversion at Nobiskrug-Werft, Rendsburg: addition of a new cabin block, 19 212 GT, 860 pass. in 280 cabins, 701 pass. unberthed / 22.4.1985 delivered as **ABEL TASMAN** / 29.6.1985–29.11.1993 service Melbourne—Devonport, then laid up in Devonport / 29.4.1994 **POLLUX**, Ventouris Ferries, Limassol / 11.7.1994 one-week cruise from Piraeus / 21.7.1994 entered service Igoumenitsa—Bari / 5.1995 **THEOFILOS**, Maritime Co. of Lesvos, Mytilene, service Piraeus—Lesvos—Chios—Thessaloniki / 28.6.2008 on a voyage from Chios to Piraeus with 475 pass. and 97 crew, ran on a reef off the island of Oinousses. The hull was torn over 20 m, one propeller and one main engine damaged, after transfer of passengers to Skaramanga for repairs. Later laid up off Salamis Island / 17.5.2009 entered service Thessaloniki—Limnos—Mytiline—Chios—Vathi—Chios—Mytiline—Limnos—Kavala / 1.2012 Disassembly of additional cabin superstructure, 12 862 GT / 16.6.2012 entered service Piraeus—Evdilos—Samos—Chios—Lesvos—Kavala / 18.1.2013 laid up in Piraeus / 12.2013 service Thessaloniki/Kavala—Lesvos—Limnos—Chios—Samos—Ikaria / 30.7.2014 laid up in Drapetsona /

MOBY DREA ex TOR BRITANNIA (photo: George Koutsoukis)

ms TOR BRITANNIA

IMO No. 7361312
Tor Line, Gothenburg
Flender Werft, Lübeck; Yard No.: 607

14 905 GRT / 3335 tdw / 182.35 m length oa / 23.60 m beam / four 12-cyl. diesels geared to 2 screws; Pielstick-Lindholmen / 45 600 bhp / 24.5 (26) kn / 845 pass. in cabins, 662 pass. unberthed / 420 cars, 910 lane metres / crew 143

10.10.1974 launched / 16.5.1975 delivered / 21.5.1975 entered service Gothenburg—Amsterdam/Felixstowe, occasionally also to Immingham / 10.11.1981 **SCANDINAVIAN STAR**, Scandinavian Seaways, Nassau, laid up in Aalborg, later in Copenhagen / 26.3.1982 **TOR BRITANNIA**, DFDS, Esbjerg. 15 794 GRT /

29.3.1982 again service Gothenburg—Amsterdam/Felixstowe / 4.1983 service Gothenburg—Amsterdam/Harwich / 10.1983 service Gothenburg—Harwich—Esbjerg / 1984 14 905 GRT / 1988 at times also short cruises Gothenburg—Copenhagen / 1989 also seasonal ferry service Gothenburg—Newcastle / 23.12.1989–15.3.1990 accomodation ship for refugees in Malmö / in summer 1990 additionally service Gothenburg—Amsterdam / 8.11.1990–11.1.1991 conversion at Blohm+Voss, Hamburg: 15 730 GRT, 2459 tdw, 1539 pass. in 433 cabins, 165 pass. unberthed, 375 cars / 20.11.1990 renamed **PRINCE OF SCANDINAVIA**, home port Copenhagen / 1.1991 partially alternating service Gothenburg—Harwich, Gothenburg—Newcastle, Gothenburg—Copenhagen, Gothenburg—Amsterdam and Esbjerg—Harwich / 27.10.1993 IJmuiden called at instead of Amsterdam / 1995 21 145 GT / 29.10.1995 laid up in Gothenburg / 28.5.–26.10.1996 service Tunis—Genoa/Marseilles under charter by Cotunav / 28.2.1997 entered service Hamburg—Harwich / 5.12.1997–14.1.1998

installation of side tanks at Remontowa, Gdansk; 22 528 GT, 184.55 m length oa, 26.90 m beam, then again service Hamburg—Harwich / 1998 also seasonal ferry services Hamburg—Newcastle and Newcastle—Gothenburg—Copenhagen / 28.1.2001 entered service IJmuiden—Newcastle / 24.10.2003 to Moby Lines, Naples / 27.11.2003 last sailing IJmuiden—Newcastle / 28.11.2003 renamed **MOBY DREA**, home port Madeira / 12.2003 conversion work in Genoa / 27.5.2004 entered service Livorno—Olbia / 12.5.2006 home port Naples / 2005 500 cars / 23.5.2007 entered service Genoa—Porto Torres / 23.5.2012 entered service Genoa—Olbia /

ms TOR SCANDINAVIA

IMO No. 7361324
Tor Line, Gothenburg
Flender Werft, Lübeck; Yard No.: 608

14 893 GRT / 3335 tdw / 182.35 m length oa / 23.62 m beam / four 12-cyl. diesels geared to 2 screws; Pielstick-Lindholmen / 45 600 bhp / 24.5 (26) kn / 845 pass. in cabins, 662 pass. unberthed / 420 cars, 816 lane metres / crew 143

4.11.1975 launched / 12.4.1976 delivered / 15.4.1976 entered service Gothenburg—Amsterdam/Felixstowe/Immingham / 10.1977 service Gothenburg—Felixstowe and Gothenburg—Amsterdam / 1.–2.1979 chartered as trade fair ship **HOLLAND EXPO** in the Persian Gulf, then renamed **TOR SCANDINAVIA** / 17.1.–6.3.1980 chartered as trade fair ship for Scan Arab Expo in the Persian Gulf, then again service for Sessan Tor Line / 16.12.1980–3.1981 chartered as trade fair ship in the Middle East, then again service for Tor Line / 10.12.1981 to DFDS, Esbjerg, then service Felixstowe—Gothenburg / 25.10.1982–25.2.1983 as trade fair ship **WORLD WIDE EXPO** to Far East, then again renamed **TOR SCANDINAVIA** / 3.3.1983 again service Gothenburg—Felixstowe/Amsterdam, 14 893 GRT / 4.1983 service Gothenburg—Amsterdam/Harwich / 10.1983 service Gothenburg—Harwich—Esbjerg / 25.9.1989 on a voyage from Gothenburg to Harwich, a fire claimed two lives, then repairs at Nobiskrug, Rendsburg / 7.12.1989 back in service / 1990 at times also short cruises Gothenburg—Copenhagen as well as seasonal ferry service Gothenburg—Newcastle /

MOBY OTTA ex TOR SCANDINAVIA (photo: Frank Lose)

17.1.–11.3.1991 conversion at Blohm+Voss, Hamburg: 15 730 GRT, 1539 pass. in 433 cabins, 165 pass. unberthed, 375 cars / 22.2.1991 renamed **PRINCESS OF SCANDINAVIA** / 3.1991 partially alternating service Gothenburg—Harwich, Gothenburg—Newcastle, Gothenburg—Copenhagen, Gothenburg—Amsterdam and Esbjerg—Harwich / 1.10.1993 fire in engine room on a voyage from Gothenburg to Amsterdam, then repairs in Esbjerg until 13.11.1993 / 1994 21 545 GT / 21.1.–11.3.1998 installation of side sponsons at Remontowa, Gdansk; 22 528 GT, 184.55 m length oa, 26.90 m beam / 2.1999 entered service Gothenburg—Kristiansand—Newcastle / 2001 22 528 GT / 10.2.–7.3.2006 service IJmuiden—Newcastle / 3.2006–30.10.2006 service Newcastle—Kristiansand—Gothenburg as well as short cruises Gothenburg—Copenhagen / 2.11.2006 **MOBY OTTA**, Moby Lines, Naples / 5.2007 service Livorno—Olbia / 23.5.2012 entered service Genoa—Olbia /

ms GREEN ARCH
IMO No. 7429669
Hiroshima Green Ferry, Hiroshima
Kanda Zosensho, Kure; Yard No.: 197

5553 GRT / 2317 tdw / 137.01 m length oa / 22.00 m beam / two 16-cyl. diesels; Pielstick-Ishikawajima / 20 800 bhp / 2 screws / 21.5 (23.77) kn / 827 pass. unberthed / 38 trucks + 104 cars / crew 53

30.5.1975 delivered, then service Hiroshima—Osaka / 3.1982 **OKUDOGO 8**, Kurushima Dock, 6135 GRT, service Kobe—Matsuyama—Oita for Diamond Ferry / 1.1991 **KYDON**, Anonymos Naftiliaki Eteria Kritis (ANEK), Chania. After conversion 110 pass. in cabins, 717 pass. unberthed, 400 cars, then service Patras—Igoumenitsa—Corfu—Ancona/Trieste / 1995 renamed **TALOS**, after conversion in Perama 5986 GRT, 357 pass. in cabins, 943 pass. unberthed, then continued service Patras—Igoumenitsa—Corfu—Ancona/Trieste / 1997 12 891 GT / 7.1999 **IERAPETRA L.**, LANE Lines, Piraeus / 4.7.1999 entered service Piraeus—Agios Nikolaos—Sitia, also to Rhodes / 7.2006 participated in evacuation operations during the war in Lebanon, then service Piraeus—Rethimnon / 5.2009 service Piraeus—Milos—Santorini—Heraklion—Kasos—Karpathos—Rhodes for ANEK Lines / 11.2010 laid up in Perama / 12.2011 again service Piraeus—Greek islands / 3.12.2012 laid up / 14.5.–13.9. 2014 service Bari—Durres / 29.11.2014 fire in engine room during a transfer voyage without pass. from Brindisi to Igoumenitsa. The fire could be extinguished with shipboard equipment after 90 minutes, then initially laid up in Brindisi, later in Perama /

ms DAISETSU
IMO No. 7394759
Taiheiyo Enkai Zosen, Nagoya
Naikai Zosen, Setoda; Yard No.: 388

11 879 GRT / 4084 tdw / 175.60 m length oa / 23.98 m beam / two 14-cyl. diesels; MAN-Mitsubishi / 27 580 bhp / 2 screws / 23 (26.21) kn / 231 pass. in cabins, 674 pass. unberthed / 130 trucks + 105 cars / crew 70

28.3.1975 launched / 20.6.1975 delivered / 25.6.1975 entered service Nagoya—Sendai—Tomokamai / 2.1980 lengthened by 12.8 m: 12 854 GRT, 5432 tdw, 188.40 m length oa, 21 kn / 1.1985 **VARUNA**, Higashi Nihon Ferry Co., Muroran, 12 789 GRT. Service Oarai—Muroran / 1987 **LATO**, Anonymos Naftiliaki Eteria Kritis

(ANEK), Chania / 1988–89 conversion in Perama: 846 pass. in 240 cabins, 718 pass. unberthed, 800 cars, 1200 lane metres, then service Patras—Igoumenitsa—Corfu—Ancona, in winter Piraeus—Chania / 1996 15 404 GRT / 1997 service Piraeus—Heraklion / 1998 25 460 GT / 6.2007–29.8.2007 service Algeria/Tunisia—Marseilles/Barcelona under charter by CNAN Maghreb Lines / 8.12.2007–2.5.2008 service Piraeus—Heraklion / 3.5.2008 entered service Piraeus—Chania / 25.5.2009 entered service Piraeus—Heraklion / 10.6.2009–4.6.2012 service Piraeus—Chania / 14.6.–4.9.2012 service Bari—Durres, then laid up in Perama / 21.4.2013 entered service Piraeus—Chania / 14.8.2014 hotel ship in Tobruk under charter by Libyan government / 6.9.2014 laid up in Souda, later in Perama /

ms WELLAMO
IMO No. 7360186
Finska Ångfartygs Ab, Helsinki
Dubigeon Normandie, Nantes; Yard No.: 142

12 348 GRT / 1719 tdw / 153.12 m length oa / 22.04 (22.30) m beam / four 12-cyl. diesels geared to 2 screws; Pielstick-Atlantique / 24 000 bhp / 20 (22) kn / 799 pass. in 327 cabins, 401 pass. unberthed / 240 cars, 468 lane metres / crew 150

IERAPETRA L. ex GREEN ARCH (photo: Frank Heine)

LATO ex DAISETSU (photo: Frank Heine)

JUPITER ex WELLAMO (photo: Jelle de Vries)

15.9.1974 launched / 15.7.1975 delivered / 17.7.1975–21.4.1981 service Helsinki—Stockholm for Silja Line / 25.5.1981 **DANA GLORIA**, DFDS, Esbjerg / 2.6.1981 entered service Esbjerg—Newcastle, in summer also Gothenburg—Newcastle / 12.10.1983 entered service Copenhagen—Oslo / 3.2.1984 renamed **SVEA CORONA** / 6.2.1984 entered service Turku—Stockholm for Silja Line under charter by Johnson Line / 21.5.1985 renamed **DANA GLORIA** / 1.6.1985–7.11.1988 service Copenhagen—Oslo for DFDS / 11.11.1988–4.2.1989 lengthening at Jos. L. Meyer, Papenburg: 20581 GT, 2857 tdw, 175.30 m length oa, 285 cars, 1175 pass. in 491 cabins, 125 pass. unberthed / 10.1.1989 renamed **KING OF SCANDINAVIA**, home port Copenhagen / 9.2.1989 again service Copenhagen—Oslo / 1.6.1990–25.7.1994 service Copenhagen—Helsingborg—Oslo / 29.7.1994 **COLOR VIKING**, Color Line, Oslo, then conversion in Sandefjord: 1122 pass. in 427 cabins, 128 pass. unberthed, 360 cars, 550 lane metres / 2.9.1994 entered service Bergen—Stavanger—Newcastle / 1.12.1998 **JUPITER**, Fjord Line, Bergen, continued service Bergen—Stavanger—Newcastle / 2003 20804 GT / 25.9.2005 laid up in Fredericia / 4.11.2005 to Troms Fylkes DS, Bergen / 14.2.2006–31.1.2007 accomodation ship in Melkøya near Hammerfest for the construction of a liquefied gas plant under charter by Statoil / 4.2007 to Jupiter Cruises, Panama / 11.2008 cruises from Vietnam / 6.2010 laid up in Van Ninh / 10.2010 home port Phnom Penh /

SIR ROBERT BOND (photo: Stefan Niederer)

ms SIR ROBERT BOND
IMO No. 7391903
Canadian National Railways, Ottawa
Port Weller Dry Docks, St. Catherines, Ontario; Yard No.: 59

10433 GRT / 3726 tdw / 135.34 m length oa / 21.33 (21.72) m beam / four 12-cyl. diesels geared to 2 screws; Ruston-Paxman / 8800 bhp / 15 kn / 12 pass. / 33 trucks, 400 lane metres, 5 rail tracks with 480 m length /

1975 launched / 10.1975 delivered, then cargo service North Sydney—Port-aux-Basques for trucks and rail wagons / 1976 to Canadian Department of Transportation, Ottawa / 1978 conversion into passenger ferry at Davie Shipbuilding in Lauzon: 11197 GRT, 200 deck pass., 60 pass. in 47 cabins, 154 cars, 42 trucks, then service Lewisporte—Cartwright—Goose Bay / 1979 under charter by CN Marine / 1987 under charter by Marine Atlantic / 1998 to Govt. of Newfoundland and Labrador / 2000 under charter by Labrador Marine Services / 11.2010 service discontinued, laid up in Lewisporte / since 2010 in winter service Blanc Sablon—Corner Brook as shipyard relief under charter by Woodward Group /

ms CUNARD PRINCESS
IMO No. 7358573
Cunard Line, Southampton
Burmeister & Wain, Copenhagen; Yard No.: 859

17496 GRT / 2499 tdw / 163.56 m length oa / 22.80 m beam / four 7-cyl. diesels geared to 2 screws; B&W / 21000 bhp / 21.3 kn / 947 pass. in 405 cabins / crew 350

12.12.1974 launched as **CUNARD CONQUEST** / 30.10.1975 delivered / 6.11.1975 arrival in La Spezia, installation of interior fittings at Industrie Navali Meccaniche Affini / 3.8.1976 in service as **CUNARD PRINCESS**. Cruises / 2.4.1977 maiden voyage from New York to Bermuda / 10.1980 home port Nassau / 24.12.1990 arrival in Bahrain, recreation centre for U.S. soldiers during Gulf War / 23.9.1991 to Valletta for overhaul / 19.10.1991 again cruises / 30.9.1992 home port London / 15.4.1995 **RHAPSODY**, StarLauro Cruises, Panama / 25.9.1995 to Mediterranean Shipping Company, Naples, 16852 GT / 2001 17095 GT / 4.2006 home port Panama / 13.4.2009 **GOLDEN IRIS**, Mano Maritime, Panama, 16852 GT /

ms CANGURO CABO SAN JORGE
IMO No. 7387718
Ybarra y Cia., Seville
Union Naval de Levante, Valencia; Yard No.: 131

7393 GRT / 2824 tdw / 137.90 m length oa / 20.55 m beam / two 16-cyl. diesels geared to 2 screws; MAN-Bazan / 15570 bhp / 22.5 kn / 750 pass. in 201 cabins, 232 pass. unberthed / 225 cars, 480 lane metres /

24.7.1975 launched / 11.6.1976 delivered / 13.6.1976 maiden voyage in service Genoa—Barcelona—Palma de Mallorca / 4.2.1981 to Cia. Trasmediterranea, then service Las Palmas de Canaria—Santa Cruz de Tenerife / 8.1981 renamed **CIUDAD DE SANTA CRUZ DE LA PALMA**, home port Seville / 2.1982 renamed **CIUDAD DE PALMA**, then service Barcelona/

GOLDEN IRIS ex CUNARD PRINCESS (photo: George Koutsoukis)

12.2.1976 launched / 30.6.1976 delivered as cargo ferry / 1984 renamed **SEAWAY HOBART**, under charter by Coastal Express Lines / 1993 **SEAWAY I**, A.K. Ventouris, Limassol, then for rebuilding to Perama / 1994 renamed **AGIA METHODIA**, delivered after conversion into passenger ferry: 10 749 GT, 4333 tdw, 57 pass. in 198 cabins, 602 pass. unberthed, 300 cars, 1050 lane metres, then service Patras—Corfu—Igoumenitsa—Brindisi / 12.4.1995 entered service Sheerness—Vlissingen under charter by Eurolink / 19.6.1995 renamed **EUROMANTIQUE**, home port Nassau, service Sheerness—Vlissingen / 1.12.1996 service discontinued / 1997 service Algeciras—Tangier under charter by ISNASA / 5.1998 laid up in Algeciras, later in Piraeus / 1.1999 **TAXIARCHIS**, Maritime Co. of Lesvos, Mytilene; service Piraeus—Mytilene / 4.2008 service Piraeus—Chios—Mythilene / 2009 service Kavala—Linmos—Agios Eystratios—Sigri—Lavrio / 10.5.2015 after bankruptcy of shipping company laid up in Lavrio /

ORIENTAL PRINCESS ex CANGURO CABO SAN JORGE (photo: Clive Harvey)

Valencia—Balearics / 1998 home port Santa Cruz de Tenerife / 27.6.2000 entered service Almeria—Melilla / 2003 11 513 GT / 23.6.–15.9.2003 service Almeria—Ghazaouet / 4.2005 **DALMATINO**, Horizon Corporate, Funafuti / 13.5.–29.9.2005 service Chioggia—Split under charter by Enermar / 1.2006 **OCEAN PRINCESS**, home port Freetown, deployment as casino ship between Hainan and Halong / 31.7.2006 home port Panama / 2008 **ORIENTAL PRINCESS**, Zhejiang Golden Road Investment, Panama / 1.2009 home port Freetown / 10.2010 home port Phnom Penh /

ms CIUDAD DE VALENCIA
IMO No. 7915802
Cia. Trasmediterranea, Valencia
Union Naval de Levante, Valencia; Yard No.: 147

7053 GRT / 2593 tdw / 138.31 m length oa / 20.52 m beam / two 16-cyl. diesels geared to 2 screws; MAN-Bazan / 17 800 bhp / 21 kn / 750 pass. in 201 cabins, 232 pass. unberthed / 225 cars, 480 lane metres / 84 crew

27.2.1982 launched / 30.10.1984 delivered / 1.11.1984 maiden voyage in service Valencia—Palma de Mallorca, later also Barcelona—Palma / 199- home port Las Palmas de Gran Canaria / 2001 11 513 GT / 2004 service Almeria/Malaga—Melilla / 10.2006 service Algeciras—Tangier / 6.2007–30.8.2008 service Almeria—Nador, then laid up / 6.2009 to M.B.R.S. Lines / 8.2009 renamed **MARY THE QUEEN**, registered for Romblon Shipping Lines, Kingstown / 3.2010 home port Manila / 10.2010 service between Manila, Cajidiocan and Romblon, later also to Masbate / 4.5.2011 grounded in storm off Manila, after repair again in service / 11.2012 laid up in Bay of Manila / 16.7.2014 stranded during typhoon Glenda off Miraveles / 19.10.2015 driven on shore in storm off Manila /

ms UNION HOBART
IMO No. 7431090
Union Shipping Australia, Sydney
Framnæs M/V, Sandefjord; Yard No.: 187

4376 GRT / 7357 tdw / 135.79 m length oa / 20.60 (26.73) m beam / two 12-cyl. diesels geared to 2 screws; Pielstick-Lindholmen / 12 000 bhp / 18.5 kn / 12 pass. in cabins / 1030 lane metres /

MARY THE QUEEN ex CIUDAD DE VALENCIA (photo: Frank Lose)

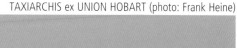

TAXIARCHIS ex UNION HOBART (photo: Frank Heine)

BRIDGE ex BASS TRADER (photo: Frank Heine)

ELLI T. ex OKUDOGU 3 (photo: Frank Heine)

2.10.1976 delivered, then service Kobe—Imabari, later Kobe—Imabari—Matsuyama / 1998 **MARIA G**, Med Link Lines, Valletta. After conversion 12 338 GT, 294 pass. in 76 cabins, 906 pass. unberthed, 1100 lane metres, 420 cars, service Brindisi—Igoumenitsa—Patras, also to Cesme / 14.3.2004 last sailing in service Brindisi—Patras / 3.2004 **ELLI T.**, Endeavor Shipping, Valletta / 5.2004–5.2006 service Patras—Igoumenitsa—Brindisi under charter by Maritime Way / 6.2006 service Patras—Kefalonia—Igoumenitsa—Brindisi for Endeavor Lines / 2008 service Igoumenitsa—Corfu—Brindisi / 26.9.2011 home port Limassol / 3.2012 under charter by Cretan Ferries / 21.7.2012 entered service Rethimnon—Piraeus / 23.9.2012 laid up with engine damage in Drapetsona, later in Ambelaki /

ms **GEDSER**
IMO No. 7500451
Gedser-Travemünde Ruten, Gedser
Schichau-Unterweser, Bremerhaven; Yard No.: 2269

4998 GRT / 4233 tdw / 118.01 m length oa / 19.89 (20.50) m beam / two 9-cyl. diesels; Stork-Werkspoor / 12 000 bhp / 18.4 kn / 48 pass. in cabins, 1200 pass. unberthed / 325 cars, 1080 lane metres /

23.8.1976 launched / 18.12.1976 delivered / 3.1.1977 maiden voyage in service Gedser—Travemünde / 7.1977 after conversion 5314 GRT, 121 pass. in cabins / 14.1.1986 last voyage in service Gedser—Travemünde / 17.2.1986 **VIKING 2**, M. Thorsviks Rederi, Nassau / 25.4.1986 entered service Ramsgate—Dunkirk under charter by Sally Line / 1.1989 **SALLY SKY**, Johnson Line, Nassau, then service Ramsgate—Dunkirk under charter by Sally Line / 19.1.–4.1990 lengthening at Humber Shiprepairers, Immingham: 14 300 GT, 4150 tdw, 143.84 m length oa, 12 pass. in 3 cabins, 1143 pass. unberthed, 300 cars, 56 trucks, 1230 lane metres / 10.4.1990 again service Ramsgate—Dunkirk / 1995 14 558 GT / 12.1996 last voyage in service Ramsgate—Dunkirk / 2.1997 renamed **EUROTRAVELLER** / 13.3.1997–20.11.1998 service Ostend—Ramsgate for Holyman Sally Ferries, then laid up in Dunkirk / 4.1999 **LARKSPUR**, Sally Line, Nassau, under charter by TransEuropa Ferries / 10.1999 to TransEuropa Ferries, then laid up in Dunkirk / 27.8.2000 entered service Ostend—Ramsgate, initially as cargo ferry / 20.6.2004 also carried pass. / 8.2011 home port Limassol / 17.2.2013 laid up in Ostend / 21.12.2013 **LARKS**, Oilchart International, Limassol / 11.7.–28.7.2014 service Brindisi—Corfu—Igoumenitsa—Kefalonia—Zante under charter by Egnatia Ferries,

ms **BASS TRADER**
IMO No. 7356252
Australian National Line, Melbourne
N.S.W. Govt. Eng. & Ship, Newcastle, N.S.W.; Yard No.: 94

6374 GRT / 7486 tdw / 141.66 m length oa / 23.26 (23.37) m beam / two 9-cyl. diesels geared to 2 screws; MAN-Kawasaki / 18 000 bhp / 18.5 kn /

8.11.1975 launched / 20.7.1976 delivered as RoRo cargo ship, then service Sydney—Hobart/Bell Bay / 31.12.1996 to Strintzis Lines, Limassol / 1997 conversion into ferry in Perama: 16 537 GT, 4050 tdw, 204 pass. in 69 cabins, 536 pass. unberthed, 51 cars, 1054 lane metres, crew 45 / 6.1997 delivered after conversion as **IONIAN BRIDGE**, then service Igoumenitsa—Corfu—Brindisi / 1999 **BLUE BRIDGE**, Blue Ferries, Limassol, service Igoumenitsa—Corfu—Brindisi / 2001 181 pass. in 62 cabins, 764 pass. unberthed / 20.5.2004 **MERCEDES DEL MAR**, Iscomar, Santa Cruz de Tenerife, entered service Barcelona—Palma de Mallorca / 26.7.2009 laid up in Valencia / 2.2010 **BRIDGE**, European Seaways, Valletta / 9.4.2010 entered service Igoumenitsa—Corfu—Brindisi / 10.2010 service Bari—Durres / 2012 service Igoumenitsa—Corfu—Bari / 4.2013 service Suez—Adabiya under charter by Sisa Shipping / 7.2013 again service Bari—Durres / 10.2015 service Bari—Durres under charter by Adria Ferries /

ms **OKUDOGO 3**
IMO No. 7432733
Ehime Hanshin Ferry, Matsuyama
Kochi Jukogyo, Kochi; Yard No.: 873

6206 GRT / 1500 tdw / 141.70 m length oa / 23.51 m beam / two 14-cyl. diesels; MAN-Kawasaki / 16 000 bhp / 2 screws / 20.5 (23.1) kn / 845 deck pass. / 100 trailers + 40 cars / crew 46

LUCKY STAR ex GEDSER (photo: Tony Davis)

then laid up with engine damage in Igoumenitsa, later in Drapetsona / 1.9.2014 renamed **LUCKY STAR** / 4.2015 laid up in Bijela /

ms **ST. COLUMBA**
IMO No. 7507019
Sealink U.K., London
Aalborg Værft, Aalborg; Yard No.:214

7836 GRT / 1945 tdw / 129.22 m length oa / 20.60 (21.24) m beam / two 16-cyl. diesels geared to 2 screws; Stork-Werkspoor / 18 000 bhp / 19.5 kn / 54 pass. in cabins, 2346 pass. unberthed / 335 cars, 648 lane metres / crew 95

17.7.1976 launched / 2.4.1977 delivered / 2.5.1977 maiden voyage in service Holyhead—Dun Laoghaire / 1990 to Sealink Stena Line / 1.—10.3.1991 conversion at Lloyd Werft, Bremerhaven: 1700 pass., incl. 62 in 16 cabins, 110 Pullman seats, then again service Holyhead—Dun Laoghaire / 3.1991 renamed **STENA HIBERNIA** / 1994 11 690 GT / 17.1.1996 renamed **STENA ADVENTURER** / 30.9.1996 laid up in Dun Laoghaire, later in Belfast / 5.1997 **EXPRESS APHRODITE**, Agapitos Express Ferries, Piraeus / 6.1997 service Piraeus—Syros—Tinos—Mykonos / 8.11.1999 to Minoan Flying Dolphins, service Piraeus—Syros—Tinos—Mykonos for Hellas Ferries / 9.2004 service Rafina—Andros—Tinos—Mykonos / 1.2005 to Hellenic Seaways, Piraeus / 15.2.2005 service Piraeus—Kythnos—Serifos—Sifnos—Kimolos—Milos / 22.9.2006 laid up in Piraeus / 1.2007 **MASARRAH**, Namma Lines, Panama / summer 2007 entered service Duba—Safaga, also service Jeddah—Port Sudan / 7.2008 home port Jeddah /

MASARRAH ex ST. COLUMBA (photo: Tony Davis)

ms **DANA ANGLIA**
IMO No. 7615414
DFDS, Copenhagen
Aalborg Værft, Aalborg; Yard No.: 210

14 399 GRT / 3440 tdw / 152.91 m length oa / 23.72 (24.19) m beam / two 18-cyl. diesels geared to 2 screws; Pielstick / 15 520 kW / 21 kn / 1249 pass. in 290 cabins, 107 pass. unberthed / 470 cars, 810 lane metres /

24.6.1977 launched / 28.4.1978 delivered / 4.5.1978 christened in London / 13.5.1978 maiden voyage in service Esbjerg—Harwich / 1.1987 short deployment in service Hoek van Holland—Harwich under charter by Sealink / 23.11.1988–11.2.1989 service Copenhagen—Oslo / 1995 19 321 GT / 1.1999 temporary service Esbjerg—Harwich—IJmuiden / 2000 19 589 GT, 26.26 m beam, 413 cars / 28.9.2002 last voyage in service Harwich—Esbjerg / 30.9.2002 renamed **DUKE OF SCANDINAVIA**, home port Copenhagen / 2.10.2002–23.11.2003 service Copenhagen—Trelleborg—Gdansk / 28.11.2003–10.2.2006 service Newcastle—IJmuiden / 6.3.2006 renamed **PONT L'ABBE**, entered service Cherbourg—Portsmouth under charter by Brittany Ferries / 30.3.2006 entered service Roscoff—Plymouth / 19.12.2007 to Brittany Ferries,

MOBY CORSE ex DANA ANGLIA (photo: Frank Lose)

Morlaix / 12.11.2008 laid up in St. Nazaire / 12.2009 **MOBY CORSE**, Moby Lines, Livorno / 20.5.2010 entered service Toulon—Bastia—Livorno / 25.2.2011 service Toulon—Bastia—Livorno, then laid up in Livorno / 1.6.–28.9.2011 service Civitavecchia—Olbia / 4.2012 service Genoa—Bastia / 1.6.2012 entered service Civitavecchia—Olbia / 30.5.–17.9.2012 service Genoa—Porto Torres / 6.6.–8.9.2013 service Genoa—Bastia / 23.9.2014–5.5.2015 accommodation ship in Esbjerg and offshore supply vessel for North Sea wind farm / 28.5.2015 again service Genoa—Bastia for Moby Lines /

ms PRINSES BEATRIX

IMO No. 7637149
Zeeland Stoomvaart Mij., Hoek van Holland
Verolme Scheepswerf Heusden, Heusden;
Yard No.: 959

9677 GRT / 1887 tdw / 131.02 m length oa / 22.56 m beam / four 8-cyl. diesels; Werkspoor / 16 182 kW / 2 screws / 21 kn / 567 pass. in 172 cabins, 1500 pass. unberthed / 320 cars, 528 lane metres /

14.1.1978 launched / 24.6.1978 delivered / 29.6.1978 maiden voyage in service Hoek van Holland—Harwich / 1.10.1985 to Brittany Ferries, continued service Hoek van Holland—Harwich under charter by SMZ / 5.1986 renamed **DUC DE NORMANDIE**, home port Morlaix / 5.6.1986 entered service Caen—Portsmouth for Brittany Ferries / 10.7.2002–30.9.2004 service Roscoff—Plymouth, then laid up in Caen / 11.2004 laid up in Gdansk, 13 505 GT / 3.2005 **WISTERIA**, TransEuropa Ferries, Limassol / 30.3.–10.2005 service Almeria—Nador under charter by Ferrimaroc / 7.11.2005 first voyage Ostend—Ramsgate for TransEuropa Ferries / 2.2006 again in service Almeria—Nador under charter by Ferrimaroc / 9.3.–16.4.2006 service Barcelona—Mahón under charter by Acciona Trasmediterrea, then again service Almeria—Nador, then under charter by Acciona Trasmediterranea / 28.7.2007 badly damaged in collision with landing stage in Almeria, then

VRONSKIY ex PRINSES BEATRIX (photo: Frank Heine)

POVL ANKER (photo: Kai Ortel)

repair / 2008 service Alicante—Melilla / 2009 service Almeria—Nador / 2010 also service Almeria—Gazaouet / 8.11.2012 service Algeciras—Tangier / 5.2013 renamed **VRONSKIY** / 6.2013 again service Almeria—Gazaouet /

ECKERÖ ex JENS KOFOED (photo: Frank Lose)

ms POVL ANKER

IMO No. 7633143
Bornholmstrafikken, Rønne
Aalborg Værft, Aalborg; Yard No.: 221

8203 GRT / 2361 tdw / 121.19 m length oa / 21.51 (21.98) m beam / four 16-cyl. diesels geared to 2 screws; Alpha / 12 480 kW / 20.5 kn / 354 pass. in 163 cabins, 1146 pass. unberthed / 270 cars, 540 lane metres / crew 107

14.4.1978 launched / 17.12.1978 delivered, then service Copenhagen—Rønne and Ystad—Rønne / 1995 12 131 GT / 16.1.1997 collision with cargo ship CESIS in Öresund, until 23.2.1997 under repair in Fredericia / 2000 490 pass. in 154 cabins, 1010 pass. unberthed / 8.10.-29.11.2001 fitting of side sponsons at Remontowa, Gdansk: 12 358 GT, 24.5 m beam / 1.10.2004 service Køge—Rønne and Ystad—Rønne, also Rønne—Sassnitz / 24.7.2008 to Nordic Ferry Services, Rønne / 1.10.2010 registered for Danske Færger, Rønne /

ms JENS KOFOED

IMO No. 7633155
Bornholmstrafikken, Rønne
Aalborg Værft, Aalborg; Yard No.: 222

8203 GRT / 2361 tdw / 121.19 m length oa / 21.51 (21.98) m beam / four 16-cyl. diesels geared to 2 screws; Alpha / 12 480 kW / 20.5 kn / 354 pass. in 163 cabins, 1146 pass. unberthed / 270 cars, 540 lane metres / crew 83

11.9.1978 launched / 1.4.1979 delivered, then service Rønne—Ystad and Rønne—Copenhagen / 1995 12 131 GT / 1997 490 pass. in 154 cabins, 1010 pass. unberthed / 22.1.–12.3.2001 fitting of side sponsons at Remontowa, Gdansk: 12 358 GT, 24.5 m beam / 1.10.2004–28.4.2005 service Rønne—Ystad and Rønne—Køge / 6.5.2005 ECKERÖ, Rederi AB Eckerö, Eckerö / 15.2.2006 first voyage in service Eckerö—Grisslehamn / 2.1.2009 home port Grisslehamn /

ADRIATICA I ex SILESIA (photo: Frank Lose)

ms SILESIA
IMO No. 7516773
Polish Baltic Shipping Co., Kolobrzeg
Stocznia Szczecinska im A. Warskiego, Szczecin;
Yard No.: B490/02

7414 GRT / 1074 tdw / 127.64 m length oa / 19.41 m beam / four 6-cyl. diesels geared to 2 screws; Sulzer / 12 360 kW / 20.25 kn / 460 pass. in 123 cabins, 523 pass. unberthed / 277 cars, 468 lane metres / crew 110

23.3.1978 launched / 26.6.1979 delivered, then service Gdansk—Karlskrona, later service Swinoujscie—Ystad and Gdansk—Nynäshamn Helsinki for Polferries / 1.7.1983 service Tunis—Genoa/Piraeus/Livorno/Valletta under charter by Cotunav / 1984 alternating Baltic services from Swinoujscie and Gdansk for Polferries / 5.1986 service Genoa—Porto Torres under charter by Grimaldi-Siosa / 10.1986 again alternating Baltic services for Polferries / 1987–88 periodic deployment in service Travemünde—Copenhagen—Swinoujscie / 1994 10 553 GT / 1995 service Swinoujscie—Malmö / 4.1997 service Swinoujscie—Copenhagen/Rønne / 1.6.1999 again service Swinoujscie—Malmö / 1999 home port Nassau / 2000 service Nynäshamn—Gdansk / 17.7.2003

again service Swinoujscie—Ystad, 426 pass. in 113 cabins, 558 pass. unberthed / 3.2005 laid up for sale in Swinoujscie / 7.2005 to GA Ferries / 9.2005 renamed FELICIA, home port Panama / 11.10.2005 to Ukrferry, Odessa / 2.2006 renamed YUZHNAYA PALMYRA, then service Odessa—Istanbul / 31.5.2008 first voyage in service Valencia—Ibiza under charter by Iscomar / 2.6.2008 entered service Denia—Ibiza / 7.2008 renamed BEGONA DEL MAR, home port Klaipeda / 11.1.2009 after end of Iscomar charter laid up in Odessa / 5.2009 renamed YUZHNAYA PALMYRA, home port Panama / 27.7.–12.9.2009 service Odessa—Istanbul, then laid up in Illichivsk / 12.2010 ADRIATICA I, South Adriatic Shipping Lines, Kingstown / 16.1.–11.9.2011 service Bari—Durres under charter by Adriatica Traghetti, then laid up with engine damage in Bari / 23.6.2012 again service Bari—Durres / 3.2013 service Tangier—Algeciras under charter by Inter-Shipping for a short time /

7.2013 under charter by Siremar, laid up in Porto Empedocle and a little later arrested /

ms ANKARA
IMO No. 7615672
Turkish Maritime Lines, Istanbul
Stocznia Szczecinska im A. Warskiego, Szczecin;
Yard No.: B490/03

10 552 GRT / 1790 tdw / 127.44 m length oa / 19.41 m beam / four 6-cyl. diesels geared to 2 screws; Zgoda-Sulzer / 12 360 kW / 20.25 kn / 463 pass. in 123 cabins, 400 pass. unberthed / 214 cars, 468 lane metres / crew 110

12.12.1981 launched as MAZOWIA for Polska Zegluga Baltycka (Polferries). While under construction handed over to Turkey as compensation payment for Polish state debts / 10.6.1983 delivered / 1.7.1983 maiden

PIRI REIS ÜNIVERSITESI ex ANKARA (photo: owner)

voyage Istanbul—Izmir, then service Izmir—Antalya—Venice / 1996 10 552 GT / 2000 289 pass. unberthed / 6.–9.2003 service Cesme—Brindisi under charter by Sancak Line / 2004 summer ferry service Cesme—Brindisi for Turkish Maritime Lines, then laid up in Istanbul / 11.2004 to Denizciler Turizm Denizcilik, Istanbul / 2006 extension of after deck superstructure, 10 870 GT / 16.6.2006 entered service Istanbul—Bodrum for Deniz Cruise & Ferry Lines / 2007 service Istanbul—Cesme—Bodrum—Izmir / 2008 also Aegaen cruises / 2009 liner service discontinued, then laid up in Istanbul / 23.2.–26.4.2011 several voyages for evacuation of foreigners during Libyan civil war / 8.7.2011 entered service Bari—Durres under charter by Adriatica Traghetti / 20.10.2011 collision off the Albanian coast with the cargo ship REINA I, which sank shortly afterwards with three crew members / 1.–7.2.2012 again service Bari—Durres / 16.2.2012 laid up in Istanbul / 7.7.2015 **PIRI REIS ÜNIVERSITESI**, Piri Reis Üniversitesi Gemisi, Istanbul; training ship /

SAMSUN (photo: Frank Heine)

ms SAMSUN
IMO No. 7615684
Turkish Maritime Lines, Istanbul
Stocznia Szczecinska im A. Warskiego, Szczecin;
Yard No.: 490/04

10 583 GRT / 1788 tdw / 127.51 m length oa / 19.41 (19.46) m beam / four 6-cyl. diesels geared to 2 screws; Zgoda-Sulzer / 12 360 kW / 19.5 kn / 463 pass. in 123 cabins, 112 pass. unberthed / 214 cars, 470 lane metres / crew 110

31.8.1984 launched / 6.1985 delivered, then service Izmir—Venice also Izmir—Cesme / 2004 laid up in Istanbul / 12.2004 to Denizciler Turizm Denizcilik, Istanbul / 2005 extension of aft deck superstructure, 10 870 GT / 16.6.2006 entered service

Istanbul—Bodrum for Deniz Cruise & Ferry Lines / 2007 service Istanbul—Cesme—Bodrum—Izmir / 2008 also Aegean cruises / 2009 laid up in Istanbul / 22.2.–30.3.2011 several voyages for evacuation of foreigners during Libyan civil war / 27.9.2011–13.1.2012 service Bari—Durres under charter by Adriatica Traghetti / 4.3.2012–10.2014 service Port Blair—Nancowry—Campbell Bay under charter by Andaman & Nancowry Administration, 340 pass. / 15.4.2015 laid up off Singapore /

ms NEW SUZURAN
IMO No. 7814046
Shin Nihonkai Ferry, Otaru
Koyo Dockyard, Mihara; Yard No.: 828

16 239 GRT / 5561 tdw / 191.80 m length oa / 29.41 (29.44) m beam / two 16-cyl. diesels geared to 2 screws; MAN-Mitsubishi / 23 870 kW / 22.5 (25.6) kn / 870 pass. unberthed / 163 trucks + 46 cars, 2268 lane metres / crew 64

22.2.1979 launched / 19.5.1979 delivered, then maiden voyage in service Tsuruga—Otaru / 1981 14 624 GRT / 1985 14 586 GRT / 1987 14 306 GRT / 1992 14 385 GRT, 189 trucks + 85 cars / 5.1996 **KRITI I**, ANEK Lines, Piraeus / 6.1997 after conversion 27 667 GT, 5498 tdw, 472 pass. in 134 cabins, 995 pass. unberthed, 600 cars, 1700 lane metres, then service Ancona—Igoumenitsa—Patras / 2.6.2001 entered service Ravenna—Catania / 10.2001–7.6.2011 service Piraeus—Heraklion/Chania, in winter also as replacement Patras—Igoumenitsa—Corfu—Venice / 1.2012–22.12.2012 only service Patras—Igoumenitsa—Corfu—Venice, then laid up in Perama / 14.6.–3.9.2013 service Olbia—Livorno/Civitavecchia under charter by Goin Sardinia / 15.9.2013 laid up in Perama / 4.7.2014–23.5.2015 service Piraeus—Heraklion / 6.6.–23.7.2015 service Piraeus—Chania / 18.10.2015 entered service Piraeus—Heraklion / 15.12.2015 laid up in Perama /

ms NEW YUKARI
IMO No. 7814058
Shin Nihonkai Ferry, Otaru
Koyo Dockyard, Mihara; Yard No.: 830

16 250 GRT / 5631 tdw / 191.80 m length oa / 29.41 (29.44) m beam / two 16-cyl. diesels geared to 2 screws; MAN-Mitsubishi / 23 870 kW / 22.5 (25.6) kn / 870 pass. unberthed / 163 trucks + 46 cars, 2268 lane metres / crew 64

30.3.1979 launched / 26.7.1979 delivered, then service Tsuruga—Otaru / 1981 14 618 GRT / 1985 14 582 GRT / 1989 14 299 GRT / 1992 14 374 GRT / 5.1996 **KRITI II**, ANEK Lines, Piraeus / 6.1997 after conversion 27 239 GT, 5339 tdw, 472 pass. in 134

KRITI I ex NEW SUZURAN (photo: Frank Lose)

KRITI II ex NEW YUKARI (photo: Frank Heine)

cabins, 995 pass. unberthed, 600 cars, 1700 lane metres, then service Ancona—Igoumenitsa—Patras / 24.4.2001 entered service Patras—Igoumenitsa—Trieste / 2002 in summer service Heraklion—Piraeus, otherwise Venice—Igoumenitsa—Patras / 17.7.–22.7.2006 two evacuation missions to Beirut under charter by a Swedish aid organisation / 7.6.2011 service Patras—Igoumenitsa—Corfu—Venice / 19.11.2012 shortly before reaching Patras badly damaged by a fire on the vehicle deck / 26.11.2012 arrival in Syros for repair, then laid up / 6.7.–5.9.2013 service Patras—Igoumenitsa—Corfu—Venice / 10.9.–2.10.2013 service Piraeus—Chania / 8.1.–5.7.2015 service Piraeus—Heraklion / 7.2014 two-month charter for Algerie Ferries could not be realised because of engine damage / 15.9.2014–28.4.2015 service Piraeus—Chania / 24.5.–17.10.2015 service Piraeus—Heraklion / 17.10.2015 laid up in Perama /

ROSELLA (photo: Marko Stampehl)

ms TURELLA
IMO No. 7807744
SF Line, Mariehamn
Wärtsilä, Turku; Yard No.: 1242

10 604 GRT / 3700 tdw / 136.12 m length oa / 24.21 m beam / four 12-cyl. diesels geared to 2 screws; Pielstick-Wärtsilä / 17 900 kW / 21.5 kn / 732 pass. in 320 cabins, 968 pass. unberthed / 535 cars, 720 lane metres / crew 140

21.11.1978 launched / 4.6.1979 delivered / 15.6.1979 maiden voyage in service Turku—Mariehamn—Stockholm for Viking Line / 6.1980–13.10.1988 service Kapellskär—Mariehamn—Naantali / 28.11.1988 STENA NORDICA, Stena Line, Gothenburg / 20.1.1989 entered service Frede-rikshavn—Moss and Frederikshavn—Gothenburg / 1990 10 549 GRT / 1995 16 630 GT / 26.4.1996 LION KING, Lion Ferry, Halmstad / 6.5.1996–6.12.1997 service Halmstad—Grenaa /

1.1998 FANTAASIA, Tallink, Tallinn / 23.2.1998 entered service Tallinn—Helsinki / 1.2001 16 405 GT, 746 pass. in 318 cabins, 954 pass. unberthed / 1.4.2002–21.3.2004 service Tallinn—Stockholm / 1.4.2004–2.1.2005 service Helsinki—Tallinn—St. Petersburg / 17.1.2005 entered service Oran—Alicante/Marseilles under charter by Algerie Ferries / 20.10.2005 laid up in Tallinn / 7.4.–12.5.2006 service Stockholm—Riga for Tallink / 23.6.2006–3.2007 service Tangier—Sète under charter by Comanav / 5.–10.2007 service Oran—Alicante/Marseilles under charter by Algerie Ferries / 11.12.2007 entered service Langesund—Hirtshals under charter by Kystlink / 30.6.2008 KONGSHAVN, Kystlink, Langesund / 1.10.–21.10.2008 service Langesund—Strömstad—Hirtshals / 31.10.2008 laid up in Sandefjord / 2010 REGINA DELLA PACE, BlueLine Ferries, Panama / 14.9.2010 entered service Split—Ancona /

ms ROSELLA
IMO No. 7901265
SF Line, Mariehamn
Wärtsilä, Turku; Yard No.: 1249

10 757 GRT / 2300 tdw / 136.11 m length oa / 24.21 m beam / four 12-cyl. diesels geared to 2 screws; Pielstick-Wärtsilä / 17 900 kW / 21.5 kn / 750 pass. in 313 cabins, 950 pass. unberthed / 555 cars, 720 lane metres / crew 140

14.8.1979 launched / 21.4.1980 delivered / 23.5.1980 maiden voyage in service Turku—Mariehamn—Stockholm for Viking Line / 13.10.1988 entered service Naantali—Mariehamn—Kapellskär / winter 1993 modernisation at Finnyards in Rauma: 16 850 GT, 1198 pass. in 453 cabins, 502 pass. unberthed, 402 cars / 1.1.1994 again service Turku—

REGINA DELLA PACE ex TURELLA (photo: Frank Heine)

Mariehamn—Stockholm / 6.1995–4.1997 from June-August service Naantali—Mariehamn—Kapellskär, from September-May service Turku—Mariehamn—Stockholm / 4.1997–11.8.2003 from August-June 24-hr cruises under marketing name "Dancing Queen" Stockholm—Mariehamn, from June-August service Kapellskär—Mariehamn—Naantali, from 6.1999 to Turku instead of Naantali / 17.8.2003–28.4.2008 service Helsinki—Tallinn / 20.5.2008 home port Norrtälje / 30.5.2008 entered service Kapellskär—Mariehamn / 6.1.–17.2.2011 conversion in Tallinn: 418 pass. in cabins, 350 cars, home port Mariehamn /

ms DOMIZIANA
IMO No. 7602089
Tirrenia di Navigazione, Naples
Italcantieri, Castellammare di Stabia; Yard No.: 4347

9485 GRT / 3250 tdw / 136.00 m length oa / 23.00 m beam / two 16-cyl. diesels geared to 2 screws; GMT / 14 120 kW / 20.5 kn / 568 pass. in 125 cabins, 160 pass. unberthed / 470 cars, 1020 lane metres / crew 105

AF FRANCESCA ex DOMIZIANA (photo: Frank Heine)

AMANAH ex EMILIA as ADRIATICA (photo: Jochen Wegener)

AURELIA (photo: Frank Heine)

19.4.1978 launched / 27.6.1979 delivered / 2.7.1979 maiden voyage in service Genoa—Porto Torres, then alternating service from the west coast of Italy to Sardinia and Sicily / 1987–88 lengthening at Fincantieri in Trieste: 12 523 GRT, 147.99 m length oa, 950 pass. in cabins, 1050 pass. unberthed, 610 cars, then again alternating services from the italian west coast to Sardinia and Sicily / 2003 service Bari—Durres under charter by Adriatica / 12.10.2010 laid up in Crotone / 6.2011 to Adria Ferries, home port Limassol, 19 811 GT / 9.7.2011 entered service Bari—Durres, also service Ancona—Durres / 10.2011 renamed AF FRANCESCA, home port Naples /

ms EMILIA
IMO No. 7602106
Tirrenia di Navigazione, Naples
Italcantieri, Castellammare di Stabia; Yard No.: 4349

9485 GRT / 3250 tdw / 136.00 m length oa / 23.00 m beam / two 16-cyl. diesels geared to 2 screws; GMT / 14 120 kW / 20.5 kn / 568 pass. in 125 cabins, 160 pass. unberthed / 470 cars, 1020 lane metres / crew 105

19.7.1978 launched / 30.11.1979 delivered / 12.1979 alternating service from the west coast of Italy to Sardinia and Sicily / 1986–87 lengthening at Fincantieri: 12 523 GRT, 147.99 m length oa, 950 pass. in cabins, 1050 pass. unberthed 610 cars / 10.2004 service Bari—Durres and Ancona—Split under charter by Adriatica, as well as at times service to Sardinia and Sicily for Tirrenia / 7.2006 to Enermar, Naples, then under charter by Tirrenia / 20.9.2006 renamed ADRIATICA, home port Naples, 19 009 GT / 2006 service Suez/Safaga—Jeddah under charter by Manafie Lines / 5.2008 to Aljoudy Maritime, home port Panama, service Suez—Jeddah / 1.2012 AL YOSEFEYAH, Namma Shipping Lines, Jeddah / 2014 renamed AMANAH, then service Duba—Safaga /

ms AURELIA
IMO No. 7602120
Tirrenia di Navigazione, Naples
Italcantieri, Castellammare di Stabia; Yard No.: 4351

9485 GRT / 3250 tdw / 136.00 m length oa / 23.04 m beam / two 16-cyl. diesels geared to 2 screws; GMT / 14 120 kW / 22 kn / 568 pass. in 125 cabins, 160 pass. unberthed / 470 cars, 1020 lane metres / crew 105

24.11.1979 launched / 20.11.1980 delivered, then alternating services from the italian west coast to Sardinia and Sicily / 1987–88 lengthening at Fincantieri, Trieste, 12 523 GRT, 147.99 m length oa, 25.4 m beam, 950 pass. in cabins, 1050 pass. unberthed 610 cars / 1987 home port Cagliari / 1992 installation of two additional passenger decks with 133 new cabins in Messina: 14 834 GRT, 2280 pass., incl. 1434 in cabins, 640 cars / 5.1992 back in service after conversion / 15.5.2002–26.3.2003 modernisation of passenger accommodation at Fincantieri, Palermo / 9.2012 laid up in Civitavecchia, then in Arbatax, only sporadic deployment in summer / 1.7.2014 entered service Bari—Durres under charter by Adria Ferries / 6.–4.11.2015 service Ancona—Split under charter by SNAV / 6.11.2015 laid up in Crotone /

ms VIKING SAGA
IMO No. 7827213
Rederi AB Sally, Mariehamn
Wärtsilä, Turku; Yard No.: 1247

13 878 GRT / 2874 tdw / 145.18 m length oa / 25.49 m beam / four 12-cyl. diesels geared to 2 screws; Pielstick-Wärtsilä / 26 000 bhp / 21.3 kn / 1223 pass. in 529 cabins, 777 pass. unberthed / 462 cars, 936 lane metres /

4.1.1980 launched / 26.6.1980 delivered / 27.6.1980 maiden voyage in service Stockholm—Helsinki for Viking Line / 2.6.1981 14 330 GRT / 24.6.1982 home port Helsinki / 14.9.1982 home port Mariehamn / 6.11.1985 14 412 GRT / 29.4.1986 last voyage in service Stockholm—Helsinki / 13.5.1986 renamed **SALLY ALBATROSS** / 16.5.1986 Baltic cruises / 21.1.1987 14 673 GRT / 6.1.–16.2.1988 conversion into cruise ship at Schichau Seebeckwerft, Bremerhaven: 15 179 GRT, 2774 tdw, 149.96 m length oa, 1016 pass. in cabins / 9.1.1990 burnt out during a shipyard overhaul at Finnboda Varf, Stockholm, constructive total loss / 25.6.–27.6.1990 towed from Stockholm to Mäntyluoto, there dismantled down to vehicle deck by Rauma-Repola / 12.7.1990 to Finnyards, Rauma / 5.9.1990 arrived in Naantali, dismantled down to double bottom, parts and engine plant were again used in newbuild **SALLY ALBATROSS** (provisionally new IMO No. 9012721) / 23.3.1992 delivered after conversion to Sally AB, Mariehamn: 25 611 GT, 1703 tdw, Yard No.: 1371, then 24-hr. cruises Helsinki—Tallinn / 4.3.1994 grounded in icy waters off Porkkala and severely damaged / 18.4. refloated and towed to Vuosaari for repairs / 21.11.1994–2.10.1995 repairs at INMA, La Spezia, renamed **LEEWARD**, then short cruises in the Caribbean under charter by Norwegian Cruise Line, home port Hamilton / 1.2000 renamed **SUPERSTAR TAURUS**, home port Panama / 3.2000–12.2001 cruises under charter by Star Cruises / 15.5.2002 **SILJA OPERA**, Silja Line, Stockholm / 29.6.2002 first cruise Helsinki—Tallinn—Visby, later Baltic cruises / 16.2.2006 laid up in Stockholm / 25.5.2006 laid up in Tilbury / 14.7.2006 renamed **OPERA**, home port Nassau / 7.2007 **CRISTAL**, Louis Cruises, Nassau / 20.7.2007 first Aegaen cruise from Piraeus / 10.2007 home port Limassol, then home port Piraeus / 6.3.2011 renamed **LOUIS CRISTAL** / 7.2.2012 home port Limassol / 16.12.2013–31.3.2014 cruises under charter by Cuba Cruise / 28.11.2014 cruise

from Piraeus to Cuba, there cruises until 30.3.2015 / 26.4.2015 first cruise Kusadasi—Aegean as **CELESTYAL CRYSTAL** for Celestyal Cruises / 11.2015 conversion in Drapetsona: 43 cabins being fitted with balconies / 27.11.2015 repositioning cruise from Piraeus to Montego Bay for Cuba cruises under charter by Cuba Cruise until 18.4.2016 /

ms SCANDINAVIA
IMO No. 7814462
Rederi AB Nordö, Malmö
Kockums Varv, Malmö; Yard No.: 569

8920 GRT / 10 500 tdw / 163.51 m length oa / 23.00 m beam / two 7-cyl. diesels; Sulzer-Kockums / 13 020 kW / 2 screws / 21 kn / 175 pass. in cabins / 2100 lane metres /

1.12.1979 launched as cargo ferry / 17.3.1980 delivered, then cargo ferry service Koper—Tartous / 1982 **TZAREVETZ**, SO Mejdunaroden Automobilen Transport (SOMAT), Bourgas / 6.1.–21.5.1987 service Malmö—Travemünde under charter by Nordö Link, then various charter services in the Mediterranean and North Sea / 13.10.1988 **FIESTA**, Sealink British Ferries, Nassau. Cargo service UK—West Africa under charter by OT Africa Line / 29.6.1989–26.2.1990 converted into passenger ferry at Lloyd Werft, Bremerhaven / 2.1990 renamed **FANTASIA**, 25 122 GT, 27.63 m beam, 1800 pass. unberthed, 650 cars, 1765 lane metres / 11.3.1990 cargo ferry service Dover—Calais, from 17.3.1990 also for passengers / 31.5.1990 to Sealink Stena Line, Nassau / 12.1990 renamed **STENA FANTASIA** / 1993 25 122 GT / 10.3.1998 service Dover—Calais for P&O Stena Line / 12.1998 renamed **P&OSL CANTERBURY** / 15.10.2002 **P O CANTERBURY**, P&O Ferries, London / 14.5.2003 laid up in Dunkirk / 22.10.2003 to GA Ferries, Piraeus / 3.2004 renamed **ALKMINI A** / 4.2004 conversion in Piraeus: 480 pass. in cabins, 520 pass. unberthed, 500 cars / 6.2004 entered service Igoumenitsa—Corfu—Brindisi /

CELESTYAL CRYSTAL ex VIKING SAGA (photo: Panagia Ektatontapiliani)

WAWEL ex SCANDINAVIA (photo: Frank Heine)

LE RIF ex GALLOWAY PRINCESS (photo: Frank Lose)

10.2004 **WAWEL**, Polferries, Nassau, conversion at Remontowa, Gdansk: 25 318 GT / 15.2.2005 entered service Swinoujscie—Ystad / 18.4.2015 entered service Gdansk—Nynäshamn /

ms GALLOWAY PRINCESS
IMO No. 7719430
Sealink (Scotland), Stranraer
Harland & Wolff, Belfast; Yard No.: 1713

6630 GRT / 1895 tdw / 129.42 m length oa /
21.00 (21.62) m beam / two 16-cyl. diesels geared to 2 screws; Pielstick-Crossley / 11 770 kW /
18.5 kn / 26 pass. in 13 cabins, 974 pass. unberthed / 309 cars, 744 lane metres /

24.5.1979 launched / 22.4.1980 delivered / 1.5.1980 entered service Stranraer—Larne / 7.1984 to Sealink British Ferries / 31.5.1990 to Sealink Stena Line, London / 2.1991 renamed **STENA GALLOWAY** / 1994 12 175 GT / 1995 to Stena Line, Stranraer / 12.11.1995—22.2.2002 service Stranraer—Belfast / 24.2.2002 **LE RIF**, International Maritime Transport Corp., Casablanca / 31.3.2002 first voyage in service Tangier—Algeciras / 21.4.2013 after bankruptcy of owner laid up in Tangier /

ms ST. ANSELM
IMO No. 7813937
Sealink British Rail, London
Harland & Wolff, Belfast; Yard No.: 1715

7003 GRT / 1755 tdw / 129.65 m length oa /
21.62 m beam / two 16-cyl. diesels geared to
2 screws; Crossley-Pielstick / 15 300 kW / 19.5 kn /
30 pass. in 15 cabins, 970 pass. unberthed /
310 cars, 744 lane metres / crew 72

5.12.1979 launched / 22.10.1980 delivered / 27.10.1980 maiden voyage in service Dover—Calais / 1982 1170 pass. unberthed / winter 1982–83 conversion at Harland & Wolff: aft decks enlarged, 7405 GRT, 30 pass. in 15 cabins, 1370 pass. unberthed / 7.1984 to Sealink British Ferries / 1.1990 registered for Sealink Stena Line / 11.2.1990 entered service Folkestone—Boulogne / 10.1990 renamed **STENA CAMBRIA** / 11.7.1991 entered service Holyhead—Dun Laoghaire / 1994 12 705 GT / 19.1.1996 again service Dover—Calais / 11.2.—24.3.1997 service Newhaven—Dieppe / 26.3.—25.4.1997 service Stranraer—Belfast, then Holyhead—Dun Laoghaire / 13.5.1997 again service

Dover—Calais / 22.4.1998–31.1.1999 service Newhaven—Dieppe for P&O Stena Line / 18.2.1999 **ISLA DE BOTAFOC**, Union Maritima Formentera Ibiza, Santa Cruz de Tenerife / 11.1999 conversion

in Gijon: 43 new cabins, 874 pass. / 18.11.1999 entered service Barcelona—Ibiza / 1.10.2003 to Balearia, Santa Cruz de Tenerife / 20.10.2003 then service Barcelona—Ibiza, later also Denia—Ibiza and Denia—Ibiza—Palma de Mallorca / 29.1.2010 laid up in Denia / 4.2010 sold for scrapping to India, renamed **WINNER 9** / 5.2010 **BARI**, Ventouris Ferries, Limassol / 24.6.2010 entered service Bari—Durres / 2015 also summer service Bari—Zante—Kefalonia /

ms ST. CHRISTOPHER
IMO No. 7813949
Sealink British Rail, London
Harland & Wolff, Belfast; Yard No.: 1716

7003 GRT / 2092 tdw / 129.62 m length oa /
21.01 (21.62) m beam / two 16-cyl. diesels geared to 2 screws; Pielstick-Crossley / 15 300 kW /
19.5 kn / 30 pass. in 15 cabins, 970 pass. unberthed / 310 cars, 744 lane metres / crew 70

20.3.1980 launched / 14.3.1981 delivered / 17.3.1981 maiden voyage in service Holyhead—Dun Laoghaire / 15.4.1981 entered service Dover—Calais / 1982 1170 pass. unberthed / 4.1983 converted at Harland & Wolff: 7399 GRT, 30 pass. in 15 cabins, 1370 pass. unberthed /

BARI ex ST. ANSELM (photo: Richard Seville)

IBN BATOUTA ex ST. CHRISTOPHER (photo: Frank Heine)

27.7.1984 to Sealink British Ferries / 1.1991 **STENA ANTRIM**, Sealink Stena Line, Stranraer / 7.4.1991 entered service Stranraer—Larne / 1994 12 711 GT / 12.11.1995 entered service Stranraer—Belfast / 7.1996 laid up in Belfast / 28.10.1996 entered service Newhaven—Dieppe / 1997 12 711 GT / 10.3.1998 entered service Dover—Calais for P&O Stena Line / 24.4.1998 laid up in Zeebrugge / 13.6.1998 **IBN BATOUTA**, Limadet, Tangier, then service Algeciras—Tangier / 2008 to Comanav, Tangier / 21.5.2012 after bankruptcy of owner laid up in Algeciras / 8.2015 to Red Star Ferries / 25.8.2015 arrival under tow in Durres / 2016 service Italy—Albania planned /

ms ST. DAVID
IMO No. 7910917
British Railways Board, London
Harland & Wolff, Belfast; Yard No.: 1717

7109 GRT / 1829 tdw / 129.65 m length oa / 21.02 (21.62) m beam / two 16-cyl. diesels geared to 2 screws; Pielstick-Crossley / 15 300 kW / 19.5 kn / 46 pass. in 23 cabins, 970 pass. unberthed / 309 cars / 744 lane metres / crew 68

25.9.1980 launched / 24.7.1981 delivered / 10.8.1981 maiden voyage in service Holyhead—Dun Laoghaire / 7.1984 to Sealink British Ferries / 21.3.–31.12.1985 service Dover—Ostend / 3.1986 service Stranraer—Larne / 1.1990 registered for Stena Sealink Line / 21.2.1991 renamed **STENA CALEDONIA**, home port Stranraer, 7196 GRT / 1994 12 619 GT / 12.11.1995 entered service Stranraer—Belfast / 23.2.–25.3.2000 fitting of sponsons at Cammell Laird in Birkenhead: 132.00 m length oa, only 30 pass. in 23 cabins, 970 pass. unberthed / 9.2000–21.11.2011 service Stranraer—Larne / 6.2012 **PORT LINK**, ASDP Ferry, Jakarta / 15.5.2013 entered service Merak—Bakauheni /

ms PRINS JOACHIM
IMO No. 7803190
Danske Statsbaner, Korsør
Nakskov Skibsværft, Nakskov; Yard No.:223

10 607 GRT / 5345 tdw / 152.00 m length oa / 22.83 (23.12) m beam / six 16-cyl. diesels geared to 2 screws; B&W-Alpha / 17 200 kW / 19 kn / 2280 pass. unberthed / 4 rail tracks with 495 m length / crew 36

25.1.1980 launched / 10.10.1980 delivered / 26.10.1980 first voyage in rail ferry service Nyborg—Korsør / 1994 16 071 GT / 1.1.1997 registered for Scandlines, Korsør / 31.5.1997 last voyage in service Korsør—Nyborg, then laid up in Nyborg / 17.7.1998 laid up in Nakskov / 12.2000–8.3.2001 conversion into car ferry in Fredericia: 1390 pass. unberthed, 220 cars, 625 lane metres / 29.3.2001 entered service Gedser—Rostock / 17.8.–18.10.2004 conversion at Blohm+Voss, Hamburg: four 8- and two 6-cyl. diesels; MaK, 23 000 kW, 21 kn / 25.10.2004 again service Rostock—Gedser / 18.6.2012 home port Rostock /

ms KRONPRINS FREDERIK
IMO No. 7803205
Danske Statsbaner, Korsør
Nakskov Skibsværft, Nakskov; Yard No.: 224

10 606 GRT / 4277 tdw / 152.00 m length oa / 22.81 (23.09) m beam / six 16-cyl. diesels geared to 2 screws; B&W-Alpha / 17 200 kW / 19 kn / 2280 pass. unberthed / 4 rail tracks with 495 m length / crew 36

PORT LINK ex ST. DAVID (photo: Suryo Anggoro)

PRINS JOACHIM (photo: Ulrich Streich)

KRONPRINS FREDERIK (photo: Marc Peper)

2.7.1980 launched / 2.4.1981 delivered / 2.5.1981 first voyage in rail ferry service Korsør—Nyborg / 1994 16 071 GT / 1.1.1997 registered for Scandlines, Korsør / 31.5.1997 laid up in Nyborg / 16.12.1997 conversion into car ferry in Nakskov: 1390 pass. unberthed, 220 cars, 625 lane metres / 26.3.1998 entered service Gedser—Rostock / 2003 1060 pass. unberthed / 26.10.–20.12.2004 conversion at Blohm+Voss, Hamburg: four 8- and two 6-cyl. diesels; MaK, 23 000 kW, 21 kn / 15.1.2005 again service Rostock—Gedser /

ms VISBY

IMO No. 7826788
Rederi AB Gotland, Visby
Öresundsvarvet, Landskrona; Yard No.: 278

14 932 GRT / 2840 tdw / 142.62 m length oa / 24.01 (24.52) m beam / four 8-cyl. diesels geared to 2 screws; B&W-Götaverken / 21 480 kW / 21 kn / 1142 pass. in 287 cabins, 872 pass. unberthed / 515 cars, 650 lane metres /

RIGEL II ex VISBY (photo: Frank Heine)

25.1.1980 floated out / 10.10.1980 delivered / 31.5.1981 entered service Visby—Nynäshamn/Oskarshamn / 1984 15 001 GRT / 1.1.1988–30.12.1989 service Visby—Nynäshamn/Oskarshamn under charter by Gotlandslinjen / 11.1.1990 renamed **FELICITY** / 5.3.1990 entered service Fishguard—Rosslare under charter by Sealink British Ferries / 12.1990 renamed **STENA FELICITY**, service Fishguard—Rosslare under charter by Stena Line / 1995 23 775 GT / 3.7.1997 after end of charter to Bremerhaven for conversion / 12.1997 renamed VISBY, 146.10 m length oa, 25.5 m beam / 1.1.1998 entered service Visby—Nynäshamn/Oskarshamn for Destination Gotland / 2000 23 842 GT /

13.1.2003 renamed **VISBORG** / 31.3.2003 laid up in Kappelshamn / 8.5.2003 laid up in Landskrona / 3.7.2003 **SCANDINAVIA**, Polferries, Nassau / 16.7.2003–17.4.2015 service Gdansk—Nynäshamn / 4.2015 **RIGEL II**, Ventouris Ferries, Limassol / 2.7.2015 entered service Bari—Durres /

ms WASA STAR

IMO No. 7826790
Rederi AB Gotland, Visby
Öresundsvarvet, Landskrona; Yard No.: 279

14 919 GRT / 2410 tdw / 142.30 m length oa / 24.01 (24.52) m beam / four 8-cyl. diesels geared to 2 screws; B&W-Götaverken / 21 470 kW / 21 kn / 1100 pass. in cabins, 448 pass. unberthed / 515 cars, 810 lane metres /

5.12.1980 floated out, originally planned as GOTLAND / 24.6.1981 delivered / 1.7.1981 service Vaasa—Sundsvall and Vaasa—Umeå under charter by Vaasanlaivat / 2.1982–31.8.1982 only service Vaasa—Umeå, then laid up in Sundsvall / 6.1983–1.10.1983 service Patras—Ancona under charter by Karageorgis

SNAV TOSCANA ex WASA STAR (photo: Frank Lose)

Lines / 15.10.1983 laid up in Landskrona / 3.3.1984 **PETER WESSEL**, Larvik-Frederikshavnferjen, Larvik, service Larvik—Frederikshavn / 27.6.1986 collision off Frederikshavn with coaster SYDFJORD, which sank shortly afterwards / 1.9.1988–27.10.1988 lengthening at Blohm+Voss, Hamburg: 29 706 GT, 3630 tdw, 168.48 m length oa, 1816 pass. in 486 cabins, 448 pass. unberthed, 600 cars, 960 lane metres / 16.4.1996–2000 in off season also service Larvik—Moss—Frederikshavn / 1.10.1996 to Color Line, Larvik / 2000 1850 pass. in 530 cabins, 350 pass. unberthed, 650 cars / 3.3.–11.4.2003 fitting of sponsons at Remontowa, Gdansk: 30 317 GT, 26.40 m beam, then again service Larvik—Frederikshavn / 3.4.2006–6.4.2008 service Larvik—Hirtshals, from

20.8.–14.10.2007 service Larvik—Frederikshavn / 16.4.2008 **SNAV TOSCANA**, SNAV, Palermo / 6.2008 service Civitavecchia—Palermo, later also Civitavecchia —Olbia / 17.1.2011 entered service Genoa—Porto Torres under charter by Grandi Navi Veloci / 2.2014 hotel ship for Olympic Games in Sochi / 7.3.–6.2015 accommodation ship in Lerwick, then again service Genoa—Porto Torres under charter by Grandi Navi Veloci / 15.12.2015-16.2.2016 service Bari—Durres /

ms DMITRIY SHOSTAKOVICH
IMO No. 7625794
Black Sea Shipping Co., Odessa
Stocznia Szczecinska, Szczecin; Yard No.: B492/01

9878 GRT /1445 tdw / 133.51 m length oa / 21.00 (21.40) m beam / four 6-cyl. diesels geared to 2 screws; Sulzer-Zgoda / 12 800 kW / 20 kn / 376 pass. in 120 cabins / crew 170

29.12.1979 launched / 22.11.1980 delivered, then liner services Black Sea—Mediterranean / 1986 modernised in Landskrona / 1991 converted at Lloyd Werft, Bremer-haven: 350 pass. in 174 cabins / 1996 12 535 GT / 1.1.1997 registered for Black Sea Shipping Co., Kingstown / 2000 conversion at Remontowa, Gdansk: 354 (400) pass. in 177 cabins / 16.4.2000 **PALO-MA**, Macro Maritime, Kingstown. European cruises under 50:50 charter by Columbus Seereisen and Neckermann / 12.2000 under charter by Hansa

OCEAN ENDEAVOUR ex KONSTANTIN SIMONOV (photo: Marko Stampehl)

NEW IMPERIAL STAR ex DMITRIY SHOSTAKOVICH (photo: Vladimir Tonic)

Touristik / 23.12.2001 **PALOMA I**, Di Maio & Partners (D&P Cruises), Kingstown. Then under charter by Hansa Touristik, 12 586 GT / 2.2007 to Everis Capital Holdings (V.Ships) / 4.2007 renamed **ROYALE STAR**, casino cruises from Singapore under charter by Everis Travel / 2.2013 short cruises China—North Korea for Chinese tourists / 18.8.2013 **NEW IMPERIAL STAR**, Arising International Holdings. After conversion in Guangzhou, deployment as casino ship in Hong Kong / 25.8.2014 home port Malakal Harbor /

ms KONSTANTIN SIMONOV
IMO No. 7625811
Baltic Shipping Co.; Leningrad
Stocznia Szczecinska, Szczecin; Yard No.: B492/03

9885 GRT / 1646 tdw / 136.61 m length oa / 21.01 (21.40) m beam / four 6-cyl. diesels geared to 2 screws; Sulzer-Zgoda / 12 799 kW / 20 kn / 376 pass. in 120 cabins / crew 170

17.4.1981 launched / 21.4.1982 delivered / 12.2.1988 arrival at Lloyd Werft, Bremerhaven, new fore ship / 1995 to Baltic Shipping Co., St. Petersburg, managed by Baltic Express Line. Service St. Petersburg—Helsinki and cruises / 30.3.1996 entered service St. Petersburg—Kiel / 28.5.1996 arrested in Kiel / 1996 12 688 GT / 7.11.1996 **FRANCESCA**, Pakartin Shipping Co. (Columbia Shipmanagement), Limassol. Not deployed in Australia as envisaged / 26.9.2000 **THE IRIS**, Silver Cruises (Mano Maritime), Valletta; for conversion to Perama / 4.2001 Mediterranean cruises. 12 825 GT, 462 (650) pass. in 231 cabins / 12.2009 under bareboat charter with involvement by Kristina Cruises / 16.1.2010 arrival in Naantali for conversion / 24.2.2010 renamed **KRISTINA KATARINA**, home port Kotka / 8.2010 12 907 GT / 31.8.2010 first cruise Helsinki—Gibraltar / 28.11.2013 bankruptcy of Kristina Cruises, laid up in Las Palmas de Gran Canaria / 8.1.2014 **OCEAN ENDEAVOUR**, Endeavour Partners Ltd. (FleetPro Ocean), Majuro. Accommodation ship for Petrofac in Lerwick / 12.2014 laid up in Portland / 14.6.2015 expedition cruises under charter by Adventure Canada and Quark Expeditions /

OCEAN ATLANTIC ex KONSTANTIN CHERNENKO (photo: Olaf Schmidt)

PREVELIS ex FERRY ORANGE NO. 2 (photo: George Koutsoukis)

ms KONSTANTIN CHERNENKO
IMO No. 8325432
Far Eastern Shipping Co., Vladiwostok
Stocznia Szczecinska, Szczecin; Yard No.: 492/06

12 798 GT / 1621 tdw / 139.55 m length oa / 21.40 m beam / four 6-cyl. diesels geared to 2 screws; Sulzer-Zgoda / 12 800 kW / 21 kn / 412 pass. in cabins / crew 170

24.1.1986 launched / 20.12.1986 delivered / 1.1987 transfer voyage from Riga to Vladivostok, then deployment in East Asia / 1988 renamed **RUSS** / 1990 376 pass. in 120 cabins / 1995 end of management by Pacific Cruise Line / 1996 transferred for cruises in the Baltic / 12.5.1997 entered service Riga—Stockholm under charter by Ferry Serviss / 10.1999 laid up in St. Petersburg / 4.2000 chartered for 17 voyages Odessa—Haifa with Jewish emigrants to Ebenezer aid fund, Mano Maritime / 2000 service Vladivostok—Fushiki / 10.2007 to Sea Ferry Shipping, Majuro / 2009 renamed **RUS** / 4.2010 renamed **SC ATLANTIC** / 2.7.2010 first Baltic cruise under charter by S-Continental / 8.2012 **OCEAN ATLANTIC**, Ocean Atlantic Partners Ltd. (International Shipping Partners), renovation work in Gdansk / 27.11.2012 laid up in Tilbury / 7.2013 under charter by Areva Wind as accommodation ship in Bremerhaven and Wilhelmshaven as well as offshore in the North Sea / 12.2014 laid up in Portland / 27.4.2015 accommodation ship for Petrofac in Lerwick /

ms FERRY ORANGE NO. 2
IMO No. 8020927
Shikoku Kaihatsu Ferry, Tokyo
Imabari Zosen, Imabari; Yard No.: 396

5683 GRT / 3300 tdw / 142.47 m length oa / 23.51 m beam / two 12-cyl. diesels; Pielstick-Ishikawajima / 15 600 bhp / 2 screws / 19.75 kn / 550 pass. / 69 trucks + 65 cars, 900 lane metres /

9.11.1980 launched / 12.1980 delivered / 27.12.1980 maiden voyage in service Tokio—Osaka / 1994 **PREVELI**, Rethymniaki Naftiliaki Touristiki, Rethimnon, after conversion 420 cars, 550 pass. in cabins, 1050 pass. unberthed / 8.1994 service Piraeus—Rethimnon / 1996 15 354 GT / 4.2000 **PREVELIS**, ANEK Lines, Chania, service Piraeus—Rhodes / 11.4.2008 entered service Piraeus—Paros—Naxos—Ios—Thira /

ms OLAU HOLLANDIA
IMO No. 7928811
Olau Line, Hamburg
AG "Weser", Werk Seebeck, Bremerhaven; Yard No.: 1028

14 981 GRT / 2875 tdw / 153.40 m length oa / 24.24 (24.71) m beam / four 8-cyl. diesels geared to 2 screws; Pielstick-Blohm+Voss / 15 300 kW / 20 kn / 938 pass. in 344 cabins, 662 pass. unberthed / 530 cars, 780 lane metres / crew 157

22.11.1980 launched / 21.3.1981 delivered / 25.3.1981 maiden voyage in service Vlissingen—Sheerness / 1984 14 981 GRT / 1985 930 pass. in 350 cabins, 670 pass. unberthed / 8.1988 to Nordström & Thulin, Visby, further service under charter by Olau Line / 2.10.1989 last voyage in service Vlissingen—Sheerness / 6.10.—14.12.1989 conversion at Schichau Seebeck, Bremerhaven. Renamed **NORD GOTLANDIA**, home port Visby, 550 cars or 65 trucks / 1.1.1990 entered service Visby—Nynäshamn/Oskarshamn / 1994 21 473 GT /

ISABELLA I ex OLAU HOLLANDIA (photo: Frank Lose)

MOBY ZAZA ex OLAU BRITANNIA as WIND PERFECTION (photo: Peter Therkildsen)

21.7.1996 fire in engine room after rupture of a fuel line, extinguished with shipboard equipment / 1997 1110 pass. unberthed / 31.12.1997 last sailing in service Visby—Nynäshamn / 7.1.1998 NORDLANDIA, Eckerö Line, Eckerö / 10.2.1998–29.3.2013 service Helsinki—Tallinn, then laid up in Tallinn / 11.6.2013 ISABELLA I, Isabella Cruise Line, Belize / 4.7.–29.9.2013 service Almeria—Nador under charter by Acciona Trasmediterranea / 7.10.2013 arrival for conversion in Perama, then laid up / 14.12.2014 single voyage Batumi—Sochi—Istanbul—Limassol—Haifa, then laid up in Limassol / 3.2015 home port Limassol / 24.4.2015 service Almeria—Nador under charter by Acciona Trasmediterranea /

ms OLAU BRITANNIA
IMO No. 8020642
Olau Line, Hamburg
AG "Weser", Werk Seebeck, Bremerhaven;
Yard No. 1031

14 985 GT / 2880 tdw / 153,40 m length oa / 24,21 m beam / four 8-cyl. diesels geared to 2 screws; Pielstick-Blohm+Voss / 15 300 kW / 21 kn / 846 pass. in cabins, 662 unberthed / 550 cars, 780 lane metres / crew 157

5.12.1981 launched / 5.5.1982 delivered / 8.5.1982 maiden voyage in service Vlissingen—Sheerness / 1984 14 983 GT, 754 pass. / 25.8.1984 on voyage Vlissingen—Sheerness collided with french RoRo ship MONT LOUIS which sank in shallow water / 8.1988 to Nordström & Thulin, Stockholm, chartered back by Olau / 5.1990 BAYARD, Fred. Olsen, Hirtshals / 22.5.–13.6.1990 conversion at Blohm+Voss, Hamburg: 938 pass. in 344 cabins, 1062 unberthed / 21.6.1990 first voyage in service Kristiansand—Hirtshals, home port Oslo / 15.12.1990 to Color Line, Oslo / 15.1.1991 renamed CHRISTIAN IV / 3.1991 service Oslo—Hirtshals and Kristiansand—Hirtshals / 29.4.1994 service only Kristiansand—Hirtshals, home port Kristiansand, 21 699 GT / 4.1.–2.2005 fitting of stern

sponsons at Remontowa, Gdansk / 10.4.–14.6.2008 service Larvik—Hirtshals / 3.7.2008 JULIA, Stella Naves Russia, Helsinki / 1.8.–7.10.2008 service Helsinki—St. Petersburg, then laid up in Kotka / 27.7.2009 to Fastnet Line, Hamilton / 10.3.2010 first voyage in service Swansea—Cork / 31.10.2011 laid up in Cork after bankruptcy of owner / 28.3.2012 WIND PERFECTION, C-Bed, Hamilton, then Offshore Accomodation ship / 15.12.2015 MOBY ZAZA, Moby Lines, Italy / 1.6.2016 service Nice—Bastia planned /

ms FINLANDIA
IMO No. 7911533
EFFOA, Helsinki
Wärtsilä, Turku; Yard No.: 1251

25 677 GRT / 3898 tdw / 166.10 m length oa / 28.46 (29.04) m beam / four 12-cyl. diesels geared to 2 screws; Pielstick-Wärtsilä / 22 950 kW / 22 kn / 1601 pass. in 647 cabins, 399 pass. unberthed / 450 cars, 1044 lane metres / crew 164

25.7.1980 launched, originally planned as SKANDIA / 27.3.1981 delivered / 1.4.1981 maiden voyage in service Helsinki—Stockholm for Silja Line / 4.1982 after conversion of fore ship 25 905 GRT / 1987 after conversion 26 671 GRT / 5.5.1990 last voyage in service Helsinki—Stockholm / 14.5.1990 QUEEN OF SCANDINAVIA, DFDS, Copenhagen, 33 575 GT, 1666 pass. in 647 cabins, 334 pass. unberthed / 1.6.1990–25.6.2001 service Copenhagen—Helsingborg—Oslo / 3.1.–18.2.2000 at Remontowa, Gdansk, new bow and sponsons installed at stern: 34 093 GT, 168.05 m length oa, 360 cars, 1022 lane metres / 28.6.2001 entered service IJmuiden—Newcastle / 29.5.2007–1.9.2008 service Newcastle—Stavanger—Haugesund—Bergen / 2.9.2008–11.2.2009 laid up in Korsør / 13.2.–18.6.2009 accommodation ship in Oskarshamn during the renovation of an atomic power station, then laid up in Klaipeda / 2.12.–22.12.2009 accommodation ship during the UN Climate Summit in Copenhagen / 10.4.2010 renamed PRINCESS MARIA,

PRINCESS MARIA ex FINLANDIA (photo: Frank Heine)

home port Valletta / 22.4.2010 entered service St. Petersburg—Helsinki under charter by St. Peter Line / 30.10.2010 service St. Petersburg—Helsinki—Tallinn / 7.11.2013 to St. Peter Line, Valletta / 7.2.–24.2.2014 hotel ship at Olympic Games in Sochi / 20.3.2014 again service St. Petersburg—Helsinki /

ms SILVIA REGINA
IMO No. 7911545
Svea Line, Helsinki
Wärtsilä, Turku; Yard No.: 1252

25 677 GRT / 3898 tdw / 166.10 m length oa / 28.41 (29.04) m beam / four 12-cyl. diesels geared to 2 screws; Pielstick-Wärtsilä / 22 950 kW / 22 kn / 1601 pass. in 647 cabins, 399 pass. unberthed / 450 cars, 1044 lane metres / crew 164

21.10.1980 launched, originally planned as SILJA STAR / 9.6.1981 delivered / 12.6.1981 maiden voyage in service Helsinki—Stockholm for Silja Line / 31.3.1982 after conversion of fore ship 25 905 GRT / 9.6.1983 home port Mariehamn / 7.1.1987 to Johnson Line,

Stockholm, 26 671 GRT / 12.3.1989 to Stena Line, Stockholm, chartered back by Johnson Line / 1990 1544 pass. in 640 cabins, 416 deck pass. / 30.5.1991 last voyage in service Helsinki—Stockholm / 3.6.1991 renamed STENA BRITANNICA / 19.6.1991–3.3.1994 service Harwich—Hoek van Holland for Stena Line / 8.3.1994 renamed STENA SAGA; 33 750 GT, entered service Frederikshavn—Oslo, also called at Gothenborg in the off season / 4.2.2000 after conversion 1666 pass. in 647 cabins, 334 pass. unberthed, fitting of sponsons at stern / 2004 33 750 GT / 2011 33 967 GT /

ms KRONPRINSESSAN VICTORIA
IMO No. 7901760
Göteborg-Frederikshavn-Linjen, Gothenburg
Götaverken Arendal, Gothenburg; Yard No.: 908

14 378 GRT / 3315 tdw / 149.05 m length oa / 26.55 (26.01) m beam / four 12-cyl. diesels geared to 2 screws; Wärtsilä / 15 150 kW / 21 kn / 616 pass. in 400 cabins, 1484 pass. unberthed / 700 cars, 1260 lane metres /

15.10.1980 launched for Göteborg-Frederikshavn-Linjen / 10.4.1981 delivered to Stena Line / 13.4.1981 maiden voyage in service Gothenburg—Frederikshavn / 3–4.1982 conversion work at Götaverken, Gothenburg: 17 062 GRT, 2710 tdw, 1374 pass. in 623 cabins, 500 cars, 900 lane metres / 7.4.1982 entered service Gothenburg—Kiel, in summer also Gothenburg—Frederikshavn / 4.1988 renamed STENA SAGA, installation of additional cabin block, 17 423 GRT / 16.5.1988 entered service Frederikshavn—Oslo, in the off season also Gothenburg—Frederikshavn / 2.1994 additional cabin block dismantled in Rotterdam, 1272 pass. in 572 cabins, 804 pass. unberthed / 4.3.1994 renamed STENA EUROPE, entered service Hoek van Holland—Harwich / 1995 24 828 GT / 2.6.1997 last voyage in service Hoek van Holland—Harwich / 10.6.1997 LION EUROPE, Lion Ferry, Nassau / 19.6.1997 entered service Karlskrona—Gdynia / 20.1.1997 home port Gdynia / 1.1.1998 STENA EUROPE, Stena Line, Gdynia / 1998 24 628 GT / 31.6.2000 home port Nassau / 22.1.–6.3.2002 conversion at Cityvarvet, Gothenburg: 24 828 GT, 452 pass. in cabins, 948 pass. unberthed, 456 cars, 1120 lane metres, home port Fishguard / 13.3.2002 entered service Fishguard—Rosslare /

ms EASY RIDER
IMO No. 7826855
Castello Hellas Shipping, Piraeus
Nuovi Cant. Apuania, Marina di Carrara; Yard No.: 2119

5072 GRT / 6235 tdw / 150.81 m length oa / 20.21 m beam / two 12-cyl. diesels geared to 2 screws; MWM / 8830 kW / 17 kn / 32 pass. in cabins / 1000 lane metres / crew 17

12.7.1980 launched / 14.5.1981 delivered, then cargo services under charter by Siosa Line, North Sea Ferries and Rederi AB Nordö / 28.5.1983 arrested in Eleusis / 30.6.1985 to Sealink UK, Hamilton / 3.4.1987 renamed SEAFREIGHT HIGHWAY, then to Marseille for conversion / 23.6.1987 entered service Dover—Zeebrugge / 1988 BOYANA, SO Mejdunaroden Automobilen Transport (SOMAT), Bourgas / 1990 to Nordström & Thulin, Stockholm, planned for Gotland service; not realised due to engine damage, then to Blæsbjerg Marine, Kalundborg; repairs at MWB, Bremerhaven / 30.11.1990 renamed AKTIV MARINE / 1991 renamed URD, conversion at PZ Dora, Gdansk: 5765 GRT, 600 pass. incl. 52 in 13 cabins, then service Aarhus—Kalundborg under charter by Danske Statsbaner, home port Kalundborg / 1994 11 030 GT / 9.1997 to Scandlines, Kalundborg / 12.6.1999 laid up in Nakskov / 21.9.1999 entered service Aarhus—Aabenraa—Klaipeda / 5.–28.9.2001 service Rostock—Liepaja / 29.9.–8.12.2001 lengthening by 20.25 m at Gdansk Shiprepair Yard "Remontowa", Gdansk: 13 144 GT, 171.05 m length oa, 1600 lane metres, 105 pass. in 43 cabins / 19.12.2001 again service Rostock—Liepaja / 1.10.2005 entered service Rostock—Ventspils / 20.12.2009–21.9.2011 service Travemünde—Ventspils, then laid up in Rostock / 3.11.2011 entered service Travemünde—Liepaja / 3.5.2012 rammed by ferry NILS HOLGERSSON while berthed in the Port of Travemünde: URD grounded as a precautionary measure to prevent uncontrolled sinking / 9.5.2012 after salvage to Fayard, Odense for repairs / 28.5.2012 again in service Liepaja—Travemünde / 1.10.2012 to SOL Continent Lines, Kalundborg, service Liepaja—Travemünde under charter by Stena Line / 15.8.2013 to Stena Line, Kalundborg / 19.10.2014 entered service Travemünde—Liepaja—Nynäshamn—Ventspils /

STENA SAGA ex SILVIA REGINA (photo: Marko Stampehl)

STENA EUROPE ex KRONPRINSESSAN VICTORIA (photo: Frank Lose)

101 pass. in 59 cabins, 79 pass. unberthed / 29.9.2001 again service Liepaja—Rostock / 2.1.–21.12.2002 service Malmö—Travemünde under charter by Nordö Link / 6.1.–10.3.2003 service Rostock—Trelleborg / 2003 GT 13 144 / 15.4.2003–30.4.2005 service Trelleborg—Travemünde under charter by Scandlines AB / 6.2005 service Barcelona/Valencia—Balearics under charter by Iscomar / 1.10.2005 entered service Rostock—Ventspils / 3.1.2009 entered service Nynäshamn—Ventspils / 9.1.–27.5.2011 service Travemünde—Liepaja/Ventspils, then laid up in Nakskov / 11.6.–27.7.2011 service Travemünde—Helsingborg under charter by SOL Continent Line, then laid up in Nakskov / 6.9.2011–22.7.2015 service Travemünde—Liepaja / 12.10.2012 to Stena Line, Aarhus / 25.7.–7.8.2015 service Gothenburg—Frederikshavn / 9.8.2015 laid up in Lysekil / 25.8.2015 again service

URD ex EASY RIDER (photo: Marko Stampehl)

STENA GOTHICA ex LUCKY RIDER (photo: Jan-Erik Andersson)

ms LUCKY RIDER

IMO No. 7826867
Castello Hellas Shipping, Piraeus
Nuovi Cant. Apaunia, Marina di Carrara;
Yard No.: 2120

5088 GRT / 6235 tdw / 150.81 m length oa / 20.20 m beam / two 12-cyl. diesels geared to 2 screws; MWM / 8830 kW / 19 kn / 32 pass. in cabins / 1000 lane metres / crew 17

16.7.1981 launched / 30.12.1981 completed / 3.1982 delivered, then cargo ferry service Koper—Patras under charter by Rederi AB Nordö / 23.10.1982 entered service Malmö—Travemünde under charter by Rederi AB Nordö / 11.1983 arrested in Malmö / 1984 STENA DRIVER, Stena Line, Nassau; then cargo ferry service Gothenburg—Travemünde / 5.1985 also service Moss—Kiel / 12.1985 SEAFREIGHT FREEWAY, Sealink UK, Nassau / 22.7.1986 entered

service Dover—Zeebrugge, later also Dover—Dunkirk / 23.5.1988 engine room fire on a voyage from Dover to Zeebrugge, one crew member killed, then repair / 16.10.1988 laid up in Falmouth / 10.1988 SERDICA, Navigation Maritime Bulgare, Bourgas / 1990 NORDIC HUNTER, Swedish Gulf Line, London / 1990 to Blæsbjerg Marine, Aarhus, then conversion at PZ Dora, Gdansk / 1991 renamed ARKA MARINE / 5.1991 renamed ASK, delivered after conversion: 5739 GRT, 4222 tdw; 23.50 (25.28) m beam, 52 pass. in 13 cabins, 548 pass. unberthed / 7.1991 service Aarhus—Kalundborg under charter by Danske Statsbaner / 8.9.–27.11.1993 installation of two new 12-cyl. diesel engines geared to 2 screws; Wärtsilä, 9870 kW / 1994 11 160 GT / 9.1997 to Scandlines, Aarhus / 1.1998 laid up in Aarhus / 1.4.1999 entered service Travemünde—Klaipeda / 11.1999 laid up in Nakskov / 4.1.2000 entered service Rostock—Liepaja / 25.5.–28.9.2001 conversion at Gdansk Shiprepair Yard "Remontowa", Gdansk: 13 294 GT, 3998 tdw, 171.05 m length oa,

Gothenburg—Frederikshavn, exclusively for freight / 28.9.2015 renamed STENA GOTHICA, home port Gothenburg / 9.1.-12.3.2016 service Ventspils—Travemünde/Ventspils /

ms ESTEREL

IMO No. 7915101
Soc. Nationale Maritime Corse Méditerranée, Marseilles
Dubigeon-Normandie, Nantes; Yard No.: 162

12 676 GRT / 2200 tdw / 145.01 m length oa / 23.80 m beam / four 16-cyl. diesels geared to 2 screws; Pielstick-Alstom / 20 550 kW / 23.5 kn / 810 pass. in cabins, 1516 pass. unberthed / 700 cars, 576 lane metres / crew 123

26.9.1980 launched / 15.5.1981 christened and delivered, then service from Marseilles and Toulon to Corsica, at times also to Algeria and Tunisia / 1984 572 pass. in

143 cabins, 1754 pass. unberthed / 3.1984 deployed for evacuation missions from Lebanon / 9.1990 deployed as troop carrier during Gulf War / 2.1997 **MISTRAL**, Cenargo, Nassau, 20 220 GT / 20.6.1997 entered service Almeria—Nador for Ferrimaroc / 2000 556 pass. in 143 cabins, 1726 pass. unberthed / 5.2005 **MISTRAL EXPRESS**, Comanav, Casablanca, further service Almeria—Nador / 15.2.2007 grounded off Nador and towed off four days later, then repair / 8.1.2012 after bankruptcy of the owner laid up in Nador /

MISTRAL EXPRESS ex ESTEREL (photo: Frank Heine)

ms CORSE
IMO No. 8003620
Soc. Nationale Maritime Corse Méditerranée, Marseilles
Dubigeon-Normandie, Nantes; Yard No.: 163

12 686 GRT / 2275 tdw / 145.01 m length oa / 23.80 m beam / four 16-cyl. diesels geared to 2 screws; Pielstick / 20 260 kW / 22.5 kn / 810 pass. in 143 cabins, 1516 pass. unberthed / 680 cars, 576 lane metres / crew 123

16.10.1982 launched / 15.6.1983 christened and delivered, then service from Marseilles and Toulon to Corsica, at times also to Algeria and Tunisia / 3.1984 deployed for evacuating personnel from Lebanon / 9.1990 deployed as troop carrier during Gulf War / 3.1992 carried troops to Yugoslavia / 4.9.1992 grounded off Ille Rousse, then repaired in Marseilles / 1997 540 pass. in 143 cabins, 1722 pass. unberthed / 2001 528 pass. in 132 cabins, 1722 pass. unberthed, 600 lane metres /

CORSE (photo: Frank Heine)

ms TRAVEMÜNDE
IMO No. 8000226
Gedser-Travemünde Ruten, Gedser
Wärtsilä, Helsinki; Yard No.: 432

9120 GRT / 4150 tdw / 137.42 m length oa / 22.31 m beam / four 12-cyl. diesels; Wärtsilä-Vaasa / 14 080 kW / 2 screws / 19.5 kn / 248 pass. in 62 cabins, 1552 pass. unberthed / 450 cars, 1152 lane metres /

30.1.1981 launched / 15.6.1981 delivered / 19.6.1981 maiden voyage in service Gedser—Travemünde / 28.4.1987 **TRAVEMÜNDE LINK**, GT-Link, Nassau / 7.11.1988 **SALLY STAR**, Sally Line, Nassau / 6.12.1988 entered service Ramsgate—Dunkirk / 20.12.1988 outbreak of fire in engine room shortly after departing Ramsgate / 21.12.1988 towed to Dunkirk for repairs / 27.1.1989 again in service Ramsgate—Dunkirk / 1994 16 829 GT / 1997 72 pass. in cabins, 1787 pass. unberthed / 25.8.1994 engine room fire shortly after departing Dunkirk, then repair at ARNO in Dunkirk / 14.10.1994 again in service Dunkirk—Ramsgate / 9.3.1997 collision with the catamaran HOLYMAN DIAMANT in the Port of Ramsgate, then repaired in Dunkirk / 13.4.1997 last voyage in service Dunkirk—Ramsgate / 8.5.–14.9.1997 service Vaasa—Umeå under charter by Silja Line with marketing name "Wasa Express" / 14.12.1997 **THJELVAR**, Rederi AB Gotland, Visby. 17 046 GT, 2840 tdw, 141.00 m length oa, 22.81 m beam, 316 pass. in 79 cabins, 1536 pass. unberthed / 1.1.1998–30.11.2003 service Visby—Nynäshamn/Oskarshamn for Destination Gotland / 5.1.2004 home port Nassau / 10.2.2004 renamed **COLOR TRAVELLER**, home port Larvik / 12.3.2004 entered service Larvik—Hirtshals under charter by Color Line, in summer Larvik—Frederikshavn, 17 098 GT / 2006 exclusively service Larvik—Hirtshals / 14.12.2006 after end of charter renamed **THJELVAR** / 28.12.2006 laid up in Visby, later in Slite / 29.12.2006 home port Visby / 27.9.2007 renamed **ROSTOCK**, home port Rostock / 14.10.2007–30.9.2008 service Rostock—Gedser under charter by Scandlines, then laid up in Sassnitz, later in Puttgarden / 6.2009–18.8.2010 service Almeria—Nador under charter by Comarit, at times also Algeciras—Tangier / 4.10.2010 renamed **THJELVAR**, home port Visby / 6.10.–13.8.2011 laid up in Norrköping / 30.8.2011 renamed **BETANCURIA** / 1.9.2011–23.8.2012 service Las Palmas de Gran Canaria—Puerto del Rosario—Arrecife under charter by Lineas Fred. Olsen, then laid up in Las Palmas / 31.10.2012 **WASA EXPRESS**, Wasa Line, Vaasa / 4.1.2013 entered service Vaasa—Umeå /

WASA EXPRESS ex TRAVEMÜNDE (photo: Marko Stampehl)

ms TROPICALE

IMO No. 7915096
Carnival Cruise Lines, Monrovia
Aalborg Værft, Aalborg; Yard No.: 234

22 919 GRT / 6654 tdw / 204.76 m length oa /
26.31 (26.45) m beam / two 7-cyl. diesels geared
to 2 screws; Sulzer / 19 570 kW / 21 kn /
1422 (1796) pass. in 511 cabins / crew 491

31.10.1980 launched / 4.12.1981 delivered / 16.1.1982
maiden cruise Miami—Caribbean; later also U.S. West
Coast up to Alaska / 1994 35 190 GT / 2000 home
port Panama / 2.2000 **COSTA TROPICALE**, Costa
Crociere, Genoa / 2..2001 conversion at T. Mariotti,
Genoa / 23.6.2001 christened, then 7-day cruises
from Venice / 10.2005 **PACIFIC STAR**, P&O Cruises
Australia, London / 18.12.2005 first cruise from
Brisbane / 7.2007 to Pullmantur Cruises, chartered
back by P&O Cruises Australia / 4.2008 renamed
OCEAN DREAM, home port Valletta / 11.5.2008 first
cruise from Barcelona / 10.2008 35 265 GT / 4.2012
Maritime Holdings Group, Panama / 8.5.2012 first
world cruise under charter by Peace Boat /

ms EUROPA

IMO No. 7822457
Hapag-Lloyd AG, Bremen
Bremer Vulkan, Vegesack; Yard No.: 1001

33 819 GRT / 6506 tdw / 199.63 m length oa /
28.55 (31.50) m beam / two 7-cyl. diesels;
MAN-Bremer Vulkan / 21 270 kW / 2 screws /
21 kn / 600 (758) pass. in 316 cabins / crew 300

22.12.1980 launched / 25.9.1981 first sea trials /
5.12.1981 delivered / 8.1.1982 maiden cruise

OCEAN DREAM ex TROPICALE (photo: Tony Davis)

Genoa—Africa / 1988 37 012 GT / 30.4.1992 330 nm east of Hong Kong collided in thick fog with the Greek container ship INCHON GLORY. Towed to Kaohsiung, where the pass. disembarked / 7.7.1992 first cruise after repair in Singapore and Bremerhaven / 5.4.1998 to Star Cruises, Nassau. Until 30.6.1999 chartered back by Hapag-Lloyd Kreuzfahrten. Then new name MEGASTAR ASIA planned / 1.7.1999 **SUPERSTAR EUROPE**, Star Cruises, Nassau / 6.7.1999 transfer to East Asia / 31.7.1999 arrival for conversion at Sembawang, Singapore incl. fitting of ducktail. 778 pass. in 339 cabins, crew 440 / 10.1999 first cruise from Laem Chabang / 2.2000 renamed **SUPERSTAR ARIES** / 3.2004 **HOLIDAY DREAM**, Pullmantur Cruceros, Nassau. After conversion at Union Naval in Barcelona: 37 301 GT / 28.6.2004 first Western Mediterranean cruise from Barcelona / 6.2006 home port Valletta / 5.2008 **BLEU DE FRANCE**, CDF Croisières de France, Valletta / 23.05.2008 first Mediterranean cruise from Marseilles / 17.11.2010 to Saga Cruises, chartered back by CDF Croisières de France until end of 2011 / 2.2012 renamed **SAGA SAPPHIRE**, home port Valletta. 37 049 GT / 3.4.2012 first cruise Southampton—Mediterranean /

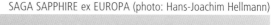

SAGA SAPPHIRE ex EUROPA (photo: Hans-Joachim Hellmann)

49

SAGA PEARL II ex ASTOR (photo: Alexander Brede)

ms ASTOR

IMO No. 8000214
Hadag Cruise Line, Hamburg
Howaldtswerke-Deutsche Werft, Hamburg;
Yard No.: 165

18 835 GRT / 2500 tdw / 164.34 m length oa /
22.61 (22.89) m beam / four 6-cyl. diesels geared
to 2 screws; MAN / 13 200 kW / 18 kn / 638 pass. /
crew 220

16.12.1980 launched. Originally planned as HAMMONIA /
14.12.1981 delivered / 14.12.1981 pre-inaugural
cruise Hamburg—Genoa / 23.12.1981 maiden cruise
Genoa—Santa Cruz de Tenerife / 12.1981 Caribbean
cruises for Astor-United Cruise / 21.10.1983 first visit in
New York / 7.2.1984 to Safmarine, Cape Town. Conversion at HDW, Hamburg: 540 pass. in 304 cabins /
4.1984 first voyage Southampton—Cape Town.
Cruises / 1.7.1984 home port Nassau / 29.8.1985 to
Deutsche West-Afrika Linie, Hamburg; immediately
afterwards ARKONA, Deutfracht/Seereederei, Rostock;
crew 250 / 15.10.1985 first cruise from Warnemünde;
cruises for the Freier Deutscher Gewerkschaftsbund
and for Western tourists, voyages to Cuba / 1990
cruises under charter by Seetours / 1990 to Deutsche
Seereederei, Rostock. 18 834 GRT, 3245 tdw / 1992
18 591 GT / 1994 managed by Deutsche Seetouristik
Rostock / 1.1.1998 home port Monrovia / 2.2001
ASTORIA, Astoria Shipping Co. (Sovcomflot), Nassau.
Full charter by Transocean Tours / 20.2.2002 first
cruise Nice—Canaries / 3.2007 to Club Cruise, then
under charter by Transocean Tours / 11.2008 short-
term cancellation of a planned 123-nights world
cruise because of engine damage, after bankruptcy of
Club Cruise arrested in Barcelona / 6.2009 towed to
Gibraltar, there laid up / 4.8.2009 to Saga Cruises /
6.9.2009 conversion at Swansea Dry Docks / 2.2010
renamed SAGA PEARL II, 18 627 GT / 15.3.2010
first cruise from Southampton / 6.5.2012 QUEST FOR
ADVENTURE, cruises for the Saga Cruises subsidiary
Spirit of Adventure / 21.11.2013 after liquidation of
Spirit of Adventure again SAGA PEARL II /

ms ASTOR

IMO No. 8506373
Marlan Corporation, Port Louis
Howaldtswerke-Deutsche Werft, Kiel; Yard No.: 218

20 606 GT / 3780 tdw / 176.26 m length oa /
22.61 m beam / two 8-cyl. and two 6-cyl. diesels
geared to 2 screws; Sulzer-Wärtsilä / 15 400 kW /
18 kn / 650 pass. in 295 cabins / crew 250

1985 ordered by South Africa Marine Corporation,
Cape Town / 1986 to Marlan Corporation, Port
Louis / 30.5.1986 floated out / 26.6.1986 christened / 14.1.1987 delivered / 31.1.1987 maiden
cruise from Hamburg via Genoa to South America
and Caribbean / 3.10.1988 FEDOR DOSTOEVSKIY,
Black Sea Shipping Co., Odessa / 23.12.1988 first
cruise from Genoa under charter by Transocean Tours /
3.1990 under five-year full charter by Neckermann

Seereisen / 1991 to Fedor Dostoevskiy Shipping Co.,
Nassau / 1.12.1995 renamed ASTOR, deployed for
Aquamarin Kreuzfahrten / 4.12.1995 first cruise
Bremerhaven—Brazil—Caribbean / 1996 to Astor
Shipping Co. (Sovcomflot), Nassau. Under ten-year
full charter by Transocean Tours / 1.2006 to Premicon
Hochseekreuzfahrt GmbH & Co. KG MS Astor, then
under charter by Transocean Tours / 11.2009 after
bankruptcy of charterer cancellation of 143-day world
cruise / 21.11.2009 laid up in Bremerhaven / 2.2010
conversion at Lloyd Werft, Bremerhaven: 20 704 GT /
1.6.2010 first cruise under charter by TransOcean
Kreuzfahrten / 5.11.2013 first cruise Civitavecchia—
Fremantle under winter charter by Cruise & Maritime
Voyages / 6.11.2014 bankruptcy of owner / 12.2014
to Global Cruise Lines, then summer charter by Trans-
Ocean Kreuzfahrten and winter charter by Cruise &
Maritime Voyages /

ASTOR ex ASTOR (photo: Alexander Brede)

ms SAGA STAR

IMO No. 7931997
Scandinavian Ferry Lines, Helsingborg
FEAB Marstrandsverken, Uddevalla; Yard No.: 153

8226 GRT / 5492 tdw / 145.96 m length oa /
24.03 m beam / four 8-cyl. diesels; Pielstick /
15 300 kW / 2 screws / 18 kn / 80 pass. in cabins /
96 cars, 1404 lane metres /

16.1.1981 aft section launched at Kalmar Varv /
9.5.1981 fore ship launched at FEAB Marstrandsverken.
The sections were joined at Götaverken, Gothen
burg and fitted out; initially planned as SAGALAND /
15.12.1981 delivered as SAGA STAR / 3.1.1982 entered
service Helsingborg—Travemünde for TT-Saga Line /
17.1.1983 entered service Trelleborg—Travemünde,
registered for Svenska Lastbil / 1.1984 registered for
Swedcarrier / 1986 service Trelleborg—Travemünde
for TT-Line / 4.1988 to CMN, Marseilles, then service
Travemünde—Trelleborg under charter by TT-Line /
23.8.1988 last voyage for TT-Line / 10.1988–2.1989
service Esbjerg/Cuxhaven/Bremerhaven—Immingham/
Harwich under charter by DFDS / 6.1989 after
conversion 9095 GRT, 5492 tdw, 154 pass. in 63

BALTIVIA ex SAGA STAR (photo: Frank Heine)

cabins, 96 pass. unberthed, renamed GIROLATA, then
service Marseilles—Bastia / 8.1993 renamed SAGA
STAR, home port Nassau / 23.8.1993 entered service

Travemünde—Trelleborg under charter by TT-Line /
5.6.1995 entered service Rostock—Trelleborg under
charter by TR-Line; 17 672 GT, 181 pass. in 76 cabins, 96
pass. unberthed / 7.1997 to TT-Line, Nassau / 15.10.–
3.11.2001 service Travemünde—Trelleborg / 11.2001
again service Rostock—Trelleborg / 8.2.2002 DIEPPE,
Transmanche Ferries, Dieppe / 5.6.2002 entered service
Dieppe—Newhaven / 2.2003 home port Rouen /
23.11.2006 BALTIVIA, Polferries, Nassau / 8.1.2007
entered service Gdansk—Nynäshamn / 21.1.2013
entered service Swinoujscie—Ystad /

ms ATLANTIC

IMO No. 7902295
Home Lines, Monrovia
Constr. Navale de la Méditerranée, La Seyne;
Yard No.: 1432

19 337 GRT / 7000 tdw / 204.81 m length oa /
27.36 m beam / two 10-cyl. diesels; GMT-Fiat /
22 070 kW / 2 screws / 23 kn / 1278 pass. in
560 cabins / crew 490

9.1.1981 launched / 2.4.1982 delivered / 17.4.1982
maiden cruise New York—Bermuda / 1984 1292
pass. in 543 cabins / 10.1988 to Premier Cruise Line,
Monrovia / 12.1988 renamed STARSHIP ATLANTIC /
13.1.1989 first cruise Port Canaveral—Bahamas / 1995
35 143 GT / 1.1997 to Mediterranean Shipping Co.,
Panama / 5.1997 renamed MELODY, Mediterranean
cruises / 2002 1550 pass. in 549 cabins / 15.9.2012 laid
up in Naples / 12.10.2013 laid up in Castellamare di
Stabia / 11.2013 QING, Sahara India Tourism Develop
ment Corporation, Mumbai / 26.11.2013 transfer
Castellamare di Stabia—Mormugao / 9.1.2014 arrival
at Western India Shipyard, Mormugao, there laid up /

QING ex ATLANTIC (photo: Christian Eckardt)

TRELLEBORG (photo: Hans-Joachim Hellmann)

ms TRELLEBORG

IMO No. 7925297
Svenska Statens Järnvägar, Trelleborg
Öresundsvarvet, Landskrona; Yard No.: 271

10 882 GRT / 3800 tdw / 170.20 m length oa /
23.78 m beam / four 8-cyl. diesels geared to
2 screws; MAN / 17 650 kW / 18.25 kn / 50 pass. in
23 cabins, 750 pass. unberthed / 15 cars, 20 trucks,
5 rail tracks with 680 m length / crew 138

19.5.1981 floated out / 16.11.1981 sea trials, Stability
problems corrected at Cityvarvet, Gothenburg /
28.5.1982 delivered / 22.6.1982 maiden voyage in

OCEAN GALA ex SCANDINAVIA as ISLAND ESCAPE (photo: Nikolaos Saratzis)

service Trelleborg—Saßnitz / 1994 to SweFerry, Trelleborg, 20 028 GT / 12.1999 to Scandlines, Trelleborg / 2001 900 pass. unberthed / 11.10.2012 to Stena Line, Trelleborg / 30.9.2014 last voyage in service Sassnitz—Trelleborg / 10.10.2014 laid up in Rostock / 19.8.2015 laid up in Uddevalla /

ms SCANDINAVIA
IMO No. 8002597
The United Steamship Co., Nassau
Dubigeon Normandie, Nantes; Yard No.: 164

26 747 GRT / 4294 tdw / 185.25 m length oa / 27.01 m beam / two 9-cyl. diesels; B&W-Atlantique / 19 850 kW / 2 screws / 20 kn / 1606 pass. in cabins / 530 cars / crew 350

16.10.1981 launched / 20.8.1982 delivered / 2.10.1982 maiden voyage in service New York—Freeport for Scandinavian World Cruises / 11.6.1983 entered service New York—Freeport—Nassau / 29.12.1983 entered service Copenhagen—Oslo / 2.4.1985 to Sundance Cruise Corp., Nassau / 29.4.1985 after conversion at Blohm+Voss, Hamburg renamed STARDANCER / 7.6.1985 first cruise on U.S. West Coast / 1986 managed by Admiral Cruises / 27.1.1990 VIKING SERENADE, Royal Caribbean Cruise Line, Nassau / 1.–4.1991 conversion into pure cruise ship at Southwest Marine, San Diego, the previous car decks being fitted with passenger cabins: 40 133 GT, 18 kn, 1514 (2104) pass. in 757 cabins, crew 610 / 24.6.1991 first cruise Los Angeles—Mexico / 1997 home port Monrovia / 1.2.2002 last cruise from Los Angeles / 26.3.2002 ISLAND ESCAPE, Island Cruises, Nassau. Mediterranean cruises in summer, in winter Brazil. 1863 pass. in 757 cabins / 2003 40 171 GT / 4.2009 to Thomson Cruises, which continued operation under the brand Island Cruises / 27.10.2015 end of last cruise in Palma de Mallorca / 27.11.2015 to Cruise Holdings Inc. / 1.12.2015 renamed OCEAN GALA / 8.12.2015 arrival at Damen Shiprepair, Brest for conversion /

CELESTYAL OLYMPIA ex SONG OF AMERICA (photo: Tony Davis)

ms SONG OF AMERICA
IMO No. 7927984
Royal Caribbean Cruise Line, Oslo
Wärtsilä, Helsinki; Yard No.: 431

37 584 GT / 5237 tdw / 214.51 m length oa / 28.41 (32.64) m beam / four 8-cyl. diesels geared to 2 screws; Sulzer-Wärtsilä / 16 480 kW / 21 kn / 1575 pass. in 633 cabins / crew 500

26.11.1981 floated out / 9.11.1982 delivered / 5.12.1982 maiden cruise Miami—West Indies / 5.1999 SUNBIRD, Airtours (later MyTravel), Nassau. After overhaul at Cammell Laird, Birkenhead, Mediterranean cruises from Limassol. 37 773 GT / 4.2003 to Louis Cruises, Limassol. Chartered back by MyTravel until 12.1.2005 / 2005 THOMSON DESTINY, Mediterranean cruises under charter by Thomson Cruises / 2005 home port Majuro / 2005 home port Limassol / 4.2012 home port Valletta / 14.5.2012 renamed LOUIS OLYMPIA / 25.5.2012 first cruise Piraeus—Aegean for Louis Cruises / 2.2014 hotel ship at the Olympic Winter Games in Sochi / 11.2014 renamed CELESTYAL OLYMPIA / 13.3.2015 first cruise Piraeus—Aegean for Celestyal Cruises /

STENA DANICA (photo: Frank Lose)

ms STENA DANICA
IMO No. 7907245
Stena Line, Gothenburg
Chantiers de France, Dunkirk; Yard No.: 309

16 494 GRT / 3100 tdw / 152.23 length oa / 28.01 (28.48) m beam / four 12-cyl. diesels geared to 2 screws; CCM-Sulzer / 26 000 kW / 21 kn / 96 pass. in 48 cabins, 2204 pass. unberthed / 550 cars, 1640 lane metres / crew 140

30.8.1980 launched / 10.2.1983 delivered / 28.2.1983 maiden voyage in service Gothenburg—Frederikshavn / 1984 after conversion 154.90 m length oa / 1985 15 899 GRT / 1994 28 727 GT /

ms NIEUW AMSTERDAM
IMO No. 8024014
Holland America Line Westours, Willemstad
Chantiers de l'Atlantique, St. Nazaire; Yard No.: V27

33 930 GT / 4217 tdw / 214.66 m length oa / 27.21 m beam / two 7-cyl. diesels; Sulzer / 21 600 kW / 2 screws / 21 kn / 1374 pass. in 605 cabins / crew 559

20.8.1982 launched / 14.5.1983 delivered / 10.7.1983 maiden voyage Le Havre—New York. U.S. cruises / 1984 home port Philipsburg / 1997 home port Rotterdam / 10.2000 PATRIOT, United States Lines (American Classic Voyages), Honolulu / 12.2000 in service after overhaul / 9.12.2000 first cruise from Honolulu around Hawaii / 27.1.2002 NIEUW AMSTERDAM, Holland America Line, Nassau / 2002 renamed SPIRIT, under charter by Louis Cruises. Conversion in Perama / 3.5.2003 THOMSON SPIRIT, cruises under charter by Thomson Cruises / 2004 home port Limassol / 5.2008 to Louis Cruises, Limassol / 2.2010 home port Valletta /

ms NOORDAM
IMO No. 8027298
Holland America Line Westours, Philipsburg
Chantiers de l'Atlantique, St. Nazaire; Yard No.: X27

33 930 GT / 4243 tdw / 214.66 m length oa / 27.22 m beam / two 7-cyl. diesels; Sulzer / 21 600 kW / 2 screws / 21 kn / 1340 pass. in 605 cabins / crew 550

21.5.1983 launched / 2.4.1984 delivered / 8.4.1984 transfer voyage from Le Havre to Tampa. U.S. cruises / 1997 home port Rotterdam. 33 933 GT / 12.11.2004 last cruise for Holland America Line / 2004 THOMSON CELEBRATION, under charter by Thomson Cruises, home port Philipsburg / 11.2008 home port Valletta /

ms NEW MIYAKO
IMO No. 8217051
Hankyu Ferry, Shimonoseki
Kanda Zosensho, Kawajiri; Yard No.: 278

11 914 GRT / 5622 tdw / 173.01 m length oa / 26.81 m beam / two 12-cyl. diesels geared to 2 screws; MAN-Mitsubishi / 17 650 kW / 21 kn / 436 pass. in cabins, 375 pass. unberthed / 136 trucks + 75 cars / crew 39

THOMSON SPIRIT ex NIEUW AMSTERDAM (photo: Alexander Brede)

THOMSON CELEBRATION ex NOORDAM (photo: Frank Lose)

26.10.1983 launched / 26.1.1984 delivered, then service Kokura—Izumiotsu / 1996 SUPERFERRY 12, WG&A Lines, Manila / 1996 service between the islands of the Philippines / 2000 116 pass. in cabins, 595 pass. unberthed / 1.2011 to Negros Navigation Co., Cebu / 2012 ST. POPE JOHN PAUL II, 2GO Travel, Cebu /

ST. POPE JOHN PAUL II ex NEW MIYAKO (photo: Irvine Kinea)

POETA LOPEZ ANGLADA ex CHAMPS ELYSEES (photo: Frank Lose)

ms ROYAL PRINCESS
IMO No. 8201480
Princess Cruises, London
Wärtsilä, Helsinki; Yard No.: 464

44 348 GT / 5580 tdw / 230.61 m length oa /
29.20 (32.21) m beam / four 6-cyl. diesels geared
to 2 screws; Pielstick-Wärtsilä / 23 200 kW / 22 kn /
1260 pass. in 600 cabins / crew 518

18.2.1984 floated out / 30.10.1984 delivered /
15.11.1984 christened in Southampton / 19.11.1984
maiden cruise Southampton—Miami / 1995
44 588 GT / 6.2005 ARTEMIS, P&O Cruises, Hamilton /
17.6.2005 first cruise from Southampton / 10.2009
to Artania Shipping (V.Ships), chartered back by P&O
Cruises / 12.4.2011 renamed ARTANIA / 28.5.2011
first cruise Hamburg—Amsterdam under charter
by Phoenix Reisen / 10.2011 44 656 GT / 9.–12.2014
conversion and fitted with new engines at Lloyd
Werft, Bremerhaven: four 12-cyl. diesels geared to
2 screws; Wärtsilä, 27 840 kW, 22 kn / 9.12.2014
first cruise Hamburg—Rotterdam after conversion /

ARTANIA ex ROYAL PRINCESS (photo: Alexander Brede)

ms SVEA
IMO No. 8306486
Svea Line, Stockholm
Wärtsilä, Helsinki; Yard No.: 470

33 830 GT / 3019 tdw / 168.03 m length oa /
27.64 (31.60) m beam / four 12-cyl. diesels geared
to 2 screws; Pielstick-Wärtsilä / 26 400 kW / 22 kn /
1625 pass. in 566 cabins, 375 pass. unberthed /
360 cars, 1080 lane metres / crew 180

28.9.1984 floated out / 7.5.1985 delivered / 13.5.1985
maiden voyage in service Stockholm—Mariehamn—
Turku for Silja Line / 15.12.1989 to Johnson Line,
Stockholm / 4.3.–7.4.1992 conversion at Lloyd
Werft, Bremerhaven: 34 417 GT, 3019 tdw, 1937
pass. in 588 cabins, 63 pass. unberthed / 31.3.1992
renamed SILJA KARNEVAL / 6.4.1994 to Color
Line, Oslo / 28.4.1994 renamed COLOR FESTIVAL /
29.4.1994–4.2.2006 service Oslo—Hirtshals /
7.4.2006–7.1.2008 service Oslo—Frederikshavn /
17.1.2008 MEGA SMERALDA, Corsica Sardinia
Ferries, Genoa, then for conversion to Perama:
400 cars / 13.6.2008 entered service Livorno—
Golfo Aranci, later also service Livorno—Bastia and
Civitavecchia—Golfo Aranci / 10.2008 service Nice/
Toulon—Ajaccio/Bastia/Ile Rousse /

ms CHAMPS ELYSEES
IMO No. 8208763
Soc. Nationale des Chemins de Fer Francais, Nantes
Dubigeon Normandie, Nantes; Yard No.: 167

15 093 GT / 2430 tdw / 130.00 m length oa /
22.51 (23.02) m beam / two 16–cyl. diesels geared
to 2 screws; SEMT-Pielstick / 15 840 kW / 18.5 kn /
4 pass. in 2 cabins, 1800 pass. unberthed /
330 cars, 850 lane metres / crew 84

21.12.1983 launched / 2.10.1984 delivered / 4.10.1984
maiden voyage in service Calais—Dover, later ocas-
sionaly also service Boulogne—Dover / 1987 home
port Calais / 22.1.1990 to SNAT, Calais / 2.7.1990
entered service Dieppe—Newhaven, home port
Dieppe / 1.5.1992 entered service Dieppe—Newhaven
under charter by Sealink Stena Line / 3.6.1992
renamed STENA PARISIEN / 9.1.1997 last voyage
Dieppe—Newhaven, end of Stena charter / 18.1.1997
SEAFRANCE MANET, Seafrance, Calais / 20.1.1997–
29.4.2008 again service Calais—Dover, then laid up
in Calais / 19.12.2008 laid up in Dunkirk / 8.7.2009
to Stena Line, London / 29.9.2009 renamed STENA
NAVIGATOR / 12.11.2009–16.11.2011 service
Belfast—Stranraer / 2.2011 to Balearia, Santa
Cruz de Tenerife / 21.03.2012 renamed DANIYA /

6.4.2012 entered service Barcelona—Ciutadella,
later service Denia—San Antonio—Barcelona /
14.11.2013 renamed POETA LOPEZ ANGLADA /
2.12.2013 entered service Ciutadella—Alcudia/
Barcelona / 21.7.2014 entered service Algeciras—
Ceuta, also Algeciras—Tangier Med. /

MEGA SMERALDA ex SVEA (photo: Frank Heine)

ms WELLAMO

IMO No. 8306498
EFFOA, Helsinki
Wärtsilä, Helsinki; Yard No.: 471

33 818 GRT / 3000 tdw / 168.03 m length oa /
27.60 (31.60) m beam / four 12-cyl. diesels geared
to 2 screws; Pielstick-Wärtsilä / 26 400 kW / 22 kn /
1625 pass. in 566 cabins, 375 pass. unberthed /
360 cars, 1200 lane metres / crew 180

15.3.1985 floated out / 9.1.1986 delivered and maiden
voyage in service Turku—Mariehamn—Stockholm
for Silja Line / 29.4.–18.11.1990 service Helsinki—
Stockholm / 18.11.1990 again service Turku—Mariehamn—Stockholm / 15.1.1992 start of conversion at
Lloyd Werft, Bremerhaven: 34 417 GT, 3720 tdw, 1937
pass. in 588 cabins, 63 pass. unberthed / 22.2.1992
renamed **SILJA FESTIVAL**, again service Turku—Mariehamn—Stockholm / 15.1.1993 home port Mariehamn /
20.3.–24.5.1995 service Vaasa—Umeå / 1.6.1993–
10.4.1994 service Lübeck—Travemünde—Malmö, from
September also to Copenhagen / 22.4.1994 entered
service Vaasa—Umeå, also Vaasa—Sundsvall, in winter
cruises Helsinki—Tallinn / 1995 GT 34 414 / 15.8.1995
entered service Helsinki—Tallinn / 2.4.1997 home port
Stockholm / 5.4.1997 entered service Stockholm—
Mariehamn—Turku / 7.1.–20.1.2001 at Finnyards in
Rauma sponsons fitted at stern / 22.7.2008 last voyage
Stockholm—Mariehamn—Turku / 2.8.2008–6.5.2013
service Stockholm—Riga for Tallink, home port Riga,
then laid up in Riga / 1.9.–19.11.2013 accommodation ship in Cadiz under charter by Disney Cruise Line,
then laid up in Tallinn / 1.3.2014–29.4.2015 hotel
ship in Kitimat under charter by Bridgemans Services /
10.6.2015 **MEGA ANDREA**, Corsica Sardinia Ferries,
Genoa / 16.7.2015 entered service Livorno—Golfo
Aranci, also service Livorno—Bastia /

ms MARIELLA

IMO No. 8320573
SF Line, Mariehamn
Wärtsilä, Turku; Yard No.: 1286

37 799 GT / 3400 tdw / 175.70 m length oa /
28.40 (29.00) m beam / four 12-cyl. diesels geared
to 2 screws; Pielstick-Wärtsilä / 23 000 kW / 22 kn /
2447 pass. in 841 cabins, 53 pass. unberthed /
580 cars, 1115 lane metres / crew 212

28.9.1984 launched / 17.5.1985 delivered / 18.5.1986
maiden voyage in service Helsinki—Stockholm for
Viking Line / 4.8.1990 fire in engine room, then repairs
in Helsinki until 9.1990 / 1.7.1999 entered service
Helsinki—Mariehamn—Stockholm / 9.2000 fitting of
sponsons at stern; 37 860 GT / 12.6.2014 in summer
also service Helsinki—Tallinn /

ms OLYMPIA

IMO No. 8414582
Rederi AB Slite, Slite
Wärtsilä, Turku; Yard No.: 1290

37 799 GT / 3420 tdw / 176.82 m length oa /
28.40 (29.00) m beam / four 12-cyl. diesels geared
to 2 screws; Pielstick-Wärtsilä / 23 000 kW / 22 kn /
2547 pass. in 841 cabins, 53 pass. unberthed /
580 cars, 1115 lane metres / crew 212

31.8.1985 launched / 26.4.1986 delivered / 29.4.1986
entered service Stockholm—Helsinki for Viking
Line / 1989 37 583 GT / 5.4.1993 last voyage in
service Stockholm—Helsinki / 22.4.1993 renamed
PRIDE OF BILBAO / 28.4.1993 entered service

MEGA ANDREA ex WELLAMO (photo: Frank Lose)

MARIELLA (photo: Frank Heine)

SPL PRINCESS ANASTASIA ex OLYMPIA (photo: Frank Heine)

Portsmouth—Bilbao also Portsmouth—Cherbourg/
Le Havre under charter by P&O European Ferries /
1.11.1993 to Irish Continental Group, Nassau,
continued under charter by P&O / 1994 home port

Portsmouth / 29.1.2005 exclusively service Portsmouth—Bilbao / 4.11.2008 home port Nassau /
27.9.2010 last voyage in service Portsmouth—Bilbao /
6.10.2010 renamed **BILBAO** / 22.10.2010 after

MAGELLAN ex HOLIDAY (photo: Hans-Joachim Hellmann)

HENNA ex JUBILEE (photo: Jonathan Boonzaier)

first cruise under charter by Cruise & Maritime Voyages /

ms JUBILEE
IMO No. 8314122
Carnival Cruise Lines, Monrovia
Kockums Varv, Malmö; Yard No.: 596

47 262 GT / 6065 tdw / 224.82 m length oa / 28.01 (28.20) m beam / two 7-cyl. diesels geared to 2 screws; Sulzer / 23 500 kW / 19 (21.7) kn / 1800 pass. in 716 cabins / crew 680

26.10.1985 floated out / 6.1986 delivered / 6.7.1986 first cruise from Miami / 1996 home port Panama / 2000 home port Nassau / 10.2004 PACIFIC SUN, P&O Cruises Australia, London / 16.11.2004 first cruise from Sydney / 9.2010 47 678 GT / 11.2011 to Triton International Investment, chartered back by P&O Cruises Australia / 15.7.2012 home port Valletta / 20.7.2012 renamed HENNA, 47 546 GT / 26.1.2013 first cruise from Sanya for HNA Cruise Co. / 17.11.2015 end of last cruise in Shanghai / 28.11.2015 arrival at Jinhai Heavy Industry, Changtu Island, for lay-up or possible conversion /

ms CELEBRATION
IMO No. 8314134
Carnival Cruise Lines, Monrovia
Kockums Varv, Malmö; Yard No.: 597

47 262 GT / 6405 tdw / 223.37 m length oa / 28.01 (28.20) m beam / two 7-cyl. diesels geared to 2 screws; Sulzer / 23 510 kW / 19 kn / 1896 pass. in 716 cabins / crew 680

9.8.1986 launched / 2.1987 delivered / 9.2.1987 transfer voyage Malmö—Miami / 14.3.1987 maiden cruise Miami—Caribbean / 10.2.1989 north of Punta Guarico collided with the Cuban cement tanker CAPITAN SAN LUIS, which sank with three dead, while the CELEBRATION was only slightly damaged / 2000 home port Panama / 6.2008 GRAND CELEBRATION,

GRAND CELEBRATION ex CELEBRATION (photo: George Koutsoukis)

end of charter back to Irish Ferries, then laid up in Falmouth / 3.12.2010 to St. Peter Line / 3.2011 SPL PRINCESS ANASTASIA, home port Valletta / 31.3.2011 entered service St. Petersburg—Tallinn—Stockholm / 4.8.2011 entered service St. Petersburg—Helsinki—Stockholm—Tallinn—St. Petersburg / 5.2.–24.2.2014 hotel ship at the Olympic Games in Sochi / 21.3.2014 again service St. Petersburg—Helsinki—Stockholm—Tallinn—St. Petersburg /

ms HOLIDAY
IMO No. 8217881
Carnival Cruise Lines, Panama
Aalborg Værft, Aalborg; Yard No.: 246

46 052 GT / 7186 tdw / 221.57 m length oa / 28.01 (28.17) m beam / two 7-cyl. diesels geared to 2 screws; Sulzer / 23 520 kW / 22 kn / 1794 pass. in 726 cabins / crew 660

10.12.1983 launched / 1.1985 first sea trials / 20.6.1985 delivered / 22.6.1985 from Aalborg to Miami / 13.7.1985 first Caribbean cruise / 2000 home port Nassau / 9.2005 chartered by U.S. government for six months as accommodation ship for persons rendered homeless by Hurricane Katrina, originally

berthed in Mobile, from 29.10.2005 in Pascagoula / 3.2006 again Caribbean cruises / 11.2009 GRAND HOLIDAY, Iberocruceros, Madeira / 2.2014 hotel ship at the Olympic Winter Games in Sochi / 1.2015 MAGELLAN, Global Cruise Lines, Nassau / 15.3.2015

Iberocruceros, Madeira / 5.2011 47 263 GT / 11.2014 COSTA CELEBRATION, Costa Crociere. Mediterranean cruises planned, not realised / 19.12.2014 to Celebration Cruise Services (FleetPro Ocean) / 1.1.2015 GRAND CELEBRATION, home port Nassau / 3.2.2015 first short cruise Palm Beach—Freeport for Bahamas Paradise Cruise Line /

ms UMSINI
IMO No. 8303264
P.T. Pelayaran Nasional Indonesia (PELNI), Sorong
Jos. L. Meyer, Papenburg; Yard No.: 612

13 853 GRT / 3434 tdw / 144.02 m length oa /
23.41 m beam / two 6-cyl. diesels geared to
2 screws; Krupp MaK / 10 890 kW / 20 kn /
pass. 40 1st, 88 2nd, 168 3rd, 1441 economy class
(total 1737) / crew 119

15.9.1984 launched / 31.1.1985 delivered, then
deployed in passenger service between the islands of
Indonesia / 2005 14 501 GRT /

ms TIDAR
IMO No. 8700292
P.T. Pelayaran Nasional Indonesia (PELNI), Semarang
Jos. L. Meyer, Papenburg; Yard No.: 617

13 888 GRT / 3200 tdw / 144.00 m length oa /
23.40 (23.70) m beam / two 6-cyl. diesels geared
to 2 screws; Krupp MaK / 12 800 kW / 20 kn /
pass. 40 1st, 88 2nd, 288 3rd, 1488 economy class
(total 1904) / crew 145

23.9.1988 floated out and christened / 30.9.1988
delivered, then deployed in passenger service between
the islands of Indonesia / 2000 14 501 GRT /

ms CIREMAI
IMO No. 9032135
P.T. Pelayaran Nasional Indonesia (PELNI), Djakarta
Jos. L. Meyer, Papenburg; Yard No.: 631

14 610 GT / 3489 tdw / 146.50 m length oa /
23.40 (26.80) m beam / two 6-cyl. diesels geared to
2 screws; Krupp MaK / 12 800 kW / 20 kn /
pass. 44 1st, 88 2nd, 288 3rd, 1553 economy class
(total 1973) / crew 145

UMSINI (photo: Suryo Anggoro)

TIDAR (photo: Jonathan Boonzaier)

CIREMAI (photo: Frank Heine)

DOBONSOLO (photo: Frank Heine)

13.8.1992 floated out / 8.5.1993 delivered, then deployed in passenger service between the islands of Indonesia / 2003 14581 GT /

ms DOBONSOLO
IMO No. 9032147
P.T. Pelayaran Nasional Indonesia (PELNI), Sorong
Jos. L. Meyer, Papenburg; Yard No.: 632

14610 GRT / 3500 tdw / 146.50 m length oa /
23.40 (23.70) m beam / two 6-cyl. diesels geared
to 2 screws; Krupp MaK / 12800 kW / 20 kn /
pass. 44 1st, 88 2nd, 288 3rd, 1554 economy class
(total 1974) / crew 145

5.5.1993 floated out / 10.10.1993 delivered, then deployed in passenger service between the islands of Indonesia / 2000 14581 GRT /

BUKIT SIGUNTANG (photo: Frank Heine)

ms BUKIT SIGUNTANG
IMO No. 9124536
P.T. Pelayaran Nasional Indonesia (PELNI), Palembang
Jos. L. Meyer, Papenburg; Yard No.: 642

14701 GT / 3686 tdw / 146.50 m length oa /
23.40 (26.50) m beam / two 6-cyl. diesels geared
to 2 screws; Krupp MaK / 12800 kW / 20.3 kn /
pass. 144 1st, 240 2nd, 355 3rd, 1264 economy
class (total 2003) / crew 147

15.5.1996 floated out / 12.10.1996 delivered, then deployed in passenger service between the islands of Indonesia / 1998 14643 GT /

ms LAMBELU
IMO No. 9124548
P.T. Pelayaran Nasional Indonesia (PELNI), Kendari
Jos. L. Meyer, Papenburg; Yard No.: 643

14701 GT / 3375 tdw / 146.50 m length oa /
23.40 (23.70) m beam / two 6-cyl. diesels geared
to 2 screws; Krupp MaK / 12800 kW / 20.3 kn /
pass. 144 1st, 240 2nd, 355 3rd, 1264 economy
class (total 2003) / crew 147

4.8.1997 delivered, then deployed in passenger service between the islands of Indonesia / 2000 14649 GT /

LAMBELU (photo: Ivan Meshkov)

SINABUNG (photo: Jonathan Boonzaier)

ms SINABUNG
IMO No. 9139672
P.T. Pelayaran Nasional Indonesia (PELNI), Belawan
Jos. L. Meyer, Papenburg; Yard No.: 644

14716 GT / 3485 tdw / 146.50 m length oa /
23.40 (23.70) m beam / two 8-cyl. diesels geared
to 2 screws; Krupp MaK / 17040 kW / 22.4 kn /
pass. 144 1st, 364 2nd, 594 3rd, 804 economy class
(total 1906) / crew 147

14.12.1997 christened and delivered / 1.1998 deployed in passenger service between the islands of Indonesia / 17.8.1998 collision in Strait of Malacca with bulk carrier WORLD NORTH: 4 killed, then under own power to Dumai / 4.2010 14716 GT /

ms KELUD
IMO No. 9139684
P.T. Pelayaran Nasional Indonesia (PELNI), Kandari
Jos. L. Meyer, Papenburg; Yard No.: 645

14 701 GT / 3375 tdw / 146.50 m length oa /
23.40 (23.70) m beam / two 6-cyl. diesels geared
to 2 screws; Krupp MaK / 12 800 kW / 22.4 kn /
pass. 144 1st, 364 2nd, 594 3rd, 804 economy class
(total 1906) / crew 157

17.7.1998 floated out / 31.10.1998 delivered, then
deployed in passenger service between the islands of
Indonesia / 2000 14 665 GT /

KELUD (photo: Tony Davis)

DORO LONDA (photo: Jonathan Boonzaier)

ms DORO LONDA
IMO No. 9226487
P.T. Pelayaran Nasional Indonesia (PELNI), Lembar
Jos. L. Meyer, Papenburg; Yard No.: 661

14 800 GT / 3686 tdw / 146.50 m length oa /
23.40 (26.50) m beam / two 8-cyl. diesels geared
to 2 screws; Krupp MaK / 17 040 kW / 22.4 kn /
pass. 104 1st, 2026 economy class (total 2130) /
crew 147

6.3.2001 floated out / 30.06.2001 delivered, then
deployed in passenger service between the islands of
Indonesia / 1.2005 14 685 GT /

ms NGGAPULU
IMO No. 9226499
P.T. Pelayaran Nasional Indonesia (PELNI), Manokwari
Jos. L. Meyer, Papenburg; Yard No.: 662

14 715 GT / 3175 tdw / 146.50 m length oa /
23.40 m beam / two 8-cyl. diesels geared to
2 screws; Krupp MaK / 17 040 kW / 22.4 kn /
pass. 104 1st, 2026 economy class (total 2130) /
crew 147

12.10.2001 floated out / 26.2.2002 delivered, then
deployed in passenger service between the islands of
Indonesia / 1.2005 14 739 GT /

NGGAPULU (photo: shipyard)

LABOBAR (photo: Jonathan Boonzaier)

ms LABOBAR
IMO No. 9281542
P.T. Pelayaran Nasional Indonesia (PELNI), Ambon
Jos. L. Meyer, Papenburg; Yard No.: 663

15 136 GT / 3482 tdw / 146.50 m length oa /
23.40 m beam / two 8-cyl. diesels geared to
2 screws; Krupp MaK / 20 000 kW / 22.4 kn /
pass. 66 1st, 1152 3rd, 1866 economy class
(total 3084) / crew 161

26.6.2004 delivered, then deployed in passenger
service between the islands of Indonesia /

COLOR VIKING ex PEDER PAARS (photo: Uwe Jakob)

ms PEDER PAARS

IMO No. 8317942
Danske Statsbaner, Aarhus
Nakskov Skibsværft, Nakskov; Yard No.: 233

11 606 GRT / 2813 tdw / 134.02 m length oa /
24.01 (24.62) m beam / two 8-cyl. diesels;
MAN B&W / 12 480 kW / 2 screws /
17.1 (19.3) kn / 144 pass. in 74 cabins, 1856 pass.
unberthed / 331 cars, 605 lane metres /

21.11.1984 launched / 14.5.1985 christened /
18.10.1985 delivered / 19.11.1985–19.5.1991 service
Aarhus—Kalundborg, 19 763 GT / 20.5.1991 STENA
INVICTA, Sealink Stena Line, Dover / 30.5.–7.1991
conversion at Lloyd Werft, Bremerhaven: 152 cars
and 30 trailers / 7.7.1991–18.2.1998 service Dover—
Calais / 3.1998 chartered by Silja Line under marketing
name "Wasa Jubilee" / 20.4.–15.9.1998 service
Vaasa—Umeå / 18.9.1998 laid up in Zeebrugge /
11.1999 to P&O Stena Line, Dover / 12.12.1999
entered service Holyhead—Dun Laoghaire under charter by Stena Line / 1.4.2000 renamed COLOR VIKING /
14.6.2000 first voyage in service Sandefjord—Strömstad under charter by Color Line / 8.5.2001 to Color
Line, Nassau / 5.2002 home port Sandefjord /

ms NIELS KLIM

IMO No. 8317954
Danske Statsbaner, Aarhus
Nakskov Skibsværft, Nakskov; Yard No.: 234

11 763 GRT / 2400 tdw / 134.00 m length oa /
24.01 (24.62) m beam / two 8-cyl. diesels; B&W /
12 480 kW / 2 screws / 17.1 (19.4) kn / 144 pass.
in 74 cabins, 1856 pass. unberthed / 331 cars,
604 lane metres /

29.5.1985 launched / 21.4.1986 delivered / 1.6.1986–
19.5.1991 service Aarhus—Kalundborg, 19 504 GT /
20.5.1991 STENA NAUTICA, Stena Line, Hamilton, then
laid up in Aarhus, later in Svendborg / 26.1.–6.3.1992

service Aarhus—Kalundborg under charter by DSB /
31.3.1992 renamed ISLE OF INNISFREE, service
Rosslare—Pembroke under charter by B+I Line /
3.5.1993 entered service Dun Laoghaire—Holyhead /
8.5.1995 LION KING, Lion Ferry, Halmstad, service
Halmstad—Grenaa / 30.4.1996 renamed LION KING
II / 5.1996 STENA NAUTICA, Stena Line, Hamilton /
24.6.–17.9.1996 service Tangier—Algeciras under
charter by Trasmediterranea, then laid up in Dunkirk /
1.1997 and 9.1997 short-term charters in the North
Sea and the Baltic, then again laid up in Dunkirk /
8.12.1997–31.1.1999 service Halmstad—Grenaa,
then service Varberg—Grenaa / 18.9.2000 passenger

capacity reduced to 100 for following winter season, in
summer 2000 pass. / 16.11.2001 home port Gothenburg / 17.12.2001–2.2002 conversion in Landskrona:
19 504 GT, 733 pass., 1110 lane metres / 4.3.2002
again service Varberg—Grenaa / 16.2.2004 on a
voyage from Grenaa to Varberg collision with cargo ship
JOANNA; the side the stern at starboard was torn over
a length of 11 m, considerable water ingress. Towed
to Grenaa for provisional repairs / 26.2.2004 arrival
in Gothenburg, later to Gdansk for repair / 24.6.2004
again service Varberg—Grenaa / 8.7.2014 collision
with landing stage in Grenaa, then repair at Fayard in
Odense / 31.7.2014 again service Varberg—Grenaa /

STENA NAUTICA ex NIELS KLIM (photo: Frank Lose)

ms VEDA
IMO No. 8602074
Higashi Nihon Ferry, Hakodate
Naikai Sb. & Eng. Co., Setoda; Yard No.:512

5087 GRT / 2917 tdw / 126.24 m length oa /
20.02 m beam / two 12-cyl. diesels;
Pielstick-Nippon / 9250 kW / 2 screws / 18.5 kn /
529 pass. unberthed / 50 trucks + 22 cars /

7.6.1986 launched / 8.1986 delivered, then service
Muroran—Aomori / 2000 10624 GT / 2.2001 ORIENTAL
PEARL II, Asia International, Panama; service
Incheon—Dandong for Dandong International Ferry
Co. / 2012 JEJU WORLD, Doowoo Shipping Co.,
Jeju / 2012 service Jeju—Samcheonpo / 7.2015 ASIA
INNOVATOR, sold to Indonesia /

ASIA INNOVATOR ex VEDA as ORIENTAL PEARL II (photo: Klas Brogren)

ms KONINGIN BEATRIX
IMO No. 8416308
Stoomvaart Mij. Zeeland, Hoek van Holland
van der Giessen-De Noord, Krimpen; Yard No.: 935

31189 GT / 3060 tdw / 161.80 m length oa /
27.61 m beam / four 8-cyl. diesels geared to 2
screws; MAN / 17900 kW / 21 kn / 1286 pass. in
539 cabins, 814 pass. unberthed / 485 cars, 990
lane metres /

9.11.1985 launched / 4.1986 delivered / 22.4.1986
maiden voyage in service Hoek van Holland—
Harwich / 1.9.1989 to Stena Line, Hoek van Holland /
1997 home port London / 3.7.1997 entered service
Fishguard—Rosslare / 2000 1296 pass. in 559
cabins, 804 pass. unberthed / 13.3.2002 renamed
STENA BALTICA, home port Nassau / 21.3.2002
entered service Karlskrona—Gdynia / 1.2.–6.2005
conversion at Remontowa, Gdansk: 31910 GT, 4272
tdw, 164.41 m length oa, 949 pass. in 379 cabins,
251 pass. unberthed, 524 cars, 1850 lane metres,
125 crew / 6.6.2005–27.6.2011 service Karlskrona—Gdynia / 29.6.2011 laid up in Landskrona,
later in Lysekil / 4.2.2013 SNAV ADRIATICO, SNAV,
Limassol / 26.4.–9.2013 service Ancona—Split /

SNAV ADRIATICO ex KONINGIN BEATRIX (photo: Frank Lose)

MARRAKECH (photo: Richard Seville)

12.2013 home port Naples / 23.4.–2.10.2014 service
Ancona—Split / 24.10.2014 entered service Colon—
Cartagena under charter by Ferry Xpress / 1.6.2015
service Barcelona—Mahón under charter by Acciona
Trasmediterranea /

ms MARRAKECH
IMO No. 8412819
Comanav, Casablanca
Chantiers de l'Atlantique, St. Nazaire; Yard No.: N28

11515 GT / 1770 tdw / 126.78 m length oa /
20.01 (20.35) m beam / two 9-cyl. diesels;
B&W Atlantique/ 9000 kW / 2 screws / 19.5 kn /
634 pass. in 185 cabins / 224 cars, 365 lane metres /

23.11.1985 launched / 2.5.1986 delivered / 21.5.1986
maiden voyage in service Tangier—Sète / 2002
summer ferry service Tangier—Genoa, otherwise
service Tangier—Sète / 6.1.2012 after bankruptcy of
shipping company arrested in Sète / 4.2014 compulsory
auction / 14.5.2014 towed from Sète to Casablanca,
and laid up /

ms HOMERIC

IMO No. 8407735
Home Lines, Panama
Jos. L. Meyer, Papenburg; Yard No.: 610

42 092 GT / 5157 tdw / 204.00 m length oa /
29.00 (29.73) m beam / two 10-cyl. diesels geared
to 2 screws; MAN B&W / 23 800 kW / 19 kn /
1132 pass. in 552 cabins / crew 468

28.9.1985 launched / 26.12.1985 first sea trials /
6.5.1986 delivered, then cruises / 27.11.1988
WESTERDAM, Holland America Line, Nassau /
30.10.1989–12.3.1990 lengthened at Jos. L. Meyer,
Papenburg: 53 872 GT, 5340 tdw, 243.20 m length
oa, 1494 (1773) pass. in 747 cabins, crew 642, then
Caribbean and Alaska cruises / 1996 home port Rotterdam / 4.2002 **COSTA EUROPA**, Costa Crociere, Genoa /
27.4.2002 first cruise from Genoa / 26.2.2010 collided

THOMSON DREAM ex HOMERIC (photo: George Koutsoukis)

with pier when berthing in Sharm El-Sheikh; three crew
members killed as a result of water ingress / 22.4.2010
THOMSON DREAM, home port Valletta, cruises under
charter by Thomson Cruises / 6.2012 54 763 GT /

ms PETER PAN

IMO No. 8502391
TT-Line, Hamburg
Seebeckwerft, Bremerhaven; Yard No.: 1058

31 356 GT / 5180 tdw / 161.53 m length oa /
27.60 (28.20) m beam / four 8-cyl. diesels geared
to 2 screws; MaK / 19 570 kW / 21.5 kn /
1320 pass. in 489 cabins, 425 pass. unberthed /
550 cars, 1410 lane metres / crew 200

30.11.1985 launched / 30.5.1986 delivered / 2.6.1986–
31.8.1993 service Travemünde—Trelleborg / 1.9.1993
SPIRIT OF TASMANIA, Transport Tasmania, Hobart /
29.11.1993 entered service Melbourne—Devonport /
2001 1279 pass. in 491 cabins, 98 pass. unberthed /
1.9.2002 last voyage in service Melbourne—Devon-
port / 7.9.2002 laid up in Sydney / 13.12.2002 to
Fjord Line, Bergen / 22.12.2002 renamed **SPIR** /
28.1.2003 arrival in Frederikshavn, conversion at
Ørskov Staalskibsværft / 30.3.2003 renamed **FJORD
NORWAY** / 8.4.2003 entered service Bergen—
Egersund—Hanstholm / 17.11.2005 entered service
Bergen—Stavanger—Newcastle, then also Bergen—
Egersund—Hanstholm / 12.10.2006 last voyage for
Fjord Line / 16.10.2006 **PRINCESS OF NORWAY**,
DFDS Seaways, Copenhagen / 9.11.2006 again service
Bergen—Haugesund—Stavanger—Newcastle /
29.5.2007 entered service Newcastle—IJmuiden /
17.2.2011 renamed **PRINCESS SEAWAYS** /

PRINCESS SEAWAYS ex PETER PAN (photo: Frank Lose)

KING SEAWAYS ex NILS HOLGERSSON (photo: Hans-Joachim Hellmann)

ms NILS HOLGERSSON

IMO No. 8502406
Swedcarrier, Trelleborg
Seebeckwerft, Bremerhaven; Yard No.: 1059

31 395 GT / 4160 tdw / 161.45 m length oa /
27.60 (32.01) m beam / four 8-cyl. diesels geared
to 2 screws; Krupp-MaK / 19 570 kW / 21 kn /
1320 pass. in 489 cabins, 280 pass. unberthed /
550 cars, 1410 lane metres / crew 205

16.8.1986 launched / 20.2.1987 delivered to
Walleniusrederierna, under charter by Swedcarrier /
26.2.1987–21.12.1992 service Travemünde—Trelleborg for TT-Line / 13.1.1993 **VAL DE LOIRE**, Brittany
Ferries, Morlaix / 5.1993 after conversion at INMA,
La Spezia: 4110 tdw, 1683 pass. in 543 cabins,
454 pass. unberthed, 570 cars, 1250 lane metres /
9.6.1993 entered service Plymouth—Santander, then
also service Plymouth—Roscoff—Cork, in winter also
Caen—Portsmouth / 2004 31 788 GT / 5.4.2004
entered service Portsmouth—Cherbourg/St. Malo /
9.2004–19.2.2006 exclusively service St. Malo—
Portsmouth / 27.2.2006 **KING OF SCANDINAVIA**,
DFDS Seaways, Copenhagen / 11.3.2006 entered
service IJmuiden—Newcastle / 27.1.2011 renamed
KING SEAWAYS /

SNAV SARDEGNA ex OLAU HOLLANDIA (photo: Kai Ortel)

SNAV LAZIO ex OLAU BRITANNIA (photo: Frank Heine)

Portsmouth—Cherbourg under charter by P&O European Ferries / 22.6.1994–30.9.2005 service Portsmouth—Le Havre / 1.10.2005 laid up in Falmouth / 30.12.2005 **SNAV LAZIO**, SNAV / 26.3.2006 home port Naples / 29.4.2006 entered service Civitavecchia—Palermo / 6.2008 service Civitavecchia—Olbia / 1.10.2010–28.7.2015 service Naples—Palermo / 31.7.–8.8.2015 service Bari—Durres, then again service Naples—Palermo /

ms MUKRAN
IMO No. 8311883
VEB Deutfracht/Seereederei, Rostock
VEB Mathias Thesen Werft, Wismar; Yard No.: 321

22 404 GT / 12 019 tdw / 190.50 m length oa / 26.00 (28.00) m beam / four 6-cyl. diesels geared to 2 screws; SKL / 10 600 kW / 16 kn / 12 pass. in 6 cabins / 10 rail tracks with 1517 m length, ca. 103 wagons / crew 46

27.8.1985 launched as rail cargo ferry / 27.8.1986 delivered / 2.10.1986 maiden voyage in service Mukran—Klaipeda / 1988 21 890 GT / 18.6.1990 to Deutsche Seereederei Rostock / 8.1990 conversion for carrying trucks / 1.1.1994 to Euroseabridge Eisenbahnfährschiffsges., Rostock / 30.1.–7.9.1995 conversion into passenger ship at Gdansk Shiprepair Yard Remontowa: 25 353 GT, 140 pass. in cabins, renamed **PETERSBURG** / 8.9.1995 entered service Travemünde—St. Petersburg / 19.3.1996 entered service Travemünde—Klaipeda / 10.8.–6.11.1996 service Kiel—St. Petersburg / 11.1996 service Travemünde—Klaipeda / 12.1996 service Mukran—Klaipeda / 17.1.1997 home port Monrovia / 1.2.1997 entered service Travemünde—Klaipeda under charter by Scandlines / 1.4.1997 entered service Klaipeda—Mukran / 1.2001 service Kiel—Klaipeda / 1.2003

PETERSBURG ex MUKRAN (photo: Frank Heine)

ms OLAU HOLLANDIA
IMO No. 8712518
Olau Line, Hamburg
Schichau Seebeckwerft, Bremerhaven; Yard No.: 1067

33 336 GT / 5083 tdw / 161.00 m length oa / 29.00 (29.60) m beam / four 8-cyl. diesels geared to 2 screws; Sulzer-Zgoda / 19 600 kW / 21.3 kn / 1720 pass. in 423 cabins / 590 cars, 1510 lane metres / crew 188

25.2.1989 launched / 2.10.1989 christened and delivered / 4.10.1989 maiden voyage in service Vlissingen—Sheerness / 6.1.1993 home port Luxembourg / 3.2.1993 home port Hamburg / 15.5.1994 service discontinued / 3.6.1994 **PRIDE OF LE HAVRE**, home port Portsmouth, then service Portsmouth—Cherbourg under charter by P&O European Ferries / 22.6.1994 entered service Portsmouth—Le Havre / 2001 1354 pass. in 411 cabins, 391 pass. unberthed / 30.9.2005 last voyage in service Le Havre—Portsmouth / 1.10.2005 laid up in Falmouth / 30.12.2005 **SNAV SARDEGNA**, SNAV / 27.3.2006 home port Naples / 15.6.2006 entered service Civitavecchia—Olbia / 1.10.2010 entered service Naples—Palermo / 4.11.2015 entered service Sète—Barcelona—Tangier /

ms OLAU BRITANNIA
IMO No. 8712520
Olau Line, Hamburg
Schichau Seebeckwerft, Bremerhaven; Yard No.: 1068

33 336 GT / 5120 tdw / 161.00 m length oa / 29.00 (29.60) m beam / four 8-cyl. diesels geared to 2 screws; Zgoda-Sulzer / 19 600 kW / 21.3 kn / 1720 pass. in 423 cabins / 590 cars, 1510 lane metres / crew 188

28.10.1989 launched / 16.5.1990 delivered / 18.5.1990 christened in Sheerness / 21.5.1990 maiden voyage in service Sheerness—Vlissingen / 6.1.1993 home port Luxembourg / 3.2.1993 home port Hamburg / 12.5.1994 last voyage in service Vlissingen—Sheerness / 31.5.1994 **PRIDE OF PORTSMOUTH**, home port Portsmouth, then service

service Karlshamn—Liepaja / 2.9.2003 on a voyage from Karlshamn to Liepaja a fire broke out in the engine room, initially towed to Karlshamn, then to Rostock for repairs / 18.12.2003 back in service after repairs / 10.2005 service Karlshamn—Ventspils / 26.10.2005–3.1.2010 service Nynäshamn—Ventspils, then laid up in Szczecin / 11.2010 to Baltic Fleet LLC, St. Petersburg / 26.11.2010 entered service Baltiysk—Ust Luga / 9.6.2012 entered service Sassnitz—Ust Luga / 28.6.2014 entered service Kerch—Novorossiysk / 15.3.2015 entered service Baltiysk—Ust Luga, occasionally also to Sassnitz /

VILNIUS SEAWAYS ex VILNIUS (photo: Frank Lose)

ms VILNIUS

IMO No. 8311900
Lithuanian Shipping Co. (LISCO), Klaipeda
VEB Mathias Thesen Werft, Wismar; Yard No.: 323

21 890 GT / 11 910 tdw / 190.93 m length oa /
28.00 (26.01) m beam / four 16-cyl. diesels geared
to 2 screws; SKL / 21 200 kW / 16.1 kn / 12 pass. in
6 cabins / 10 rail tracks with 1517 m length,
ca. 103 wagons / crew 46

16.4.1987 launched as VILNYUS / 30.10.1987 delivered as VILNIUS, then service Mukran—Klaipeda /
16.7.1993 back in service after conversion at Schooner
Marine, Liverpool: 21 800 GT, 100 pass. in 50 cabins,
20 pass. unberthed, 9 rail tracks with 1290 m length /
6.10.1993 entered service Kiel—Klaipeda / 2000
22 341 GT / 21.6.2003 entered service Riga—Lübeck
under charter by Latlines / 9.7.2006 entered service
Klaipeda—Sassnitz / 4.2007 weekly service Sassnitz—
Baltijsk / 9.1.2011 VILNIUS SEAWAYS, DFDS Seaways,
Klaipeda / 24.7.2012 entered service Kiel—Ust Luga /
23.6.2013 entered service Illichivsk—Poti under charter
by Ukrferry / 2.2014 service Illichivsk—Haydarpasa
(Istanbul) /

ms GREIFSWALD

IMO No. 8311912
VEB Deutfracht/Seereederei, Rostock
VEB Mathias Thesen Werft, Wismar; Yard No.: 324

21 890 GT / 12 019 tdw / 190.90 m length oa /
26.00 (28.00) m beam / four 6-cyl. diesels geared to
2 screws; SKL. / 10 600 kW / 16.4 (17) kn / 12 pass.
in 6 cabins / 10 rail tracks with 1517 m length,
ca. 103 wagons / crew 46

31.5.1988 launched / 25.11.1988 delivered as rail
cargo ferry, then ferry service Mukran—Klaipeda /
8.6.1990 to Deutsche Seereederei, Rostock / 1.1.1994
to Euroseabridge, Rostock / 12.4.1994 delivered
after conversion into freight ferry at Gryfia Shipyard, Szczecin: 24 084 GT, 96 pass. in 48 cabins,
48 trucks + 54 wagons / 13.4.1994 again service
Mukran—Klaipeda / 10.1.1997 home port Monrovia /
13.4.1997 entered service Klaipeda—Travemünde /
12.1.—26.3.1999 service Gothenburg—Kiel under
charter by Stena Line / 2.11.1999 entered service
Kiel—Klaipeda / 3.2001 service Aarhus—Halmstad

GREIFSWALD (photo: Olaf Kuhnke)

under charter by Transocean Shipping / 23.5.2001
laid up in Aarhus / 22.8.2001 entered service Kiel—
St. Petersburg under charter by TransRussia Express /
29.11.2001 entered service Kiel—Klaipeda under
charter by Scandlines / 22.12.2002 laid up in Rostock /
2003 service Illichivsk—Poti under charter by Ukrferry,
home port Batumi / 10.2005 to Ukrferry / 4.2011
home port Panama /

ms KAUNAS

IMO No. 8311924
Lithuanian Shipping Co. (LISCO), Klaipeda
VEB Mathias-Thesen-Werft, Wismar; Yard No.: 325

21 934 GT / 12 020 tdw / 190.93 m length oa /
26.00 (28.00) m beam / four 6-cyl. diesels geared
to 2 screws; SKL / 10 600 kW / 16.1 kn / 12 pass.
in 6 cabins / 10 rail tracks with 1517 m length,
ca. 103 wagons /

13.5.1989 launched / 20.10.1989 delivered as rail
cargo ferry, 21 934 GRT / 1989 service Mukran—
Klaipeda / 8.1990 conversion for carrying trucks on
lower rail deck / 5.4.—6.1994 conversion into RoRo
ferry at Blohm+Voss, Hamburg: 25 606 GT, 210 pass.
in cabins, 460 cars, 9 rail tracks with 1290 m length /
1994 service Kiel—Klaipeda / 2000 162 pass. in 69
cabins, 40 pass. unberthed / 4.2002 service Klaipeda—
Karlshamn / 2003 226 pass. in 77 cabins, 63 pass.
unberthed / 3.2.2004 entered service Lübeck—Riga
under charter by DFDS Tor Line / 1.2005 service

KAUNAS SEAWAYS ex KAUNAS (photo: Frank Lose)

Karlshamn—Klaipeda / 6.2009 laid up in Klaipeda /
25.10.2009—26.1.2010 service Riga—Travemünde /
2.5.—21.12.2010 entered service Liepaja—Travemünde
under charter by Scandlines / 10.3.—10.5.2011 service
Ventspils—Kapellskär under charter by Baltic Scandinavian Lines / 25.5.2011 entered service Kiel—Ust Luga /
5.2012 renamed KAUNAS SEAWAYS / 5.2012 service
Klaipeda—Sassnitz / 30.9.2013 last voyage in service
Sassnitz—Klaipeda, service discontinued / 4.10.2013
entered service Paldiski—Kapellskär / 6.2014 entered
service Ust Luga—Sassnitz—Copenhagen under charter
by Black Sea Ferry & Investments (Russian Railways) /
20.3.2015 laid up in Klaipeda / 5.8.2015 entered service
Illichivsk—Batumi under charter by Ukrferry /

OSCAR WILDE ex KRONPRINS HARALD (photo: Frank Heine)

ms KRONPRINS HARALD
IMO No. 8506311
Jahre Line, Sandefjord
Wärtsilä Marine, Turku; Yard No.: 1292

31 122 GT / 5250 tdw / 166.30 m length oa /
28.41 m beam / two 12-cyl. and two 6-cyl. diesels
geared to 2 screws; Sulzer-Wärtsilä / 19 800 kW /
22 kn / 1440 pass. in 468 cabins / 583 cars,
1220 lane metres / crew 122

31.8.1986 floated out / 19.3.1987 delivered / 26.3.1987
entered service Oslo—Kiel / 5.1989 installation of a
conference centre on the top deck at HDW, Kiel:
31 914 GT, 1481 pass. in 468 cabins / 10.1990 to
Color Line, Oslo / 15.7.1999 grounded in Oslo Fjord.
The ship could free itself, then unloaded in Moss, later
for repairs to Emden / 19.7.1999 back in service
Oslo—Kiel / 2000 1414 pass. in 468 cabins, 50 pass.
unberthed / 22.01.2007 to Irish Ferries, chartered
back by Color Line / 31.8.2007 last voyage Kiel—
Oslo / 10.9.2007 renamed **OSCAR WILDE**, home
port Nassau / 30.11.2007 entered service Rosslare—
Cherbourg/Roscoff /

ms NEW HAMANASU
IMO No. 8604266
Shin Nihonkai Ferry, Otaru
Ishikawajima-Harima H.I., Aioi; Yard No.: 2961

17 261 GRT / 6965 tdw / 184.51 m length oa /
26.51 m beam / two 9-cyl. diesels geared to
2 screws; Pielstick-Ishikawajima / 21 850 kW /
22.5 kn / 172 pass. in 46 cabins, 748 pass.
unberthed / 103 cars, 1350 lane metres / crew 58

11.11.1986 launched / 20.3.1987 completion, then
service Niigata—Otaru / 17 304 GRT / 1999 service
Tomakomai—Akita—Niigata—Tsuruga / 2001
17 311 GRT / 10.2002 **UTOPIA**, Orient Ferry, service
Shimonoseki—Tsingtao, 26 906 GT, 6473 tdw / 9.2006
service Shimonoseki—Taicang, 26 933 GT, later again
service Shimonoseki—Tsingtao / 26.12.2015 ferry
service discontinued / 12.2015 laid up /

ms NEW SHIRAYURI
IMO No. 8604278
Shin Nihonkai Ferry, Otaru
Ishikawajima-Harima H.I., Aioi; Yard No.: 2948

17 261 GRT / 6965 tdw / 184.51 m length oa /
26.51 m beam / two 9-cyl. diesels geared
to 2 screws; Pielstick-Ishikawajima /
19 670 kW / 22.6 kn / 172 pass. in 47 cabins,
748 pass. unberthed / 103 cars, 1350 lane metres /
crew 58

5.2.1987 launched / 20.4.1987 delivered, then service
Otaru—Niigata / 1999 service Tomakomai—Akita—
Niigata—Tsuruga / 2001 17 309 GRT / 2002 laid
up / 6.2005 **UTOPIA 2**, Shanghai-Shimonoseki Ferry,
Panama, then service Shimonoseki—Shanghai /
7.10.2009 laid up in Aioi /

UTOPIA ex NEW HAMANASU (photo: Richard Seville)

UTOPIA 2 ex NEW SHIRAYURI (photo: Osamu Taniguchi)

NISSOS SAMOS ex NEW AKASHIA as IONIAN QUEEN (photo: Frank Lose)

OCEAN GRAND ex FERRY LAVENDER (photo: Jonathan Boonzaier)

FERRY AZALEA (photo: Tsuyoshi Ishiyama)

FERRY SHIRAKABA (photo: Tsuyoshi Ishiyama)

ms NEW AKASHIA

IMO No. 8712635
Shin Nihonkai Ferry, Otaru
Ishikawajima-Harima H.I., Kure; Yard No.: 2972

19 796 GRT / 7622 tdw / 192.90 m length oa /
29.40 m beam / two 8-cyl. diesels geared to
2 screws; Pielstick / 17 480 kW / 21.8 kn / 220 pass.
in cabins, 580 pass. unberthed / 80 cars,
1860 lane metres / crew 59

27.4.1988 launched / 1988 delivered, then service
Maizuru—Otaru / 11.2004 **IONIAN GLORY**, Endeavor
Lines, Kingstown / 4.2005 renamed **IONIAN QUEEN**,
home port Limassol, 30 708 GT / 20.8.2005 entered
service Patras—Corfu—Igoumenitsa—Bari, later
service Patras—Kefalonia—Igoumenitsa—Corfu—
Brindisi / 2009 30 435 GT / 11.9.2012 after bankruptcy
of shipping company arrested in Patras / 12.2015
auctioned to Hellenic Seaways, Piraeus / 12.2015
renamed **NISSOS SAMOS**, service Piraeus—Chios—
Mytilene planned /

ms FERRY LAVENDER

IMO No. 9006629
Shin Nihonkai Ferry, Otaru
Ishikawajima-Harima H.I., Tokyo; Yard No.: 3012

19 904 GRT / 7689 tdw / 192.91 m length oa /
29.40 m beam / two 8-cyl. diesels geared to
2 screws; Pielstick / 17 480 kW / 21.8 kn / 316 pass.
in 85 cabins, 480 pass. unberthed / 226 cars /
crew 57

1.3.1991 launched / 21.9.1991 completion, then service
Maizuru—Otaru / 11.2004 **IONIAN KING**, Agoudimos
Lines, Piraeus / 22.8.2005 home port Limssol, 30 413 GT,
entered service Patras—Corfu—Igoumenitsa—Bari,
later service Patras—Kefalonia—Igoumenitsa—
Corfu—Brindisi / 16.9.2011 **VICTORY STEP**, Shenghao
Marine Hong Kong, Panama / 17.10.2011 **OCEAN
ROSE**, Huis Ten Bosch, Panama / 29.2.–13.10.2012
service Nagasaki—Shanghai / 1.2013 conversion in
Busan / 8.8.2013 renamed **OCEAN GRAND**, stationary
casino ship at Batam, Indonesia /

ms FERRY AZALEA

IMO No. 9066772
Shin Nihonkai Ferry, Otaru
Ishikawajima-Harima H.I., Tokyo; Yard No.: 3039

20 554 GT / 7440 tdw / 195.46 m length oa /
29.40 m beam / two 9-cyl. diesels geared to
2 screws; Pielstick-Diesel United / 23 800 kW /
22.7 kn / 638 pass. in 135 cabins, 288 pass.
unberthed / 80 cars, 1860 lane metres / crew 70

1.10.1993 launched / 15.4.1994 delivered, then
service Niigata—Otaru / 2002 service Tomakomai—
Akita—Niigata—Tsuruga / 2003 20 558 GT /

ms FERRY SHIRAKABA

IMO No. 9066784
Shin Nihonkai Ferry, Otaru
Ishikawajima-Harima H.I., Tokyo; Yard No.: 3040

20 552 GT / 7427 tdw / 195.46 m length oa /
29.40 m beam / two 9-cyl. diesels geared to
2 screws; Pielstick-Diesel United / 23 800 kW /
22.7 kn / 638 pass. in 118 cabins, 288 pass.
unberthed / 180 trucks + 80 cars / crew 70

13.1.1994 launched / 7.1994 delivered, then service
Niigata—Otaru / 2002 service Tomakomai—Akita—
Niigata—Tsuruga / 2003 20 558 GT /

PRIDE OF BRUGES ex NORSUN (photo: Frank Lose)

PRIDE OF YORK ex NORSEA (photo: Frank Heine)

ms NORSEA

IMO No. 8501957
North Sea Ferries, Hull
Govan Shipbuilders, Glasgow; Yard No.: 265

31 785 GT / 6403 tdw / 179.20 m length oa /
25.09 (25.40) m beam / two 9-cyl. and two
6-cyl. diesels geared to 2 screws; Wärtsilä-Sulzer /
18 390 kW / 18.5 kn / 1124 pass. in 268 cabins,
134 pass. unberthed / 850 cars, 2250 lane metres /
crew 107

9.9.1986 launched / 2.5.1987 delivered / 8.5.1987
maiden voyage in service Hull—Rotterdam / 1998 to
P&O North Sea Ferries, Hull / 1.12.2001 last voyage
Hull—Rotterdam / 1.3.2002 entered service Hull—
Zeebrugge / 2.9.2002 fire in engine room extinguished
with shipboard equipment / 9.9.2002 after repair again
in service Hull—Zeebrugge / 22.01.2003 renamed
PRIDE OF YORK / 29.11.2011 home port Nassau /

ms FERRY DIAMOND

IMO No. 8604333
Diamond Ferry, Oita
Kurushima Dockyard Co., Onishi; Yard No.: 2472

9023 GRT / 4000 tdw / 150.88 m length oa /
25.01 m beam / two 8-cyl. diesels geared to
2 screws; MAN-Mitsubishi / 17 652 kW /
22 (24.6) kn / 98 pass. in 36 cabins, 867 pass.
unberthed / 50 cars, 105 trucks /

5.8.1986 launched / 11.1986 delivered, then service
Kobe—Imabari—Matsuyama—Oita / 12.2007 **CHINA
DIAMOND**, Bright Searoad Corp., Panama / 3.2011
SECHANG CORDELIA, Se Chang Shipping, Jeju;
15 561 GT, service Pyeongtaek—Jeju / 3.2013 **PORT
LINK III**, ASDP Indonesia Ferry, Panama, service
Merak—Bakauheni /

ms NORSUN

IMO No. 8503797
North Sea Ferries, Rotterdam
Nippon Kokan, Yokohama; Yard No.: 1033

31 589 GT / 6403 tdw / 179.35 m length oa /
25.09 (25.35) m beam / two 9-cyl. and two
6-cyl. diesels geared to 2 screws; Sulzer-Wärtsilä /
19 200 kW / 18.5 kn / 1138 pass. in 264 cabins,

152 pass. unberthed / 850 cars, 2250 lane metres /
crew 107

29.8.1986 launched / 31.3.1987 delivered / 2.4.1987
transfer voyage to Rotterdam with 800 export cars /
12.5.1987 maiden voyage in service Rotterdam—Hull /
1998 to P&O North Sea Ferries, Rotterdam / 29.4.2001
last voyage Hull—Rotterdam / 2.7.2001 entered service
Zeebrugge—Hull / 15.1.2003 renamed **PRIDE OF BRUGES** /

PORT LINK III ex FERRY DIAMOND as CHINA DIAMOND (photo: Olaf Schmidt)

ST. MICHAEL THE ARCHANGEL ex BLUE DIAMOND (photo: Irvine Kinea)

ms BLUE DIAMOND
IMO No. 9000455
Diamond Ferry, Oita
Shin Kurushima Dockyard, Onishi; Yard No.: 2671

9447 GRT / 3773 tdw / 150.87 m length oa /
25.00 m beam / two 14-cyl. diesels geared to
2 screws; Sulzer-Hitachi / 21 420 bhp / 22.2 kn /
98 pass. in 24 cabins, 844 pass. unberthed /
50 cars, 900 lane metres /

19.4.1990 launched / 17.7.1990 delivered, then
service Kobe—Imabari—Matsuyama—Oita / 2008
QUEEN MARY, Sea World Express Ferry, Mokpo, after
conversion 1650 pass., then service Jeju—Mokpo /
1.2011 QUEEN, Negros Navigation, Phnom-Penh /
2011 home port Cebu / 3.2011 renamed ST. MICHAEL
THE ARCHANGEL; 17 781 GT, then service Manila—
Iloilo, also service Bacolod—Cagayan de Oro /

ms STAR DIAMOND
IMO No. 8847595
Diamond Ferry, Oita
Kurushima Dockyard, Onishi; Yard No.: 2672

9463 GRT / 3781 tdw / 150.87 m length oa /
25.00 m beam / two 14-cyl. diesels geared to
2 screws; Hitachi Zosen / 21 420 bhp / 22.2 kn /
485 pass. in cabins, 457 pass. unberthed /
260 cars, 900 lane metres /

1.1991 delivered, then service Kobe—Oita / 1.2008
JIADONG PEARL, Weihai Jiadong Intl. Shipping,
Panama, then service Weihai—Pyeongtaek / 29.6.2009
entered service Sokcho—Niigata—Troitsa / 9.2009
GWANGYANG BEECH, Gwangyang Ferry Co., Jeju;

ST. FRANCIS XAVIER ex STAR DIAMOND (photo: Mike Baylon)

15 071 GT / 23.1.2011 entered service Gwangyang—
Shimonoseki—Moji / 3.2011 service Gwangyang—
Shimonoseki / 1.2014 ST. FRANCIS XAVIER, 2Go
Travel, Cebu / 2014 service Manila—Cebu /

ms SUN FLOWER NISHIKI
IMO No. 9042764
Kansai Kisen Kaisha, Osaka
Kanasahi Co. Ltd., Toyohashi; Yard No.: 3285

9684 GRT / 3520 tdw / 150.87 m length oa /
25.00 m beam / two 14-cyl. diesels geared to
2 screws; Sulzer-Hitachi / 21 420 bhp / 22.1 kn /
942 pass. unberthed / 60 cars, 100 trucks /

6.9.1992 launched / 12.1992 delivered / 19.12.1992–
1.2010 service Osaka—Beppu / 3.2010 SUPERFERRY
21, Aboitiz Transport System, Manila; 19 468 GT /
1.2011 to Negros Navigation Co., Manila / 2012
ST. LEO THE GREAT, 2Go Travel, Manila /

ST. LEO THE GREAT ex SUN FLOWER NISHIKI (photo: Irvine Kinea)

ms STENA GERMANICA

IMO No. 7907659
Stena Line, Gothenburg
Stocznia im. Komuny Paryskiej, Gdansk;
Yard No.: B494/01

24 967 GRT / 4500 tdw / 175.37 m length oa /
28.52 (29.04) m beam / four 16-cyl. diesels geared
to 2 screws; Sulzer-Zgoda / 29 420 kW / 21.5 kn /
2204 pass. in 610 cabins, 196 pass. unberthed /
700 cars, 1700 lane metres / crew 145

22.8.1981 launched as **STENA SCANDINAVICA** /
11.1986 renamed **STENA GERMANICA** / 4.1987
delivery with delay of four years / 7.4.1987 entered
service Gothenburg—Kiel, in summer also Gothenburg—Frederikshavn / 2–4.1988 conversion work
at Cityvarvet, Gothenburg: 26 071 GRT, 2372 pass. /
1.1993 conversion at HDW, Kiel: additional cabin
section for 42 pass. / 1995 GT 38 772 / 22.2.–26.3.1999
conversion at Cityvarvet, Gothenburg: removal of
80 cabins for additional stowage space in car deck
(additional 18 trucks), fitting of sponsons, 39 178 GT /
beam 30.46 (30.82) m / 30.8.2010 last voyage in
service Gothenburg—Kiel / 7.9.2010 renamed **STENA
VISION**, home port Karlskrona / 2.11.2010 after conversion at Cityvarvet, Gothenburg 39 191 GT, 1854 pass.
in 489 cabins, 360 cars, 2300 lane metres / 4.11.2010
entered service Gdynia—Karlskrona /

ms STENA SCANDINAVICA

IMO No. 7907661
Stena Line, Gothenburg
Stocznia Gdanska im. Lenina, Gdansk;
Yard No.: B494/02

26 088 GRT / 4500 tdw / 175.39 m length oa /
28.49 (29.01) m beam / four 16-cyl. diesels geared
to 2 screws; Sulzer-Zgoda / 29 420 kW / 18.5 kn /
2204 pass. in 610 cabins, 196 pass. unberthed /
700 cars, 1700 lane metres / crew 145

16.4.1983 launched as **STENA GERMANICA** / 11.1986
renamed **STENA SCANDINAVICA** / 1.12.1987 arrival
for remaining work at Citivarvet, Gothenburg /
1.1988 completion / 10.2.1988 christened in Kiel /
29.2.1988 maiden voyage in service Gothenburg—
Kiel, in summer also Gothenburg—Frederikshavn /
1.1992 installation of additional cabin section for 42
pass.; 26 593 GRT / 1995 38 756 GT / 12.1.–13.2.1999

STENA VISION ex STENA GERMANICA (photo: Frank Lose)

STENA SPIRIT ex STENA SCANDINAVICA (photo: Frank Heine)

removal of 80 cabins on upper car deck at Öresundsvarvet, Landskrona to create space for additional 18
trucks, fitting of sponsons; 39 169 GT / 18.4.2011
last voyage in service Kiel—Gothenburg / 22.6.2011
renamed **STENA SPIRIT**, home port Nassau /
11.06.2011 delivered after conversion at Cityvarvet,

Gothenburg: 39 191 GT, 1854 pass. in 489 cabins, 360
cars, 2214 lane metres / 27.6.2011 entered service
Karlskrona—Gdynia /

ms EL. VENIZELOS

IMO No. 7907673
ANEK Lines, Chania
Stocznia im. Komuny Paryskiej, Gdansk;
Yard No.: 494/03

38 261 GT / 4500 tdw / 175.40 m length oa /
28.50 m beam / four 16-cyl. diesels geared to
2 screws; Sulzer-Zgoda / 34 130 kW / 20 kn /
1600 pass. in 650 cabins, 1400 pass. unberthed /
750 cars, 1650 lane metres /

28.10.1984 launched, originally planned as STENA
POLONICA. Work on the ship ordered by Stena Line
in 1979 was discontinued in summer 1984; the launch
served merely to clear the slipway / 1988 sale of
unfinished ship to Fred. Olsen, renamed **BONANZA**,
then laid up in Poland / 1989 to ANEK Lines, Chania /
16.2.1989 arrival under tow in Eleusis, then laid
up / 11.1989 towed for further construction work to
Perama / 6.1990 renamed **KYDON II** / 18.7.1990 for
further construction to Avlis Shipyard, Chalkis / 6.1992
delivered as **EL. VENIZELOS** / 8.7.1992 entered service
Patras—Igoumenitsa—Corfu—Trieste, in winter
service Piraeus—Heraklion / 6.2000 whole-year service

EL. VENIZELOS (photo: Frank Heine)

SEOKYUNG PARADISE ex FERRY MUROTO (photo: Vladimir Tonic)

Piraeus—Heraklion / from 11.2002 mainly in winter service Piraeus—Chania, interrupted by service / summer 2003 service Patras—Igoumenitsa—Corfu—Trieste / 22.6.–17.9.2004 service Tunis—Genoa/Marseilles under charter by Cotunav / 10.1.–5.2005 service Patras—Igoumenitsa—Corfu—Venice / 2005–2011 in winter service Piraeus—Chania for ANEK Lines, in summer service Tunis—Genoa/Marseilles under charter by Cotunav / 4.6.2012–25.5.2013 service Piraeus—Chania / 25.5.–6.10.2013 service Marseilles—Tunis under charter by SNCM Ferryterranee, occasionally also service Marseilles—Corsica, then laid up in Perama / 15.7.–28.8.2014 service Livorno—Olbia under charter by Goin Sardinia / 2.9.–14.9.2014 service Piraeus—Chania, then laid up in Perama / 14.8.2015 first voyage carrying refugees from Kos and Mytilene to Piraeus /

ms FERRY MUROTO
IMO No. 8705319
Muroto Kisen, Kochi
Kurushima Dockyard Co., Kurushima; Yard No.: 2516

6472 GRT / 2713 tdw / 127.41 m length oa / 23.02 m beam / two 7-cyl. diesels geared to 2 screws; Pielstick-Ishikawajima / 16402 kW / 2 screws / 21 kn / 332 pass. in cabins, 535 pass. unberthed / 48 cars, 63 trucks /

7.1987 delivered, then service Kobe—Ashizuri / 2002 FERRY COSMO, Cosmo Shipping, Panama / 2002 renamed HUADONG PEARL, service Shidao—Incheon under charter by Huadong Ferry / 2006 NEW DONG CHUN, Dong Chun Ferry, Panama, 12961 GT / 4.2006 service Vladivostok—Zarubino—Sokcho / 2014 SEOKYUNG PARADISE, Seo Kyung Shipping, Busan, service Busan—Jeju / 3.7.2015 laid up in Busan /

ms VARUNA
IMO No. 8616336
Higashi Nihon Ferry, Muroran
Mitsubishi H.I., Shimonoseki; Yard No.: 899

16725 GRT / 6005 tdw / 187.13 m length oa / 27.01 m beam / two 8-cyl. diesels geared to 2 screws; MAN-Mitsubishi / 21180 kW / 2 screws / 23.5 kn / 448 pass. in 88 cabins, 232 pass. unberthed / 116 cars, 1760 lane metres / crew 50

31.3.1987 launched / 10.7.1987 delivered, then service Oarai—Muroran / 1989 service Sendai—Tomakomai /

1998 SUPERFERRY HELLAS, Strintzis Lines, Piraeus, after conversion in Perama 27230 GT, 532 pass. in 172 cabins, 144 Pullman, 824 pass. unberthed, 900 cars, crew 80 / 6.1.1999 entered service Patras—Igoumenitsa—Corfu—Ancona, also to Venice /

BLUE HORIZON ex VARUNA (photo: Frank Heine)

2000 BLUE HORIZON, Blue Ferries, Piraeus / 9.2003 service Patras—Igoumenitsa—Bari / 10.2009 service Piraeus—Santorini—Kos—Rhodes / 4.2010 service Piraeus—Chania / 28.4.2011 laid up in Drapetsona, later in Syros / 11.4.2013 again service Piraeus—Santorini—Kos—Rhodes / 5.2015 service Piraeus—Heraklion /

ms VICTORY
IMO No. 8814263
Higashi Nihon Ferry, Muroran
Mitsubishi H.I., Kobe; Yard No.: 1174

17113 GRT / 6737 tdw / 187.13 m length oa / 27.00 m beam / two 8-cyl. diesels geared to 2 screws; MAN-Mitsubishi / 21180 kW / 23.5 kn / 448 pass. in 88 cabins, 232 pass. unberthed / 116 cars, 1760 lane metres / crew 50

19.3.1989 launched / 10.7.1989 delivered, then service Muroran—Oarai / 9.1998 to Grandi Navi Veloci, Palermo / 16.10.1998 arrival at T. Mariotti, Genoa for conversion: 27100 GT, 406 pass. in 110 cabins, 544 deck pass., 1600 lane metres / 3.1999 service Livorno—Palermo / 8.2.2003 entered service Genoa—Tunis / 2003 27362 GT / 15.9.2007 entered

CARIBBEAN FANTASY ex VICTORY (photo: Michael Segeth)

service Genoa—Barcelona—Tangier / 8.2.2008
CHIHUAHUA STAR, Baja Ferries, La Paz / 2008 service
La Paz—Topolobampo/Mazatlan / 16.3.2010 entered
service Santo Domingo—Mayaguez—San Juan as
cargo ferry under charter by America Cruise Ferries /
1.6.2011 also for passengers / 7.2011 renamed
CARIBBEAN FANTASY, home port Panama /

ms KISO
IMO No. 8704406
Taiheiyo Ferry, Nagoya
Mitsubishi H.I., Shimonoseki; Yard No.: 902

13 608 GRT / 7150 tdw / 192.51 m length oa /
27.01 (27.28) m beam / two 8-cyl. diesels geared to
2 screws; MAN-Mitsubishi / 17 210 kW / 21.5 kn /
252 pass. in 62 cabins, 598 pass. unberthed /
110 cars, 165 trucks / crew 59

NISSOS RODOS ex KISO (photo: Tony Davis)

KITAKAMI (photo: Tsuyoshi Ishiyama)

1.7.1987 launched / 20.10.1987 delivered, then service
Nagoya—Sendai—Tomakomai / 1991 13 691 GRT /
1993 13 730 GRT / 8.2004 **OCEAN TRAILER**, Hellas
Ferries, Limassol / 1.2005 to Hellenic Seaways, Piraeus,
cargo ferry service Corinth—Porto Marghera / 4.6.2005
entered service Genoa—Barcelona under charter by
Grandi Navi Veloci / 2007 service Livorno—Palermo /
10.2007 end of Grandi Navi Veloci charter / 29.10.2007
renamed **HELLENIC VOYAGER** / 11.2007 cargo ferry
service Corinth—Porto Marghera for Hellenic Seaways /

11.6.2010 first voyage in passenger ferry service
Piraeus—Rhodes—Kos; 29 733 GT, 6148 tdw, 176
pass. in 62 cabins, 1524 pass. unberthed, 103 cars,
2105 lane metres / 13.3.2011 laid up in Perama /
1.9.2012–23.5.2013 service Iskenderun—Port Said
under charter by Sisa Shipping / 6.7.2013 laid up in
Perama / 11.9.2013 again cargo ferry service Corinth—
Porto Marghera / 15.6.2015 entered service Piraeus—
Syros—Mykonos—Patmos—Ag. Kirykos—Vathi—
Chios—Mytilene—Limnos—Kavala /

ms KITAKAMI
IMO No. 8815073
Taiheiyo Ferry, Nagoya
Mitsubishi H.I., Shimonoseki; Yard No.: 926

13 818 GRT / 6748 tdw / 192.50 m length oa /
27.00 (27.26) m beam / two 8-cyl. diesels geared to
2 screws; MAN-Mitsubishi / 21 190 kW / 21.5 kn /
242 pass. in 62 cabins, 598 pass. unberthed /
147 cars, 165 trucks / crew 60

22.4.1989 launched / 12.10.1989 delivered, then
service Nagoya—Sendai—Tomakomai / 1995
13 937 GRT /

ms SOVEREIGN OF THE SEAS
IMO No. 8512281
Royal Caribbean Cruise Line, Oslo
Chantiers de l'Atlantique, St. Nazaire; Yard No.: A29

73 192 GT / 7283 tdw / 268.33 m length oa /
32.21 m beam / four 9-cyl. diesels geared to
2 screws; Pielstick-Alstom / 20 480 kW / 21 kn /
2276 (2524) pass. in 1138 cabins / crew 750

4.4.1987 floated out / 19.12.1987 delivered / 21.12.1987
transfer voyage St. Nazaire—Miami / 15.1.1988 christened in Miami / 16.1.1988 first cruise from Miami /
2005 home port Nassau / 7.11.2008 **SOVEREIGN**,
Pullmantur Cruises, Valletta; 73 529 GT / 13.12.2008
first cruise to Brazil under charter by CVC / 23.3.2009
first Mediterranean cruise for Pullmantur Cruises /

SOVEREIGN ex SOVEREIGN OF THE SEAS (photo: Frank Lose)

ms MONARCH OF THE SEAS
IMO No. 8819500
Royal Caribbean Cruise Line, Oslo
Chantiers de l'Atlantique, St. Nazaire; Yard No.: A30

73 937 GT / 8600 tdw / 268.32 m length oa /
32.00 (36.00) m beam / four 9-cyl. diesels geared to
2 screws; Pielstick-Alstom / 21 680 kW / 21.25 kn /
2354 (2744) pass. in 1177 cabins / crew 780

21.9.1990 floated out / 3.12.1990 delivery delayed
by six months due to a major fire caused by welding
work / 10.1991 completion, then Caribbean cruises /
2005 home port Nassau / 29.3.2013 last cruise
Port Canaveral—Bahamas / 3.4.2013 MONARCH,
Pullmantur Cruises, Valletta / 27.4.2013 first cruise
Colon—Caribbean /

MONARCH ex MONARCH OF THE SEAS (photo: Cees Bustraan)

MAJESTY OF THE SEAS (photo: Andy Hernandez)

ms MAJESTY OF THE SEAS
IMO No. 8819512
Royal Caribbean Cruise Line, Oslo
Chantiers de l'Atlantique, St. Nazaire; Yard No.: B30

73 937 GT / 8600 tdw / 268.32 m length oa /
32.20 (36.00) m beam / four 9-cyl. diesels geared to
2 screws; Pielstick-Atlantique / 21 840 kW / 20 kn /
2354 (2524) pass. in 1177 cabins / crew 780

29.8.1991 floated out / 27.3.1992 delivered / 26.4.1992
christened in Miami, then Caribbean cruises / 2005
home port Nassau / 2009 74 077 GT /

ms OSADO MARU
IMO No. 8705747
Sado Kisen, Ryotsu
Kanda Zosensho, Kawajiri; Yard No.: 308

10 811 GRT / 1506 tdw / 131.91 m length oa /
21.01 m beam / two 9-cyl. diesels geared to
2 screws; Pielstick-Niigata / 8840 kW / 20 kn /
1525 pass. unberthed / 190 cars, 360 lane metres /

9.9.1987 launched / 27.1.1988 delivered, then service
Ryotsu—Niigata / 1996 11 085 GRT / 2009 5973 GRT /
2014 SAGITA, Brother Stars Maritime SA, Malakal

Harbor / 2014 renamed MARIA, home port Tanjung
Priok / 2014 service Merak—Bakauheni / 8.2015
renamed SMS SAGITA, home port Jakarta, 5373 GT /

SMS SAGITA ex OSADO MARU as OSADO MARU (photo: Hiroyuki Yoshimoto)

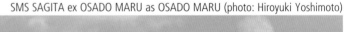

SUPERSTAR LIBRA ex SEAWARD (photo: Jonathan Boonzaier)

ms SEAWARD
IMO No. 8612134
Kloster Cruise, Nassau
Wärtsilä, Turku; Yard No.: 1294

42 276 GT / 3500 tdw / 216.17 m length oa /
32.63 m beam / four 8-cyl. diesels geared to 2
screws; Wärtsilä-Sulzer / 18 476 kW / 20 kn /
1798 pass. in 774 cabins / crew 609

14.11.1987 launched / 16.5.1988 delivered / 26.5.1988
christened in New York, then Caribbean cruises /
1997 **NORWEGIAN SEA**, Norwegian Cruise Line,
Nassau / 9.2005 **SUPERSTAR LIBRA**, Star Cruises,
Nassau / 2.10.2005 first cruise Mumbai—Goa /
1.2006 42 285 GT /

ms CROWN ODYSSEY
IMO No. 8506294
Royal Cruise Line, Piraeus
Jos. L. Meyer, Papenburg; Yard No.: 616

34 242 GT / 5186 tdw / 187.71 m length oa /
28.21 m beam / two 8-cyl. and two 6-cyl. diesels
geared to 2 screws; MaK / 21 300 kW / 22.5 kn /
1209 pass. in 526 cabins / crew 443

1.11.1987 floated out / 14.5.1988 christened / 6.1988
delivered / 4.6.1988 transfer voyage Emden—Tilbury /
7.6.1988 first Baltic cruise from Tilbury / 1990 home
port Nassau / 1996 to Kloster Cruise, Nassau / 5.1996
NORWEGIAN CROWN, Norwegian Cruise Line, Nassau /
5.2000 **CROWN ODYSSEY**, managed by Orient Lines /
2.2003 renamed **NORWEGIAN CROWN**, conversion
at Singapore Technologies Marine: spa area enlarged,
installation of further balconies / 15.9.2003 first cruise
for NCL from Baltimore to New England / 5.2006 to Fred.
Olsen Cruise Lines, chartered back by NCL / 5.11.2007
renamed **BALMORAL** / 16.11.2007–24.1.2008
lengthening by 30 m at Blohm+Voss, Hamburg:
43 537 GT, 217.91 m length oa, 20 kn, 1402 pass. in
746 cabins / 13.2.2008 first cruise Dover—Caribbean /

ms NEW SETO
IMO No. 8618152
Hankyu Ferry, Kobe
Kanda Zosensho, Kawajiri; Yard No.: 306

12 589 GRT / 4926 tdw / 174.50 m length oa /
26.80 m beam / two 8-cyl. diesels geared to
2 screws; MAN-Mitsubishi / 18 000 kW / 22.6 kn /
432 pass. in cabins, 768 pass. unberthed /
75 cars, 1500 lane metres / crew 39

2.4.1988 launched / 23.6.1988 delivered, then service
Kobe—Kokura / 1991 service Kobe—Shin Moji / 1995
service Izumiotsu—Shin Moji / 9.2003 **SUPERFERRY 18**,
WG&A, Manila, 336 pass. in cabins / 2.2004 deployed
on various ferry services between the islands of the
Philippines / 1.2007 **ASIA PEARL**, PacificAsia Shipping,
Panama / 3.2008 **HUADONG PEARL VI**, Huadong Ferry,
Panama, 19 534 GT, service Shidao—Incheon /

BALMORAL ex CROWN ODYSSEY (photo: Alexander Brede)

HUADONG PEARL VI ex NEW SETO (photo: Klas Brogren)

ms VENILIA
IMO No. 8718471
Higashi Nihon Ferry, Hakodate
Mitsubishi H.I., Shimonoseki; Yard No.: 915

6340 GRT / 3334 tdw / 134.60 m length oa /
21.00 (21.35) m beam / two 14-cyl. diesels
geared to 2 screws; Pielstick-Nippon / 11 380 kW /
20.75 kn / 600 pass. unberthed / 20 cars,
900 lane metres / crew 33

2.4.1988 launched / 2.7.1988 delivered, then service
Hakodate—Aomori / 1994 6327 GRT / 1995 **DA-IN**,
Da-In Ferry, Panama, 12 365 GT / 7.10.1995 entered
service Dalian—Incheon / 2015 **MUTIARA SENTOSA 1**,
Atosim Lampung Pelayaran, Panjang / 7.2015 service
Panjang—Tanjung Perak /

MUTIARA SENTOSA ex VENILIA as DA-IN (photo: collection Ton Grootenboer)

AMORELLA (photo: Frank Lose)

ms AMORELLA
IMO No. 8601915
SF Line, Mariehamn
Brodogradevna Industrija Split, Split; Yard No.: 356

34 384 GT / 3690 tdw / 169.40 m length oa /
27.61 (28.20) m beam / four 12-cyl. diesels
geared to 2 screws; Pielstick-Wärtsilä / 23 760 kW /
21.5 kn / 2112 pass. in 564 cabins, 88 pass.
unberthed / 450 cars, 970 lane metres /

11.7.1987 launched / 28.9.1988 delivered / 14.10.1988
entered service Turku—Mariehamn—Stockholm for
Viking Line / 1.2.1993 ran aground in the Stockholm
archipelago, then to Turku for repairs / 12.4.1995
to Viking Line, Mariehamn / 2003 1986 pass. in
564 cabins, 434 pass. unberthed / 14.12.2013 ran
aground off Långnäs, on same day to Rauma for
repairs / 22.12.2013 again in service Stockholm—
Mariehamn—Turku /

ISABELLE ex ISABELLA (photo: Frank Heine)

ms ISABELLA
IMO No. 8700723
SF Line, Mariehamn
Brodogradevna Industrija Split, Split; Yard No.: 357

34 384 GT / 3680 tdw / 169.40 m length oa /
27.60 (28.20) m beam / four 12-cyl. diesels
geared to 2 screws; Pielstick-Wärtsilä / 23 760 kW /
21.5 kn / 2112 pass. in 564 cabins, 88 pass.
unberthed / 364 cars, 970 lane metres /

13.8.1988 launched / 6.1989 delivered / 4.7.1989
maiden voyage in service Stockholm—Naantali for
Viking Line / 13.8.1990 entered service Helsinki—
Muuga (Tallinn) / 1993 34 937 GT / 7.10.1994 entered
service Helsinki—Stockholm / 12.4.1995 registered
for Viking Line, Mariehamn / 1.5.1997 entered service
Turku—Mariehamn—Stockholm / 1999 34 386 GT /
4.2000 after installation of sponsons at the stern
35 154 GT / 11.2.2013 laid up in Turku / 22.4.2013
ISABELLE, Tallink, Riga / 6.5.2013 entered service
Riga—Stockholm /

ms FRANS SUELL
IMO No. 8917601
Euroway, Malmö
Brodogradevna Industrija Split, Split; Yard No.: 372

35 285 GT / 2962 tdw / 169.40 m length oa /
27.60 (28.20) m beam / four 12-cyl. diesels
geared to 2 screws; Pielstick-Alstom / 23 750 kW /
21.5 kn / 2188 pass. in 678 cabins, 212 pass.
unberthed / 400 cars, 970 lane metres /

23.1.1991 launched / 5.5.1992 delivered / 19.5.1992
maiden voyage in service Malmö—Travemünde,
in winter service Malmö—Travemünde—Lübeck /
1.9.1993–12.3.1994 service Copenhagen—Malmö—
Travemünde—Lübeck / 3.1994 after fitting of sponsons
at stern: 35 492 GT, 171.32 m length oa / 30.3.1994
renamed SILJA SCANDINAVIA / 31.3.1994–3.4.1997
service Turku—Mariehamn—Stockholm under charter
by Silja Line / 4.1997 GABRIELLA, Viking Line,
Mariehamn / 17.4.1997 entered service Helsinki—
Stockholm / 30.6.1999 entered service Helsinki—
Mariehamn—Stockholm / 2001 2170 pass. in 678
cabins, 230 pass. unberthed / from 2014 in summer
additional service Helsinki—Tallinn /

GABRIELLA ex FRANS SUELL (photo: Frank Lose)

ms CROWN OF SCANDINAVIA
IMO No. 8917613
DFDS, Copenhagen
Brodogradevna Industrija Split, Split; Yard No.:373

35 285 GT / 2940 tdw / 169.40 m length oa /
27.60 (28.20) m beam / four 12-cyl. diesels geared
to 2 screws; Pielstick / 23 760 kW / 18 kn / 2026
pass. in 637 cabins, 110 pass. unberthed / 450 cars,
970 lane metres /

6.4.1992 launched for Euroway, originally planned
as THOMAS MANN for service Malmö—Lübeck /
7.6.1994 delivered to DFDS Seaways, Copenhagen /
16.6.–23.7.1994 final fitting out at Lloyd Werft,
Bremerhaven / 26.7.1994 christened in Copenhagen,
then maiden voyage in service Copenhagen—Helsingborg—Oslo / 15.10.2006 service Copenhagen—Oslo /
14.1.2012 renamed CROWN SEAWAYS /

CROWN SEAWAYS ex CROWN OF SCANDINAVIA (photo: Frank Lose)

HUCKLEBERRY FINN ex NILS DACKE (photo: Frank Lose)

ms NILS DACKE
IMO No. 8618358
Scandinavian Ferry Lines, Trelleborg
Schichau Seebeckwerft, Bremerhaven; Yard No.: 1063

24 745 GT / 7426 tdw / 177.20 m length oa /
26.00 (26.50) m beam / two 6-cyl. and two
8-cyl. diesels geared to 2 screws; MAN B&W /
14 810 kW / 20 kn / 284 pass. in 122 cabins /
2250 lane metres, 5 rail tracks with 790 m length /
crew 40

9.4.1988 launched / 28.10.1988 delivered to Rederi
AB Swedcarrier / 31.10.1988 maiden voyage in service
Travemünde—Trelleborg for TT-Line / 1.1.1992 to
Rederi AB Gotland, continued service for TT-Line /
1.1.1993 to TT-Line, home port Nassau / 17.5.–
27.8.1993 conversion into passenger ferry at Kværner
Masa-Yards, Turku: 30 825 GT, 1020 pass. in 307
cabins, 24 pass. unberthed, 80 trucks, renamed
PETER PAN / 1.9.1993 again service Travemünde—
Trelleborg / 27.10.2001 renamed PETER PAN IV /
10.11.2001–1.2002 converted back into cargo ferry
in Bremerhaven: 26 478 GT, 6176 tdw, 14 800 kW,
20 kn, 2000 lane metres, 400 pass. in 134 cabins, crew
36, renamed HUCKLEBERRY FINN / 17.1.2002 home
port Trelleborg / 19.1.2002 entered service Rostock—
Trelleborg / 7.1.2014 also service Trelleborg—Travemünde and Trelleborg—Swinoujscie /

ms ROBIN HOOD

IMO No. 8703232
TT-Line, Hamburg
Schichau Seebeckwerft, Bremerhaven; Yard No.: 1064

24 728 GT / 8900 tdw / 177.20 m length oa /
26.00 (26.50) m beam / two 6-cyl. and two
8-cyl. diesels geared to 2 screws; MAN B&W /
14 800 kW / 20 kn / 284 pass. in 122 cabins /
2250 lane metres, 5 rail tracks with 790 m length /
crew 40

10.9.1988 launched / 28.1.1989 maiden voyage
in service Travemünde—Trelleborg / 7.12.1992–
30.3.1993 conversion into passenger ferry at Kværner
Masa-Yards, Turku: 30 740 GT, 1020 pass. in 307
cabins, 25 pass. unberthed, 98 trucks, renamed
NILS HOLGERSSON / 2.4.1993–23.7.2001 service
Travemünde—Trelleborg / 29.7.2001–12.10.2001
converted back into cargo ferry in Bremerhaven:
26 478 GT, 6176 tdw, 2000 lane metres, 400 pass.
in 134 cabins, crew 36, renamed **TOM SAWYER** /
15.10.2001 entered service Rostock—Trelleborg /
12.2010 home port Rostock / 7.1.2014 also
service Trelleborg—Travemünde and Trelleborg—
Swinoujscie /

TOM SAWYER ex ROBIN HOOD (photo: Frank Lose)

ms ROYAL VIKING SUN

IMO No. 8700280
Royal Viking Line, Nassau
Wärtsilä, Turku; Yard No.: 1296

37 845 GT / 6150 tdw / 204.00 m length oa /
28.90 (32.32) m beam / four 8-cyl. diesels geared
to 2 screws; Sulzer-Wärtsilä / 21 120 kW / 21.8 kn /
768 pass. in 383 cabins / crew 469

5.1988 floated out / 26.11.1988 delivered / 8.1.1989
christened in San Francisco, then cruises / 1994 to Cunard
Line, Nassau / 4.4.1996 after grounding in Red Sea
sprang a leak, towed to Sharm El-Sheikh, later arrested
because of destruction of a fish-breeding reef / 22.4.1996
departed to Valletta for repairs / 12.6.1996 again in
service / 26.11.1999 **SEABOURN SUN**, Seabourn Cruise
Line, Nassau / 23.4.2002 to Holland America Line, Rotterdam / 3.6.2002 renamed **PRINSENDAM** / 13.6.2002 first
cruise from Southampton / 2004 37 983 GT / 1.2010
after conversion at Grand Bahama Shipyard, Freeport
39 051 GT, 835 pass. in 419 cabins /

PRINSENDAM ex ROYAL VIKING SUN (photo: Kai Ortel)

PACIFIC PEARL ex STAR PRINCESS (photo: Clyde Dickens)

NEW BLUE OCEAN ex NEW ORION as NEW QINGDAO (photo: Jukka Huotari)

ms STAR PRINCESS
IMO No. 8611398
Princess Cruises, Monrovia
Chantiers de l'Atlantique, St. Nazaire;
Yard No.: B29

63 524 GT / 7506 tdw / 245.60 m length oa /
32.20 m beam / four 8-cyl. diesels with 38 880 kW;
MAN B&W / four generators connected to two
elec. motors / 24 000 kW / 2 screws / 19.5 (21) kn /
1621 pass. in 735 cabins / crew 634

28.5.1988 launched as **SITMAR FAIRMAJESTY** for
Sitmar Cruises / 1.9.1988 to P&O Cruises / 4.3.1989
delivered / 23.3.1989 christened **STAR PRINCESS** in
Fort Lauderdale, then cruises / 23.6.1995 grounded
during an Alaska cruise and later repaired in Portland
until 8.1995 / 11.1997 conversion at Harland & Wolff,
Belfast: 63 524 GT, 1500 (1650) pass. in 748 cabins,
crew 650 / 12.1997 **ARCADIA**, P&O Cruises, London /
3.–4.2003 conversion at Lloyd Werft, Bremerhaven,
renamed **OCEAN VILLAGE** / 6.5.2003–21.10.2010
cruises for Ocean Village / 11.–12.2010 conversion
at Sembawang, Singapore / 21.12.2010 **PACIFIC**

PEARL, P&O Cruises Australia, London; 63 786 GT.
South Pacific cruises /

ms OHKOH MARU (no photo)
IMO No. 8817057
Satokuni Kisen, Kobe
Imbari Zosen, Imabari; Yard No.: 473

4575 GRT / 5132 tdw / 135.74 m length oa /
20.00 m beam / one 7-cyl. diesel; B&W / 6782 kW /
1 screw / 18 kn / 62 trucks, paper reels /

26.9.1988 launched / 19.11.1988 delivered as
RoRo cargo ship to Satokuni Kisen, service Tokyo—
Hitachi—Tomakomai under charter by Kawasaki
Kinkai Kinsen / 1.2000 **YING HUA**, Shadong Bohai
Ferry, Yantai / 2008 conversion into ferry: 10 903 GT,
653 pass., 62 cars, 940 lane metres / 2008 service
Dalian—Yantai /

ms NEW ORION
IMO No. 8800755
K.K. Meimon Taiyo Ferry, Osaka
Onomichi Zosen, Onomichi; Yard No.: 332

9317 GRT / 4429 tdw / 160.00 m length oa /
25.00 m beam / two 8-cyl. diesels geared to
2 screws; Ishikawajima Harima / 19 418 kW /
2 screws / 22.9 (26) kn, 828 pass. unberthed /
410 cars, 1400 lane metres /

22.11.1988 launched / 11.3.1989 delivered, then
service Osaka—Shin Moji / 12.1993 renamed **FERRY
FUKUOKA** / 7.2002 **SUPERFERRY 16**, WG&A, Manila /
6.2007 **NEW QINGDAO**, Chang Myung Shipping,
Panama, then service Qingdao—Kwangyang / 2008
16 485 GT / 7.2008 renamed **QUEEN QINGDAO** /
28.7.2009 entered service Sokcho—Niigata—
Zarubino under charter by Northeast Asia Ferry /
3.2013 renamed **NEW BLUE OCEAN** / 21.3.2013
entered service Sokcho—Zarubino—Vladivostok
under charter by Dae Stena Line / 6.2014 laid up in
Sokcho / 11.2015 to 2Go Travel, Cebu / 2016 renamed
ST. THERESE OF THE CHILD JESUS /

SASSNITZ (photo: Frank Lose)

YONG XIA ex ERIMO MARU as NEW GOLDEN BRIDGE VI (photo: Klas Brogren)

ms ERIMO MARU

IMO No. 8806840
Nippon Enkai Ferry, Tokyo
Ishikawajima-Harima H.I., Tokyo ; Yard No.: 2979

11 272 GRT / 5729 tdw / 178.00 m length oa /
25.00 (26.70) m beam / two 9-cyl. diesels geared
to 2 screws; Pielstick-IHI / 21 840 kW / 23 kn /
634 pass. unberthed / 105 cars, 1961 lane metres /
crew 50

25.10.1988 launched / 17.3.1989 delivered, then
service Tokyo—Tomakomai / 1.11.1990 to Blue
Highway Line, Tokyo / 22.1.1991 renamed **SUN
FLOWER ERIMO** / 1997 service Osaka—Shibushi /
9.2003 **FERRY COSMO 5**, Cosmo Shipping, Panama,
15 139 GT / 4.2004 **SHUTTLE OITA**, Shuttle Highway
Line, Yokosuka, service Oita—Kurihama / 6.2005
renamed **SHUTTLE YOKOSUKA** / 2007 **NGB 6**, Vision
Sea, Panama / 4.2008 **NEW GOLDEN BRIDGE VI**,
Weidong Ferry Co., Panama, then service Incheon—
Qingdao / 9.2009 **YONG XIA**, Rongcheng Great
Dragon Shipping, Panama, 25 151 GT, then service
Pyeongtaek—Longyan (Rongcheng) for Dalong Ferry /
11.2014 home port Jeju /

ms PALLADIO

IMO No. 8705694
Adriatica di Navigazione, Venice
Fincantieri-Cant. Nav. Italiani, Ancona; Yard No.: 5864

10 977 GT / 2501 tdw / 122.88 m length oa /
19.41 m beam / two 6-cyl. diesels geared to
2 screws; GMT Fincantieri / 6180 kW / 17 kn /
348 pass. in 172 cabins, 752 pass. unberthed /
276 cars, 400 lane metres / crew 55

20.10.1988 launched / 18.3.1989 delivered, then
service Brindisi—Corfu—Igoumenitsa—Patras, later
alternating Adriatic service between Italy, Croatia,
Albania and Greece / 2000 334 pass. in 138 cabins,
754 pass. unberthed / 11.2004 to Sicilia Regionale
Marittima (SI.RE.MAR), Venice / 2005 home port
Palermo, sporadic service Naples—Aeolian Islands—
Milazzo, otherwise laid up /

PALLADIO (photo: Frank Heine)

ms SASSNITZ

IMO No. 8705383
Deutsche Reichsbahn, Saßnitz
Aalborg Værft, Aalborg; Yard No.: 690

20 276 GRT / 5050 tdw / 171.50 m length oa /
23.80 (24.05) m beam / four 12-cyl. diesels geared
to 2 screws; S.K.L-Halberstadt / 18 000 kW /
17.8 (20) kn / 56 pass. in 24 cabins, 744 pass.
unberthed / 140 cars or 24 trucks, 5 rail tracks
with 711 m length for approx. 56 freight or
23 passenger wagons / crew 110

24.6.1988 launched, then to Frederikshavn for final
fitting out / 25.11.1988 christened / 19.3.1989
maiden voyage in service Saßnitz—Trelleborg /
1.1.1993 to DFO Deutsche Fährgesellschaft Ostsee,
Rostock / 2.3.–25.3.1994 modernised at Lloyd Werft,
Bremerhaven: 20 445 GT / 1995 21 154 GT / 4.11.1995
on a voyage from Sassnitz to Trelleborg improperly
secured rail wagons broke free during a storm and
nearly caused the ship to capsize, significant damage /
1997 to Scandlines, Sassnitz / 1.7.2001 a fire in the
engine room could be extinguished with shipboard
equipment, then to Sassnitz for repairs / 18.7.2001
again in service Sassnitz—Trelleborg; 3100 tdw, 819
pass. unberthed / 11.10.2012 to Stena Line, Sassnitz /

SANSOVINO ex SANSOVINO (photo: Frank Lose)

LAURANA (photo: Frank Heine)

MARIA I, G-Lines, Monrovia / 12.2007 service Bari—Durres / 8.2008 laid up with engine damage off Elefsina / 6.2009 again service Bari—Durres / 21.7.–19.11.2009 service Barletta/Bari—Durres, then laid up in Bari, later in Drapetsona and Elefsina with engine damage / 10.11.2010 to Ricardo Shipping, Monrovia / 24.11.2010 renamed **ADRIATICA KING** / 7.2011 after repair service Bari—Durres / 8.2011 laid up with engine damage in Durres / 14.8.–10.2012 service Bari—Durres, then again laid up in Durres / 6.2014 **SANSOVINO**, Siremar, Limassol / 8.2014 service Porto Empedocle—Linosa—Lampedusa /

ms LAURANA
IMO No. 9011014
Adriatica di Navigazione, Venice
Fincantieri-Cant. Nav. Italiani, Palermo;
Yard No.: 5908

10 977 GT / 2523 tdw / 122.00 m length oa / 19.40 m beam / two 6-cyl. diesels geared to 2 screws; GMT Fincantieri/ 7060 kW / 17 kn / 348 pass. in 138 cabins, 752 pass. unberthed / 276 cars, 400 lane metres / crew 55

15.2.1992 launched / 26.9.1992 delivered, then service Brindisi—Corfu—Igoumenitsa—Patras, later alternating Adriatic service between Italy, Croatia, Albania and Greece / 11.2004 to Sicilia Regionale Marittima (SI.RE.MAR), Venice / 2005 home port Palermo / 7.2005 service Milazzo—Aeolian Islands—Naples /

ms FUJI MARU
IMO No. 8700474
Mitsui O.S.K. Passenger Line, Tokyo
Mitsubishi H.I., Kobe; Yard No.: 1177

23 340 GT / 4613 tdw / 167.00 m length oa / 24.00 (27.00) m beam / two 8-cyl. diesels; Mitsubishi / 13 390 kW / 2 screws / 20 kn / 603 pass. in 163 cabins / crew 135

10.9.1988 launched / 19.4.1989 delivered / 29.4.1989 maiden cruise from Tokyo / 2000 23 235 GT/ 10.2001 to Nippon Charter Cruise, Tokyo / 10.12.2013 **MIRA 1**, Mira Cruise Co., Panama / 11.12.2013 arrival at Tsuneishi Shipbuilding, conversion into floating health clinic / 4.2015 commissioning planned but not realised /

MIRA 1 ex FUJI MARU as FUJI MARU (photo: Hiroyuki Yoshimoto)

ms SANSOVINO
IMO No. 8705709
Adriatica di Navigazione, Venice
Fincantieri-Cant. Nav. Italiani, Ancona;
Yard No.:5865

10 977 GT / 2300 tdw / 122.80 m length oa / 19.41 m beam / two 6-cyl. diesels geared to 2 screws; GMT Fincantieri / 6180 kW / 17 kn / 334 pass. in 138 cabins, 754 pass. unberthed / 275 cars, 400 lane metres / crew 55

23.3.1989 launched / 9.1989 delivered, then service in the Adriatic Seas / 7.2003 service Porto Empedocle—Lampedusa under charter by Siremar / 11.2004 to Sicilia Regionale Marittima (SI.RE.MAR), Venice / 7.2005 service Porto Empedocle—Linosa—Lampedusa, home port Palermo / 11.2007 **SANTA**

Star Cruises, Panama / 10.1993 converted into cruise ship at Sembawang Shipyard, Singapore: 40022 GT / 12.1993 renamed **LANGKAPURI STAR AQUARIUS**, then short cruises from Singapore / 1999 cruises from Keelung to Ishigaki and Naha / 26.2.2001 **AQUARIUS**, DFDS, Copenhagen, then conversion in Aalborg and Hamburg: 40039 GT, 178.4 m length oa, 2166 pass. in 703 cabins, 350 cars, 1008 lane metres / 7.5.2001 renamed **PEARL OF SCANDINAVIA** / 26.6.2001 entered service Copenhagen—Helsingborg—Oslo / 15.10.2006 only service Copenhagen—Oslo / 19.1.2011 renamed **PEARL SEAWAYS** / 1.2014 conversion at Fayard, Lindø: 40231 GT /

PEARL SEAWAYS ex ATHENA (photo: Raoul Fiebig)

ms **KALYPSO**
IMO No. 8710857
Rederi AB Slite, Slite
Masa-Yards, Turku; Yard No.: 1298

40012 GT / 2800 tdw / 176.75 m length oa / 29.61 (34.00) m beam / four 9-cyl. diesels geared to 2 screws; Wärtsilä-Sulzer / 23760 kW / 22 kn / 1950 pass. in 650 cabins, 250 pass. unberthed / 490 cars, 1120 lane metres /

27.9.1989 launched / 30.4.1990 delivered / 1.5.1990 entered service Stockholm—Mariehamn—Turku for Viking Line / 7.4.1993 after bankruptcy of owner charted by Viking Line and continued in service / 31.12.1994 last voyage for Viking Line, then conversion at Finnyards, Rauma / 13.1.1994 **STAR PISCES**, Star Cruises, Panama, then short cruises from Hong Kong / 2003 40053 GT, 2165 pass. in 829 cabins / 1.2014 home port Nassau /

ms **ATHENA**
IMO No. 8701674
Rederi AB Slite, Slite
Wärtsilä Marine, Turku; Yard No.: 1297

40012 GT / 2800 tdw / 176.60 m length oa / 29.60 (34.00) m beam / four 9-cyl. diesels geared to 2 screws; Wärtsilä-Sulzer / 23760 kW / 21.3 kn /

1728 pass. in 573 cabins, 472 pass. unberthed / 620 cars, 1120 lane metres /

22.10.1988 floated out / 21.4.1989 delivered / 18.4.1989 maiden voyage to Slite / 24.4.1989–16.8.1993 24-hr. cruises Stockholm—Mariehamn for Viking Line / 16.8.1993 after bankruptcy of owner laid up in Stockholm / 23.9.1993 **STAR AQUARIUS**,

STAR PISCES ex KALYPSO (photo: Vladimir Tonic)

ms DANIELLE CASANOVA
IMO No. 8705395
Soc. Nationale Maritime Corse Méditerranée, Ajaccio
Chantiers de l'Atlantique, St. Nazaire;
Yard No.: C29

21 317 GRT / 3452 tdw / 165.54 m length oa /
27.40 (29.40) m beam / four 18-cyl. diesels geared
to 2 screws; Pielstick-Atlantique / 35 770 kW /
23 kn / 1836 pass. in 539 cabins, 936 pass.
unberthed / 804 cars, 800 lane metres / crew 169

15.12.1988 launched / 5.1989 delivered, then
service Marseilles/Nice/Toulon—Corsica / 9.1990
troop carrier in Gulf War, 30 985 GT / 2000 1832
pass. in 539 cabins, 600 pass. unberthed / 5.2002
renamed **MEDITERRANEE** / 24.6.2002 entered service
Marseilles—Tunis /

MEDITERRANEE ex DANIELLE CASANOVA (photo: Frank Heine)

SHIDAO ex ORANGE ACE as ORANGE ACE (photo: shipyard)

ms ORANGE ACE
IMO No. 88189158
Shikoku Kaihatsu Ferry K.K., Toyo
Imabari Zosen K.K., Imabari;
Yard No.: 478

7318 GRT / 2902 tdw / 147.22 m length oa /
23.50 m beam / two 12-cyl. diesels geared to
2 screws; Ishikawajima-Harima H.I. / 13 240 kW /
21 (23.59) kn / 204 pass. in cabins, 400 pass.
unberthed / 214 cars, 1000 lane metres /

7.1989 delivered, then service Osaka/Kobe—
Toyo—Niihama / 3.2005 **FERRY NADESHIKO 3**, Asia
International Ferry, Panama / 9.2005 renamed
HUADONG PEARL II, then service Incheon—Shidao /
2008 **SHIDAO**, Chang Myung Shipping, Jeju / 2008
17 022 GT, service Shidao—Gunsan for Shidao Int.
Ferry /

BRETAGNE (photo: Frank Lose)

ms BRETAGNE
IMO No. 8707329
Brittany Ferries, Morlaix
Chantiers de l'Atlantique, St. Nazaire;
Yard No.: D29

25 015 GRT / 2950 tdw / 151.20 m length oa /
26.00 (29.25) m beam / four 12-cyl. diesels;
Wärtsilä-Crepelle / 18 020 kW / 2 screws / 19.5 kn /
1146 pass. in 367 cabins, 910 pass. unberthed /
580 cars, 745 lane metres /

4.2.1989 launched / 13.7.1989 delivered / 16.7.1989
maiden voyage in service Plymouth—Santander, also
service Plymouth—Roscoff and Roscoff—Cork /
14.6.1993 entered service St. Malo—Portsmouth, until
1997 in winter also service Portsmouth—Santander /
1994 24 534 GT /

ms CINDERELLA

IMO No. 8719188
SF Line, Mariehamn
Wärtsilä Marine, Turku; Yard No.: 1302

46 398 GT / 4228 tdw / 191.00 m length oa /
29.00 (35.84) m beam / four 12-cyl. diesels geared
to 2 screws; Sulzer-Wärtsilä / 28 780 kW / 22 kn /
2734 pass. in 876 cabins / 480 cars, 1130 lane
metres / crew 224

15.4.1989 floated out / 7.11.1989 delivered / 8.11.1989
maiden voyage in service Helsinki—Stockholm for
Viking Line / 1993 2766 pass. in 914 cabins, 44
Pullman / 1.10.1994–1996 in winter day cruises
Helsinki—Muuga (Tallinn), in summer service Turku—
Mariehamn—Stockholm / 20.8.1996–16.8.2003

VIKING CINDERELLA ex CINDERELLA (photo: Marko Stampehl)

WIND SURF ex CLUB MED 1 (photo: Frank Heine)

CLUB MED 2 (photo: Frank Heine)

service Helsinki—Muuga / 1.9.2003 renamed **VIKING
CINDERELLA**, home port Stockholm / 4.9.2003 24-hr.
cruises Stockholm—Mariehamn /

ms CLUB MED 1

IMO No. 8700785
Services et Transports Cruise Line
(Club Méditerranée), Nassau
Ateliers et Chantiers du Havre, Le Havre;
Yard No.: 274

14 745 GT / 1654 tdw / 187.20 m length oa /
20.00 m beam / 2500 m² sail area / four 6-cyl.
diesels with 9720 kW; Wärtsilä-Duvant Crepelle /
four generators connected to two elec.
motors geared to 2 screws / 3680 kW / 15 kn
(10 under sail) / 402 (409) pass. in 201 cabins /
crew 207

23.12.1988 launched as **LA FAYETTE** / 29.12.1989
delivered as **CLUB MED 1**, then cruises / 4.1997 to
Windstar Cruises, Nassau / 4.1998 renamed **WIND
SURF**, 312 (366) pass. in 156 cabins, crew 163 /
11.2006 home port Rotterdam / 3.2007 home port
Nassau /

ms CLUB MED 2

IMO No. 9007491
Services et Transports Cruise Line
(Club Méditerranée), Le Havre
Ateliers et Chantiers du Havre, Le Havre;
Yard No.: 282

14 983 GT / 1674 tdw / 187.20 m length oa /
20.00 m beam / 2500 m² sail area / four 6-cyl.
diesels with 9720 kW; Wärtsilä-Duvant Crepelle /
four generators connected to two elec. motors
geared to 2 screws / 3680 kW / 15 kn (10 under
sail) / 402 (409) pass. in 201 cabins / crew 207

12.7.1991 launched / 25.9.1992 delivered / 10.10.1992
pre-inaugural voyage to Brest / 10.1992 maiden
voyage to New Caledonia, then cruises / 1994 home
port Mata-Utu / 1.1998 deployment in the Caribbean
and the Mediterranean / 2000 in summer for the first
time cruises in Northern Europe /

ms FANTASY

IMO No. 8700773
Carnival Cruise Lines, Monrovia
Masa-Yards, Helsinki; Yard No.: 479

70 367 GT / 7200 tdw / 260.60 m length oa /
31.50 (36.00) m beam / two 8-cyl. and four
12-cyl. diesels with 42 240 kW; Sulzer-Wärtsilä /
six generators connected to two elec. motors
geared to 2 screws / 28 000 kW / 18 kn /
2634 pass. in 1024 cabins / crew 980

9.12.1988 launched / 26.8.1989 christened / 26.1.1990
delivered / 2.3.1990 first cruise from Miami / 4.2000
home port Panama / 12.2007 renamed **CARNIVAL
FANTASY** /

CARNIVAL FANTASY ex FANTASY (photo: Marko Stampehl)

CARNIVAL ECSTASY ex ECSTASY (photo: Marcus Puttich)

ms ECSTASY

IMO No. 8711344
Carnival Cruise Lines, Monrovia
Kværner Masa-Yards, Helsinki; Yard No.: 480

70 367 GT / 7200 tdw / 262.00 m length oa /
31.50 m beam / two 8-cyl. and four 12-cyl. diesels
with 42 240 kW; Sulzer-Wärtsilä / six generators
connected to two elec. motors geared to 2 screws /
28 000 kW / 18 kn / 2634 pass. in 1022 cabins /
crew 980

21.10.1989 floated out / 18.4.1991 delivered /
24.4.1991 transfer voyage to New York / 11.5.1991
christened in New York / 9.6.1991 maiden cruise
from Miami / 20.7.1998 after departing Miami a
fire started in the laundry and spread through the
ventilation system to the aft mooring deck causing
heavy damage, 60 injuries / 18.10.1998 back in
service after repairs / 4.2000 home port Panama /
9.2005 chartered by U.S. government for six months
as accommodation ship for people made homeless by
Hurricane Katrina in New Orleans / 11.2007 renamed
CARNIVAL ECSTASY / 19.9.–17.10.2009 conversion
at Grand Bahama Shipyard, Freeport: 98 cabins being
fitted with balconies / 3.2011 70 526 GT /

CARNIVAL SENSATION ex SENSATION (photo: Jürgen Pfarre)

ms SENSATION

IMO No. 8711356
Carnival Cruise Lines, Panama
Kværner Masa-Yards, Helsinki; Yard No.: 484

70 367 GT / 6870 tdw / 262.00 m length oa /
31.50 m beam / four 12-cyl. and two 8-cyl. diesels
with 42 240 kW; Sulzer-Wärtsilä / six generators
connected to two elec. motors geared to 2 screws /
28 000 kW / 18 (22.1) kn / 2634 pass. in
1024 cabins / crew 900

23.10.1992 floated out / 18.10.1993 delivered /
13.11.1993 christened in Miami / 21.11.1993 maiden
cruise Miami—Caribbean / 2000 home port Nassau /
9.2005 chartered by U.S. government for six months
as accommodation ship for people made homeless by
Hurricane Katrina in New Orleans / 10.2007 renamed
CARNIVAL SENSATION / 8.1.–12.2.2009 conversion
at Grand Bahama Shipyard, Freeport: 98 cabins being
fitted with balconies / 8.2010 70 538 GT /

ms FASCINATION
IMO No. 9041253
Carnival Cruise Lines, Panama
Kværner Masa-Yards, Helsinki; Yard No.: 487

70367 GT / 7180 tdw / 260.80 m length oa /
31.50 m beam / four 12-cyl. and two 8-cyl. diesels
with 42240 kW; Sulzer-Wärtsilä / six generators
connected to two elec. motors geared to 2 screws /
28000 kW / 18 kn / 2624 pass. in 1020 cabins /
crew 980

27.6.1994 delivered, then cruises / 2000 home
port Nassau / 10.2007 renamed CARNIVAL
FASCINATION / 4.1.–31.1.2010 conversion at Grand
Bahama Shipyard, Freeport: 98 cabins being fitted
with balconies; 70538 GT /

CARNIVAL FASCINATION ex FASCINATION (photo: Tony Davis)

CARNIVAL IMAGINATION ex IMAGINATION (photo: Tony Davis)

CARNIVAL INSPIRATION ex INSPIRATION (photo: Hans-Jürgen Amberg)

ms IMAGINATION
IMO No. 9053878
Carnival Cruise Lines, Panama
Kværner Masa-Yards, Helsinki; Yard No.: 488

70367 GT / 7200 tdw / 262.00 m length oa /
31.53 (36.00) m beam / four 12-cyl. and two
8-cyl. diesels with 42240 kW; Sulzer-Wärtsilä /
six generators connected to two elec. motors geared
to 2 screws / 28000 kW / 18 kn / 2624 pass. in
1020 cabins / crew 900

10.1994 floated out / 8.6.1995 delivered / 2.7.1995
christened in Miami, then maiden Caribbean cruise /
2.2000 home port Nassau / 10.2007 renamed CARNIVAL
IMAGINATION /

ms INSPIRATION
IMO No. 9087489
Carnival Cruise Lines, Panama
Kværner Masa-Yards, Helsinki; Yard No.: 489

70367 GT / 7180 tdw / 262.00 m length oa /
31.50 (36.01) m beam / four 12-cyl. and two 8-cyl.
diesels with 42240 kW; Sulzer-Wärtsilä /
six generators connected to two elec. motors
geared to 2 screws / 28000 kW / 22 kn /
2634 pass. in 1020 cabins / crew 920

24.5.1995 floated out / 22.2.1996 delivered / 16.3.1996 christened in Miami, then pre-inaugural cruise / 4.1996 Caribbean cruises from San Juan / 2000 home port Nassau / 10.2007 renamed **CARNIVAL INSPIRATION** /

CARNIVAL ELATION ex ELATION (photo: Marko Stampehl)

ms ELATION
IMO No. 9118721
Carnival Cruise Lines, Panama
Kværner Masa-Yards, Helsinki; Yard No.: 491

70 390 GT / 7498 tdw / 262.00 m length oa /
31.50 (36.01) m beam / six 12-cyl. diesels
with 47 520 kW; Sulzer-Wärtsilä / six generators
connected to two elec. motors / 28 000 kW /
2 Azipod VO / 19.5 (22.3) kn / 2634 pass. in
1020 cabins / crew 920

3.7.1997 floated out / 24.2.1998 delivered / 20.3.1998 first cruise Miami—Los Angeles, then 7-day voyages Los Angeles—Mexico / 12.2007 renamed **CARNIVAL ELATION** /

CARNIVAL PARADISE ex PARADISE (photo: Christina Heinrich)

ms PARADISE
IMO No. 9120877
Carnival Cruise Lines, Panama
Kværner Masa-Yards, Helsinki; Yard No.: 494

70 390 GT / 6894 tdw / 262.00 m length oa /
31.50 (36.10) m beam / six 12-cyl. diesels with
47 520 kW; Sulzer-Wärtsilä / six generators
connected to two elec. motors / 28 000 kW /
2 Azipod VO / 18 (22.5) kn / 2040 (2624) pass.
in 1020 cabins / crew 920

29.1.1998 floated out / 29.10.1998 delivered / 6.12.1998 first 7-day cruise from Miami / 2004 transferred to U.S. West Coast / 10.2007 renamed **CARNIVAL PARADISE** /

HORIZON ex HORIZON (photo: Frank Lose)

ms HORIZON
IMO No. 8807088
Celebrity Cruises, Monrovia
Jos. L. Meyer, Papenburg; Yard No.: 619

46 811 GT / 5550 tdw / 208.00 m length oa /
29.00 (29.32) m beam / two 9-cyl. and two
6-cyl. diesels geared to 2 screws; MAN B&W /
19 980 kW / 22 kn / 1798 pass. in 677 cabins /
crew 642

19.11.1989 floated out / 11.4.1990 christened / 30.4.1990 delivered, then Bermuda- and Caribbean cruises / 2003 home port Nassau / 11.2005 **ISLAND STAR**, Island Cruises, Nassau. Conversion at Grand Bahama Shipyard, Freeport: 47 427 GT, 1875 pass. in 745 cabins, crew 573 / 12.2005 cruises from Rio de Janeiro / 25.3.2006 first Mediterranean cruise from Palma de Mallorca / 3.2009 **PACIFIC DREAM**, Pullmantur Cruises, Valletta / 31.5.2009 first cruise from Lisbon / 13.8.2010 serious engine damage near Lisbon / 11.2010 renamed **HORIZON** / 5.12.2010 first South America cruise under charter by CVC / 8.4.2012 first Mediterranean cruise under charter by CDF Croisières de France /

ZENITH (photo: Frank Heine)

NEW GOLDEN BRIDGE II ex SABRINA (photo: Jonathan Boonzaier)

TIAN REN ex BLUE ZEPHYR (photo: Jukka Huotari)

EMPRESS OF THE SEAS ex NORDIC EMPRESS as EMPRESS (photo: Hans-Joachim Hellmann)

ms ZENITH
IMO No. 8918136
Celebrity Cruises, Monrovia
Jos. L. Meyer, Papenburg; Yard No.: 620

47 255 GT / 4915 tdw / 208.00 m length oa /
29.00 (29.33) m beam / two 9-cyl. and two
6-cyl. diesels geared to 2 screws; MAN B&W /
19 980 kW / 21.4 kn / 1774 pass. in 687 cabins /
crew 640

15.2.1992 undocked / 22.2.1992 sea trials / 2.3.1992
delivered / 4.4.1992 first cruise from Florida / 2004
home port Nassau / 13.4.2007 last cruise for
Celebrity Cruises from Tampa to Bayonne / 6.2007 to
Pullmantur Cruises, Valletta. 47 413 GT / 11.6.2007
first cruise from Barcelona / 25.6.2013 engine
room fire in the Adriatic Sea, towed to Marg hera /
1.7.–21.7.2013 repair at Fincantieri, Trieste /
22.4.2014 first Mediterranean cruise under charter
by CDF Croisières de France /

ms SABRINA
IMO No. 8902345
Kinkai Yusen, Tokyo
Kanda Zosensho, Kawajiri; Yard No.: 330

12 521 GRT / 6281 tdw / 186.50 m length oa /
24.80 (24.98) m beam / two 9-cyl. diesels geared
to 2 screws; Pielstick-Diesel United / 17 530 kW /
23.5 kn / 64 pass. in 32 cabins, 630 pass.
unberthed / 170 trucks + 140 cars / crew 53

13.12.1989 launched / 5.1990 delivered, then service
Tokyo—Kushiro / 2000 NEW GOLDEN BRIDGE II,
Weidong Ferry, Panama / 2000 service Incheon—
Weihai; 26 463 GT /

ms BLUE ZEPHYR
IMO No. 9802357
Kinkai Yusen, Tokyo
Kanda Zosensho, Kawajiri; Yard No.: 331

12 521 GRT / 6000 tdw / 186.50 m length oa /
24.50 (24.98) m beam / two 9-cyl. diesels geared
to 2 screws; Pielstick-Diesel United / 17 530 kW /
23 kn / 64 pass. in 32 cabins, 630 pass. unberthed /
170 trucks + 140 cars / crew 53

27.3.1990 launched / 1990 delivered, then service
Tokyo—Kushiro / 1996 12 524 GRT / 1999 TIAN REN,
Jinchon Ferry, Panama, service Incheon—Xingang /
2000 26 463 GT /

ms NORDIC EMPRESS
IMO No. 8716899
Royal Caribbean Cruise Line, Monrovia
Chantiers de l'Atlantique, St. Nazaire; Yard No.: G29

48 563 GT / 4978 tdw / 210.81 m length oa /
30.70 (34.40) m beam / two 8-cyl. diesels geared
to 2 screws; Wärtsilä-Duvant Crepelle / 16 200 kW /
19.5 kn / (2284) pass. in 805 cabins / crew 640

25.8.1989 launched, originally ordered as FUTURE
SEAS by Admiral Cruises / 31.5.1990 delivered /
25.6.1990 first cruise Miami—Bahamas / 2002
home port Nassau / 5.2004 renamed EMPRESS OF
THE SEAS / 24.3.2008 EMPRESS, Pullmantur Cruises,
Valletta / 15.3.2008 first Caribbean cruise from
Oranjestad / 2.2016 EMPRESS OF THE SEAS, Royal
Caribbean International / 30.3.2016 first short cruise
from Miami after conversion planned /

PACIFIC JEWEL ex CROWN PRINCESS (photo: Clyde Dickens)

Ordered by Sitmar Cruises / 1988 to P&O / 25.5.1989 floated out / 29.6.1990 delivered / 8.7.1990 first Mediterranean cruise from Piraeus / 13.9.1990 transfer voyage Southampton—New York / 10.1990 first Caribbean cruise / 1992 to Princess Cruises, Monrovia / 2000 home port Hamilton; 70 825 GT / 6.5.–11.6.2002 conversion at Lloyd Werft, Bremerhaven, renamed **A'ROSA BLU**, Seetours, London / 15.6.2002 first cruise Hamburg—Oslo / 4.2004 **AIDABLU**, Aida Cruises, London / 13.–27.4.2004 conversion at Blohm+Voss, Hamburg: 34 new cabins, larger theatre / 27.4.2004 transfer cruise Hamburg—Kiel / 1.5.2004 first cruise from Kiel / 1.11.2004 home port Genoa / 4.2007 **OCEAN VILLAGE TWO**, Ocean Village, London; 70 310 GT / 25.4.2007 first Mediterranean cruise from Southampton / 12.2009 **PACIFIC JEWEL**, P&O Cruises Australia, London / 13.12.2009 first cruise from Sydney /

ms CROWN PRINCESS

IMO No. 8521220
P&O Cruises, Palermo
Fincantieri, Monfalcone; Yard No.: 5839

69 845 GT / 6995 tdw / 245.08 m length oa / 32.25 m beam / four 8-cyl. diesels with 38 880 kW; MAN B&W / four generators connected to two elec. motors / 24 000 kW / 2 screws / 19.5 (22.5) kn / 1900 pass. in 798 cabins / crew 678

ms REGAL PRINCESS

IMO No. 8521232
P&O Cruises, Palermo
Fincantieri, Monfalcone; Yard No.: 5840

69 845 GT / 6896 tdw / 245.10 m length oa / 32.20 (36.00) m beam / four 8-cyl. diesels with 38 880 kW; MAN B&W / four generators connected to two elec. motors / 24 000 kW / 2 screws / 19.5 (22.5) kn / 1900 pass. in 798 cabins / crew 680

29.3.1990 launched. Originally ordered by Sitmar Cruises / 5.6.1991 first sea trials / 20.7.1991 delivered / 1992 to Princess Cruises, Monrovia / 2000 70 285 GT / 2002 home port London / 9.2004 home port Hamilton / 2.11.2007 **PACIFIC DAWN**, P&O Cruises Australia, London / 3.11.2007 first cruise from Sydney /

ms CRYSTAL HARMONY

IMO No. 8806204
Crystal Cruises, Nassau
Mitsubishi H.I., Nagasaki; Yard No.: 2100

48 621 GT / 8642 tdw / 240.90 m length oa / 29.60 (29.84) m beam / four 8-cyl. diesels with 34 560 kW; MAN-Mitsubishi / four generators connected to two elec. motors / 24 000 kW / 2 screws / 22 kn / 960 pass. in 480 cabins / crew 505

30.9.1989 launched / 7.1990 delivered, then worldwide cruises / 26.2.2006 **ASUKA II**, NYK Cruises, Yokohama; 50 142 GT /

PACIFIC DAWN ex REGAL PRINCESS (photo: Dale E. Crisp)

ASUKA II ex CRYSTAL HARMONY (photo: Hiroyuki Yoshimoto)

CRYSTAL SYMPHONY (photo: Tsuyoshi Ishiyama)

AEGEAN PARADISE ex ORIENT VENUS (photo: George Koutsoukis)

26.1.1990 launched / 8.7.1990 delivered, then Pacific cruises / 1992 21 884 GRT / 1994 transferred to Shin Nihonkai Ferry, then managed by Japan Cruise Line / 10.2001 to Nippon Charter Cruise / 2.2002 laid up for sale in Aioi / 9.2005 **CRUISE ONE**, First Cruise One, Nassau / 26.11.2005 start of conversion in Perama / 2006 renamed **DELPHIN VOYAGER** / 15.4.2007 delivered after conversion: 23 287 GT, 4863 tdw, 652 pass. in 326 cabins / 19.5.2007 first cruise from Hamburg under charter by Delphin Kreuzfahrten, some cruises marketed by Hansa Kreuzfahrten / 13.10.2010 end of last cruise for Delphin Kreuz-fahrten after bankruptcy of the company, then laid up in Perama / 21.12.2010 transfer via Suez Canal to CSSC Guangzhou Logxue Shipbuilding in China, there conversion work / 1.2011 **HAINAN EMPRESS**, Hainan Cruise Enterprises, Nassau / 3.2.2011 for two weeks cruises in China for the owner / 3.2011 renamed **HAPPY DOLPHIN** / 30.5.2011 first cruise Venice—Greece under charter by Happy Cruises / 25.9.2011 after bankruptcy of charterer laid up in Venice / 30.09.2011 laid up in Perama / 5.2012 renamed **AEGEAN PARADISE**, Mediterranean cruises under charter by Etstur / 26.9.2015 end of last cruise in Piraeus / 31.10.2015 arrival at Singa-pore Technologies Marine, Singapore for conversion into casino ship / 3.11.2015 to New Century Group Hong Kong Ltd. /

ms NIPPON MARU
IMO No. 8817631
Mitsui O.S.K. Passenger Line, Tokyo
Mitsubishi H.I., Kobe; Yard No.: 1188

21 903 GT / 4840 tdw / 166.65 m length oa / 24.00 (28.00) m beam / two 8-cyl. diesels; Mitsubishi / 15 370 kW / 2 screws / 18 (21.6) kn / 404 (607) pass. in 202 cabins / crew 160

8.3.1990 launched / 22.9.1990 delivered / 27.9.1990 first cruise to Hong Kong and Taiwan / 2001 first world cruise / 6.2010 22 472 GT, 398 (524) pass. /

NIPPON MARU (photo: Hiroyuki Yoshimoto)

ms CRYSTAL SYMPHONY
IMO No. 9066667
Crystal Cruises, Nassau
Kværner Masa-Yards, Turku; Yard No.: 1323

51 044 GT / 4500 tdw / 238.01 m length oa / 30.20 (30.60) m beam / six 9-cyl. diesels with 36 330 kW; Wärtsilä-Sulzer / six generators connected to two elec. motors / 23 000 kW / 2 screws / 22 kn / 975 pass. in 480 cabins / crew 550

8.7.1994 floated out / 18.4.1995 delivered / 2.5.1995 christened in New York / 4.5.1995 maiden cruise through the Panama Canal to San Francisco /

ms ORIENT VENUS
IMO No. 8902333
Japan Cruise Line, Osaka
Ishikawajima-Harima H.I., Tokyo ; Yard No.: 2987

21 906 GRT / 4277 tdw / 174.00 m length oa / 24.00 m beam / two 12-cyl. diesels geared to 2 screws; Pielstick-United / 12 600 kW / 21 (22.56) kn / 626 pass. in 194 cabins / crew 120

VOYAGER ex CROWN MONARCH (photo: Alexander Brede)

cabins, 410 cars / 15.1.1993 home port Mariehamn / 17.3.1993–8.1.1995 service Stockholm—Mariehamn—Turku / 8.1.1995 again service Helsinki—Stockholm / 9.1998 2852 pass. in cabins / 5.6.1999 entered service Helsinki—Mariehamn—Stockholm /

ms SILJA SYMPHONY
IMO No. 8803769
Silja Line, Stockholm
Kværner Masa-Yards, Turku; Yard No.: 1309

58 377 GT / 5340 tdw / 203.03 m length oa / 31.50 (31.93) m beam / four 9-cyl. diesels geared to 2 screws; Wärtsilä-Vaasa / 32 560 kW / 21 kn / 2500 pass. in 952 cabins / 470 cars, 950 lane metres / crew 264

15.11.1990 floated out / 30.5.1991 delivered / 31.5.1991 maiden voyage in service Helsinki—Stockholm / 1.1994 2700 pass. in 985 cabins, 410 cars / 7.2.1996 grounded off Vaxholm, after repair again in service / 5.1998 2852 pass. in cabins / 5.6.1999 entered service Helsinki—Mariehamn—Stockholm /

ms CROWN MONARCH
IMO No. 8709573
Commodore Cruise Line, Panama
Union Naval de Levante, Valencia; Yard No.: 185

15 271 GT / 1384 tdw / 150.72 m length oa / 20.60 (19.80) m beam / four 9-cyl. diesels geared to 2 screws; Normo-Bergen / 13 240 kW / 18 kn / 556 pass. in 265 cabins /

30.10.1989 launched / 25.10.1990 delivered / 1.12.1990 first cruise from Palm Beach / 1.1993 managed by Cunard / 1994 NAUTICAN, Crown Cruise Line (Commodore Cruise Line), Panama. Cruises from Singapore / 1996 renamed WALRUS, casino cruises from Hong Kong; 15 343 GT / 6.2006 to Club Cruise, conversion work in Genoa / 4.2007 renamed JULES VERNE, home port Nassau / 28.5.2007 first Mediterranean cruise under charter by Vision Cruceros / 4.2008 under charter by Phoenix Reisen, renamed ALEXANDER VON HUMBOLDT / 1.5.2008 first cruise for Phoenix Reisen / 12.2008 after bankruptcy of the owner arrested in Bremerhaven / 7.9.2009 towed from Bremerhaven to Tilbury / 10.11.2009 auctioned off to All Leisure Group / 9.5.–30.10.2010 again cruises under charter by Phoenix Reisen / 11.2010–5.2011 conversion in Genoa incl. additional balconies, 15 396 GT / 6.–9.2011 Mediterranean cruises under charter by Bamtur / 9.2011 renamed VOYAGER / 6.2012 laid up in Genoa / 31.10.2012 arrival for conversion of interior fittings in Portland / 4.12.2012 first cruise for Voyages of Discovery /

ms SILJA SERENADE
IMO No. 8715259
Silja Line, Helsinki
Masa-Yards, Turku; Yard No.: 1301

58 376 GT / 4648 tdw / 203.03 m length oa / 31.50 (31.93) m beam / four 9-cyl. diesels geared to 2 screws; Wärtsilä-Vaasa / 32 560 kW / 21 kn / 2500 pass. in 952 cabins / 450 cars, 950 lane metres / crew 264

6.11.1989 floated out / 2.4.1990 christened / 15.11.1990 delivered / 17.11.1990 maiden voyage in service Helsinki—Stockholm / 1.1992 2700 pass. in 985

SILJA SERENADE (photo: Marko Stampehl)

SILJA SYMPHONY (photo: Marko Stampehl)

ms KAPTAN BURHANETTIN ISIM

IMO No. 8818300
Turkish Cargo Lines, Istanbul
Fosen Mek. Verksteder, Rissa; Yard No.: 43

18 653 GT / 6934 tdw / 158.00 m length oa /
24.00 (24.33) m beam / two 6-cyl. diesels geared
to 2 screws; Sulzer-Wärtsilä / 7920 kW / 17.7 kn /
120 pass. in 60 cabins / 1800 lane metres /

10.3.1990 launched / 21.12.1990 delivered / 1992
service Derince—Trieste / 18.5.–12.2002 service
Lübeck—Riga under charter by Latlines / 22.6.2003
entered service Travemünde—Ventspils under charter
by JSC Latvian Shipping Co. / 2.8.2004 GRYF, Unity
Line, Valletta / 9.2004 home port Nassau / 3.1.2005
entered service Swinoujscie—Ystad / 5.2.2007 entered
service Swinoujscie—Trelleborg /

GRYF ex KAPTAN BURHANETTIN ISIM (photo: Uwe Jakob)

LEIF ERICSON ex STENA CHALLENGER (photo: Marko Stampehl)

BO HAI MING ZHU ex KAPTAN ABIDIN DORAN (photo: ShipPax Information)

ms STENA CHALLENGER

IMO No. 8917388
Stena Line, Dover
Fosen Mek. Verksteder, Rissa; Yard No.: 50

18 523 GT / 4598 tdw / 154.00 m length oa /
24.00 (24.30) m beam / two 8-cyl. diesels geared
to 2 screws; Sulzer-Wärtsilä / 10 560 kW / 19 kn /
92 pass. in cabins, 500 pass. unberthed /
1560 lane metres /

26.6.1990 launched at Bruce Shipyard, Landskrona,
then towed to Rissa for completion / 25.5.1991
delivered / 27.6.1991 entered service Dover—Calais /
1992 service Dover—Dunkirk / 13.3.1994 again
service Dover—Calais / 19.9.1995 stranded in storm
1.5 nm west of Calais, towed off next day, then to
Newcastle for repair / 23.10.1995 after repair again
service Dover—Calais / 17.9.1996 entered service
Holyhead—Dublin / 4.2001 LEIF ERICSON, Marine
Atlantic, St. John's / 1.6.2001 entered service North
Sydney—Port-aux-Basques / 4.1.2011 after conversion
used for cargo transport only /

ms KAPTAN ABIDIN DORAN

IMO No. 8818312
Turkish Cargo Lines, Istanbul
Fosen Mek. Verksteder, Rissa; Yard No.: 44

18 685 GT / 6934 tdw / 158.00 m length oa /
24.00 (24.33) m beam / two 6-cyl. diesels geared
to 2 screws; Sulzer Wärtsilä / 7920 kW / 17 kn /
120 pass. in 60 cabins / 1800 lane metres /

24.10.1991 launched / 1992 delivered, then service
Derince—Trieste / 2002 BO HAI MING ZHU,
Shandong Bohai Ferry, Yantai / 2002 after conversion
20 403 GT, 1162 pass., 1600 lane metres, then service
Dalian—Yantai /

ms STENA TRAVELLER

IMO No. 8917390
Stena Line, Gothenburg
Fosen Mek. Verksteder, Rissa; Yard No.: 51

18 332 GT / 4758 tdw / 153.60 m length oa /
24.00 (24.33) m beam / two 8-cyl. diesels geared
to 2 screws; Sulzer-Wärtsilä / 8980 kW / 18 kn /
120 pass. in 50 cabins / 1800 lane metres /

26.3.1991 launched at Bruce Shipyard, Landskrona,
then towed to Rissa for completion / 2.1992 delivered /

PATRIA SEAWAYS ex STENA TRAVELLER (photo: Micke Asklander)

additionally one weekly voyage in service Klaipeda—Baltijsk—Karlshamn / 1.2006 entered service Klaipeda—Kiel / 11.5.–13.9.2011 service Paldiski—Kapellskär under charter by Baltic Scandinavia Line / 14.9.2011 entered service Paldiski—Kapellskär for DFDS Seaways / 1.2012 **PATRIA SEAWAYS**, DFDS Seaways, Klaipeda / 5.10.2014 last voyage in service Kapellskär—Paldiski / 4.11.–4.12.2014 service Fredericia—Copenhagen—Klaipeda / 5.12.2014 overhaul in Gdansk, then laid up / 27.3.2015 laid up in Klaipeda / 9.4.–6.5.2015 cargo ferry service Klaipeda—Fredericia—Copenhagen / 7.5.2015 accommodation ship for offshore workers in the North Sea under charter by SweOffshore / 16.11.2015–1.1.2016 service Kiel—Klaipeda / 4.1.2016 entered service Zeebrugge—Hull under charter by P&O Ferries /

ms BERGEN
IMO No. 9058995
Fjord Line, Bergen
Fosen Mek. Verksteder, Rissa; Yard No.: 52

16 551 GT / 3318 tdw / 134.50 m length oa / 24.00 m beam / two 8-cyl. diesels geared to 2 screws; Sulzer-Wärtsilä / 11 520 kW / 19 kn / 542 pass. in 145 cabins, 358 pass. unberthed / 350 cars /

29.1.1993 launched at Bruces Shipyard, Landskrona, then towed to Rissa for completion / 19.6.1993

1.4.1992 entered service Hoek van Holland—Harwich for Sealink Stena Line / 5.–16.9.1992 service Southampton—Cherbourg / 12.1992 renamed **TT-TRAVELLER** / 5.12.1992–29.10.1995 service Travemünde—Trelleborg under charter by TT-Line / 11.11.1995 after end of charter renamed **STENA TRAVELLER** / 23.11.1995–16.9.1996 service Holyhead—Dublin for Stena Line, then several short-term charters / 2.1997 renamed **TT-TRAVELLER** /

11.2.1997 entered service Rostock—Trelleborg under charter by TT-Line / 12.1999–2.2000 conversion of passenger facilities at Flender-Werft, Lübeck: 204 pass. in 83 cabins / 13.1.2002 last voyage in service Rostock—Trelleborg / 20.1.2002 renamed **STENA TRAVELLER**, entered service Karlskrona—Gdynia / 10.5.2004 **LISCO PATRIA**, Lisco, Klaipeda / 17.5.2004 entered service Klaipeda—Karlshamn / 11.6.2005

OSLOFJORD ex BERGEN (photo: Marko Stampehl)

delivered / 27.6.1993 maiden voyage in service Bergen—Stavanger—Hanstholm, then also service Hanstholm—Egersund / 1997 conversion: 16 794 GT, 3200 tdw, 559 pass. in 184 cabins, 341 pass. unberthed / 2000 conversion: 698 pass. in 211 cabins, 184 pass. unberthed / 10.4.2003 renamed **DUCHESS OF SCANDINAVIA**, home port Copenhagen / 17.4.2003—6.11.2005 service Cuxhaven—Harwich under charter by DFDS / 15.11.2005 renamed **ATLANTIC TRAVELLER** / 17.11.2005 again service Bergen—Stavanger—Egersund—Hanstholm for Fjord Line / 8.1.2008 renamed **BERGENSFJORD**, home port Hanstholm / 24.1.2008 also service Kristiansand—Hanstholm / 26.10.2008 entered service Bergen—Risavika—Hirtshals / 6.3.2009 home port Hirtshals / 14.7.—22.12.2013 service Hirtshals—Stavanger/Langesund / 16.1.2014 renamed **OSLOFJORD** / 15.1.—30.5.2014 conversion at STX Finland, Rauma: 17 851 GT, 2400 tdw, 1814 pass. unberthed, 370 cars / 20.6.2014 entered service Sandefjord—Strömstad /

MUTIARA PERSADA III ex WAKANATSU OKINAWA as ASIA INNOVATOR (photo: Olaf Schmidt)

ms WAKANATSU OKINAWA
IMO No. 9004592
Ryukyu Kaiun, Naha
Saiki Jukogoyo, Saiki; Yard No.: 1012

8052 GRT / 3900 tdw / 138.03 m length oa / 23.00 m beam / one 9-cyl. diesel geared to 2 screws; Pielstick / 16 200 bhp / 21 kn / 50 pass. in 17 cabins, 100 pass. unberthed / 180 cars, 42 trucks /

21.10.1990 launched / 2.1991 delivered, then service Japan—Okinawa / 2006 **ASIA INNOVATOR**, Asiana Lines Inc., Panama, 15 380 GT / 2.2015 **MUTIARA PERSADA III**, Pt. Atosim Lampung Pelayaran, Panjang / 2015 service Panjang—Tanjung Perak/

SEA STAR CRUISE ex NEW NAGATO (photo: Frank Lose)

ms NEW NAGATO
IMO No. 9001291
Hankyu Ferry, Kobe
Kanda Zosensho, Kawajiri; Yard No.: 332

14 988 GRT / 5155 tdw / 185.50 m length oa / 26.80 m beam / two 9-cyl. diesels geared to 2 screws; Pielstick-Diesel United / 20 260 kW / 22.9 kn / 368 pass. in 109 cabins, 698 pass. unberthed / 110 cars, 1530 lane metres / crew 39

3.1991 delivered, then service Shin Moji—Kobe / 1.2011 **SEA STAR CRUISE**, Sea World Express Ferry, Mokpo, 15 089 GRT, then service Mokpo—Jeju /

GRAND PEACE ex NEW AKASHI as NEW AKASHI (photo: Hiroyuki Yoshimoto)

ms NEW AKASHI
IMO No. 9001306
Hankyu Ferry, Kobe
Kanda Zosensho, Kawajiri; Yard No.: 333

14 988 GRT / 5156 tdw / 185.50 m length oa / 26.80 m beam / two 9-cyl. diesels geared to 2 screws; Pielstick-Diesel United / 20 260 kW / 22.9 kn / 386 pass. in 109 cabins, 698 pass. unberthed / 110 cars, 1530 lane metres / crew 39

16.1.1991 launched / 15.3.1991 delivered, then service Shin Moji—Kobe / 8.2010 **GRAND PEACE**, Weihai Jiaodong Ferries, Panama, then service Weihai—Pyeongtaek /

ms ISHIKARI

IMO No. 8922163
Taiheiyo Ferry (Pacific Ferry Co.), Nagoya
Mitsubishi Heavy Industries, Kobe; Yard No.: 1183

14 257 GRT / 6938 tdw / 192.50 m length oa /
27.00 m beam / 6.92 m draught / two 14-cyl.
diesels geared to 2 screws; MAN-Mitsubishi /
18 460 kW / 21.5 kn / 260 pass. in 71 cabins,
594 pass. unberthed / 151 cars, 88 trucks / crew 54

8.11.1990 launched / 18.3.1991 delivered, then service
Nagoya—Sendai—Tomakomai / 2003 534 pass.
unberthed / 3.2011 **GRAND SPRING**, Weihai Jiadong
International Shipping, Panama, then service Weihai—
Pyeongtaek / 26.8.2015 laid up in Weihai /

ms MONTE D'ORO

IMO No. 8911516
Soc. Nationale Maritime Corse Méditerranée, Bastia
Soc. Nouvelle of the At. & Ch. du Havre, Le Havre;
Yard No.: 280

22 070 GT / 4155 tdw / 145.00 m length oa /
25.70 m beam / four 12-cyl. diesels geared to
2 screws; Wärtsilä-Duvant Crepelle / 14 800 kW /
19 kn / 514 pass. in 203 cabins / 135 cars,
1630 lane metres / crew 47

21.8.1990 launched / 5.1991 delivered, then service
Marseilles—Corsica, in summer also service Livorno/
Genoa—Corsica / 2001 508 pass. in 203 cabins /
27.7.1998 on a voyage from Marseilles to Porto
Vecchio a fire broke out in the engine room, could be
extinguished with shipboard equipment, then repairs
in Marseilles /

ms NICOBAR (no photo)

IMO No. 8606161
The Shipping Corporation of India, Mumbai
Stocznia Szczecinska im. A. Warskiego, Szczecin;
Yard No.: B561/01

14 195 GT / 4963 tdw / 157.00 m length oa /
20.10 (21.00) m beam / two 6-cyl. diesels;
B&W-Cegielski / 5220 kW / 2 screws / 15.5 kn /
300 pass. in 63 cabins, 900 Pullman / crew 110

12.4.1990 launched / 5.8.1991 delivered / 10.1991
passenger service Kolkata/Chennai—Port Blair /

ms NANCOWRY

IMO No. 8606434
The Shipping Corporation of India, Mumbai
Stocznia Szczecinska im. A. Warskiego, Szczecin;
Yard No.: B561/02

14 176 GT / 5014 tdw / 157.00 m length oa /
20.10 (21.00) m beam / two 6-cyl. diesels;
B&W-Cegielski / 5215 kW / 2 screws / 15.5 kn /
300 pass. in 63 cabins, 900 Pullman / crew 110

5.10.1992 launched / 31.3.1992 delivered, then
passenger service Kolkata/Chennai—Port Blair also
voyages for pilgrims to Jeddah /

GRAND SPRING ex ISHIKARI as ISHIKARI (photo: Tsuyoshi Ishiyama)

MONTE D'ORO (photo: Frank Heine)

NANCOWRY (photo: Dieter Streich)

ms SWARAJ DWEEP (no photo)

IMO No. 9101168
The Shipping Corporation of India, Mumbai
Hindustan Shipyard, Vishakapatnam; Yard No.: 11101

14 239 GT / 4701 tdw / 156.97 m length oa /
20.10 (21.00) m beam / two 6-cyl. diesels;
MAN B&W / 5280 kW / 2 screws / 16 kn / 300
pass. in 63 cabins, 900 pass. unberthed / crew 111

11.12.1996 launched / 6.12.1999 delivered, then
passenger service Kolkata/Chennai/Vishakapatnam—
Port Blair also voyages for pilgrims to Jeddah /

ms HERMES

IMO No. 8916607
Highashi Nihon Ferry, Iwanai
Mitsubishi H.I., Shimonoseki; Yard No.: 937

13 384 GRT / 6987 tdw / 192.00 m length oa /
27.00 (29.00) m beam / two 12-cyl. diesels geared
to 2 screws; Pielstick-Nippon / 26 180 kW /
24.00 (26.21) kn / 252 pass. in 76 cabins, 548 pass.
unberthed / 154 trucks + 77 cars / crew 49

29.3.1990 launched / 11.7.1991 delivered, then
service Iwanai—Naoetsu / 11.1998 to ANEK Lines,
Chania / 1999 renamed SOFOKLIS VENIZELOS /
6.1999 after conversion in Perama: 29 378 GT, 644
pass. in cabins, 956 deck pass., 1100 cars, 1934
lane metres, renamed SOPHOCLES VENIZELOS,
shortly afterwards SOPHOCLES V. / 2.7.1999 entered
service Patras—Igoumenitsa—Corfu—Trieste /
2001 29 991 GT, 637 pass. in 180 cabins, 1413
pass. unberthed, 1890 lane metres / 10.1.2005–
15.2.2012 service Patras—Igoumenitsa—Corfu—
Venice / 6.2012 chartered to Jeju Cruise Line, Jeju /
9.2012 renamed ELISABETH L., planned for service
to Jeju not realised, laid up in Busan / 11.2013
renamed SOPHOCLES V. / 13.12.2013 after return
from Asia laid up in Perama / 1.6.–14.7.2014 service
Livorno—Olbia/Arbatax under charter by Goin
Sardinia / 17.7.–9.2014 service Oran—Alicante
under charter by Algerie Ferries / 7.2015 renamed
KYDON / 22.7.2015 entered service Piraeus—
Chania / 2.2016 service Patras—Igoumenitsa—
Corfu—Venice planned /

BLUE GALAXY ex HERCULES (photo: Frank Heine)

ms HERCULES

IMO No. 9035876
Higashi Nihon Ferry, Iwanai
Mitsubishi H.I.,Shimonoseki; Yard No.: 954

13 403 GRT / 6911 tdw / 192.00 m length oa /
27.00 (29.00) m beam / two 12-cyl. diesels geared
to 2 screws; Pielstick-Nippon / 26 180 kW / 24 kn /
250 pass. in 76 cabins, 550 pass. unberthed /
154 trucks + 77 cars / crew 49

22.11.1991 launched / 15.4.1992 delivered, then
service Naoetsu—Muroran/Iwanai / 1999 KRITI V,
ANEK Lines, Chania / 6.2000 renamed LEFKA ORI,
delivered after conversion in Perama: 29 429 GT,
448 pass. in 182 cabins, 255 pass. unberthed /
3.7.2000 entered service Patras—Igoumenitsa—
Corfu—Trieste / 10.1.2005 entered service Patras—
Igoumenitsa—Corfu—Venice / 9.–10.2007 service
Marseilles—Algeria under charter by CNAN Maghreb
Lines / 12.2007 again service Patras—Igoumenitsa—
Corfu—Venice for ANEK Lines, sometimes also to
Ancona / 6.2012 chartered to Jeju Cruise Line, Jeju /
9.2012 renamed ANTONIOS L., planned for service to

Jeju not realised, laid up in Busan / 11.2013 renamed
LEFKA ORI / 10.12.2013 after return from Asia laid
up in Perama / 3.2015 renamed BLUE GALAXY /
24.4.2015 entered service Piraeus—Chania under
charter by Blue Star Ferries /

ms HESTIA

IMO No. 9061590
Higashi Nippon Ferry & Hayashi Marine, Muroran
Mitsubishi H.I., Shimonoseki; Yard No.: 979

13 539 GRT / 6805 tdw / 192.00 m length oa /
27.00 (29.00) m beam / two 12-cyl. diesels geared
to 2 screws; Pielstick-Nippon / 26 180 kW / 24 kn /
292 pass. in 88 cabins, 391 pass. unberthed /
460 cars, 1750 lane metres /

8.7.1993 launched / 18.11.1993 entered service
Muroran—Oarai / 2002 service Tomakomai—Oarai /
1.2007 SUN FLOWER FURANO, Shosen Mitsui Ferry,
then service Tomakomai—Oarai /

KYDON ex HERMES (photo: Frank Heine)

SUN FLOWER FURANO ex HESTIA (photo: Hiroyuki Yoshimoto)

ms TYCHO BRAHE
IMO No. 9007116
Danske Statsbaner, Helsingør
Langsten Slip & Båtbyggeri, Tomrefjord; Yard No.: 156

10 845 GT / 2500 tdw / 111.20 m length oa /
27.60 (28.20) m beam / four 6-cyl. diesels with
9860 kW; Wärtsilä / four generators connected to
four elec. motors / 6000 kW / 4 screws / 13.5 kn /
1250 pass. unberthed / 238 cars, 535 lane metres,
3 rail tracks with 260 m length /

19.1.1991 launched at Tangen Verft, Kragerø, then
to Tomrefjord for completion / 1.10.1991 delivered /
5.11.1991 maiden voyage in service Helsingør—
Helsingborg / 6.11.1991 serious collision with berth
in Helsingør, 54 pass. injured / 17.12.1991 after repair
back in service / 1998 to Scandlines, Helsingør / 2001
11 148 GT / 5.12.2011 11 223 GT / 1.2015 to HH
Ferries Helsingør, Helsingør /

TYCHO BRAHE (photo: Frank Heine)

AURORA AF HELSINGBORG (photo: Frank Lose)

ms AURORA AF HELSINGBORG
IMO No. 9007128
Swedish Ferry Lines (SweFerry), Helsingborg
Langsten Slip & Båtbyggeri, Tomrefjord; Yard No.: 157

10 918 GT / 2300 tdw / 111.20 m length oa /
27.60 (28.22) m beam / four 6-cyl. diesels with
9860 kW; Wärtsilä / four generators connected to
four elec. motors / 6000 kW / 4 screws / 13.5 kn /
1250 pass. unberthed / 238 cars, 535 lane metres,
3 rail tracks with 260 m length /

6.7.1991 launched at Tangen Verft, Kragerø, then
to Tomrefjord for completion / 5.3.1992 delivered /
5.4.1992 maiden voyage in service Helsingborg—
Helsingør / 1998 to Scandlines, Helsingborg / 1.2015
to HH Ferries, Helsingborg /

AMADEA ex ASUKA (photo: Alexander Brede)

COSTA NEOCLASSICA ex COSTA CLASSICA (photo: Tony Davis)

to 2 screws; Sulzer-Grandi Motori / 21 180 kW / 19.2 (20.2) kn / 1766 (1905) pass. in 654 cabins / crew 607

2.2.1991 floated out / 6.1991 first sea trials / 7.12.1991 christened and delivered / 17.12.1991 first cruise, deployed in Europe and the Caribbean / 1994 home port Monrovia / 2000 home port Genoa / 11.2000 planned lengthening of ship at Cammell Laird, Birkenhead, not realised despite the already launched midships section / 12.2006 first Costa cruise from Dubai / 4.2009 cruises from Chinese ports / 18.10.2010 collided in the mouth of the Yangtze with the bulk carrier LOWLANDS LONGEVITY, the hull being torn open over a length of about 60 m, then repair in Singapore / 11.–12.2014 conversion at San Giorgio del Porto, Genoa: 53 015 GT / 18.12.2014 first cruise as **COSTA NEOCLASSICA** /

ms COSTA ROMANTICA

IMO No. 8821046
Costa Crociere, Naples
Fincantieri, Monfalcone; Yard No.: 5899

53 700 GT / 7781 tdw / 220.52 m length oa / 30.79 m beam / four 8-cyl. diesels geared to 2 screws; Sulzer-Fincantieri / 21 180 kW / 19.75 kn / 1600 (1782) pass. in 654 cabins / crew 607

28.11.1992 floated out / 22.9.1993 delivered / 7.10.1993 maiden cruise Genoa—Canaries / 20.10.1993 transfer Genoa—Miami / 21.11.1993 first Caribbean cruise / 1995 53 049 GT / 2000 home port Genoa / 25.2.2009 blackout after engine room fire off Punta del Este, Uruguay. The pass. were taken ashore in local boats. After emergency repair in Montevideo, transfer without passengers to shipyard in Genoa / 7.4.2009 after repairs back in operation / 10.2011–2.2012 conversion at Giorgio del Porto, Genoa / 2.2012 returned as **COSTA NEOROMANTICA**: 57 150 GT, 1578 (1894) pass. in 789 cabins / 2.3.2012 first cruise from Savona / 9.2012 56 769 GT /

COSTA NEOROMANTICA ex COSTA ROMANTICA (photo: Marko Stampehl)

ms ASUKA

IMO No. 8913162
NYK Cruises, Tokyo
Mitsubishi H.I., Nagasaki; Yard No.: 2050

28 717 GT / 2248 tdw / 192.82 m length oa / 24.70 m beam / two 7-cyl. diesels geared to 2 screws; MAN-Mitsubishi / 15 560 kW / 21 kn / 584 (604) pass. in 292 cabins / crew 243

6.4.1991 launched / 12.1991 delivered / 24.12.1991 maiden cruise Yokohama—Taiwan, then cruises in East Asia and Australia / 2000 28 856 GT / 27.2.2006 to Amadea Shipping (V.Ships) / 1.3.2006 renamed **AMADEA**, home port Nassau, cruises under charter by Phoenix Reisen / 6.2010 29 008 GT /

ms COSTA CLASSICA

IMO No. 8716502
Costa Crociere, Naples
Fincantieri, Monfalcone; Yard No.: 5877

52 926 GT / 7781 tdw / 222.61 m length oa / 30.80 (32.78) m beam / four 8-cyl. diesels geared

ms EUROPEAN PATHWAY

IMO No. 9007295
P&O European Ferries, Dover
Schichau Seebeckwerft, Bremerhaven; Yard No.: 1076

22 986 GT / 7550 tdw / 179.40 m length oa /
27.80 (28.28) m beam / four 8-cyl. diesels geared to
2 screws; Sulzer-Jugoturbina / 21 120 kW / 21 kn /
200 pass. in 81 cabins / 1925 lane metres /

10.8.1991 launched / 29.12.1991 delivered / 4.1.1992
entered service Dover—Zeebrugge / 10.3.1998
to P&O Stena Line, Dover / 15.10.2002 to P&O
Ferries, Dover / 11.2002 conversion into passenger
ferry at Lloyd Werft, Bremerhaven / 3.2003 renamed
PRIDE OF CANTERBURY / 2.5.2003 delivered
after conversion: 30 635 GT, 4203 tdw, 179.70 m
length oa, 2000 pass. unberthed, 520 cars, crew
200 / 12.5.2003 entered service Dover—Calais /
31.1.2008 after grounding off Dover, one propeller
and shaft were damaged, resulted in only sporadic
deployment / 6.2008 laid up in Dunkirk / 11.3.2009
after repairs back in service Dover—Calais /

PRIDE OF CANTERBURY ex EUROPEAN PATHWAY (photo: Frank Lose)

PRIDE OF KENT ex EUROPEAN HIGHWAY (photo: Frank Lose)

ms EUROPEAN HIGHWAY

IMO No. 9015266
P&O European Ferries, Dover
Schichau Seebeckwerft, Bremerhaven; Yard No.: 1077

22 986 GT / 7550 tdw / 179.40 m length oa /
27.80 (28.28) m beam / four 8-cyl. diesels geared to
2 screws; Sulzer-Jugoturbina / 21 120 kW / 21 kn /
200 pass. in 81 cabins / 1925 lane metres /

14.12.1991 launched / 12.6.1992 delivered / 16.6.1992
entered service Dover—Zeebrugge / 10.3.1998 to P&O
Stena Line, Dover / 15.10.2002 to P&O Ferries, Dover /
17.12.2002 arrival for conversion into passenger ferry
at Lloyd Werft, Bremerhaven / 2003 renamed **PRIDE
OF KENT** / 6.6.2003 delivered after conversion:
30 635 GT, 4203 tdw, 179.70 m length oa, 2000 pass.
unberthed, 520 cars, crew 200 / 14.6.2003 entered
service Dover—Calais /

PRIDE OF BURGUNDY ex PRIDE OF BURGUNDY (photo: Frank Lose)

ms PRIDE OF BURGUNDY

IMO No. 9015254
P&O European Ferries, Dover
Schichau Seebeckwerft, Bremerhaven; Yard No.: 1078

28 138 GT / 5875 tdw / 179.40 m length oa /
27.80 (28.30) m beam / four 8-cyl. diesels geared to
2 screws; Sulzer-Jugoturbina / 21 120 kW / 21 kn /
196 pass. in 79 cabins, 1320 pass. unberthed /
600 cars, 1925 lane metres /

16.5.1992 launched; planned as cargo ferry EUROPEAN
CAUSEWAY / 26.3.1993 delivered / 5.4.1993 maiden
voyage in service Dover—Calais / 10.3.1998 to P&O
Stena Line / 12.1998 renamed **P&OSL BURGUNDY** /
15.10.2002 **P O BURGUNDY**, P&O Ferries, Dover /
3.2003 renamed **PRIDE OF BURGUNDY**, continued
in service Dover—Calais /

ms BARFLEUR

IMO No. 9007130
Truckline Ferries, Cherbourg
Kværner Masa-Yards, Helsinki; Yard No.: 485

20 133 GT / 5175 tdw / 157.65 m length oa /
23.30 m beam / four 8-cyl. diesels geared to
2 screws; Wärtsilä / 11 990 kW / 19.5 kn / 268 pass.
in 72 cabins, 944 pass. unberthed / 550 cars,
1530 lane metres / crew 58

26.7.1991 floated out / 11.1991 lengthened by 7.9 m
because of stability problems / 27.3.1992 delivered /
15.4.1992 entered service Cherbourg—Poole /
1.1999 to Brittany Ferries, Cherbourg / 16.3.2005
also service Cherbourg—Portsmouth / 31.1.2010
last voyage in service Cherbourg—Poole, then laid
up in Ouistreham / 27.2.2010–3.11.2011 again
service Cherbourg—Poole / 15.10.2011 laid up
in Caen / 24.4.2012 renamed **DEAL SEAWAYS** /
27.4.–6.11.2012 service Calais—Dover under charter
by DFDS Seaways / 11.2012 after end of charter
renamed **BARFLEUR** / 21.3.2013 again service
Cherbourg—Poole /

BARFLEUR ex BARFLEUR (photo: Richard Seville)

SU ZHOU HAO ex LU XUN (photo: Osamu Taniguchi)

ms LU XUN

IMO No. 9030632
Shanghai Ferry, Panama
Shin Kurushima Dockyard, Onishi; Yard No.: 2721

14 410 GT / 3721 tdw / 154.73 m length oa /
22.00 m beam / two 7-cyl. diesels geared to 2
screws; Mitsubishi / 10 500 kW / 21 kn / 322 pass. /
200 cars /

3.12.1991 launched / 13.4.1992 delivered / 1.10.1992
entered service Yokohama—Shanghai / 1993 **SU
ZHOU HAO**, Shanghai Ferry, Shanghai, then service
Shanghai—Osaka /

CHINA STAR ex RADISSON DIAMOND (photo: Gerolf Drebes)

ms RADISSON DIAMOND

IMO No. 9008407
Diamond Cruise, Helsinki
Finnyards, Rauma; Yard No.: 310

18 400 GT / 1676 tdw / 131.20 m length oa /
31.96 m beam / two 8-cyl. and two 6-cyl. diesels
geared to 2 screws; Wärtsilä / 11 340 kW / 12.5 kn /
354 pass. in 176 cabins / crew 177

20.6.1991 launched / 20.2.1992 first sea trials /
30.4.1992 delivered, first SWATH (Small Water-
plane Area Twin Hull) design cruise ship / 28.5.1992
christened in Greenwich / until 5.7.1992 presentation
in European ports, then Caribbean cruises / 1994
20 205 GT / 1997 to Radisson Seven Seas Cruises,
Nassau / 1999 20 295 GT / 6.2005 **OMAR STAR**,
Treasure Ocean, Nassau / 7.2005 renamed **ASIA STAR**,
casino cruises from Hong Kong / 8.2009 casino cruises
from Singapore / 7.2011 to China Cruises Company /
10.2011 renamed **CHINA STAR** / 8.3.2012 first cruise
from Hong Kong. Mostly stationary casino ship in Hong
Kong roads /

ms CROWN JEWEL
IMO No. 9000687
Commodore Cruise Line, Panama
Union Naval de Levante, Valencia; Yard No.: 197

19 154 GT / 1800 tdw / 163.81 m length oa /
22.50 m beam / four 8-cyl. diesels geared to 2 screws;
Wärtsilä-Echevarria / 12 945 kW / 19 (21.5) kn /
820 (916) pass. in 410 cabins / crew 304

30.5.1991 launched / 5.1992 delivered, then accommodation ship at the Olympic Games in Barcelona /
11.8.1992 transfer voyage to New York / 5.9.1992 first
cruise New York—Canada, then Caribbean cruises /
1.1993 Cunard management, planned renaming as
CUNARD CROWN JEWEL not realised / 1993 19 089 GT,
916 pass. in 410 cabins / 1995 SUPERSTAR GEMINI,
Star Cruises, Panama. Cruises from Singapore / 1998
19 093 GT / 9.2007 to Clipper Group, chartered back
by Star Cruises until 12.2008 / 1.2009 renamed VISION
STAR / 3.2009 home port Valletta / 4.2009 renamed
GEMINI, Mediterranean cruises under charter by Quail
Cruises / 30.9.2011 after bankruptcy of charterer laid
up in Genoa / 26.10.2011 laid up in Tilbury / 7.8.2012
accommodation ship at the Olympic Games in London,
then again laid up in Tilbury / 12.7.2014 accommodation ship for Petrofac in Lerwick / 20.12.2015 arrival at
Besiktas, Yalova, for conversion / 2.2016 Mediterranean
cruises under charter by Celestyal Cruises as CELESTYAL
NEFELI planned /

ms CROWN DYNASTY
IMO No. 9000699
Commodore Cruise Line, Panama
Union Naval de Levante, Valencia; Yard No.: 198

19 089 GT / 1800 tdw / 163.81 m length oa /
22.50 m beam / four 8-cyl. diesels geared to
2 screws; Wärtsilä-Echevarria / 13 110 kW /
18.5 kn / 820 (916) pass. in 410 cabins / crew 304

31.1.1992 launched / 23.2.1993 fire in dining room
delayed completion envisaged for 2.1993 by about
three months / 25.6.1993 delivered / 3.7.1993 from
Southampton to U.S. East Coast / 17.7.1993 maiden
cruise / 12.1994 Cunard management / 3.1997
CROWN MAJESTY, under charter by Majesty Cruise

CELESTYAL NEFELI ex CROWN JEWEL as GEMINI (photo: Tony Davis)

BRAEMAR ex CROWN DYNASTY (photo: Hans-Joachim Hellmann)

Line / 1997 NORWEGIAN DYNASTY, Norwegian
Cruise Line, Panama / 10.1999 CROWN DYNASTY,
Commodore Cruise Line, Panama / 18.12.1999 cruises

from Oranjestad for Crown Cruises of Panama /
2.2000 after bankruptcy of the owner under charter
by Apple Vacations / 11.5.2001 BRAEMAR, Fred. Olsen
Cruise Lines, Panama / 20.6.–22.7.2001 conversion
at Blohm+Voss, Hamburg: e.g. ducktail, only 750
pass. / 11.8.2001 first cruise from Dover / 5.2003
home port Nassau / 10.5.2008 arrival for lengthening
at Blohm+Voss, Hamburg / 24.6.2008 delivered after
conversion: 24 344 GT, 2978 tdw, 195.92 m length oa,
984 pass. in 503 cabins, crew 348 /

CALAIS SEAWAYS ex PRINS FILIP (photo: Frank Lose)

ms PRINS FILIP
IMO No. 8908466
Regie voor Maritiem Transport, Ostend
Boelwerf, Tamise; Yard No.: 1534

28 833 GT / 4000 tdw / 163.40 m length oa /
27.00 (27.70) m beam / four 8-cyl. diesels geared to
2 screws; Sulzer-Jugoturbina / 21 120 kW / 21 kn /
252 pass. in 126 cabins, 916 pass. unberthed /
710 cars, 1745 lane metres /

1.2.1991 floated out / 4.5.1992 delivered / 12.5.1992
maiden voyage in service Ostend—Dover / 1.1.1994
entered service Ostend—Ramsgate / 14.9.1994
collapse of a gangway in Ramsgate, six pass. fatally
injured / 29.4.1997 laid up in Dunkirk / 2.7.1998
STENA ROYAL, Stena Ferries, Hamilton / 20.11.1998
first voyage in freight service Dover—Zeebrugge

under charter by P&O Stena Line / 5.1999 renamed
P&OSL AQUITAINE, home port Dover / 7.11.1999
first voyage in passenger ferry service Dover—Calais /
15.10.2002 **P O AQUITAINE**, P&O Ferries, Dover /
3.2002 renamed **PRIDE OF AQUITAINE** / 7.6.2005
laid up in Dunkirk / 13.9.2005 **NORMAN SPIRIT**, LD
Lines, Dover / 3.10.2005 entered service Le Havre—
Portsmouth / 15.6.2006 home port Southampton /
12.2006 after conversion in Dunkirk additional 80
beds in 20 cabins / 11.11.2009–16.3.2010 service
Boulogne—Dover / 27.3.2010 renamed **OSTEND
SPIRIT**, home port Ramsgate / 27.3.2010–13.3.2011
service Ostend—Ramsgate / 4.2011 renamed **NORMAN
SPIRIT**, home port Le Havre / 2.5.–28.11.2011 service
Le Havre—Portsmouth / 1.12.2011–6.1.2012 service
Dunkirk—Dover under charter by DFDS Seaways /
17.1.2012 entered service Dover—Calais / 11.3.2013
renamed **CALAIS SEAWAYS** /

ms NORMANDIE
IMO No. 9006253
Brittany Ferries, Caen
Kværner Masa-Yards, Turku; Yard No.: 1315

27 541 GT / 5229 tdw / 161.40 m length oa /
26.00 m beam / four 12-cyl. diesels geared to
2 screws; Wärtsilä / 17 760 kW / 20.5 kn / 774 pass.
in 217 cabins, 1384 pass. unberthed / 680 cars,
1720 lane metres / crew 141

5.10.1991 launched / 5.5.1992 delivered / 14.5.1992
christened in Rotterdam / 18.5.1992 maiden voyage
in service Caen—Portsmouth / 2000 780 pass. in 220
cabins, 1340 pass. unberthed /

ms VIA LIGURE
IMO No. 9019054
Viamare di Navigazione, Palermo
van der Giessen-De Noord, Krimpen; Yard No.: 957

14 398 GT / 5535 tdw / 150.43 m length oa /
23.40 m beam / two 8-cyl. diesels geared to 2
screws; Sulzer-Fincantieri / 11 520 kW / 19 kn /
50 pass. in 25 cabins / 1850 lane metres / crew 18

11.3.1992 launched / 6.1992 delivered / 7.7.1992
maiden voyage in service Termini Imerese—Voltri /
3.1994 renamed **IONIAN STAR**, conversion in Perama:

NORMANDIE (photo: Kai Ortel)

SCANDOLA ex VIA LIGURE (photo: Frank Lose)

19 308 GT, 1050 pass., incl. 259 in 80 cabins, 141 trailers,
crew 60 / 17.6.1994 entered service Patras—Ancona
under charter by Strintzis Lines / 10.1996 to Strintzis Lines,
home port Piraeus, then service Patras—Igoumenitsa—
Corfu—Ancona / 30.3.1999 **SCANDOLA**, Cie. Mérdi-
onale de Nav., Ajaccio / 31.3.1999–24.12.2011 service
Marseilles—Ajaccio, then laid up in Marseilles /
23.7.2012 home port Limassol / 5.8.2012–22.1.2013
service Tarragona—Vado Ligure under charter by
ASA Line, then laid up in Naples / 4.3.2013 entered
service Valencia—Ibiza under charter by Acciona
Trasmediterreanea /

ms ROYAL MAJESTY
IMO No. 8814744
Majesty Cruise Line, Panama
Kværner Masa-Yards, Turku; Yard No.: 1312

32 396 GT / 2700 tdw / 173.50 m length oa /
33.20 (27.60) m beam / four 6-cyl. diesels geared
to 2 screws; Wärtsilä / 21 120 kW / 20.8 kn /
1056 pass. in 528 cabins / crew 549

THOMSON MAJESTY ex ROYAL MAJESTY (photo: Raoul Fiebig)

SUPERSTAR GEMINI ex DREAMWARD (photo: Jonathan Boonzaier)

maiden cruise to Bermuda / 3–5.1998 lengthened at Lloyd Werft, Bremerhaven : 50764 GT, 6731 tdw, 229.84 m length oa, 1748 (2100) pass. in 847 cabins / 12.5.1998 returned as **NORWEGIAN DREAM** / 24.8.1999 while proceeding from Zeebrugge to Dover with 1726 pass. on board, NORWEGIAN DREAM hit the port side of the Taiwanese container ship EVER DECENT, which had the right of way. 20 persons were slightly injured on the NORWEGIAN DREAM, the bow was severely damaged. The container ship caught fire, the NORWEGIAN DREAM could continue to Dover / 4.9.–4.10.1999 repair at Lloyd Werft, Bremerhaven / 9.11.2008 laid up in Freeport, after a planned sale to Louis Cruises did not materialise / 6.2009 laid up at Piraeus roads, later in Kalamata and Syros / 4.2011 transferred to Singapore and laid up / 23.5.2012 laid up in Penang / 3.10.2012 arrival for conversion at Sembawang, Singapore / 2.1.2013 first cruise Penang—Phuket as **SUPERSTAR GEMINI** for Star Cruises /

1989 keel-laying for Birka Line, Mariehamn by Wärtsilä. After the yard's bankruptcy in 1989 Birka Line acquired a stake worth the value of the half-finished hull in the succeeding firm Kværner Masa-Yards / 27.2.1990 Birka returned ship and shareholding to shipyard. The order was then assumed by Majesty Cruise Line / 15.11.1991 launched / 2.7.1992 delivered / 7.7.1992 maiden voyage Southampton—New York / 21.7.1992 christened in New York, then cruises / 5.1997 to Norwegian Cruise Line, Nassau / 11.1997 renamed **NORWEGIAN MAJESTY** / 16.1.–1.4.1999 lengthened at Lloyd Werft, Bremerhaven: 40876 GT, 207.26 m length oa, 1462 (1800) pass. in 731 cabins. crew 570 / 11.2009 **LOUIS MAJESTY**, Louis Cruises, Valletta / 4.12.2009 first Mediterranean cruise from Genoa / 3.3.2010 several front windows destroyed by violent wave impact, two killed / 12.3.2010 after repair back in operation / 4.5.2012 first cruise as **THOMSON MAJESTY** under charter by Thomson Cruises / 10.2.2013 life boat crashed during a drill in Santa Cruz de Tenerife, killing five crew members /

ms DREAMWARD
IMO No. 9008419
Kloster Cruise, Nassau
Chantiers de l'Atlantique, St. Nazaire; Yard No.: C30

39217 GT / 5589 tdw / 190.04 m length oa / 28.50 (32.10) m beam / two 8- and two 6-cyl. diesels geared to 2 screws; MAN B&W / 18640 kW / 21 kn / 1260 (1505) pass. in 630 cabins / crew 495

24.2.1992 floated out / 4.11.1992 delivered / 5.12.1992 christened in Fort Lauderdale / 6.12.1992

ms WINDWARD
IMO No. 9008421
Kloster Cruise, Nassau
Chantiers de l'Atlantique, St. Nazaire; Yard No.: D30

39217 GT / 4800 tdw / 190.04 m length oa / 28.85 (32.10) m beam / two 8- and two 6-cyl. diesels geared to 2 screws; MAN B&W / 18650 kW / 18.5 (20.5) kn / 1246 (1505) pass. in 623 cabins / crew 482

14.11.1992 floated out / 4.5.1993 delivered / 14.5.1993 maiden voyage Fort Lauderdale—San Francisco, then Caribbean and Alaska cruises / 14.1.–3.1998 lengthening at Lloyd Werft, Bremerhaven / 14.3.1997 return after conversion as **NORWEGIAN WIND**: 50760 GT, 6731 tdw, 229.85 m length oa, 1748 (2100) pass. in 874 cabins, crew 700 / 6.2007 **SUPERSTAR AQUARIUS**, Star Cruises, Nassau; 51309 GT / 22.6.2007 cruises in Asia /

SUPERSTAR AQUARIUS ex WINDWARD (photo: Jonathan Boonzaier)

BAJA STAR ex PACIFIC EXPRESS as PACIFIC EXPRESS (photo: Hiroyuki Yoshimoto)

ms PACIFIC EXPRESS

IMO No. 9035096
Marine Express, Tokyo
Mitsubishi H.I., Shimonoseki; Yard No.:962

11 582 GRT / 5809 tdw / 170.00 m length oa / 25.00 m beam / two 14-cyl. diesels geared to 2 screws; Pielstick-Nippon / 30 580 kW / 26.2 kn / 80 pass. in 26 cabins, 580 pass. unberthed / 90 cars, 1400 lane metres / crew 50

16.6.1992 launched / 12.11.1992 delivered / 20.11.1992 maiden voyage in service Kawasaki—Hyuga / 2002 service Kawasaki—Nachikatsuura—Kochi—Hyuga / 2.2005 to Miyazaki Car Ferry / 6.2005 sold to KC Line after route was closed / 2006 renamed **KC RAINBOW**, service Rizhao—Pyongtaek, 24 946 GT / 17.5.2010 renamed **SECO MARU**, entered service Busan—Moji under charter by Grand Ferry / 2011 **RI ZHAO DONG FANG**, Rizhao Port Shipping, Panama, then service Rizhao—Pyeongtaek / 10.2015 **BAJA STAR**, Baja Ferries, Panama /

ms PHOENIX EXPRESS

IMO No. 9035101
Marine Express, Tokyo
Mitsubishi H.I., Shimonoseki; Yard No.: 963

11 578 GRT / 5802 tdw / 170.00 m length oa / 25.00 (25.02) m beam / two 14-cyl. diesels geared to 2 screws; Pielstick-Nippon / 30 580 kW / 26.2 kn / 80 pass. in 26 cabins, 580 pass. unberthed / 90 cars, 1400 lane metres / crew 50

29.1.1993 launched / 1993 delivered, then service Kawasaki—Hyuga / 2002 service Kawasaki—Nachikatsuura—Kochi—Hyuga / 6.2005 to Miyazaki Car Ferry, service Kaizuka—Miyazaki / 9.2006 **MEGA EXPRESS FIVE**, Corsica-Sardinia Ferries, Genoa / 22.10.2006 arrival in Messina for conversion / 3.8.–7.8.2008 towed from Messina to Genoa for further conversion / 4.2009 delivered after conversion: 27 711 GT, 5106 tdw, 177.7 m length oa, 1078 beds in 275 pass., 922 deck pass., 568 cars, 810 lane metres, crew 130 / 6.4.2009 maiden voyage in service Savona—Bastia, then service Toulon/Nice—Corsica /

MEGA EXPRESS FIVE ex PHOENIX EXPRESS (photo: Nikolaos Saratzis)

SUN FLOWER SATSUMA (photo: Hiroyuki Yoshimoto)

ms SUN FLOWER SATSUMA

IMO No. 9035113
Blue Highway Line, Tokyo
Mitsubishi H.I., Shimonoseki; Yard No.: 964

12 436 GRT / 5814 tdw / 186.00 m length oa / 25.50 (27.50) m beam / two 12-cyl. diesels geared to 2 screws; Pielstick-Nippon / 21 380 kW / 22.85 (25.74) kn / 711 pass. in cabins, 71 pass. unberthed / 140 cars, 2208 lane metres / crew 50

14.11.1992 launched / 14.3.1993 delivered / 24.3.1993 maiden voyage in service Osaka—Shibu-shi / 1997 service Tokyo—Tomakomai / 9.1997 service Oarai—Tomakomai / 1998 12 415 GRT / 1999 service Osaka—Shibushi /

ms SUN FLOWER KIRISHIMA

IMO No. 9035125
Blue Highway Line, Tokyo
Mitsubishi H.I., Shimonoseki; Yard No.: 965

12 439 GRT / 5790 tdw / 186.00 m length oa / 25.50 (27.51) m beam / two 12-cyl. diesels

geared to 2 screws; Pielstick-Nippon / 25 160 kW /
22.8 kn / 711 pass. in cabins, 71 pass. unberthed /
140 cars, 2208 lane metres / crew 50

9.4.1993 launched / 8.1993 delivered, then service
Osaka—Shibushi / 1997 service Oarai—Tomakomai /
1999 service Osaka—Shibushi / 2000 12 418 GRT /

ms SUN FLOWER MITO
IMO No. 9073440
Blue Highway Line, Tokyo
Mitsubishi H.I., Shimonoseki; Yard No.: 981

11 782 GRT / 6045 tdw / 186.00 m length oa /
25.50 (27.51) m beam / two 12-cyl. diesels
geared to 2 screws; Pielstick-Nippon / 25 160 kW /
22.85 kn / 126 pass. in 42 cabins, 388 pass.
unberthed / 140 cars, 2208 lane metres /

28.9.1993 launched / 9.12.1993 delivered, then service
Oarai—Tomakomai / 2001 to Shosen Mitsui Ferry,
Tokyo / 2.2007 **PANSTAR SUNNY**, PanStar Ferry, Jeju,
service Osaka—Busan / 6.2009 **COSCO STAR**, China
Ocean Shipping Co. (COSCO), Hong Kong; 26 847 GT /
6.9.2009 entered service Xiamen—Taichung / 2015
also service Xiamen—Keelung—Damaiyu Island /

ms STATENDAM
IMO No. 8919245
Holland America Line, Nassau
Fincantieri, Monfalcone; Yard No.: 5881

55 451 GT / 7637 tdw / 219.21 m length oa /
30.80 m beam / two 12-cyl. and three 8-cyl. diesels
with 34 560 kW; Sulzer-Grandi Motori /
five generators connected to two elec. motors /
24 000 kW / 2 screws / 20 (22.6) kn / 1260 (1512)
pass. in 630 cabins / crew 588

3.4.1992 floated out / 5.1.1993 delivered and transfer
voyage to Fort Lauderdale, maiden cruise to Los
Angeles / 1996 home port Rotterdam / 6.2005
55 819 GT / 21.9.2015 last cruise Seattle—Singapore
for Holland America Line / 22.10.–3.11.2015 conversion at Sembcorp Marine Admiralty Yard, Singapore /
11.2015 **PACIFIC EDEN**, P&O Cruises Australia,
London / 15.11.2015 first cruise Fremantle—Sydney /

SUN FLOWER KIRISHIMA (photo: Osamu Taniguchi)

COSCO STAR ex SUN FLOWER MITO (photo: Ivan Meshkov)

PACIFIC EDEN ex STATENDAM (photo: Dale E. Crisp)

MAASDAM (photo: Tony Davis)

ms MAASDAM
IMO No. 8919257
Holland America Line, Nassau
Fincantieri, Monfalcone; Yard No.: 5882

55451 GT / 7406 tdw / 219.21 m length oa /
30.80 m beam / two 12-cyl. and three 8-cyl.
diesels with 34560 kW; Sulzer-Grandi Motori /
five generators connected to two elec. motors /
24000 kW / 2 screws / 20 (22) kn / 1258 (1510)
pass. in 629 cabins / crew 588

12.12.1992 floated out / 26.10.1993 delivered /
3.12.1993 commissioned in Fort Lauderdale /
17.17.1993 first Caribbean cruise / 1996 home port
Rotterdam / 1998 55575 GT /

ms RYNDAM
IMO No. 8919269
Holland America Line, Nassau
Fincantieri, Monfalcone; Yard No.: 5883

55451 GT / 7447 tdw / 219.21 m length oa /
30.80 m beam / two 12-cyl. and three 8-cyl. diesels
with 34560 kW; Sulzer-Grandi Motori /
five generators connected to two elec. motors/

24000 kW / 2 screws / 20 kn / 1260 (1512) pass.
in 630 cabins / crew 588

1.11.1993 launched / 9.9.1994 delivered / 20.10.1994
maiden cruise from Fort Lauderdale / 1997 home
port Rotterdam / 2004 55819 GT / 3.10.2015 last
cruise Venice—Singapore for Holland America Line /

31.10.–12.11.2015 conversion at Sembcorp Marine
Admiralty Yard, Singapore / 11.2015 **PACIFIC ARIA**,
P&O Cruises Australia, London / 25.11.2015 first cruise
Sydney—Brisbane /

ms VEENDAM
IMO No. 9102992
Holland America Line, Nassau
Fincantieri, Marghera; Yard No.: 5954

55451 GT / 6604 tdw / 219.21 m length oa /
30.80 m beam / three 8-cyl. and two 12-cyl. diesels
with 34560 kW; Sulzer-Grandi Motori /
five generators connected to two elec. motors /
24000 kW / 2 screws / 20 (22) kn / 1258 (1510)
pass. in 629 cabins / crew 588

25.5.1996 launched / 23.4.1996 delivered / 28.4.1996
from Venice to Malaga / 25.5.1996 first cruise from
Fort Lauderdale / 10.1.2006 home port Rotterdam /
2.4.2009 start of conversion at Grand Bahama Shipyard, Freeport, fitting of a ducktail and an additional
cabin block aft, 57092 GT, 1350 (1620) pass. in 675
cabins / 1.5.2009 again in operation /

VEENDAM (photo: Peter Knego)

PACIFIC ARIA ex RYNDAM (photo: Clyde Dickens)

ms SPIRIT OF BRITISH COLUMBIA
IMO No. 9015668
British Columbia Ferry Corp., Victoria
I.F.C. (Integrated Ferry Construction), Victoria B.C.;
Yard No.: 20 / 254

18 747 GT / 2925 tdw / 167.50 m length oa /
26.60 (27.21) m beam / two 6-cyl. diesels geared
to 2 screws; MAN / 13 600 kW / 19.25 kn /
2000 pass. unberthed / 470 cars /

Fore ship was built at Allied Shipbuilders in North
Vancouver (Yard No.: 254), aft ship at Integrated Ferry
Constr. in Victoria (Yard No.: 20) and the superstructure
at Pacific Rim Shipbuilders, assembled in Esquimalt
drydock, Victoria / 17.4.1992 launch of aft ship /
4.3.1993 delivered / 3.1993 service Tsawwassen—
Swartz Bay /

SPIRIT OF BRITISH COLUMBIA (photo: Scott Arkell)

SPIRIT OF VANCOUVER ISLAND (photo: Scott Arkell)

ms SPIRIT OF VANCOUVER ISLAND
IMO No. 9030682
British Columbia Ferry Corp., Victoria
I.F.C. (Integrated Ferry Construction), Victoria B.C.;
Yard No.: 21 / 255

18 747 GT / 2925 tdw / 167.50 m length oa /
26.60 (27.21) m beam / four 6-cyl. diesels geared
to 2 screws; MAN / 13 600 kW / 19.25 kn /
2000 pass. unberthed / 470 cars /

14.2.1993 aft ship launched; fore ship delivered from
Allied Shipbuilders in North Vancouver / 13.12.1993
sea trials / 17.3.1994 maiden voyage in service Swartz
Bay—Tsawwassen /

SILJA EUROPA (photo: Jukka Huotari)

ms SILJA EUROPA
IMO No. 8919805
Silja Line, Mariehamn
Jos. L. Meyer, Papenburg; Yard No.: 627

59 912 GT / 5380 tdw / 201.78 m length oa /
32.00 (32.60) m beam / four 6-cyl. diesels geared
to 2 screws; MAN B&W / 31 800 kW / 23 kn /
2746 pass. in 1196 cabins, 267 pass. unberthed /
400 cars, 932 lane metres /

23.1.1993 floated out as EUROPA for Rederi AB Slite /
5.3.1993 delivered as SILJA EUROPA / 14.3.1993
entered service Helsinki—Stockholm / 11.1.1995
entered service Stockholm—Mariehamn—Turku /
1998 3123 pass. in 1158 cabins / 1.3.2001 in winter
service Kapellskär—Mariehamn—Turku / 2003
59 912 GT, 4650 tdw / 1.1.2008–20.1.2013 service
Turku—Mariehamn—Stockholm / 22.1.2013 home
port Tallinn / 23.1.2013–6.8.2014 service Helsinki—
Tallinn / 22.10.2014–30.12.2015 accommodation ship
off Barrow Island, Western Australia, under charter by
Bridgemans Services for LNG production /

OKESA MARU (photo: Hiroyuki Yoshimoto)

ms OKESA MARU
IMO No. 9052616
Sado Kisen, Ryotsu
Kanda Zosensho, Kawajiri; Yard No.: 350

12 419 GT / 3250 tdw / 134.70 m length oa /
20.30 (23.40) m beam / two 12-cyl. diesels
geared to 2 screws; Pielstick-Niigata / 12 500 kW /
22.5 kn / 1520 pass. unberthed / 48 cars +
32 buses, 850 lane metres / crew 45

11.11.1992 launched / 4.1993 delivered, then
service Niigata—Ryotsu /

ms LAS PALMAS DE GRAN CANARIA
IMO No. 9031997
Cia. Trasmediterranea, Santa Cruz de Tenerife
Union Naval de Levante, Valencia; Yard No.: 216

10 473 GT / 2901 tdw / 116.79 m length oa /
20.70 m beam / two 12-cyl. diesels geared to
2 screws; MAN-Bazan / 5280 kW / 16 kn / 78 pass.
in 31 cabins, 300 pass. unberthed / 280 cars,
993 lane metres / crew 39

5.1993 delivered, then service Las Palmas—Santa
Cruz / 1996 conversion at Empresa Nacional Bazan:
800 pass. unberthed / 1999 service Barcelona—Palma
de Mallorca / 2000 service Algeciras—Tangier, 378
pass. unberthed /

LAS PALMAS DE GRAN CANARIA (photo: Frank Lose)

SEOKYUNG ISLAND ex SANTA CRUZ DE TENERIFE (photo: Frank Lose)

ms SANTA CRUZ DE TENERIFE
IMO No. 9032006
Cia. Trasmediterranea, Las Palmas
Union Naval de Levante, Valencia; Yard No.: 217

10 473 GT / 2663 tdw / 116.79 m length oa /
20.70 m beam / two 12-cyl. diesels geared to
2 screws; MAN-Bazan / 5280 kW / 16 kn / 78 pass.
in 31 cabins, 300 pass. unberthed / 280 cars,
993 lane metres / crew 39

20.5.1993 launched / 1994 delivered, then service Las
Palmas—Santa Cruz / 1997 enlargement of facilities to
800 pass. unberthed at Empresa Nacional Bazan / 2005
service Alicante/Almeria—Oran / 2011–9.11.2012
service Tangier Med.—Algeciras / 19.11.2012 to Seo
Kyung Co, Ltd., home port Funafuti / 1.2.2013 renamed
SEOKYUNG ISLAND, home port Busan / 2014 service
Busan—Jeju / 21.3.2015 laid up in Busan /

MAJESTIC (photo: Frank Lose)

ms MAJESTIC
IMO No. 9015735
Grandi Navi Veloci, Palermo
Nuovi Cant. Apuania, Marina di Carrara;
Yard No.: 1159

32 746 GT / 6875 tdw / 188.22 m length oa /
26.80 (27.60) m beam / four 8-cyl. diesels geared to
2 screws; Sulzer / 23 040 kW / 23 kn / 1205 pass.
in 339 cabins, 236 pass. unberthed / 760 cars,
1725 lane metres / crew 169

8.12.1992 launched / 11.5.1993 delivered, then
service Genoa—Palermo / 1.1997 service Livorno—
Palermo / 1998 seasonal alternating service from
Genoa, Livorno, Palermo and Porto Torres / 2008
service Genoa—Barcelona—Tangier / 19.1.2016
service Naples—Palermo planned /

SPLENDID (photo: Frank Lose)

ms SPLENDID
IMO No. 9015747
Grandi Navi Veloci, Palermo
Nuovi Cant. Apuania, Marina di Carrara;
Yard No.: 1160

32 731 GT / 6875 tdw / 188.22 m length oa /
26.80 (27.60) m beam / four 8-cyl. diesels geared
to 2 screws; Sulzer / 23 040 kW / 23 kn /
1250 pass. in 339 cabins, 236 pass. unberthed /
700 cars, 1725 lane metres /

18.12.1993 launched / 6.1994 delivered, then service
Palermo—Genoa / 2.7.1994 entered service Genoa—
Porto Torres / 9.1995 service Genoa—Palermo—
Tunis—Valletta / 10.–12.1996 lengthened in Palermo:

39 109 GT, 8707 tdw, 214.14 m length oa, 1639 pass. in 440 cabins, 679 Pullman, crew 198 / 1.1997 service Genoa—Palermo and Genoa—Porto Torres / 2015 service Civitavecchia—Palermo /

ms FANTASTIC
IMO No. 9100267
Grandi Navi Veloci, Palermo
Nuovi Cant. Apuania, Marina di Carrara;
Yard No.: 1182

25 186 GT / 7037 tdw / 188.22 m length oa / 26.80 (28.00) m beam / four 9-cyl. diesels geared to 2 screws; Sulzer / 25 920 kW / 23 kn / 1389 pass. in 373 cabins, 311 pass. unberthed / 760 cars, 1725 lane metres /

25.5.1996 delivered / 14.6.1996 three cruises Genoa—Malaga—Palma de Mallorca—Lisbon / 28.6.1996 entered service Genoa—Porto Torres / 22.9.1998 entered service Genoa—Barcelona / 26.5.2012 entered service Sète—Tangier/Nador /

ms JUAN J. SISTER
IMO No. 9039391
Cia. Trasmediterranea, Las Palmas
Kværner Masa-Yards, Turku; Yard No.: 1319

22 409 GT / 5567 tdw / 151.10 m length oa / 26.00 m beam / four 8-cyl. diesels geared to 2 screws; Wärtsilä / 10 800 kW / 18 kn / 406 pass. in 142 cabins, 150 pass. unberthed / 150 cars, 1680 lane metres /

24.11.1992 launched / 12.5.1993 delivered, then service Cadiz—Canaries / 1.10.2006 entered service Melilla—Almeria/Malaga / 26.4.2015 entered service Valencia—Ibiza, also service Barcelona—Ibiza /

ms KONG HARALD
IMO No. 9039119
Troms Fylkes D/S (TFDS), Tromsø
Volkswerft Stralsund, Stralsund; Yard No.: 101

11 204 GT / 902 tdw / 121.80 m length oa / 19.20 (23.40) m beam / two 6-cyl. diesels geared to 2 screws; MaK / 9000 kW / 18 kn / 483 pass. in 227 cabins, 208 pass. unberthed / 45 cars / crew 59

28.11.1992 launched / 25.6.1993 delivered / 6.7.1993 entered liner service Bergen—Kirkenes / 2000 460 pass. in 230 cabins / 3.2006 to Hurtigruten, Narvik /

FANTASTIC (photo: Frank Lose)

JUAN J. SISTER (photo: Frank Lose)

KONG HARALD (photo: Tom Gulbrandsen)

13.8.1993 launched / 3.1994 delivered / 4.4.1994 maiden voyage in liner service Bergen—Kirkenes / 3.2006 to Hurtigruten, Tromsø / 15.9.2011 on a voyage from Torvik to Ålesund shortly before reaching Ålesund explosion and fire in the engine room, two crew members killed. Towed to Alesund, fire extinguished there / 20.3.2012 back in liner service Bergen—Kirkenes after repairs /

ms POLARLYS
IMO No. 9107796
Troms Fylkes D/S (TFDS), Tromsø
Ulstein Verft, Ulsteinvik; Yard No.: 223

11 341 GT / 850 tdw / 123.00 m length oa / 19.50 m beam / four 9-cyl. diesels geared to 2 screws; Normo-Ulstein / 11 260 kW / 15.5 kn /

RICHARD WITH (photo: Tom Gulbrandsen)

ms RICHARD WITH
IMO No. 9040429
Ofotens og Vesteraalens D/S, Narvik
Volkswerft Stralsund, Stralsund; Yard No.: 103

11 205 GT / 850 tdw / 121.80 m length oa / 19.20 (23.40) m beam / two 6-cyl. diesels geared to 2 screws; MaK / 9000 kW / 15 kn / 466 pass. in 219 cabins, 225 pass. unberthed / 45 cars / crew 59

14.2.1993 launched / 23.11.1993 delivered / 30.11.1993 christened in Narvik, then liner service Bergen—Kirkenes / 3.2006 to Hurtigruten, Narvik / 11.2013 home port Tromsø /

NORDLYS (photo: Uwe Jakob)

ms NORDLYS
IMO No. 9048914
Troms Fylkes D/S (TFDS), Tromsø
Volkswerft Stralsund, Stralsund; Yard No.: 102

11 204 GT / 860 tdw / 121.66 m length oa / 19.20 (23.78) m beam / two 6-cyl. diesels geared to 2 screws; MaK / 9000 kW / 18 kn / 475 pass. in 223 cabins, 216 pass. unberthed / 45 cars / crew 59

POLARLYS (photo: Uwe Jakob)

479 pass. in 225 cabins, 258 pass. unberthed / 35 cars / crew 59

1995 launched / 23.3.1995 christened / 17.4.1996 maiden voyage in liner service Bergen—Kirkenes / 3.2006 to Hurtigruten, Tromsø /

ms NORDKAPP
IMO No. 9107772
Ofotens og Vesteraalens D/S, Narvik
Kværner Kleven, Ulsteinvik; Yard No.: 265

11 386 GT / 1104 tdw / 123.30 m length oa / 19.50 (24.20) m beam / two 6-cyl. diesels geared to 2 screws; MaK / 9000 kW / 15 (18) kn / 464 pass. in 218 cabins, 227 pass. unberthed / 45 cars / crew 59

18.8.1995 launched / 23.3.1996 christened / 2.4.1996 maiden voyage in liner service Bergen—Kirkenes / 3.2006 to Hurtigruten, Narvik / 11.12.2013 home port Tromsø /

NORDKAPP (photo: Tom Gulbrandsen)

NORDNORGE (photo: Mike Louagie)

ms NORDNORGE
IMO No. 9107784
Ofotens og Vesteraalens D/S, Narvik
Kværner Kleven, Ulsteinvik; Yard No.: 266

11384 GT / 1171 tdw / 123.30 m length oa /
19.50 (24.50) m beam / two 6-cyl. diesels geared to
2 screws; MaK / 9000 kW / 15 (18) kn / 457 pass. in
214 cabins, 234 pass. unberthed / 45 cars / crew 59

1996 launched / 19.3.1997 delivered, then promotional cruises in the Baltic / 28.4.1997 maiden
voyage in liner service Bergen—Kirkenes /
29.11.2002–spring 2008 winter cruises from Chile
to Antarctica / 3.2006 to Hurtigruten, Narvik /
20.12.2008–13.8.2009 accommodation ship
for construction of a LNG platform near Venice /
1.4.2010 again liner service Bergen—Kirkenes /
11.2013 home port Tromsø /

KALLISTE (photo: Frank Lose)

ms KALLISTE
IMO No. 9050618
Cie Méridionale de Navigation, Bastia
Finnyards, Rauma; Yard No.: 403

29575 GT / 9710 tdw / 165.00 m length oa /
29.00 m beam / four 16-cyl. diesels geared to
2 screws; Wärtsilä / 19700 kW / 19 kn / 196 pass.
in 95 cabins / 121 cars, 2200 lane metres /

24.1.1993 launched / 19.7.1993 delivered / 29.7.1993
entered service Marseilles—Bastia /

ms QUEEN CORAL

IMO No. 9066710
Marix Line, Kagoshima
Hayashikane Dockyard, Nagasaki; Yard No.: 1001

4924 GRT / 1300 tdw / 140.01 m length oa /
20.50 m beam / two 9-cyl. diesels; Nippon Kokkan /
9930 kW / 2 screws / 20.2 (22.4) kn / 246 pass. in
cabins, 254 pass. unberthed / 66 cars + 27 trucks,
300 lane metres /

9.1993 delivered / 7.10.1993 entered service
Kagoshima—Amami—Naha / 1.2009 EASTERN
DREAM, DBS Cruiseferry, Panama; 11 478 GT / 4.2009
service Donghae—Vladivostok—Sakaiminato /

EASTERN DREAM ex QUEEN CORAL (photo: Osamu Taniguchi)

SILVER CLOUD (photo: Alexander Brede)

ms SILVER CLOUD

IMO No. 8903923
Silversea Cruises, Venice
Cantiere Navale Visentini, Donada (hull);
Soc. Esercizio, Viareggio; Yard No.: 775

16 927 GT / 1564 tdw / 155.81 m length oa /
21.40 m beam / two 6-cyl. diesels geared to
2 screws; Wärtsilä / 11 700 kW / 17.5 (20.5) kn /
314 pass. in 153 cabins / crew 185

6.3.1993 launched, then final fitting out at T. Mariotti,
Genoa / 3.1994 delivered / 2.4.1994 maiden cruise
from Civitavecchia / 1996 home port Nassau / 8.2017
conversion into ice-strengthened expedition cruise ship
for Silversea Expeditions planned /

ms SILVER WIND

IMO No. 8903935
Silversea Cruises, Palermo
Cantiere Navale Visentini, Donada (hull);
Soc. Esercizio, Viareggio; Yard No.: 776

16 927 GT / 1790 tdw / 155.81 m length oa /
21.40 m beam / two 6-cyl. diesels geared to
2 screws; Wärtsilä / 11 700 kW / 17.5 (20.5) kn /
314 pass. in 153 cabins / crew 185

16.10.1993 launched, then final fitting out at T.
Mariotti, Genoa / 1.1995 delivered, then cruises / 2000
home port Nassau / 6.2010 17 235 GT /

SILVER WIND (photo: Frank Heine)

AF MARINA ex TOSCANA (photo: Frank Heine)

ms TOSCANA

IMO No. 9059107
Tirrenia di Navigazione, Naples
Cantiere Navale Visentini, Donada; Yard No.: 163

12 790 GT / 6550 tdw / 166.20 m length oa /
22.00 m beam / one 16-cyl. diesel geared to
1 screw; New Sulzer / 11 520 kW / 20 kn /
170 pass. in 58 cabins / 1676 lane metres /

16.7.1994 launched / 1994 delivered, then service
Naples—Palermo / 1996 converted in Messina:
13 885 GT, 474 pass. in 119 cabins, 126 pass.
unberthed / 1999 service Cagliari—Genoa/Palermo /
2004 laid up in Naples / 2005 in winter service
Cagliari—Naples, Cagliari—Palermo and Cagliari—
Trapani, in summer service Ancona—Split / 15.11.2012
AF MARINA, Adria Ferries, Valletta / 15.12.2012
entered service Ancona—Durres, also Durres—Trieste/
Bari / 5.2013 home port Naples /

ms PAGLIA ORBA
IMO No. 9059107
Soc. Nationale Maritime Corse Méditerranée,
Marseilles
Soc. Nouvelle of the At. & Ch. du Havre, Le Havre;
Yard No.: 290

29 718 GT / 6325 tdw / 165.80 m length oa /
29.00 m beam / four 16-cyl. diesels geared to
2 screws; Wärtsilä / 19 720 kW / 19 kn / 196 pass.
in 95 cabins / 120 cars / 2330 lane metres /

3.6.1993 launched / 12.5.1994 delivered, then service
Marseilles—Bastia /

PAGLIA ORBA (photo: Frank Lose)

ms XIN JIAN ZHEN
IMO No. 9065376
China-Japan International Ferry Co., Shanghai
Onomichi Zosen, Onomichi; Yard No.: 372

14 543 GT / 3750 tdw / 156.67 m length oa /
23.00 m beam / two 14-cyl. diesels geared to
2 screws; Pielstick-Nippon / 11 032 kW / 21 kn /
68 pass. in 22 cabins, 287 pass. unberthed /
crew 61

12.1.1994 launched / 4.1994 delivered, then service
Osaka/Kobe—Shanghai /

XIN JIAN ZHEN (photo: Frank Lose)

ms FINNHANSA
IMO No. 9010151
Finnlines, Helsinki
Stocznia Gdanska, Gdansk; Yard No.: B501/01

32 531 GT / 11 602 tdw / 183.00 m length oa /
28.70 (29.90) m beam / four 8-cyl. diesels geared
to 2 screws; Sulzer-Zgoda / 23 040 kW / 21.3 kn /
112 pass. in 34 cabins / 3380 lane metres / crew 21

14.9.1993 launched / 3.8.1994 delivered / 10.8.1994
maiden voyage in service Helsinki—Lübeck /
1.10.2001 entered service Helsinki—Travemünde /
25.4.2009 renamed EUROFERRY SICILIA, home
port Palermo; entered service Genoa/Civitavecchia
—Catania—Valletta under charter by Grimaldi
Ferries / 16.7.2010 renamed TRANSRUSSIA, home
port Rostock / 28.7.2010 entered service Lübeck—
Sassnitz—Ventspils—St. Petersburg / 22.2.–
4.10.2012 service Aarhus—Helsinki / 6.10.2012
again service Lübeck—Sassnitz—Ventspils—St.
Petersburg / 30.1.2014 renamed FINNHANSA, then
service Lübeck—Sassnitz—Ventspils—St. Petersburg /
11.2014 EUROFERRY EGNAZIA, Grimaldi Ferries,
Palermo / 12.2014 after conversion 33 400 GT, 1000
pass. / 28.12.2014 entered service Patras—Igoumenitsa—Brindisi /

EUROFERRY EGNAZIA ex FINNHANSA (photo: Frank Heine)

FINNPARTNER (photo: Frank Lose)

ms FINNPARTNER
IMO No. 9010163
Finnlines, Helsinki
Stocznia Gdanska, Gdansk; Yard No.: B501/02

32 534 GT / 11 558 tdw / 183.00 m length oa /
28.70 (29.90) m beam / four 8-cyl. diesels geared
to 2 screws; Sulzer-Zgoda / 23 040 kW / 21.25 kn /
112 pass. in 34 cabins / 3380 lane metres / crew 21

15.7.1994 launched / 12.2.1995 delivered / 18.2.1995
maiden voyage in service Helsinki—Lübeck / 1.10.2001
entered service Helsinki—Travemünde / 8.2007
delivered after conversion in Gdansk: 33 313 GT, 9993
tdw, 270 pass. in cabins, 3052 lane metres / 28.8.2007
entered service Malmö—Travemünde /

ms TRANSEUROPA
IMO No. 9010175
Poseidon Schiffahrt, Lübeck
Stocznia Gdanska, Gdansk; Yard No.: B501/03

32 534 GT / 11 682 tdw / 183.00 m length oa /
28.70 (29.90) m beam / four 8-cyl. diesels geared
to 2 screws; Sulzer-Zgoda / 23 040 kW / 21.3 kn /
90 pass. in 34 cabins / 3200 lane metres / crew 20

29.12.1994 launched / 31.5.1995 delivered / 12.6.1995
maiden voyage in service Lübeck—Helsinki / 2001
to Finnlines, Lübeck / 1.10.2001 entered service
Helsinki—Travemünde / 14.2.2009 entered service
Lübeck—St. Petersburg for the Finnlines subsidiary
TransRussia Express / 12.2013 **EUROFERRY OLYMPIA**,

EUROFERRY OLYMPIA ex TRANSEUROPA (photo: Frank Lose)

Grimaldi Ferries, Palermo / 27.2.2014 entered service
Patras—Igoumenitsa—Ravenna / 24.7.–10.9.2014
entered service Trieste—Ravenna—Igoumenitsa
—Patras / 4.10.2014 entered service Brindisi—
Igoumenitsa—Patras /

ms FINNTRADER
IMO No. 9017769
Finnlines, Helsinki
Stocznia Gdanska, Gdansk; Yard No.: B501/04

32 534 GT / 11 600 tdw / 183.00 m length oa /
28.70 (29.90) m beam / four 8-cyl. diesels geared
to 2 screws; Sulzer-Zgoda / 23 040 kW / 21.25 kn /
112 pass. in 34 cabins / 3380 lane metres / crew 21

7.4.1995 launched / 26.10.1995 delivered /
3.11.1995 maiden voyage in service Helsinki—
Lübeck / 1.10.2001–4.8.2006 entered service
Helsinki—Travemünde / 7.8.2006 home port Malmö /
13.2.2007 delivered after conversion in Gdansk:
33 313 GT, 9035 tdw, 304 pass. in 194 cabins, 3052
lane metres, crew 30 / 19.2.2006 entered service
Malmö—Travemünde /

FINNTRADER (photo: Frank Lose)

ORIANA (photo: George Koutsoukis)

ms ORIANA
IMO No. 9050137
P&O Cruises, London
Jos. L. Meyer, Papenburg; Yard No.: 636

69 153 GT / 6715 tdw / 260.00 m length oa /
32.20 m beam / two 9-cyl. and two 6-cyl. diesels
geared to 2 screws; MAN B&W / 39 750 kW /
24 kn / 1975 (2108) pass. in 914 cabins / crew 760

30.6.1994 floated out / 2.4.1995 delivered / 6.4.1995
christened by Queen Elizabeth II. in Southampton /
9.4.1995 maiden cruise Southampton—Canaries /
12.2006 home port Hamilton / 11–12.2011 conversion
at Blohm+Voss, Hamburg: 69 840 GT /

SKANIA ex SUPERFAST I (photo: Frank Lose)

ms SUPERFAST I
IMO No. 9086588
SuperFast Ferries, Patras
Schichau Seebeckwerft, Bremerhaven; Yard No.: 1087

23 663 GT / 5717 tdw / 173.70 m length oa /
24.00 (28.70) m beam / four 12-cyl. diesels geared
to 2 screws; Sulzer-Zgoda / 31 680 kW / 27 kn /
626 pass. in 200 cabins, 784 pass. unberthed /
830 cars, 1675 lane metres / crew 103

30.7.1994 launched / 25.3.1995 christened / 6.4.1995
delivered / 15.4.1995 maiden voyage in service
Patras—Ancona / 16.3.1998 entered service Bari—
Patras / 26.2.2004 **EUROSTAR ROMA**, Grimaldi Ferries,
Palermo / 14.3.2004 entered service Civitavecchia—
Barcelona / 5.2008 **SKANIA**, Unity Line, Nassau /
1.9.2008 entered service Swinoujscie—Ystad /

MEGA EXPRESS FOUR ex SUPERFAST II (photo: Nikolaos Saratzis)

ms SUPERFAST II
IMO No. 9086590
SuperFast Ferries, Patras
Schichau Seebeckwerft, Bremerhaven; Yard No.: 1088

23 663 GT / 5717 tdw / 173.70 m length oa /
24.00 (28.70) m beam / four 12-cyl. diesels geared
to 2 screws; Sulzer-Zgoda / 31 680 kW / 27 kn /
626 pass. in 200 cabins, 784 pass. unberthed /
830 cars, 1675 lane metres / crew 103

14.1.1995 launched / 25.3.1995 christened / 31.5.1995
delivered / 11.6.1995 maiden voyage in service
Patras—Ancona / 10.4.1998 entered service Bari—
Patras / 30.9.2003 **SPIRIT OF TASMANIA III**, TT
Line Co., Devonport / 13.1.2004–27.8.2006 service
Sydney—Devonport / 6.9.2006 **MEGA EXPRESS
FOUR**, Corsica Sardinia Ferries, Genoa / 6.11.2006
entered service Savona—Bastia, later service Toulon
—Corsica / 10.1.–30.4.2007 conversion in Perama:
25 710 GT, 909 pass. in 252 cabins, 1056 pass.
unberthed, 550 cars, 1400 lane metres, crew 115 /
4.5.2007 entered service Nice/Toulon—Corsica /

LEGEND OF THE SEAS (photo: Alexander Brede)

ms LEGEND OF THE SEAS
IMO No. 9070620
Royal Caribbean Cruise Line, Monrovia
Chantiers de l'Atlantique, St. Nazaire; Yard No.: A31

69 130 GT / 5200 tdw / 264.26 m length oa /
32.00 (37.00) m beam / five 12-cyl. diesels with
58 800 kW; Wärtsilä / five generators connected
to two elec. motors / 40 000 kW / 2 screws /
24 (24.9) kn / 1804 (2064) pass. in 902 cabins /
crew 735

4.9.1994 floated out / 28.4.1995 delivered / 16.5.1995
maiden voyage Miami—Los Angeles, then worldwide
cruises / 29.11.1996 grounded with 2500 persons on
board off Isla Catalina, Dominican Republic; refloated
after twelve hours / 3.2003 home port Nassau /
1.–2.2013 conversion at Sembawang, Singapore:
69 472 GT, 1830 (2196) pass. in 915 cabins /

ms SPLENDOUR OF THE SEAS
IMO No. 9070632
Royal Caribbean Cruise Line, Oslo
Chantiers de l'Atlantique, St. Nazaire; Yard No.: B31

69 130 GT / 5200 tdw / 264.26 m length oa /
32.00 (36.30) m beam / five 12-cyl. diesels with
58 500 kW; Wärtsilä / five generators connected to
two elec. motors / 40 000 kW / 2 screws / 24 kn /
1804 (2066) pass. in 902 cabins / crew 735

17.6.1995 floated out / 15.3.1996 delivered / 29.3.1996
christened in Southampton / 31.3.1996 maiden cruise
Southampton—Barcelona / 12.2004 home port
Nassau / 25.10.–24.11.2011 conversion at Navantia,
Cadiz: 69 472 GT, 1830 (2196) pass. in 915 cabins /
2.3.2015 with delivery 4.2016 to TUI Cruises / 4.4.2016
last cruise Dubai—Venice for Royal Caribbean International planned / 11.6.2016 first cruise Palma de
Mallorca—Mediterranean as **THOMSON DISCOVERY**
under charter by Thomson Cruises planned /

SPLENDOUR OF THE SEAS (photo: Richard Seville)

POLONIA (photo: Frank Lose)

ms POLONIA
IMO No. 9107942
Unity Line, Nassau
Langsten Slip & Båtbyggeri, Tomrefjord; Yard No.: 163

29 875 GT / 7250 tdw / 169.90 m length oa /
28.00 m beam / four 6-cyl. diesels; Stork-Wärtsilä /
15 840 kW / 2 screws / 21 kn / 584 pass. in 204
cabins, 414 pass. unberthed / 172 cars, 2200 lane
metres, 5 rail tracks with 740 m length / crew 82

26.5.1995 delivered / 31.5.1995 maiden voyage in
service Swinoujscie—Ystad /

KAITAKI ex ISLE OF INNISFREE (photo: Clyde Dickens)

ms ISLE OF INNISFREE
IMO No. 9107942
Irish Ferries, Dublin
van der Giessen-De Noord, Krimpen; Yard No.: 963

22 365 GT / 5794 tdw / 181.60 m length oa /
23.40 (23.90) m beam / four 8-cyl. diesels geared
to 2 screws; Sulzer-Adria / 23 040 kW / 21 kn /
132 pass. in 34 cabins, 1650 pass. unberthed /
600 cars, 1780 lane metres /

27.1.1995 launched / 15.5.1995 delivered /
23.5.1995–3.3.1997 service Dublin—Holyhead /
22.3.1997 entered service Rosslare—Fishguard /
18.4.1997 entered service Rosslare—Pembroke Dock /
2001 132 pass. in 36 cabins, 1518 pass. unberthed /
17.5.2001 laid up in Dublin / 14.6.2001 laid up in Le
Havre / 1.7.2002 under charter by P&O Ferries, home
port Portsmouth. Conversion in Falmouth / 12.8.2002
renamed **PRIDE OF CHERBOURG** / 12.9.2002–
14.1.2005 service Portsmouth—Cherbourg / 2005
renamed **STENA CHALLENGER** / 12.2.–7.6.2005
service Karls-krona—Gdynia under charter by Stena
Line / 6.2005 renamed **CHALLENGER** / 22.8.2005
entered service Wellington—Picton under charter by
Interisland Line / 17.4.2007 renamed **KAITAKI** /

ms ARETOUSA
IMO No. 9088859
Minoan Lines, Heraklion
Fosen Mek. Verksteder, Rissa; Yard No.: 56

28 417 GT / 5850 tdw / 177.30 m length oa /
27.00 m beam / four 8-cyl. diesels geared to
2 screws; MAN B&W / 31 200 kW / 23.8 kn /
500 pass. in 125 cabins, 1000 pass. unberthed /
634 cars, 2250 lane metres /

15.12.1994 launched at Bruces Shipyard in Landskrona,
then towed to Rissa for completion / 9.6.1995
delivered / 8.7.1995 maiden voyage in service
Patras—Igoumenitsa—Ancona / 14.1.1998 entered
service Patras—Igoumenitsa—Corfu—Venice / 2002
GIROLATA, Compagnie Meridionale de Navigation,
Bastia / 11.3.2002 entered service Marseilles—Corsica /

GIROLATA ex ARETOUSA (photo: Frank Heine)

ORIENTAL PEARL 6 ex CRUISE FERRY HIRYU as CRUISE FERRY HIRYU (photo: Hiroyuki Yoshimoto)

ms CRUISE FERRY HIRYU
IMO No. 9112246
Arimura Sangyo, Naha
Mitsubishi H.I., Shimonoseki; Yard No.: 1007

10 342 GRT / 3606 tdw / 167.00 m length oa /
22.00 m beam / two 18-cyl. diesels geared to
2 screws; Pielstick-Nippon / 19 860 kW / 24.9 kn /
430 pass. in 80 cabins / 143 trucks + 72 cars /
crew 39

16.4.1995 launched / 29.6.1995 delivered / 1.7.1995
entered service Nagoya—Osaka—Naha—Miyako—
Ishigaki—Keelung—Kaohsiung / 1997 10 351 GT /
6.6.2008 service discontinued, ship laid up in Naha /
11.7.2008 shipping company wound up, then laid up
in Fukuyama / 4.2010 **PYEONG SAN**, Panama Arro
Shipping, Panama, 16 445 GT, service Pyeongtaek—
Weihai chartered by Weihai Jiadong Ferries / 12.2010
ORIENTAL PEARL 6, Doowoo Shipping, Jeju, Panama,
service Dandong—Incheon / 1.2011 to Dandong International
Ferry, Panama, service Dandong—Incheon
for Dandong International Ferry / 2015 16 537 GT /

ms BANG CHUI DAO
IMO No. 9110781
Dalian Marine Transport, Dalian
van der Giessen-De Noord, Krimpen; Yard No.: 965

15 560 GT / 6883 tdw / 134.80 m length oa /
23.40 m beam / two 9-cyl. diesels geared to
2 screws; Stork-Wärtsilä / 11 520 kW / 20 kn /
937 pass. in 169 cabins / 226 cars, 830 lane metres /

13.5.1995 launched / 5.9.1995 delivered, then service
Dalian—Yantai / 2001 to China Shipping Passenger
Liner, Dalian /

BANG CHUI DAO (photo: Marko Stampehl)

HAI YANG DAO (photo: Ton Grootenboer)

ms HAI YANG DAO
IMO No. 9110793
Dalian Marine Transport, Dalian
van der Giessen-de Noord, Krimpen; Yard No.: 966

15 560 GT / 3250 tdw / 134.80 m length oa /
23.40 m beam / two 9-cyl. diesels geared to
2 screws; Stork-Wärtsilä / 11 520 kW / 20 kn /
937 pass. in 169 cabins / 226 cars, 900 lane metres /

16.9.1995 launched / 15.12.1995 delivered, then
service Dalian—Xingang, also Dalian—Yantai / 2001
to China Shipping Passenger Liner, Dalian /

ms PU TUO DAO
IMO No. 9305154
China Shipping Passenger Liner, Dalian
Jiangnan Shipyard, Shanghai; Yard No.: H2307

16 234 GT / 3996 tdw / 137.30 m length oa /
23.40 m beam / two 9-cyl. diesels geared to
2 screws; Wärtsilä / 11 600 kW / 19 kn / 940 pass.
in 170 cabins / 835 lane metres /

22.4.2005 delivered, then service Dalian—Yantai /

PU TUO DAO (photo: Marko Stampehl)

ms HU LU DAO
IMO No. 9305166
China Shipping Passenger Liner, Dalian
Jiangnan Shipyard, Shanghai; Yard No.: H2308

16 234 GT / 3873 tdw / 137.30 m length oa /
23.40 m beam / two 9-cyl. diesels geared to
2 screws; Wärtsilä / 11 600 kW / 19 kn / 940 pass.
in 170 cabins / 835 lane metres /

29.8.2005 delivered, then service Dalian—Yantai /

HU LU DAO (photo: Marko Stampehl)

ms ROBIN HOOD
IMO No. 9087465
TT-Line, Hamburg
Finnyards, Rauma; Yard No.: 410

NILS DACKE ex ROBIN HOOD (photo: Frank Lose)

26 796 GT / 6538 tdw / 177.20 m length oa /
27.20 (27.53) m beam / four 6-cyl. diesels with
18 000 kW; Krupp MaK / four generators
connected to two elec. motors / 13 000 kW /
2 screws / 18.5 kn / 308 pass. in 154 cabins /
2428 lane metres / crew 35

21.12.1994 floated out / 14.5.1995 delivery delayed
by defective elec. motor / 2.10.1995 delivered /
9.10.1995 maiden voyage in service Travemünde—
Trelleborg / 6.9.2003 additional weekly round trip
Travemünde—Helsingborg / 15.12.2014 renamed
NILS DACKE, home port Limassol / 16.12.2014 entered
service Trelleborg—Swinoujscie /

ms NILS DACKE
IMO No. 9087477
TT-Line, Nassau
Finnyards, Rauma; Yard No.: 411

ROBIN HOOD ex NILS DACKE (photo: Ulrich Streich)

26 790 GT / 6538 tdw / 179.30 m length oa /
27.20 (27.53) m beam / four 6-cyl. diesels with
18 000 kW; Krupp MaK / four generators
connected to two elec. motors / 13 000 kW /
2 screws / 18.5 kn / 308 pass. in 154 cabins /
2428 lane metres / crew 35

19.5.1995 floated out / 28.11.1995 delivery delayed
by problems with elec. motor / 4.12.1995 maiden
voyage in service Travemünde—Trelleborg / 6.9.2003
additional weekly round trip Travemünde—Helsingborg / 19.8.2004 home port Trelleborg / 2.1.2014
home port Szczecin / 7.1.2014 entered service
Trelleborg—Swinoujscie / 15.12.2014 renamed
ROBIN HOOD, home port Lübeck, service Trelleborg—
Travemünde, also Trelleborg—Rostock / 12.2014
home port Emden /

ms TARIQ IBN ZIYAD

IMO No. 9109768
Entreprise Nationale de Transport Maritime
de Voyageurs (E.N.T.M.V.), Algiers
Union Naval de Levante, Valencia; Yard No.: 211

21659 GT / 5125 tdw / 153.26 m length oa /
25.20 m beam / two 12-cyl. diesels geared to
2 screws; Wärtsilä / 22 200 kW / 21.5 kn / 804 pass.
in 178 cabins, 508 pass. unberthed / 446 cars,
780 lane metres /

12.1995 delivered / 12.1995 service Algiers/Oran—
Marseilles/Alicante /

TARIQ IBN ZIYAD (photo: Frank Lose)

ms SUN PRINCESS

IMO No. 9000259
Princess Cruises, Monrovia
Fincantieri, Monfalcone; Yard No.: 5909

77 441 GT / 8270 tdw / 261.31 m length
oa / 32.25 m beam / four 16-cyl. diesels with
46 080 kW; Sulzer-Grandi Motori / four generators
connected to two elec. motors / 28 000 kW /
2 screws / 19.5 (21.4) kn / 2022 (2342) pass. in
1011 cabins / crew 814

21.1.1995 floated out / 11.11.1995 delivered / 1.12.1995
christened in Fort Lauderdale / 8.12.1995 maiden
voyage from Fort Lauderdale / 2000 home port London /
8.2004 home port Hamilton /

SUN PRINCESS (photo: Frank Lose)

ms DAWN PRINCESS

IMO No. 9103996
Princess Cruises, Monrovia
Fincantieri, Monfalcone; Yard No.: 5955

77 441 GT / 8251 tdw / 261.31 m length
oa / 32.25 m beam / four 16-cyl. diesels with
46 080 kW; Sulzer-Grandi Motori / four generators
connected to two elec. motors / 28 000 kW /
2 screws / 19.5 (21.4) kn / 2022 (2342) pass. in
1011 cabins / crew 814

11.7.1996 floated out / 19.4.1997 delivered, then
Alaska and Caribbean cruises / 2000 home port
London / 7.2004 home port Hamilton / 5.2017 new
name **PACIFIC EXPLORER** and transfer to P&O Cruises
Australia planned /

DAWN PRINCESS (photo: Frank Lose)

ms SEA PRINCESS

IMO No. 9150913
Princess Cruises, Monrovia
Fincantieri, Monfalcone; Yard No.: 5998

77 499 GT / 8251 tdw / 261.31 m length
oa / 32.25 m beam / four 16-cyl. diesels with
46 080 kW; Sulzer-Grandi Motori / four generators
connected to two elec. motors / 28 000 kW /
2 screws / 19.5 (21.4) kn / 2016 (2342) pass. in
1008 cabins / crew 814

23.1.1998 floated out / 27.11.1998 delivered /
17.12.1998 christened in Fort Lauderdale / 19.12.1998
maiden Caribbean cruise from Fort Lau-derdale / 2000
home port London / 5.2003 renamed **ADONIA**,
deployment for P&O Cruises / 4.2005 home port
Hamilton / 29.4.2005 renamed **SEA PRINCESS**. First
Mediterranean cruise from Southampton for Princess
Cruises /

SEA PRINCESS ex SEA PRINCESS (photo: Clyde Dickens)

ms OCEAN PRINCESS

IMO No. 9169550
Princess Cruises, Monrovia
Fincantieri, Monfalcone; Yard No.: 6044

77 499 GT / 8293 tdw / 261.22 m length
oa / 32.25 m beam / four 16-cyl. diesels with
46 080 kW; Sulzer-Grandi Motori / four generators
connected to two elec. motors / 28 000 kW /
2 screws / 21 kn / 2016 (2272) pass. in
1008 cabins / crew 814

29.4.1999 floated out / 29.1.2000 delivered /
15.2.2000 home port London / 16.2.2000 christened
in Fort Lauderdale, then cruises from San Juan /
10.2002 OCEANA, P&O Cruises, London / 1.11.2002
first Caribbean cruise from Fort Lauderdale / 5.2005
home port Hamilton /

OCEANA ex OCEAN PRINCESS (photo: Luis Miguel Correia)

XIN YU JIN XIANG ex YU JIN XIANG (photo: collection Ton Grootenboer)

ms YU JIN XIANG

IMO No. 9110810
Shanghai Hai Xing Shipping Co., Shanghai
De Merwede, Hardinxveld; Yard No.: 667

12 304 GT / 4590 tdw / 148.20 m length oa /
22.70 m beam / two 9-cyl. diesels geared to
2 screws; Sulzer / 12 960 kW / 20 kn / 348 pass.
in 95 cabins / crew 93

20.5.1995 launched / 22.11.1995 delivered, then
service Shanghai—Kobe / 1998 service Tsingtao—
Yokohama / 3.2001 service Shanghai—Incheon, for
Incheon International Ferry Co. / 16.4.2004 entered
service Qinhuangdao—Incheon for Qin-In Ferry Co. /
5.2008 renamed XIN YU JIN XIANG /

ms ARAFURA LILY

IMO No. 9110822
Shanghai Hai Xing Shipping Co., Panama
De Merwede, Hardinxveld; Yard No.: 668

12 307 GT / 5696 tdw / 148.20 m length oa /
22.70 m beam / two 9-cyl. diesels geared to
2 screws; Sulzer / 12 960 kW / 20 kn / 348 pass.
in 95 cabins / crew 95

25.11.1995 launched as ZI THING XIANG, planned for
service Shanghai—Kobe / 5.1996 delivered, then liner
service Brisbane—Singapore under charter by Southern
Cross Line. After two voyages arrested in Singapore,
then service Hong Kong—Fuzhou for Shanghai Hai
Xing / 1998 service Lianyungang—Tsingtao—Japan /
3.2001 service Shanghai—Incheon for Incheon International Ferry Co. / 2.2002 service Incheon—Yingkou for
Pan Korea Yingkou Ferry / 9.2014 home port Majuro /

ARAFURA LILY (photo: Ulrich Streich)

ms CENTURY

IMO No. 9072446
Celebrity Cruises, Monrovia
Jos. L. Meyer, Papenburg; Yard No.: 637

70 606 GT / 7260 tdw / 248.52 m length oa /
32.20 m beam / two 6-cyl. and two 9-cyl. diesels
geared to 2 screws; MAN B&W / 29 250 kW /
21.5 kn / 1778 pass. in 889 cabins / crew 858

2.10.1995 floated out / 26.10.1995 christened /
30.11.1995 delivered / 6.12.1995 transfer voyage
Southampton—New York, then Caribbean cruises
from Fort Lauderdale / 11.2002 home port Nassau /
5.2006 redelivered after conversion at Fincantieri,
Palermo: 72 458 GT, 1814 (2253) pass. in 907
cabins, / 2.2008 renamed **CELEBRITY CENTURY**,
home port Valletta / 29.9.2014 to Exquisite Marine /
5.4.2015 last cruise Dubai—Singapore for Celebrity
Cruises / 19.4.–7.5.2015 conversion at Sembawang,
Singapore / 15.5.2015 first cruise Shanghai—
Hakata—Shanghai as **SKYSEA GOLDEN ERA** for
SkySea Cruise Line /

SKYSEA GOLDEN ERA ex CENTURY (photo: Vladimir Tonic)

MEIN SCHIFF 1 ex GALAXY (photo: Frank Lose)

ms GALAXY

IMO No. 9106297
Celebrity Cruises, Monrovia
Jos. L. Meyer, Papenburg; Yard No.: 638

76 522 GT / 6500 tdw / 259.70 m length oa /
32.20 m beam / two 9-cyl. and two 6-cyl. diesels
geared to 2 screws; MAN B&W / 29 250 kW /
21.5 kn / 1896 pass. in 948 cabins / crew 908

14.9.1996 floated out / 20.11.1996 delivered /
21.12.1996 maiden cruise from Fort Lauderdale, after
the ship was presented in various U.S. ports / 12.2002
home port Nassau / 2.2008 renamed **CELEBRITY
GALAXY**, home port Valletta / 2.3.2009 last cruise
for Celebrity Cruises, then conversion at Lloyd Werft,
Bremerhaven / 5.2009 **MEIN SCHIFF**, TUI Cruises,
Valletta; 76 998 GT, 262.50 m length oa, 1924 pass.
in 962 cabins, crew 780 / 23.5.2009 first Baltic cruise
from Kiel / 7.11.2010 renamed **MEIN SCHIFF 1** /

MEIN SCHIFF 2 ex MERCURY (photo: Alexander Brede)

ms MERCURY

IMO No. 9106302
Celebrity Cruises, Panama
Jos. L. Meyer, Papenburg; Yard No.: 639

76 522 GT / 5700 tdw / 259.70 m length oa /
32.20 m beam / two 6-cyl. and two 9-cyl. diesels
geared to 2 screws; MAN B&W / 29 250 kW /
21.5 kn / 1896 pass. in 948 cabins / crew 909

11.7.1997 floated out / 15.10.1997 delivered /
27.10.1997 christened in New York, then maiden
Caribbean cruise from Fort Lauderdale / 8.2002 home
port Nassau / 2.2008 renamed **CELEBRITY MERCURY**,
home port Valletta / 3.–5.2011 conversion at Lloyd
Werft, Bremerhaven: 77 302 GT, 262.50 m length oa,
1912 pass. in 956 cabins, crew 780 / 4.2011 **MEIN
SCHIFF 2**, TUI Cruises, Valletta / 15.5.2011 first cruise
from Hamburg to European metropolises /

ms FERRY SETTSU

IMO No. 9117351
Hankyu Ferry, Kobe
Kanda Zosensho, Setoda; Yard No.: 511

15 188 GRT / 5634 tdw / 189.00 m length oa /
27.00 m beam / two 9-cyl. diesels geared to 2
screws; Pielstick-Diesel United / 12 000 kW / 23kn /
194 pass. in 74 cabins, 616 pass. unberthed /
77 cars + 219 trucks (8 tons) / crew 41

28.7.1995 launched / 8.12.1995 delivered / 21.12.1995
entered service Kobe—Shin Moji / 1.6.2008 entered
service Izumiotsu—Shin Moji / 2011 service Kobe—
Shin Moji / 3.2015 laid up / 4.2015 **HANIL CARFERRY
2**, Hanil Express Co Ltd., Yeosu / 6.2015 renamed
HANIL GOLD STELLA / 2015 service Yeosu—Jeju /

ms FERRY SUOU

IMO No. 9117363
Hankyu Ferry, Kobe
Kanda Zosensho, Kawajiri; Yard No.: 365

15 188 GRT / 5599 tdw / 189.00 m length oa /
27.00 m beam / two 9-cyl. diesels geared to 2
screws; Pielstick-Diesel United / 23 830 kW / 23 kn /
194 pass. in 74 cabins, 616 pass. unberthed /
77 cars + 219 trucks (8 tons) / crew 41

24.10.1995 launched / 12.03.1996 delivered /
15.3.1996 entered service Kobe—Shin Moji / 1.6.2008
entered service Izumiotsu—Shin Moji / 2011 service
Kobe—Shin Moji / 7.2015 **SANTA LUCINO**, Sea World
Express Ferry, Mokpo / 13.10.2015 entered service
Mokpo—Jeju /

ts STENA EXPLORER

IMO No. 9080194
Stena Line, London
Aker Finnyards, Rauma; Yard No.: 404

19 638 GT / 1500 tdw / 126.60 m length oa /
40.00 m beam / four gas turbines geared to
2 screws; GEC Kværner / 80 000 kW / 4 waterjets /
40 kn / 1520 pass. unberthed / 375 cars,
775 lane metres / crew 51

16.2.1996 delivered / 10.4.1996 maiden voyage
in service Dun Laoghaire—Holyhead / 14.9.1996
christened in Dun Laoghaire / 4.2010 only seasonal
service April-September, remaining time laid up in
Holyhead / 9.2014 no longer in service / 10.2015 **ONE
WORLD KARADENIZ**, Karadeniz Black Sea Holding,
Monrovia / 1.11.2015 towed from Holyhead to Yalova /

ms XIANG XUE LAN

IMO No. 9086904
China National Transport, Shanghai
MTW, Wismar; Yard No.: 162

16 071 GT / 6526 tdw / 150.54 m length oa /
24.00 m beam / two 6-cyl. diesels geared to
2 screws; Krupp MaK / 15 000 kW / 20 kn /
392 pass. in 122 cabins / crew 95

3.11.1995 launched / 25.3.1996 delivered, then
service Shanghai—Hong Kong, home port Panama /
23.11.1996 entered service Incheon—Tsingtao under
charter by Weidong Ferry / 3.2002 service Incheon—
Yantai for C&K Ferry Lines (Zhong Han Yantai Ferry
Co.) / 2003 to China Shipping Passenger Liner, Panama,
still deployed under charter by C&K Ferry Lines /

HANIL GOLD STELLA ex FERRY SETTSU (photo: Hanil Express)

SANTA LUCINO ex FERRY SUOU as FERRY SUOU (photo: Hiroyuki Yoshimoto)

ONE WORLD KARADENIZ ex STENA EXPLORER as STENA EXPLORER (photo: Frank Heine)

XIANG XUE LAN (photo: collection Ton Grootenboer)

ms ZI YU LAN

IMO No. 9086899
China National Transport, Shanghai
MTW, Wismar; Yard No.: 161

16071 GT / 6526 tdw / 150.54 m length oa /
24.00 m beam / two 6-cyl. diesels geared to
2 screws; Krupp MaK / 15000 kW / 20 kn /
392 pass. in 122 cabins / crew 95

17.2.1995 launched / 31.8.1996 delivered, then
service Shanghai—Kobe / 2001 service Busan—
Yantai / 23.6.2003 entered service Incheon—Tsingtao for Weidong Ferry / 30.12.2004 entered service
Lianyungang—Incheon for Lianyungang C-K Ferry Co. /

ZI YU LAN (photo: collection Ton Grootenboer)

ARIADNE ex RAINBOW BELL (photo: Frank Lose)

ms RAINBOW BELL

IMO No. 9135262
Kyuetsu Ferry, Fukuoka
Mitsubishi H.I., Shimonoseki; Yard No.: 1020

13597 GRT / 6203 tdw / 195.95 m length oa /
27.00 (29.01) m beam / two 14-cyl. diesels
geared to 2 screws; Pielstick-Nippon / 33980 kW /
24.9 kn / 350 pass. in cabins / 77 cars, 154 trucks /
crew 46

8.12.1995 launched / 28.3.1996 delivered / 9.4.1996
entered service Hakata—Naoetsu / 7.2001 to Higashi
Nihon Ferry, service Naoetsu—Muroran / 9.2001
laid up / 1.2004 FERRY HIMUKA, Marine Express,
service Kaizuka—Hyuga—Miyazaki / 10.2004 service
Kaizuka—Hyuga / 3.2005 laid up / 6.2005 service
Kaizuka—Miyazaki / 11.2006 ARIADNE, Hellenic
Seaways, Piraeus / 2.1.–9.2007 conversion in Perama:
30882 GT, 4981 tdw, 459 pass. in 145 cabins, 1386
pass. unberthed, 700 cars, 2050 lane metres, crew
90 / 25.9.2007 entered service Piraeus—Chania /
2008 service Patras—Venice/Ancona under charter
by Minoan Lines / 5.2008 service Piraeus—Chania
under charter by ANEK Lines / 20.6.2009–9.2013 in
summer service Algeria—Marseilles under charter by
Algerie Ferries / 21.10.2013 entered service Piraeus—
Chios—Mytilene /

NEW GOLDEN BRIDGE V ex RAINBOW LOVE (photo: Vladimir Tonic)

ms RAINBOW LOVE

IMO No. 9145047
Kyuetsu Ferry, Fukuoka
Mitsubishi H.I., Shimonoseki; Yard No.: 1021

13621 GRT / 6203 tdw / 195.95 m length oa /
27.00 (29.01) m beam / two 14-cyl. diesels
geared to 2 screws; Pielstick-Nippon / 28890 kW /
24.9 kn / 350 pass. in cabins / 77 cars, 154 trucks /
crew 46

17.10.1996 launched / 24.2.1997 delivered / 4.3.1997
entered service Hakata—Naoetsu / 7.2001 to Higashi
Nihon Ferry, service Naoetsu—Muroran / 9.2001 laid
up / 10.2003 NEW GOLDEN BRIDGE V, Weidong Car
Ferry, Panama, 29554 GT / 2.2004 service Incheon—
Tsingtao /

ms CRUISE FERRY HIRYU 21
IMO No. 9135250
Arimura Sangyo K.K., Naha
Mitsubishi H.I., Shimonoseki; Yard No.: 1019

9225 GRT / 3692 tdw / 167.00 m length oa /
22.00 m beam / two 18-cyl. diesels geared to
2 screws; Pielstick-Nippon / 17 654 kW / 24.3 kn /
330 pass. in cabins / 335 cars + 123 trucks,
52 10 ft. containers /

27.1.1996 launched / 30.3.1996 delivered / 1.4.1996
entered service Naha—Miyako—Ishigaki—Keelung—
Kaoshsiung / 1997 service Nagoya—Osaka—Naha—
Miyako—Ishigaki—Keelung—Kaohsiung / 5.6.2008
out of service / 20.8.2008 laid up off Fukuyama /
27.1.2010 to Marue Ferry, Naha / 3.2010 service
Tokyo—Okinawa / 2014 **BIRYONG**, Da-In Ferry,
Panama, 14 614 GT, then service Dalian—Incheon /

BIRYONG ex CRUISE FERRY HIRYU 21 as CRUISE FERRY HIRYU 21 (photo: Hiroyuki Yoshimoto)

MINERVA ex MINERVA (photo: Olaf Kuhnke)

ms MINERVA
IMO No. 9144196
Swan Hellenic Cruises (V.Ships), Nassau
Okean Shipyard, Nikolaiew, Yard No.: 1

12 331 GT / 1500 tdw / 133.00 m length oa /
20.00 m beam / two 6-cyl. diesels geared to
2 screws; Pielstick-Eriksbergs / 6920 kW /
16 (17.5) kn / 398 (428) pass. in 194 cabins /
crew 156

30.3.1989 keel-laying as Soviet research ship / 1990
construction discontinued / 1994 to V.Ships Leisure /
10.12.1994 launched / 1.1995 arrival in Genoa for
completion as passenger ship at T. Mariotti under Yard
No.: 595 / 25.4.1996 delivered / 29.4.1996 maiden
cruise Genoa—Mediterranean under charter by Swan
Hellenic Cruises / 7.6.1996 christened in London /
1.5.2003 **SAGA PEARL**, under charter by Saga Cruises,
however in the winter months 2003–2008 Antarctica
charter voyages for Abercrombie & Kent as **EXPLORER
II** / 6.3.2005 **ALEXANDER VON HUMBOLDT**, Phoenix
Reisen charter replacing Saga Cruises charter in the
summer months / 2008 **MINERVA**, Swan Hellenic
Cruises, Nassau / 31.5.2008 first cruise from Dover /
30.1.–7.4.2010 cruises under charter by Phoenix
Reisen / 7.12.2011–28.2.2012 conversion at Lloyd
Werft, Bremerhaven: 12 892 GT /

RHAPSODY ex NAPOLEON BONAPARTE (photo: Frank Heine)

ms NAPOLEON BONAPARTE
IMO NO. 9104835
Soc. Nationale Maritime Corse Méditerranée,
Marseilles
Chantiers de l'Atlantique, St. Nazaire;
Yard No.: D31

44 307 GT / 3538 tdw / 172.00 m length oa /
30.40 (36.86) m beam / four 18-cyl. diesels
geared to 2 screws; Pielstick-Alstom / 45 360 kW /
23.8 kn / 2220 pass. in 555 cabins, 703 pass.
unberthed / 716 cars, 697 lane metres / crew 162

16.9.1995 launched / 4.1996 delivered / 24.4.1996
service Marseilles—Corsica / 2001 242 pass. unberthed /
27.10.2012 in Marseilles pressed against a quay in
heavy storm, after water ingress sank to the bottom /
10.1.2013 after salvage docking in Marseilles / 2.2014
sold to insurance company / 4.2014 **RHAPSODY**, SNAV,
Valletta / 8.5.2014 towed from Marseilles to Naples for
repairs / 8.8.2015 entered service Bari—Durres under
charter by Grandi Navi Veloci / 19.12.-30.1.2016 service
Genoa—Barcelona—Tangier / 16.2.2016 service
Bari—Durres planned /

ms GOTLAND

IMO No. 9010814
Rederi AB Gotland, Visby
P.T. Dok & Perkapalan Kodja Bahari, Jakarta;
Yard No.: 1005

25 996 GT / 6124 tdw / 168.15 m length oa /
27.70 (28.34) m beam / four 6-cyl. diesels geared
to 2 screws; Sulzer-Zgoda / 14 700 kW / 21 kn /
200 pass. in 94 cabins / 800 cars, 2400 lane metres /

28.9.1992 launched / 19.4.1996 delivered, then laid
up in Kappelshamn / 2.1997–16.3.1997 cargo ferry
service Gothenburg—Gent under charter by Tor Line /
11.4.1997 entered service Oxelösund—St. Petersburg under charter by Nordic Trucker Line / 9.6.1997
entered service Stockholm—Turku under charter by
SeaWind Line / 17.12.1997 FINNARROW, Finnlines,
Helsinki / 31.12.1997–26.5.1998 service Helsinki
—Travemünde / 2.7.1998 entered service Kapellskär
—Naantali for Finnlink / 2.1.2003 to Nordö Link,
Malmö, then service Malmö—Travemünde / 3.1.2005
entered service Kapellskär—Naantali / 2.1.2006–
30.3.2007 service Malmö—Travemünde / 31.3.2007
entered service Rostock—Ventspils under charter by
Scandlines / 7.5.2007 entered service Karlskrona—
Gdynia under charter by Stena Line / 10.12.2010–
28.2.2011 service Hoek van Holland—Killingholme
under charter by Stena Line / 9.3.2011 again service
Malmö—Travemünde / 9.9.–13.10.2011 service
Lübeck—Ventspils—St. Petersburg / 17.10.2011
again service Naantali—Kapellskär / 17.9.2012 home
port Helsinki / 17.1.–2.3.2013 service Holyhead—
Dublin under charter by Stena Line / 16.2.2013 badly
damaged during berthing manoeuvre in Holyhead
due to extended stabiliser, towed to Greenock for
repair / 22.3.2013 after repair again in service /
3.4.–12.2013 service Travemünde—Ventspils under
charter by Stena Line / 4–6.2013 installation of
additional passenger accommodation at Besiktas, Yalova:
29 289 GT, 206 pass. in reclining chairs, 2212 lane
metres / 29.6.2013 EUROFERRY BRINDISI, Grimaldi
Ferries, Palermo / 20.7.2013 service Palermo/Salerno/
Civitavecchia—Tunis / 18.12.2013 entered service
Patras—Igoumenitsa—Ravenna / 25.2.–15.12.2014
service Patras—Igoumenitsa—Brindisi / 19.12.2014
MAZOVIA, Polferries, Nassau / 16.6.2015 entered
service Swinoujscie—Ystad /

MAZOVIA ex GOTLAND (photo: Frank Lose)

KATTEGAT ex MAREN MOLS (photo: Frank Lose)

ms MAREN MOLS

IMO No. 9112765
Mols-Linien, Odden Færgehavn
Ørskov Christensens Stålskibsværft, Frederikshavn;
Yard No.: 191

14 221 GT / 3790 tdw / 136.40 m length oa /
24.00 (24.60) m beam / two 9-cyl. diesels;
MAN B&W / 11 200 kW / 2 screws / 18 kn /
616 pass. unberthed / 344 cars, 1240 lane metres /
crew 20

6.10.1995 launched / 19.4.1996 delivered / 1.5.1996
maiden voyage in service Ebeltoft—Sjællands Odden /
3.1.2000 entered service Aarhus—Kalundborg / 2004
14 379 GT / 14.9.2011 last voyage in service Kalundborg—Aarhus / 16.9.2011 KATTEGAT, Kattegat Ruten,
Limassol / 20.9.2011–11.10.2013 service Aarhus—
Kalundborg, then laid up in Kalundborg / 22.1.2014
to FRS Maroc, Limassol / 25.3.2014 entered service
Algeciras—Tangier under marketing name "Maroc
Express" / 1.2016 service Motril—Tanger Med. planned /

ms METTE MOLS

IMO No. 9112777
Mols-Linien, Ebeltoft
Ørskov Christensens Stålskibsværft, Frederikshavn;
Yard No.: 192

14 221 GT / 3790 tdw / 136.40 m length oa /
24.00 (24.60) m beam / two 9-cyl. diesels; MAN B&W /
11 200 kW / 2 screws / 18 kn / 616 pass. unberthed /
344 cars, 1240 lane metres / crew 20

2.2.1996 launched / 28.6.1996 delivered / 1.7.1996
maiden voyage in service Ebeltoft—Sjællands Odden /
3.1.2000 entered service Aarhus—Kalundborg /
2004 14 379 GT / 22.7.2011 last voyage in service
Kalundborg—Aarhus / 25.7.2011 **TANGER EXPRESS**,
FRS Iberia, Limassol / 30.11.2011 entered service
Algeciras—Tangier / 16.2.2012 home port Tangier /

ms STENA JUTLANDICA III

IMO No. 9125944
Stena Line, Gothenburg
van der Giessen-De Noord, Krimpen; Yard No.: 967

29 691 GT / 6559 tdw / 182.35 m length oa /
27.80 (28.43) m beam / four 9-cyl. diesels geared
to 2 screws; MAN B&W / 25 920 kW / 22 kn /
176 pass. in 64 cabins, 1326 pass. unberthed /
550 cars, 2720 lane metres, 5 rail tracks with
571 m length / crew 92

2.3.1996 launched / 11.5.1996 delivered / 25.6.1996
maiden voyage in service Gothenburg—Frederikshavn / 8.1996 renamed **STENA JUTLANDICA** /

ms ISLE OF INISHMORE

IMO No. 9142605
Irish Ferries, Dublin
van der Giessen-De Noord, Krimpen; Yard No.: 968

34 031 GT / 5860 tdw / 182.50 m length oa /
27.80 (28.90) m beam / four 8-cyl. diesels geared
to 2 screws; Sulzer-Adria / 23 040 kW / 21 kn /
208 pass. in 60 cabins, 1992 pass. unberthed /
800 cars, 2890 lane metres /

4.10.1996 launched / 15.2.1997 delivered / 2.3.1997
entered service Dublin—Holyhead / 16.5.2001 entered
service Rosslare—Pembroke Dock / 3.2006 home port
Limassol /

TANGER EXPRESS ex METTE MOLS (photo: Frank Heine)

STENA JUTLANDICA ex STENA JUTLANDICA III (photo: Frank Lose)

ISLE OF INISHMORE (photo: Frank Lose)

ms SUZURAN
IMO No. 9116266
Shin Nihonkai Ferry, Otaru
Ishikawajima-Harima H.I., Tokyo ; Yard No.: 3062

17 345 GRT / 5440 tdw / 199.45 m length oa /
25.00 m beam / two 18-cyl. diesels geared to
2 screws; Pielstick / 47 700 kW / 29.4 kn /
475 pass. in 106 cabins, 32 pass. unberthed /
80 cars + 122 trucks (8 tons) / crew 50

12.7.1995 launched / 30.5.1996 delivered / 11.6.1996
entered service Tsuruga—Otaru / 9.2002 service
Tomakomai—Tsuruga / 20.6.2012 laid up in Sakaide /
10.2013 renamed **HAKUOU**, under charter by Japanese
Armed Forces /

HAKUOU ex SUZURAN (photo: Osamu Taniguchi)

SUISEN (photo: Tsuyoshi Ishiyama)

ms SUISEN
IMO No. 9116278
Shin Nihonkai Ferry, Otaru
Ishikawajima-Harima H.I., Tokyo ; Yard No.: 3063

17 329 GRT / 5861 tdw / 199.45 m length oa /
25.00 m beam / two 18-cyl. diesels geared to
2 screws; Pielstick / 47 700 kW / 29.4 kn /
475 pass. in 106 cabins, 32 pass. unberthed /
80 cars + 122 trucks (8 tons) / crew 50

26.10.1995 launched / 30.5.1996 delivered / 11.6.1996
entered service Tsuruga—Otaru / 9.2002 service
Tomakomai—Tsuruga / 2.7.2012 laid up in Sakaide /

ms AIDA
IMO No. 9112789
Deutsche Seereederei Touristik, Rostock
Kværner Masa-Yards, Turku; Yard No.: 1337

38 531 GT / 3752 tdw / 193.34 m length oa /
27.60 (32.60) m beam / four 6-cyl. diesels geared
to 2 screws; MAN B&W / 21 720 kW / 21 kn /
1186 (1250) pass. in 593 cabins / crew 366

16.2.1996 floated out / 4.6.1996 delivered / 7.6.1996
christened in Warnemünde / 11.6.1996 maiden
voyage Bremerhaven—Palma de Mallorca, then
Mediterranean cruises, in winter Caribbean cruises /
8.1997 to Norwegian Cruise Line, Monrovia.
Chartered back by DSR Touristik / 8.1999 bought back
by DSR successor Arkona Touristik / 9.1999 to Aida
Cruises / 11.2001 renamed **AIDACARA** / 5.4.2002
to Seetours, London / 1.11.2004 to Aida Cruises,
Genoa / 18.4.–1.5.2005 conversion at Neptun
Industrie, Rostock: 38 557 GT, 1298 pass. /

AIDACARA ex AIDA (photo: Alexander Brede)

COSTA VICTORIA (photo: Tsuyoshi Ishiyama)

ms COSTA VICTORIA
IMO No. 9109031
Costa Crociere, Genoa
Bremer Vulkan, Vegesack; Yard No.: 1107

75 051 GT / 8039 tdw / 252.91 m length oa /
32.15 (36.10) m beam / three 6-cyl. and three 7-cyl.
diesels with 50 700 kW; MAN B&W / six generators
connected to two elec. motors / 30 000 kW /
2 screws / 22.8 kn / 1928 (2274) pass. in
964 cabins / crew 850

2.9.1995 floated out / 10.7.1996 delivered / 13.7.1996
christened / 28.7.1996 maiden cruise from Venice /
10.11.1996 first Caribbean cruise / 1997 75 166 GT /
12.1.–5.2.2004 conversion at Lloyd Werft, Bremerhaven: 246 cabins fitted with balconies /

NORWEGIAN SKY ex NORWEGIAN SKY (photo: Andy Hernandez)

ms NORWEGIAN SUN
IMO No. 9218131
Norwegian Cruise Line, Nassau
Lloyd Werft, Bremerhaven; Yard No.: 109, hull under
subcontract by Aker MTW, Wismar; Yard No.: 005

78 309 GT / 7100 tdw / 259.99 m length oa /
32.25 (36.00) m beam / three 6-cyl. and three 7-cyl.
diesels with 51 700 kW; MAN B&W / six generators
connected to two elec. motors / 30 700 kW /
2 screws / 22.6 (23.6) kn / 1936 (2450) pass. in
968 cabins / crew 950

23.9.2000 floated out / 31.8.2001 delivered / 3.9.2001
short cruise to Southampton / 10.9.2001 maiden cruise
to New York / 20.11.2001 christened in Miami, then
cruises /

NORWEGIAN SUN (photo: Cees Bustraan)

ms CARNIVAL DESTINY
IMO No. 9070058
Carnival Cruise Lines, Panama
Fincantieri, Monfalcone; Yard No.: 5941

101 353 GT / 11 142 tdw / 272.35 m length oa /
35.50 m beam / four 16-cyl. and two 12-cyl. diesels
with 63 360 kW; Sulzer-Grandi Motori / six generators
connected to two elec. motors / 40 000 kW /
2 screws / 18 (23) kn / 2642 (3336) pass. in
1321 cabins / crew 1060

15.11.1995 floated out / 19.10.1996 delivered as
first passenger ship with more than 100 000 GT /
23.10.1996 christened in Venice / 24.11.1996 maiden
cruise from Miami / 2000 home port Nassau / 2.–4.2013
conversion at Fincantieri, Trieste: 103 881 GT, 3012
(3765) pass. in 1506 cabins, renamed **CARNIVAL
SUNSHINE** / 5.5.2013 first cruise Venice—Barcelona
after conversion /

CARNIVAL SUNSHINE ex CARNIVAL DESTINY (photo: Marcus Puttich)

ms NORWEGIAN SKY
IMO No. 9128532
Norwegian Cruise Line, Nassau
Bremer Vulkan, Vegesack; Yard No.: 1108

77 104 GT / 8800 tdw / 258.60 m length oa /
32.25 (36.00) m beam / three 6-cyl. and three 7-cyl.
diesels with 50 700 kW; MAN B&W / six generators
connected to two elec. motors / 30 000 kW /
2 screws / 23 (23.8) kn / 2002 (2450) pass. in
1001 cabins / crew 814

1996 after bankruptcy of builders, construction discontinued on the approx. 35 % completed newbuild,
due to be delivered in 1997 as COSTA OLYMPIA /
6.10.1996 floated out. Put up for sale / 8.3.1998 transferred to Lloyd Werft, Bremerhaven for completion as
NORWEGIAN SKY for Norwegian Cruise Line as Yard
No. 108 / 17.6.1999 sea trials / 28.7.1999 delivered /
4.8.1999 pre-inaugural cruise Bremerhaven—Dover /
9.8.1999 maiden cruise to Norway / 7.6.2004 **PRIDE
OF ALOHA**, NCL America, Honolulu, maiden cruise
from Los Angeles / 4.7.2004 christened in Honolulu,
then first Hawaii cruise / 14.7.2008 **NORWEGIAN
SKY**, Nassau, Bahamas cruises for Norwegian Cruise
Line from Miami /

CARNIVAL TRIUMPH (photo: Marko Stampehl)

2 screws / 19 (23) kn / 2642 (3480) pass. in 1379 cabins / crew 1080

25.9.1998 floated out / 11.7.1999 delivered / 19.7.1999 promotional voyage New York—Hamilton / 25.7.1999 christened in New York / 27.7.1999 maiden cruise New York—Canada / 10.1999 first seven-day cruise Miami—Caribbean / 2000 home port Nassau / 10.2.2013 engine room fire with power failure in Gulf of Mexico / 14.2.2013 arrival under tow in Mobile, Alabama for repairs at BAE Systems / 3.4.2013 in a storm the disabled ship tore away from the shipyard pier and collided with two other vessels, two persons killed / 13.6.2013 after repair again in service /

ms CARNIVAL TRIUMPH
IMO No. 9138850
Carnival Cruise Lines, Panama
Fincantieri, Monfalcone; Yard No.: 5979

101 509 GT / 10 984 tdw / 272.82 m length oa / 35.50 m beam / four 16-cyl. and two 12-cyl. diesels with 57 600 kW; Sulzer-Fincantieri / six generators connected to two elec. motors / 40 000 kW /

ms CARNIVAL VICTORY
IMO No. 9172648
Carnival Cruise Lines, Panama
Fincantieri, Monfalcone; Yard No.: 6045

101 509 GT / 11 774 tdw / 272.20 m length oa / 35.42 (35.54) m beam / two 12-cyl. and four 16-cyl. diesels with 63 360 kW; Sulzer-Fincantieri / six generators connected to two elec. motors / 40 000 kW / 2 screws / 22 (23) kn / 2758 (3480) pass. in 1379 cabins / crew 1080

31.12.1999 floated out / 29.7.2000 delivered / 18.8.2000 maiden cruise from New York /

CARNIVAL VICTORY (photo: Jürgen Pfarre)

COSTA FORTUNA (photo: Luis Miguel Correia)

ms COSTA FORTUNA
IMO No. 9239783
Costa Crociere, Genoa
Fincantieri; Sestri Ponente; Yard No.: 6086

102 587 GT / 8200 tdw / 272.20 m length oa /
35.50 (38.00) m beam / four 16-cyl. and two
12-cyl. diesels with 63 360 kW; Sulzer-Fincantieri /
six generators connected to two elec. motors /
40 000 kW / 2 screws / 20 (23) kn / 2702 (3470)
pass. in 1358 cabins / crew 1027

11.1.2002 launched / 14.11.2003 delivered /
18.11.2003 promotional voyage Genoa—Barcelona
—Marseilles—Genoa / 22.11.2003 christened in
Genoa / 25.11.2003 maiden cruise from Savona to
Spain and Morocco /

ms COSTA MAGICA
IMO No. 9239795
Costa Crociere, Genoa
Fincantieri, Sestri Ponente; Yard No.: 6087

102 587 GT / 9859 tdw / 272.20 m length oa /
35.50 (38.00) m beam / four 16-cyl. and two
12-cyl. diesels with 63 360 kW; Sulzer-Fincantieri /
six generators connected to two elec. motors /
40 000 kW / 2 screws / 20 (22) kn / 2702 (3470)
pass. in 1359 cabins / crew 1027

2.2002 launch of a section built in Palermo, which was
towed to Sestri / 14.11.2003 floated out / 3.11.2004
delivered / 6.11.2004 christened in Barcelona /
8.11.2004 two-day promotional voyage from Savona /
10.11.2004 maiden Mediterranean cruise from Savona /

ms GRANDEUR OF THE SEAS
IMO No. 9102978
Royal Caribbean Cruise Line, Monrovia
Kværner Masa-Yards, Helsinki; Yard No.: 492

73 817 GT / 7000 tdw / 279.10 m length oa /
32.20 (36.00) m beam / four 12-cyl. diesels with
50 400 kW; MAN B&W / four generators connected
to two elec. motors / 34 000 kW / 2 screws /
22 (23.5) kn / 1950 (2440) pass. in 975 cabins /
crew 776

1.3.1996 floated out / 20.11.1996 delivered /
13.12.1996 christened in Miami / 14.12.1996 maiden
cruise Miami—Caribbean / 3.2003 home port Nassau /
5.–6.2012 conversion at Navantia, Cadiz: 1994 (2393)
pass. in 997 cabins / 27.5.2013 fire on the aft mooring
deck, which spread to further decks. The ship reached
Freeport under own power. Repair at Grand Bahama
Shipyard, Freeport / 12.7.2013 first cruise Baltimore—
Bermuda after repairs /

COSTA MAGICA (photo: George Koutsoukis)

GRANDEUR OF THE SEAS (photo: Andy Hernandez)

RHAPSODY OF THE SEAS (photo: George Koutsoukis)

ms RHAPSODY OF THE SEAS

IMO No. 9116864
Royal Caribbean Cruise Line, Oslo
Chantiers de l'Atlantique, St. Nazaire; Yard No.: E31

78 491 GT / 8439 tdw / 278.94 m length oa / 32.20 (35.64) m beam / four 12-cyl. diesels with 50 480 kW; Wärtsilä / four generators connected to two elec. motors / 34 000 kW / 2 screws / 22.3 (23.5) kn / 2014 (2435) pass. in 1007 cabins / crew 787

9.8.1996 floated out / 22.4.1997 delivered / 5.1997 two three-day cruises from New York / 19.5.1997 first cruise Miami—Alaska / 2.2005 home port Nassau / 2.–3.2012 conversion at Sembawang, Singapore: 78 878 GT, 2026 (2431) pass. in 1013 cabins /

ms ENCHANTMENT OF THE SEAS

IMO No. 9111802
Royal Caribbean International, Oslo
Kværner Masa-Yards, Helsinki; Yard No.: 493

74 136 GT / 7000 tdw / 279.60 m length oa / 32.20 m beam / four 12-cyl. diesels with 50 400 kW; MAN B&W / four generators connected to two elec. motors / 34 000 kW / 2 screws / 22.3 (23.5) kn / 1995 (2430) pass. in 975 cabins / crew 760

20.11.1996 floated out / 4.7.1997 delivered / 17.7.1997 first Mediterranean cruise / 19.10.1997 first Caribbean cruise / 1.2005 home port Nassau / 15.5.–23.6.2005 lengthening at Keppel Verolme Yard, Rotterdam: 81 278 GT, 301.80 m length oa, 2295 (2750) pass. in 1126 cabins, crew 864 / 7.7.2005 first Caribbean cruise after conversion / 2007 82 910 GT /

ms VISION OF THE SEAS

IMO No. 9116876
Royal Caribbean International, Monrovia
Chantiers de l'Atlantique, St. Nazaire; Yard No.: F31

78 340 GT / 6300 tdw / 279.00 m length oa / 32.20 (35.60) m beam / four 12-cyl. diesels with 50 400 kW; Wärtsilä / four generators connected to two elec. motors / 34 000 kW / 2 screws / 22 kn / 2014 (2416) pass. in 1007 cabins / crew 787

ENCHANTMENT OF THE SEAS (photo: Cees Bustraan)

VISION OF THE SEAS (photo: Alexander Brede)

26.9.1997 floated out / 15.4.1998 delivered /
26.4.1998 christened in Southampton, then cruises
in Europe and USA / 4.2003 home port Nassau /
9.–10.2013 conversion at Navantia, Cadiz: 78 717 GT,
2036 (2443) pass. in 1018 cabins /

ms MIYAZAKI EXPRESS
IMO No. 9145865
Marine Express, Tokyo
Mitsubishi H.I., Shimonoseki; Yard No.: 1022

11 931 GRT / 5884 tdw / 170.00 m length oa /
27.00 (27.32) m beam / two 12-cyl. diesels geared
to 2 screws; Pielstick-Nippon / 26 220 kW / 25 kn /
518 pass. in 80 cabins, 108 pass. unberthed /
85 cars + 130 trucks (8 tons) / 1560 lane metres /
crew 42

MIYAZAKI EXPRESS (photo: Frank Lose)

KOBE EXPRESS ex OSAKA EXPRESS (photo: Osamu Taniguchi)

20.8.1996 launched / 25.11.1996 delivered /
2.12.1996 entered service Osaka—Miyazaki / 2004
to Miyazaki Car Ferry / 1.10.2014 entered service
Kobe—Miyazaki /

ms OSAKA EXPRESS
IMO No. 9162124
Marine Express, Tokyo
Mitsubishi H.I., Shimonoseki; Yard No.: 1023

11 933 GRT / 5857 tdw / 170.00 m length oa /
27.00 (27.32) m beam / two 12-cyl. diesels geared
to 2 screws; Pielstick-Nippon / 26 220 kW / 25 kn /
518 pass. in 80 cabins, 108 pass. unberthed /
85 cars + 130 trucks (8 tons) / crew 42

12.5.1997 launched / 22.7.1997 delivered / 28.7.1997
entered service Osaka—Miyazaki / 2005 to Miyazaki
Car Ferry / 6.2014 renamed KOBE EXPRESS / 1.10.2014
entered service Kobe—Miyazaki /

ms MECKLENBURG-VORPOMMERN
IMO No. 9131797
Deutsche Fährgesellschaft Ostsee, Rostock
Schichau Seebeckwerft, Bremerhaven; Yard No.: 1092

36 185 GT / 7520 tdw / 199.95 m length oa /
28.20 (28.90) m beam / four 6-cyl. diesels geared
to 2 screws; MAN B&W / 25 200 kW / 21 kn /
396 pass. in 150 cabins, 491 pass. unberthed /
90 cars, 2151 lane metres, 6 rail tracks with
945 m length / crew 63

27.7.1996 launched / 13.12.1996 delivered in Rostock /
16.12.1996 maiden voyage in service Rostock—
Trelleborg / 15.12.2002 conversion at Remontowa,
Gdansk: one passenger deck converted into cargo
deck / 7.3.2003 delivered after conversion: 37 987 GT,
410 pass. in 158 cabins, 3100 lane metres, crew 54 /
10.3.2003 continued service Rostock—Trelleborg /
11.10.2012 to Stena Line, Rostock, continued service
Rostock—Trelleborg /

MECKLENBURG-VORPOMMERN (photo: Hans-Joachim Hellmann)

PRINS RICHARD (photo: Frank Heine)

ms PRINS RICHARD
IMO No. 9144419
Scandlines, Rødby Havn
Ørskov Christensens Stålskibsværft, Frederikshavn;
Yard No.: 193

14 621 GT / 2490 tdw / 142.00 m length oa /
24.80 (25.40) m beam / five 8-cyl. diesels with
17 600 kW; Krupp MaK / five generators connected
to four elec. motors / 16 320 kW / 4 screws / 18.5 kn /
900 pass. unberthed / 294 cars, 586 lane metres, 1
rail track with 114 m length / crew 13

20.12.1996 launched / 7.5.1997 christened / 22.5.1997
delivered / 6.6.1997 maiden voyage in service Rødby
Havn—Puttgarden / 2004 installation of mezzanine
car deck: 14 822 GT, 1040 pass. unberthed, 365 cars /
16.4.2010 14 810 GT /

ms PRINSESSE BENEDIKTE
IMO No. 9144421
Scandlines, Rødby Havn
Ørskov Christensens Stålskibsværft, Frederikshavn;
Yard No.: 194

14 621 GT / 2490 tdw / 142.00 m length oa /
24.80 (25.40) m beam / five 8-cyl. diesels with
17 600 kW; Mak / five generators connected to four
elec. motors / 16 320 kW / 4 screws / 18.5 kn /
900 pass. unberthed / 286 cars / 586 lane metres,
1 rail track with 114 m length / crew 13

17.10.1997 delivered / 1.11.1997 maiden voyage
in service Rødby Havn—Puttgarden / 10.2003 installation of mezzanine car deck: 14 822 GT, 1040 pass.
unberthed, 365 cars / 11.3.2015 during a shipyard
overhaul at Remontowa, Gdansk capsized in floating
dock, considerably damaged / 10.7.2015 again service
Rødby Havn—Puttgarden /

ms HAMLET
IMO No. 9150030
Scandlines, Helsingør
Aker Finnyards, Rauma; Yard No.: 412

10 067 GT / 2864 tdw / 111.20 m length oa /
27.60 (28.22) m beam / four 9-cyl. diesels geared
to 4 screws; Wärtsilä / 6 120 kW / 14.6 kn /
1000 pass. unberthed / 240 cars, 553 lane metres /

14.3.1997 launched / 12.6.1997 delivered / 1.7.1997
entered service Helsingør—Helsingborg / 1.2015 to
HH Ferries Helsingør, Helsingør /

PRINSESSE BENEDIKTE (photo: Frank Heine)

HAMLET (photo: Frank Heine)

ms C. COLUMBUS

IMO No. 9138329
Conti Reederei, Nassau
MTW Schiffswerft, Wismar; Yard No.: 451

14903 GT / 1378 tdw / 145.00 m length oa /
21.50 m beam / four 6-cyl. diesels geared to
2 screws; Wärtsilä / 10560 kW / 18.5 kn /
420 pass. in 205 cabins / crew 169

30.10.1996 launched as **COLUMBUS** / 17.6.1997
christened and delivered as **C. COLUMBUS**, home port
Hamburg, same day home port changed to Nassau /
29.6.1997 maiden cruise Bremen—North Cape under
charter by Hapag-Lloyd Kreuzfahrten / 9.–10.1997 first
visit of an oceangoing cruise ship to the Great Lakes /
5.2001 conversion of the stern: ducktail, 15067 GT /
7.5.2012 end of last cruise under charter by Hapag-
Lloyd / 25.5.2012 first cruise as **HAMBURG** under
charter by Plantours Kreuzfahrten / 11.5.2015 grounded
off Tobermory, Inner Hebrides and seriously damaged,
initially for provisional repairs to Harland & Wolff,
Belfast / 3.6.2015 arrival at Lloyd Werft, Bremerhaven
for final repairs / 10.8.2015 back in service /

HAMBURG ex C. COLUMBUS (photo: Alexander Brede)

ms SUN FLOWER KUROSHIO

IMO No. 9162150
Blue Highway Line, Tokyo
Mitsubishi H.I., Shimonoseki; Yard No. 1034

9723 GT / 4249 tdw / 160.00 m length oa /
25.00 (26.60) m beam / two 18-cyl. diesels geared
to 2 screws; Pielstick-Nippon / 16882 kW /
22.7 kn / 450 pass. in 139 cabins, 80 pass.
unberthed / 280 cars, 1275 lane metres /

21.3.1997 launched / 18.6.1997 delivered, then
service Tokyo—Nachikatsuura—Kochi / 2001 laid
up / 5.2002 **PANSTAR DREAM**, PanStar Ferry, Jeju,
21535 GT / 2002 service Busan—Osaka /

PANSTAR DREAM ex SUN FLOWER KUROSHIO (photo: Frank Lose)

ms MERSEY VIKING

IMO No. 9136022
Levantina Trasporti, Bari
Cantiere Navale Visentini, Porto Viro; Yard No.: 180

21856 GT / 8000 tdw / 186.00 m length oa /
25.60 (26.00) m beam / two 8-cyl. diesels geared to
2 screws; Wärtsilä / 15600 kW / 24 kn / 340 pass.
in 72 cabins / 100 cars, 2460 lane metres / crew 22

7.12.1997 launched / 12.7.1997 entered service
Liverpool—Belfast under charter by Norse Irish
Ferries / 1997 home port Bari / 3.2001 to Norse
Merchant Ferries / 17.6.2002 entered service Birkenhead—Belfast / 29.6.2004 home port Belfast /
12.9.2005 renamed **DUBLIN VIKING** / 15.11.2005
entered service Birkenhead—Dublin / 12.7.2010
to DFDS Seaways / 2.8.2010 renamed **DUBLIN
SEAWAYS**, home port Belfast / 29.1.2011 last voyage
in service Dublin—Birkenhead / 1.4.2011 to Stena
RoRo / 15.4.2011 renamed **STENA FERONIA**, home
port Glasgow / 13.5.–29.9.2011 service Klaipeda
—Karlshamn under charter by DFDS Seaways /
23.1.–6.2.2012 service Gdynia—Karlshamn for Stena
Line / 7.2.–12.2.2012 service Gothenburg—Kiel for
Stena Line / 20.2.–3.2012 service Belfast—Liverpool
for Stena Line / 28.3.2012 entered service Klaipeda
—Karlshamn under charter by DFDS Seaways /
30.4.–21.5.2012 service Kiel—Sassnitz—Ust Luga
under charter by DFDS Seaways / 18.6.2012 entered
service Algeciras—Tangier under charter by FRS
Iberia / 18.11.2012 entered service Algeciras—
Tangier under charter by Inter Line / 7.2013 home port

Limassol / 20.11.2014 service Belfast—Birkenhead
under charter by Stena Line / 26.12.2014 laid up in
Lysekil / 25.1.–25.3.2015 service Gothenburg—Kiel /

31.3.2015 to Strait Shipping, Wellington / 2.4.2015
renamed **STRAIT FERONIA** / 17.6.2015 entered
service Wellington—Picton /

STRAIT FERONIA ex MERSEY VIKING (photo: Stephen Berry)

LIVERPOOL SEAWAYS ex LAGAN VIKING (photo: Frank Heine)

ms LAGAN VIKING
IMO No. 9136034
Levantina Trasporti, Bari
Cantiere Navale Visentini, Porto Viro; Yard No.: 182

21 856 GT / 8000 tdw / 186.00 m length oa /
25.60 (26.00) m beam / two 8-cyl. diesels geared to
2 screws; Wärtsilä / 15 600 kW / 24 kn / 340 pass.
in 72 cabins / 100 cars, 2460 lane metres / crew 22

29.10.1997 delivered / 16.11.1997 entered service
Liverpool—Belfast under charter by Norse Irish Ferries /
3.2001 to Norse Merchant Ferries / 30.6.2004 home
port Belfast / 8.1.2005 renamed **LIVERPOOL VIKING** /
20.7.2005 entered service Liverpool—Dublin /
12.7.2010 to DFDS Seaways / 26.8.2010 renamed
LIVERPOOL SEAWAYS, home port Belfast / 29.1.2011
final voyage in service Birkenhead—Dublin / 22.2.2011
home port Klaipeda / 1.3.2011 entered service Klaipeda
—Karlshamn / 9.1.–30.12.2014 service Hanko—
Paldiski under charter by Navirail / 10.1.2015 entered
service Paldiski—Kapellskär /

SCHLESWIG-HOLSTEIN (photo: Marko Stampehl)

ms SCHLESWIG-HOLSTEIN
IMO No. 9151539
Deutsche Fährgesellschaft Ostsee, Rostock
van der Giessen-De Noord, Krimpen; Yard No.: 969

15 187 GT / 2836 tdw / 143.00 m length oa /
24.80 (25.40) m beam / three 8-cyl. and two 6-cyl.
diesels with 17 600 kW; Krupp MaK / five generators
connected to four elec. motors / 16 320 kW /
4 screws / 18.5 kn / 900 pass. unberthed / 295 cars,
480 lane metres, 1 rail track with 118 m length /
crew 16

3.5.1997 launched / 25.7.1997 delivered / 2.8.1997
maiden voyage in service Puttgarden—Rødby Havn /
10.1998 to Scandlines Germany, Puttgarden / 2004
fitting of mezzanine car deck: 1200 pass. unberthed,
365 cars /

ms DEUTSCHLAND
IMO No. 9151541
Deutsche Fährgesellschaft Ostsee, Puttgarden
van der Giessen-De Noord, Krimpen; Yard No.: 970

15 187 GT / 2904 tdw / 143.00 m length oa /
24.80 (25.40) m beam / three 8-cyl. and two 6-cyl.
diesels with 17 600 kW; Krupp MaK / five generators
connected to four elec. motors / 16 320 kW /
4 screws / 18.5 kn / 900 pass. unberthed / 294 cars,
1 rail track with 120 m length / crew 16

1.7.1997 launched / 7.10.1997 delivered / 9.10.1997
christened in Puttgarden / 11.10.1997 maiden voyage
in service Puttgarden—Rødby Havn / 10.1998 to
Scandlines, Puttgarden / 2004 installation of mezzanine
car deck: 1200 pass. unberthed, 365 cars /

DEUTSCHLAND (photo: Uwe Jakob)

TACOMA (photo: Brandon Swan)

ms TACOMA
IMO No. 9133977
State of Washington
(Department of Transportation), Seattle
Todd Pacific Shipyards Corp, Seattle, WA; Yard No.: 91

4340 GRT / 1393 tdw / 138.00 m length oa /
26.73 (27.00) m beam / four 16-cyl. diesels with
10 592 kW; General Motors / four generators
connected to two elec. motors / 8830 kW /
2 screws / 18 kn / 2500 pass. unberthed / 216 cars /

29.08.1996 floated out / 18.8.1997 delivered / 9.1997
service Seattle—Bainbridge Island for Washington
State Ferries / 2003 12 684 GT /

WENATCHEE (photo: Brandon Swan)

ms WENATCHEE
IMO No. 9137351
State of Washington
(Department of Transportation), Seattle
Todd Pacific Shipyards Corp, Seattle, WA; Yard No.: 92

4998 GRT / 1393 tdw / 138.00 m length oa /
26.73 (27.00) m beam / four 16-cyl. diesels with
10 592 kW; General Motors / four generators
connected to two elec. motors / 8830 kW /
2 screws / 18 kn / 2500 pass. unberthed / 216 cars /

21.8.1997 floated out / 26.5.1998 delivered / 9.1998
service Seattle—Bainbridge Island for Washington
State Ferries / 2003 12 689 GT /

PUYALLUP (photo: Brandon Swan)

ms PUYALLUP
IMO No. 9137363
State of Washington
(Department of Transportation), Seattle
Todd Pacific Shipyards Corp, Seattle, WA; Yard No.: 93

4998 GRT / 1393 tdw / 138.00 m length oa /
26.73 (27.00) m beam / four 16-cyl. diesels with
10 592 kW; General Motors / four generators
connected to two elec. motors / 8830 kW /
2 screws / 18 kn / 2500 pass. unberthed / 216 cars /

12.6.1998 floated out / 24.12.1998 delivered / 1999
service Edmonds—Kingston for Washington State
Ferries / 2003 12 689 GT /

ms PAUL GAUGUIN
IMO No. 9111319
Services et Transports Tahiti, Mata-Utu
Chantiers de l'Atlantique, St. Nazaire; Yard No.: G31

19 170 GT / 2208 tdw / 153.66 m length oa /
22.00 (27.10) m beam / two 9-cyl. and two 6-cyl.
diesels with 12 600 kW; MAN B&W / four generators
connected to two elec. motors / 9000 kW /
2 screws / 19 kn / 320 pass. in 160 cabins /
crew 203

25.4.1996 launched, originally planned as TAHITI
NUI / 1.12.1997 delivered / 2.12.1997 transfer voyage
from St. Nazaire to the South Pacific via the U.S. /
18.12.1997 named in Fort Lauderdale / 19.12.1997
first cruise Fort Lauderdale—San Diego / 31.1.1998
first cruise to the Society Islands under charter by
Radisson Seven Seas Cruises / 10.2004 to Grand
Circle Corp., Nassau; under charter by Regent Seven
Seas Cruises (RSSC) / 12.2009 end of RSSC charter,
continued deployment in South Pacific under charter
by Paul Gauguin Cruises /

PAUL GAUGIN (photo: Gerald Zinnecker)

ROTTERDAM (photo: Frank Lose)

ms ROTTERDAM
IMO No. 9122552
Holland America Line, Rotterdam
Fincantieri, Marghera; Yard No.: 5980

59 652 GT / 6354 tdw / 237.95 m length oa /
32.25 m beam / five 16-cyl. diesels with 57 670 kW;
Sulzer-Fincantieri / five generators connected to two
elec. motors / 37 500 kW / 2 screws / 22.5 (25) kn /
1620 (1668) pass. in 660 cabins / crew 644

21.12.1996 floated out / 7.11.1997 delivered /
11.11.1997 maiden cruise Barcelona—Mediterranean—Transatlantic / 2005 after extension of spa area:
59 885 GT / 18.11.–16.12.2009 conversion at Grand
Bahama Shipyard, Freeport: 61 849 GT, 1404 (1685)
pass. in 702 cabins /

VOLENDAM (photo: Tsuyoshi Ishiyama)

ms VOLENDAM
IMO No. 9156515
Holland America Line, Rotterdam
Fincantieri, Marghera; Yard No.: 6035

60 906 GT / 6150 tdw / 237.00 m length oa /
32.25 m beam / five 12-cyl. diesels with 43 200 kW;
Sulzer-Fincantieri / five generators connected to two
elec. motors / 26 000 kW / 2 screws / 22 (23) kn /
1440 pass. in 720 cabins / crew 645

18.9.1998 floated out / 25.10.1999 delivered /
12.11.1999 maiden cruise / 3.2006 61 214 GT /

ZAANDAM (photo: Clyde Dickens)

ms ZAANDAM
IMO No. 9156527
Holland America Line, Nassau
Fincantieri, Marghera; Yard No.: 6036

60 906 GT / 6150 tdw / 237.00 m length oa /
32.25 m beam / five 12-cyl. diesels with 43 200 kW;
Sulzer-Fincantieri / five generators connected to two
elec. motors / 26 000 kW / 2 screws / 22 (23) kn /
1440 (1846) pass. in 720 cabins / crew 647

30.4.1999 floated out / 8.4.2000 delivered / 6.5.2000
maiden Caribbean cruise from Fort Lauderdale / 2004
61 396 GT, home port Rotterdam /

AMSTERDAM (photo: Cees Bustraan)

ms AMSTERDAM
IMO No. 9188037
Holland America Line, Nassau
Fincantieri, Marghera; Yard No.: 6052

60 874 GT / 7381 tdw / 237.86 m length oa /
32.25 m beam / two 16-cyl. and three 12-cyl.
diesels with 48 960 kW; Sulzer-GMT / five generators
connected to two elec. motors / 22 800 kW /
2 Azipod VO / 22.5 (24.5) kn / 1380 (1738) pass.
in 690 cabins / crew 647

7.1.2000 floated out / 30.9.2000 delivered / 10.2000
christened in Boston / 30.10.2000 first cruise from Fort
Lauderdale / 2.2001 home port Rotterdam / 6.2006
62 735 GT /

ms IKARUS
IMO No. 9144811
Minoan Lines, Heraklion
Fosen Mek. Verksteder, Rissa; Yard No.: 57

30 010 GT / 5150 tdw / 200.65 m length oa /
25.80 m beam / four 8-cyl. diesels geared to
2 screws; MAN B&W / 44 480 kW / 26.4 kn /
700 pass. in 193 cabins, 800 pass. unberthed /
975 cars, 2185 lane metres / crew 118

IKARUS PALACE ex IKARUS (photo: Frank Lose)

5.5.1997 launched at Bruces Shipyard, Landskrona
(Yard No.: 201), then towed to Rissa for completion /
5.12.1997 delivered / 21.12.1997 maiden voyage
in service Patras—Igoumenitsa—Ancona / 12.2001
renamed **IKARUS PALACE** / 22.10.2001–3.7.2010
service Patras—Igoumenitsa—Corfu—Venice /
7.7.2010 entered service Civitavecchia—Trapani—
Tunis, also Salerno—Palermo—Tunis under charter by
Grimaldi Ferries / 8.2010 laid up with damaged crank-
shaft in Naples, then repair in Messina / 19.12.2010
entered service Livorno—Valencia—Tangier, also Livorno
—Barcelona / 16.3.2011 entered service Livorno—
Barcelona—Tangier / 9.12.2012–1.2013 service Piraeus
—Heraklion for Minoan Lines / 19.1.2013 entered
service Livorno—Barcelona—Tangier for Grimaldi Lines /

JEAN NICOLI ex PASIPHAE (photo: Frank Lose)

ms PASIPHAE
IMO No. 9161948
Minoan Lines, Heraklion
Fosen Mek. Verksteder, Rissa; Yard No.: 67

30 018 GT / 5742 tdw / 200.65 m length oa /
25.80 m beam / four 8-cyl. diesels geared to
2 screws; MAN B&W / 44 480 kW / 26.4 kn /
704 pass. in 195 cabins, 796 pass. unberthed /
975 cars, 2195 lane metres / crew 118

23.12.1997 launched at Bruces Shipyard, Landskrona /
12.1.1998 arrived at Rissa for completion / 13.6.1998
christened and delivered / 4.7.1998 maiden voyage in
service Patras—Ancona / 12.2001 renamed **PASIPHAE
PALACE** / 22.10.2001–15.3.2009 service Patras—
Igoumenitsa—Corfu—Venice / 3.2009 **JEAN NICOLI**,
SNCM Ferryterranee, Ajaccio / 8.5.2009 entered service
Marseilles—Porto Vecchio /

ms SUN FLOWER TSUKUBA
IMO No. 9178599
Blue Highway Line, Tokyo
Mitsubishi H.I., Shimonoseki; Yard No.: 1035

12 325 GRT / 7210 tdw / 192.00 m length oa /
27.00 m beam / two 16-cyl. diesels geared to
2 screws; Pielstick / 26 180 kW / 23 kn / 292 pass.
in 68 cabins, 50 pass. unberthed / 111 cars +
216 trucks (8 tons) /

19.1.1998 delivered, then service Oarai–Tomakomai /
7.2001 to Shosen Mitsui Ferry / 1.2007 **FERRY TSUKUBA**,
Higashi Nihon Ferry; laid up in Muroran / 24.7.2007
ELYROS, ANEK, Chania / 9.2008 after conversion in
Keratsini 32 623 GT, 5590 tdw, 780 pass. in 237 cabins,
1094 pass. unberthed, 620 cars, 1940 lane metres /
28.9.2008 entered service Piraeus—Chania / 3.9.2014
chartered by Libyan government, laid up in Tobruk /
25.9.2014–5.6.2015 service Piraeus—Chania / 23.6.–
21.9.2015 service Oran/Algiers—Marseilles/Alicante /
29.9.2015 laid up in Perama / 4.12.2015 continued
service Piraeus—Chania /

ms VARUNA
IMO No. 9184574
Blue Highway Line, Muroran
Mitsubishi H.I., Shimonoseki; Yard No.: 1056

13 654 GRT / 6511 tdw / 192.00 m length oa /
27.00 m beam / two 16-cyl. diesels geared to
2 screws; Pielstick / 26 190 kW / 24 kn / 330 pass.
in cabins, 300 pass. unberthed / 154 trucks +
77 cars /

28.10.1998 delivered / 3.11.1998 entered service
Oarai—Tomakomai / 2001 to Shosen Mitsui Ferry,
then service Oarai—Tomakomai / 1.2005 renamed
SUN FLOWER SAPPORO /

ELYROS ex SUN FLOWER TSUKUBA (photo: George Koutsoukis)

SUNFLOWER SAPPORO ex VARUNA (photo: Tsuyoshi Ishiyama)

SPIRIT OF TASMANIA II ex SUPERFAST III (photo: Dale E. Crisp)

SPIRIT OF TASMANIA I ex SUPERFAST IV (photo: Dale E. Crisp)

New Syros Shipyards, Syros: 886 pass. unberthed / 1.9.2002 entered service Melbourne—Devonport / 11.2005 29 338 GT /

ms PACIFIC VENUS
IMO No. 9160011
Japan Cruise Line, Osaka
Ishikawajima-Harima H.I., Tokyo; Yard No.: 3095

26 518 GT / 4202 tdw / 183.4 m length oa / 25.0 m beam / four 12-cyl. diesels geared to 2 screws; Pielstick-Diesel United / 26 000 kW / 20.8 (21.6) kn / 532 (720) pass. in 266 cabins / crew 180

29.9.1997 launched / 31.3.1998 delivered / 12.4.1998 40-day maiden cruise Tokyo—South-East Asia—Tokyo / 12.2008 26 594 GT /

ms KENNICOTT
IMO No. 9145205
Alaska Marine Highways, Juneau
Halter Marine Group, Moss Point; Yard No.: 1510

12 635 GT / 1695 tdw / 116.43 m length oa / 25.91 m beam / two 12-cyl. diesels geared to 2 screws; Wärtsilä / 9850 kW / 16.75 kn / 314 pass. in 109 cabins, 434 pass. unberthed / 120 cars, 20 trucks /

9.12.1997 launched / 2.6.1998 delivered / 7.1998 service Skagway—Haines—Juneau—Sitka—Petersburg—Wrangell—Ketchikan—Prince Rupert /

ms SUPERFAST III
IMO No. 9158434
SuperFast Ferries, Patras
Kværner Masa-Yards, Turku; Yard No.: 1340

29 067 GT / 5651 tdw / 194.33 m length oa / 25.00 m beam / four 16-cyl. diesels; Wärtsilä-Sulzer / 42 240 kW / 28.5 kn / 750 pass. in 222 cabins, 654 pass. unberthed / 1000 cars, 1464 lane metres /

1.2.1998 christened / 12.2.1998 delivered / 16.3.1998 maiden voyage in service Patras—Igoumenitsa—Ancona / 1.11.1999 caught fire while on a voyage from Patras to Ancona shortly after departing Patras. The fire was extinguished with on board equipment. 14 stowaways hiding in a truck were killed, ship badly damaged / 3.12.1999–2.2000 repair at Blohm+Voss, Hamburg / 3.3.2000 back in service / 10.5.2002 **SPIRIT OF TASMANIA II**, TT Line Co., Devonport, conversion until 6.2002 at Neorion New Syros Shipyards, Syros: 886 deck pass. / 1.9.2002 entered service Melbourne—Devonport / 11.2005 29 338 GT /

PACIFIC VENUS (photo: Ulrich Streich)

ms SUPERFAST IV
IMO No. 9158446
SuperFast Ferries, Patras
Kværner Masa-Yards, Turku; Yard No.: 1341

29 067 GT / 5600 tdw / 194.30 m length oa / 25.00 m beam / four 16-cyl. diesels; Wärtsilä / 42 240 kW / 2 screws / 28.5 kn / 750 pass. in 222 cabins, 654 pass. unberthed / 1000 cars, 1464 lane metres /

1.2.1998 christened / 1.4.1998 delivered / 10.4.1998–1.5.2002 service Patras—Igoumenitsa—Ancona / 10.5.2002 **SPIRIT OF TASMANIA I**, TT Line Co., Devonport, conversion until late June at Neorion

KENNICOTT (photo: Richard Seville)

ms GRAND PRINCESS

IMO No. 9104005
Princess Cruises, Monrovia
Fincantieri, Monfalcone; Yard No.: 5956

108 806 GT / 8418 tdw / 289.51 m length oa /
36.00 (40.20) m beam / six 16-cyl. diesels with
69 120 kW; Sulzer-Grandi Motori / six generators
connected to two elec. motors / 42 000 kW /
2 screws / 22.5 (24) kn / 2592 (3300) pass. in
1296 cabins / crew 1200

22.5.1997 floated out / 12.1997 first sea trials /
3.5.1998 delivered / 14.5.1998 maiden cruise
cancelled, as fittingout out was not completed /
19.5.1998 delivered again / 26.5.1998 maiden cruise
Istanbul—Barcelona / 29.9.1998 christened in New
York / 2000 home port Hamilton / 11.4.–4.5.2011
conversion at Grand Bahama Shipyard, Freeport:
removal of night club superstructure at stern,
107 517 GT, 2602 (3122) pass. in 1301 cabins /

GRAND PRINCESS (photo: Hans-Jürgen Amberg)

GOLDEN PRINCESS (photo: Marc Piché)

ms GOLDEN PRINCESS

IMO No. 9192351
Princess Cruises, Hamilton
Fincantieri, Monfalcone; Yard No.: 6050

108 865 GT / 8418 tdw / 289.51 m length oa /
36.00 (40.20) m beam / four 16-cyl. and two 12-cyl.
diesels with 63 360 kW; Sulzer-Grandi Motori /
six generators connected to two elec. motors /
38 000 kW / 2 screws / 22.5 (24) kn / 2632 (3158)
pass. in 1316 cabins / crew 1200

31.8.2000 floated out / 4.2001 first sea trials /
28.4.2001 delivered, then some short cruises from
Southampton / 16.5.2001 maiden Mediterranean
cruise from Southampton /

STAR PRINCESS (photo: Frank Heine)

ms STAR PRINCESS

IMO No. 9192363
Princess Cruises, Hamilton
Fincantieri, Monfalcone; Yard No.: 6051

108 977 GT / 10 852 tdw / 289.51 m length oa /
36.00 m beam / four 16-cyl. and two 12-cyl. diesels
with 63 360 kW; Sulzer-Grandi Motori / six generators
connected to two elec. motors / 38 000 kW /
2 screws / 22.5 (24) kn / 2596 (3115) pass. in
1298 cabins / crew 1200

10.5.2001 floated out / 25.1.2002 delivered /
16.3.2002 cruises from Los Angeles to Mexico, in
summer to Alaska / 23.3.2006 caught fire on a cabin
balcony on a voyage from Grand Cayman to Jamaica.
One person killed, more than 100 cabins destroyed /
9.4.2006 arrival for repairs at Lloyd Werft, Bremerhaven / 15.5.2006 first cruise from Copenhagen
after repairs /

CARIBBEAN PRINCESS (photo: Egidio Ferrighi)

ms CARIBBEAN PRINCESS
IMO No. 9215490
Princess Cruises, Hamilton
Fincantieri, Monfalcone; Yard No.: 6067

112 894 GT / 8418 tdw / 289.61 m length oa /
36.00 m beam / four 16-cyl. and two 12-cyl. diesels
with 63 360 kW; Sulzer-Fincantieri / six generators
connected to two elec. motors / 38 000 kW /
2 screws / 21.7 (23) kn / 3130 (3756) pass. in
1565 cabins / crew 1205

4.7.2003 launched / 22.3.2004 delivered / 19.3.2004
transfer voyage to Fort Lauderdale / 2.4.2004
christened / 3.4.2004 maiden Caribbean cruise from
Fort Lauderdale /

ms CROWN PRINCESS
IMO No. 9293399
Princess Cruises, Hamilton
Fincantieri, Monfalcone; Yard No.: 6100

113 651 GT / 13 294 tdw / 288.63 m length oa /
36.01 (36.05) m beam / four 12-cyl. and two 8-cyl.
diesels with 67 200 kW; Wärtsilä / six generators
connected to two elec. motors / 42 000 kW /
2 screws / 21.7 (22.5) kn / 3062 (3674) pass. in
1531 cabins / crew 1205

9.9.2005 floated out / 27.5.2006 delivered / 14.6.2006
maiden Caribbean voyage from New York /

ms EMERALD PRINCESS
IMO No. 9333151
Princess Cruises, Hamilton
Fincantieri, Monfalcone; Yard No.: 6131

113 561 GT / 8400 tdw / 290.00 m length oa /
36.00 m beam / four 12-cyl. and two 8-cyl. diesels
with 67 200 kW; Wärtsilä / six generators
connected to two elec. motors / 42 000 kW /
2 screws / 21.7 kn / 3060 (3672) pass. in
1530 cabins / crew 1205

1.6.2006 floated out / 24.3.2007 delivered / 11.4.2007
maiden Mediterranean voyage from Civitavecchia /

CROWN PRINCESS (photo: Andy Hernandez)

EMERALD PRINCESS (photo: Jürgen Pfarre)

ms VENTURA
IMO No. 9333175
P&O Cruises, Hamilton
Fincantieri, Monfalcone; Yard No.: 6132

116 017 GT / 8044 tdw / 289.60 m length oa /
36.00 m beam / four 12-cyl. and two 8-cyl. diesels
with 67 200 kW; Wärtsilä / six generators connected
to two elec. motors / 42 000 kW / 2 screws /
21.7 (23.5) kn / 3106 (3727) pass. in 1553 cabins /
crew 1239

10.6.2007 floated out / 31.3.2008 delivered /
18.4.2008 maiden Mediterranean voyage from
Southampton /

VENTURA (photo: Olaf Schmidt)

ms RUBY PRINCESS
IMO No. 9378462
Princess Cruises, Hamilton
Fincantieri, Monfalcone; Yard No.: 6150

113 651 GT / 8044 tdw / 289.60 m length oa /
36.00 m beam / four 12-cyl. and two 8-cyl. diesels
with 67 200 kW; Wärtsilä / six generators
connected to two elec. motors / 42 000 kW /
2 screws / 21.7 kn / 3060 (3672) pass. in
1530 cabins / crew 1205

1.2.2008 floated out / 23.10.2008 delivered /
8.11.2008 maiden Caribbean cruise from Fort
Lau-derdale /

RUBY PRINCESS (photo: Andy Hernandez)

ms AZURA
IMO No. 9424883
P&O Cruises, Southampton
Fincantieri, Monfalcone; Yard No.: 6166

115 055 GT / 8044 tdw / 289.61 m length oa /
36.00 m beam / four 12-cyl. and two 8-cyl. diesels
with 67 200 kW; Wärtsilä / six generators connected
to two elec. motors / 42 000 kW / 2 screws /
21.7 (22.2) kn / 3096 (3737) pass. in 1557 cabins /
crew 1226

26.6.2009 floated out / 26.3.2010 delivered /
12.4.2010 maiden Mediterranean voyage from
Southampton / 11.2011 home port Hamilton /

AZURA (photo: Olaf Schmidt)

WORLD ODYSSEY ex DEUTSCHLAND (photo: Hans-Joachim Hellmann)

ms DEUTSCHLAND
IMO No. 9141807
Peter Deilmann Reederei, Neustadt in Holstein
Howaldtswerke-Deutsche Werft, Kiel; Yard No.: 328

22 496 GT / 3460 tdw / 175.30 m length oa /
23.00 m beam / two 6-cyl. and two 8-cyl. diesels
geared to 2 screws; MaK-DMR / 12 320 kW /
20 (21) kn / 620 (650) pass. in 318 cabins / crew 270

16.1.1998 floated out / 11.5.1998 christened and
delivered, then pre-inaugural cruise / 13.5.1998
presentation in Hamburg / 16.5.1998 maiden cruise
from Kiel to Norway / 1998 conversion: 520 pass.
in 282 cabins / 5.1999 guarantee docking at HDW
Rendsburg; replacement of noisy gears, conversion
of 80 double cabins for single use: 520 pass. in
314 cabins / 6.2009 bankruptcy of Peter Deilmann
Reederei, ship operation continued / 1.2010 management assumed by newly founded Reederei Peter
Deilmann / 23.5.2010 engine room fire in Eidfjord /
2.6.2010 arrival under tow at Blohm+Voss, Hamburg /
3.7.2010 back in service after repairs / 29.10.2014
bankruptcy of Reederei Peter Deilmann / 11.11.2014
end of last cruise in Lisbon / 14.11.2014 laid up in
Algeciras roads, five days later off Gibraltar and put
up for sale / 19.5.2015 to Absolute Nevada (V.Ships),
home port Nassau / 9.6.–10.8.2015 under charter by
Plantours Kreuzfahrten / 28.8.2015 renamed **WORLD
ODYSSEY** / 13.9.2015 first world cruise as floating
campus under charter by the Institute for Shipboard
Education (Semester at Sea) / 14.5.–7.9.2016 cruises
under five-year summer charter by Phoenix Reisen as
DEUTSCHLAND planned /

ms EXCELLENT
IMO No. 9143441
Grandi Navi Veloci, Palermo
Nuovi Cant. Apuania, Marina di Carrara;
Yard No.: 1206

39 739 GT / 7300 tdw / 202.83 m length oa /
26.80 m beam / four 8-cyl. diesels geared to
2 screws; Wärtsilä / 25 950 kW / 23 kn / 1456 pass.
in 387 cabins, 544 pass. unberthed / 800 cars,
2520 lane metres /

1.1998 launched / 8.6.1998 delivered / 10.6.1998
maiden cruise from Genoa to Israel and Cyprus /
25.6.1998 entered service Genoa—Olbia. Shortly

after departing the port, the engines break down, ship
towed back for repairs to Genoa / 20.9.1998 entered
service Genoa—Palermo, then seasonally alternating
service from Genoa, Livorno, Palermo and Porto Torres /
26.5.2012 also service Sète—Tangier/Nador /

ms EXCELSIOR
IMO No. 9184419
Grandi Navi Veloci, Palermo
Sestri Cant. Nav., Genoa-Sestri

39 739 GT / 7300 tdw / 202.78 m length oa /
226.80 m beam / four 8-cyl. diesels geared to
2 screws; Wärtsilä / 28 960 kW / 24 kn / 1456 pass.
in 387 cabins, 544 pass. unberthed 800 cars,
2520 lane metres /

17.1.1999 launched at Nuovi Cant. Apunia, Carrara,
yard no. 1209, completed in Genoa / 7.5.1999
delivered, then service Genoa—Porto Torres, alternating service from Genoa, Livorno, Palermo and Porto
Torres / 5.2011 39 777 GT / 23.2.2013 entered service
Marseilles—Tunis under charter by SNCM, then laid
up in Marseille because of problems with the Italian
Register / 4.2013 home port Marseilles / 19.4.2013
entered service Marseilles—Ajaccio / 9.2014 after end
of charter home port Palermo / 6.12.2014 entered
service Genoa—Barcelona—Tangier /

EXCELLENT (photo: Frank Heine)

EXCELSIOR (photo: Frank Lose)

ms DISNEY MAGIC

IMO No. 9126807
Disney Cruise Line, Nassau
Fincantieri, Marghera; Yard No.: 5989

83 338 GT / 8452 tdw / 294.06 m length oa /
32.25 m beam / five 16-cyl. diesels with 57 670 kW;
Sulzer-Fincantieri / five generators connected to
two elec. motors / 38 000 kW / 2 screws /
21.5 (25.36) kn / 1754 (2456) pass. in 877 cabins /
crew 954

17.4.1997 floated out / 21.6.1998 delivered /
30.7.1998 christened and departed for first 7-day
cruise from Port Canaveral / 2005 deployed in the
summer months on Mexican Riviera / 2007 for the
first time Mediterranean cruises / 2010 first cruises in
Northern Europe / 9.–10.2013 conversion at Navantia,
Cadiz: 83 969 GT /

DISNEY MAGIC (photo: Christina Heinrich)

DISNEY WONDER (photo: Frank Heine)

ms DISNEY WONDER

IMO No. 9126819
Disney Cruise Line, Nassau
Fincantieri, Marghera; Yard No.: 5990

83 308 GT / 8604 tdw / 294.00 m length oa /
32.25 m beam / five 16-cyl. diesels with 57 670 kW;
Sulzer-Fincantieri / five generators connected to two
elec. motors / 38 000 kW / 2 screws / 21.5 (24) kn /
1754 (2456) pass. in 877 cabins / crew 945

23.2.1998 floated out / 1.7.1999 delivered / 15.8.1999
maiden Bahamas cruise from Port Canaveral /

SKÅNE (photo: Frank Lose)

ms SKÅNE

IMO No. 9133915
Scandlines, Trelleborg
Astilleros Espanoles, Puerto Real; Yard No.: 77

42 705 GT / 7290 tdw / 200.00 m length oa /
29.00 (29.60) m beam / four 8-cyl. diesels; MAN
B&W geared to 2 screws / 28 980 kW / 21 kn /
290 pass. in 145 cabins, 310 pass. unberthed /
500 cars, 110 trucks, 3295 lane metres, 6 rail tracks
with 1110 m length / crew 40

9.8.1997 launched / 22.6.1998 delivered / 7.8.1998
maiden voyage in service Rostock—Trelleborg /
11.10.2012 to Stena Line, Trelleborg, continued service
Rostock—Trelleborg /

ms R ONE
IMO No. 9156462
Renaissance Cruises, Monrovia
Chantiers de l'Atlantique, St. Nazaire; Yard No.: H31

30 277 GT / 2700 tdw / 181.00 m length oa /
25.46 m beam / four 12-cyl. diesels with 19 440 kW;
Wärtsilä / four generators connected to two
elec. motors / 13 500 kW / 2 screws / 18 (20) kn /
698 (803) pass. in 349 cabins / crew 372

24.1.1998 floated out / 25.6.1998 delivered / 17.7.1998
first voyage St. Nazaire—Dover—Amsterdam /
1.8.1998 first Mediterranean cruise from Piraeus /
25.9.2001 Renaissance Cruises filed for bankruptcy /
7.10.2001 arrested in Gibraltar / 28.11.2001 to Cruiseinvest, Majuro / 1.2002 laid up in Marseilles / 20.2.2003
renamed REGATTA, under charter by Oceania Cruises /
15.6.2003 renamed INSIGNIA, until 10.2003 cruises in
sub charter of TMR under marketing name "Vaisseau
Renaissance" / 3.4.2004 first cruise for Oceania
Cruises / 12.2006 to Oceania Cruises / 16.4.2012–
21.4.2014 cruises as COLUMBUS 2 under charter by
Hapag-Lloyd Kreuzfahrten / 8.5.2014 again in service
as INSIGNIA for Oceania Cruises / 11.12.2014 engine
room fire in Castries, St. Lucia, three persons killed /
22.12.2014 arrival under tow for repairs in San Juan /
18.2.2015 after repairs without pass. from San Juan
to Singapore / 22.3.2015 first cruise from Singapore /

INSIGNIA ex R ONE (photo: Tony Davis)

ms R TWO
IMO No. 9156474
Renaissance Cruises, Monrovia
Chantiers de l'Atlantique, St. Nazaire; Yard No.: I31

30 277 GT / 2700 tdw / 181.00 m length oa /
25.46 m beam / four 12-cyl. diesels with 19 440 kW;
Wärtsilä / four generators connected to two elec.
motors / 13 500 kW / 2 screws / 18 (20) kn /
698 (803) pass. in 349 cabins / crew 372

22.5.1998 floated out / 24.11.1998 delivered, then
Mediterranean cruises / 25.9.2001 Renaissance Cruises
filed for bankruptcy / 7.10.2001 arrested in Gibraltar /
28.11.2001 to Cruiseinvest, Majuro / 1.2002 laid up
in Marseilles / 20.2.2003 renamed INSIGNIA, under
charter by Oceania Cruises / 4.2003–6.2003 cruises
under sub-charter by TMR with marketing name
"Vaisseau Renaissance" / 15.6.2003 renamed REGATTA /
5.7.2003 first cruise from Barcelona for Oceania
Cruises / 12.2006 to Oceania Cruises /

REGATTA ex R TWO (photo: Nikolaos Saratzis)

PACIFIC PRINCESS ex R THREE (photo: Kai Ortel)

ms R THREE
IMO No. 9187887
Renaissance Cruises, Gibraltar
Chantiers de l'Atlantique, St. Nazaire; Yard No.: N31

30 277 GT / 2700 tdw / 181.00 m length oa /
25.46 m beam / four 12-cyl. diesels with 19 440 kW;
Wärtsilä / four generators connected to two elec.
motors / 13 500 kW / 2 screws / 18 (20) kn /
684 (702) pass. in 342 cabins / crew 372

12.3.1999 floated out / 28.7.1999 delivered / 12.1999
cruises Tahiti—South Pacific from Papeete / 25.9.2001
Renaissance Cruises filed for bankruptcy / 9.2001 arrested in Uturoa / 10.2002 renamed PACIFIC PRINCESS,
under charter by P&O Princess Cruises / 18.11.2002
first cruise from Sydney / 2004 to P&O Princess Cruises,
Gibraltar / 5.2006 home port Hamilton /

ms R FOUR

IMO No. 9187899
Renaissance Cruises, Gibraltar
Chantiers de l'Atlantique, St. Nazaire; Yard No.: O31

30 277 GT / 2700 tdw / 181.00 m length oa /
25.46 m beam / four 12-cyl. diesels with 19 440 kW;
Wärtsilä / four generators connected to two elec.
motors / 13 500 kW / 2 screws / 18 (20) kn /
684 (702) pass. in 342 cabins / crew 372

12.5.1999 floated out / 22.10.1999 delivered /
12.1999 christened in Fort Lauderdale, then cruises
Tahiti—South Pacific from Papeete / 25.9.2001 Renaissance Cruises filed for bankruptcy / 9.2001 arrested
in Uturoa / 10.2002 renamed **TAHITIAN PRINCESS**,
under charter by P&O Princess Cruises / 21.12.2002
christened in Papeete / 2004 to P&O Princess Cruises /
6.2006 home port Hamilton / 11.2009 renamed
OCEAN PRINCESS / 25.11.2014 to Oceania Cruises,
chartered back to Princess Cruises until 3.2016 /
27.4.2016 first cruise Barcelona—Venice as **SIRENA**
for Oceania Cruises planned /

SIRENA ex R FOUR as OCEAN PRINCESS (photo: George Koutsoukis)

NAUTICA ex R FIVE (photo: George Koutsoukis)

ms R FIVE

IMO No. 9200938
Renaissance Cruises, Monrovia
Chantiers de l'Atlantique, St. Nazaire; Yard No.: P31

30 277 GT / 2700 tdw / 181.00 m length oa /
25.46 m beam / four 12-cyl. diesels with 19 440 kW;
Wärtsilä / four generators connected to two elec.
motors / 13 500 kW / 2 screws / 18 (20) kn /
684 (702) pass. in 342 cabins / crew 372

31.7.1999 floated out / 29.1.2000 christened and
delivered / 1.2.2000 first Mediterranean cruise /
25.9.2001 Renaissance Cruises filed for bankruptcy /
10.2001 arrested in Gibraltar / 12.2001 to Cruiseinvest, Majuro / 1.2002 laid up in Marseilles / 6.2002
Mediterranean cruises under charter by Pullmantur with
marketing name "Blue Dream" / 28.3.2004 renamed
NAUTICA, under charter by Oceania Cruises / 3.4.2004
first cruise under sub charter by TMR / 20.3.2005
under sub charter by Pullmantur using marketing name
"Blue Dream" / 22.11.2005 first cruise under charter
by Oceania Cruises / 12.2006 to Oceania Cruises /

AZAMARA JOURNEY ex R SIX (photo: Ton Grootenboer)

ms R SIX

IMO No. 9200940
Renaissance Cruises, Monrovia
Chantiers de l'Atlantique, St. Nazaire;
Yard No.: Q31

30 277 GT / 2700 tdw / 181.00 m length oa /
25.46 m beam / four 12-cyl. diesels with 19 440 kW;
Wärtsilä / four generators connected to two elec.
motors / 13 500 kW / 2 screws / 18 (20) kn /
712 (777) pass. in 356 cabins / crew 372

17.1.2000 floated out / 24.6.2000 delivered, then
worldwide cruises / 25.9.2001 Renaissance Cruises
filed for bankruptcy / 6.10.2001 arrested in Gibraltar /
12.2001 to Cruiseinvest, Majuro / 1.2002 laid up
in Marseilles / 6.2003 under charter by Pullmantur,
marketed as "Blue Star", at times also as "Blue
Dream" / 7.7.2004 **BLUE DREAM**, Pullmantur
Cruises, Nassau / 6.2006 home port Valletta / 5.2007
AZAMARA JOURNEY, Azamara Cruises / 5.5.2007
first cruise Bayonne—Bermuda / 8.12.2009 owner
renamed Azamara Club Cruises /

ms R SEVEN
IMO No. 9210218
Renaissance Cruises, Monrovia
Chantiers de l'Atlantique, St. Nazaire; Yard No.: Y31

30 277 GT / 2700 tdw / 181.00 m length oa /
25.46 m beam / four 12-cyl. diesels with 19 440 kW;
Wärtsilä / four generators connected to two elec.
motors / 13 500 kW / 2 screws / 18 (20) kn /
712 (777) pass. in 356 cabins / crew 372

24.3.2000 floated out / 28.9.2000 delivered, then
European cruises / 25.9.2001 Renaissance Cruises
filed for bankruptcy / 9.2001 arrested in Dover,
then in Tilbury / 12.2001 to Cruiseinvest, Majuro /
1.2002 laid up in Marseilles / 20.5.2003 **DELPHIN
RENAISSANCE**, in charter with purchase option to
Delphin Renaissance, Majuro / 26.6.2003 first cruise
for Delphin Seereisen from Nice / 4.7.2003 first arrival
in Hamburg for conversion and fitting out / 21.7.2003
christened in Hamburg / 22.7.2003 first cruise from

AZAMARA QUEST ex R SEVEN (photo: Alexander Brede)

ADONIA ex R EIGHT (photo: Alexander Brede)

BEN-MY-CHREE (photo: Frank Lose)

Bremerhaven / 24.5.2006 **BLUE MOON**, Pullmantur
Cruises, Valletta / 8.2007 **AZAMARA QUEST**, Azamara
Cruises / 22.10.2007 first Caribbean cruise from
Miami / 8.12.2009 owner renamed Azamara Club
Cruises / 30.3.2012 engine room fire off the coast
of Borneo, six persons injured / 24.4.2012 back in
service after repairs /

ms R EIGHT
IMO No. 9210220
Renaissance Cruises, Monrovia
Chantiers de l'Atlantique, St. Nazaire; Yard No.: Z31

30 277 GT / 2700 tdw / 181.00 m length oa /
25.46 m beam / four 12-cyl. diesels with 19 440 kW;
Wärtsilä / four generators connected to two elec.
motors / 13 500 kW / 2 screws / 18 (20) kn /
712 (777) pass. in 356 cabins / crew 372

16.9.2000 floated out / 1.2.2001 delivered, then
European cruises / 25.9.2001 Renaissance Cruises
filed for bankruptcy / 10.2001 arrested in Gibraltar /
11.2001 to Cruiseinvest, Majuro / 1.2002 laid up
in Marseilles / 4.2003 renamed **MINERVA II**, under
charter by Swan Hellenic Cruises / 4.2007 **ROYAL
PRINCESS**, Princess Cruises, Hamilton / 19.4.2007
first cruise Barcelona—Mediterranean / 18.6.2009
engine room fire off Port Said / 26.6.2009 arrival for
repairs at Hellenic Shipyards, Skaramanga / 7.7.2009
back in service / 21.5.2011 **ADONIA**, P&O Cruises,
Hamilton / 10.4.2016 first development aid cruise in
charter by fathom planned /

ms BEN-MY-CHREE
IMO No. 9170705
Isle of Man Steam Packet, Douglas
van der Giessen-De Noord, Krimpen; Yard No.: 971

12 504 GT / 2200 tdw / 125.20 m length oa /
23.40 (23.84) m beam / two 9-cyl. diesels geared
to 2 screws; MaK / 8640 kW / 19 kn / 80 pass. in
20 cabins, 332 pass. unberthed / 1235 lane metres /
crew 22

4.4.1998 launched / 3.7.1998 delivered / 31.7.1998
entered service Douglas—Heysham / 2001 420 pass.
unberthed / 6.1.–5.2.2004 conversion of passenger
facilities at Northwestern Ship Repairers, Birkenhead:
500 pass. unberthed / 7.2.2004 back in service
Douglas—Heysham /

ms COMMODORE CLIPPER

IMO No. 9201750
Commodore Shipping Co., Nassau
van der Giessen-De Noord, Krimpen; Yard No.: 975

13 465 GT / 2500 tdw / 129.14 m length oa /
23.40 m beam / two 9-cyl. diesels geared to
2 screws; MaK / 8640 kW / 18.8 kn / 160 pass.
in 40 cabins, 364 pass. unberthed / 279 cars,
1265 lane metres /

8.5.1999 launched / 17.9.1999 delivered / 27.9.1999
entered service Portsmouth—St. Helier—St. Peter
Port / 11.2003 to Condor Ferries, Nassau; continued
service Portsmouth—St. Helier—St. Peter Port /

ms DUEODDE

IMO No. 9323704
Bornholmstrafikken, Rønne
Bodewes, Harlingen, Yard No.: 579

13 906 GT / 3630 tdw / 124.90 m length oa /
23.40 m beam / two 9-cyl. diesels geared to
2 screws; Caterpillar-MaK / 8640 kW / 18.5 kn /
108 pass. in 60 cabins, 292 pass. unberthed /
200 cars, 1235 lane metres / crew 10

24.3.2005 floated out / 18.4.2005 delivered /
1.5.2005–10.10.2010 service Rønne—Køge, also
Rønne—Ystad / 18.10.2010 STRAITSMAN, Straits
Shipping, Wellington / 9.12.2010 entered service
Wellington—Picton /

ms HAMMERODDE

IMO No. 9323699
Bornholmstrafikken, Rønne
Merwede Shipyard, Hardinxveld-Giessendam,
Yard No.:702

13 906 GT / 3630 tdw / 124.90 m length oa /
23.40 m beam / two 9-cyl. diesels geared to
2 screws; Caterpillar-MaK / 8640 kW / 18.5 kn /
108 pass. in 60 cabins, 292 pass. unberthed /
200 cars, 1235 lane metres / crew 10

COMMODORE CLIPPER (photo: Kai Ortel)

STRAITSMAN ex DUEODDE (photo: Michael Pryce)

HAMMERODDE (photo: Frank Lose)

7.1.2005 launched / 20.4.2005 delivered / 1.5.2005
maiden voyage in service Rønne—Køge, also service
Rønne—Ystad / 21.1.–26.3.2010 conversion at STX
Finland, Helsinki: new vehicle deck and additional
passenger accommodation: 14 551 GT, 3096 tdw, 58
sleeperettes, 1548 lane metres / 14.1.2011 to Danske
Færger, Rønne, service Rønne—Køge, in summer also
Rønne—Sassnitz /

ms HAMAYUU

IMO No. 9184562
Kampu Ferry, Shimonoseki
Mitsubishi H.I., Shimonoseki; Yard No.: 1052

16 187 GT / 4045 tdw / 162.00 m length oa /
23.60 m beam / two 8-cyl. diesels; Daihatsu /
8830 kW / 2 screws / 18 kn / 460 pass. in
70 cabins / 30 cars, 150 TEU /

27.4.1998 launched / 27.8.1998 delivered / 28.8.1998
entered service Shimonoseki—Busan /

HAMAYUU (photo: Osamu Taniguchi)

Barcelona—Palma de Mallorca/Mahón under charter by Balearia / 12.2008 renamed **AVE LUEBECK**, intended service Liepaja—Travemünde under charter by AVE Logistics not realised / 4.2009 renamed **T REX** / 18.4.–3.11.2009 service Voltri—Termini Imerese under charter by T-Link / 11.1.2010 laid up in Cadiz / 14.4.2010 entered service Birkenhead—Dublin under charter by Norfolk Line / 30.5.–5.9.2010 service Dover—Boulogne under charter by LD Lines as **NORMAN TRADER** / 5.1.–15.2.2011 service Le Havre—Portsmouth / 5.4.–5.2011 service Liverpool—Dublin under charter by P&O Ferries / 10.6.–22.6.2011 service Holyhead—Dublin under charter by Stena Line / 2.7.2011 laid up in Falmouth / 6.2013 **STENA ALEGRA**, Stena Line, London / 8.7.2013 entered service Gdynia—Karls-krona / 28.10.2013 grounded in heavy storm off Karlskrona, towed off one day later, then to Gdynia for repair / 13.1.–30.6.2014 service Wellington—Picton under charter by Interisland / 28.7.2014 laid up off Singapore / 9.2015 renamed **KAIARAHI**, 22 160 GT, 7012 tdw / 12.10.2015 entered service Wellington—Picton under charter by Interisland Line /

KAIARAHI ex DAWN MERCHANT (photo: Nigel Kirby)

ms **NORTHERN MERCHANT**
IMO No. 9181091
Merchant Ferries, Dover
Astilleros Espanoles, Seville; Yard No.: 289

22 152 GT / 7477 tdw / 179.93 m length oa / 24.30 (25.00) m beam / four 9-cyl. diesels geared to 2 screws; Wärtsilä-NSD / 23 760 kW / 22.5 kn / 114 pass. in 57 cabins, 136 pass. unberthed / 2130 lane metres /

15.5.1999 launched / 26.2.2000 delivered / 20.3.2000–4.3.2006 service Dover—Dunkirk under charter by Norfolk Line / 30.4.2006 entered service Barcelona—Palma de Mallorca under charter by Acciona Trasmediterranea, also Valencia—Palma de Mallorca—Mahón / 7.2006 **ZURBARAN**, Acciona Trasmediterranea, Santa Cruz de Tenerife /

ZURBARAN ex NORTHERN MERCHANT (photo: Frank Lose)

ms **DAWN MERCHANT**
IMO No. 9147291
Merchant Ferries, London
Astilleros Espanoles, Seville; Yard No.: 287

22 152 GT / 7360 tdw / 179.93 m length oa / 24.30 (25.24) m beam / four 9-cyl. diesels geared to 2 screws; Wärtsilä-NSD / 23 760 kW / 24 kn / 114 pass. in 57 cabins, 136 pass. unberthed / 2000 lane metres /

15.11.1997 launched / 1.9.1998 delivered / 10.1998–1.1999 cargo ferry service Istanbul—Trieste under charter by UND RoRo / 15.2.1999 entered service Liverpool—Dublin, home port Douglas / 15.9.2002 entered service Dunkirk—Dover under charter by Norfolk Line / 2003 home port Liverpool / 10.2005 service Liverpool—Dublin for Norse Merchant Ferries / 11.2005 **EUROPAX APPIA**, New Paragon Investments, Liverpool / 11.1.2006 renamed **PAU CASALS**, then service Palma de Mallorca—Barcelona under charter by Balearia / 7.–10.2008 service Salerno—Messina under charter by Caronte & Tourist / 10.2008 service

EUROPEAN ENDEAVOUR ex MIDNIGHT MERCHANT (photo: Frank Lose)

DRUJBA ex MURILLO as MURILLO (photo: Dieter Streich)

NORWEGIAN SPIRIT ex SUPERSTAR LEO (photo: Nikolaos Saratzis)

SUPERSTAR VIRGO (photo: Jonathan Boonzaier)

ms MIDNIGHT MERCHANT
IMO No. 9181106
Merchant Ferries, Dover
Astilleros Espanoles, Seville; Yard No.: 290

22 152 GT / 7396 tdw / 179.95 m length oa /
24.30 (25.24) m beam / four 9-cyl. diesels geared
to 2 screws; Wärtsilä-NSD / 23 760 kW / 23.3 kn /
114 pass. in 57 cabins, 136 pass. unberthed /
2130 lane metres /

26.11.1999 launched / 12.9.2000 delivered /
5.10.2000–27.7.2006 service Dover—Dunkirk under
charter by Norfolk Line / 14.8.2006 EL GRECO, Acciona
Trasmediterranea, Santa Cruz de Tenerife / 8.2006–
19.9.2007 service Palma de Mallorca—Barcelona/
Valencia / 9.10.2007 EUROPEAN ENDEAVOUR, P&O
Ferries, Dover / 6.11.2007 entered service Liverpool—
Dublin / 11.1.2008 entered service Dover—Calais /
4.5.2010 laid up in Tilbury / 1.8.–8.9.2010 service
Liverpool—Dublin/Belfast under charter by DFDS
Seaways / 23.9.2010 laid up in Dunkirk / 22.2.2011
again service Liverpool—Dublin / 4.2011 home port
Nassau /

ms MURILLO
IMO No. 9237242
Cia. Trasmediterranea, Santa Cruz de Tenerife
IZAR, Seville; Yard No.: 291

25 028 GT / 8058 tdw / 180.50 m length oa /
24.30 (26.00) m beam / four 9-cyl. diesels geared
to 2 screws; Wärtsilä-NSD / 23 760 kW / 22.8 kn /
396 pass. in 123 cabins, 154 pass. unberthed /
2196 lane metres / crew 53

19.9.2001 launched / 14.3.2002 delivered / 22.3.2002
entered service Palma de Mallorca—Barcelona/
Valencia / 6.2009–9.2010 in summer service Cadiz—
Canaries, in winter Balearics service / 6.2014 DRUJBA,
Port Bulgaria West EAD, Burgas / 10.2014 service
Burgas—Poti—Novorossiysk—Batumi /

ms SUPERSTAR LEO
IMO No. 9141065
Star Cruises, Panama
Jos. L. Meyer, Papenburg; Yard No.: 646

75 338 GT / 8530 tdw / 268.60 m length oa /
32.20 m beam / four 14-cyl. diesels with
58 800 kW; MAN B&W / four generators connected
to two elec. motors / 40 000 kW / 2 screws /
24 (25.2) kn / 1964 (3350) pass. in 982 cabins /
crew 1125

14.7.1998 floated out / 25.9.1998 delivered / 17.10.1999
first cruise from Hong Kong to Vietnam and China /
5.2004 NORWEGIAN SPIRIT, Norwegian Cruise Line,
Nassau / 1.2008 75 904 GT, 2012 (2414) pass. in
1006 cabins /

ms SUPERSTAR VIRGO
IMO No. 9141077
Star Cruises, Panama
Jos. L. Meyer, Papenburg; Yard No.: 647

75 338 GT / 8530 tdw / 268.60 m length oa /
32.20 m beam / four 14-cyl. diesels with 58 800 kW;
MAN B&W / four generators connected to two elec.
motors / 40 000 kW / 2 screws / 24 (25.2) kn /
1964 (3350) pass. in 982 cabins / crew 1125

17.4.1999 floated out / 2.8.1999 delivered / 20.8.1999
maiden cruise Mumbai—Singapore / 3.10.1999 first
cruise from Singapore / 1.2014 home port Nassau /

ARATERE (photo: Stephen Berry)

FINNCLIPPER (photo: Ulrich Streich)

ms ARATERE
IMO No. 9174828
Tranz Rail, Nassau
Hijos de J. Barreras, Vigo; Yard No.: 1570

12 596 GT / 3977 tdw / 150.00 m length oa /
20.25 (20.50) m beam / four 8-cyl. diesels with
13 430 kW; Wärtsilä / four generators connected
to two elec. motors / 10 400 kW / 2 screws /
19.5 kn / 20 pass. in 10 cabins, 345 pass. unberthed /
70 cars, 1005 lane metres, 4 rail tracks with
425 m length / crew 31

8.9.1998 launched / 12.1998 delivered / 1.2.1999
maiden voyage in service Wellington—Picton / 28.4.–
10.9.2011 lengthening by 30 m at Sembawang,
Singapore: 17 816 GT, 5464 tdw, 183.89 m length oa,
600 pass. unberthed, 18 pass. in 6 cabins, 270 cars, 28

wagons, 30 trucks, crew 35 / 3.10.2011 again service
Wellington—Picton / 5.11.2013 on a voyage from
Picton to Wellington the ship lost a propeller, laid up in

Wellington / 10.12.–23.12.2013 service Wellington—
Picton with only one engine / 23.12.2013 laid up in
Wellington / 2.3.–14.6.2014 repairs at Keppel Shipyard, Singapore, propellers and new rudder blades
fitted / 7.7.2014 back in service Wellington—Picton /

ms FINNCLIPPER
IMO No. 9137997
Stena Rederi, Lübeck
Astilleros Espanoles, Puerto Real; Yard No.: 78

29 841 GT / 8681 tdw / 188.30 m length oa /
28.70 (29.30) m beam / four 8-cyl. diesels geared
to 2 screws; Sulzer / 23 040 kW / 22 kn / 440 pass.
in 191 cabins / 2459 lane metres /

1.2.1998 floated out / 19.5.1999 delivered to Stena
Rederi, same day sold to Finnlines, Lübeck / 10.6.1999
entered service Travemünde—Helsinki for Finncarriers /
19.12.2001 home port Helsinki / 7.1.2003 entered
service Naantali—Kapellskär for Finnlink / 3.1.2005
entered service Malmö—Travemünde for Nordö
Link, home port Malmö / 2.1.2006 entered service
Naantali—Kapellskär for Finnlink / 26.12.2006–
14.3.2007 conversion at Remontowa, Gdansk: additional truck deck, 33 958 GT, 3079 lane metres /
21.2.2012–12.5.2015 service Travemünde—Malmö,
also Lübeck—Mukran—Ventspils—St. Petersburg /
14.5.2015 entered service Naantali—Kapellskär /

ms FINNEAGLE
IMO No. 9138006
Stena Ferries, Lübeck
Astilleros Espanoles, Puerto Real; Yard No.: 79

29 841 GT / 8383 tdw / 188.00 m length oa /
28.70 (29.30) m beam / four 8-cyl. diesels geared
to 2 screws; Sulzer / 23 040 kW / 22 kn / 440 pass.
in 191 cabins / 2459 lane metres /

6.10.1995 ordered by Stena Ferries, London /
18.4.1998 floated out / 5.10.1999 delivered to
Stena Ferries, same day sold to Finnlines, Lübeck /
29.10.1999 to Finnlines, Stockholm, 120 pass. in
cabins / 1.11.1999 entered service Naantali—
Kapellskär for Finnlink / 15.4.2009–9.3.2011 service
Travemünde—Malmö for Nordö Link / 13.3.–1.9.2011
service Naantali—Kapellskär / 3.9.2011–10.2012
service Malmö—Travemünde / 3.10.2012 home port
Helsinki / 13.11.2012 entered service Naantali—
Kapellskär / 1.10.2013 Långnäs also called at /
8.10.2014 home port Mariehamn / 15.8.2015
first voyage in freight service Hanko—Rostock /
12.9.–10.10.2015 service Malmö—Travemünde /
19.10.–8.11.2015 service Naantali—Mariehamn—
Kapellskär / 21.11.–22.12.2015 service Salerno—
Catania under Charter by Grimaldi Ferries /

FINNEAGLE (photo: Frank Heine)

ms STENA BRITANNICA

IMO No. 9145164
Stena Line, London
Astilleros Espanoles, Puerto Real; Yard No.: 80

33 769 GT / 6155 tdw / 188.30 m length oa /
28.70 m beam / four 8-cyl. diesels geared to
2 screws; Wärtsilä-Grandi Motori / 23 040 kW /
22 kn / 452 pass. in 192 cabins / 2500 lane metres /

21.12.1999 launched / 25.8.2000 delivered / 3.10.2000
entered service Harwich—Hoek van Holland / 3.3.2003
FINNFELLOW, Finnlines, Stockholm / 3.4.2003 entered
service Travemünde—Helsinki / 5.1.2004 entered
service Kapellskär—Naantali for Finnlink / 17.1.2013
home port Helsinki / 1.10.2013 Långnäs also called
at / 15.10.2014 home port Mariehamn /

ms STENA HOLLANDICA

IMO No. 9145176
Stena Line, Hoek van Holland
Astilleros Espanoles, Puerto Real; Yard No.: 81

33 769 GT / 6155 tdw / 188.30 m length oa /
28.70 m beam / four 8-cyl. diesels geared to
2 screws; Wärtsilä-Grandi Motori / 23 040 kW /
22 kn / 452 pass. in 192 cabins / 2500 lane metres /

6.5.2000 floated out / 5.2.2001 delivered / 9.3.2001
maiden voyage in service Hoek van Holland—
Harwich / 12.3.–8.5.2007 lengthening by 50 m
midships section at Lloyd Werft, Bremerhaven:
44 372 GT, 10 670 tdw, 240.10 m length oa, 1067
pass. in 400 cabins, 4000 lane metres / 15.5.2007
again service Hoek van Holland—Harwich /
15.5.2010 last voyage in service Harwich—
Hoek van Holland / 5.2010–18.8.2010 conversion at Remontowa, Gdansk: renamed STENA
GERMA-NICA III, 51 837 GT, 1375 pass. in 490
cabins, crew 77 / 31.8.2010 entered service Gothenburg—Kiel / 8.9.2010 renamed STENA GERMAN-
ICA / 26.1.–24.3.2015 engines converted for
methanol at Remontowa, Gdansk / 26.3.2015 again
service Gothenburg—Kiel /

FINNFELLOW ex STENA BRITANNICA (photo: Jukka Huotari)

STENA GERMANICA ex STENA HOLLANDICA (photo: Hans-Joachim Hellmann)

CARTHAGE (photo: Frank Lose)

ms CARTHAGE

IMO No. 9185396
Cotunav, La Goulette
Fosen Mek. Verksteder, Rissa; Yard No.: 68

32 298 GT / 4100 tdw / 180.00 m length oa /
27.50 m beam / four 12-cyl. diesels geared to
2 screws; Sulzer / 34 560 kW / 23.5 kn / 1908 pass.
in 479 cabins, 308 pass. unberthed / 666 cars,
866 lane metres / crew 123

17.12.1998 launched at Bruces Shipyard, Landskrona /
1.6.1999 delivered / 15.6.1999 entered service Tunis—
Genoa/Marseilles / 2000 31 657 GT /

ms CAPRICORN

IMO No. 9179658
"Tirrenia" di Navigazione, Naples
Fincantieri-Cant. Nav. Italiani, Riva Trigoso;
Yard No.: 6046

11 347 GT / 1200 tdw / 145.60 m length oa /
22.00 m beam / four 20-cyl. diesels with 26 800 kW;
MTU; two gas turbines with 44 396 kW; GE Marine,
all geared to 4 waterjets / 40 kn / 1800 pass.
unberthed / 460 cars, 350 lane metres / crew 34

12.12.1998 launched / 7.6.1999 delivered / 15.6.1999
entered service Genoa—Olbia, also service Genoa—
Porto Torres / 2003 service Fiumicino—Golfo Aranci /
20.7.2011 flag of Sierra Leone / 29.7.2011 arrived
for scrapping at Aliaga, then to Avid Ltd., Freetown /
10.10.2011 towed to Tuzla, conversion planned / 2014
towed to Lamjane Shipyard, Zadar /

CAPRICORN (photo: Jürgen Pfarre)

TERA JET ex SCORPIO (photo: George Koutsoukis)

ms SCORPIO

IMO No. 9179660
"Tirrenia" di Navigazione, Naples
Fincantieri-Cant. Nav. Italiani, Riva Trigoso;
Yard No.: 6047

11 347 GT / 1200 tdw / 145.60 m length
oa / 22.00 m beam / four 20-cyl. diesels with
26 800 kW; MTU; two gas turbines with 44 396 kW;
GE Marine, all geared to 4 waterjets / 40 kn / 1800
pass. unberthed / 460 cars,
350 lane metres / crew 34

17.3.1999 launched / 4.6.1999 delivered / 19.6.1999
entered service Civitavecchia—Olbia / 6.—9.2005
service Naples—Milazzo under charter by Siremar /
13.6.—9.2008 service Livorno—Golfo Aranci under
charter by Corsica Sardinia Ferries / 9.2008 laid up
in Cagliari / 22.7.2011 to Karina Shipping, Funafuti /
8.2011 renamed **SCORPIO I**, home port Tuvalu /
6.2012 renamed **RONKE**, home port Dominica, laid
up in Eleusis / 8.2012 renamed **SEA BREEZE III**, home
port Panama / 6.2014 **TERA JET**, Seajets, Limassol,
11 374 GT / 7.7.2014 entered service Heraklion—
Santorini /

COSTA NEORIVIERA ex MISTRAL (photo: Kai Ortel)

ms MISTRAL

IMO No. 9172777
Festival Cruises, Mata-Utu
Chantiers de l'Atlantique, St. Nazaire; Yard No.: J31

47 276 GT / 4225 tdw / 216.00 m length oa / 28.80
(32.00) m beam / four 12-cyl. diesels with 31 700 kW;
Wärtsilä / four generators connected to two
elec. motors / 18 000 kW / 2 screws / 20 (22.5) kn /
1196 (1667) pass. in 598 cabins / crew 450

28.2.1997 keel-laying for Services et Transports;
cancelled, then to Festival Cruises / 2.1.1999 floated
out / 25.6.1999 christened and delivered, then promotional voyage to Northern European ports / 17.7.1999
first cruise from Genoa / 19.1.2004 arrested in
Marseilles / 10.6.2004 auctioned off to Auro Shg.
(builders), Majuro / 2005 **GRAND MISTRAL**, Iberojet,
Majuro / 30.5.2005 first Mediterranean cruise from
Barcelona / 2007 conversion of stern: 48 200 GT,
1248 (1498) pass. in 624 cabins / 14.9.2007 to
Iberocruceros, Genoa / 12.2009 home port Madeira /
11.2013 **COSTA NEORIVIERA**, Costa Crociere, Genoa /
25.11.2013 first cruise for Costa from Dubai /

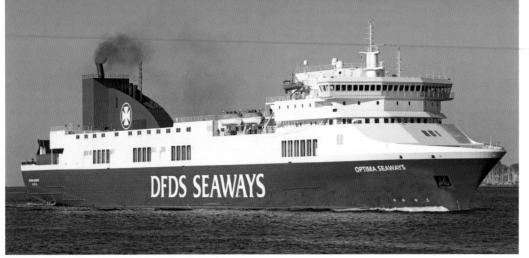

OPTIMA SEAWAYS ex ALYSSA (photo: Frank Lose)

LISCO OPTIMA, DFDS Lisco, Klaipeda / 8.5.2006 entered service Klaipeda—Kiel / 26.5.2009 entered service Klaipeda—Karlshamn / 21.2.2011 entered service Klaipeda—Kiel / 30.9.2011 entered service Klaipeda—Karlshamn / 4.2012 renamed OPTIMA SEAWAYS / 21.10.2014 entered service Klaipeda—Kiel / 7.7.2016 entered service Klaipeda—Karlshamn / 31.8.2015 entered service Klaipeda—Kiel / 5.10.2015 entered service Klaipeda—Karlshamn / 12.2015 entered service Klaipeda—Kiel /

CALIFORNIA STAR ex STENA FORWARDER (photo: ShipPax Information)

ms STENA FORWARDER

IMO No. 9243435
Levantina Trasporti, Bari
Cantiere Navale Visentini, Porto Viro; Yard No.: 195

24 418 GT / 7500 tdw / 186.00 m length oa / 25.60 m beam / two 9-cyl. diesels geared to 2 screws; Wärtsilä / 18 900 kW / 22 kn / 308 pass. in 93 cabins, 642 pass. unberthed / 2100 lane metres /

28.10.2000 launched / 3.2001 delivered / 12.4.2001– 13.4.2003 service Dublin—Holyhead under charter by Stena Line / 14.4.2003 renamed CALIFORNIA STAR / 2003 service Topolobampo—La Paz under charter by Baja Ferries / 3.2007 to Baja Ferries, La Paz /

ms CARTOUR

IMO No. 9243447
Caronte Shipping, Reggio Calabria
Cantiere Navale Visentini, Porto Viro; Yard No.: 196

24 418 GT / 7500 tdw / 186.00 m length oa / 25.60 m beam / two 9-cyl. diesels geared to 2 screws; MAN B&W / 18 900 kW / 22.5 (23) kn / 304 pass. in 76 cabins, 696 pass. unberthed / 2100 lane metres /

8.4.2001 launched / 28.9.2001 delivered / 6.10.2001 entered service Messina—Salerno under charter by Caronte & Tourist / 10.2007 VINASHIN PRINCE, Vinashin Ocean Shipping, Vietnam / 13.12.2007 entered service Hon Gai—Hue-Nha Rong (Ho Chi Minh City) / 12.2007 renamed HOA SEN / 2.2012 service Incheon—China under charter by Lianyungang CK Ferry / 11.2013 STENA EGERIA, Stena RoRo, Limassol / 7.2014 service Yantai—Pyeongtaek under charter by Yantai Bohai International Ferry Co. /

ms ALYSSA

IMO No. 9188427
Levantina Trasporti, Bari
Cantiere Navale Visentini, Porto Viro; Yard No.: 185

25 206 GT / 7500 tdw / 186.00 m length oa / 25.60 m beam / two 9-cyl. diesels geared to 2 screws; MAN B&W / 18 900 kW / 21.5 kn / 240 pass. in 78 cabins / 221 cars, 172 trucks / crew 28

19.12.1998 launched / 30.6.1999 delivered / 8.1999– 2.2000 service Tunis—Marseilles under charter by Cotunav / 3.3.2000 entered service Valencia—Palma de Mallorca under charter by Trasmediterranea / 9.7.2001 SVEALAND, entered service Gothenburg—Travemünde under charter by Stena Line / 26.7.2001 entered service Trelleborg—Travemünde under charter by Scandlines / 17.4.2003 entered service Kiel—Klaipeda / 8.2004 home port Nassau / 1.2006 service Travemünde—Trelleborg under charter by TT-Line / 4.2006

STENA EGERIA ex CARTOUR as HOA SEN (photo: Jelle de Vries)

ms PARTENOPE
IMO No. 9243423
TTT Lines, Naples
Cantiere Navale Visentini, Porto Viro; Yard No.: 193

24 409 GT / 7500 tdw / 186.00 m length oa /
25.60 m beam / two 9-cyl. diesels geared to
2 screws; MAN B&W / 18 900 kW / 22.5 kn /
1000 pass. in 208 cabins / 75 cars,
2050 lane metres /

29.12.2001 launched / 13.5.2002 delivered, then
service Naples—Catania / 10.2013 to Stena RoRo,
chartered back by TTT Lines / 4.4.2015 last voyage in
service Naples—Catania / 5.2015 renamed **NAPOLES**,
home port Limassol / 11.5.2015 entered service Barcelona—Ibiza under charter by Balearia, also service
Barcelona—Palma de Mallorca /

ms TRINACRIA
IMO No. 9261542
TTT Lines, Naples
Cantiere Navale Visentini, Porto Viro; Yard No.: 194

24 409 GT / 7500 tdw / 186.00 m length oa /
25.60 m beam / two 9-cyl. diesels geared to
2 screws; Wärtsilä / 18 900 kW / 22.5 kn /
1000 pass. in 308 cabins / 75 cars,
2050 lane metres /

15.11.2002 delivered / 12.12.2002 entered service
Naples—Catania / 10.2013 to Stena RoRo, chartered
back by TTT Lines / 14.4.2015 last voyage in service
Naples—Catania / 26.4.2015 renamed **SICILIA**, home
port Limassol / 19.5.2015 entered service Algeciras—
Tangier Med. under charter by Balearia / 7.9.2015
entered service Valencia—Palma de Mallorca under
charter by Balearia /

ms EUROSTAR VALENCIA
IMO No. 9264312
Grimaldi Ferries, Palermo
Cantiere Navale Visentini, Porto Viro; Yard No.: 197

25 984 GT / 7150 tdw / 186.50 m length oa /
25.60 m beam / two 9-cyl. diesels geared to
2 screws; Wärtsilä / 18 900 kW / 22.5 (24) kn /
370 pass. in 93 cabins, 580 pass. unberthed /
160 cars, 2240 lane metres /

18.1.2003 launched / 16.6.2003 delivered / 5.7.2003
entered service Salerno—Valencia, also service Salerno—
Valletta—Tunis / 27.1.2005 entered service Civitavecchia—Toulon / 13.11.2006 renamed **SORRENTO** /
3.2008 service Civitavecchia—Trapani—Tunis /
14.7.2009 entered service Livorno—Valencia /
11.4.2012–24.2.2014 service Brindisi—Igoumenitsa—
Patras / 3.3.2014 entered service Valencia—Palma de
Mallorca under charter by Acciona Trasmediterranea /
28.4.2015 caught fire on vehicle deck while on a
voyage from Palma de Mallorca to Valenica. Passengers
and crew evacuated. / 6.5.2015 arrived under tow in
Sagunto and laid up /

ms EUROSTAR SALERNO
IMO No. 9261554
Grimaldi Ferries, Palermo
Cantiere Navale Visentini, Porto Viro; Yard No.: 200

25 995 GT / 7150 tdw / 186.50 m length oa /
25.60 m beam / two 9-cyl. diesels geared to
2 screws; Wärtsilä / 18 900 kW / 22.5 (24) kn /
370 pass. in 93 cabins, 580 pass. unberthed /
160 cars, 2240 lane metres /

NAPOLES ex PARTENOPE (photo: Frank Lose)

SICILIA ex TRINACRIA (photo: Frank Lose)

SORRENTO ex EUROSTAR VALENCIA (photo: Manuel Hernandez Lafuente)

28.6.2003 launched / 12.11.2003 delivered / 26.11.2003 entered service Salerno—Valletta / 2005 service Civitavecchia/Livorno/Salerno—Palermo/Tunis/Valletta / 16.6.2008 entered service Barcelona—Livorno / 2009 renamed **CATANIA** / 5.2.2009 entered service Genoa—Civitavecchia—Catania—Valletta / 28.4.2009 entered service Civitavecchia—Catania / 2010 service Livorno—Valencia / 28.5.2011 entered service Civitavecchia—Catania—Valletta / 11.2011 service Genoa—Catania—Corinth—Patras / 2012 service Civitavecchia/Naples—Palermo/Trapani/Tunis / 1.2013 service Brindisi—Igoumenitsa—Patras / 10.2014 service Ancona—Igoumenitsa—Patras / 16.2.–4.4.2015 service Ravenna—Igoumenitsa—Patras, once weekly also from Trieste / 17.4.2015 entered service Catania—Naples under charter by TTT Lines / 23.12.2015 entered service Palermo—Tunis/Salerno/Civitavecchia /

CATANIA ex EUROSTAR SALERNO (photo: Frank Lose)

SEVEN SEAS NAVIGATOR (photo: Tony Davis)

ms **SEVEN SEAS NAVIGATOR**
IMO No. 9064126
Radisson Seven Seas Cruises, Hamilton
T. Mariotti, Genoa; Yard No.: 6125

28550 GT / 3470 tdw / 170.69 m length oa / 24.80 m beam / four 8-cyl. diesels geared to 2 screws; Wärtsilä-NSD / 15536 kW / 19.5 (22) kn / 506 (557) pass. in 253 cabins / crew 325

23.8.1991 launched at Admiralty Shipyard, Leningrad. Originally planned as Soviet satellite tracking and guidance vessel AKADEMIK NIKOLAY PILYUGIN, construction discontinued / 1996 to V.Ships, then for reconstruction into cruise ship towed to T. Mariotti, Genoa / 25.8.1999 delivered / 19.10.1999 christened in Fort Lauderdale, then worldwide cruises / 3.2006 owner operating as Regent Seven Seas Cruises / 10.2011 home port Nassau / 1.2014 28803 GT /

ms **EUROPA**
IMO No. 9183855
Hapag-Lloyd Kreuzfahrten, Nassau
Kværner Masa-Yards, Helsinki; Yard No.: 495

28437 GT / 3252 tdw / 198.52 m length oa / 24.00 m beam / two 8-cyl. and two 7-cyl. diesels

EUROPA (photo: Olaf Kuhnke)

VINCENZO FLORIO (photo: Frank Lose)

RAFFAELE RUBATTINO (photo: Frank Heine)

19.7.1997 launched / 10.1999 delivered / 7.10.1999 maiden voyage in service Naples—Palermo / 28.5.2009 caught of fire on vehicle deck on a voyage from Naples to Palermo. The passengers were evacuated and the ship was towed to Palermo, where the fire was extinguished / 5.2009 laid up in Palermo, later repair at Fincantieri, Palermo / 2.5.2012 again service Palermo—Naples /

ms RAFFAELE RUBATTINO
IMO No. 9144744
"Tirrenia" di Navigazione, Naples
Cant. Nav. "Ferrari", La Spezia; Yard No.: 226

30 650 GT / 7300 tdw / 180.30 m length oa / 26.80 m beam / two 12-cyl. diesels geared to 2 screws; Wärtsilä / 25 200 kW / 23 kn / 980 pass. in 289 cabins, 220 pass. unberthed / 608 cars, 2000 lane metres / crew 80

18.8.1998 launched / 18.10.2000 delivered. After bankruptcy of builders, completion at Nuovi Cantieri Apuania, Marina di Carrara / 10.2001 service Naples—Palermo /

ms VOYAGER OF THE SEAS
IMO No. 9161716
Royal Caribbean International, Monrovia
Kværner Masa-Yards, Turku; Yard No.: 1344

137 276 GT / 11 132 tdw / 311.12 m length oa / 38.60 (47.44) m beam / six 12-cyl. diesels with 75 600 kW; Wärtsilä / six generators connected to three elec. motors / 42 000 kW / 3 Azipod VO / 22 kn / 3114 (3840) pass. in 1557 cabins / crew 1176

27.11.1998 floated out / 29.6.1999 sea trials / 29.10.1999 delivered / 19.11.1999 christened in Miami / 21.11.1999 pre-inaugural cruise / 11.1999 cruises Miami—Caribbean / 11.2001 home port Nassau / 2006 Mediterranean cruises from Barcelona / 6.2012 cruises from Shanghai / 17.10.–24.11.2014 conversion at Sembawang, Singapore: 138 194 GT, 3282 (3938) pass. in 1641 cabins / 25.11.2014 first cruise Singapore—Sydney after conversion /

with 21 510 kW; MAN B&W / four generators connected to two elec. motors / 13 300 kW / 2 Azipod VO / 21 kn / 408 pass. in 204 cabins / crew 261

4.3.1999 floated out / 9.9.1999 delivered / 15.9.1999 christened in Hamburg and pre-inaugural cruise / 17.9.1999 maiden cruise Hamburg—Malaga / 1.2006 28 890 GT /

ms VINCENZO FLORIO
IMO No. 9144732
"Tirrenia" di Navigazione, Naples
Cant. Nav. "Ferrari", La Spezia; Yard No.: 225

30 757 GT / 7300 tdw / 180.30 m length oa / 26.80 m beam / two 12-cyl. diesels geared to 2 screws; Wärtsilä / 25 200 kW / 23 kn / 980 pass. in 289 cabins, 220 pass. unberthed / 608 cars, 2000 lane metres / crew 80

VOYAGER OF THE SEAS (photo: Hiroyuki Yoshimoto)

EXPLORER OF THE SEAS (photo: Dale E. Crisp)

ms EXPLORER OF THE SEAS

IMO No. 9161728
Royal Caribbean International, Monrovia
Kværner Masa-Yards, Turku; Yard No.: 1345

137 308 GT / 10 937 tdw / 311.12 m length oa /
38.60 (49.10) m beam / six 12-cyl. diesels with
75 600 kW; Wärtsilä / six generators connected
to three elec. motors / 42 000 kW / 3 Azipod VO /
23 kn / 3114 (3844) pass. in 1557 cabins / crew 1176

4.11.1999 floated out / 29.9.2000 delivered / 2.10.2000 transfer from Helsinki to New York / 21.10.2000 christened in New York / 28.10.2000 maiden cruise from Miami / 11.2001 home port Nassau / 22.3.–20.4.2015 conversion at Navantia, Cadiz: 138 194 GT, 3282 (3938) pass. in 1641 cabins / 24.4.2015 first cruise Southampton—Canaries after conversion /

ms ADVENTURE OF THE SEAS

IMO No. 9167227
Royal Caribbean International, Monrovia
Kværner Masa-Yards, Turku; Yard No.: 1346

137 276 GT / 11 033 tdw / 311.12 m length oa /
38.60 (49.10) m beam / six 12-cyl. diesels with
75 600 kW; Wärtsilä / six generators connected
to three elec. motors / 42 000 kW / 3 Azipod VO /

23 kn / 3114 (3844) pass. in 1557 cabins /
crew 1176

5.1.2001 floated out / 26.10.2001 delivered / 5.11.2001 presentation in Boston / 10.11.2001 christened in New York, where the ADVENTURE OF THE SEAS had called as first cruise ship after September 11th 2001. Then departure on a three-day appreciation cruise for helpers and their families after the terrorist attacks / 13.11.2001 transfer from New York to San Juan / 18.11.2001 maiden cruise from San Juan / 11.2001 home port Nassau /

ms NAVIGATOR OF THE SEAS

IMO No. 9227508
Royal Caribbean International, Nassau
Kværner Masa-Yards, Turku; Yard No.: 1347

138 279 GT / 9616 tdw / 311.12 m length oa /
38.60 (49.04) m beam / six 12-cyl. diesels with
74 544 kW; Wärtsilä / six generators connected to
three elec. motors / 42 000 kW / 3 Azipod VO /
22 (23) kn / 3114 (3807) pass. in 1557 cabins /
crew 1181

25.1.2002 floated out / 18.11.2002 delivered / 6.12.2002 christened in Miami / 14.12.2002 maiden Caribbean cruise from Miami / 1.–2.2014 conversion at Grand Bahama Shipyard, Freeport: 139 570 GT, 3272 (3926) pass. in 1636 cabins / 5.2.2014 first cruise Galveston—Caribbean after conversion /

ADVENTURE OF THE SEAS (photo: Frank Lose)

NAVIGATOR OF THE SEAS (photo: Marko Stampehl)

ms MARINER OF THE SEAS

IMO No. 9227510
Royal Caribbean International, Nassau
Kværner Masa-Yards, Turku; Yard No.: 1348

138 279 GT / 9616 tdw / 311.12 m length oa /
38.60 (49.10) m beam / six 12-cyl. diesels with
75 600 kW; Wärtsilä / six generators connected
to three elec. motors / 42 000 kW / 3 Azipod VO /
22 (23) kn / 3114 (3840) pass. in 1557 cabins /
crew 1181

28.2.2003 floated out / 29.10.2003 delivered /
16.11.2003 maiden Caribbean cruise from Port
Canaveral / 3.2009 via South America to the U.S. West
Coast. Year-round cruises along the Mexican Riviera /
1.2011 via South America back to U.S. East Coast /
6.2013 cruises from Shanghai /

MARINER OF THE SEAS (photo: Olaf Schmidt)

ms AURORA

IMO No. 9169524
P&O Cruises, London
Jos. L. Meyer, Papenburg; Yard No.: 640

76 152 GT / 8486 tdw / 270.00 m length oa /
32.20 (32.60) m beam / four 14-cyl. diesels with
58 800 kW; MAN B&W / four generators connected
to two elec. motors / 40 000 kW / 2 screws /
24 (29) kn / 1874 (2290) pass. in 939 cabins /
crew 936

8.1.2000 floated out / 15.4.2000 delivered /
27.4.2000 christened by Princess Anne in Southampton, then one-day pre-inaugural cruise /
1.5.2000 first cruise Southampton—Mediterranean,
which had to be discontinued on 2.5.2000 because
of an overheated shaft bearing. The passengers
disembarked in Southampton / 5.5.—13.5.2000
repairs at Blohm+Voss, Hamburg / 15.5.2000
maiden voyage from Southampton / 1.2005 owing
to a defective propulsion motor a just started round-
the-world-cruise had be cancelled. / 28.1.—19.5.2005
both propulsion motors replaced at Lloyd Werft,
Bremerhaven / 12.2007 home port Hamilton /

AURORA (photo: Richard Seville)

FUNDY ROSE ex BLUE STAR ITHAKI (photo: Shipfax/Mac Mackay)

ms BLUE STAR ITHAKI

IMO No. 9203916
Blue Star Ferries, Piraeus
Daewoo Shipbuilding & Marine Engineering, Okpo;
Yard No.: 7504

10 193 GT / 1410 tdw / 123.80 m length oa /
18.90 m beam / four 9-cyl. diesels geared to
2 screws; Wärtsilä / 16 560 kW / 24 kn / 20 pass.
in 5 cabins, 1293 pass. unberthed / 245 cars,
365 lane metres / crew 40

24.11.1999 launched / 12.5.2000 delivered / 6.2000
maiden voyage in service Rafina—Syros—Paros—
Naxos—Ios—Santorini / 1.6.2011—9.2014 in summer
service Rafina—Andros—Tinos—Mykonos / 7.11.2014
CANADA 2014, Transport Canada, Ottawa / 7.2015
renamed **FUNDY ROSE** / 28.7.2015 entered service
Digby—Saint John /

ms BLUE STAR PAROS

IMO No. 9241774
Blue Star Ferries, Piraeus
Daewoo Shipbuilding & Marine Engineering, Okpo;
Yard No.: 7507

10 438 GT / 1391 tdw / 123.80 m length oa /
18.90 m beam / four 6-cyl. diesels geared to
2 screws; Wärtsilä / 17 400 kW / 24.5 (24.7) kn /
120 pass. in 35 cabins, 1380 pass. unberthed /
204 cars, 365 lane metres / crew 65

15.11.2001 launched / 18.4.2002 delivered / 10.5.2002
maiden voyage in service Piraeus—Paros—Naxos—
Santorini / 14.11.2011 last voyage in service Pirae-
us—Paros—Naxos—Santorini, then laid up / 1.2012
service Piraeus—Astypalaia—Patmos—Leipsoi—
Leros—Kalymnos—Kos—Nisyros—Tilos—Symi—
Rhodes—Kastellorizo / 1.6.2012 service Piraeus—
Syros—Paros—Naxos—Santorini—Amorgos
—Iraklia—Schoussa—Koufonissi—Donousa—
Astyplalaia—Kalymnos /

BLUE STAR PAROS (photo: Frank Heine)

ms BLUE STAR NAXOS

IMO No. 9241786
Blue Star Ferries, Piraeus
Daewoo Shipbuilding & Marine Engineering, Okpo;
Yard No.: 7508

10 438 GT / 1391 tdw / 124.20 m length oa /
18.90 m beam / four 6-cyl. diesels geared to
2 screws; Wärtsilä / 17 400 kW / 24.5 (24.7) kn /
120 pass. in 35 cabins, 1380 pass. unberthed /
204 cars, 365 lane metres / crew 65

28.2.2002 launched / 7.6.2002 delivered / 1.7.2002
maiden voyage in service Piraeus—Paros—Naxos—
Santorini / 6.2011 service Piraeus—Syros—Tinos—
Mykonos /

BLUE STAR NAXOS (photo: Frank Heine)

BLUE STAR 1 (photo: Frank Lose)

ms BLUE STAR 1

IMO No. 9197105
Blue Star Ferries, Piraeus
van der Giessen-De Noord, Krimpen; Yard No.: 976

29 415 GT / 4563 tdw / 176.10 m length oa /
25.70 m beam / four 8-cyl. diesels geared to
2 screws; MAN B&W / 44 480 kW / 27 kn /
430 pass. in 161 cabins, 1170 pass. unberthed /
640 cars, 1745 lane metres / crew 112

18.12.1999 launched / 6.6.2000 delivered / 13.6.2000
maiden voyage in service Patras—Brindisi—Ancona /
1.1.2001 entered service Patras—Igoumenitsa—
Ancona / 22.7.2002 entered service Piraeus—Patmos—
Leros—Kos—Rhodes / 4.3.2005 entered service
Patras—Igoumenitsa—Bari / 29.1.2007–13.9.2008
service Zeebrugge—Rosyth / 9.2008 service Piraeus—
Rhodes / 27.3.2011 entered service Piraeus—
Syros—Santorini—Patmos—Leros—Kos—Rhodes /
18.1.2013 entered service Piraeus—Heraklion /
15.11.–8.12.2013 service Patras—Igoumenitsa—
Ancona / 11.1.–30.3.2014 service Piraeus—
Chios—Mytilene / 4.2014 service Piraeus—Syros—
Santorini—Patmos—Leros—Kos—Rhodes /

BLUE STAR 2 (photo: George Koutsoukis)

ms OLYMPIA EXPLORER

IMO No. 9183518
Royal Olympic Cruises, Gibraltar
Blohm+Voss, Hamburg; Yard No.: 962

24 318 GT / 2490 tdw / 180.40 m length oa /
25.50 m beam / four 9-cyl. diesels geared to
2 screws; Wärtsilä / 37 800 kW / 28 (30.5) kn /
800 (836) pass. in 400 (416) cabins / crew 360

19.5.2000 floated out as OLYMPIC EXPLORER /
9.3.2001 sea trials / 4.2001 renamed OLYMPIA
EXPLORER, registered under Greek flag in Gibraltar /
24.4.2001 guest voyage for B+V employees /
27.4.2001 Royal Olympic Cruises refused delivery of
the ship for pretextual reasons. / 25.4.2002 delivered,
transfer Hamburg—Piraeus / 4.5.2002 first Mediterranean cruise / 7.6.2002 christened in Piraeus / 8.2002

ms BLUE STAR 2

IMO No. 9207584
Blue Star Ferries, Piraeus
van der Giessen-de Noord, Krimpen; Yard No.: 978

29 415 GT / 4563 tdw / 176.10 m length oa /
25.70 m beam / four 8-cyl. diesels geared to
2 screws; MAN B&W / 44 480 kW / 27 kn /
430 pass. in 161 cabins, 1170 pass. unberthed /
640 cars, 1745 lane metres / crew 112

25.3.2000 launched / 6.7.2000 delivered / 14.7.2000
maiden voyage in service Patras—Brindisi—Ancona /
1.1.2001 entered service Patras—Igoumenitsa—
Ancona / 4.3.2003 entered service Piraeus—Chania /
2003 29 560 GT / 3.2003 service Piraeus—Patmos—
Leros—Kos—Rhodes /

CHINESE TAISHAN ex OLYMPIC VOYAGER (photo: Wei-Lin Chen)

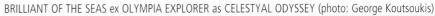

BRILLIANT OF THE SEAS ex OLYMPIA EXPLORER as CELESTYAL ODYSSEY (photo: George Koutsoukis)

ms OLYMPIC VOYAGER

IMO No. 9183506
Royal Olympic Cruises, Piraeus
Blohm+Voss, Hamburg; Yard No.: 961

24 391 GT / 2352 tdw / 180.40 m length oa /
25.50 m beam / four 9-cyl. diesels geared to
2 screws; Wärtsilä / 37 800 kW / 28 (30.6) kn /
800 (836) pass. in 400 (416) cabins / crew 360

14.7.1999 floated out / 15.6.2000 delivered / 22.6.2000
christened in Piraeus / 24.6.2000 first seven-day cruise
from Piraeus. In winter from Fort Lauderdale, e.g. to
the Amazon River / 2001 cruises from Houston / 2001
renamed OLYMPIA VOYAGER / 12.2003 arrested
in Charlotte Amalie / 2.1.2004 pass. disembarked
in Fort Lauderdale, then laid up in Miami / 3.2004
purchased at auction by German bank Kreditanstalt
für Wiederaufbau / 5.2004 VOYAGER, Horizon Navigation Inc., Nassau / 28.6.2004 first Mediterranean
cruise from Valencia under charter by Iberojet /
14.2.2005 en route from Tunis to Barcelona serious
damage after wave impact (blown-in windows on
bridge) / 15.2.2005 arrival in Cagliari, where pass.
disembarked / 12.2005 renamed GRAND VOYAGER /
4.2008 to Iberocruceros, Genoa / 11.2011 COSTA
VOYAGER, Costa Crociere, Genoa / 6.11.2013 laid
up in Genoa / 3.2014 CHINESE TAISHAN, Bohai
Cruise Company, Panama / 29.3.2014 transfer from
Genoa to Shidao and initially laid up in Shidao roads /
26.8.2014 first cruise Yantai—South Korea /

CELEBRITY MILLENNIUM ex MILLENNIUM (photo: Hiroyuki Yoshimoto)

CELEBRITY INFINITY ex INFINITY (photo: Peter Knego)

home port Piraeus / 12.2003 after bankruptcy of owner laid up in Long Beach / 3.2004 sold at auction to German bank Kreditanstalt für Wiederaufbau / 6.2004 renamed **EXPLORER**, home port Nassau. Chartered for 15 years with purchase option by The Institute for Shipboard Education of the University of Pittsburgh under the Semester at Sea programme / 17.6.2004 first cruise for students from Seattle into the Pacific / 27.1.2005 badly damaged by wave impact, which blew in a bridge window / 31.1.2005 the EXPLORER reached Honolulu with only two functioning main engines, where the students left the ship. After repair without passengers to Ho Chi Minh City / 16.5.2015 transferred to KfW Bankengruppe / 4.2015 renamed **CELESTYAL ODYSSEY** / 5.2015 first Aegean cruise from Izmir under charter by Celestyal Cruises / 10.2015 charter prematurely terminated / 28.10.2015 to Diamond Cruise International / 29.11.2015 arrival at Shanghai Huarun Dadong Dockyard, Chongming Dao, for conversion / 3.2016 first cruise from Shanghai as **BRILLIANT OF THE SEAS** planned /

CELEBRITY INFINITY ex INFINITY (photo: Peter Knego)

ts MILLENNIUM
IMO No. 9189419
Celebrity Cruises, Monrovia
Chantiers de l'Atlantique, St. Nazaire; Yard No.: R31

90 228 GT / 11 928 tdw / 294.00 m length oa / 32.20 (32.30) m beam / two gas turbines and one exhaust steam turbine (COGES) with 50 000 kW; GE Marine / two generators connected to two elec. motors / 38 000 kW / 2 Mermaid pods / 24 (26.5) kn / 1950 (2460) pass. in 975 cabins / crew 999

7.11.1999 floated out / 31.5.2000 delivery planned, not accepted; maiden voyage planned for 17.5. cancelled / 22.6.2000 delivered / 1.7.2000 maiden cruise Amsterdam—Baltic / 11.-12.2000 stern conversion at Newport News Shipbuilding, Newport News / 7.2002 home port Nassau / 2.2008 home port Valletta / 6.2009 renamed **CELEBRITY MILLENNIUM** / 21.4.–11.5.2012 conversion at Grand Bahama Shipyard, Freeport: 90 963 GT, 2158 (2590) pass. in 1079 cabins / 12.5.2012 first cruise Miami—Caribbean after conversion /

ts INFINITY
IMO No. 9189421
Celebrity Cruises, Monrovia
Chantiers de l'Atlantique, St. Nazaire; Yard No.: S31

90 228 GT / 11 778 tdw / 294.00 m length oa / 32.20 (32.30) m beam / two gas turbines and one exhaust steam turbine (COGES) with 50 000 kW; GE Marine / two generators connected to two elec. motors / 38 000 kW / 2 Mermaid pods / 24 kn / 1950 (2449) pass. in 1019 cabins / crew 1000

9.6.2000 floated out / 23.2.2001 delivered / 3.3.2001 maiden cruise Fort Lauderdale—San Diego / 8.2002 home port Nassau / 6.2007 renamed **CELEBRITY INFINITY** / 2.2008 home port Valletta / 11.–12.2011 conversion at Grand Bahama Shipyard, Freeport: 90 940 GT, 2170 (2604) pass. in 1085 cabins / 3.12.2011 first cruise Fort Lauderdale—Valparaiso after conversion /

ts SUMMIT
IMO No. 9192387
Celebrity Cruises, Monrovia
Chantiers de l'Atlantique, St. Nazaire; Yard No.: T31

90 280 GT / 11 788 tdw / 294.00 m length oa / 32.20 (32.30) m beam / two gas turbines and one exhaust steam turbine (COGES) with 50 000 kW; GE Marine / two generators connected to two elec. motors / 38 000 kW / 2 Mermaid pods / 24 kn / 1950 (2449) pass. in 1019 cabins / crew 1000

9.3.2001 floated out / 1.10.2001 delivered, then cruises / 1.2003 home port Nassau / 2.2008 home port

CELEBRITY SUMMIT ex SUMMIT (photo: Tony Davis)

CELEBRITY CONSTELLATION ex CONSTELLATION (photo: Hans-Joachim Hellmann)

Barcelona / 2003 home port Nassau / 5.2007 renamed **CELEBRITY CONSTELLATION** / 2.2008 home port Valletta / 4.–5.2013 conversion at Grand Bahama Shipyard, Freeport: 90 940 GT, 2158 (2590) pass. in 1079 cabins / 5.5.2013 first cruise Miami—Amsterdam after conversion /

ms COSTA ATLANTICA
IMO No. 9187796
Costa Crociere, Genoa
Kværner Masa-Yards, Helsinki; Yard No.: 498

85 619 GT / 8600 tdw / 292.56 m length oa / 32.20 (38.78) m beam / six 9-cyl. diesels with 62 370 kW; Wärtsilä / six generators connected to two elec. motors / 35 200 kW / 2 Azipod VO / 22 (24) kn / 2114 (2537) pass. in 1057 cabins / crew 902

11.11.1999 floated out / 30.6.2000 delivered / 4.7.2000 transfer to Venice / 16.7.2000 maiden cruise Venice—Eastern Mediterranean / 1.2015 conversion at Shanghai Huarun Dadong Dockyard: 2218 (2680) pass. in 1109 cabins /

COSTA ATLANTICA (photo: Alexander Brede)

ms CARNIVAL SPIRIT
IMO No. 9188647
Carnival Cruise Lines, Panama
Kværner Masa-Yards, Helsinki; Yard No.: 499

85 920 GT / 7200 tdw / 292.56 m length oa / 32.20 (38.80) m beam / six 9-cyl. diesels with 62 370 kW; Wärtsilä / six generators connected to two elec. motors / 35 200 kW / 2 Azipod VO / 22 (24) kn / 2124 (2549) pass. in 1062 cabins / crew 961

17.7.2000 floated out / 11.4.2001 delivered / 12.4.2001 transfer from Helsinki to Miami / 29.4.2001 maiden cruise Miami—Los Angeles / 6.2012 home port Valletta /

Valletta / 4.2008 renamed **CELEBRITY SUMMIT** / 1.2012 conversion at Grand Bahama Shipyard, Freeport: 90 940 GT, 2158 (2590) pass. in 1079 cabins / 28.1.2012 first cruise San Juan—Caribbean after conversion /

ts CONSTELLATION
IMO No. 9192399
Celebrity Cruises, Monrovia
Chantiers de l'Atlantique, St. Nazaire; Yard No.: U31

90 280 GT / 11 763 tdw / 294.00 m length oa / 32.20 (37.40) m beam / two gas turbines and one exhaust steam turbine (COGES) with 50 000 kW; GE Marine / two generators connected to two elec. motors / 38 000 kW / 2 Mermaid pods / 24 kn / 2038 (2450) pass. in 1019 cabins / crew 999

31.10.2001 floated out / 30.4.2002 delivered / 5.5.2002 first cruise (charter) cancelled because of pod problems / 12.5.2002 maiden cruise from

CARNIVAL SPIRIT (photo: Clyde Dickens)

ms CARNIVAL PRIDE
IMO No. 9223954
Carnival Cruise Lines, Panama
Kværner Masa-Yards, Helsinki; Yard No.: 500

85 920 GT / 7200 tdw / 292.50 m length oa /
32.80 (38.80) m beam / six 9-cyl. diesels with
62 370 kW; Wärtsilä / six generators connected
to two elec. motors / 35 200 kW / 2 Azipod VO /
22 (24) kn / 2124 (2549) pass. in 1062 cabins /
crew 961

29.3.2001 floated out / 12.12.2001 delivered /
30.12.2001 New Year's cruise / 7.1.2002 christened
in Port Canaveral, then pre-inaugural cruise / 9.1.2002
three-day Bahamas cruise / 12.1.2002 after two
promotional voyages first Caribbean cruise from Port
Canaveral /

ms CARNIVAL LEGEND
IMO No. 9224726
Carnival Cruise Lines, Panama
Kværner Masa-Yards, Helsinki; Yard No.: 501

85 942 GT / 7089 tdw / 292.56 m length oa /
32.20 (38.80) m beam / six 9-cyl. diesels with
62 370 kW; Wärtsilä / six generators connected to
two elec. motors / 35 200 kW / 2 Azipod VO /
22 (24) kn / 2124 (2549) pass. in 1062 cabins /
crew 961

17.12.2001 floated out / 14.8.2002 delivered /
21.8.2002 christened in Harwich, then three-day cruise
to Amsterdam and a twelve-day voyage to the North
Cape / 8.2014 home port Valletta /

ms COSTA MEDITERRANEA
IMO No. 9237345
Costa Crociere, Genoa
Kværner Masa-Yards, Helsinki; Yard No.: 502

85 619 GT / 7500 tdw / 292.50 m length oa /
32.20 (38.80) m beam / six 9-cyl. diesels with
62 370 kW; Wärtsilä / six generators connected
to two elec. motors / 35 200 kW / 2 Azipod VO /
22 kn / 2114 (2537) pass. in 1057 cabins / crew 902

24.9.2002 floated out / 22.5.2003 delivered / 7.6.2003
christened / 16.6.2003 maiden Mediterranean cruise
from Genoa /

CARNIVAL PRIDE (photo: Hans-Jürgen Amberg)

CARNIVAL LEGEND (photo: Kai Ortel)

COSTA MEDITERRANEA (photo: Alexander Brede)

ms CARNIVAL MIRACLE
IMO No. 9237357
Carnival Cruise Lines, Panama
Kværner Masa-Yards, Helsinki; Yard No.: 503

85 942 GT / 7089 tdw / 292.56 m length oa /
32.20 (38.80) m beam / six 9-cyl. diesels with
62 370 kW; Wärtsilä / six generators connected to
two elec. motors / 35 200 kW / 2 Azipod VO /
22 (24) kn / 2124 (2549) pass. in 1062 cabins /
crew 961

5.6.2003 floated out / 11.2003 sea trials / 17.1.2004
delivered / 9.2.1004 transfer from Helsinki to Jacksonville / 27.2.2004 christened in Jacksonville, then
maiden Caribbean cruise /

CARNIVAL MIRACLE (photo: Cees Bustraan)

ms **EUROPEAN CAUSEWAY**
IMO No. 9208394
P&O Ferries, Nassau
Mitsubishi H.I., Shimonoseki; Yard No.: 1065

20 646 GT / 4331 tdw / 159.20 m length oa /
23.40 (25.72) m beam / four 12-cyl. diesels geared
to 2 screws; Wärtsilä / 31 680 kW / 22.7 kn /
410 pass. unberthed / 375 cars, 1750 lane metres /
crew 61

20.3.2000 launched / 14.7.2000 delivered / 14.8.2000
maiden voyage in service Cairnryan—Larne /

EUROPEAN CAUSEWAY (photo: Frank Lose)

MALO SEAWAYS ex EUROPEAN AMBASSADOR (photo: Frank Lose)

ms **EUROPEAN AMBASSADOR**
IMO No. 9215505
P&O Ferries, Nassau
Mitsubishi H.I., Shimonoseki; Yard No.: 1068

24 206 GT / 4884 tdw / 170.51 m length oa /
24.00 (25.82) m beam / two 18-cyl. and two 12-cyl.
diesels geared to 2 screws; Wärtsilä / 39 600 kW /
25.7 kn / 222 pass. in 80 cabins, 222 pass.
unberthed / 375 cars, 1948 lane metres /

18.8.2000 launched / 12.2000 delivered / 8.1.2001
entered service Liverpool—Dublin / 11.2001–4.4.2002
service Mostyn—Dublin / 8.4.2004 laid up in Liverpool /
21.4.2004 **STENA NORDICA**, Stena Line, Gothenburg;
22 206 GT / 6.5.2004–20.10.2008 service Gdynia—
Karlskrona / 12.11.2008–8.3.2015 service Dublin—
Holyhead / 24.3.2009 home port London / 9.4.2015
renamed **MALO SEAWAYS** / 14.4.2015 entered service
Dover—Calais under charter by DFDS Seaways /

ms EUROPEAN HIGHLANDER

IMO No. 9244116
P&O Ferries Irish Sea, Nassau
Mitsubishi H.I., Shimonoseki; Yard No.: 1069

21 188 GT / 4276 tdw / 162.70 m length oa /
23.40 (25.72) m beam / four 12-cyl. diesels geared
to 2 screws; Wärtsilä / 31 680 kW / 22.6 (25) kn /
331 pass. in 82 cabins, 79 pass. unberthed /
375 cars, 1750 lane metres / crew 61

18.1.2002 launched / 31.5.2002 delivered / 3.7.2002
maiden voyage in service Larne—Cairnryan /

EUROPEAN HIGHLANDER (photo: Frank Lose)

SILVER SHADOW (photo: Hiroyuki Yoshimoto)

SILVER WHISPER (photo: Cees Bustraan)

ms SILVER SHADOW

IMO No. 9192167
Silversea Cruises, Nassau
Cantiere Navale Visentini, Porto Viro (hull),
T. Mariotti, Genoa; Yard No.: 981

28 258 GT / 2980 tdw / 182.00 m length oa /
24.80 m beam / two 8-cyl. diesels geared to
2 screws; Wärtsilä / 15 600 kW / 20.5 kn /
388 (466) pass. in 194 cabins / crew 295

19.10.1999 floated out / 2.9.2000 delivered / 14.9.2000
christened in Civitavecchia / 15.9.2000 maiden
voyage from Civitavecchia via Lisbon to New York,
then worldwide cruises /

ms SILVER WHISPER

IMO No. 9192179
Silversea Cruises, Nassau
Cantiere Navale Visentini, Porto Viro (hull),
T. Mariotti, Genoa; Yard No.: 982

28 258 GT / 2980 tdw / 182.00 m length oa /
24.80 m beam / two 8-cyl. diesels geared to
2 screws; Wärtsilä / 15 600 kW / 20.5 kn / 388
(466) pass. in 194 cabins / crew 295

9.2.2000 floated out / 11.6.2001 delivered, then
worldwide cruises /

ms OLYMPIC CHAMPION

IMO No. 9216028
ANEK Lines, Chania
Fosen Mek. Verksteder, Rissa; Yard No.: 69

32 694 GT / 6524 tdw / 204.10 m length oa /
25.80 (26.12) m beam / four 12-cyl. diesels geared
to 2 screws; Wärtsilä-NSD / 50 400 kW / 27.5 kn /
808 pass. in 236 cabins, 1042 pass. unberthed /
654 cars, 2028 lane metres /

14.4.2000 launched as KRITI III at Bruces Shipyard,
Landskrona, Yard No.: 243 / 16.10.2000 delivered as
OLYMPIC CHAMPION / 11.2000 service Piraeus
—Chania / 20.2.2001 entered service Patras—
Igoumenitsa—Ancona / 8.6.2011 entered service
Piraeus—Heraklion / 19.1.2015 entered service Patras—
Igoumenitsa—Venice, also Patras—Igoumenitsa
—Ancona /

OLYMPIC CHAMPION (photo: Frank Heine)

HELLENIC SPIRIT (photo: Frank Lose)

ms HELLENIC SPIRIT

IMO No. 9216030
ANEK Lines, Chania
Fosen Mek. Verksteder, Rissa; Yard No.: 70

32 694 GT / 6524 tdw / 204.10 m length oa /
25.80 (26.12) m beam / four 12-cyl. diesels geared
to 2 screws; Wärtsilä-NSD / 50 400 kW / 27.5 kn /
808 pass. in 236 cabins, 1042 pass. unberthed /
654 cars, 2028 lane metres /

30.8.2000 launched at Bruces Shipyard, Landskrona,
Yard No.: 244. Planned as KRITI IV, then as OLYMPIC
SPIRIT / 7.5.2001 delivered as HELLENIC SPIRIT /
18.5.2001 maiden voyage in service Patras—
Igoumenitsa—Ancona /

ms KNOSSOS PALACE

IMO No. 9204063
Minoan Lines, Heraklion
Fincantieri, Sestri Ponente; Yard No.: 6059

37 482 GT / 5850 tdw / 214.00 m length oa /
26.40 m beam / four 16-cyl. diesels geared to
2 screws; Wärtsilä-Grandi Motori / 67 200 kW /
29.5 kn / 758 pass. in 216 cabins, 1430 pass.
unberthed / 660 cars, 1560 lane metres /

1.7.2000 floated out / 25.11.2000 delivered /
12.2000 maiden voyage in service Heraklion—
Piraeus /

KNOSSOS PALACE (photo: Richard Seville)

FESTOS PALACE (photo: Frank Heine)

ms FESTOS PALACE

IMO No. 9204568
Minoan Lines, Heraklion
Fincantieri, Sestri Ponente; Yard No.: 6060

37 482 GT / 5850 tdw / 214.00 m length oa /
26.40 m beam / four 16-cyl. diesels geared to
2 screws; Wärtsilä-Grandi Motori / 67 200 kW /
29.5 kn / 758 pass. in 216 cabins, 1430 pass.
unberthed / 660 cars, 1560 lane metres /

16.11.2000 floated out / 19.4.2001 delivered /
5.5.2001 maiden voyage in service Heraklion—
Piraeus /

BONARIA ex OLYMPIA PALACE (photo: Frank Lose)

ms OLYMPIA PALACE
IMO No. 9220330
Minoan Lines, Heraklion
Fincantieri, Sestri Ponente; Yard No.: 6073

36825 GT / 5500 tdw / 214.00 m length oa /
26.40 m beam / four 16-cyl. diesels geared to
2 screws; Wärtsilä / 67200 kW / 29.5 (32) kn /
744 pass. in 190 cabins, 1136 pass. unberthed /
821 cars, 2000 lane metres /

14.6.2001 floated out / 11.12.2001 delivered /
21.12.2001 maiden voyage in service Patras—
Igoumenitsa—Ancona / 10.2009 service Patras—
Corfu—Igoumenitsa—Venice / 1.11.2011 laid up
in Perama / 27.7.2012 renamed **BONARIA**, home
port Cagliari / 30.7.2012 entered service Cagliari—
Civitavecchia under charter by Tirrenia /

AMSICORA ex EUROPA PALACE (photo: Frank Heine)

ms EUROPA PALACE
IMO No. 9220342
Minoan Lines, Heraklion
Fincantieri, Sestri Ponente; Yard No.: 6074

36825 GT / 5500 tdw / 214.00 m length oa /
26.40 m beam / four 16-cyl. diesels geared to
2 screws; Wärtsilä / 67200 kW / 29.5 (32) kn /
744 pass. in 190 cabins, 1136 pass. unberthed /
821 cars, 2000 lane metres /

26.10.2001 floated out / 11.5.2002 delivered /
14.5.2002 maiden voyage in service Patras—
Igoumenitsa—Ancona / 3.7.2010–15.7.2012 service
Patras—Igoumenitsa—Corfu—Venice / 26.7.2012
renamed **AMSICORA**, home port Cagliari / 31.7.2012
entered service Cagliari—Civitavecchia under charter
by Tirrenia /

ms SUPERFAST VI
IMO No. 9198939
SuperFast Ferries, Patras
Howaldtswerke-Deutsche Werft, Kiel; Yard No.: 356

32728 GT / 6515 tdw / 203.90 m length oa /
25.00 m beam / four 16-cyl. diesels geared to
2 screws; Wärtsilä-NSD / 46080 kW / 28 kn /
842 pass. in 244 cabins, 766 pass. unberthed /
712 cars, 1926 lane metres / crew 110

11.3.2000 floated out / 6.2.2001 delivered / 2.3.2001–
2.4.2013 service Patras—Igoumenitsa—Ancona /
5.4.2013 **BIMINI SUPERFAST**, Genting Group,
Panama / 20.7.2013 entered service Miami—Bimini /
10.1.2016 service suspended /

BIMINI SUPERFAST ex SUPERFAST VI (photo: Ton Grootenboer)

CAP FINISTERE ex SUPERFAST V (photo: Frank Lose)

ms SUPERFAST V
IMO No. 9198927
SuperFast Ferries, Patras
Howaldtswerke-Deutsche Werft, Kiel; Yard No.: 355

32728 GT / 6515 tdw / 203.90 m length oa /
25.00 m beam / four 16-cyl. diesels geared to
2 screws; Wärtsilä-NSD / 46080 kW / 28 kn /
842 pass. in 244 cabins, 766 pass. unberthed /
712 cars, 1926 lane metres / crew 110

11.3.2000 floated out / 24.8.2000 sea trials discontinued after gear problems / 6.4.2001 delivered / 12.4.2001
maiden voyage in service Patras—Igoumenitsa—
Ancona / 2.2010 **CAP FINISTERE**, Brittany Ferries,
Morlaix / 22.3.2010 entered service Portsmouth—
Cherbourg and Portsmouth—Santander / 27.3.2011
weekly round voyage in service Portsmouth—Santander
and two round voyages Portsmouth—Bilbao /

ms ULYSSES
IMO No. 9214991
Irish Ferries, Dublin
Aker Finnyards, Rauma; Yard No.: 429

50 938 GT / 9665 tdw / 209.02 m length oa /
31.84 (31.20) m beam / four 9-cyl. diesels geared
to 2 screws; MaK / 31 200 kW / 22 kn / 228 pass. in
117 cabins, 1647 pass. unberthed / 1342 cars,
4076 lane metres /

1.9.2000 floated out / 28.2.2001 delivered / 25.3.2001
maiden voyage in service Dublin—Holyhead / 1.2006
home port Limassol /

ULYSSES (photo: Frank Lose)

MEGA EXPRESS (photo: Frank Heine)

ms MEGA EXPRESS
IMO No. 9203174
Corsica Ferries, Genoa
Cantiere Navale Fratelli Orlando, Livorno;
Yard No.: 273

26 400 GT / 3500 tdw / 172.70 m length oa /
24.80 m beam / four 12-cyl. diesels geared to
2 screws; Wärtsilä-NSD / 50 400 kW / 28 kn /
1176 pass. in 299 cabins, 580 pass. unberthed /
550 cars, 900 lane metres /

25.3.2000 launched / 29.3.2001 delivered / 2.4.2001
maiden voyage in service Toulon—Ajaccio, then
alternating services from France and Italy to Sardinia
and Corsica /

MEGA EXPRESS TWO (photo: Nikolaos Saratzis)

ms MEGA EXPRESS TWO
IMO No. 9203186
Corsica Ferries, Genoa
Cantiere Navale Fratelli Orlando, Livorno;
Yard No.: 274

26 400 GT / 3500 tdw / 172.70 m length oa /
24.80 m beam / four 12-cyl. diesels geared to
2 screws; Wärtsilä-NSD / 50 400 kW / 28 kn /
1176 pass. in 299 cabins, 580 pass. unberthed /
550 cars, 900 lane metres /

23.9.2000 launched / 1.6.2001 delivered / 15.6.2001
alternating services from France and Italy to Sardinia
and Corsica /

SEVEN SEAS MARINER (photo: Frank Lose)

ms SEVEN SEAS MARINER
IMO No. 9210139
Radisson Seven Seas Cruises, Mata-Utu
Chantiers de l'Atlantique, St. Nazaire; Yard No.: K31

48 075 GT / 4700 tdw / 216.00 m length oa /
28.80 m beam / four 12-cyl. diesels with 33 600 kW;
Wärtsilä / four generators connected to two elec.
motors / 17 000 kW / 2 Mermaid pods / 20 (21) kn /
708 (779) pass. in 354 cabins / crew 431

8.9.2000 floated out / 8.3.2001 delivered / 22.5.2001
christened in Los Angeles, then worldwide cruises /
3.2006 owner operates as Regent Seven Seas Cruises /
12.2006 home port Nassau /

ts RADIANCE OF THE SEAS
IMO No. 9195195
Royal Caribbean International, Monrovia
Jos. L. Meyer, Papenburg; Yard No.: 655

90 090 GT / 10 759 tdw / 293.20 m length oa /
32.20 (39.80) m beam / two gas turbines and one
exhaust steam turbine (COGES) with 57 800 kW;

GE Marine / two generators connected to two elec.
motors / 40 120 kW / 2 Azipod VO / 24 (24.7) kn /
2110 (2501) pass. in 1055 cabins / crew 858

12.10.2000 floated out / 1.2001 sea trials / 9.3.2001
delivered / 6.4.2001 christened in Fort Lauderdale /
7.4.2001 maiden cruise Fort Lauderdale—Panama
Canal—Los Angeles / 11.2001 home port Nassau /
5.–6.2011 conversion at Victoria Shipyards, Victoria:
2122 (2546) pass. in 1061 cabins /

ts BRILLIANCE OF THE SEAS
IMO No. 9195200
RCL UK, Nassau
Jos. L. Meyer, Papenburg; Yard No.: 656

90 090 GT / 10 759 tdw / 293.20 m length oa /
32.20 (39.80) m beam / two gas turbines and one
exhaust steam turbine (COGES) with 57 800 kW;
GE Marine / two generators connected to two elec.
motors / 40 120 kW / 2 Azipod VO / 24 (24.7) kn /
2110 (2501) pass. in 1055 cabins / crew 858

31.5.2002 floated out / 5.7.2002 delivered / 13.7.2002
christened in Harwich / 15.7.2002 maiden cruise
Harwich—Norway in 25-year charter by Royal Caribbean
International / 4.–5.2013 conversion at Navantia,
Cadiz: 2150 (2580) pass. in 1075 cabins / 12.12.2014
termination of charter and purchase of ship by Royal
Caribbean International /

BRILLIANCE OF THE SEAS (photo: Frank Heine)

RADIANCE OF THE SEAS (photo: Clyde Dickens)

ts SERENADE OF THE SEAS
IMO No. 9228344
Royal Caribbean International, Monrovia
Jos. L. Meyer, Papenburg; Yard No.: 657

90 090 GT / 11 936 tdw / 293.20 m length oa /
32.20 (39.80) m beam / two gas turbines and one
exhaust steam turbine (COGES) with 57 800 kW;
GE Marine / two generators connected to two elec.
motors / 40 120 kW / 2 Azipod VO / 24 (24.7) kn /
2110 (2501) pass. in 1055 cabins / crew 858

20.6.2003 floated out / 30.7.2003 delivered / 4.8.2003
transfer voyage Amsterdam—Boston / 8.2003 home
port Nassau / 25.8.2003 maiden cruise New York—
New England / 11.–12.2012 conversion at Navantia,
Cadiz: 2150 (2580) pass. in 1075 cabins /

ts JEWEL OF THE SEAS
IMO No. 9228356
Royal Caribbean International, Nassau
Jos. L. Meyer, Papenburg; Yard No.: 658

90 090 GT / 11 936 tdw / 293.20 m length oa /
32.20 (39.80) m beam / two gas turbines and one
exhaust steam turbine (COGES) with 57 800 kW;
GE Marine / two generators connected to two elec.
motors / 40 120 kW / 2 Azipod VO / 24 (24.7) kn /
2110 (2501) pass. in 1055 cabins / crew 858

13.3.2004 floated out / 22.4.2004 delivered / 25.4.2004
promotional voyage from Hamburg / 28.4.2004 first
short cruise Hamburg—Oslo, then short trips from
Oslo / 7.5.2004 christened in Southampton, then
maiden cruise Southampton—Baltic /

ms PROMETHEUS
IMO No. 9208071
Minoan Lines, Heraklion
Samsung H.I., Koje; Yard No.: 1279

26 995 GT / 6200 tdw / 212.00 m length oa /
25.00 m beam / four 12-cyl. diesels geared to
2 screws; Wärtsilä / 50 400 kW / 28.5 kn / 200 pass.
in 52 cabins, 800 pass. unberthed / 100 cars,
2000 lane metres /

12.8.2000 launched / 14.3.2001 delivered / 6.4.2001
maiden voyage in service Patras—Igoumenitsa—
Venice / 13.6.–20.9.2003 service Patras—Igoumenitsa
—Corfu—Bari / 10.9.2003–10.1.2004 service
Livorno—Catania under charter by Caronte & Tourist /
17.1.2004 to Caronte & Tourist, Reggio Calabria /
16.2.2004 entered service Salerno—Catania /
11.2004 **EUROSTAR BARCELONA**, Grimaldi Ferries,

SERENADE OF THE SEAS (photo: Cees Bustraan)

JEWEL OF THE SEAS (photo: Uwe Jakob)

Palermo; 30 860 GT / 2.5.2005 entered service
Civitavecchia—Barcelona / 11.10.2008 entered

ZEUS PALACE ex PROMETHEUS (photo: Frank Heine)

service Patras—Igoumenitsa—Corfu—Venice/Ancona
under charter by Minoan Lines / 4.2.2009 entered
service Civitavecchia—Trapani—Tunis, also Salerno—
Palermo—Tunis for Grimaldi Ferries / 3.2009 renamed
ZEUS PALACE / 15.3.2009 entered service Patras—
Igoumenitsa—Corfu—Venice under charter by Minoan
Lines / 9.11.2009 one voyage Civitavecchia—Porto
Torres—Barcelona, then service Civitavecchia/
Palermo—Tunis / 24.2.2010 entered service Genoa—
Palermo under charter by Grandi Navi Veloci / 10.3.–
28.9.2012 service Palermo—Civitavecchia under
charter by Grandi Navi Veloci / 4.10.–1.12.2012 service
Patras—Igoumenitsa—Ancona for Minoan Lines /
1.2013 service Civitavecchia/Salerno—Palermo/
Tunis/Trapani / 19.7.2013 entered service Ancona—
Igoumenitsa—Corfu—Patras, also Trieste—Ancona—
Igoumenitsa—Corfu—Patras / 19.12.2013 entered
service Civitavecchia/Salerno—Palermo/Tunis /
11.1.2016 entered service Livorno—Olbia

ms OCEANUS
IMO No. 9208083
Minoan Lines, Heraklion
Samsung H.I., Koje; Yard No.: 1280

26995 GT / 6200 tdw / 212.00 m length oa /
25.00 m beam / four 12-cyl. diesels geared to
2 screws; Wärtsilä / 50400 kW / 28.5 kn /
200 pass. in 52 cabins, 800 pass. unberthed /
100 cars, 2000 lane metres /

13.1.2001 floated out / 5.7.2001 delivered / 5.8.2001
maiden voyage in service Patras—Igoumenitsa—
Venice / 5.2002 renamed **ARIADNE PALACE I** /
31.5.2002 entered service Genoa—Tunis, once weekly
also Tunis—Valletta—Genoa / 10.1.2003 laid up in
Piraeus / 1.2003 **ARIADNE PALACE ONE**, Corsica
Sardinia Ferries, Genoa / 13.6.—20.9.2003 service
Patras—Igoumenitsa—Corfu—Bari under charter by
Minoan Lines / 4.2004 delivered after conversion at
NCA, Marina di Carrara: 29650 GT, 5590 tdw, 1446
pass. in 374 cabins, 660 pass. unberthed, 680 cars,
1093 lane metres, renamed **MEGA EXPRESS THREE** /
19.5.2004 entered service Livorno—Golfo Aranci /

MEGA EXPRESS THREE ex OCEANUS (photo: Frank Lose)

MOBY TOMMY ex ARIADNE PALACE (photo: Frank Lose)

ms ARIADNE PALACE
IMO No. 9221310
Minoan Lines S.A., Heraklion
Samsung H.I., Koje; Yard No.: 1281

28007 GT / 6075 tdw / 211.94 m length oa /
25.00 m beam / four 12-cyl. diesels geared to
2 screws; Wärtsilä / 50400 kW / 28.5 (31.5) kn /
408 pass. in 105 cabins, 842 pass. unberthed /
580 cars, 1916 lane metres /

28.5.2001 floated out as **ARIADNE** / 9.10.2002 delivered
as **ARIADNE PALACE** / 11.2002 maiden voyage in
service Patras—Igoumenitsa—Ancona / 2.2003
entered service Patras—Igoumenitsa—Venice /
19.12.2007 **MOBY TOMMY**, Moby Lines, Naples /
5.2007 service Livorno/Piombino—Olbia, also service
Olbia—Civitavecchia /

PRIDE OF ROTTERDAM (photo: George Koutsoukis)

ms PRIDE OF ROTTERDAM
IMO No. 9208617
P&O North Sea Ferries, Rotterdam
Fincantieri, Marghera; Yard No.: 6065

59925 GT / 8850 tdw / 215.00 m length oa /
31.50 m beam / four 9-cyl. diesels geared to
2 screws; Wärtsilä / 37800 kW / 22 kn / 1360 pass.
in 546 cabins, 136 pass. unberthed / 250 cars,
3300 lane metres / crew 136

29.9.2000 floated out / 12.4.2001 delivered / 30.4.2001
maiden voyage in service Rotterdam—Hull /

ms SUPERFAST VIII

IMO No. 9198953
SuperFast Ferries, Piraeus
Howaldtswerke-Deutsche Werft, Kiel; Yard No.: 358

30 285 GT / 5295 tdw / 203.30 m length oa /
25.00 (25.40) m beam / four 16-cyl. diesels
geared to 2 screws; Sulzer-Fincantieri / 46 000 kW /
28.6 kn / 610 pass. in 176 cabins, 107 pass.
unberthed / 653 cars, 1891 lane metres /

11.7.2001 christened and delivered / 16.7.2001 maiden
voyage in service Rostock—Hanko / 10.4.2006
Tallink, Tallinn, service Rostock—Paldiski—Hanko /
9.6.2006 service Hanko—Rostock / 1.1.2007 entered
service Rostock—Helsinki / 11.1.2007 entered service
Tallinn—Helsinki—Rostock / 1.9.2008 service reduced
to Helsinki—Rostock / 24.12.2009 laid up in Tallinn /
26.4.–2.9.2010 service Helsinki—Rostock / 1.4.–
12.8.2011 service Helsinki—Rostock / 22.8.2011
conversion in Gdansk: renamed **STENA SUPERFAST
VIII**, home port Belfast, 194 pass. in 51 cabins, 1006
pass. unberthed, crew 72 / 21.11.2011 entered service
Cairnryan—Belfast under charter by Stena Line /

PRIDE OF HULL (photo: Frank Lose)

ms PRIDE OF HULL

IMO No. 9208629
P&O North Sea Ferries, Hull
Fincantieri, Marghera; Yard No.: 6066

59 925 GT / 8850 tdw / 215.00 m length oa /
31.50 m beam / four 9-cyl. diesels geared to
2 screws; Wärtsilä / 37 800 kW / 22 kn / 1360 pass.
in 546 cabins, 136 pass. unberthed / 250 cars,
3300 lane metres / crew 136

11.4.2001 floated out / 16.11.2001 delivered / 11.2001
maiden voyage in service Hull—Rotterdam /

ms SUPERFAST VII

IMO No. 9198941
SuperFast Ferries, Piraeus
Howaldtswerke-Deutsche Werft, Kiel; Yard No.: 357

30 285 GT / 5295 tdw / 203.30 m length oa /
25.00 (25.40) m beam / four 16-cyl. diesels geared
to 2 screws; Sulzer-Fincantieri / 46 000 kW /
28.6 kn / 610 pass. in 176 cabins, 107 pass.
unberthed / 653 cars, 1891 lane metres /

18.11.2000 floated out / 8.5.2001 delivered / 15.5.2001
maiden voyage in service Rostock—Hanko / 10.4.2006
to Tallink, Tallinn, service Rostock—Paldiski—Hanko /
9.6.2006 service Hanko—Rostock / 1.1.2007 entered
service Rostock—Helsinki / 11.1.2007 entered service
Tallinn—Helsinki—Rostock / 1.9.2008 service
reduced to Helsinki—Rostock / 3.1.2010 laid up in
Tallinn / 26.4.–2.9.2010 service Helsinki—Rostock /
1.4.–14.8.2011 service Helsinki—Rostock / 22.8.–
9.11.2011 conversion in Gdansk: renamed **STENA
SUPERFAST VII**, home port Belfast, 194 pass. in 51
cabins, 1006 pass. unberthed, crew 72 / 21.11.2011
entered service Cairnryan—Belfast under charter by
Stena Line /

STENA SUPERFAST VII ex SUPERFAST VII (photo: Frank Lose)

STENA SUPERFAST VIII ex SUPERFAST VIII (photo: Nikolaos Saratzis)

ATLANTIC VISION ex SUPERFAST IX (photo: Marko Stampehl)

ms SUPERFAST IX

IMO No. 9211509
SuperFast Ferries, Piraeus
Howaltswerke-Deutsche Werft, Kiel; Yard No.: 359

30 285 GT / 5915 tdw / 203.30 m length oa /
25.00 (25.40) m beam / four 16-cyl. diesels geared
to 2 screws; Sulzer-Fincantieri / 46 000 kW /
29.2 kn / 678 pass. in 193 cabins, 39 pass.
unberthed / 653 cars, 1891 lane metres /

18.11.2000 floated out / 8.1.2002 delivered / 10.1.2002
maiden voyage in service Rostock—Södertälje /
17.5.2002 entered service Rosyth—Zeebrugge /
10.11.2005 entered service Rostock—Hanko /
12.4.2006 to Tallink, Tallinn, service Rostock—
Paldiski—Hanko / 9.6.2006 service Hanko—
Rostock / 1.1.–10.1.2007 service Rostock—Helsinki /
11.1.2007–31.8.2008 service Tallinn—Helsinki—
Rostock / 9.2008 under charter by Marine Atlantic,
conversion work in Naantali / 14.11.2008 renamed
ATLANTIC VISION, home port Limassol / 6.6.2009
homeport St. John's / 1.4.2009 entered service North
Sydney—Argentia /

ms SUPERFAST X

IMO No. 9211511
SuperFast Ferries, Piraeus
Howaltswerke-Deutsche Werft, Kiel; Yard No.: 360

30 285 GT / 5295 tdw / 203.30 m length oa /
25.00 (25.40) m beam / four 16-cyl. diesels geared
to 2 screws; Sulzer-Fincantieri / 46 000 kW /
28.6 (30.4) kn / 678 pass. in 193 cabins, 39 pass.
unberthed / 653 cars, 1920 lane metres /

18.11.2000 floated out / 26.2.2002 delivered /
27.2.2002 maiden voyage in service Rostock—Hanko /
17.5.2002–27.1.2007 service Rosyth—Zeebrugge /

12.2.2007 **JEAN NICOLI**, SNCM, Ajaccio, then laid
up in Marseilles / 8.9.–30.11.2007 service Patras—
Igoumenitsa—Corfu—Venice under charter by ANEK
Lines / 24.12.2007 to Seafrance, Calais / 2008
renamed **SEAFRANCE MOLIERE**, after conversion
in Dunkirk: 480 cars, 1900 lane metres, 1200 pass.
unberthed, crew 80 / 19.8.2008 maiden voyage in
service Calais—Dover / 16.11.2011 after Seafrance
bankruptcy laid up in Calais, later in Dunkirk / 3.7.2012
renamed **MOLIERE**, home port Valletta / 20.7.2012 laid
up in Tilbury / 2012 30 551 GT, 6920 tdw / 30.10.2012
renamed **DIEPPE SEAWAYS**, home port Le Havre /
6.11.2012 entered service Calais—Dover under
charter by DFDS Seaways / 2.2014 under charter by
Stena RoRo, then DFDS Seaways / 10.12.2014–3.2015
conversion at Gdynska Stocznia Remontowa "Nauta",
Gdynia / 3.2015 renamed **STENA SUPERFAST X**,

home port Cardiff / 8.3.2015 entered service Holyhead—Dublin /

ms SOROLLA

IMO No. 9217125
Cia. Trasmediterranea, Santa Cruz de Tenerife
Hijos de J. Barreras, Vigo; Yard No.: 1580

26 916 GT / 5000 tdw / 172.60 m length oa /
26.20 m beam / four 8-cyl. diesels geared to
2 screws; Wärtsilä / 28 960 kW / 23.5 kn / 748 pass.
in 203 cabins, 252 pass. unberthed / 350 cars,
1809 lane metres /

25.10.2000 launched / 10.5.2001 delivered / 17.5.2001
maiden voyage in service Barcelona—Palma de
Mallorca, then service Barcelona/Valencia—Palma

STENA SUPERFAST X ex SUPERFAST X (photo: Frank Lose)

SOROLLA (photo: Frank Lose)

TRASMEDITERRANEA

FORTUNY (photo: Frank Lose)

de Mallorca/Ibiza/Mahón / 9.2006 service Cadiz—Canaries / 2.2007 service Barcelona—Balearics / 8.4.2012 entered service Almeria—Melilla /

ms FORTUNY
IMO No. 9216585
Cia. Trasmediterranea, Santa Cruz de Tenerife
Astilleros Espanoles, Puerto Real; Yard No.: 86

26 916 GT / 5000 tdw / 172.60 m length oa / 26.20 m beam / four 8-cyl. diesels geared to 2 screws; Wärtsilä / 28 960 kW / 23.5 kn / 748 pass. in 203 cabins, 252 pass. unberthed / 350 cars, 1809 lane metres /

9.12.2000 launched / 8.6.2001 delivered, then service Barcelona/Valenica—Palma de Mallorca/Ibiza/Mahón / 16.5.2006–25.1.2007 service Bilbao—Portsmouth / 1.2007 service Cadiz—Canaries / 6.–9.2009 service Barcelona—Ibiza/Mahón / 23.4.2015 entered service Almeria—Melilla, also service Malaga—Melilla /

ms MOBY WONDER
IMO No. 9214367
Moby Lines, Naples
Daewoo Shipbuilding & Marine Engineering Co., Okpo; Yard No.: 7505

36 093 GT / 5500 tdw / 179.00 m length oa / 27.00 m beam / four 12-cyl. diesels geared to 2 screws; Wärtsilä / 51 470 kW / 27 kn / 1190 pass. in 298 cabins, 690 pass. unberthed / 665 cars, 1950 lane metres /

3.10.2000 floated out / 4.5.2001 delivered / 30.5.2001 services Genoa—Bastia, Genoa—Olbia and Olbia—Civitavecchia / 10.2012 exclusively service Livorno—Olbia /

MOBY WONDER (photo: Frank Lose)

ms MOBY FREEDOM

IMO No. 9214379
Moby Lines, Naples
Daewoo Shipbuilding & Marine Engineering Co.,
Okpo; Yard No.: 7506

36 093 GT / 5500 tdw / 179.00 m length oa /
27.00 m beam / four 12-cyl. diesels geared to
2 screws; Wärtsilä / 51 470 kW / 27 kn / 1190 pass.
in 298 cabins, 690 pass. unberthed / 665 cars,
1950 lane metres /

23.12.2000 floated out / 25.6.2001 delivered /
25.7.2001 service Genoa—Bastia, Genoa—Olbia
and Olbia—Civitavecchia / 14.2.2011 last voyage in
service Olbia—Livorno, docking in Genoa / 8.3.2012
FREEDOM, Eckerö Line, Eckerö / 24.9.2012 renamed
FINLANDIA, after conversion in Landskrona and Tallinn
36 365 GT, 982 pass. in cabins, 1098 pass. unberthed,
610 cars, 1796 lane metres, crew 92 / 31.12.2012
entered service Helsinki—Tallinn /

FINLANDIA ex MOBY FREEDOM (photo: Frank Heine)

ms MOBY AKI

IMO No. 9299393
Moby Lines, Naples
Fincantieri, Ancona; Yard No.: 6116

36 284 GT / 5628 tdw / 174.99 m length oa /
27.60 m beam / four 12-cyl. diesels geared to
2 screws; Wärtsilä / 50 400 kW / 27 kn / 1256 pass.
in 320 cabins, 764 pass. unberthed / 665 cars,
1950 lane metres / crew 120

20.11.2005 launched / 15.5.2005 delivered /
20.5.2005 maiden voyage in service Livorno—Olbia /
2007 service Livorno/Piombino—Olbia /

ms SUPERSTAR

IMO No. 9365398
Tallink, Tallinn
Fincantieri; Ancona; Yard No.: 6140

36 227 GT / 5370 tdw / 176.95 m length oa /
27.60 m beam / four 12-cyl. diesels geared to
2 screws; Wärtsilä / 50 400 kW / 27.00 (27.80) kn /
735 pass. in 185 cabins, 1345 pass. unberthed /
665 cars, 1930 lane metres / crew 120

5.10.2007 launched / 8.4.2008 delivered / 21.4.2008
maiden voyage in service Tallinn—Helsinki / 1.12.2015
to Corsica Sardinia Ferries, chartered back to Tallink and
continued service Tallinn—Helsinki / 2017 planned, for
service France-Corsica as **MEGA EXPRESS SIX** /

SUPERSTAR (photo: Kai Ortel)

MOBY AKI (photo: Nikolaos Saratzis)

ms EUROPEAN VISION

IMO No. 9210141
Festival Cruises, Genoa
Chantiers l'Atlantique, St. Nazaire; Yard No.: V31

58 625 GT / 4500 tdw / 251.25 m length
oa / 28.80 m beam / four 12-cyl. diesels with
31 680 kW; Wärtsilä / four generators connected to
two elec. motors / 20 000 kW / 2 Mermaid pods /
20.8 kn / 1566 pass. in 783 cabins / crew 760

1.12.2000 floated out / 22.6.2001 christened and
delivered, then promotional voyages until 29.6.2001 /
1.7.2001 maiden cruise Genoa—Mediterranean /
7.2001 hotel ship for G8 summit in Genoa / 19.1.2004
arrested in Santo Domingo / 23.1.2004 laid up
in Bridgetown / 17.4.2004 MSC ARMONIA, MSC
Crociere, Panama / 30.5.2004 first cruise from Venice /
31.8.–17.11.2014 lengthened at Fincantieri, Palermo:
65 542 GT, 6909 tdw, 274.90 m length oa, 1952
(2680) pass. in 976 cabins / 19.11.2014 first cruise
Genoa—Las Palmas de Gran Canaria after conversion /

MSC ARMONIA ex EUROPEAN VISION (photo: Hans-Jürgen Amberg)

MSC SINFONIA ex EUROPEAN STARS (photo: Hans-Joachim Hellmann)

ms EUROPEAN STARS

IMO No. 9210153
Festival Cruises, Genoa
Chantiers l'Atlantique, St. Nazaire; Yard No.: X31

58 625 GT / 6980 tdw / 251.20 m length
oa / 28.80 m beam / four 12-cyl. diesels with
31 680 kW; Wärtsilä / four generators connected
to two elec. motors / 20 000 kW / 2 Mermaid pods /
21 kn / 1566 pass. in 783 cabins / crew 763

24.3.2001 floated out as EUROPEAN DREAM /
18.4.2002 delivered as EUROPEAN STARS /
25.4.2002 maiden Western Mediterranean cruise
from Barcelona / 19.1.2003 arrested in Barcelona,
later laid up in Marseilles / 16.7.2004 sold by auction
to MSC Crociere, Panama / 3.2005 first cruise as
MSC SINFONIA / 12.1.–25.3.2015 lengthened at
Fincantieri, Palermo: 65 542 GT, 274.90 m length
oa, 1952 (2680) pass. in 976 cabins / 27.3.2015
first cruise Genoa—Western Mediterranean after
conversion /

MSC LIRICA (photo: Alexander Brede)

ms MSC LIRICA

IMO No. 9246102
MSC Crociere, Panama
Chantiers de l'Atlantique, St. Nazaire; Yard No.: K32

59 058 GT / 5138 tdw / 251.25 m length
oa / 28.80 m beam / four 12-cyl. diesels with
30 600 kW; Wärtsilä / four generators connected to
two elec. motors / 20 000 kW / 2 Mermaid pods /
20.8 (21.70) kn / 1588 (1906) pass. in 794 cabins /
crew 760

8.2002 floated out / 27.3.2003 delivered / 12.4.2003
christened in Naples / 13.4.2003 maiden cruise from
Genoa / 31.8.–2.11.2015 lengthened at Fincantieri,
Palermo: 65 591 GT, 6563 tdw, 274.90 m length oa,
1976 (2371) pass. in 988 cabins / 4.11.2015 first cruise
Genoa—Rio de Janeiro after conversion /

MSC OPERA (photo: George Koutsoukis)

ms MSC OPERA
IMO No. 9250464
MSC Crociere, Panama
Chantiers de l'Atlantique, St. Nazaire; Yard No.: L32

59 058 GT / 6561 tdw / 251.25 m length oa /
28.80 (32.20) m beam / four 12-cyl. diesels with
30 600 kW; Wärtsilä / four generators connected to
two elec. motors / 20 000 kW / 2 Mermaid pods /
20.8 kn / 1756 (2107) pass. in 878 cabins /
crew 760

11.9.2003 floated out / 9.6.2004 delivered /
26.6.2004 christened in Genoa / 27.6.2004 maiden
Western Mediterranean cruise from Genoa / 2.5.–
4.7.2015 lengthened at Fincantieri, Palermo:
65 591 GT, 274.90 m length oa, 2142 (2570) pass.
in 1071 cabins / 6.7.2015 first cruise Venice—Black
Sea after conversion /

ms NEW RAINBOW LOVE
IMO No. 9236705
Kyuetsu Ferry Co., Fukuoka
Mitsubishi H.I., Shimonoseki; Yard No.: 1079

11 401 GT / 6277 tdw / 190.00 m length oa /
26.40 m beam / two 12-cyl. diesels geared to
2 screws; Pielstick-Nippon Kokan / 29 160 kW /
24.9 kn / 150 pass. in cabins / 62 cars + 7 trucks
(8 tons), 154 trailers / crew 26

14.3.2001 launched / 29.6.2001 delivered / 9.7.2001
entered service Muroran—Naoetsu—Hakata /
21.3.2007 SUN FLOWER DAISETSU, Shosen Mitsui
Ferry / service Tomakomai—Oarai / 31.7.2015 on a
voyage from Oarai to Tomakomai 27 nm off Tomakomai
caught fire on the vehicle deck, one crew member
killed. Ship then towed to Tomakomai, severe damage /

ms NEW RAINBOW BELL
IMO No. 9236717
Kyuetsu Ferry Co., Fukuoka
Mitsubishi H. I., Shimonoseki; Yard No.: 1080

11 410 GRT / 6277 tdw / 190.00 m length oa /
26.40 m beam / two 12-cyl. diesels geared to
2 screws; Pielstick-Nippon Kokan / 29 160 kW /
24.9 kn / 150 pass. in cabins / 62 cars + 7 trucks
(8 tons), 154 trailers / crew 26

14.6.2001 launched / 28.9.2001 delivered / 5.10.2001
entered service Muroran—Naoetsu—Hakata /
6.3.2007 SUN FLOWER SHIRETOKO, Shosen Mitsui
Ferry / 3.2007 service Tomakomai—Oarai /

SUN FLOWER DAISETSU ex NEW RAINBOW LOVE (photo: Hiroyuki Yoshimoto)

SUN FLOWER SHIRETOKO ex NEW RAINBOW BELL (photo: Hiroyuki Yoshimoto)

ms BITHIA
IMO No. 9222522
"Tirrenia" di Navigazione, Naples
Fincantieri, Castellammare di Stabia;
Yard No.: 6069

36 475 GT / 4600 tdw / 214.60 m length oa /
26.40 m beam / four 12-cyl. diesels geared to
2 screws; Wärtsilä-Fincantieri / 51 360 kW /
28.9 (31) kn / 1230 pass. in 324 cabins, 1470 pass.
unberthed / 620 cars, 832 lane metres / crew 77

10.2.2001 launched / 9.7.2001 delivered / 27.7.2001
entered service Genoa—Porto Torres /

BITHIA (photo: Frank Lose)

JANAS (photo: Frank Heine)

ms JANAS
IMO No. 9222534
"Tirrenia" di Navigazione, Naples
Fincantieri Sestri Cantieri Navale, Genoa;
Yard No.: 6070

36 475 GT / 4600 tdw / 214.60 m length oa /
26.40 m beam / four 12-cyl. diesels geared to
2 screws; Wärtsilä-Fincantieri / 51 360 kW /
28.9 (31) kn / 1230 pass. in 324 cabins, 1470 pass.
unberthed / 620 cars, 832 lane metres / crew 77

22.9.2001 launched / 9.4.2002 delivered, then service
Genoa—Porto Torres /

ms ATHARA
IMO No. 9263655
"Tirrenia" di Navigazione, Naples
Fincantieri, Castellammare di Stabia;
Yard No.: 6096

35 736 GT / 4700 tdw / 213.96 m length oa /
26.40 m beam / four 12-cyl. diesels geared to
2 screws; Wärtsilä-Fincantieri / 51 360 kW /
28.9 (29.5) kn / 1230 pass. in 324 cabins,
1470 pass. unberthed / 620 cars, 832 lane metres /
crew 77

14.1.2003 launched / 18.6.2003 delivered, then
service Genoa—Olbia, also Genoa—Porto Torres /

ATHARA (photo: Frank Lose)

NURAGHES (photo: Frank Lose)

ms NURAGHES
IMO No. 9293404
"Tirrenia" di Navigazione, Naples
Fincantieri, Castellammare di Stabia;
Yard No.: 6113

39 798 GT / 5000 tdw / 213.96 m length oa /
26.40 m beam / four 12-cyl. diesels geared to
2 screws; Wärtsilä-Fincantieri / 51 360 kW /
28.9 (31) kn / 1218 pass. in 320 cabins, 1692 pass.
unberthed / 620 cars, 1900 lane metres / crew 77

24.1.2004 launched / 5.7.2004 delivered, then service
Civitavecchia—Olbia / 21.6.2006 collision with MOBY
FANTASY off Olbia, both ships considerably damaged,
then for repair to Naples /

ms SHARDEN

IMO No. 9305269
"Tirrenia" di Navigazione, Naples
Fincantieri, Castellammare di Stabia; Yard No.: 6114

39 798 GT / 7031 tdw / 213.96 m length oa /
26.40 m beam / four 12-cyl. diesels geared to
2 screws; Wärtsilä-Fincantieri / 51 360 kW /
28.9 (31) kn / 1218 pass. in 320 cabins, 1692 pass.
unberthed / 620 cars, 1900 lane metres / crew 77

25.9.2004 launched / 21.3.2005 delivered, then
service Civitavecchia—Olbia /

SHARDEN (photo: Frank Lose)

ms NILS HOLGERSSON

IMO No. 9217230
TT-Line, Lübeck
Schichau Seebeckwerft, Bremerhaven; Yard No.: 2000

36 468 GT / 6475 tdw / 190.77 m length oa /
29.50 m beam / two 7-cyl., two 8-cyl. and one
6-cyl. diesels with 29 880 kW; MaK / five generators
connected to two elec. motors / 22 000 kW / 2 SSP
pods / 22 kn / 640 pass. in 220 cabins, 104 pass.
unberthed / 540 cars, 2613 lane metres / crew 56

19.8.2000 launched / 16.7.2001 delivered / 23.7.2001 maiden voyage in service Travemünde—Trelleborg / 3.5.2012 collision during a turning manoeuvre with moored ferry URD in Travemünde. The NILS HOLGERSSON was slightly damaged in the bow area, while the URD was grounded after water ingress to prevent uncontrolled sinking. / 5.5.2012 arrival in Landskrona for repairs / 25.5.2012 back in service Travemünde—Trelleborg / 7.1.2014 also service Travemünde—Rostock—Trelleborg /

NILS HOLGERSSON (photo: Frank Lose)

ms PETER PAN

IMO No. 9217242
TT-Line, Nassau
Schichau Seebeckwerft, Bremerhaven;
Yard No.: 2001

36 468 GT / 6654 tdw / 190.77 m length oa /
29.50 m beam / two 7-cyl., two 8-cyl. and one
6-cyl. diesels with 29 880 kW; MaK / five generators
connected to two elec. motors / 22 000 kW / 2 SSP
pods / 22 kn / 640 pass. in 220 cabins, 104 pass.
unberthed / 540 cars, 2613 lane metres / crew 56

3.3.2001 launched / 10.2001 delivered / 11.2001
maiden voyage in service Travemünde—Trelleborg /
7.1.2014 also service Travemünde—Rostock—
Trelleborg /

PETER PAN (photo: Frank Lose)

ms AEOLOS KENTERIS

IMO No. 9244350
NEL Lines, Mytilene
Alstom Leroux Naval, Lorient; Yard No.: 825

11 705 GT / 2680 tdw / 140.00 m length oa /
21.80 m beam / two gas turbines ; GE Marine /
36 778 kW / two 20-cyl. diesels; SEMT-Pielstick /
16 200 kW / 4 waterjets / 40 kn / 1742 pass.
unberthed / 442 cars, 30 trucks /

26.3.2001 launched / 3.8.2001 delivered, then service
Piraeus—Chios—Lesvos / 2002 also service Piraeus—
Kalymnos—Kos—Rhodes / 2006 new engines installed
at Fincantieri, Palermo, identical type / 8.2006 service
Piraeus—Paros—Naxos / 2006 service in the Red Sea
under charter by Namma Lines / 2.2007 **RED SEA 1**,
Pictor Shipping, Valletta / 8.2009 renamed **AEOLOS
KENTERIS** / 22.6.–4.9.2011 service Bari—Durres /
5.9.2011 laid up in Ambelaki /

AEOLOS KENTERIS (photo: Frank Heine)

ms NORWEGIAN STAR

IMO No. 9195157
Norwegian Cruise Line, Nassau
Jos. L. Meyer, Papenburg; Yard No.: 648

91 470 GT / 7500 tdw / 294.13 m length oa /
32.20 m beam / four 14-cyl. diesels with 58 800 kW;

MAN B&W / four generators connected to two
elec. motors / 39 000 kW / 2 Azipod VO / 24.6 kn /
2240 (4066) pass. in 1120 cabins / crew 1318

6.7.2001 floated out, originally ordered by Star Cruises
as SUPERSTAR LIBRA / 31.10.2001 delivered /
20.11.2001 christened in Miami / 16.12.2001 maiden

cruise from Honolulu, 7-day Hawaii cruises / 2.4.2002
rescued 11 crew members of the Indonesian coastal
tanker INSIKO 1907. They had been drifting for
three weeks on the disabled ship after an engine
room explosion / 16.2.–2.3.2010 conversion at
Victoria Shipyards, Victoria: 2344 (2813) pass. in
1172 cabins /

NORWEGIAN STAR (photo: Marko Stampehl)

ms NORWEGIAN DAWN

IMO No. 9195169
Norwegian Cruise Line, Nassau
Jos. L. Meyer, Papenburg; Yard No.: 649

91 470 GT / 7500 tdw / 294.13 m length oa /
32.20 (38.10) m beam / four 14-cyl. diesels with
58 800 kW; MAN B&W / four generators connected
to two elec. motors / 39 000 kW / 2 Azipod VO /
25 kn / 2256 pass. in 1128 cabins / crew 1130

27.10.2002 floated out, originally ordered by Star
Cruises as SUPERSTAR CAPRICORN / 3.12.2002
delivered / 7.12.2002 maiden cruise Southampton—
New York / 16.12.2002 christened in New York; then
promotional voyages / 21.12.2002 first Caribbean
cruise from Miami / 1.5.–27.5.2011 conversion at
Grand Bahama Shipyard, Freeport: 92 250 GT, 2340
(2808) pass. in 1170 cabins /

NORWEGIAN DAWN (photo: Marcus Puttich)

ms NORWEGIAN JEWEL
IMO No. 9304045
Norwegian Cruise Line, Nassau
Jos. L. Meyer, Papenburg; Yard No.: 667

93502 GT / 7500 tdw / 294.13 m length oa /
32.20 (37.88) m beam / five 12-cyl. diesels with
72000 kW; MAN B&W / five generators connected
to two driving motors / 39000 kW / 2 Azipod VO /
25 kn / 2376 pass. in 1188 cabins / crew 1100

12.6.2005 floated out / 4.8.2005 delivered / 5.8.2005
short cruise / 10.8.2005 maiden Mediterranean cruise
from Dover, then transfer to New York /

ms PRIDE OF HAWAI'I
IMO No. 9304057
NCL America, Honolulu
Meyer Werft, Papenburg; Yard No.: 668

93558 GT / 7500 tdw / 294.14 m length oa /
32.20 (37.88) m beam / five 12-cyl. diesels with
73550 kW; MAN B&W / five generators connected
to two elec. motors / 39000 kW / 2 Azipod VO /
24.6 (25) kn / 2376 pass. in 1188 cabins / crew 1317

14.2.2006 floated out / 12.4.2006 delivered / 5.6.2006
maiden voyage from Honolulu around Hawaii / 2.2008
NORWEGIAN JADE, Norwegian Cruise Line, Nassau /
16.2.2008 first cruise Los Angeles—Miami /

ms NORWEGIAN PEARL
IMO No. 9342281
Norwegian Cruise Line, Nassau
Meyer Werft, Papenburg; Yard No.: 669

93530 GT / 10000 tdw / 294.13 m length oa /
32.20 (32.30) m beam / five 12-cyl. diesels with
73550 kW; MAN B&W / five generators connected
to two elec. motors / 39000 kW / 2 Azipod VO /
24.6 kn / 2394 (2400) pass. in 1197 cabins /
crew 1331

15.10.2006 floated out / 28.11.2006 delivered /
30.11.2006 maiden cruise Rotterdam—Southampton,
then transfer to Miami / 16.12.2006 christened in
Miami, then Caribbean cruises /

NORWEGIAN JEWEL (photo: Christina Heinrich)

NORWEGIAN JADE ex PRIDE OF HAWAI'I (photo: Nikolaos Saratzis)

NORWEGIAN PEARL (photo: Andy Hernandez)

NORWEGIAN GEM (photo: Andy Hernandez)

ms NORWEGIAN GEM
IMO No. 9355733
Norwegian Cruise Line, Nassau
Meyer Werft, Papenburg; Yard No.: 670

93 530 GT / 10 000 tdw / 294.13 m length oa /
32.20 m beam / five 12-cyl. diesels with 73 550 kW;
MAN B&W / five generators connected to two elec.
motors / 39 000 kW / 2 Azipod VO / 24.6 kn /
2394 (2400) pass. in 1197 cabins / crew 1331

12.8.2007 floated out / 1.10.2007 delivered / 8.10.2007
maiden Mediterranean cruise from Dover /

ms SEAFRANCE RODIN
IMO No. 9232527
Seafrance, Calais
Aker Finnyards, Rauma; Yard No.: 437

33 796 GT / 5700 tdw / 185.00 m length oa /
28.00 m beam / two 12-cyl. and two 8-cyl. diesels
geared to 2 screws; Wärtsilä / 39 000 kW / 25 kn /
1900 pass. unberthed / 700 cars, 2000 lane metres /

19.5.2001 floated out / 13.11.2001 delivered /
29.11.2001 maiden voyage in service Calais—Dover /
16.11.2011 laid up in Calais / 11.6.2012 to Eurotransmanche, Calais / 18.7.2012 renamed RODIN /
20.8.2012 entered service Calais—Dover under charter
by My Ferry Link / 29.6.2015 laid up in Calais due to
strike / 15.9.2015 under charter by DFDS Seaways /
12.2015 renamend COTE DES DUNES / 2.2016 service
Calais—Dover planned /

COTE DES DUNES ex SEAFRANCE RODIN as RODIN (photo: Frank Lose)

COTE DES FLANDRES ex SEAFRANCE BERLIOZ as BERLIOZ (photo: Frank Lose)

ms SEAFRANCE BERLIOZ
IMO No. 9305843
Seafrance, Calais
Chantiers de l'Atlantique, St. Nazaire; Yard No.: 032

33 940 GT / 5700 tdw / 185.00 m length oa /
27.70 m beam / two 8-cyl. and two 12-cyl. diesels
geared to 2 screws; Wärtsilä / 39 000 kW / 25 kn /
1900 pass. unberthed / 714 cars, 2000 lane metres /

15.10.2004 floated out / 28.3.2005 delivered /
4.4.2005 maiden voyage in service Calais—Dover /
16.11.2011 laid up in Calais / 11.6.2012 to Eurotransmanche, Calais / 18.7.2012 renamed BERLIOZ /
20.8.2012 entered service Calais—Dover under charter
by My Ferry Link / 29.6.2015 laid up in Calais due to
strike / 15.9.2015 under charter by DFDS Seaways,
conversion at Dunkerque / 12.2015 renamed COTE DES
FLANDRES / 2.2016 service Calais—Dover planned /

ms LILAC
IMO No. 9257424
Shin Nihonkai Ferry Co., Otaru
Ishikawajima-Harima H.I., Yokohama; Yard No.: 3145

18 225 GRT / 6800 tdw / 199.90 m length oa /
26.50 m beam / two 8-cyl. diesels geared to 2
screws; Pielstick-Diesel United / 21 200 kW / 22.7
(25.09) kn / 414 pass. in 150 cabins, 478 pass.
unberthed / 58 cars + 146 trucks (8 tons) /

20.9.2001 launched / 29.3.2002 delivered / 5.4.2002
maiden voyage in service Otaru—Niigata /

LILAC (photo: Richard Seville)

YUUKARI (photo: Tsuyoshi Ishiyama)

ms YUUKARI
IMO No. 9257436
Shin-Nihonkai Ferry Co., Otaru
Ishikawajima-Harima H.I., Yokohama; Yard No.:
3146

18 229 GRT / 6800 tdw / 199.90 m length oa /
26.50 m beam / two 8-cyl. diesels geared to
2 screws; Pielstick-Diesel United / 21 200 kW /
22.7 (25.09) kn / 414 pass. in cabins, 478 pass.
unberthed / 58 cars + 146 trucks (8 tons) /

18.12.2001 launched / 1.2003 delivered / 2.2.2003
maiden voyage Otaru—Niigata /

ms THE WORLD
IMO No. 9219331
ResidenSea, Nassau
Bruces Shipyard, Landskrona; Yard No.: 247 (hull),
Fosen Mek. Verksteder, Rissa; Yard No.: 71

43 188 GT / 4558 tdw / 196.35 m length oa /
29.20 (29.80) m beam / two 12-cyl. diesels geared
to 2 screws; Wärtsilä / 11 880 kW / 17 (19) kn /
396 (1042) pass. in 198 suites / crew 343

28.2.2001 launched, then towed to Rissa for completion /
12.3.2002 delivered as first cruise ship with owned
apartments / 29.3.2002 start of promotional voyage
to Amsterdam, Hamburg, London, Lisbon and Funchal,
then worldwide cruises / 17.11.2005 transferred to the
residential community ResidenSea II Ltd. /

THE WORLD (photo: Mike Louagie)

ms LA SUPERBA
IMO No. 9214288
Grandi Navi Veloci, Palermo
Nuovi Cantieri Apuania, Marina di Carrara;
Yard No.: 1220

49 257 GT / 9750 tdw / 211.50 m length oa /
30.40 m beam / four 16-cyl. diesels geared to
2 screws; Wärtsilä / 67 200 kW / 28.5 kn / 2148
pass. in 567 cabins, 852 pass. unberthed / 719 cars,
2300 lane metres / crew 252

26.5.2001 launched / 18.3.2002 delivered / 24.3.–
28.3.2002 maiden cruise / 3.2002 maiden voyage in service
Genoa—Palermo, / 10.2003 also services Palermo—
Civitavecchia, Palermo—Genoa, Genoa—Tunis /

LA SUPERBA (photo: Frank Heine)

ms LA SUPREMA

IMO No. 9214276
Grandi Navi Veloci, Palermo
Nuovi Cantieri Apuania, Marina di Carrara;
Yard No.: 1221

49 270 GT / 9720 tdw / 211.50 m length oa /
30.40 m beam / four 16-cyl. diesels geared to
2 screws; Wärtsilä / 67 200 kW / 29 kn / 2148 pass.
in 567 cabins, 852 pass. unberthed / 719 cars,
2800 lane metres / crew 252

21.8.2002 launched / 13.5.2003 delivered / 29.5.2003
maiden voyage in service Genoa—Porto Torres /
10.2003 also services Palermo—Civitavecchia,
Palermo—Genoa, Genoa—Tunis /

LA SUPREMA (photo: Frank Lose)

SEONG HEE (photo: Jukka Huotari)

ms SEONG HEE

IMO No. 9241700
Pukwan Ferry Co., Jeju
Hyundai Mipo Dockyard, Ulsan; Yard No.: 0027

16 875 GT / 3750 tdw / 162.00 m length oa /
23.60 m beam / two 8-cyl. diesels geared to
2 screws; Daihatsu / 8826 kW / 18 (20.5) kn /
560 pass. in cabins / 150 cars, 760 lane metres /

9.12.2001 launched / 30.3.2002 delivered / 23.5.2002
maiden voyage in service Busan—Shimonoseki /

ms FINNMARKEN

IMO No. 9231951
Ofotens og Vesteraalens D/S, Narvik
Kværner Kleven, Ulsteinvik; Yard No.: 292

15 690 GT / 904 tdw / 138.50 m length oa /
21.50 m beam / two 9-cyl. and two 6-cyl. diesels
geared to 2 screws; Wärtsilä / 13 800 kW /
15 (18) kn / 628 pass. in 275 cabins, 372 pass.
unberthed / 47 cars / crew 85

15.9.2001 launched / 4.4.2002 delivered /
6.4.2002 maiden cruise / 20.4.2002 maiden voyage
in liner service Bergen—Kirkenes / 3.2006 to
Hurtigruten, Narvik / 7.11.2009 last sailing in liner
service Bergen—Kirkenes / 28.2.2009–30.10.2011
accommodation ship at Barrow Island, Western
Australia / 16.2.2012 again liner service Bergen—
Kirkenes /

FINNMARKEN (photo: Mike Louagie)

AIDAVITA (photo: Frank Heine)

AIDAAURA (photo: Nikolaos Saratzis)

ms AIDAAURA
IMO No. 9221566
Seetours, London
Aker MTW, Wismar; Yard No.: 004

42 289 GT / 4157 tdw / 202.90 m length oa /
28.10 (35.53) m beam / two 12-cyl., one 8-cyl.
and one 6-cyl. diesels with 27 550 kW; Wärtsilä /
four generators connected to two elec. motors /
18 800 kW / 2 screws / 19.7 (21.8) kn /
1266 (1582) pass. in 633 cabins / crew 384

2.3.2003 floated out / 3.4.2003 delivered / 12.4.2003
christened in Warnemünde / 13.4.2003 pre-inaugural
cruise to Hamburg / 15.4.2003 maiden cruise
Hamburg—Palma de Mallorca; then 7-day cruises from
Heraklion. In winter Caribbean cruises / 1.11.2004 to
Aida Cruises, Genoa /

ms TROLLFJORD
IMO No. 9233258
Troms Fylkes D/S (TFDS), Tromsø
Fosen Mek. Verksteder, Rissa; Yard No.: 72

16 140 GT / 1180 tdw / 135.75 m length oa /
21.50 m beam / two 9-cyl. diesels geared to
2 screws; Wärtsilä / 8280 kW / 2 Aquamaster rudder
propellers / 16 (18) kn / 646 pass. in 301 cabins,
176 pass. unberthed / 45 cars / crew 74

10.10.2001 launched at Bruces Shipyard, Landskrona,
Yard No. 246 / 6.5.2002 delivered / 18.5.2002 maiden
voyage in liner service Bergen—Kirkenes / 3.2006 to
Hurtigruten, Tromsø /

ms MIDNATSOL
IMO No. 9247728
Troms Fylkes D/S (TFDS), Tromsø
Fosen Mek. Verksteder, Rissa; Yard No.: 73

16 151 GT / 1184 tdw / 135.75 m length oa /
21.50 m beam / two 9-cyl. diesels geared to
2 screws; Wärtsilä / 8280 kW / 2 Aquamaster rudder
propellers / 16 (18) kn / 644 pass. in 302 cabins,
178 pass. unberthed / 45 cars / crew 74

26.4.2002 launched at Bruces Shipyard, Landskrona.
Towed to Rissa for completion / 12.3.2003 delivered /
4.4.2003 maiden voyage in liner service Bergen—
Kirkenes / 3.2006 to Hurtigruten, Tromsø /

TROLLFJORD (photo: Tom Gulbrandsen)

ms AIDAVITA
IMO No. 9221554
Seetours, London
Aker MTW, Wismar; Yard No.: 003

42 289 GT / 4232 tdw / 202.85 m length oa /
28.10 (35.53) m beam / two 12-cyl., one 8-cyl.
and one 6-cyl. diesels with 27 550 kW; Wärtsilä /
four generators connected to two elec. motors /
18 800 kW / 2 screws / 19.4 (21.5) kn / 1266
(1582) pass. in 633 cabins / crew 384

15.9.2001 floated out / 26.1.2002 first sea trials /
2.5.2002 delivered / 4.5.2002 christened in Warnemünde,
then pre-inaugural cruise / 6.5.2001 presentation in Kiel /
10.5.–17.5.2002 three introductory short cruises from
Hamburg / 17.5.2002 transfer cruise Hamburg—Mediterranean; then 7-day cruises from Heraklion. In winter
Caribbean cruises / 1.11.2004 to Aida Cruises, Genoa /

MIDNATSOL (photo: Tom Gulbrandsen)

ms ROMANTIKA
IMO No. 9237589
Tallink, Tallinn
Aker Finnyards, Rauma; Yard No.: 433

40 803 GT / 4500 tdw / 192.90 m length oa /
29.00 (35.20) m beam / four 16-cyl. diesels geared
to 2 screws; Wärtsilä / 26 240 kW / 22 kn /
2178 pass. in 727 cabins, 982 pass. unberthed /
300 cars, 1000 lane metres /

14.12.2001 floated out / 10.5.2002 delivered /
21.5.2002 maiden voyage in service Tallinn—Helsinki /
6.5.2006 entered service Tallinn—Mariehamn—
Stockholm / 8.5.2009 entered service Stockholm—
Riga, home port Riga / 7.8.2014 service Stockholm—
Mariehamn—Tallinn / 10.5.2015 home port Tallinn /

ROMANTIKA (photo: Frank Heine)

VICTORIA I (photo: Marko Stampehl)

ms VICTORIA I
IMO No. 9281281
Tallink, Tallinn
Aker Finnyards, Rauma; Yard No.: 434

40 975 GT / 4930 tdw / 192.90 m length oa /
29.00 (35.20) m beam / four 16-cyl. diesels geared
to 2 screws; Wärtsilä / 26 240 kW / 22 (23.9) kn /
2246 pass. in 739 cabins, 254 pass. unberthed /
300 cars, 1030 lane metres / crew 146

16.10.2003 floated out as **VICTORIA** / 9.3.2004
delivered as **VICTORIA I** / 22.3.2004 maiden voyage in
service Tallinn—Stockholm / 1.5.2004 entered service
Tallinn—Mariehamn—Stockholm /

DANIELLE CASANOVA (photo: Frank Lose)

ms DANIELLE CASANOVA
IMO No. 9230476
Soc. Nationale Maritime Corse Méditeranée
(S.N.C.M.), Ajaccio
Fincantieri, Ancona; Yard No.: 6081

41 447 GT / 3400 tdw / 175.00 m length oa /
30.40 m beam / four 9-cyl. diesels geared to
2 screws; Wärtsilä / 37 800 kW / 24 (24.8) kn /
1880 pass. in 470 cabins, 324 pass. unberthed /
700 cars, 1000 lane metres / crew 171

28.11.2001 launched as **MEDITERRANEE** / 26.6.2002
delivered as **DANIELLE CASANOVA** / 2.7.2002 entered
service Marseilles—Corsica, also service Marseilles—
Tunis/Algiers /

ms SUPERFAST XI
IMO No. 9227417
SuperFast Ferries, Piraeus
Flender Werft, Lübeck; Yard No.: 682

30 902 GT / 6574 tdw / 199.90 m length oa /
25.00 m beam / four 12-cyl. diesels geared to
2 screws; Wärtsilä / 48 000 kW / 29.2 (31.5) kn /
714 pass. in 198 cabins, 725 pass. unberthed /
653 cars, 1915 lane metres / crew 118

3.8.2001 launched / 10.7.2002 delivered / 20.7.2002
maiden voyage in service Patras—Igoumenitsa—
Ancona /

SUPERFAST XI (photo: Frank Lose)

ms SUPERFAST XII
IMO No. 9227429
SuperFast Ferries, Piraeus
Flender Werft, Lübeck; Yard No.: 683

30 902 GT / 6578 tdw / 199.90 m length oa /
25.20 m beam / four 12-cyl. diesels geared to
2 screws; Wärtsilä / 48 000 kW / 29.2 (31.5) kn /
774 pass. in 198 cabins, 655 pass. unberthed /
653 cars, 1915 lane metres / crew 118

7.12.2001 launched / 2.10.2002 delivered / 12.10.2002
maiden voyage in service Patras—Igoumenitsa—
Ancona / 2004 additional service Patras—Igoumenitsa—
Bari / 3.2009 service Piraeus—Heraklion / 30.3.2015
entered service Piraeus—Syros—Patmos—Leros—
Kos—Rhodes /

SUPERFAST XII (photo: Frank Heine)

ms HJALTLAND
IMO No. 9244958
NorthLink Orkney and Shetland Ferries Ltd., Lerwick
Aker Finnyards, Rauma; Yard No.: 438

11 486 GT / 1831 tdw / 125.00 m length oa /
19.50 (20.05) m beam / four 6-cyl. diesels geared
to 2 screws; Mak / 21 600 kW / 24 (24.2) kn /
292 pass. in 96 cabins, 308 pass. unberthed /
125 cars, 450 lane metres / crew 42

8.3.2002 floated out / 12.8.2002 delivered / 1.10.2002
maiden voyage in service Aberdeen—Kirkwall—
Lerwick / 2007 after conversion 356 pass. in 118
cabins / 2009 11 720 GT, installation of 32 couchettes
in Fredericia /

ms HROSSEY
IMO No. 9244960
NorthLink Orkney and Shetland Ferries Ltd., Kirkwall
Aker Finnyards, Rauma; Yard No.: 439

11 486 GT / 1563 tdw / 125.00 m length oa /
19.50 (20.05) m beam / four 6-cyl. diesels geared
to 2 screws; MaK / 21 600 kW / 24 (24.2) kn /
292 pass. in 96 cabins, 308 pass. unberthed /
125 cars, 450 lane metres / crew 42

19.4.2002 floated out / 6.9.2002 delivered / 1.10.2002
maiden voyage in service Aberdeen—Kirkwall—
Lerwick / 25.2.–18.3.2007 installation of additional
cabins in Birkenhead: 356 pass. in 118 cabins / 2009
11 720 GT, installation of 32 couchettes in Fredericia /

ms CARNIVAL CONQUEST
IMO No. 9198355
Carnival Cruise Lines, Panama
Fincantieri, Monfalcone; Yard No.: 6057

110 239 GT / 10 000 tdw / 290.20 m length oa /
35.50 (35.54) m beam / four 16-cyl. and two 12-cyl.
diesels with 63 360 kW; Sulzer-Wärtsilä / six generators connected to two elec. motors / 40 000 kW /
2 screws / 19.6 (22.5) kn / 2966 (3783) pass. in
1483 cabins / crew 1170

1.2.2002 floated out / 25.10.2002 delivered / 15.11.2002
maiden cruise from New Orleans to Mexico /

HJALTLAND (photo: Frank Heine)

HROSSEY (photo: Frank Heine)

CARNIVAL CONQUEST (photo: Cees Bustraan)

CARNIVAL GLORY (photo: Marc Piché)

27.3.2004 floated out / 27.11.2004 delivered / 1.12.2004 transfer to Miami / 12.2004 two pre-inaugural cruises Miami—Bahamas / 17.12.2004 christened / 19.12.2004 first 7-day Caribbean cruise from Miami /

ms CARNIVAL LIBERTY
IMO No. 9278181
Carnival Cruise Lines, Panama
Fincantieri, Monfalcone; Yard No.: 6111

110 320 GT / 13 294 tdw / 290.2 m length oa / 35.5 m beam / six 12-cyl. diesels with 75 600 kW; Wärtsilä / six generators connected to two elec. motors / 40 000 kW / 2 screws / 20.2 (23) kn / 2974 (3540) pass. in 1487 cabins / crew 1182

ms CARNIVAL GLORY
IMO No. 9198367
Carnival Cruise Lines, Panama
Fincantieri, Monfalcone; Yard No.: 6058

110 239 GT / 11 100 tdw / 290.20 m length oa / 35.50 (35.54) m beam / four 16-cyl. and two 12-cyl. diesels with 63 360 kW; Sulzer-Wärtsilä / six generators connected to two elec. motors / 40 000 kW / 2 screws / 22.5 kn / 2974 (3783) pass. in 1487 cabins / crew 1118

30.10.2002 floated out / 27.6.2003 delivered / 19.7.2003 maiden Caribbean cruise from Port Canaveral /

ms CARNIVAL VALOR
IMO No. 9236389
Carnival Cruise Lines, Panama
Fincantieri, Monfalcone; Yard No.: 6082

110 239 GT / 13 294 tdw / 290.20 m length oa / 35.50 (35.54) m beam / four 16-cyl. and two 12-cyl. diesels with 63 360 kW; Sulzer-Wärtsilä / six generators connected to two elec. motors / 40 000 kW / 2 screws / 22.5 kn / 2974 (3540) pass. in 1487 cabins / crew 1118

CARNIVAL VALOR (photo: Marcus Puttich)

CARNIVAL LIBERTY (photo: Andy Hernandez)

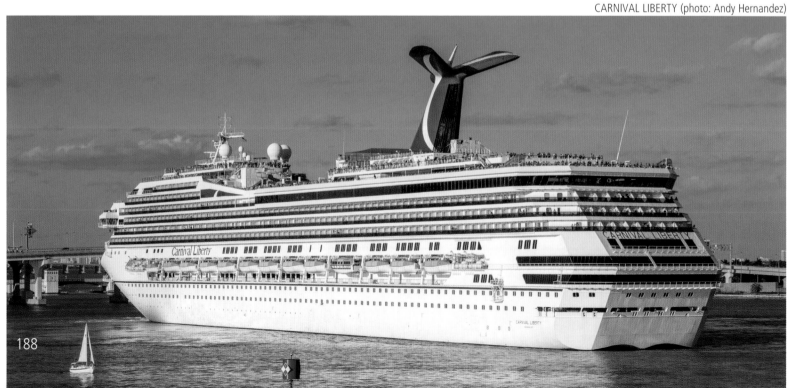

2.12.2004 floated out / 15.7.2005 delivered / 16.7.2005 pre-inaugural cruise to Civitavecchia; christened there / 20.7.2005 maiden Mediterranean cruise /

ms CARNIVAL FREEDOM
IMO No. 9333149
Carnival Cruise Lines, Panama
Fincantieri, Marghera; Yard No.: 6129

110 320 GT / 12 870 tdw / 290.23 m length oa / 35.50 m beam / six 12-cyl. diesels with 75 600 kW; Wärtsilä / six generators connected to two elec. motors / 40 000 kW / 2 screws / 19.6 kn / 2974 (3700) pass. in 1487 cabins / crew 1160

28.4.2006 floated out / 28.2.2007 delivered / 5.3.2007 maiden Mediterranean cruise from Venice /

CARNIVAL FREEDOM (photo: Marko Stampehl)

COSTA SERENA (photo: Frank Lose)

ms COSTA SERENA
IMO No. 9343132
Costa Crociere, Genoa
Fincantieri, Sestri Ponente; Yard No.: 6130

114 147 GT / 8900 tdw / 290.20 m length oa / 35.50 m beam / six 12-cyl. diesels with 75 600 kW; Wärtsilä / six generators connected to two elec. motors / 42 000 kW / 2 screws / 19.6 (23.2) kn / 3014 (3617) pass. in 1507 cabins / crew 1090

4.8.2006 floated out / 14.5.2007 delivered / 26.5.2007 maiden voyage from Venice to Greece /

ms CARNIVAL SPLENDOR
IMO No. 9333163
Carnival Cruise Lines, Panama
Fincantieri, Sestri Ponente; Yard No.: 6135

113 323 GT / 11 843 tdw / 290.20 m length oa / 35.50 m beam / six 12-cyl. diesels with 75 600 kW; Wärtsilä / six generators connected to two elec. motors / 42 000 kW / 2 screws / 19.6 (22.5) kn / 3006 (3607) pass. in 1503 cabins / crew 1160

3.8.2007 floated out / 30.6.2008 delivered / 10.7.2008 maiden voyage from Dover /

CARNIVAL SPLENDOR (photo: Raoul Fiebig)

ms COSTA PACIFICA
IMO No. 9378498
Costa Crociere, Genoa
Fincantieri, Sestri Ponente; Yard No.: 6148

114 288 GT / 10 000 tdw / 290.20 m length oa /
35.50 m beam / six 12-cyl. diesels with 75 600 kW;
Wärtsilä / six generators connected to two elec.
motors / 42 000 kW / 2 screws / 19.6 kn (23.2) /
3014 (3617) pass. in 1507 cabins / crew 1090

16.7.2007 floated out / 28.5.2009 delivered / 6.6.2009
maiden Mediterranean cruise from Savona / 11.2014
114 425 GT /

COSTA PACIFICA (photo: Alexander Brede)

ms COSTA FAVOLOSA
IMO No. 9479852
Costa Crociere, Genoa
Fincantieri, Marghera; Yard No.: 6188

113 216 GT / 10 000 tdw / 290.20 m length oa /
35.50 m beam / six 12-cyl. diesels with 75 600 kW;
Wärtsilä / six generators connected to two elec.
motors / 42 000 kW / 2 screws / 19.6 kn (23.2) /
3014 (3617) pass. in 1507 cabins / crew 1110

6.8.2010 floated out / 30.7.2011 delivered / 4.7.2011
maiden Mediterranean cruise from Venice /

COSTA FAVOLOSA (photo: Alexander Brede)

ms COSTA FASCINOSA
IMO No. 9479864
Costa Crociere, Genoa
Fincantieri, Marghera; Yard No.: 6189

113 321 GT / 10 000 tdw / 290.20 m length oa /
35.50 m beam / six 12-cyl. diesels with 75 600 kW;
Wärtsilä / six generators connected to two elec.
motors / 42 000 kW / 2 screws / 19.6 kn (23.2) /
3014 (3617) pass. in 1507 cabins / crew 1110

29.7.2011 floated out / 5.5.2012 delivered / 11.5.2012
maiden Mediterranean cruise from Savona /

COSTA FASCINOSA (photo: Frank Lose)

ZUIDERDAM (photo: Cees Bustraan)

ms ZUIDERDAM
IMO No. 9221279
Holland America Line, Willemstad
Fincantieri, Marghera; Yard No.: 6075

81 769 GT / 10 965 tdw / 285.28 m length oa /
32.25 m beam / three 16-cyl. and two 12-cyl.
diesels with 51 840 kW; Sulzer-Wärtsilä, one
gas turbine with 23 000 kW; GE Marine, overall
74 840 kW (IEP) / six generators connected to
two elec. motors / 35 200 kW / 2 Azipod VO /
22 (24) kn / 1848 (2388) pass. in 924 cabins /
crew 812

14.12.2001 floated out / 15.11.2002 delivered /
14.12.2002 maiden Caribbean cruise from Fort
Lauderdale / 30.12.2002 home port Rotterdam /
5.2008 after conversion at Finantieri, Palermo:
82 305 GT, 1920 (2304) pass. in 960 cabins / 1.4.–
13.4.2015 conversion at Fincantieri, Palermo:
82 820 GT, 1970 (2364) pass. in 985 cabins /

ms OOSTERDAM
IMO No. 9221281
Holland America Line, Rotterdam
Fincantieri, Marghera; Yard No.: 6076

81 769 GT / 10 965 tdw / 285.24 m length oa /
32.22 m beam / three 16-cyl. and two 12-cyl.
diesels with 51 840 kW; Sulzer-Wärtsilä, one
gas turbine with 23 000 kW; GE Marine, overall
74 840 kW (IEP) / six generators connected to
two elec. motors / 35 200 kW / 2 Azipod VO /
22 (24) kn / 1848 (2388) pass. in 924 cabins /
crew 866

18.11.2002 floated out / 11.7.2003 delivered /
30.7.2003 christened in Rotterdam / 3.8.2003 maiden
Baltic cruise from Harwich / 4.2009 after conversion
at Fincantieri, Palermo: 82 305 GT, 1920 (2304) pass.
in 960 cabins /

ms WESTERDAM
IMO No. 9226891
Holland America Line, Rotterdam
Fincantieri, Marghera; Yard No.: 6077

81 811 GT / 10 965 tdw / 285.22 m length oa /
32.21 m beam / three 16-cyl. and two 12-cyl.
diesels with 51 840 kW; Sulzer-Wärtsilä, one

gas turbine with 23 000 kW; GE Marine, overall
74 840 kW (IEP) / six generators connected to two
elec. motors / 35 200 kW / 2 Azipod VO /
22 (24) kn / 1848 (2388) pass. in 924 cabins /
crew 866

OOSTERDAM (photo: Clyde Dickens)

16.7.2003 floated out / 19.4.2004 delivered /
25.4.2004 christened in Venice, then maiden cruise
Venice—Eastern Mediterranean / 5.2007 after
conversion at Fincantieri, Palermo: 82 348 GT, 1920
(2304) pass. in 960 cabins /

WESTERDAM (photo: Ian Shiffman)

ms ARCADIA

IMO No. 9226906
P&O Cruises, Hamilton
Fincantieri, Marghera; Yard No.: 6078

82 972 GT / 10 939 tdw / 285.11 m length oa /
32.24 m beam / three 16-cyl. and two 12-cyl.
diesels with 51 840 kW; Sulzer-Wärtsilä / five
generators connected to two elec. motors /
35 200 kW / 2 Azipod VO / 22 kn / 1952 (2388)
pass. in 976 cabins / crew 1068

Keel-laying as QUEEN VICTORIA for Cunard Line;
originally ordered by Holland America Line / 2004
continued construction as ARCADIA for P&O Cruises /
26.5.2004 floated out / 12.2004 first sea trials / 24.3.2005
delivered / 12.4.2005 christened in Southampton /
14.4.2005 maiden cruise Southampton—Mediterranean / 26.11.–20.12.2008 conversion at Lloyd Werft,
Bremerhaven: additional cabins aft, 83 781 GT, 2016
(2388) pass. in 1010 cabins /

ARCADIA (photo: Jürgen Saupe)

ms NOORDAM

IMO No. 9230115
Holland America Line, Rotterdam
Fincantieri, Marghera; Yard No.: 6078

82 318 GT / 10 939 tdw / 285.24 m length oa /
32.21 m beam / three 16-cyl. and two 12-cyl.
diesels with 51 840 kW; Sulzer-Wärtsilä, one
gas turbine with 23 000 kW; GE Marine, overall
74 840 kW (IEP) / six generators connected to two
elec. motors / 35 200 kW / 2 Azipod VO / 22 kn /
1968 (2368) pass. in 984 cabins / crew 866

1.4.2005 floated out / 31.1.2006 delivered /
22.2.2006 maiden Caribbean cruise from New York /
4.–20.4.2013 conversion at Fincantieri, Palermo:
82 897 GT /

ms QUEEN VICTORIA

IMO No. 9320556
Cunard Line, Southampton
Fincantieri, Marghera; Yard No.: 6127

90 049 GT / 7685 tdw / 294.00 m length oa /
32.25 m beam / four 16-cyl. and two 12-cyl. diesels
with 67 200 kW; Sulzer-Wärtsilä / six generators
connected to two elec. motors / 35 200 kW /
2 Azipod VO / 21.7 (24.3) kn / 2014 (2144) pass.
in 1007 cabins / crew 818

15.1.2007 floated out / 24.11.2007 delivered /
11.12.2007 maiden cruise from Southampton /
10.2011 home port Hamilton /

NOORDAM (photo: Dale E. Crisp)

QUEEN VICTORIA (photo: Frank Heine)

ms EURODAM
IMO No. 9378448
Holland America Line, Rotterdam
Fincantieri, Marghera; Yard No.: 6149

86 273 GT / 9125 tdw / 285.30 m length oa /
32.25 m beam / four 12-cyl. and two 8-cyl. diesels
with 64 000 kW; MaK / six generators connected to
two elec. motors / 35 200 kW / 2 Azipod VO /
21.9 (23.9) kn / 2104 (2611) pass. in 1052 cabins /
crew 929

28.9.2007 floated out / 16.6.2008 delivered / 5.7.2008
maiden voyage from Copenhagen to Norway /

EURODAM (photo: Andy Hernandez)

COSTA LUMINOSA (photo: Raoul Fiebig)

ms COSTA LUMINOSA
IMO No. 9398905
Costa Crociere, Genoa
Fincantieri, Marghera; Yard No.: 6155

92 720 GT / 7600 tdw / 294.00 m length oa /
32.25 m beam / four 12-cyl. and two 8-cyl. diesels
with 64 000 kW; Mak / six generators connected to
two elec. motors / 35 200 kW / 2 Azipod VO /
21.6 (23.6) kn / 2260 (2826) pass. in 1130 cabins /
crew 934

27.5.2008 floated out / 28.4.2009 delivered / 5.5.2009
maiden Mediterranean cruise from Venice /

ms COSTA DELIZIOSA
IMO No. 9398917
Costa Crociere, Genoa
Fincantieri, Marghera; Yard No.: 6164

92 720 GT / 7500 tdw / 294.00 m length oa /
32.25 m beam / four 12-cyl. and two 8-cyl. diesels
with 64 000 kW; Mak / six generators connected
to two elec. motors / 35 200 kW / 2 Azipod VO /
21.6 (23.6) kn / 2260 (2826) pass. in 1130 cabins /
crew 934

12.3.2009 floated out / 30.1.2010 delivered / 5.2.2010
maiden cruise from Savona to Dubai /

COSTA DELIZIOSA (photo: George Koutsoukis)

NIEUW AMSTERDAM (photo: Andy Hernandez)

ms NIEUW AMSTERDAM

IMO No. 9378450
Holland America Line, Rotterdam
Fincantieri, Marghera; Yard No.: 6181

86 273 GT / 8754 tdw / 285.30 m length oa /
32.21 (32.26) m beam / four 12-cyl. and two
8-cyl. diesels with 64 000 kW; MaK / six generators
connected to two elec. motors / 35 200 kW /
2 Azipod VO / 21.9 kn / 2106 (2611) pass. in
1053 cabins / crew 929

30.10.2009 floated out / 2.7.2010 delivered / 4.7.2010
maiden Mediterranean cruise from Venice /

QUEEN ELIZABETH (photo: Hans-Joachim Hellmann)

ms QUEEN ELIZABETH

IMO No. 9477438
Cunard Line, Southampton
Fincantieri, Marghera; Yard No.: 6187

90 901 GT / 7685 tdw / 294.00 m length oa /
32.25 (32.29) m beam / four 12-cyl. and two
8-cyl. diesels with 64 000 kW; MaK / six generators
connected to two elec. motors / 35 200 kW /
2 Azipod VO / 21.7 kn / 2092 pass. in 1046 cabins /
crew 996

5.1.2010 floated out / 4.10.2010 delivered / 11.10.2010
christened in Southampton by Queen Elizabeth II. /
12.10.2010 maiden cruise Southampton—Canaries /
24.10.2011 home port Hamilton /

ms YUE HAI TIE 1 HAO

IMO No. 9255866
Yuehai Railway Co., Haikou
Jiangnan Shipyard, Shanghai; Yard No.: 2279

14 381 GT / 5600 tdw / 165.40 m length oa /
22.60 m beam / two 6-cyl. diesels geared to
2 screws; Wärtsilä / 5760 kW / 15.2 kn / 1230 pass.
unberthed / 150 cars, 40 wagons /

27.7.2002 launched / 20.11.2002 delivered / 28.12.2002
entered service Haikou—Hainan /

YUE HAI TIE 1 HAO (photo: ShipPax Information)

YUE HAI TIE 2 HAO (photo: ShipPax Information)

the customers refused to accept the still uncompleted ship / 2.7.2002 to DFDS, Copenhagen. Conversion and increase in passenger capacity / 27.11.2002 delivered as **DANA SIRENA**, then for conversion to Remontowa, Gdansk: 22 382 GT, 5625 tdw, 199.40 m length oa, 661 pass. in 196 cabins / 17.6.2003 entered service Esbjerg—Harwich / 3.2004 installation of a mezzanine deck, additional 41 cars / 11.3.2013 renamed **SIRENA SEAWAYS** / 22.6.2013 collision with landing stage in Harwich, considerably damaged, then repairs in Bremerhaven / 5.7.2013 again service Esbjerg—Harwich / 28.9.2014 last voyage in service Harwich—Esbjerg / 6.10.2014–8.1.2015 service Paldiski—Kapellskär / 10.2.2015 entered service Klaipeda—Karlshamn / 8.4.2015 renamed **BAIE DE SEINE** / 7.5.2015 entered service Le Havre—Portsmouth under charter by Brittany Ferries, also service Portsmouth—Bilbao /

BAIE DE SEINE ex DANA SIRENA (photo: Frank Lose)

ms MONT ST MICHEL

IMO No. 9238337
Brittany Ferries, Caen
van der Giessen-De Noord, Krimpen;
Yard No.: 1702

35 586 GT / 5579 tdw / 173.40 m length oa / 28.50 (29.10) m beam / four 6-cyl. diesels geared to 2 screws; MaK-Caterpillar / 21 600 kW / 21 (21.8) kn / 796 pass. in 224 cabins, 1324 pass. unberthed / 874 cars, 2246 lane metres / crew 151

16.3.2002 launched / 10.12.2002 delivered / 20.12.2002 maiden voyage in service Caen—Portsmouth /

MONT ST MICHEL (photo: Frank Heine)

ms YUE HAI TIE 2 HAO

IMO No. 9274692
Yuehai Railway Co., Haikou
Jiangnan Shipyard, Shanghai; Yard No.: 2280

14 381 GT / 5600 tdw / 165.40 m length oa / 22.60 m beam / two 6-cyl. diesels geared to 2 screws; Wärtsilä / 5760 kW / 15.2 kn / 1230 pass. unberthed / 150 cars, 40 wagons /

18.11.2002 launched / 11.6.2003 delivered, then service Haikou—Hainan /

ms DANA SIRENA

IMO No. 9212163
DFDS, Esbjerg
Stocznia Szczecinska im. A. Warskiego, Szczecin; Yard No.: 59112

17 150 GT / 7300 tdw / 196.90 m length oa / 23.40 (25.00) m beam / two 9-cyl. diesels geared to 2 screws; Wärtsilä / 19 080 kW / 22 (23.2) kn / 154 pass. in cabins / 2400 lane metres /

22.4.2001 launched as **GOLFO DEI DELFINI** for Lloyd Sardegna. After completion was considerably delayed due to the shipyard's financial difficulties,

195

CORAL PRINCESS (photo: Tony Davis)

ms **CORAL PRINCESS**
IMO No. 9229659
Princess Cruises, Hamilton
Chantiers de l' Atlantique, St. Nazaire; Yard No.: C32

91 627 GT / 8015 tdw / 294.00 m length oa /
32.20 (32.31) m beam / two 16-cyl. diesels
with 33 600 kW; Wärtsilä, one gas turbine with
29 080 kW; GE Marine, overall 62 680 kW (IEP) /
three generators connected to two elec. motors /
40 000 kW / 2 screws / 21.5 (24) kn / 1974 (2581)
pass. in 987 cabins / crew 900

3.2.2002 floated out / 23.12.2002 delivered / 3.1.2003
first cruise from Fort Lauderdale / 17.1.2003 christened
in the Panama Canal /

ms **ISLAND PRINCESS**
IMO No. 9230402
Princess Cruises, Hamilton
Chantiers de l'Atlantique, St. Nazaire; Yard No.: D32

91 627 GT / 8015 tdw / 294.00 m length oa /
32.20 (32.31) m beam / two 16-cyl. diesels
with 33 600 kW; Wärtsilä, one gas turbine with
29 080 kW; GE Marine, overall 62 680 kW (IEP) /
three generators connected to two elec. motors /
40 000 kW / 2 screws / 21.5 (24) kn / 1974 (2581)
pass. in 987 cabins / crew 900

2.7.2002 floated out / 18.6.2003 delivered / 11.7.2003
christened in Vancouver / 12.7.2003 maiden cruise
from Vancouver / 7.4.–20.5.2015 conversion at
Fincantieri, Trieste: 92 822 GT, 2214 (2657) pass. in
1107 cabins / 22.5.2015 first cruise Venice—Barcelona
after conversion /

ms **STENA BRITANNICA II**
IMO No. 9235517
Stena Line, Harwich
Hyundai H. I., Ulsan; Yard No.: 1392

43 487 GT / 9673 tdw / 211.56 m length oa /
29.30 (29.88) m beam / four 9-cyl. diesels geared to
2 screws; MAN B&W / 25 920 kW / 22 (23.6) kn /
602 pass. in 246 cabins, 298 pass. unberthed /
3517 lane metres /

7.9.2002 floated out / 1.2003 delivered / 25.2.2003
maiden voyage in service Hoek van Holland—Harwich /
17.3.2003 renamed STENA BRITANNICA / 20.1.–
9.3.2007 lengthening at Lloyd Werft, Bremerhaven:
55 050 GT, 12 200 tdw, 240.00 m length oa, 1040 pass.
in 398 cabins, 4220 lane metres, crew 76 / 11.3.2007
again service Hoek van Holland—Harwich / 21.9.2010
renamed BRITANNICA / 9.10.2010 last voyage in
service Harwich—Hoek van Holland / 9.11.2011
caught fire during conversion in Gdansk, blaze brought
under control but delivery delayed by two months /
11.4.2011 renamed STENA SCANDINAVICA IV, home
port Gothenburg; 57 958 GT / 19.4.2011 entered

STENA SCANDINAVICA ex STENA BRITANNICA II (photo: Frank Lose)

ISLAND PRINCESS (photo: George Koutsoukis)

196

service Gothenburg—Kiel / 17.5.2011 renamed STENA SCANDINAVICA /

ms STENA ADVENTURER
IMO No. 9235529
Stena Line, London
Hyundai H. I., Ulsan; Yard No.: 1393

43 532 GT / 9673 tdw / 211.56 m length oa /
29.30 (29.88) m beam / four 9-cyl. diesels geared
to 2 screws; MAN B&W / 25 920 kW / 22 kn /
364 pass. in 148 cabins, 1136 pass. unberthed /
3517 lane metres /

6.10.2002 floated out / 16.5.2003 delivered / 1.7.2003
maiden voyage in service Dublin—Holyhead /

ms VISBY
IMO No. 9223784
Rederi AB Gotland, Visby
Guangzhou Shipyard, Guangzhou;
Yard No.: 9130004

29 746 GT / 4730 tdw / 196.00 m length oa /
25.00 (25.64) m beam / four 12-cyl. diesels geared
to 2 screws; Wärtsilä / 50 400 kW / 28.5 (29.5) kn /
316 pass. in 119 cabins, 1184 pass. unberthed /
520 cars, 1800 lane metres / crew 82

3.7.2001 launched / 25.1.2003 delivered / 28.3.2003
maiden voyage in service Visby—Nynäshamn/
Oskarshamn /

ms GOTLAND
IMO No. 9223796
Rederi AB Gotland, Visby
Guangzhou Shipyard, Guangzhou; Yard No.:
9130005

29 746 GT / 4730 tdw / 195.80 m length oa /
25.00 (25.64) m beam / four 12-cyl. diesels geared
to 2 screws; Wärtsilä / 50 400 kW / 28.5 (30) kn /
316 pass. in 119 cabins, 1184 pass. unberthed /
500 cars, 1800 lane metres / crew 82

31.12.2001 launched / 8.10.2003 delivered / 28.3.2003
maiden voyage in service Visby—Nynäshamn/
Oskarshamn /

STENA ADVENTURER (photo: Frank Lose)

VISBY (photo: Uwe Jakob)

GOTLAND (photo: Frank Lose)

197

SEVEN SEAS VOYAGER (photo: Mike Louagie)

ms SEVEN SEAS VOYAGER
IMO No. 9247144
Radisson Seven Seas Cruises (V.Ships), Nassau
Cantiere Navale Visentini, Porto Viro (hull),
T. Mariotti, Genoa; Yard No.: MAR 001

41500 GT / 5400 tdw / 206.50 m length oa /
28.80 m beam / four 6-cyl. diesels with 23760 kW;
Wärtsilä / four generators connected to two elec.
motors / 14000 kW / 2 Dolphin pods / 20 kn /
706 (777) pass. in 353 cabins / crew 451

22.9.2001 launched / 27.2.2003 delivered / 1.4.2003
maiden cruise from Monte Carlo / 12.2003 42363 GT /
3.2006 owner renamed as Regent Seven Seas Cruises /

YAMATO (photo: Frank Lose)

ms YAMATO
IMO No. 9263150
Hankyu Ferry, Kobe
Mitsubishi H.I., Shimonoseki; Yard No.: 1090

13353 GRT / 6445 tdw / 195.00 m length oa /
26.40 m beam / two 16-cyl. diesels geared to
2 screws; Wärtsilä / 20152 kW / 23.5 (25.8) kn /
652 pass. in cabins, 15 pass. unberthed / 128 cars
+ 229 trucks /

4.12.2002 launched / 25.3.2003 delivered / 27.3.2003
maiden voyage in service Izumiotsu—Shin Moji /
1.6.2008 entered service Kobe—Shin Moji / 2011
service Izumiotsu—Shin Moji / 3.2015 service Kobe—
Shin Moji /

ms TSUKUSHI
IMO No. 9263162
Hankyu Ferry Co., Kobe
Mitsubishi H.I., Shimonoseki; Yard No.: 1091

13353 GRT / 5560 tdw / 195.00 m length oa /
26.40 m beam / two 16-cyl. diesels geared to
2 screws; Wärtsilä / 20152 kW / 23.5 kn / 652 pass.
in cabins, 15 pass. unberthed / 128 cars +
229 trucks /

20.2.2003 launched / 5.6.2003 delivered, then service
Izumiotsu—Shin Moji / 1.6.2008 entered service
Kobe—Shin Moji / 2011 service Izumiotsu—Shin
Moji / 3.2015 service Kobe—Shin Moji /

TSUKUSHI (photo: Hiroyuki Yoshimoto)

NORRÖNA (photo: Frank Lose)

ms NORRÖNA
IMO No. 9227390
Smyril Line, Tórshavn
Flender Werft, Lübeck; Yard No.: 694

35966 GT / 6350 tdw / 165.74 m length oa /
30.00 (34.23) m beam / four 6-cyl. diesels geared
to 2 screws; MaK-Caterpillar / 21600 kW /
20.8 (22) kn / 1020 pass. in 318 cabins, 462 pass.
unberthed / 634 cars, 1870 lane metres /
crew 118

24.8.2002 launched / 7.4.2003 delivered / 10.4.2003
entered service Hanstholm—Tórshavn—Bergen—
Seydisfjördur / 4.2.2008 entered service Esbjerg—
Tórshavn—Seydisfjördur; from June-August to
Hanstholm instead of Esbjerg / 1.10.2010 Danish
port of call exclusively Hirtshals /

ms PASCAL PAOLI
IMO No. 9247510
SNCM Ferryterranée, Bastia
van der Giessen-De Noord, Krimpen; Yard No.: 988

35 760 GT / 9304 tdw / 176.00 m length oa /
30.50 m beam / four 9-cyl. diesels geared to
2 screws; Wärtsilä / 37 800 kW / 23 (24) kn /
544 pass. in 160 cabins, 114 pass. unberthed /
135 cars, 2300 lane metres /

26.10.2002 launched / 16.5.2003 delivered / 27.5.2003
entered service Marseilles—Corsica /

PASCAL PAOLI (photo: Frank Heine)

CRYSTAL SERENITY (photo: Hiroyuki Yoshimoto)

ms CRYSTAL SERENITY
IMO No. 9243667
Crystal Cruises, Nassau
Chantiers de l'Atlantique, St. Nazaire; Yard No.: H32

68 870 GT / 10 810 tdw / 250.00 m length oa /
32.20 (32.30) m beam / six 12-cyl. diesels with
52 200 kW; Wärtsilä / six generators connected to
two elec. motors / 27 000 kW / 2 Mermaid pods /
22 (22.72) kn / 1090 (1254) pass. in 545 cabins /
crew 655

8.11.2003 floated out / 30.6.2003 delivered / 7.7.2003
maiden cruise from Southampton /

QUEEN MARY 2 (photo: Alexander Brede)

ms QUEEN MARY 2
IMO No. 9241061
Cunard Line, Southampton
Chantiers de l'Atlantique, St. Nazaire; Yard No.: G32

148 528 GT / 19 189 tdw / 345.03 m length
oa / 41.00 m beam / four 16-cyl. diesels with
67 200 kW; Wärtsilä, two gas turbines with
59 660 kW; GE Marine, overall 126 870 kW (IEP) /
six generators connected to four elec. motors /
86 000 kW / 4 Mermaid pods / 26.5 (30) kn /
2626 (3151) pass. in 1313 cabins / crew 1254

21.3.2003 floated out / 25–29.9.2003 sea trials /
15.11.2003 A gangway with 50 persons collapsed
into the drydock during a guided tour on the ship. 15
killed, 32 seriously injured / 22.12.2003 delivered /
26.12.2003 first arrival in Southampton, several short
promotional trips / 8.1.2004 christened by Queen
Elizabeth II. / 12.1.2004 maiden voyage Southampton
—Canaries—Fort Lauderdale / 25.4.2005 entered
liner service New York—Southampton, occasionally
extended to Hamburg, also deployed for cruises /
10.1.2007 first 81-day world cruise from Southampton /
12.2011 home port Hamilton /

DIAMOND PRINCESS (photo: Tsuyoshi Ishiyama)

ms DIAMOND PRINCESS
IMO No. 9228198
Princess Cruises, Hamilton
Mitsubishi H.I., Nagasaki; Yard No.: 2181

115 875 GT / 14 274 tdw / 290.00 m length oa /
37.50 (37.75) m beam / two 9-cyl. and two 8-cyl.
diesels with 35 700 kW; Wärtsilä, one gas turbine
with 25 000 kW; GE Marine, overall 60 700 kW
(IEP) / five generators connected to two elec.
motors / 40 000 kW / 2 screws / 23 kn /
2706 (3247) pass. in 1353 cabins / crew 1238

12.4.2003 floated out, original planned as SAPPHIRE
PRINCESS / 26.2.2004 delivered and christened /
13.3.2004 maiden cruise Los Angeles—Mexico /
4.2014 home port London; 115 906 GT /

ms SAPPHIRE PRINCESS
IMO No. 9228186
Princess Cruises, Hamilton
Mitsubishi H.I., Nagasaki; Yard No.: 2180

115 875 GT / 14 274 tdw / 290.00 m length oa /
37.50 (37.75) m beam / two 9-cyl. and two 8-cyl.
diesels with 35 700 kW; Wärtsilä, one gas turbine
with 25 000 kW; GE Marine, overall 60 700 kW
(IEP) / five generators connected to two elec.
motors / 40 000 kW / 2 screws / 23 kn /
2678 (3214) pass. in 1339 cabins / crew 1238

25.5.2002 floated out as DIAMOND PRINCESS /
1.10.2002 burnt out at shipyard, 40 % of superstructure destroyed; taken again into the construction
dock for repair / 11.2002 renamed SAPPHIRE
PRINCESS / 13.9.2003 again floated out / 27.5.2004
delivered / 10.6.2004 christened in Seattle /
13.6.2004 maiden cruise Seattle—Alaska / 4.2014
home port London /

ms PONT-AVEN
IMO No. 9268708
Brittany Ferries, Morlaix
Jos. L. Meyer, Papenburg; Yard No.: 650

41 748 GT / 4803 tdw / 184.30 m length oa /
30.90 m beam / four 12-cyl. diesels geared to
2 screws; MaK / 43 200 kW / 27 kn / 2012 pass.
in 652 cabins, 388 pass. unberthed / 650 cars,
1188 lane metres / crew 183

13.9.2003 floated out / 27.2.2004 delivered / 24.3.2004
entered service Plymouth—Santander, also service
Plymouth—Roscoff and Roscoff—Cork / 18.3.2009
also a weekly round trip Santander—Portsmouth /

PONT-AVEN (photo: Frank Lose)

SAPPHIRE PRINCESS (photo: Dale E. Crisp)

FLORENCIA ex GOLFO ARANCI (photo: Frank Lose)

ALBAYZIN ex GOLFO DEGLI ANGELI (photo: Frank Lose)

AKASHIA (photo: Tsuyoshi Ishiyama)

16.1.2014 entered service Savona—Barcelona /
22.12.2015 entered service Napoles—Catania under
charter by TTT Lines /

ms GOLFO DEGLI ANGELI
IMO No. 9304631
Lloyd Sardegna, Cagliari
Cantiere Navale Visentini, Porto Viro; Yard No.: 210

26 302 GT / 7500 tdw / 186.00 m length oa /
25.60 m beam / two 9-cyl. diesels geared to
2 screws; MAN B&W / 21 600 kW / 24 kn /
400 pass. in cabins, 600 pass. unberthed / 150 cars,
2200 lane metres /

12.6.2004 launched / 20.9.2004 delivered / 17.10.2004
maiden voyage in service Piombino—Olbia / 1.2007
MARIA GRAZIA ON., Moby Lines, Livorno, then
service Piombino—Olbia / winter 2007 and 2008
service Messina—Salerno under charter by Caronte &
Tourist / 10.2009–24.2.2010 service Genoa Voltri—
Termini Imerese under charter by T-Link / 12.3.2010
entered service Barcelona—Tangier under charter by
Acciona Trasmediterranea as **ALBAYZIN** / 5.10.2010
entered service Cadiz—Las Palmas de Gran Canaria—
Santa Cruz de la Palma—Santa Cruz de Tenerife /
13.02.2013 entered service Valencia—Palma de
Mallorca, also Ibiza / 2014 service Cadiz—Las Palmas
de Gran Canaria—Santa Cruz de la Palma—Santa
Cruz de Tenerife / 2015 to Acciona Trasmediterranea /

ms AKASHIA
IMO No. 9288617
Shin Nihonkai Ferry, Otaru
Mitsubishi H.I., Nagasaki; Yard No.: 2192

16 810 GT / 6649 tdw / 224.82 m length oa /
26.00 m beam / two 12-cyl. diesels; Wärtsilä /
25 200 kW / 1 screw, 1 Azipod VC / 30.5 (32.04) kn /
820 pass. in 180 cabins / 65 cars + 158 trucks
(8 tons) /

21.3.2004 launched / 21.6.2004 delivered / 1.7.2004
entered service Maizuru—Otaru

ms GOLFO ARANCI
IMO No. 9287584
Lloyd Sardegna, Cagliari
Cantiere Navale Visentini, Porto Viro; Yard No.: 209

26 302 GT / 7500 tdw / 186.00 m length oa /
25.60 m beam / two 9-cyl. diesels geared to
2 screws; MAN B&W / 21 600 kW / 24 kn /
400 pass. in cabins, 600 pass. unberthed / 150 cars,
2200 lane metres /

20.12.2003 launched / 30.4.2004 delivered / 17.5.2004
maiden voyage in service Piombino—Olbia / 5.2007
FLORENCIA, Grimaldi Ferries, Palermo / 4.6.2007
entered service Livorno—Barcelona / 2.7.2012 entered
service Brindisi—Igoumenitsa—Patras, once a week
also to Corfu / 12.9.–2.10.2012 service Ancona—
Igoumenitsa—Patras / 3.10.2012 again service
Brindisi—Igoumenitsa—Patras / 30.1.2013–4.1.2014
service Civitavecchia—Termini Imerese, also Civitavecchia—Palermo under charter by Grandi Navi Veloci /

ms HAMANASU

IMO No. 9288605
Shin Nihonkai Ferry, Osaka
Mitsubishi H.I., Nagasaki; Yard No.: 2191

16 810 GT / 6649 tdw / 224.82 m length oa /
26.00 m beam / two 12-cyl. diesels; Wärtsilä /
25 200 kW / 1 screw, 1 Azipod VC / 30.5 (32.04) kn /
820 pass. in 180 cabins / 65 cars + 158 trucks
(8 tons) /

17.1.2004 launched / 25.6.2004 delivered / 1.7.2004
entered service Maizuru—Otaru /

HAMANASU (photo: Tsuyoshi Ishiyama)

NEW CAMELLIA (photo: Osamu Taniguchi)

ms NEW CAMELLIA

IMO No. 9304497
Camellia Line, Tokyo
Mitsubishi H.I., Shimonoseki; Yard No.: 1104

19 961 GT / 4642 tdw / 170.00 m length oa /
24.00 m beam / two 18-cyl. diesels geared to
2 screws; Pielstick / 19 800 kW / 2 screws /
23.5 (25.9) kn, / 221 pass. in cabins, 301 pass. in
23 dormitories / 30 cars, 220 TEU / crew 49

20.2.2004 launched / 28.6.2004 delivered / 5.7.2004
entered service Hakata—Busan /

VOLCAN DE TAMASITE (photo: Frank Heine)

ms VOLCAN DE TAMASITE

IMO No. 9281322
Naviera Armas, Las Palmas de Gran Canaria
Astillero Barreras, Vigo; Yard No.: 1625

17 343 GT / 3500 tdw / 142.45 m length oa /
24.20 m beam / two 8-cyl. diesels; Wärtsilä /
16 800 kW / 2 screws / 21 (22.3) kn / 34 pass. in
26 cabins, 1466 pass. unberthed / 395 cars,
1220 lane metres /

8.3.2004 launched / 17.6.2004 delivered / 17.7.2004
entered service Las Palmas de Gran Canaria—Morro
Jable / 6.2013 service Motril—Nador/Al Hoceima /

VOLCAN DE TIMANFAYA (photo: Dieter Streich)

ms VOLCAN DE TIMANFAYA

IMO No. 9281334
Naviera Armas, Las Palmas de Gran Canaria
Astillero Barreras, Vigo; Yard No.: 1626

17 343 GT / 3500 tdw / 142.45 m length oa /
24.20 m beam / two 8-cyl. diesels; Wärtsilä /
16 800 kW / 2 screws / 21 kn / 206 pass. in
56 cabins, 794 pass. unberthed / 395 cars,
1270 lane metres /

11.11.2004 launched / 31.3.2005 delivered / 11.4.2005
entered service Las Palmas de Gran Canaria—Puerto
del Rosario / 5.2005 service Santa Cruz de Tenerife—
Arrecife / 12.7.2011–28.5.2012 service Motril—
Mellila / 6.2012 service Santa Cruz de Tenerife—Las
Palmas de Gran Canaria /

ms TASSILI II
IMO No. 9265419
Algerie Ferries, Algiers
IZAR, Seville; Yard No.: 293

19 955 GT / 145.00 m length oa / 24.00 m beam /
two 12-cyl. diesels geared to 2 screws, Wärtsilä /
25 200 kW / 22 kn / 728 pass. in 209 cabins,
572 pass. unberthed / 300 cars, 500 lane metres /
crew 130

27.10.2003 launched / 7.10.2004 delivered / 4.11.2004
maiden voyage in service Algiers—Marseilles, then
service Algiers/Oran—Alicante/Marseilles /

TASSILI II (photo: Frank Lose)

EL-DJAZAIR II (photo: Frank Heine)

ms EL-DJAZAIR II
IMO No. 9265421
Algerie Ferries, Algiers
IZAR, Seville; Yard No.: 294

20 124 GT / 145.00 m length oa / 24.00 m beam /
two 12-cyl. diesels geared to 2 screws; Wärtsilä /
25 200 kW / 22 kn / 728 pass. in 209 cabins,
572 pass. unberthed / 300 cars, 500 lane metres /
crew 130

4.6.2004 launched / 24.5.2005 delivered, then service
Algiers—Marseilles, then service Algiers/Oran—
Alicante/Marseilles /

ms BIRKA PARADISE
IMO No. 9273727
Birka Line, Mariehamn
Aker Finnyards, Rauma; Yard No.: 442

34 728 GT / 4020 tdw / 176.85 m length oa /
28.00 m beam / four 6-cyl. diesels geared to
2 screws; Wärtsilä / 23 390 kW / 21 kn / 1468
(1800) pass. in 734 cabins / crew 219

16.4.2004 floated out / 8.11.2004 delivered /
10.11.2004 christened / 14.11.2004 maiden cruise
Stockholm—Mariehamn / 3.6.2009 home port
Stockholm; 34 924 GT / 13.1.2013 renamed BIRKA
STOCKHOLM /

BIRKA STOCKHOLM ex BIRKA PARADISE (photo: Hans-Joachim Hellmann)

COLOR FANTASY (photo: Marko Stampehl)

ms COLOR FANTASY
IMO No. 9278234
Color Line, Oslo
Kværner Masa-Yards, Turku; Yard No.: 1351

75 027 GT / 6133 tdw / 223.90 m length oa /
35.00 (41.35) m beam / four 8-cyl. diesels geared
to 2 screws; Wärtsilä / 31 200 kW / 22.1 kn /
2750 pass. in 968 cabins / 750 cars, 1270
lane metres / crew 250

1.5.2004 floated out / 3.12.2004 delivered / 10.12.2004
maiden voyage in service Oslo—Kiel /

COLOR MAGIC (photo: Frank Heine)

ms COLOR MAGIC
IMO No. 9349863
Color Line, Oslo
Aker Finnyards, Rauma; Yard No.: 1355

75 156 GT / 6133 tdw / 223.90 m length oa /
35.00 (41.40) m beam / four 8-cyl. diesels geared
to 2 screws; Wärtsilä / 31 200 kW / 22.3 (23) kn /
2775 pass. in 1021 cabins / 550 cars, 1265
lane metres /

15.12.2006 floated out in Turku / 16.12.2006 towed from
Turku to Rauma for completion / 6.9.2007 delivered /
17.9.2007 maiden voyage in service Oslo—Kiel /

ms KISO
IMO No. 9294317
Taiheiyo Ferry, Nagoya
Mitsubishi H.I., Shimonoseki; Yard No.: 1103

15 795 GRT / 7042 tdw / 199.90 m length oa /
27.00 m beam / two 9-cyl. diesels geared to 2 screws;
Mitsubishi / 25 020 kW / 23 (26.55) kn / 800 pass.
in 178 cabins / 113 cars, 2071 lane metres /
crew 78

22.7.2004 launched / 5.1.2005 delivered / 9.1.2005
maiden voyage in service Nagoya—Sendai—
Tomakomai /

ms ORANGE HOPE
IMO No. 9089085
Shikoku Kaihatsu Ferry, Toyo
Imabari Zosen, Imabari; Yard No.: 606

15 732 GT / 5144 tdw / 175.21 m length oa /
27.50 m beam / one 14-cyl. diesel; Pielstick /
18 550 kW / 1 screw / 22.2 (25.76) kn /
218 pass. in cabins / 175 trucks (8 tons) / crew 20

13.1.2005 delivered, then service Niihama—Kobe /

ORANGE HOPE (photo: Osamu Taniguchi)

ms PRIDE OF AMERICA
IMO No. 9209221
NCL America, Honolulu
Lloyd Werft, Bremerhaven; Yard No.: 7672

80 439 GT / 8260 tdw / 282.50 m length oa /
32.21 m beam / six 8-cyl. diesels with 50 400 kW;
Wärtsilä / six generators connected to two
elec. motors / 25 000 kW / 2 Mermaid pods /
22 kn / 2146 (2300) pass. in 1073 cabins /
crew 900

3.1999 ordered with a sister ship for United States
Lines (American Classic Voyages) from Ingalls Shipbuilding, Pascagoula (Yard No.: 7671) / 10.2001 bankruptcy of shipping company, construction discontinued,
to U.S. Maritime Administration / 2002 to Norwegian
Cruise Line / 5.11.2002 towed from Pascagoula to
Bremerhaven / 13.12.2002 arrival at Lloyd Werft,
Bremerhaven for further construction, hull lengthened
by 24.56 m / 14.1.2004 sunk during a storm after
listing / 15.2.2004 refloated / 7.6.2005 delivered /
17.6.2005 christened in New York / 25.6.2005 first
cruise from Miami to Los Angeles / 23.7.2005 first
seven-day Hawaii cruise from Honolulu / 3.–4.2013
conversion at Pearl Harbor Naval Shipyard, Honolulu:
2192 (2630) pass. in 1096 cabins /

KISO (photo: Hiroyuki Yoshimoto)

PRIDE OF AMERICA (photo: Olaf Schmidt)

STENA LAGAN ex LAGAN VIKING (photo: Frank Lose)

STENA LAGAN ex LAGAN VIKING (photo: Frank Lose)

ms LAGAN VIKING
IMO No. 9329849
Levantina Trasporti, Bari
Cantiere Navale Visentini, Porto Viro; Yard No.: 212

27 510 GT / 7000 tdw / 186.46 m length oa /
25.60 m beam / two 9-cyl. diesels geared to
2 screws; MAN B&W / 21 600 kW / 24.1 kn /
480 pass. in cabins / 170 cars, 2270 lane metres /

5.2.2005 launched / 2.7.2005 delivered / 19.7.2005
maiden voyage in service Belfast—Birkenhead under
charter by Norse Merchant Ferries / 7.2008 to Norfolk
Line, Belfast / 12.7.2010 to DFDS Seaways, Belfast,
continued service Belfast—Birkenhead / 12.8.2010
renamed LAGAN SEAWAYS / 1.12.2010 to Stena
Line, Belfast, continued service Belfast—Birkenhead /
1.8.2011 renamed STENA LAGAN /

STENA MERSEY ex MERSEY VIKING (photo: Frank Lose)

ms MERSEY VIKING
IMO No. 9329851
Levantina Trasporti, Bari
Cantiere Navale Visentini, Porto Viro; Yard No.: 213

27 510 GT / 7000 tdw / 186.58 m length oa /
25.60 m beam / two 9-cyl. diesels geared to
2 screws; MAN B&W / 21 600 kW / 24.1 kn /
480 pass. in cabins / 170 cars, 2270 lane metres /

12.2005 delivered / 12.2005 maiden voyage in
service Belfast—Birkenhead under charter by Norse
Merchant Ferries / 11.2008 to Norfolk Line, Belfast /
12.7.2010 to DFDS Seaways, Belfast, continued service
Belfast—Birkenhead / 3.8.2010 renamed MERSEY
SEAWAYS / 1.12.2010 to Stena Line, Belfast, continued
service Belfast—Birkenhead / 8.8.2011 renamed
STENA MERSEY /

ms DOKTER WAGEMAKER
IMO No. 9294070
Teso, Texel
Royal Schelde, Vlissingen (hull Santierul Naval
Galatz, Galatz); Yard No.: 557051

13 256 GT / 6837 tdw / 130.40 m length oa /
22.15 (22.70) m beam / four 8-cyl. diesels geared
to 2 screws with 11 076 kW; Caterpillar / four
generators connected to four elec. motors /
8972 kW / 4 screws / 14.8 (15.2) kn / 1750 pass.
unberthed / 204 cars, 704 lane metres / crew 8

26.11.2004 launched / 17.1.2005 to Vlissingen for
completion / 5.9.2005 delivered / 16.9.2005 maiden
voyage in service Texel—Den Helder /

DOKTER WAGEMAKER (photo: Frank Lose)

DUNKERQUE SEAWAYS ex MAERSK DUNKERQUE (photo: Frank Lose)

DELFT SEAWAYS ex MAERSK DELFT (photo: Frank Lose)

ms MAERSK DUNKERQUE
IMO No. 9293076
Norfolk Line, Dover
Samsung H. I., Koje; Yard No.: 1523

35 923 GT / 6160 tdw / 186.65 m length oa /
28.40 (29.12) m beam / four 8-cyl. diesels geared
to 2 screws; MAN B&W / 40 000 kW / 25.8 kn /
780 pass. unberthed / 200 cars, 2000 lane metres /
crew 70

29.12.2004 floated out / 27.9.2005 delivered / 3.11.2005
maiden voyage in service Dover—Dunkirk / 3.2008
1000 pass. unberthed / 18.07.2010 DUNKERQUE
SEAWAYS, DFDS Seaways, Dover, then service Dover—
Dunkirk /

ms MAERSK DELFT
IMO No. 9293088
Norfolk Line, Dover
Samsung H. I., Koje; Yard No.: 1524

35 923 GT / 6164 tdw / 186.65 m length oa /
28.40 (29.12) m beam / four 8-cyl. diesels geared
to 2 screws; MAN B&W / 38 400 kW / 25.8 kn /
780 pass. unberthed / 200 cars, 2000 lane metres /
crew 70

7.5.2005 floated out / 25.1.2006 delivered / 27.2.2006
maiden voyage in service Dover—Dunkirk / 3.2008
1000 pass. unberthed / 3.8.2010 DELFT SEAWAYS,
DFDS Seaways, Dover, then service Dunkirk—Dover /

ms MAERSK DOVER
IMO No. 9318345
Norfolk Line, Dover
Samsung H. I., Koje; Yard No.: 1574

35 923 GT / 6874 tdw / 186.65 m length oa /
28.40 (29.12) m beam / four 8-cyl. diesels geared
to 2 screws; MAN B&W / 38 400 kW / 25.8 kn /
780 pass. unberthed / 200 cars, 2000 lane metres /
crew 70

12.11.2005 floated out / 19.6.2006 delivered / 23.7.2006 maiden voyage in service Dover—Dunkirk / 3.2008 1000 pass. unberthed / 27.7.2010 **DOVER SEAWAYS**, DFDS Seaways, Dover, then service Dover—Dunkirk /

DOVER SEAWAYS ex MAERSK DOVER (photo: Andreas Wörteler)

ms SUPER LINER OGASAWARA
IMO No. 9287950
Ogasawara Kaiun, Tokyo
Mitsui Eng. & SB., Tamano; Yard No.: 1560

13 923 GT / 925 tdw / 140.00 m length oa / 29.80 m beam / two gas turbines; GE Marine / 50 360 kW / 2 water jets / 38 (42.8) kn / 742 pass. unberthed / 250 cars /

11.2004 launched / 10.2005 delivered, planned for service Tokyo—Chichijima, not accepted because of excessive costs. Ship laid up at builders /

SUPER LINER OGASAWARA (photo: Hiroyuki Yoshimoto)

ms SMYRIL
IMO No. 9275218
Strandfaraskip Landsins, Tvøroyri
IZAR, San Fernando; Yard No.: 399

12 320 GT / 2100 tdw / 135.00 m length oa / 22.70 m beam / four 7-cyl. diesels geared to 2 screws; MAN B&W-Izar / 13 440 kW / 21 kn / 98 pass. in 34 cabins, 877 pass. unberthed / 200 cars, 540 lane metres / crew 22

20.3.2004 launched / 15.10.2005 delivered / 31.10.2005 entered service Tvøroyri—Tórshavn /

SMYRIL (photo: Jürgen Pfarre)

COTE D'ALBATARE (photo: Frank Lose)

ms COTE D'ALBATARE
IMO No. 9320128
Transmanche Ferries, Rouen
Astillero Barreras, Vigo; Yard No.: 1645

18 425 GT / 3608 tdw / 142.45 m length oa /
24.20 m beam / two 9-cyl. diesels geared to
2 screws; Wärtsilä-Bermeo / 18 900 kW /
22 (24) kn / 192 pass. in 51 cabins, 408 pass.
unberthed / 224 cars, 750 lane metres / crew 44

21.7.2005 launched / 2.2006 delivered / 5.3.2006
maiden voyage in service Dieppe—Newhaven /
1.5.2007 also service Le Havre—Newhaven / 12.2.2009
again Dieppe—Newhaven, Dieppe—Dover, Dover—
Boulogne / 29.6.2009 only service Boulogne—Dover /
13.9.2009 entered service Le Havre—Portsmouth /
2.5.2010 laid up in Le Havre / 22.5.2011 again service
Dieppe—Newhaven / 23.9.2011 laid up in Dieppe /
16.2.2014 again service Dieppe—Newhaven /

ms SEVEN SISTERS
IMO No. 9320130
Transmanche Ferries, Dieppe
Astilleros Barreras; Yard No.: 1646

18 425 GT / 3608 tdw / 142.45 m length oa /
24.20 m beam / two 9-cyl. diesels geared to 2
screws; Wärtsilä-Bermeo / 18 900 kW / 22 (24) kn /

196 pass. in 51 cabins, 404 pass. unberthed /
224 cars, 750 lane metres / crew 44

21.3.2006 launched / 21.10.2006 delivered / 2.11.2006
maiden voyage in service Dieppe—Newhaven / 1.5.–
9.2007 service Le Havre—Newhaven, then again service

Dieppe—Newhaven / 22.5.2011 laid up in Dieppe /
23.9.2011–7.1.2013 service Dieppe—Newhaven, then
laid up in Dieppe / 2.5.–13.6.2013 service Dieppe—
Newhaven, then laid up in Dieppe / 10.3.–30.12.2014
service Le Havre—Portsmouth under charter by DFDS
Seaways, then laid up in Le Havre / 1.5.2015 again
service Dieppe—Newhaven /

ms VOLCAN DE TABURIENTE
IMO No. 9348558
Naviera Armas, Las Palmas de Gran Canaria
Astillero Barreras, Vigo; Yard No.: 1650

12 895 GT / 1400 tdw / 130.45 m length oa /
21.60 m beam / four 9-cyl. diesels geared to
2 screws; Caterpillar / 18 000 kW / 22.50
(23.25) kn / 1500 pass. unberthed / 103 cars,
448 lane metres / crew 34

1.12.2005 launched / 9.6.2006 delivered / 25.6.2006
maiden voyage in service Los Cristianos—San Sebastián
de La Gomera—Puerto de La Estaca /

VOLCAN DE TABURIENTE (photo: Frank Lose)

SEVEN SISTERS (photo: Marc Peper)

ms GALAXY
IMO No. 9333694
Tallink, Tallinn
Aker Finnyards, Rauma; Yard No.: 435

48 915 GT / 4850 tdw / 212.10 m length oa /
29.00 (35.20) m beam / four 16-cyl. diesels geared
to 2 screws; Wärtsilä / 26 240 kW / 22 kn /
2500 pass. in 927 cabins, 300 pass. unberthed /
420 cars, 1130 lane metres / crew 130

1.12.2005 floated out / 18.4.2006 delivered / 2.5.2006–
15.7.2008 service Tallinn—Helsinki / 7.2008 home
port Stockholm / 23.07.2008 entered service Turku—
Mariehamn—Stockholm for Silja Line /

GALAXY (photo: Frank Heine)

ms BALTIC PRINCESS
IMO No. 9354284
Tallink, Tallinn
Aker Finnyards, Helsinki; Yard No.: 1361

48 915 GT / 6287 tdw / 212.10 m length oa /
29.00 (35.20) m beam / four 16-cyl. diesels geared
to 2 screws; Wärtsilä / 26 240 kW / 22 (24.5) kn /
2500 pass. in 1057 cabins, 300 pass. unberthed /
420 cars, 1130 lane metres / crew 130

14.11.2006 keel-laying in St. Nazaire, then completion
in Rauma / 10.7.2008 delivered / 15.7.2008 maiden
voyage in service Tallinn—Helsinki / 23.1.2013 home
port Mariehamn / 1.2.2013 entered service Turku—
Mariehamn—Stockholm for Silja Line /

BALTIC PRINCESS (photo: Frank Heine)

BALTIC QUEEN (photo: Frank Lose)

ms BALTIC QUEEN
IMO No. 9443255
Tallink, Tallinn
STX Finland, Rauma; Yard No.: 1365

48 915 GT / 6287 tdw / 212.10 m length oa /
29.00 (35.20) m beam / four 16-cyl. diesels geared
to 2 screws; Wärtsilä / 26 240 kW / 22 (24.5) kn /
2500 pass. in 1057 cabins, 300 pass. unberthed /
420 cars, 1130 lane metres / crew 130

9.12.2008 floated out / 16.4.2009 delivered / 24.4.2009
maiden voyage in service Tallinn—Mariehamn—Stockholm / 7.9.2014 entered service Tallinn—Helsinki /

ms FREEDOM OF THE SEAS
IMO No. 9304033
Royal Caribbean International, Nassau
Aker Finnyards, Turku; Yard No.: 1352

154 407 GT / 10 500 tdw / 338.77 m length oa /
38.59 (39.03) m beam / six 12-cyl. diesels with
75 624 kW; Wärtsilä / six generators connected to
three elec. motors / 42 000 kW / 3 Azipod VO /
21 (23) kn / 3634 (4375) pass. in 1817 cabins /
crew 1396

19.8.2005 floated out / 23.4.2006 delivered / 4.6.2006
maiden Caribbean cruise from Miami / 7.1.–31.1.2015
conversion at Grand Bahama Shipyard, Freeport: 3784
(4541) pass. in 1892 cabins /

FREEDOM OF THE SEAS (photo: Hans-Joachim Hellmann)

LIBERTY OF THE SEAS (photo: Andy Hernandez)

INDEPENDENCE OF THE SEAS (photo: Frank Heine)

ms LIBERTY OF THE SEAS

IMO No. 9330032
Royal Caribbean International, Nassau
Aker Yards, Turku; Yard No.: 1353

154 407 GT / 10 500 tdw / 338.92 m length oa /
38.60 (39.03) m beam / six 12-cyl. diesels with
75 624 kW; Wärtsilä / six generators connected to
three elec. motors / 42 000 kW / 3 Azipod VO /
21.6 (23.6) kn / 3634 (4375) pass. in 1817 cabins /
crew 1396

3.8.2006 floated out / 18.4.2007 delivered / 19.5.2007
maiden Caribbean cruise from Miami /

ms INDEPENDENCE OF THE SEAS

IMO No. 9349681
Royal Caribbean International, Nassau
Aker Yards, Turku; Yard No.: 1354

INDEPENDENCE OF THE SEAS (photo: Frank Heine)

154 407 GT / 10 500 tdw / 338.72 m length oa /
38.60 (39.03) m beam / six 12-cyl. diesels with
75 624 kW; Wärtsilä / six generators connected to
three elec. motors / 42 000 kW / 3 Azipod VO /
21.6 (23.5) kn / 3634 (4375) pass. in 1817 cabins /
crew 1396

20.9.2007 floated out / 17.4.2008 delivered / 2.5.2008
maiden cruise from Southampton /

Genoa—Porto Torres, later service Genoa—Tunis under
charter by Grandi Navi Veloci / 22.10.2011 entered
service Rosslare—Cherbourg under charter by Celtic

Link Ferries as **CELTIC HORIZON** / 31.3.2014 continued
service Rosslare—Cherbourg, now under charter by
Stena Line / 15.4.2014 renamed **STENA HORIZON** /

ms CARTOUR BETA

IMO No. 9332559
Levantina Trasporti, Bari
Cantiere Navale Visentini, Porto Viro; Yard No.: 214

27 522 GT / 7000 tdw / 186.40 m length oa /
25.60 m beam / two 9-cyl. diesels geared to
2 screws; MAN B&W / 21 600 kW / 24.5 kn /
480 pass. in 120 cabins, 520 pass. unberthed /
170 cars, 2275 lane metres /

12.12.2005 launched / 24.5.2006 delivered / 5.2006
maiden voyage in service Salerno—Messina under
charter by Caronte & Tourist / 18.11.2008–4.2009
service Messina—Civitavecchia / 4.2009 again
service Salerno—Messina / 9.11.2011 entered service
Salerno—Termini Imerese / 21.6.2011 entered service

STENA HORIZON ex CARTOUR BETA (photo: Frank Heine)

ms CARTOUR GAMMA
IMO No. 9349758
Levantina Trasporti, Bari
Cantiere Navale Visentini, Porto Viro; Yard No.: 215

27 522 GT / 7000 tdw / 186.62 m length oa /
25.60 m beam / two 9-cyl. diesels geared to
2 screws; MAN B&W / 21 600 kW / 24.5 kn /
480 pass. in 120 cabins, 520 pass. unberthed /
170 cars, 2275 lane metres /

8.11.2006 delivered / 10.12.2006 maiden voyage in
service Salerno—Messina under charter by Caronte &
Tourist / 10.4.2015 entered service Naples—Catania
under charter by TTT Lines /

ms BORJA
IMO No. 9349760
Stena Ro/Ro, Bari
Cantiere Navale Visentini, Porto Viro; Yard No.: 216

27 414 GT / 7000 tdw / 186.50 m length oa /
25.60 m beam / two 9-cyl. diesels geared to
2 screws; MAN B&W / 21 600 kW / 24.5 kn /
480 pass. in cabins, 372 pass. unberthed /
170 cars, 2275 lane metres /

18.12.2006 launched / 11.5.2007 delivered / 20.5.2007
maiden voyage in service Barcelona—Palma de
Mallorca under charter by Balearia / 26.3.2010
renamed **BALTIC AMBER** / 9.4.2010 entered service
Travemünde—Ventspils under charter by Ave Line /
16.4.2010 entered service Travemünde—Riga under
charter by Ave Line / 17.10.2010 entered service
Klaipeda—Kiel under charter by DFDS Seaways /
3.3.2010 entered service Marseilles—Tunis under
charter by LD Lines / 18.4.2011 entered service
St. Nazaire—Gijon under charter by LD Lines / 6.2011
renamed **NORMAN ASTURIAS** / 3.11.2013 entered
service Santander—Poole under charter by LD Lines /
10.1.2014 services Poole—Santander, Poole—Gijon
and Gijon—St. Nazaire / 27.9.2014 entered service
Algeciras—Tangier Med. under charter by Interlines /
27.1.2015 home port Frederikshavn /

ms BORJA DOS
IMO No. 9349772
Stena RoRo, Bari
Cantiere Navale Visentini, Porto Viro; Yard No.: 217

27 105 GT / 7000 tdw / 186.50 m length oa /
25.60 m beam / two 9-cyl. diesels geared to
2 screws; MAN B&W / 21 600 kW / 24.5 kn /
480 pass. in cabins, 372 pass. unberthed /
170 cars, 2275 lane metres /

28.6.2007 launched / 19.10.2007 delivered /
28.10.2007–16.4.2009 service Valencia—Palma
de Mallorca under charter by Balearia / 23.4.2009
entered service Genoa Voltri—Termini Immerese under
charter by T Link Line / 6.2009 renamed **T REX UNO** /
22.2.2010–13.6.2011 service Barcelona—Palma de
Mallorca under charter by Balearia / 6.2011 renamed
DIMONIOS / 22.6.–15.9.2011 service Vado Ligure—
Porto Torres under charter by Saremar / 16.9.2011
laid up in Livorno / 16.1.–15.9.2012 service Civitavecchia—Olbia under charter by Saremar / 5.10.2012
entered service Catania—Naples under charter by TTT
Lines / 15.11.–14.12.2012 service Genoa—Palermo
under charter by Grandi Navi Veloci / 28.12.2012
entered service Cagliari—Livorno under charter
by Tirrenia / 31.5.2013 service Cagliari—Naples/
Palermo/Trapani / 10.2014 only service Cagliari—
Naples/Palermo /

CARTOUR GAMMA (photo: Frank Lose)

NORMAN ASTURIAS ex BORJA (photo: Frank Lose)

DIMONIOS ex BORJA DOS (photo: Frank Lose)

STENA FLAVIA ex WATLING STREET (photo: Frank Lose)

LD Lines / 1.12.2011 entered service Le Havre—Portsmouth under charter by LD Lines / 21.3.2012 home port Le Havre / 10.2013 to Stena RoRo, Le Havre, then service Le Havre—Portsmouth under charter by LD Lines / 11.3.2014 renamed **ETRETAT** / 21.3.2014 entered service Portsmouth—Santander, also Portsmouth—Le Havre under charter by Brittany Ferries /

ms SCOTTISH VIKING
IMO No. 9435454
Epic Shipping, Bari
Cantiere Navale Visentini, Porto Viro; Yard No.: 221

26 904 GT / 7800 tdw / 186.44 m length oa / 25.60 m beam / two 9 cyl. diesels geared to 2 screws; MAN B&W / 21 600 kW / 24.2 kn / 428 pass. in 107 cabins, 452 pass. unberthed / 195 cars, 2250 lane metres /

31.5.2009 delivered / 18.5.2009–23.12.2010 service Zeebrugge—Rosyth under charter by Norfolk Line / 3.1.2011 entered service Nynäshamn—Ventspils under charter by Scandlines / 11.10.2011 continued service Nynäshamn—Ventspils under charter by Stena Line /

ms WATLING STREET
IMO No. 9417919
Epic Shipping, London
Cantiere Navale Visentini, Porto Viro; Yard No.: 218

26 904 GT / 5587 tdw / 186.46 m length oa / 25.60 m beam / two 9 cyl. diesels geared to 2 screws; MAN B&W / 21 600 kW / 24 kn / 432 pass. in cabins, 420 pass. unberthed / 170 cars, 2255 lane metres /

20.12.2007 launched / 28.5.2008 delivered / 6.2008 renamed **PILAR DEL MAR** / 19.6.2008–18.9.2009 service Barcelona/Valencia—Palma de Mallorca under charter by Iscomar / 2.2010 renamed **WATLING STREET** / 22.2.2010–25.4.2011 service Voltri—Termini Imerese under charter by T Link Line / 28.5.2011 entered service Travemünde—Ventspils under charter by Scandlines / 11.10.2011 continued service Travemünde—Ventspils under charter by Stena Line / 9.4.2013 renamed **STENA FLAVIA** / 30.3.2014 two round voyages Ventspils—Travemünde, one round voyage Ventspils—Nynäshamn weekly / 28.9.2015 home port Frederikshavn /

ETRETAT ex NORMAN VOYAGER (photo: Frank Heine)

ms NORMAN VOYAGER
IMO No. 9420423
Epic Shipping, Bari
Cantiere Navale Visentini, Porto Viro; Yard No.: 220

26 904 GT / 7000 tdw / 186.42 m length oa / 25.60 m beam / two 9-cyl. diesels geared to 2 screws; MAN B&W / 21 600 kW / 24.2 kn / 432 pass. in 109 cabins, 452 pass. unberthed / 195 cars, 2250 lane metres / crew 39

21.9.2008 delivered / 6.11.2008 maiden voyage in service Le Havre—Portsmouth, also one weekly round voyage Le Havre—Rosslare / 12.2008 home port London / 13.9.2009 last voyage in service Portsmouth—Le Havre / 19.9.2009 entered service Cherbourg—Rosslare / 5.10.2009 entered service Cherbourg—Portsmouth under charter by Celtic Link Ferries, also service Cherbourg—Rosslare / 21.11.2009 exclusively service Rosslare—Cherbourg / 9.11.2011 entered service St. Nazaire—Gijon under charter by

SCOTTISH VIKING (photo: Frank Heine)

ms AKEMAN STREET
IMO No. 9435466
Epic Shipping, Bari
Cantiere Navale Visentini, Porto Viro; Yard No.: 222

26 904 GT / 7800 tdw / 186.45 m length oa /
25.60 m beam / two 9 cyl. diesels geared to
2 screws; MAN B&W / 21 600 kW / 24.2 kn /
428 pass. in 107 cabins, 452 pass. unberthed /
195 cars, 2250 lane metres /

18.6.2009 launched / 2.11.2009 delivered, then laid
up in Trieste / 26.2.2010–30.4.2011 service Genoa
Voltri—Termini Imerese under charter by T-Link
Ferries / 6.2011 renamed **SCINTU** / 15.6.–16.9.2011
service Civitavecchia—Golfo Aranci under charter by
Saremar / 16.1.–16.9.2012 service Civitavecchia—
Golfo Aranci under charter by Saremar / 10.1.2013
entered service Genoa—Palermo under charter by
Grandi Navi Veloci / 6.4.–25.10.2013 service Genoa—
Olbia under charter by Moby Lines / 3.11.2013
entered service St. Nazaire—Gijon under charter by
LD Lines / 1.2014 renamed **NORMAN ATLANTIC** /
10.1.2014 service Gijon—St. Nazaire/Rosslare /
23.9.–10.12.2014 service Messina—Salerno under

NORMAN ATLANTIC ex AKEMAN STREET (photo: Frank Heine)

charter by Caronte & Tourist / 19.12.2014 entered
service Patras—Igoumenitsa—Ancona under charter
by ANEK Lines / 28.12.2014 caught fire while on a
voyage from Igoumenitsa to Ancona north-west of
Corfu, 477 persons rescued, 11 killed, 18 missed /
2.1.2015 arrival under tow in Brindisi / 14.2.2015
arrival under tow in Bari /

SHENG SHENG 1 (photo: Klas Brogren)

ms SHENG SHENG 1
IMO No. 8741545
Weihai Haida Passenger, Weihai
Shandong Huanghai Shipbuilding, Shidao

10 347 GT / 2541 tdw / 120.00 m length oa /
20.40 m beam / two 8-cyl. diesels geared to
2 screws; Daihatsu / 5000 kW / 16.3 kn /
1026 pass. unberthed / 124 cars /

6.2006 delivered / 11.6.2006 maiden voyage in service
Dalian—Weihai /

MSC MUSICA (photo: Frank Heine)

ms MSC MUSICA
IMO No. 9320087
MSC Crociere, Panama
Aker Yards, St. Nazaire; Yard No.: Q32

92 409 GT / 10 000 tdw / 293.80 m length oa /
32.30 m beam / five 16-cyl. diesels with 58 000 kW;
Wärtsilä / five generators connected to two elec.
motors / 35 000 kW / 2 screws / 22 (23) kn /
2550 (3060) pass. in 1275 cabins / crew 987

15.10.2005 floated out / 19.6.2006 delivered /
29.6.2006 maiden Eastern Mediterranean cruise
from Venice /

MSC ORCHESTRA (photo: Ulrich Streich)

MSC POESIA (photo: Alexander Brede)

MSC MAGNIFICA (photo: Alexander Brede)

ms MSC ORCHESTRA
IMO No. 9320099
MSC Crociere, Panama
Aker Yards, St. Nazaire; Yard No.: R32

92 409 GT / 10 000 tdw / 293.80 m length oa /
32.30 m beam / five 16-cyl. diesels with 58 000 kW;
Wärtsilä / five generators connected to two
elec. motors / 35 000 kW / 2 screws / 22 (23) kn /
2550 (3060) pass. in 1275 cabins / crew 987

9.9.2006 floated out / 3.5.2007 delivered / 2.6.2007
maiden cruise from Venice /

ms MSC POESIA
IMO No. 9387073
MSC Crociere, Panama
Aker Yards, St. Nazaire; Yard No.: S32

92 409 GT / 10 561 tdw / 293.80 m length oa /
32.20 m beam / five 16-cyl. diesels with 58 000 kW;
Wärtsilä / five generators connected to two
elec. motors / 36 050 kW / 2 screws / 22 (23) kn /
2550 (3060) pass. in 1275 cabins / crew 987

30.8.2007 floated out / 27.03.2008 delivered /
6.4.2008 maiden voyage from Dover to Venice /
6.2011 92 627 GT /

ms MSC MAGNIFICA
IMO No. 9387085
MSC Crociere, Panama
STX France Cruise, St. Nazaire; Yard No.: T32

95 128 GT / 9429 tdw / 293.80 m length oa /
32.30 m beam / five 16-cyl. diesels with 58 000 kW;
Wärtsilä / five generators connected to two
elec. motors / 35 000 kW / 2 screws / 22 (23) kn /
2506 (3007) pass. in 1253 cabins / crew 987

14.1.2009 floated out / 23.2.2010 delivered / 7.3.2010
maiden voyage Hamburg—Venice /

ms FINNSTAR
IMO No. 9319442
Finnlines, Helsinki
Fincantieri, Castellammare di Stabia; Yard No.: 6123

45 923 GT / 9653 tdw / 218.77 m length oa /
30.50 (32.52) m beam / four 9-cyl. diesels geared
to 2 screws; Wärtsilä-Fincantieri / 48 000 kW /
25 kn / 573 pass. in 201 cabins / 62 cars,
4223 lane metres /

1.8.2005 launched / 27.7.2006 delivered / 6.8.2006
maiden voyage in service Helsinki—Travemünde /
2.6.2009 also service Helsinki—Gdynia—Rostock /
1.10.2012 exclusively service Helsinki—Travemünde /

ms FINNMAID
IMO No. 9319466
Finnlines, Helsinki
Fincantieri, Ancona; Yard No.: 6125

45 923 GT / 9653 tdw / 218.80 m length oa /
30.50 (32.52) m beam / four 9-cyl. diesels geared to
2 screws; Wärtsilä-Fincantieri / 48 000 kW / 25 kn /
573 pass. in 201 cabins / 4223 lane metres /

28.10.2005 floated out / 7.8.2006 delivered /
19.8.2006 maiden voyage in service Travemünde—
Helsinki / 2.6.2009 also service Helsinki—Gdynia—
Rostock / 1.10.2012 exclusively service Helsinki—
Travemünde /

ms FINNLADY
IMO No. 9336268
Finnlines, Helsinki
Fincantieri, Ancona; Yard No.: 6133

45 923 GT / 9653 tdw / 218.80 m length oa /
30.50 (32.52) m beam / four 9-cyl. diesels geared to
2 screws; Wärtsilä-Fincantieri / 48 000 kW / 25 kn /
573 pass. in 201 cabins / 4223 lane metres /

16.6.2006 floated out as **EUROPALINK** / 9.2.2007
delivered as **FINNLADY** / 22.2.2007 maiden voyage in
service Travemünde—Helsinki / 2.6.2009 also service
Helsinki—Gdynia—Rostock / 1.10.2012 exclusively
service Helsinki—Travemünde /

ms EUROPALINK
IMO No. 9319454
Finnlines, Malmö
Fincantieri, Castellammare di Stabia; Yard No.: 6124

45 923 GT / 9653 tdw / 218.80 m length oa /
30.50 (32.52) m beam / four 9-cyl. diesels geared to
2 screws; Wärtsilä-Fincantieri / 48 000 kW / 25 kn /
573 pass. in 201 cabins / 4223 lane metres /

3.6.2006 launched as **FINNLADY** / 5.3.2007 delivered
as **EUROPALINK** / 30.3.2007 maiden voyage in
service Travemünde—Malmö / 16.4.2009 entered
service Travemünde—Helsinki / 2.6.2009 also
service Helsinki—Gdynia—Rostock / 4.10.2012
last voyage in service Helsinki—Gdynia—Rostock /
2.12.2012 entered service Ancona—Igoumenitsa—
Patras under charter by Minoan Lines, home port
Palermo / 10.12.2012 also service Trieste—Ancona—
Igoumenitsa—Patras / 24.7.–10.9.2014 service
Trieste—Ravenna—Igoumenitsa—Patras / 21.9.2014
on a voyage from Igoumenitsa to Corfu grounded
north of Corfu, Corfu called at as port of distress /
9.10.2014–20.9.2015 repair in Yalova / 29.9.2015
entered service Livorno—Palermo /

FINNSTAR (photo: Frank Heine)

FINNMAID (photo: Ulrich Streich)

FINNLADY (photo: Frank Heine)

EUROPALINK (photo: Frank Lose)

ms NORDLINK

IMO No. 9336256
Finnlines, Malmö
Fincantieri, Ancona; Yard No.: 6134

45 923 GT / 9300 tdw / 218.80 m length oa /
30.50 (32.52) m beam / four 9-cyl. diesels geared to
2 screws; Wärtsilä-Fincantieri / 48 000 kW / 25 kn /
573 pass. in 201 cabins / 4223 lane metres /

16.9.2006 floated out / 6.7.2007 delivered / 24.7.2007
maiden voyage in service Malmö—Travemünde /
13.2.2009 entered service Travemünde—Helsinki /
2.6.2009 also service Helsinki—Gdynia—Rostock /
4.10.2012 entered service Malmö—Travemünde /
27.11.2014–7.4.2015 service Helsinki—Travemünde /
13.5.2015 again service Malmö—Travemünde /

NORDLINK (photo: Frank Lose)

BLUE PUTTEES ex STENA TRADER (photo: Andreas Wörteler)

ms STENA TRAVELLER

IMO No. 9331189
Stena Line, Hoek van Holland
Fosen Mek Verksted., Rissa; Yard No.: 75

26 663 GT / 10.466 tdw / 212.00 m length oa /
26.70 (31.62) m beam / two 9-cyl. diesels geared
to 2 screws; MAN B&W / 21 600 kW / 22 (23) kn /
204 pass. in 100 cabins, 96 pass. unberthed /
3100 lane metres /

8.12.2006 launched at Baltijsky Zavod Shipyard,
St. Petersburg / 16.1.2007 towed from St. Petersburg to Rissa for completion / 12.6.2007 delivered /
20.6.2007–9.12.2010 service Hoek van Holland—
Killingholme / 24.2.2011 delivered after conversion
by Lloyd Werft, Bremerhaven as **HIGHLANDERS**:
28 460 GT, 7634 tdw, 200.00 m length oa, 301 pass.
in 96 cabins, 624 pass. unberthed, 2741 lane metres /
24.3.2011 home port St. John's / 21.4.2011 entered
service North Sydney—Port aux Basques under charter
by Marine Atlantic /

HIGHLANDERS ex STENA TRAVELLER (photo: Marko Stampehl)

ms STENA TRADER

IMO No. 9331177
Stena Line, Hoek van Holland
Fosen Mek Verksted., Rissa; Yard No.: 74

26 663 GT / 7500 tdw / 212.00 m length oa /
26.70 (31.62) m beam / two 9-cyl. diesels geared
to 2 screws; MAN B&W / 21 600 kW / 22 (23) kn /
204 pass. in 100 cabins, 100 pass. unberthed /
3100 lane metres /

21.12.2005 launched at Baltijsky Zavod Shipyard, St.
Petersburg. Towed to Rissa for completion / 4.8.2006
delivered / 12.8.2006–29.9.2010 service Hoek van
Holland—Killingholme / 22.12.2010 delivered after
conversion by Lloyd Werft, Bremerhaven as **BLUE
PUTTEES**: 28 460 GT, 7634 tdw, 200.00 m length oa,
301 pass. in 96 cabins, 624 pass. unberthed, 2741 lane
metres / 19.2.2011 home port St. John's / 9.3.2011
entered service North Sydney—Port aux Basques under
charter by Marine Atlantic /

BO HAI JIN ZHU (photo: owner)

ms BO HAI JIN ZHU
IMO No. 9486219
Bo Hai Ferry Co., Yantai
Shandong Huanghai Shipbuilding, Shidao

19 847 GT / 5700 tdw / 161.20 m length oa /
24.80 m beam / two diesels; MAN / 12 000 kW /
19.2 kn / 1351 pass. unberthed / 200 cars /
1929 lane metres /

10.9.2006 launched, then delivered / 20.9.2006
maiden voyage in service Dalian—Yantai /

BO HAI YIN ZHU (photo: owner)

ms BO HAI YIN ZHU
IMO No. 9486219
Bo Hai Ferry Co., Yantai
Shandong Huanghai Shipbuilding, Shidao

19 847 GT / 5700 tdw / 161.20 m length oa /
24.80 m beam / two diesels; MAN / 12 000 kW /
19.2 kn / 1351 pass. unberthed / 200 cars /
1929 lane metres /

4.2.2007 delivered, then service Dalian—Yantai /

ms ZHONG TIE BO HAI 1 HAO
IMO No. 9383390
Sinorail Bohai Train Ferry, Yantai
Xingang Shipyard, Tianjin; Yard No.: 3461

24 975 GT / 7200 tdw / 182.60 m length oa /
24.80 m beam / four 9-cyl. diesels with 11 520 kW;
MaK / four generators connected to two elec.
motors / 8000 kW / 2 Azipod CO / 18 kn /
281 pass. in 138 cabins, 199 pass. unberthed /
1200 lane metres, 50 trucks + 25 cars, 5 rail tracks
with 768 m length, 50 wagons / crew 63

10.9.2006 launched / 10.2006 delivered, then service
Lushun—Yantai /

ZHONG TIE BO HAI 1 HAO (photo: owner)

ZHONG TIE BO HAI 2 HAO (photo: Klas Brogren)

ms ZHONG TIE BO HAI 2 HAO
IMO No. 9383405
Sinorail Bohai Train Ferry, Yantai
Xingang Shipyard, Tianjin; Yard No.: 3462

24 975 GT / 7200 tdw / 182.60 m length oa /
24.80 m beam / four 9-cyl. diesels with 11 520 kW;
MaK / four generators connected to two elec.
motors / 8000 kW / 2 Azipod CO / 18 kn /
281 pass. in 138 cabins, 199 pass. unberthed /
1200 lane metres, 50 trucks + 25 cars, 5 rail tracks
with 768 m length, 50 wagons / crew 63

1.2007 delivered, then service Lushun—Yantai /

25 058 GT / 8500 tdw / 199.14 m length oa / 26.60 m beam / two 12-cyl. diesels geared to 2 screws; Wärtsilä / 34 262 kW / 23.7 (26) kn / 265 pass. in 68 cabins, 130 pass. unberthed / 2623 lane metres / crew 63

6.6.2007 launched / 2.10.2007 delivered / 5.10.2007 maiden voyage in service Genoa—Barcelona / 7.10.2008–30.9.2010 service Valencia/Barcelona—Palma de Mallorca under charter by Acciona Trasmediterranea / 6.6.–5.7.2011 service Valenica—Palma de Mallorca under charter by Acciona Trasmediterranea / 2.–9.2012 service Pendik—Konstanza under charter by UN RoRo / 8.11.2012–7.11.2013 service Augusta—Salerno for Grimaldi Holding / 28.6.2012 also service Augusta—Valletta / 15.11.2013–25.11.2014 service Patras—Igoumenitsa—Corfu—Venice under charter by ANEK Lines / 12.2014 **RIZHAO ORIENT**, Rizhao Haitong Ferry, Panama / 2015 service Rizhao—Pyeongtaek /

ZHONG TIE BO HAI 3 HAO (photo: Olaf Schmidt)

ms ZHONG TIE BO HAI 3 HAO
IMO No. 9399375
Sinorail Bohai Train Ferry, Yantai
Xingang Shipyard, Tianjin; Yard No.: 3463

25 380 GT / 7200 tdw / 182.60 m length oa / 24.80 m beam / four 9-cyl. diesels with 11 520 kW; MaK / four generators connected to two elec. motors / 8000 kW / 2 Azipod CO / 18 kn / 281 pass. in 138 cabins, 331 pass. unberthed / 1200 lane metres, 50 trucks + 25 cars, 5 rail tracks with 768 m length, 50 wagons / crew 63

10.7.2008 delivered, then service Lushun—Yantai /

ms CORAGGIO
IMO No. 9350680
Grimaldi Holding, Palermo
Nuovi Cantieri Apuania, Marina di Carrara;
Yard No.: 1237

25 058 GT / 8500 tdw / 199.14 m length oa / 26.60 m beam / two 12-cyl. diesels geared to 2 screws; Wärtsilä / 34 262 kW / 23.7 (26) kn / 265 pass. in 68 cabins, 235 pass. unberthed / 2593 lane metres / crew 63

24.11.2006 launched / 24.3.2007 delivered / 29.3.2007 maiden voyage in service Genoa—Valletta—Tunis under charter by Navi Grandi Veloci / 12.6.2007 entered service Genoa—Barcelona / 16.10.2007 entered service Palermo—Livorno / 7.2010 conversion at Nuova Cantieri Apuania: 900 pass. / 30.9.2010–6.11.2011 service Hoek van Holland—Killingholme under charter by Stena Line / 1.6.–16.9.2012 service Vado Ligure—Porto Torres under charter by Saremar / 15.11.2012–13.11.2013 service Venice—Igoumenitsa—Corfu—Patras under charter by ANEK Lines / 11.2013 renamed **ATHENA SEAWAYS**, home port Klaipeda / 8.1.2014 entered service Klaipeda—Kiel under charter by DFDS Seaways / 7.7.2014 entered service Klaipeda—Karlshamn / 5.10.2015 again entered service Klaipeda—Kiel / 12.2015 again service Klaipeda—Karlshamn /

ATHENA SEAWAYS ex CORAGGIO (photo: Uwe Jakob)

RIZHAO ORIENT ex AUDACIA as AUDACIA (photo: Nikolaos Saratzis)

ms AUDACIA
IMO No. 9350692
Grimaldi Holding, Palermo
Nuovi Cantieri Apuania, Marina di Carrara;
Yard No.: 1238

TENACIA (photo: Frank Lose)

ms TENACIA
IMO No. 9350707
Grimaldi Holding, Palermo
Nuovi Cantieri Apuania, Marina di Carrara;
Yard No.: 1239

25 058 GT / 8500 tdw / 199.14 m length oa /
26.60 m beam / two 12-cyl. diesels geared to
2 screws; Wärtsilä / 24 000 kW / 23.7 (26) kn /
265 pass. in 68 cabins, 208 pass. unberthed /
2623 lane metres / crew 63

4.4.2008 delivered / 5.4.2008 maiden voyage in
service Genoa—Barcelona under charter by Grandi
Navi Veloci / 2010 increase in passenger capacity at
Nuova Cantieri Apunia: 25 993 GT, 470 pass. in 118
cabins, 430 pass. unberthed / 5.12.2011 entered
service Barcelona—Palma de Mallorca under charter
by Acciona Trasmediterranea /

ms SUPERFAST I
IMO No. 9350719
SuperFast Ferries, Piraeus
Nuovi Cantieri Apuania, Marina di Carrara;
Yard No.: 1240

25 757 GT / 8500 tdw / 199.14 m length oa /
26.60 m beam / two 12-cyl. diesels geared to
2 screws; Wärtsilä / 34 262 kW / 23 (24.5) kn /
375 pass. in 103 cabins, 625 pass. unberthed /
120 cars, 2623 lane metres /

12.6.2008 launched, originally ordered as FORZA by
Grimaldi Holding / 6.10.2008 delivered / 13.10.2008
maiden voyage in service Patras—Igoumenitsa—Bari /

ms LISCO MAXIMA
IMO No. 9350721
DFDS Tor Line, Klaipeda
Nuovi Cantieri Apuania, Marina di Carrara;
Yard No.: 1241

25 518 GT / 8500 tdw / 199.14 m length oa /
26.60 m beam / two 12-cyl. diesels geared to
2 screws; Wärtsilä / 34 262 kW / 23 (24.5) kn /
448 pass. in 107 cabins, 452 pass. unberthed /
120 cars, 2623 lane metres /

3.12.2008 floated out, originally ordered by Grimaldi
Holding / 12.3.2009 delivered to DFDS Tor Line /

SUPERFAST I (photo: Frank Lose)

VICTORIA SEAWAYS ex LISCO MAXIMA (photo: Ulrich Streich)

11.5.2009 maiden voyage in service Klaipeda—Kiel /
3.2012 VICTORIA SEAWAYS, DFDS Seaways, Klaipeda /
8.1.2012 entered service Klaipeda—Karlshamn /

7.7.2014 entered service Klaipeda—Kiel / 10.2014
service Klaipeda—Karlshamn / 8.2015 service Klaipeda—
Kiel / 31.8.2015 again service Klaipeda—Karlshamn /

SUPERFAST II (photo: Richard Seville)

ms SUPERFAST II
IMO No. 9458511
SuperFast Ferries, Piraeus
Nuovi Cantieri Apuania, Marina di Carrara;
Yard No.: 1242

25 760 GT / 8500 tdw / 199.14 m length oa /
26.60 m beam / two 12-cyl. diesels geared to
2 screws; Wärtsilä / 34 262 kW / 23 (24.5) kn /
375 pass. in 103 cabins, 625 pass. unberthed /
85 cars, 2623 lane metres /

2.10.2009 delivered, originally ordered by Grimaldi
Holding / 6.10.2009 maiden voyage in service Patras—
Igoumenitsa—Bari /

FORZA (photo: Frank Lose)

ms FORZA
IMO No. 9458523
Grimaldi Holding, Palermo
Nuovi Cantieri Apuania, Marina di Carrara;
Yard No.: 1243

25 518 GT / 8500 tdw / 198.99 m length oa /
26.60 m beam / two 12-cyl. diesels geared to
2 screws; Wärtsilä / 25 200 kW / 24 kn / 448 pass.
in 112 cabins, 452 pass. unberthed / 120 cars,
2600 lane metres /

3.2010 delivered / 27.3.2010 maiden voyage in
service Livorno—Palermo under charter by Grandi
Navi Veloci / 2.6.2010 laid up in Genoa / 28.5.2011
entered service Palermo—Civitavecchia under charter
by Grand Navi Veloci / 22.7.2011 service Civita-
vecchia/Genoa—Termini Imerese under charter by
Grandi Navi Veloci / 19.10.2011 entered service
Livorno—Termini Imerese under charter by Grandi
Navi Veloci / 21.12.2012–2.2.2016 service Patras—
Igoumenitsa—Corfu—Venice under charter by ANEK
Lines /

REGINA SEAWAYS ex ENERGIA (photo: Hans-Joachim Hellmann)

ms ENERGIA
IMO No. 9458535
Grimaldi Holding, Palermo
Nuovi Cantieri Apuania, Marina di Carrara;
Yard No.: 1244

25 518 GT / 8500 tdw / 198.99 m length oa /
26.60 m beam / two 12-cyl. diesels geared to
2 screws; Wärtsilä / 25 200 kW / 24.5 kn / 448 pass.
in 112 cabins, 452 pass. unberthed / 120 cars,
2600 lane metres /

13.8.2010 delivered, then laid up in Viareggio / 9.2011
renamed REGINA SEAWAYS / 26.9.2011 maiden
voyage in service Klaipeda—Kiel under charter by
DFDS Seaways, home port Genoa / 7.11.2011 home
port Klaipeda / 10.2014 service Klaipeda—Karlshamn /
8.2015 service Klaipeda—Kiel / 31.08.2015 entered
service Klaipeda—Karlshamn / 12.2015 service
Klaipeda—Kiel /

STAR (photo: Marko Stampehl)

ms STAR
IMO No. 9364722
Tallink, Tallinn
Aker Finnyards, Helsinki; Yard No.: 1356

36 249 GT / 4700 tdw / 186.00 m length oa /
27.70 m beam / four 12-cyl. diesels geared to
2 screws; MaK / 48 000 kW / 27 (29) kn / 520 pass.
in 131 cabins, 1380 pass. unberthed / 300 cars,
1085 lane metres /

23.11.2006 floated out / 10.4.2007 delivered /
12.4.2007 maiden voyage in service Tallinn—Helsinki /

AIDADIVA (photo: Frank Heine)

AIDABELLA (photo: Hans-Jürgen Amberg)

69 203 GT / 8765 tdw / 251.89 m length oa /
32.20 m beam / four 9-cyl. diesels with 36 000 kW;
MaK / four generators connected to two elec.
motors / 25 000 kW / 2 screws / 21.8 (22.5) kn /
2050 (2566) pass. in 1025 cabins / crew 588

19.10.2007 floated out / 14.4.2008 delivered /
23.4.2008 christened in Warnemünde / 24.4.2008
maiden cruise Warnemünde—Norway /

ms AIDALUNA
IMO No. 9334868
Aida Cruises, Genoa
Meyer Werft, Papenburg; Yard No.: 660

69 203 GT / 8654 tdw / 251.89 m length oa /
32.20 m beam / four 9-cyl. diesels with 36 000 kW;
MaK / four generators connected to two elec.
motors / 25 000 kW / 2 screws / 21.8 (22.5) kn /
2050 (2566) pass. in 1025 cabins / crew 588

6.10.2008 floated out / 16.3.2009 delivered / 22.3.2009
maiden cruise Hamburg—Palma de Mallorca /

AIDALUNA (photo: Alexander Brede)

ms AIDADIVA
IMO No. 9334856
Aida Cruises, Genoa
Meyer Werft, Papenburg; Yard No.: 659

69 203 GT / 8810 tdw / 251.89 m length oa /
32.20 m beam / four 9-cyl. diesels with 36 000 kW;
MaK / four generators connected to two elec.
motors / 25 000 kW / 2 screws / 21.8 (22.5) kn /
2050 (2566) pass. in 1025 cabins / crew 588

2.3.2007 floated out / 16.4.2007 delivered / 30.4.2007
maiden cruise Hamburg—Palma de Mallorca /

ms AIDABELLA
IMO No. 9362542
Aida Cruises, Genoa
Meyer Werft, Papenburg; Yard No.: 666

ms AIDABLU
IMO No. 9398888
Aida Cruises, Genoa
Meyer Werft, Papenburg; Yard No.: 680

71304 GT / 7889 tdw / 253.33 m length oa /
32.20 m beam / four 9-cyl. diesels with 36000 kW;
MaK / four generators connected to two elec.
motors / 25000 kW / 2 screws / 21 (21.8) kn /
2192 (2686) pass. in 1096 cabins / crew 609

11.7.2009 floated out / 4.2.2010 delivered / 9.2.2010
maiden cruise Hamburg—Palma de Mallorca /

AIDABLU (photo: Marko Stampehl)

AIDASOL (photo: Alexander Brede)

AIDAMAR (photo: Marko Stampehl)

ms AIDASOL
IMO No. 9490040
Aida Cruises, Genoa
Meyer Werft, Papenburg; Yard No.: 689

71304 GT / 7891 tdw / 253.33 m length oa /
32.20 m beam / four 9-cyl. diesels with 36000 kW;
MaK / four generators connected to two elec.
motors / 25000 kW / 2 screws / 21 (21.8) kn /
2194 (2686) pass. in 1097 cabins / crew 609

27.2.2011 floated out / 31.3.2011 delivered / 9.4.2011
maiden cruise Kiel—Hamburg /

ms AIDAMAR
IMO No. 9490052
Aida Cruises, Genoa
Meyer Werft, Papenburg; Yard No.: 690

71304 GT / 7757 tdw / 253.22 m length oa /
32.20 m beam / four 9-cyl. diesels with 36000 kW;
MaK / four generators connected to two elec.
motors / 25000 kW / 2 screws / 21 (21.8) kn /
2194 (2686) pass. in 1097 cabins / crew 609

1.4.2012 floated out / 3.5.2012 delivered / 12.5.2012
maiden cruise Hamburg—North Sea /

AIDASTELLA (photo: George Koutsoukis)

ms **AIDASTELLA**
IMO No. 9601132
Aida Cruises, Genoa
Meyer Werft, Papenburg; Yard No.: 695

71 304 GT / 7833 tdw / 253.26 m length oa /
32.20 m beam / four 9-cyl. diesels with 36 000 kW;
MaK / four generators connected to two elec.
motors / 25 000 kW / 2 screws / 21 (21.8) kn /
2194 (2700) pass. in 1097 cabins / crew 609

25.1.2013 floated out / 11.3.2013 delivered / 12.5.2012
maiden cruise Warnemünde—Hamburg /

ms **FRAM**
IMO No. 9370018
Hurtigruten, Narvik
Fincantieri, Monfalcone; Yard No.: 6144

11 647 GT / 984 tdw / 113.72 m length oa /
20.20 m beam / four 6-cyl. diesels with 7924 kW;
MaK / four generators connected to two
elec. motors / 4620 kW / 2 Aquamaster rudder
propellers / 15 (16) kn / 272 (318) pass. in
136 cabins, 182 pass. unberthed / 25 cars / crew 70

18.11.2006 floated out / 23.4.2007 delivered / 30.4.2007
maiden cruise Barcelona—Oslo / 19.5.2007 christened
in Oslo, then in summer Greenland cruises, in winter
Antarctica cruises /

FRAM (photo: Tom Gulbrandsen)

VOLCAN DE TAMADABA (photo: Frank Lose)

VOLCAN DE TIJARAFE (photo: Tony Davis)

ms **VOLCAN DE TAMADABA**
IMO No. 9360506
Naviera Armas, Las Palmas de Gran Canaria
Astillero Barreras, Vigo; Yard No.: 1653

19 976 GT / 3350 tdw / 154.51 m length oa /
24.20 m beam / two 12-cyl. diesels geared to
2 screws; Wärtsilä / 23 406 kW / 21.7 (23) kn /
206 pass. in 56 cabins, 760 pass. unberthed /
174 cars, 1870 lane metres / crew 34

9.10.2006 launched / 18.5.2007 delivered / 29.5.2007
entered service Las Palmas de Gran Canaria—Arrecife /

ms **VOLCAN DE TIJARAFE**
IMO No. 9398890
Naviera Armas, Santa Cruz de Tenerife
Astillero Barreras, Vigo; Yard No.: 1654

19 976 GT / 3400 tdw / 154.51 m length oa /
24.20 m beam / two 12-cyl. diesels geared to
2 screws; Wärtsilä / 23 400 kW / 21.7 (23) kn /
206 pass. in 56 cabins, 760 pass. unberthed /
174 cars, 1870 lane metres / crew 34

30.8.2007 launched / 28.4.2008 delivered / 5.5.2008
service between the Canaries /

BAHAMA MAMA ex SF ALHUCEMAS (photo: Manuel Hernandez Lafuente)

ms **SF ALHUCEMAS**
IMO No. 9441142
Balearia, Santa Cruz de Tenerife
Astillero Barreras, Vigo; Yard No.: 1662

20 238 GT / 3230 tdw / 154.51 m length oa /
24.20 m beam / two 9-cyl. diesels geared to
2 screws; MaK / 18 006 kW / 21.4 (23) kn /
206 pass. in 56 cabins, 760 pass. unberthed /
400 cars, 1413 lane metres /

27.4.2009 launched / 22.12.2009 delivered / 28.1.2010
maiden voyage in service Denia—Ibiza—Palma de
Mallorca / 8.2010 home port Valletta / 6.2011 in
summer service Algeciras—Tangier, in winter Denia—
Ibiza—Palma de Mallorca / 05.11.2013 exclusively
service Palma de Mallorca—Ibiza—Denia / 12.2014
renamed **BAHAMA MAMA**, service Fort Lauderdale—
Freeport / 5.10.2015 entered service Barcelona—Ibiza /
18.12.2015 entered service Algeciras—Tangier /

NATCHAN RERA (photo: Tsuyoshi Ishiyama)

ms NATCHAN RERA
IMO No. 9294238
Higashi Nihon Ferry, Hakodate
Incat, Hobart; Yard No.: 064

10 841 GT / 1360 tdw / 112.60 m length oa /
30.50 m beam / four 20-cyl. diesels geared to
2 screws; MAN B&W / 36 000 kW / 4 waterjets /
40 (45.4) kn / 797 pass. unberthed / 355 cars,
450 lane metres /

30.6.2007 floated out / 8.8.2007 delivered / 1.9.2007
maiden voyage in service Aomori—Hakodate /
11.2008 laid up / 10.2012 to Tsugaru Strait Ferry,
Keelung / 7.8.2013 entered service Suao—Hualien /
27.5.2014 additional two weekly round trips in service
Taipan—Pingtan /

ms NATCHAN WORLD
IMO No. 9383649
Higashi Nihon Ferry, Hakodate
Incat, Hobart; Yard No.: 065

10 841 GT / 1380 tdw / 112.60 m length oa /
30.50 m beam / four 20-cyl. diesels geared to
2 screws; MAN B&W / 36 000 kW / 4 waterjets /
40 kn / 797 pass. unberthed / 355 cars,
450 lane metres /

22.2.2008 floated out / 9.4.2008 delivered / 2.5.2008
maiden voyage in service Aomori—Hakodate / 11.2008
laid up / 18.7.–30.9.2009 again service Aomori—
Hakodate, then laid up in Hakodate /

ms NORMAN ARROW
IMO No. 9501590
MGC Chartering, London
Incat Tasmania, Hobart; Yard No.: 066

10 503 GT / 1450 tdw / 112.60 m length oa /
30.50 m beam / four 20-cyl. diesels geared to
2 screws; MAN B&W / 36 000 kW / 4 waterjets /
40 kn / 1200 pass. unberthed / 195 cars,
567 lane metres / crew 28

8.2.2009 floated out / 30.4.2009 delivered / 6.6.–
10.11.2009 service Boulogne—Dover under charter by
LD Lines, then laid up in Boulogne / 26.3.2010 entered

NATCHAN WORLD (photo: Hiroyuki Yoshimoto)

KATEXPRESS 1 ex NORMAN ARROW (photo: Andreas Wörteler)

KATEXPRESS 2 (photo: Ulrich Streich)

service Le Havre—Portsmouth / 12.9.2011 laid up in Rouen / 11.4.2012 home port Nassau / 30.4.2012 renamed **KATEXPRESS 1**, home port Aarhus / 9.5.2012 entered service Sjællands Odden—Ebeltoft/Aarhus under charter by Mols-Linien /

ms KATEXPRESS 2
IMO No. 9561356
Mols-Linien, Nassau
Incat Tasmania, Hobart; Yard No.: 067

10 503 GT / 1450 tdw / 112.60 m length oa / 30.20 (30.50) m beam / four 20-cyl. diesels geared to 2 screws; MAN B&W / 36 000 kW / 4 waterjets / 40.00 (42.10) kn / 1000 pass. unberthed / 417 cars, 567 lane metres / crew 28

25.2.2013 floated out / 26.3.2013 delivered / 29.4.2013 home port Aarhus / 2.5.2013 maiden voyage in service Aarhus—Sjællands Odden under charter by Mols-Linien / 27.3.2014 10 500 GT /

Sister ship **KATEXPRESS 3** is due for delivery in 5.2017.

ms COASTAL RENAISSANCE
IMO No. 9332755
BC Ferries, Victoria
Flensburger Schiffbau-Gesellschaft, Flensburg;
Yard No.: 733

21 777 GT / 2410 tdw / 160.00 m length oa / 28.20 (27.60) m beam / four 8-cyl. diesels with 16 000 kW; MaK / four generators connected to two elec. motors / 23 300 kW / 2 screws / 21 (22) kn / 1650 pass. unberthed / 371 cars, 480 lane metres / crew 35

19.3.2007 launched / 27.10.2007 delivered / 9.3.2008 maiden voyage in service Horseshoe Bay—Departure Bay /

ms COASTAL CELEBRATION
IMO No. 9332779
BC Ferries, Victoria
Flensburger Schiffbau-Gesellschaft, Flensburg;
Yard No.: 735

21 777 GT / 2410 tdw / 160.00 m length oa / 28.20 (27.60) m beam / four 8-cyl. diesels with 16 000 kW; MaK / four generators connected to two elec. motors / 23 300 kW / 2 screws / 21 (22) kn / 1650 pass. unberthed / 372 cars, 480 lane metres / crew 35

14.12.2007 launched / 9.5.2008 delivered / 21.11.2008 maiden voyage in service Swartz Bay—Tsawwassen /

ms COASTAL INSPIRATION
IMO No. 9332767
BC Ferries, Vancouver
Flensburger Schiffbau-Gesellschaft, Flensburg;
Yard No.: 734

21 777 GT / 2410 tdw / 160.00 m length oa / 28.20 (27.60) m beam / four 8-cyl. diesels with 16 000 kW; MaK / four generators connected to two

COASTAL CELEBRATION (photo: Scott Arkell)

COASTAL RENAISSANCE (photo: Scott Arkell)

COASTAL INSPIRATION (photo: Scott Arkell)

elec. motors / 23 300 kW / 2 screws / 21 (22) kn /
1650 pass. unberthed / 372 cars, 480 lane metres /
crew 35

31.8.2007 launched / 18.1.2008 delivered / 16.6.2008
maiden voyage in service Duke Point—Tsawwassen /

ms COTENTIN
IMO No. 9364978
Brittany Ferries, Cherbourg
Aker Finnyards, Helsinki; Yard No.: 1357

19 909 GT / 6200 tdw / 167.88 m length oa / .
26.80 m beam / two 12-cyl. diesels geared to
2 screws; Mak / 24 000 kW / 23 (27.6) kn /
240 pass. in 120 cabins / 2188 lane metres /
crew 43

STENA BALTICA ex COTENTIN (photo: Frank Heine)

ARMORIQUE (photo: Frank Lose)

12.4.2007 floated out / 9.11.2007 delivered / 26.11.2007–
29.9.2013 service Cherbourg—Poole, also Poole—
Santander / 11.2013 STENA BALTICA, Stena Line,
London / 24.11.2013 entered service Gdynia—Karlskrona /

ms ARMORIQUE
IMO No. 9364980
Brittany Ferries, Morlaix
STX Europe, Helsinki; Yard No.: 1362

29 468 GT / 4700 tdw / 168.37 m length oa /
26.80 m beam / two 12-cyl. diesels geared to
2 screws; MaK / 24 000 kW / 23 (25) kn / 788 pass.
in 248 cabins, 712 pass. unberthed / 235 cars,
985 lane metres / crew 120

7.8.2008 floated out / 26.1.2009 delivered / 10.2.2009
maiden voyage in service Roscoff—Plymouth /

ms **SUNFLOWER GOLD**
IMO No. 9376335
Diamond Ferry, Oita
Mitsubishi H.I., Shimonoseki; Yard No.: 1124

11 178 GRT / 4458 tdw / 165.50 m length oa /
27.00 m beam / two 12-cyl. diesels; JFE-Pielstick /
18 000 kW / 2 screws / 23.2 kn / 748 pass. in
219 cabins / 75 cars + 147 trucks (8 tons) /
crew 34

15.11.2007 delivered / 21.11.1997 entered service
Kobe—Oita /

SUNFLOWER GOLD (photo: Hiroyuki Yoshimoto)

SUNFLOWER PEARL (photo: Osamu Taniguchi)

ms **SUNFLOWER PEARL**
IMO No. 9376347
Diamond Ferry, Oita
Mitsubishi H.I., Shimonoseki; Yard No.: 1125

11 177 GRT / 4458 tdw / 165.50 m length oa /
27.00 m beam / two 12-cyl. diesels; JFE-Pielstick /
18 000 kW / 2 screws / 23.2 kn / 748 pass. in
219 cabins / 75 cars + 147 trucks (8 tons) /
crew 34

11.1.2008 delivered / 16.1.2008 entered service Oita—
Kobe /

SUPERSPEED 1 (photo: Frank Lose)

ms **SUPERSPEED 1**
IMO No. 9374519
Color Line, Kristiansand
Aker Yards, Rauma; Yard No.: 1359

34 231 GT / 5525 tdw / 212.80 m length oa /
25.80 m beam / four 9-cyl. diesels geared to
2 screws; Wärtsilä / 38 400 kW / 27 kn / 74 pass.
in 54 cabins, 1854 pass. unberthed / 860 cars,
2036 lane metres /

3.8.2007 floated out / 27.2.2008 delivered / 28.2.2008
maiden voyage in service Kristiansand—Hirtshals /
29.12.2010–29.1.2011 conversion at STX Finland,
Helsinki: 36 822 GT, 2315 pass. unberthed / 1.2.2011
again service Kristiansand—Hirtshals /

SUPERSPEED 2 (photo: Frank Lose)

ms **SUPERSPEED 2**
IMO No. 9378682
Color Line, Kristiansand
Aker Yards, Rauma; Yard No.: 1360

34 231 GT / 5525 tdw / 211.30 m length oa /
25.80 m beam / four 9-cyl. diesels geared to
2 screws; Wärtsilä / 38 400 kW / 27 kn / 74 pass.
in 54 cabins, 1854 pass. unberthed / 860 cars,
2036 lane metres /

20.1.2008 floated out / 5.6.2008 delivered / 16.6.2008
maiden voyage in service Larvik—Hirtshals /

ms CRUISE ROMA

IMO No. 9351476
Grimaldi Ferries, Palermo
Fincantieri, Castellammare di Stabia;
Yard No.: 6136

54 310 GT / 8381 tdw / 225.00 m length oa /
30.40 m beam / four 12-cyl. diesels geared to
2 screws; Wärtsilä / 55 440 kW / 27.5 (30.6) kn /
1912 pass. in 478 cabins, 231 pass. unberthed /
209 cars, 3060 lane metres / crew 157

22.6.2007 launched / 13.3.2008 delivered / 17.3.2008
maiden voyage in service Civitavecchia—Barcelona /
1.3.2009 entered service Civitavecchia—Porto
Torres—Barcelona /

CRUISE ROMA (photo: Frank Lose)

CRUISE BARCELONA (photo: Frank Lose)

ms CRUISE EUROPA

IMO No. 9351490
Grimaldi Ferries, Palermo
Fincantieri, Castellammare di Stabia;
Yard No.: 6138

54 919 GT / 8550 tdw / 225.00 m length oa /
30.40 m beam / four 12-cyl. diesels geared to
2 screws; Wärtsilä / 55 440 kW / 27.5 (30) kn /
1912 pass. in 478 cabins, 231 pass. unberthed /
209 cars, 3060 lane metres / crew 157

14.3.2009 launched / 9.10.2009 delivered / 15.10.2009
maiden voyage in service Patras—Igoumenitsa—Ancona
under charter by Minoan Lines / 10.12.2012 entered
service Patras—Igoumenitsa—Ancona—Trieste /

CRUISE EUROPA (photo: Frank Lose)

ms CRUISE BARCELONA

IMO No. 9351488
Grimaldi Ferries, Palermo
Fincantieri, Castellammare di Stabia;
Yard No.: 6137

54 310 GT / 8550 tdw / 225.00 m length oa /
30.40 m beam / four 12-cyl. diesels geared to
2 screws; Wärtsilä / 55 440 kW / 27.5 (30) kn /
1912 pass. in 478 cabins, 231 pass. unberthed /
209 cars, 3060 lane metres / crew 157

16.2.2008 launched / 2.9.2008 delivered / 6.9.2008
maiden voyage in service Civitavecchia—Barcelona /
1.3.2009 entered service Civitavecchia—Porto
Torres—Barcelona /

CRUISE OLYMPIA (photo: Frank Heine)

ms CRUISE OLYMPIA
IMO No. 9351505
Grimaldi Ferries, Palermo
Fincantieri, Castellammare di Stabia; Yard No. 6139

54310 GT / 8351 tdw / 225.00 m length oa /
30.40 m beam / four 12-cyl. diesels geared to
2 screws; Wärtsilä / 55440 kW / 27.5 (30) kn /
1912 pass. in 478 cabins, 231 pass. unberthed /
209 cars, 3060 lane metres / crew 157

14.11.2009 launched / 30.6.2010 delivered / 2.7.2010
maiden voyage in service Patras—Igoumenitsa—Ancona
under charter by Minoan Lines / 10.12.2012 entered
service Patras—Igoumenitsa—Ancona—Trieste /

ms VIKING XPRS
IMO No. 9375654
Viking Line, Mariehamn
Aker Finnyards, Helsinki; Yard No.: 1358

35778 GT / 4372 tdw / 185.70 m length oa /
27.70 m beam / four 8-cyl. diesels geared to
2 screws; Wärtsilä / 40000 kW / 25 (28) kn /
736 pass. in 238 cabins, 1764 pass. unberthed /
550 cars, 995 lane metres / crew 105

19.9.2007 floated out / 21.4.2008 delivered /
22.4.2008 home port Norrtälje / 28.4.2008 maiden
voyage in service Helsinki—Tallinn / 2009 in spring
installation of additional lounge on the aft deck:
35918 GT, 5184 tdw / 22.1.2014 home port Tallinn /

ms WAN RONG HAI
IMO No. 8741569
Dalian Wantong Ronghai Shipping, Dalian
Huanghai Shipbuilding, Rongcheng; Yard No.: K-04

11585 GT / 3252 tdw / 129.90 m length oa /
20.40 m beam / two 8-cyl. diesels geared to
2 screws; Daihatsu / 5000 kW / 15.7 kn /
900 pass. in 164 cabins, 200 pass. unberthed /
733 lane metres /

4.6.2008 delivered, then service Dalian—Yantai /

VIKING XPRS (photo: Marko Stampehl)

WAN RONG HAI (photo: Marko Stampehl)

WAN TONG HAI (photo: Marko Stampehl)

ms CELEBRITY SOLSTICE
IMO No. 9362530
Celebrity Cruises, Valletta
Meyer Werft, Papenburg; Yard No.: 675

121 878 GT / 9500 tdw / 317.19 m length oa /
36.79 (36.90) m beam / four 16-cyl. diesels with
67 200 kW; Wärtsilä / four generators connected to
two elec. motors / 41 000 kW / 2 Azipod VO /
24 (25) kn / 2850 (3420) pass. in 1425 cabins /
crew 1271

10.8.2008 floated out / 24.10.2008 delivered /
23.11.2008 maiden Caribbean cruise from Fort
Lauderdale /

ms DE YIN HAI (no photo)
IMO No. 8670148
Dalian Shipping, Dalian
Huanghai Shipbuilding, Rongcheng; Yard No.: K-10

11 585 GT / 3199 tdw / 129.40 m length oa /
20.40 m beam / two 8-cyl. diesels geared to
2 screws; Daihatsu / 5000 kW / 900 pass. in
164 cabins, 142 pass. unberthed / 155 cars,
733 lane metres / crew 67

10.2009 delivered, then service Dalian—Yantai /

ms WAN TONG HAI
IMO No. 9622497
Dalian Ronghai Shipping, Dalian
Huanghai Shipbuilding Co., Rongcheng;
Yard No.: K-07

24 105 GT / 7646 tdw / 163.95 m length oa /
25.00 m beam / two 12-cyl. diesels geared to
2 screws; Wärtsilä / 12 000 kW / 15.7 kn /
1650 pass. unberthed / 192 cars, 2000 lane metres /

19.6.2010 launched / 29.11.2010 delivered, then
service Dalian—Yantai /

GUNUNG DEMPO (photo: Jonathan Boonzaier)

CELEBRITY SOLSTICE (photo: Tony Davis)

ms GUNUNG DEMPO
IMO No. 9401324
P.T. Pelni, Palembang
Meyer Werft, Papenburg; Yard No.: 664

14 030 GT / 3650 tdw / 146.80 m length oa /
23.40 m beam / two 6-cyl. diesels geared to
2 screws; Caterpillar / 12 000 kW / 20 kn /
pass. 96 I., 1487 economy class (total 1583) /
crew 141

15.3.2008 floated out / 21.6.2008 delivered, then
deployed in passenger service between the islands
of Indonesia /

CELEBRITY EQUINOX (photo: George Koutsoukis)

Spain after air traffic was suspended all over Europe due to the eruption of the volcano Eyjafjallajökull in Iceland / 29.4.2010 maiden voyage from Southampton to Ireland /

ms CELEBRITY SILHOUETTE

IMO No. 9451094
Celebrity Cruises, Valletta
Meyer Werft, Papenburg; Yard No.: 679

122 210 GT / 9500 tdw / 319.00 m length oa / 36.80 m beam / four 14-cyl. diesels with 67 200 kW; MAN Diesel & Turbo / four generators connected to two elec. motors / 41 000 kW / 2 Azipod VO / 24 (25) kn / 2886 (3463) pass. in 1443 cabins / crew 1271

2.6.2011 floated out / 18.7.2011 delivered / 27.7.2011 maiden voyage from Hamburg to Civitavecchia /

ms CELEBRITY EQUINOX

IMO No. 9372456
Celebrity Cruises, Valletta
Meyer Werft, Papenburg; Yard No.: 676

121 878 GT / 9500 tdw / 317.20 m length oa / 36.80 m beam / four 16-cyl. diesels with 67 200 kW; Wärtsilä / four generators connected to two elec. motors / 41 000 kW / 2 Azipod VO / 24 (25) kn / 2850 (3420) pass. in 1425 cabins / crew 1271

6.6.2009 floated out / 16.7.2009 delivered / 31.7.2009 maiden voyage from Southampton to Norway /

28.2.2010 floated out / 16.4.2010 delivered / 20.4.–22.4.2010 round-trip Southampton—Bilbao for about 2000 British tourists, which were stranded in

CELEBRITY SILHOUETTE (photo: Marko Stampehl)

ms CELEBRITY ECLIPSE

IMO No. 9404314
Celebrity Cruises, Valletta
Meyer Werft, Papenburg; Yard No.: 677

121 878 GT / 9500 tdw / 317.14 m length oa / 36.80 m beam / four 16-cyl. diesels with 67 200 kW; Wärtsilä / four generators connected to two elec. motors / 41 000 kW / 2 Azipod VO / 24 (25) kn / 2850 (3420) pass. in 1425 cabins / crew 1271

CELEBRITY ECLIPSE (photo: Jürgen Pfarre)

ms CELEBRITY REFLECTION
IMO No. 9506459
Celebrity Cruises, Valletta
Meyer Werft, Papenburg; Yard No.: 691

125 366 GT / 9500 tdw / 319.00 m length oa /
37.40 m beam / two 14-cyl. and two 12-cyl. diesels
with 62 400 kW; MAN Diesel & Turbo /
four generators connected to two elec. motors /
35 000 kW / 2 Azipod XO / 23 (25) kn /
3046 (3655) pass. in 1523 cabins / crew 1271

11.8.2012 floated out / 9.10.2012 delivered /
12.10.2012 maiden voyage from Amsterdam to
Barcelona /

ms MSC FANTASIA
IMO No. 9359791
MSC Crociere, Panama
STX France Cruise, St. Nazaire; Yard No.: A33

137 936 GT / 15 000 tdw / 333.33 m length oa /
37.92 m beam / two 16-cyl. and three 12-cyl.
diesels with 71 400 kW; Wärtsilä / five generators
connected to two elec. motors / 40 400 kW /
2 screws / 22.3 (23.3) kn / 3247 (3959) pass. in
1637 cabins / crew 1332

8.2.2008 floated out / 11.12.2008 delivered /
20.12.2008 maiden Mediterranean cruise from
Genoa / 3.2011 after conversion at Fincantieri,
Palermo 4363 pass. (max.), crew 1370 /

ms MSC SPLENDIDA
IMO No. 9359806
MSC Crociere, Panama
STX France Cruise, St. Nazaire; Yard No.: B33

137 936 GT / 13 413 tdw / 333.33 m length oa /
37.92 m beam / two 16-cyl. and three 12-cyl.
diesels with 71 400 kW; Wärtsilä / five generators
connected to two elec. motors / 40 400 kW /
2 screws / 22.3 (23.3) kn / 3247 (3959) pass. in
1637 cabins / crew 1332

22.7.2008 floated out, originally planned as MSC
SERENATA / 2.7.2009 delivered / 4.7.2009 maiden
voyage from St. Nazaire to Toulon /

CELEBRITY REFLECTION (photo: George Koutsoukis)

MSC FANTASIA (photo: Frank Heine)

MSC SPLENDIDA (photo: Alexander Brede)

233

ms MSC DIVINA

IMO No. 9585285
MSC Crociere, Panama
STX France Cruise, St. Nazaire; Yard No.: U32

139 072 GT / 13 188 tdw / 333.33 m length oa /
37.92 m beam / two 16-cyl. and three 12-cyl.
diesels with 71 400 kW; Wärtsilä / five generators
connected to two elec. motors / 43 700 kW /
2 screws / 22.3 (23.7) kn / 3502 (4202) pass. in
1751 cabins / crew 1388

3.9.2011 floated out, originally planned as MSC
FANTASTICA / 16.5.2012 delivered / 27.5.2012 maiden
Mediterranean cruise from Genoa /

MSC DIVINA (photo: Egidio Ferrighi)

MSC PREZIOSA (photo: Frank Heine)

ms MSC PREZIOSA

IMO No. 9595321
MSC Crociere, Panama
STX France Cruise, St. Nazaire; Yard No.: X32

139 072 GT / 13 188 tdw / 333.33 m length oa /
37.92 m beam / two 16-cyl. and three 12-cyl.
diesels with 71 400 kW; Wärtsilä / five generators
connected to two elec. motors / 43 600 kW /
2 screws / 22.3 (23.7) kn / 3502 (4378) pass. in
1751 cabins / crew 1388

4.6.2010 ordered as PHOENICIA by General National
Maritime Transport Corporation (GNMTC), Tripolis /
6.2011 order cancelled by the shipyard as a result of
overdue payments after the outbreak of the Libyan
civil war / 25.2.2012 floated out / 13.3.2012 to MSC
Crociere / 14.3.2013 delivered and maiden voyage
from St. Nazaire to Genoa /

ms MARTIN I SOLER

IMO No. 9390367
Balearia, Santa Cruz de Tenerife
Astillero Barreras, Vigo; Yard No.: 1655

24 761 GT / 4370 tdw / 165.30 m length oa /
25.60 m beam / two 9-cyl. diesels geared to
2 screws; MaK / 18 000 kW / 21.4 (22) kn /
172 pass. in 46 cabins, 1028 pass. unberthed /
330 cars, 1720 lane metres / crew 36

5.6.2008 launched / 15.1.2009 delivered / 19.1.2009
maiden voyage in service Barcelona—Ibiza/Mahón /
17.2.2009 entered service Valencia—Palma de Mallorca /
10.2011 in winter service Algeciras—Tangier, in
summer service Palma de Mallorca/Ciutadella—
Alcudia—Barcelona /

MARTIN I SOLER (photo: Frank Lose)

NORTHERN EXPEDITION (photo: Scott Arkell)

ms NORTHERN EXPEDITION

IMO No. 9408413
BC Ferries, Victoria
Flensburger Schiffbau Gesellschaft, Flensburg;
Yard No.: 748

17 729 GT / 1853 tdw / 151.78 m length oa /
23.00 m beam / two 9-cyl. diesels geared to
2 screws; Caterpillar / 9000 kW / 20.5 kn /
110 pass. in 55 cabins, 490 pass. unberthed /
130 cars, 285 lane metres / crew 60

25.9.2008 launched / 30.1.2009 delivered / 18.5.2009
maiden voyage in service Port Hardy—Prince Rupert /

BO HAI ZHEN ZHU (photo: ShipPax Information)

ms BO HAI ZHEN ZHU

IMO No. 9508328
Shandong Bohai Ferry Co., Yantai
Huanghai Shipbuilding, Rongcheng; Yard No. K-05

24 024 GT / 7535 tdw / 163.90 m length oa /
25.00 m beam / two 12-cyl. diesels geared to
2 screws; MAN / 12 000 kW / 18.5 (19) kn /
1427 pass. in 267 cabins, 220 pass. unberthed /
200 cars, 2025 lane metres / crew 81

30.10.2008 launched / 17.4.2009 delivered, then
service Dalian—Yantai /

ms BO HAI YU ZHU

IMO No. 9508330
Shandong Bohai Ferry Co., Yantai
Huanghai Shipbuilding, Rongcheng; Yard No.: K-06

24 024 GT / 7535 tdw / 163.95 m length oa /
25.00 m beam / two 12-cyl. diesels geared to
2 screws; MAN B&W / 12 000 kW / 18.5 (19.2) kn /
1426 pass. in 268 cabins, 174 pass. unberthed /
1929 lane metres /

21.7.2009 delivered, then entered service Dalian—
Yantai /

BO HAI YU ZHU (photo: ShipPax Information)

BO HAI FEI ZHU (photo: owner/Shippax Information)

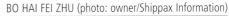

ms BO HAI FEI ZHU

IMO No. 9508366
Shandong Bohai Ferry Co., Yantai
Huanghai Shipbuilding, Rongcheng; Yard No.: K-09

24 024 GT / 7592 tdw / 163.95 m length oa /
25.00 m beam / two 12-cyl. diesels geared to
2 screws; MAN B&W / 12 000 kW / 18.5 (19.2) kn /
1426 pass. in 268 cabins, 174 pass. unberthed /
200 cars, 2006 lane metres /

5.2010 delivered / 1.6.2010 maiden voyage in service
Dalian—Yantai /

SEABOURN ODYSSEY (photo: George Koutsoukis)

ms SEABOURN ODYSSEY
IMO No. 9417086
Seabourn Cruise Line, Nassau
T. Mariotti, Genoa; Yard No.: 62

32 346 GT / 5000 tdw / 198.15 m length oa / 25.60 m beam / four 12-cyl. diesels with 23 040 kW; Wärtsilä / four generators connected to two elec. motors / 15 000 kW / 2 screws / 19 kn / 450 (540) pass. in 225 cabins / crew 335

27.5.2008 arrival of hull built by San Giorgio di Nogaro in Genoa for fitting out / 19.6.2009 delivered / 24.6.2009 maiden cruise from Venice / 2014 32 477 GT /

ms SEABOURN SOJOURN
IMO No. 9417098
Seabourn Cruise Line, Nassau
T. Mariotti, Genoa; Yard No.: 63

32 346 GT / 5000 tdw / 198.15 m length oa / 25.60 m beam / four 12-cyl. diesels with 23 040 kW; Wärtsilä / four generators connected to two elec. motors / 15 000 kW / 2 screws / 19 kn / 450 (540) pass. in 225 cabins / crew 335

7.2009 arrival of hull built by San Giorgio di Nogaro in Genoa for fitting out / 28.5.2010 delivered / 6.6.2010 maiden Baltic cruise from London /

SEABOURN SOJOURN (photo: Ulrich Streich)

ms SEABOURN QUEST
IMO No. 9483126
Seabourn Cruise Line, Nassau
T. Mariotti, Genoa; Yard No.: 64

32 346 GT / 5000 tdw / 198.15 m length oa / 25.60 m beam / four 12-cyl. diesels with 23 040 kW; Wärtsilä / four generators connected to two elec. motors / 15 000 kW / 2 screws / 19 kn / 450 (540) pass. in 225 cabins / crew 335

8.2010 arrival of hull built by San Giorgio di Nogaro in Genoa for fitting out / 31.5.2011 delivered / 24.6.2011 maiden cruise from Barcelona to Piraeus / 3.2014 32 477 GT /

SEABOURN QUEST (photo: Hans-Joachim Hellmann)

ms BO HAI BAO ZHU (no photo)
IMO No. 9508342
Shandong Bohai Ferry Co., Yantai
Huanghai Shipbuilding, Rongcheng; Yard No.: K-08

24 024 GT / 7618 tdw / 163.95 m length oa / 25.00 m beam / two 12-cyl. diesels geared to 2 screws; MAN B&W / 12 000 kW / 18.5 kn / 1426 pass. in 268 cabins, 174 pass. unberthed / 200 cars, 2006 lane metres /

18.10.2009 launched / 28.1.2010 delivered, then service Dalian—Yantai /

CARNIVAL DREAM (photo: Jürgen Pfarre)

ms CARNIVAL DREAM
IMO No. 9378474
Carnival Cruise Lines, Panama
Fincantieri; Monfalcone; Yard No.: 6151

128 251 GT / 13 815 tdw / 306.00 m length oa /
37.00 m beam / six 12-cyl. diesels with 75 600 kW;
Wärtsilä / six generators connected to two elec.
motors / 44 000 kW / 2 screws / 20 (22) kn / 3626
(4533) pass. in 1813 cabins / crew 1369

24.10.2008 floated out / 17.9.2009 delivered /
21.9.2009 maiden Mediterranean cruise from Venice /

ms CARNIVAL MAGIC
IMO No. 9378486
Carnival Cruise Lines, Panama
Fincantieri; Monfalcone; Yard No.: 6167

CARNIVAL MAGIC (photo: Marko Stampehl)

CARNIVAL BREEZE (photo: Andy Hernandez)

128 048 GT / 13 073 tdw / 306.00 m length oa /
37.00 m beam / six 12-cyl. diesels with 75 600 kW;
Wärtsilä / six generators connected to two
elec. motors / 44 000 kW / 2 screws / 20 (22) kn /
3690 (4428) pass. in 1845 cabins / crew 1386

27.8.2010 floated out / 27.4.2011 delivered / 1.5.2011
maiden Mediterranean cruise from Venice /

ms CARNIVAL BREEZE
IMO No. 9555723
Carnival Cruise Lines, Panama
Fincantieri; Monfalcone; Yard No.: 6201

128 052 GT / 10 250 tdw / 305.60 m length oa /
37.20 m beam / six 12-cyl. diesels with 75 600 kW;
Wärtsilä / six generators connected to two
elec. motors / 44 000 kW / 2 screws / 20 (22.5) kn /
3690 (4428) pass. in 1845 cabins / crew 1386

19.9.2011 floated out / 29.5.2012 delivered / 3.6.2012
maiden cruise from Venice to Barcelona /

COSTA DIADEMA (photo: Egidio Ferrighi)

ms COSTA DIADEMA
IMO No. 9636888
Costa Crociere, Genoa
Fincantieri; Marghera; Yard No.: 6203

133 019 GT / 11 118 tdw / 306.00 m length oa /
37.20 m beam / four 12-cyl. and two 8-cyl. diesels
with 67 200 kW; Wärtsilä / six generators connected
to two elec. motors / 42 000 kW / 2 screws /
20 (22.5) kn / 3772 (4526) pass. in 1886 cabins /
crew 1253

15.11.2013 floated out / 29.10.2014 delivered /
1.11.2014 maiden cruise from Trieste to Genoa /

OASIS OF THE SEAS (photo: Andy Hernandez)

ms OASIS OF THE SEAS
IMO No. 9383936
Royal Caribbean International, Nassau
STX Finland, Turku; Yard No.: 1363

225 282 GT / 15 000 tdw / 360.00 m length oa /
47.00 (60.50) m beam / three 16-cyl. and three
12-cyl. diesels with 88 200 kW; Wärtsilä /
six generators connected to three elec. motors /
60 000 kW / 3 Azipod VO / 22.6 kn / 5396 (6296)
pass. in 2698 cabins / crew 2150

21.11.2008 floated out / 28.10.2009 delivered /
1.12.2009 maiden Caribbean cruise from Fort
Lauderdale / 10.2014 after conversion at Keppel
Verolme, Rotterdam 5484 (6307) pass. in 2742 cabins /

ms ALLURE OF THE SEAS
IMO No. 9383948
Royal Caribbean International, Nassau
STX Finland, Turku; Yard No.: 1364

225 282 GT / 19 750 tdw / 360.00 m length oa /
47.00 (60.50) m beam / three 16-cyl. and three
12-cyl. diesels with 88 200 kW; Wärtsilä /
six generators connected to three elec. motors /
60 000 kW / 3 Azipod VO / 22.6 kn / 5404
(6215) pass. in 2702 cabins / crew 2150

20.11.2009 floated out / 28.10.2010 delivered /
1.12.2010 maiden Caribbean cruise from Fort
Lauderdale / 5.2015 after conversion at Navantia,
Cadiz 5490 (6314) pass. in 2745 cabins /

The sister ship HARMONY OF THE SEAS is due for
delivery by the shipyard STX France Cruise in 5.2016,
another sister ship being due for delivery in 2018.

ALLURE OF THE SEAS (photo: Frank Lose)

SILVER SPIRIT (photo: Kai Ortel)

ms SILVER SPIRIT
IMO No. 9437866
Silversea Cruises, Nassau
Fincantieri, Ancona; Yard No.: 6178

36 009 GT / 3882 tdw / 195.80 m length oa /
26.50 m beam / four 9-cyl. diesels with 26 100 kW;
Wärtsilä / four generators connected to two
elec. motors / 17 000 kW / 2 screws / 21.5 kn /
540 (648) pass. in 270 cabins / crew 376

27.2.2009 floated out / 12.12.2009 delivered /
23.12.2009 maiden voyage from Barcelona to Lisbon /

The sister ship SILVER MUSE is due for delivery in
4.2017.

ms ABEL MATUTES
IMO No. 9441130
Balearia, Valletta
Hijos de J. Barreras, Vigo; Yard No.: 1661

29 670 GT / 5300 tdw / 190.50 m length oa /
26.00 m beam / two 9-cyl. diesels geared to
2 screws; Caterpillar MAK / 18 006 kW /
21.4 (23) kn / 364 pass. in 92 cabins, 536 pass.
unberthed / 247 cars, 2238 lane metres /

15.4.2010 delivered, hull from Lisnave, Setubal, fitting
out at Estaleiros Navais de Viana do Castelo, final
fitting out at Barreras / 2.5.2010 maiden voyage in
service Palma de Mallorca—Ibiza—Valencia, also
service Palma de Mallorca—Barcelona / 3.2015 home
port Santa Cruz de Tenerife /

ABEL MATUTES (photo: Frank Lose)

VISEMAR ONE (photo: Frank Heine)

ms VISEMAR ONE
IMO No. 9498743
Visemar di Navigazione, Bari
Cantiere Navale Visentini, Porto Viro; Yard No.: 223

26 375 GT / 8702 tdw / 186.40 m length oa /
25.60 m beam / two 9-cyl. diesels geared to
2 screws; MAN B&W / 21 600 kW / 23.5 kn /
276 pass. in 70 cabins, 291 pass. unberthed /
2860 lane metres / crew 38

21.4.2010 delivered / 20.5.2010–5.6.2011 service
Venice—Tartous—Alexandria / 14.6.2011 entered
service Palma de Mallorca—Barcelona under charter
by Balearia /

CARTOUR DELTA (photo: Frank Lose)

ms CARTOUR DELTA
IMO No. 9539042
Caronte & Tourist, Bari
Cantiere Navale Visentini, Porto Viro; Yard No.: 227

26 375 GT / 8398 tdw / 186.60 m length oa /
25.60 m beam / two 9-cyl. diesels geared to
2 screws; MAN B&W / 21 600 kW / 23.5 (24.2) kn /
276 pass. in 70 cabins, 212 pass. unberthed /
74 cars, 2860 lane metres /

24.9.2010 delivered / 19.10.2010 entered service
Salerno—Messina /

ms CARTOUR EPSILON

IMO No. 9539054
Caronte & Tourist, Bari
Cantiere Navale Visentini, Porto Viro; Yard No.: 228

26 375 GT / 8615 tdw / 186.44 m length oa /
25.60 m beam / two 9-cyl. diesels geared to
2 screws; MAN B&W / 21 600 kW / 23.5 (24.1) kn /
276 pass. in 70 cabins, 212 pass. unberthed /
74 cars, 2860 lane metres /

5.2011 delivered / 3.5.2011 maiden voyage in service
Salerno—Termini Imerese / 20.11.2012 entered service
Termini Imerese—Civitavecchia / 21.6.–15.9.2013
service Genoa—Palermo under charter by Grandi Navi
Veloci / 17.12.2013 entered service Dublin—Holyhead
under charter by Irish Ferries / 18.1.2014 also one
weekly round voyage Dublin—Cherbourg / 2.2014
renamed EPSILON /

EPSILON ex CARTOUR EPSILON (photo: Frank Heine)

LE BOREAL (photo: Cees Bustraan)

ms LE BOREAL

IMO No. 9502506
Compagnie du Ponant, Mata-Utu
Fincantieri, Ancona; Yard No.: 6192

10 944 GT / 1400 tdw / 142.10 m length oa /
18.00 m beam / four 8-cyl. diesels with 6400 kW;
Wärtsilä / four generators connected to two
elec. motors / 4600 kW / 2 screws / 16 (17.4) kn /
264 pass. in 132 cabins / crew 146

1.10.2009 floated out / 27.4.2010 delivered / 6.5.2010
maiden Mediterranean cruise from Marseilles /

ms L'AUSTRAL

IMO No. 9502518
Compagnie du Ponant, Mata-Utu
Fincantieri, Ancona; Yard No.: 6193

10 944 GT / 1400 tdw / 142.10 m length oa /
18.00 m beam / four 8-cyl. diesels with 6400 kW;
Wärtsilä / four generators connected to two
elec. motors / 4600 kW / 2 screws / 16 (17.4) kn /
264 pass. in 132 cabins / crew 146

8.4.2010 floated out / 20.4.2011 delivered / 27.4.2011
maiden voyage from Marseilles to Lisbon /

L'AUSTRAL (photo: Mike Louagie)

ms LE SOLEAL

IMO No. 9641675
Compagnie du Ponant, Mata-Utu
Fincantieri, Ancona; Yard No.: 6229

10 992 GT / 1400 tdw / 142.10 m length oa /
18.00 m beam / four 8-cyl. diesels with 6400 kW;
Wärtsilä / four generators connected to two
elec. motors / 4600 kW / 2 screws / 16 (17.4) kn /
264 pass. in 132 cabins / crew 139

6.12.2012 floated out / 28.6.2013 delivered / 1.7.2013
maiden voyage from Venice to Barcelona /

ms LE LYRIAL

IMO No. 9704130
Compagnie du Ponant, Mata-Utu
Fincantieri, Ancona; Yard No.: 6230

10 992 GT / 1400 tdw / 142.10 m length oa /
18.00 m beam / four 8-cyl. diesels with 6400 kW;
Wärtsilä / four generators connected to two
elec. motors / 4600 kW / 2 screws / 16 (17.4) kn /
244 pass. in 122 cabins / crew 139

23.10.2014 floated out / 11.4.2015 delivered / 9.5.2015
maiden voyage Venice—Adriatic /

LE SOLEAL (photo: Mike Louagie)

LE LYRIAL (photo: George Koutsoukis)

ms STENA HOLLANDICA
IMO No. 9419163
Stena Line, Hoek van Holland
Nordic Yards, Wismar; Yard No.: 159

64039 GT / 11600 tdw / 240.87 m length oa /
32.00 (33.02) m beam / two 6-cyl. and two
8-cyl. diesels geared to 2 screws; MAN B&W /
33600 kW / 22.5 kn / 1376 pass. in 538 cabins /
230 cars, 5566 lane metres /

22.9.2008 keel-laying of fore ship at Nordic
Yards, Warnemünde, originally intended as STENA
BRITANNICA / 6.6.2009 floated out / 7.5.2010
delivered / 16.5.2010 maiden voyage in service Hoek
van Holland—Harwich /

STENA HOLLANDICA (photo: Marc Peper)

STENA BRITANNICA (photo: Frank Lose)

ms STENA BRITANNICA
IMO No. 9419175
Stena Line, London
Nordic Shipyards, Wismar; Yard No.: 164

64039 GT / 11600 tdw / 240.00 m length oa /
32.00 (33.02) m beam / two 6-cyl. and two
8-cyl. diesels geared to 2 screws; MAN B&W /
33600 kW / 22 kn / 1376 pass. in 538 cabins /
230 cars, 5566 lane metres /

24.4.2010 floated out, fore ship from Nordic Yards
Warnemünde, Rostock / 28.9.2010 delivered /
9.10.2010 maiden voyage in service Hoek van
Holland—Harwich / 11.11.2010 when the ship was
entering Hoek van Holland, the tug FAIRPLAY 22 called
for support capsized, two crew members killed /

NORWEGIAN EPIC (photo: Jürgen Pfarre)

ms NORWEGIAN EPIC
IMO No. 9410569
Norwegian Cruise Line, Nassau
STX France Cruise, St. Nazaire; Yard No.: C33

155873 GT / 10850 tdw / 329.45 m length oa /
40.64 m beam / three 16-cyl. and three 12-cyl.
diesels with 79800 kW; MaK / six generators
connected to two elec. motors / 48000 kW /
2 screws / 22.5 (24) kn / 4100 (5074) pass. in
2114 cabins / crew 1730

10.7.2009 floated out / 17.6.2010 delivered /
24.6.2010 maiden voyage Southampton—New York /

LONG XING DAO (photo: shipyard/ShipPax Information)

ms LONG XING DAO
IMO No. 9517317
China Shipping Gang Lian Maritme, Dalian
Guangzhou Shipyard International, Guangzhou;
Yard No.: 08130001

24572 GT / 7744 tdw / 167.50 m length oa /
25.20 m beam / two 12-cyl. diesels geared to
2 screws; Wärtsilä / 12000 kW / 19 kn / 1193 pass.
in 190 cabins, 207 pass. unberthed / 600 cars,
2045 lane metres /

12.2010 delivered, then service Dalian—Yantai /

DISNEY DREAM (photo: Tony Davis)

ms QING SHAN DAO (no photo)
IMO No. 9520285
China Shipping Passenger Liner, Dalian
Guangzhou Shipyard International, Guangzhou;
Yard No.: 08130003

24 572 GT / 7683 tdw / 167.50 m length oa /
25.20 m beam / two 12-cyl. diesels geared to
2 screws; Wärtsilä / 12 000 kW / 19 kn / 940 pass.
in 170 cabins, 460 pass. unberthed / 600 cars,
2052 lane metres / crew 71

12.2011 delivered / 12.1.2012 maiden voyage in
service Dalian—Yantai /

ms CHANG SHAN DAO (no photo)
IMO No. 9520297
China Shipping Passenger Liner, Dalian
Guangzhou Shipyard International, Guangzhou;
Yard No.: 08130004

24 572 GT / 7670 tdw / 167.50 m length oa /
25.20 m beam / two 12-cyl. diesels geared to
2 screws; Wärtsilä / 12 000 kW / 18.5 kn / 940 pass.
in 170 cabins, 460 pass. unberthed / 600 cars,
2000 lane metres / crew 71

5.2012 delivered / 18.7.2012 maiden voyage in service
Dalian—Yantai /

ms DISNEY DREAM
IMO No. 9434254
Disney Cruise Line, Nassau
Meyer Werft, Papenburg; Yard No.: 687

129 690 GT / 9800 tdw / 339.80 m length oa /
37.00 m beam / three 14-cyl. and two 12-cyl.
diesels with 76 800 kW; MAN Diesel & Turbo /
five generators connected to two elec. motors /
42 000 kW / 2 screws / 22 (23.5) kn / 2500
(3500) pass. in 1250 cabins / crew 1458

30.10.2010 floated out / 9.12.2010 delivered /
26.1.2011 maiden voyage Port Canaveral—Bahamas /

ms DISNEY FANTASY
IMO No. 9445590
Disney Cruise Line, Nassau
Meyer Werft, Papenburg; Yard No.: 688

129 750 GT / 9500 tdw / 339.80 m length oa /
37.00 m beam / three 14-cyl. and two 12-cyl.
diesels with 76 800 kW; MAN Diesel & Turbo /
five generators connected to two elec. motors /
42 000 kW / 2 screws / 22 (23.5) kn / 2500
(3500) pass. in 1250 cabins / crew 1458

8.1.2012 floated out / 9.2.2012 delivered / 31.3.2012
maiden voyage Port Canaveral—Caribbean /

DISNEY FANTASY (photo: Hans-Jürgen Amberg)

SPIRIT OF BRITAIN (photo: Frank Lose)

ms SPIRIT OF BRITAIN

IMO No. 9524231
P&O Ferries, Dover
STX Finland, Rauma; Yard No.: 1367

47 592 GT / 9500 tdw / 212.97 m length oa /
30.80 (31.40) m beam / four 7-cyl. diesels geared
to 2 screws; MAN B&W / 30 400 kW / 22 (25) kn /
2000 pass. unberthed / 194 cars, 2741 lane metres /

8.6.2010 floated out / 5.1.2011 delivered / 21.1.2011
maiden voyage in service Dover—Calais /

ms SPIRIT OF FRANCE

IMO No. 9533816
P&O Ferries, Dover
STX Finland, Rauma; Yard No.: 1368

47 592 GT / 9884 tdw / 212.00 m length oa /
30.80 (31.40) m beam / four 7-cyl. diesels geared
to 2 screws; MAN B&W / 30 400 kW / 22 (25) kn /
1750 pass. unberthed / 200 cars, 2700 lane metres /

17.2.2011 floated out / 24.1.2012 delivered / 9.2.2012
maiden voyage in service Dover—Calais /

SPIRIT OF FRANCE (photo: Frank Lose)

ms VOLCAN DEL TEIDE

IMO No. 9506289
Naviera Armas, Santa Cruz de Tenerife
Hijos de J. Barreras, Vigo; Yard No.: 1666

29 514 GT / 11 980 tdw / 175.70 m length oa /
26.40 m beam / four 7-cyl. diesels geared to
2 screws; MAN B&W / 33 600 kW / 24 (26) kn /
484 pass. in 124 cabins, 1016 pass. unberthed /
600 cars, 2010 lane metres /

26.7.2010 launched / 9.1.2011 delivered / 1.2011
service Santa Cruz de Tenerife—Las Palmas de Gran
Canaria / 31.3.2011 also service Las Palmas de Gran
Canaria—Huelva /

VOLCAN DEL TEIDE (photo: Frank Lose)

ms YUE HAI TIE 3 HAO (no photo)

IMO No. 9633111
Yuehai Railway Co., Haikou
Tianjin Xingang Shipbuilding Industry, Tianjin;
Yard No.: 2279

23 217 GT / 6557 tdw / 188.00 m length oa /
23.00 m beam / two 8-cyl. diesels geared to
2 screws; Guangzhou / 7104 kW / 17 kn /
1398 pass. / 1000 lane metres, 44 wagons /
crew 26

29.9.2010 launched / 11.01.2011 delivered, then
service Haikou—Hainan /

ms YUE HAI TIE 4 HAO (no photo)

IMO No. 9647538
Yuehai Railway Co., Haikou
Tianjin Xingang Shipbuilding Industry, Tianjin

23 217 GT / 6525 tdw / 188.00 m length oa /
23.00 m beam / two 8-cyl. diesels geared to
2 screws; Guangzhou / 7104 Kw / 17 kn /
1398 pass. / 1000 lane metres, 44 wagons /
crew 26

24.5.2011 delivered, then service Haikou—Hainan /

VOLCAN DE TINAMAR (photo: Frank Lose)

ms VOLCAN DE TINAMAR
IMO No. 9506291
Naviera Armas, Las Palmas de Canaria
Hijos de J. Barreras, Vigo; Yard No.: 1667

29 514 GT / 11 980 tdw / 175.70 m length oa /
26.40 m beam / four 7-cyl. diesels geared to
2 screws; MAN B&W / 33 600 kW / 24 (26) kn /
484 pass. in 124 cabins, 1016 pass. unberthed /
600 cars, 2010 lane metres /

21.1.2011 launched / 3.6.2011 delivered / 6.2011
service Las Palmas de Gran Canaria—Santa Cruz de
Tenerife—Funchal—Portimao / 28.5.2012 entered
service Mellila—Motril /

MARINA (photo: Mike Louagie)

ms MARINA
IMO No. 9438066
Oceania Cruises, Majuro
Fincantieri, Sestri Ponente; Yard No.: 6194

66 084 GT / 6000 tdw / 239.30 m length oa /
32.20 m beam / two 12-cyl. and two 8-cyl. diesels
with 42 000 kW; Wärtsilä / four generators
connected to two elec. motors / 24 000 kW /
2 screws / 20 (21.68) kn / 1258 (1447) pass. in
629 cabins / crew 780

26.2.2010 floated out / 15.1.2011 delivered /
22.1.2011 maiden voyage Barcelona—Miami /

RIVIERA (photo: Nikolaos Saratzis)

ms RIVIERA
IMO No. 9438078
Oceania Cruises, Majuro
Fincantieri, Sestri Ponente; Yard No.: 6195

66 172 GT / 7662 tdw / 239.30 m length oa /
32.20 m beam / two 12-cyl. and two 8-cyl. diesels
with 42 000 kW; Wärtsilä / four generators
connected to two elec. motors / 24 000 kW /
2 screws / 20 (21.68) kn / 1258 (1447) pass. in
629 cabins / crew 780

19.7.2011 floated out / 27.4.2012 delivered /
16.5.2012 maiden voyage Venice—Piraeus /

YONG XING DAO (photo: Marko Stampehl)

ms YONG XING DAO
IMO No. 9517329
China Shipping Gang Lian Maritime Co. Ltd.,
Dalian Guangzhou Shipyard International Co. Ltd.,
Guangzhou; Yard No.: 08130002

24 572 GT / 7662 tdw / 167.50 m length oa /
25.20 m beam / two 12-cyl. diesels geared to
2 screws; Wärtsilä / 12 000 kW / 18.5 kn /
940 pass. in 170 cabins, 440 pass. unberthed /
600 cars, 2052 lane metres / crew 71

3.2011 delivered, then service Dalian—Yantai /

ms ISHIKARI
IMO No. 9526655
Taiheiyo Ferry, Nagoya
Mitsubishi H.I., Shimonoseki; Yard No.: 1145

15 762 GRT / 6150 tdw / 199.90 m length oa /
27.00 m beam / two 16-cyl. diesels geared to
2 screws; Pielstick / 23 680 kW / 23 (26.5) kn /
783 pass. in 156 cabins / 96 cars, 2358 lane
metres / crew 73

26.8.2010 launched / 8.3.2011 delivered / 23.3.2011
maiden voyage as cargo ferry in service Tomakomai—Nagoya / 11.4.2011 entered service Nagoya—
Sendai—Tomakomai /

ISHIKARI (photo: Hiroyuki Yoshimoto)

ms LEONORA CHRISTINA
IMO No. 9557848
Danske Færger, Rønne
Austal Ships, Fremantle; Yard No.: 246

10 371 GT / 975 tdw / 112.60 m length oa /
26.20 (27.50) m beam / four 20 cyl. diesels geared
to 2 screws; MAN B&W / 36 000 kW / 4 waterjets /
40 kn / 1400 pass. unberthed / 359 cars,
300 lane metres / crew 35

28.1.2011 launched / 17.5.2011 delivered / 22.6.2011
maiden voyage in service Rønne—Ystad /

LEONORA CHRISTINA (photo: Ulrich Streich)

ms BLUE STAR DELOS
IMO No. 9565039
Blue Star Ferries, Piraeus
Daewoo Shipbuilding & Heavy Machinery, Okpo;
Yard No.: 7509

18 498 GT / 2775 tdw / 145.50 m length oa /
23.20 m beam / four 16-cyl. diesels geared to
2 screws; MAN B&W / 32 000 kW / 25.5 (26) kn /
118 pass. in 32 cabins, 2278 pass. unberthed /
431 cars, 600 lane metres / crew 87

18.10.2011 delivered / 15.11.2011 maiden voyage
in service Piraeus—Paros—Naxos—Ios—Santorini /

ms BLUE STAR PATMOS
IMO No. 9565041
Blue Star Ferries, Piraeus
Daewoo Shipbuilding & Heavy Machinery, Okpo;
Yard No.: 7510

18 498 GT / 2775 tdw / 145.90 m length oa /
23.20 m beam / four 16-cyl. diesels geared to
2 screws; MAN B&W / 32 000 kW / 25.5 kn /
330 pass. in 90 cabins, 2070 pass. unberthed /
427 cars, 600 lane metres / crew 87

12.6.2012 delivered / 10.7.2012 maiden voyage in
service Piraeus—Chios—Mytilene /

ms PIANA
IMO No. 9526332
Compagnie Meridionale Navigation, Marseilles
Brodosplit-Brodogradiliste Specijalnih Objekekata,
Split; Yard No.: 468

42 180 GT / 7569 tdw / 179.99 m length oa /
30.50 m beam / four 8-cyl. diesels geared to
2 screws; Wärtsilä / 38 400 kW / 21 (27.6) kn /
700 pass. in 200 cabins, 50 pass. unberthed /
2473 lane metres / crew 56

24.11.2010 launched / 13.12.2011 delivered /
26.12.2011 maiden voyage in service Marseilles—
Bastia /

BLUE STAR DELOS (photo: George Koutsoukis)

BLUE STAR PATMOS (photo: George Koutsoukis)

PIANA (photo: Frank Heine)

ms S.A. AGULHAS II

IMO No. 9577135
Republic of South Africa – Department of
Environmental Affairs, Cape Town
STX Finland Rauma Shipyard, Rauma;
Yard No.: 1369

12897 GT / 4780 tdw / 134.20 m length oa /
21.70 (22.00) m beam / four 6-cyl. diesels with
12000 kW; Wärtsilä / four generators connected
to two elec. motors / 9000 kW / 2 screws / 14 kn /
100 pass. in 46 cabins / crew 44

4.4.2012 delivered, then research voyages with
passengers to Antarctica /

ms SILVER PRINCESS

IMO No. 9597616
Kawasaki K.K., Hachinohe
Mitsubishi H.I., Shimonoseki; Yard No.: 1158

10536 GRT / 4724 tdw / 150.00 m length oa /
25.00 m beam / two 12-cyl. diesels geared to
2 screws; Pielstick / 18000 kW / 20.5 kn /
500 pass. in 176 cabins / 30 cars + 92 trucks
(8 tons) / crew 30

11.11.2011 launched / 5.4.2012 delivered / 8.4.2012
entered service Hachinohe—Tomakomai /

ms TANIT

IMO No. 9598579
Cotunav, La Goulette
Daewoo Shipbuilding & Marine Engineering, Okpo;
Yard No.: 7511

52645 GT / 6189 tdw / 210.00 m length oa /
30.00 (35.30) m beam / four 12-cyl. diesels with
56000 kW; MAN B&W / four generators connected
to two elec. motors / 2 screws / 27.50 (28.60) kn /
2400 pass. in 653 cabins, 800 pass. unberthed /
1060 cars, 1365 lane metres / crew 285

S.A. AGULHAS II (photo: Ian Shiffman)

SILVER PRINCESS (photo: Tsuyoshi Ishiyama)

TANIT (photo: Frank Lose)

26.11.2011 floated out / 25.5.2012 delivered / 21.6.2012 maiden voyage in service Tunis—Marseilles, also Tunis—Genoa /

ms SUZURAN
IMO No. 9606895
Shin Nihonkai Ferry, Otaru
Mitsubishi H.I., Nagasaki; Yard No.: 2276

17 382 GRT / 7891 tdw / 224.50 m length oa / 26.00 m beam / two 12-cyl. diesels with 17 400 kW; Wärtsilä / two generators connected to two elec. motors / 12 900 kW / 2 screws / 27.5 (29.4) kn / 613 pass. in 128 cabins / 58 cars + 158 trucks (8 tons) /

14.6.2012 delivered / 20.6.2012 entered service Tomakomai—Tsuruga /

ms SUISEN
IMO No. 9607057
Shin Nihonkai Ferry, Otobe
Mitsubishi H.I., Nagasaki; Yard No.: 2277

17 382 GRT / 7891 tdw / 224.50 m length oa / 26.00 m beam / two 12-cyl. diesels with 17 400 kW; Wärtsilä / two generators connected to two elec. motors / 12 900 kW / 2 screws / 27.5 (29.4) kn / 613 pass. in 128 cabins / 58 cars + 158 trucks (8 tons) /

1.7.2012 delivered / 1.7.2012 entered service Tomakomai—Tsuruga /

ms BO HAI CUI ZHU (no photo)
IMO No. 9584803
Shandong Bohai Ferry Co., Yantai
Huanghai Shipbuilding Co., Rongcheng; Yard No.: K-11

34 222 GT / 7587 tdw / 178.80 m length oa / 28.00 (28.60) m beam / two 16-cyl. diesels geared to 2 screws; MAN B&W / 16 000 kW / 20 kn / 2296 pass. / 2500 lane metres /

20.1.2012 launched / 5.7.2012 delivered / 8.8.2012 maiden voyage in service Yantai—Dalian /

ms BO HAI JING ZHU
IMO No. 9584815
Shandong Bohai Ferry Co., Yantai
Huanghai Shipbuilding Co., Rongcheng; Yard No.: K-12

34 222 GT / 7598 tdw / 178.81 m length oa / 28.00 (28.60) m beam / two 16-cyl. diesels geared to 2 screws; MAN B&W / 16 000 kW / 20 kn / 2296 pass. / 2500 lane metres /

18.6.2012 launched / 8.10.2012 delivered, then service Yantai—Dalian /

ms BO HAI ZUAN ZHU (no photo)
IMO No. 9713533
Shandong Bohai Ferry Co., Yantai
Huanghai Shipbuilding Co., Rongcheng

33 458 GT / 7481 tdw / 178.81 m length oa / 28.00 m beam / two 16-cyl. diesels geared to 2 screws; MAN B&W / 16 000 kW / 20 kn / 2296 pass. / 2500 lane metres /

12.9.2014 launched / 1.2015 delivered, then service Yantai—Dalian /

SUZURAN (photo: Hiroyuki Yoshimoto)

SUISEN (photo: Hiroyuki Yoshimoto)

BO HAI JING ZHU (photo: shipyard)

ms BO HAI MA ZHU (no photo)
IMO No. 9723461
Shandong Bohai Ferry Co., Yantai
Huanghai Shipbuilding Co., Rongcheng

33458 GT / 7503 tdw / 178.81 m length oa /
28.00 m beam / two 16-cyl. diesels geared to
2 screws; MAN B&W / 16000 kW / 20 kn /
2296 pass. / 2500 lane metres /

6.11.2014 launched / 3.2015 delivered, then service
Yantai—Dalian

VIKING GRACE (photo: Krzysztof Brzoza)

NORWEGIAN BREAKAWAY (photo: Frank Lose)

ms VIKING GRACE
IMO No. 9606900
Viking Line, Mariehamn
STX Finland, Turku; Yard No.: 1376

57565 GT / 6107 tdw / 213.00 m length oa /
31.80 (32.42) m beam / four 8-cyl. dual fuel diesels
with 30400 kW; Wärtsilä / four generators
connected to two elec. motors / 21000 kW /
2 screws / 21.8 kn / 2800 pass. in 880 cabins /
531 cars, 1275 lane metres / crew 200

10.8.2012 floated out / 10.1.2013 delivered /
15.1.2013 entered service Turku—Mariehamn—
Stockholm /

ms NORWEGIAN BREAKAWAY
IMO No. 9606912
Norwegian Cruise Line, Nassau
Meyer Werft, Papenburg; Yard No.: 678

145655 GT / 11000 tdw / 325.64 m length oa /
39.70 m beam / two 14-cyl. and two 12-cyl.
diesels with 62400 kW; MAN Diesel & Turbo /
four generators connected to two elec. motors /
35000 kW / 2 Azipod XO / 21.5 kn / 3957 (4819)
pass. in 2008 cabins / crew 1595

23.2.2013 floated out / 25.4.2013 delivered /
30.4.2013 maiden voyage Southampton—New York /

NORWEGIAN GETAWAY (photo: Andy Hernandez)

ms NORWEGIAN GETAWAY
IMO No. 9606924
Norwegian Cruise Line, Nassau
Meyer Werft, Papenburg; Yard No.: 692

145655 GT / 11110 tdw / 325.65 m length oa /
39.73 (44.39) m beam / two 14-cyl. and two 12-cyl.
diesels with 62400 kW; MAN Diesel & Turbo /
four generators connected to two elec. motors /
35000 kW / 2 Azipod XO / 21.5 kn / 3957 (4819)
pass. in 2008 cabins / crew 1595

2.11.2013 floated out / 10.1.2014 delivered / 16.1.2014
maiden voyage Southampton—New York /

ms NORWEGIAN ESCAPE

IMO No. 9677076
Norwegian Cruise Line, Nassau
Meyer Werft, Papenburg; Yard No.: 693

165 157 GT / 11 700 tdw / 325.90 m length oa /
41.40 (46.50) m beam / two 14-cyl. and three
12-cyl. diesels with 76 800 kW; MAN Diesel & Turbo /
five generators connected to two elec. motors /
39 000 kW / 2 Azipod XO / 21.5 kn / 4266 (5218)
pass. in 2174 cabins / crew 1750

15.8.2015 floated out / 22.10.2015 delivered /
25.10.2015 maiden voyage Hamburg—Southampton /
9.11.2015 christened in Miami, then Caribbean cruises /

Three sister ships are due for delivery in spring 2017/
spring 2018/autumn 2019.

NORWEGIAN ESCAPE (photo: Marko Stampehl)

ms EUROPA 2

IMO No. 9616230
Hapag-Lloyd Kreuzfahrten, Valletta
STX France Cruise, St. Nazaire; Yard No.: H33

42 830 GT / 5285 tdw / 225.62 m length oa /
26.70 m beam / four 6-cyl. diesels with 18 000 kW;
MaK / four generators connected to two
elec. motors / 14 500 kW / 2 Mermaid pods /
18 (21.4) kn / 516 pass. in 258 cabins / crew 375

6.7.2012 floated out / 26.4.2013 delivered to Omison
S.A. / 11.5.2013 maiden voyage Hamburg—Lisbon
under charter by Hapag-Lloyd Kreuzfahrten / 1.2015
to Hapag-Lloyd Kreuzfahrten /

ms SHENG SHENG 2 (no photo)

IMO No. 8673293
Weihai Haida Passenger, Weihai
Huanghai Shipbuilding Co., Rongcheng

20 472 GT / 5493 tdw / 165.00 m length oa /
24.00 m beam / two 9-cyl. diesels; MAN /
2160 pass. / 320 cars, 1100 lane metres /

5.2013 delivered, then service Weihai—Dalian /

EUROPA 2 (photo: Peter Knego)

ROYAL PRINCESS (photo: Raoul Fiebig)

ms ROYAL PRINCESS

IMO No. 9584712
Princess Cruises, Hamilton
Fincantieri, Monfalcone; Yard No.: 6223

142 714 GT / 12 512 tdw / 330.00 m length oa /
38.40 m beam / two 14-cyl. and two 12-cyl.
diesels with 62 000 kW; Wärtsilä / four generators
connected to two elec. motors / 36 000 kW /
2 screws / 22.5 kn / 3560 (4272) pass. in 1780
cabins / crew 1350

16.8.2012 floated out / 30.5.2013 delivered / 16.6.2013
maiden voyage Southampton—Mediterranean /

REGAL PRINCESS (photo: Hans-Joachim Hellmann)

14.2.2014 floated out / 22.2.2015 delivered / 14.3.2015 maiden voyage Southampton—Mediterranean /

The sister ship **MAJESTIC PRINCESS** for Princess Cruises is due for delivery in 2017, another ship in late 2019.

ms STAVANGERFJORD
IMO No. 9586605
Fjord Line, Hirtshals
Bergen Group Fosen, Rissa; Yard No.: 87

31 678 GT / 3620 tdw / 170.00 m length oa /
27.50 m beam / four 12-cyl. diesels; Rolls Royce
Bergen / 21 600 kW / 2 screws / 21.5 kn /
1181 pass. in 303 cabins, 99 pass. unberthed /
600 cars, 1366 lane metres / crew 100

12.4.2012 launched at Gdansk Shipyard, Gdansk /
20.6.2013 delivered / 15.7.2013 maiden voyage in
service Bergen—Stavanger—Hirtshals—Langesund /

ms REGAL PRINCESS
IMO No. 9584724
Princess Cruises, Hamilton
Fincantieri, Monfalcone; Yard No.: 6224

142 714 GT / 12 193 tdw / 330.00 m length oa /
38.40 m beam / two 14-cyl. and two 12-cyl. diesels
with 62 000 kW; Wärtsilä / four generators
connected to two elec. motors / 36 000 kW /
2 screws / 22.5 kn / 3560 (4272) pass. in 1780
cabins / crew 1350

26.3.2013 floated out / 11.5.2014 delivered / 20.5.2014
maiden voyage Venice—Mediterranean /

ms BRITANNIA
IMO No. 9614036
P&O Cruises, Southampton
Fincantieri, Monfalcone; Yard No.: 6231

143 730 GT / 10 500 tdw / 330.00 m length oa /
38.40 m beam / two 14-cyl. and two 12-cyl.
diesels with 62 000 kW; Wärtsilä / four generators
connected to two elec. motors / 36 000 kW /
2 screws / 22.5 kn / 3645 (4406) pass. in
1836 cabins / crew 1398

BRITANNIA (photo: Micke Asklander)

STAVANGERFJORD (photo: Frank Lose)

BERGENSFJORD (photo: Frank Lose)

ms BERGENSFJORD
IMO No. 9586617
Fjord Line, Hirtshals
Bergen Group Fosen, Rissa; Yard No.: 88

31678 GT / 3900 tdw / 170.00 m length oa /
27.48 m beam / four 12-cyl. diesels; Rolls Royce
Bergen / 20000 kW / 2 screws / 21.5 kn /
1180 pass. in 303 cabins, 320 pass. unberthed /
600 cars, 1350 lane metres / crew 100

1.3.2013 launched at Gdansk Shipyard, Gdansk /
3.2.2014 delivered / 9.3.2014 maiden voyage in
service Bergen—Stavanger—Hirtshals—Langesund /

ms NOVA STAR
IMO No. 9462067
Singapore Technologies Marines (ST Marine), Nassau
ST Marine, Singapore; Yard No.: BOA19

27744 GT / 4145 tdw / 161.00 m length oa /
25.60 (26.20) m beam / four 10 cyl. diesels geared
to 2 screws; MAN / 22400 kW / 19 (22) kn /
648 pass. in 160 cabins, 567 pass. unberthed /
200 cars, 1500 lane metres / crew 85

8.10.2009 launched as **NORMAN LEADER** for LD
Lines, planned for service Le Havre—Portsmouth /
18.11.2011 order cancelled owing to long delay and
insufficient capacity / 3.2014 delivered as **NOVA STAR** /
15.05.2014 entered service Portland—Yarmouth under
charter by Nova Ferries / 15.11.2014 laid up for winter
in Shelbourne / 19.1.2015 transferred to Charleston /
1.6.—13.10.2015 service Portland—Yarmouth, then
laid up / 30.10.2015 arrested in Portland / 13.12.2015
laid up in Freeport /

NOVA STAR (photo: Marko Stampehl)

ms MEIN SCHIFF 3
IMO No. 9641730
TUI Cruises, Valletta
STX Finland, Turku; Yard No.: 1383

99526 GT / 7900 tdw / 293.20 m length oa /
35.80 (42.20) m beam / two 12-cyl. and two 8-cyl.
diesels with 48000 kW; Wärtsilä / four generators
connected to two elec. motors / 28000 kW /
2 screws / 21.7 kn / 2506 (2790) pass. in
1253 cabins / crew 1000

7.11.2013 floated out / 22.5.2014 delivered / 13.6.2014
maiden voyage Hamburg—Palma de Mallorca /

MEIN SCHIFF 3 (photo: Frank Lose)

ms MEIN SCHIFF 4
IMO No. 9678408
TUI Cruises, Valletta
Meyer Turku, Turku; Yard No.: 1384

99 526 GT / 7900 tdw / 293.20 m length oa /
35.80 (42.30) m beam / two 12-cyl. and two 8-cyl.
diesels with 48 000 kW; Wärtsilä / four generators
connected to two elec. motors / 28 000 kW /
2 screws / 21.7 kn / 2506 (2790) pass. in
1253 cabins / crew 1000

10.10.2014 floated out / 8.5.2015 delivered / 6.6.2015
maiden voyage Kiel—Baltic /

Sister ships **MEIN SCHIFF 5** due for delivery in 7.2016,
MEIN SCHIFF 6 in 2017, **MEIN SCHIFF 7** in 2018 and
MEIN SCHIFF 8 in 2019.

MEIN SCHIFF 4 (photo: Krzysztof Brzoza)

QUANTUM OF THE SEAS (photo: Hans-Joachim Hellmann)

ANTHEM OF THE SEAS (photo: Hans-Joachim Hellmann)

ms QUANTUM OF THE SEAS
IMO No. 9549463
Royal Caribbean International, Nassau
Meyer Werft, Papenburg; Yard No.: 697

168 666 GT / 12 000 tdw / 347.08 m length oa /
41.40 (49.47) m beam / two 16-cyl. and two 12-cyl.
diesels with 67 200 kW; Wärtsilä / four generators
connected to two elec. motors / 41 000 kW /
2 Azipod XO / 22 kn / 4162 (4819) pass. in
2095 cabins / crew 1550

13.8.2014 floated out / 28.10.2014 delivered / 2.11.2014
maiden voyage Southampton—Bayonne /

ms ANTHEM OF THE SEAS
IMO No. 9656101
Royal Caribbean International, Nassau
Meyer Werft, Papenburg; Yard No.: 698

168 666 GT / 12 000 tdw / 347.08 m length oa /
41.40 m beam / two 16-cyl. and two 12-cyl.
diesels with 67 200 kW; Wärtsilä / four generators
connected to two elec. motors / 41 000 kW /
2 Azipod XO / 22 kn / 4162 (4819) pass. in
2095 cabins / crew 1550

SAN SHA 1 HAO (photo: Knud E. Hansen)

21.2.2015 floated out / 10.4.2015 delivered / 22.4.2015 maiden voyage Southampton—Western Europe /

The sister ship **OVATION OF THE SEAS** is due for delivery in 4.2016, further sister ships in spring 2019 and autumn 2020.

ms **SAN SHA 1 HAO**
IMO No. 9722883
CS Marine
Bo Hai Shipyard, Huludao;
Yard No.: BH423–1

12 545 GT / 2495 tdw / 122.30 m length oa / 21.00 m beam / two 9-cyl. diesels; MAN / 2 screws / 18 kn / 444 pass. in 145 cabins / 350 lane metres / crew 81

12.2014 delivered / 1.1.2015 maiden voyage in service Hainan—Sansha /

ms **LIU LIAN LING** (no photo)
IMO No. 9738442
Hainan Strait Shipping Co.
Taizhou Kouan Shipyard, Taizhou; Yard No.: TK0514

10 982 GT / 2555 tdw / 123.90 m length oa / 20.50 m beam / diesel / 999 pass. /

15.12.2014 delivered, then service Haikou—Hainan /

ms **HAI TANG WAN** (no photo)
IMO No. 9756406
Hainan Strait Shipping Co.

10 124 GT / 2773 tdw /

12.2014 delivered, then service Haikou—Hainan /

IZUMI (photo: Osamu Taniguchi)

ms **IZUMI**
IMO No. 9726906
Hankyu Ferry, Kobe
Misubishi Heavy Industries, Shimonoseki;
Yard No.: 1177

15 897 GRT / 6756 tdw / 195.00 m length oa / 29.60 m beam / two 12-cyl. diesels; Wärtsilä / 17 400 kW / 23,5 kn / 366 pass. in 172 cabins / 188 cars / 1800 lane metres / 35 crew

31.7.2014 launched / 15.1.2015 delivered / 22.1.2015 maiden voyage in service Izumiotsu—Shin Moji /

HIBIKI (photo: Osamu Taniguchi)

ms **HIBIKI**
IMO No. 9726786
Hankyu Ferry, Kobe
Misubishi Heavy Industries, Shimonoseki;
Yard No.: 1178

15 897 GRT / 6756 tdw / 195.00 m length oa / 29.60 m beam / two 12-cyl. diesels; Wärtsilä / 17 400 kW / 23,5 kn / 366 pass. in 172 cabins / 188 cars / 1800 lane metres / 35 crew

25.11.2015 launched / 16.4.2015 delivered / 21.4.2015 maiden voyage in service Izumiotsu—Shin Moji /

ms F.-A.-GAUTHIER
IMO No. 9669861
Societe des Traversiers du Quebec, Quebec
Fincantieri, Castellammare di Stabia; Yard No.: 6239

15 901 GT / 3000 tdw / 133.20 m length oa /
22.40 m beam / four 12-cyl. dual fuel diesels;
Wärtsilä / 20 880 kW / 2 screws / 20 kn / 800 pass.
unberthed / 180 cars / crew 22

28.6.2014 launched / 1.4.2015 delivered / 13.7.2015
maiden voyage in service Matane—Baie Comeau/
Godbout /

ms VIKING STAR
IMO No. 9650418
Viking Ocean Cruises, Bergen
Fincantieri, Marghera; Yard No.: 6236

47 842 GT / 3640 tdw / 227.20 m length oa /
28.80 m beam / two 12-cyl. and two 9-cyl.
diesels with 23 520 kW; MAN Diesel & Turbo /
four generators connected to two elec. motors /
14 500 kW / 2 screws / 20 kn / 930 pass. in
465 cabins / crew 465

23.6.2014 floated out / 28.3.2015 delivered /
11.4.2015 maiden voyage Istanbul—Venice /

The sister ships **VIKING SEA** and **VIKING SKY** are due
for delivery in 3.2016 and 2.2017, two further sister
ships are due for delivery in mid-2018 and end-2020,
a further ship is ordered with no delivery date set yet.

ms FERRY OSAKA II
IMO No. 9726932
Meimon Taiyo Ferry, Osaka
Mitsubishi H.I., Shimonoseki; Yard No. 1182

14 920 GRT / 5600 tdw / 183.00 m length oa /
27.00 m beam / two 12-cyl. diesels / 14 000 kW /
23.2 kn / 713 pass. in cabins / 105 cars +
146 trucks (12 tons) /

23.3.2015 launched / 9.2015 delivered / 16.9.2015
maiden voyage in service Osaka—Shin Moji /

F.-A.-GAUTHIER (photo: shipyard)

VIKING STAR (photo: Alexander Brede)

FERRY OSAKA II (photo: Osamu Taniguchi)

FERRY KITAKYUSHU 2 (photo: Osamu Taniguchi)

ms AIDAPRIMA
IMO No. 9636955
AIDA Cruises, Genoa
Mitsubishi H.I., Nagasaki; Yard No.: 2300

116 500 GT / 9200 tdw / 300.00 m length oa /
37.60 m beam / three 12-cyl. diesels and one
12-cyl. dual fuel diesel with 43 200 kW; MaK /
four generators connected to two elec. motors /
28 000 kW / 2 Azipod XO / 16.0 (21.5) kn /
3286 (3500) pass. in 1643 cabins / crew 900

3.4.2014 floated out / 2016 delivery planned /

A sister ship was due to be delivered in 3.2016, but
delivery will be significantly delayed.

ms FERRY KITAKYUSHU II
IMO No. 9726982
Meimon Taiyo Ferry, Osaka
Mitsubishi H.I., Shimonoseki; Yard No. 1183

14 920 GRT / 5600 tdw / 183.00 m length oa /
27.00 m beam / two 12-cyl. diesels / 14 000 kW /
23.2 kn / 713 pass. / 105 cars + 146 trucks (12 tons) /

2.7.2015 launched / 11.2015 delivered / 29.11.2015
maiden voyage in service Osaka—Shin Moji /

ms ARANUI 5
IMO No. 9677492
Compagnie Polynesienne de Transport Maritime,
Papeete
Huanghai Shipbuilding Co., Rongcheng; Yard No.: K-19

11 468 GT / 3300 tdw / 126.10 m length oa /
22.20 m beam / two 8-cyl. diesels; MaK /
8000 kW / 2 screws / 15 kn / 206 (254) pass.
in 103 cabins / crew 104

8.2.2015 launched / 16.10.2015 delivered / 23.10.2015
transfer from Rongcheng to Papeete / 12.12.2015
entered liner service Papeete—Fakarava—Nuku
Hiva—Ua Pou—Tahuata—Hiva Oa—Fatu Hiva—Hiva
Oa—Ua Huka—Nuku Hiva—Ua Pou—Rangiroa—
Bora Bora—Papeete /

AIDAPRIMA (photo: Vladimir Tonic)

ARANUI 5 (photo: owner)

ms BERLIN
IMO No. 9587855
Scandlines, Gedser
Fayard, Odense; Yard No.: 502

25 527 GT / 4200 tdw / 169.50 m length oa /
24.80 m beam / two 9-cyl. diesels; MAK /
15 800 kW / 20.5 kn / 1300 pass. unberthed /
480 cars, 1600 lane metres /

1.12.2011 floated out / 27.11.2012 after numerous
technical problems, the order was cancelled at
the insolvent P&S Werft in Stralsund. The ship was
planned for the service Rostock—Gedser with delivery
5.2012 / 12.2012 home port Stralsund / 12.3.2014 to
Scandlines, Gedser / 16.5.2014 towed from Stralsund
to Blohm+Voss, Hamburg / 16.7.2014 towed from
Hamburg to Fayard, Odense for conversion / 2016
delivery planned, home port Rostock / 2016 service
Rostock—Gedser planned /

BERLIN (photo: Peter Therkildsen)

ms COPENHAGEN
IMO No. 9587867
Scandlines, Gedser
Fayard, Odense; Yard No.: 503

25 000 GT / 4200 tdw / 169.50 m length oa /
24.80 m beam / two 9-cyl. diesels; MAK /
15 800 kW / 20.5 kn / 1300 pass. unberthed /
480 cars, 1600 lane metres /

4.4.2012 floated out / 27.11.2012 after numerous
technical problems, the order was cancelled at
the insolvent P&S Werft in Stralsund. The ship was
envi-saged for the service Rostock—Gedser with
delivery 5.2012 / 12.3.2014 to Scandlines, Gedser /
3.6.2014 towed from Stralsund to Blohm+Voss,
Hamburg / 16.7.2014 towed from Hamburg to Fayard,
Odense for conversion / 2016 delivery planned / 2016
service Rostock—Gedser planned /

COPENHAGEN (photo: Peter Therkildsen)

Appendix 1
Cargo ferries and temporary passenger ships

The vessels are presented in chronological order.

ms SVEALAND
IMO No. 7128332
Rederi AB Svea, Helsingborg
Helsingør Skibsværft og Maskinbyggeri, Helsingør;
Yard No.: 397

3987 GRT / 4100 tdw / 118.01 m length oa /
20.90 m beam / four 9-cyl. diesels geared to
2 screws; Ruston-Paxman diesel / 10000 bhp /
18.5 kn / 36 pass. in cabins / 600 lane metres /

17.11.1971 launched / 11.3.1972 delivered / 17.3.1972
entered service Travemünde—Copenhagen—Helsingborg for Trave Line / 10.1976 service Malmö—Travemünde
under charter by Saga Linjen / 1.1.1981 entered service
Travemünde—Trelleborg under charter by TT-Saga-
Line / 28.12.1982 to Svenska Lastbil, Helsingborg /
9.1984 lengthening by Fosen Mek. Verksted, Trondheim:
13893 GT, 2635 tdw, 154.41 m length oa, four 8-cyl.
diesels geared to 2 screws; Krupp-MaK, 10000 bhp,
18 kn, 77 pass. in cabins, 1270 lane metres / 10.9.1984
renamed SAGA WIND / 22.9.1984 again service Travemünde—Trelleborg under charter by TT-Saga-Line /
8.12.1986 to AB Swedcarrier, Helsingborg / 12.1986
conversion at Seebeck, Bremerhaven: 14422 GT, 4166
tdw, 140 pass. / 29.1.–18.4.1989 conversion into rail
ferry at Blohm+Voss, Hamburg: 15879 GT, 2635 tdw,
363 pass. in 102 cabins, 60 cars, 1270 lane metres, 4
rail tracks with 550 m length, 26 wagons, renamed SEA
WIND / 21.4.1989 entered service Turku—Stockholm
under charter by Sea Wind Line, home port Stockholm /
20.1.1993 to Sea Wind Line, Stockholm / 5.3.1997
grounded in the Stockholm archipelago, 107 pass.
evacuated / 6.3.1997 refloated under own power, then
to Turku for a four-week repair / 1.7.1999 entered
service Stockholm—Långnäs—Turku / 1.1.2008 cargo
ferry service Stockholm—Turku / 8.9.2008 to Tallink,
Stockholm / 2.12.2008 On a voyage from Turku to
Stockholm caught fire in the engine room it the Åland
archipelago. Extinguished after an hour, then repair in
Turku / 8.1.2009 back in service Turku—Stockholm /
1.1.2012 transport of rail cars ceased / 21.12.2014
last voyage in service Turku—Stockholm / 7.1.2015
home port Tallinn / 8.1.2015 entered service Helsinki—
Tallinn /

ms BAYARD
IMO No. 7382366
Fred. Olsen, Oslo
Ankerløkken Verft, Florø; Yard No.: 99

3974 GRT / 5650 tdw / 136.91 m length oa /
20.99 m beam / two 12-cyl. diesels; Pielstick /
12000 bhp / 2 screws / 18.5 kn / 12 pass.
in cabins / 1724 lane metres /

9.1974 launched / 1.1975 delivered, then North Sea
ferry services from Norway / 1981 lengthening at

Frederikshavn Værft: 5722 GRT, 10320 tdw, 167.52 m
length oa, 1724 lane metres / 1987 ISOLA DELLE
STELLE, Sardegna Compagnia di Navigazione, Cagliari;
154 pass. in cabins, then service Livorno—Olbia / 1996

12618 GT, service Piombino—Olbia / 2004 service
Livorno—Olbia / 1.2007 GIUSEPPE SA., Moby Lines
Cargo, Cagliari, then service Livorno—Olbia, also
Piombino—Olbia /

SEA WIND ex SVEALAND (photo: Jukka Huotari)

GIUSEPPE SA. ex BAYARD (photo: Rob de Visser)

LUIGI PA. ex BOHEMUND (photo: Frank Lose)

27.2.1975 launched / 6.1975 delivered, then North
Sea ferry services from Norway / 1981 lengthening at
Frederikshavn Værft: 5722 GRT, 10 320 tdw, 167.52 m
length oa, 1724 lane metres / 1987 **ISOLA DELLE
PERLE**, Sardegna Compagnia di Navigazione, Cagliari;
154 pass. in cabins, then service Livorno—Olbia /
1996 12 804 GT, service Piombino—Olbia / 2004
service Livorno—Olbia / 1.2007 **LUIGI PA.**, Moby
Lines Cargo, Cagliari, then service Livorno—Olbia,
also Piombino—Olbia /

ms BOHEMUND
IMO No. 7382378
Fred. Olsen, Oslo
Ankerløkken Verft, Florø; Yard No.: 100

3974 GRT / 5650 tdw / 136.91 m length oa /
20.99 m beam / two 12-cyl. diesels; Pielstick /
12 000 bhp / 18.5 kn / 12 pass. in cabins /
1440 lane metres /

ms ROSTOCK
IMO No. 7527887
Deutsche Reichsbahn, Saßnitz
Bergens Mek. Verksted., Bergen; Yard No.: 779

6111 GRT / 3132 tdw / 158.35 m length oa /
21.63 (22.60) m beam / four 8-cyl. diesels geared to
2 screws; MAN B&W / 9680 bhp / 18 kn / 36 pass.
in cabins, 34 pass. unberthed / 1275 lane metres,
5 rail tracks with 606 m length /

7.3.1977 launched / 7.1977 delivered / 25.7.1977
maiden voyage in service Saßnitz—Trelleborg / 1.1993
to DFO Deutsche Fährgesellschaft Ostsee, Rostock /
1.3.1993 start of conversion at Neptun Industrie,
Rostock: 13 788 GT, 400 pass. unberthed / 8.4.1993
back in service / 6.1994 service Rostock—Trelleborg /
2.1999 **STAR WIND**, SeaWind Line, Stockholm /
5.1999 service Stockholm—Turku / 17.10.2002
entered service Helsinki—Tallinn / 5.–8.2005 service
Stockholm—Turku / 10.2005 **VIRONIA**, Euro Shipping,
Tallinn / 21.3.2006-18.10.2007 service Kotka—
Sillamäe / 6.11.2007 **KOPERNIK**, Unity Line, Szczecin /
3.4.2008 entered service Swinoujscie—Ystad /

KOPERNIK ex ROSTOCK (photo: Frank Lose)

ms ALPHA ENTERPRISE
IMO No. 7528635
Stena Line, London
Hyundai H.I., Ulsan; Yard No.: 649

5466 GRT / 8672 tdw / 151.01 m length oa /
21.67 m beam / two 12-cyl. diesels geared to
2 screws; Pielstick-Nippon / 11 480 kW / 17 kn /
12 pass. in cabins /

1.2.1978 launched / 31.5.1978 delivered as cargo
ferry, then worldwide cargo services under charter
by Arghiris Lines / 15.5.–14.7.1979 heightened by
one deck at Lloyd Werft, Bremerhaven: 6455 GRT,
8704 tdw, 25.28 m beam, 144 pass. in cabins /
9.1979 renamed **SYRIA**, service Volos—Tartous
under charter by Hellas Ferries / 15.11.–23.12.1981
lengthened at Lloyd Werft, Bremerhaven: 8596 GRT,
8794 tdw, 184.61 m length oa, 210 pass. in cabins /
5.1982–4.1983 service Felixstowe—Rotterdam
under charter by European Ferries / 1983 **STENA
TRANSPORTER**, Stena Line, Gothenburg / 1985
renamed **CERDIC FERRY**, service Felixstowe—
Rotterdam under charter by European Ferries /
22.10.1987 now under charter by P&O European
Ferries / 3.1.1992 renamed **EUROPEAN FREEWAY** /
4.1994 to P&O European Ferries, London; 21 162 GT,
180 pass. in 45 cabins / 2001 166 pass. in 45
cabins / 1.8.2002 **FREEWAY**, Stena Line, London,
service Rotterdam—Felixstowe / 15.9.2002 entered
service Rotterdam—Harwich / 2003 renamed **STENA
PARTNER** / 19.12.2010 last voyage in service
Harwich—Rotterdam / 21.12.2010 **SEA PARTNER**,
Brax Shipholding, London / 24.2.2011 entered service
Illichivsk—Istanbul under charter by Sea Lines /
11.2012 home port Panama / 12.2012 now under
charter by Stena Sea Line /

SEA PARTNER ex ALPHA ENTERPRISE (photo: Olaf Kuhnke)

ms MERZARIO ESPANIA

IMO No. 7528659
Stena Line, London
Hyundai H.I., Ulsan; Yard No.: 651

5466 GRT / 8672 tdw / 151.01 m length oa /
21.67 m beam / two 12-cyl. diesels geared to
2 screws; Pielstick-Nippon / 11 640 kW / 17 kn /
12 pass. in cabins /

20.3.1978 launched / 31.7.1978 delivered as cargo
ferry, then worldwide ferry services under charter
by Merzario Lines / 1978 renamed **MERZARIO
HISPANIA** / 1979 renamed **NORDIC FERRY**, service
Felixstowe—Rotterdam under charter by Townsend
Thoresen / 16.12.1980–7.2.1981 conversion at Lloyd
Werft, Bremerhaven: 6455 GRT, 8704 tdw, 23.58 m
beam / 3.5.–29.7.1982 troop carrier in Falklands War /
25.8.1982 again service Felixstowe—Rotterdam /
12.1984 to Townsend Thoresen, London / 3.–6.1986
conversion into passenger ferry at Wilton Fijenoord,
Schiedam: 18 732 GRT, 4952 tdw, 258 pass. in 111
cabins, 424 pass. unberthed, 207 cars / 6.1986 service
Felixstowe—Zeebrugge / 19.1.1987 to P&O Ferries,
London / 2.1992 renamed **PRIDE OF FLANDERS** /
23.10.1995 service Felixstowe—Rotterdam / 11.1995
conversion into cargo ferry at Harland & Wolff, Belfast:

LA PAZ STAR ex MERZARIO ESPANIA as STRADA CORSA (photo: Frank Heine)

16 776 GT, 5455 tdw, 124 pass. in cabins, 66 deck pass.,
110 trailers / 24.7.2002 **FLANDERS**, Stena Line, London,
then service Rotterdam—Felixstowe / 15.9.2002
entered service Rotterdam—Harwich / 23.9.–10.2002
service Trelleborg—Travemünde under charter by
Scandlines / 11.2002 renamed **STENA TRANSPORTER** /
23.11.2002–28.2.2009 service Rotterdam—Harwich,
then laid up in Rotterdam / 23.6.2009 **STRADA CORSA**,
Strade Blu, London / 8.7.2009 entered service Livorno—
Olbia / 4.2011–20.9.2013 service Livorno—Olbia under

charter by Moby Lines / 9.2013 **LA PAZ STAR**, Baja
Ferries, La Paz, then service Topolobampo—Mazatlan /

ms GEROITE NA ODESSA

IMO No. 7529964
Navigation Maritime Bulgare, Varna
AS Fredrikstad Mek. Verksted, Fredrikstad;
Yard No.: 433

9610 GRT / 12 900 tdw / 185.45 m length oa /
26.01 (26.70) m beam / two 10-cyl. diesels;
B&W-Fredrikstad / 12 495 kW / 2 screws / 19 kn /
50 pass. in cabins / 10 rail tracks with
1650 m length /

2.1978 launched / 6.1978 delivered, then service
Varna—Illichivsk / 1994 19 518 GT /

ms GEROITE NA SEVASTOPOL

IMO No. 7529976
Navigation Maritime Bulgare, Varna
AS Framnæs Mek. Verksted, Sandefjord;
Yard No.: 188

9610 GRT / 12 900 tdw / 185.45 m length oa /
26.01 (26.70) m beam / two 10-cyl. diesels;
B&W-Fredrikstad / 12 945 kW / 2 screws / 19 kn /
50 pass. in cabins / 10 rail tracks with 1650 m
length /

15.9.1977 launched / 25.8.1978 delivered, then
service Varna—Illichivsk / 1994 19 518 GT / 5.2012
service Kerch—Illichivsk under charter by Ukrferry /
2013 service Varna—Batumi—Illichivsk /

GEROITE NA ODESSA (photo: Olaf Kuhnke)

GEROITE NA SEVASTOPOL (photo: Olaf Kuhnke)

GEROI SHIPKI (photo: Uwe Jakob)

ms GEROI SHIPKI

IMO No. 7605770
Black Sea Shipping Co., Illichivsk
Brodogradiliste "Uljanik", Pula; Yard No.: 312

10 095 GRT / 12 900 tdw / 184.21 m length
oa / 26.01 (26.78) m beam / two 10-cyl. diesels;
B&W-Uljanik / 12 945 kW / 2 screws / 20.8 kn /
50 pass. in cabins / 10 rail tracks with
1650 m length /

24.12.1977 launched / 10.1978 delivered, then service
Varna—Illichivsk / 10.1995 to Ukrferry State Shipping
Co., Illichivsk / 1997 19 019 GT / 2013 service Derince
—Constanta—Poti /

GEROI PLEVNY (photo: Olaf Kuhnke)

ms GEROI PLEVNY

IMO No. 7605782
Black Sea Shipping Co., Illichivsk
Brodogradiliste "Uljanik", Pula; Yard No.: 313

10 095 GRT / 12 889 tdw / 184.21 m length
oa / 26.01 (26.78) m beam / two 10-cyl. diesels;
B&W-Uljanik / 12 944 kW / 2 screws / 19.5 kn /
50 pass. in cabins / 10 rail tracks with
1650 m length /

25.2.1978 launched / 23.12.1978 delivered, then
service Varna—Illichivsk / 10.1995 to Ukrferry State
Shipping Co., Illichivsk / 1997 19 019 GT / 2013 service
Poti—Illichivsk /

ms PORTO CARDO

IMO No. 7902726
Cie Méridionale de Navigation, Marseilles
Soc. Nouvelle des At. & Ch. du Havre, Le Havre;
Yard No.: 253

4681 GRT / 3314 tdw / 126.50 m length oa /
21.01 m beam / two 12-cyl. diesels geared to
2 screws; Pielstick-Atlantique / 11 040 kW / 18 kn /
96 pass. in cabins / 1120 lane metres /

15.10.1979 launched / 20.5.1980 delivered, then
service Marseilles—Corsica / 7.1999 **MALTA EXPRESS**,
Grimaldi Ferries, Valletta; 11 457 GT / 7.7.1999 entered
service Salerno—Valletta—Valencia / 15.7.2003

entered service Livorno—Valencia / 6.2006 renamed
WARRIOR SPIRIT, service Port of Spain—Scarborough
under charter by Port Authority of Trinidad & Tobago,
home port Nassau / 9.2008 home port Basseterre /

WARRIOR SPIRIT ex PORTO CARDO (photo: Olaf Schmidt)

ms MONTE CINTO
IMO No. 8120686
Soc. Nationale Maritime Corse Méditerranée,
Marseilles
Soc. Nouvelle des At. & Ch. du Havre,
Le Havre; Yard No.: 263

13 977 GT / 3400 tdw / 136.02 m length oa /
20.50 m beam / two 8-cyl. diesels geared to
2 screws; Pielstick-Atlantique / 11 550 kW / 18 kn /
36 pass. in cabins / 1308 lane metres /

11.6.1983 launched / 6.6.1984 delivered, then service
Marseilles—Corsica / 1994 14 798 GT, 140 pass. in
cabins / 10.2010 **MAZATLAN STAR**, Baja Ferries, La
Paz / 2011 service Topolobampo—Mazatlan / 2.2014
EDEN, Navimag, Valparaiso / 14.2.2014 entered service
Puerto Montt—Puerto Eden—Puerto Natales /

EDEN ex MONTE CINTO as MONTE CINTO (photo: Frank Heine)

ms SANTA REGINA
IMO No. 8314562
Cie. Méridionale de Navigation, Ajaccio
Soc. Nouvelle des At. & Ch. du Havre, Le Havre;
Yard No.: 266

6570 GT / 3750 tdw / 136.02 m length oa /
22.51 m beam / two 9-cyl. diesels geared to 2
screws; Pielstick / 7640 kW / 18.5 kn / 36 pass. in
cabins / 48 cars, 1350 lane metres /

31.7.1984 launched / 1985 delivered, then service
Marseilles—Corsica / 1986 13 558 GT, 46 pass. / 1990
140 pass. / 1995 110 pass. / 22.11.2002 to Strait
Shipping, Wellington / 26.12.2002 entered service
Wellington—Picton / 10.2003 14 588 GT, 130 pass. /
23.5.2015 last voyage in service Picton—Wellington,
laid up in Wellington / 9.9.2015 to Putera Master
Sarana Lines, Jakarta / 27.9.2015 arrival in Cilegon
for conversion work /

SANTA REGINA (photo: Stephen Berry)

ms FINNROSE
IMO No. 7822859
Skärhamns Oljetransport, Skärhamn
Oskarshamns Varv, Oskarshamn; Yard No.: 428

13 375 GRT / 18 541 tdw / 192.59 m length
oa / 27.03 m beam / two 6-cyl. diesels; Sulzer /
15 900 kW / 2 screws / 19 kn / 12 pass. in cabins /
2712 lane metres /

OLYMPUS ex FINNROSE (photo: Frank Heine)

22.1.1980 launched / 27.7.1980 delivered as RoRo
cargo ship, then service Europe—North America under
charter by Atlantic Cargo Services / 29.12.1981 to
Finnlines, Helsinki / 2.9.1985 home port Nassau /
20.9.1989 to Nordö-Link, Gibraltar, conversion into
cruise ferry for service Malmö—Lübeck planned,
not realised / 23.12.1989–23.4.1990 conversion
into rail/truck ferry at Polish Marin Yard, Gdynia:
33 163 GT, 10 600 tdw, 214 pass. in 102 cabins, 26
pass. unberthed, 3058 lane metres, 6 rail tracks with
900 m length / 23.4.1990 **LÜBECK LINK**, Nordö-Link,
Malmö / 4.1990–8.2007 service Malmö—Travemünde / 8.2007 arrival for conversion at Cammell
Laird, Birkenhead / 9.2007 **ROPAX 2**, Channel Ferries,
London / 10.2009 entered service Ravenna—Corinth
under charter by Adriatic Lines / 1.12.2009 entered
service Ravenna—Bari—Corinth under charter by
Adriatic Lines / 2.12.2010 entered service Vlore—
Trieste under charter by NEL Lines / 3.2011 renamed
OLYMPUS / 17.3.2011 entered service Igoumenitsa—
Bari under charter by Ventouris Ferries / 8.2012 service
Suez—Adabiya under charter by Sisa Shipping /
13.6.2013 laid up off Adabiya /

ms FINNHAWK

IMO No. 7822861
Skärhamns Oljetransport, Skärhamn
Oskarshamns Varv, Oskarshamn; Yard No.: 429

13 341 GRT / 18 451 tdw / 192.59 m length
oa / 27.03 m beam / two 6-cyl. diesels; Sulzer /
15 900 kW / 2 screws / 19 kn / 12 pass. in cabins /
2712 lane metres /

13.8.1980 launched / 12.12.1980 delivered as RoRo
cargo ship, then service Europe—North America under
charter by Atlantic Cargo Services / 30.12.1981 to
Finnlines, Helsinki / 27.8.1985 home port Nassau /
21.10.1989 to Nordö-Link, Gibraltar / 21.10.1989
home port Malmö, conversion into cruise ferry for
service Malmö—Lübeck planned, not realised /
1.12.1989–6.5.1990 conversion into rail/truck ferry
at Polish Marin Yard, Gdynia: 33 163 GT, 10 600 tdw,
192.48 m length oa, 214 pass. in 102 cabins, 26 pass.
unberthed, 3058 lane metres, 6 rail tracks with 900 m
length / 6.5.1990 **MALMÖ LINK**, home port Malmö /
5.1990–24.7.2007 service Malmö—Travemünde /
28.7.2007 arrival for conversion at Cammell Laird,
Birkenhead / 23.8.2007 **ROPAX 1**, Channel Ferries,
London / 2008 to Ropax 1 K/S, London / 10.2009
service Ravenna—Corinth under charter by Adriatic
Lines / 1.12.2009 service Ravenna—Bari—Corinth
under charter by Adriatic Lines / 7.12.2010 entered
service Corinth—Ancona under charter by NEL Lines /
5.2011 renamed **AQUA HERCULES** / 30.11.2011
entered service Igoumenitsa—Bari / 8.11.2012
entered service Mersin—Damietta under charter
by Salem Al Makrani Cargo / 10.7.2013 laid up off
Iskenderun /

ms KAPITAN KHLEBNIKOV

IMO No. 7824417
Far Eastern Shipping Co., Vladivostok
Wärtsilä, Helsinki; Yard No.: 430

10 471 GRT / 4418 tdw / 129.42 m length oa /
26.51 (26.70) m beam / six 9-cyl. diesels with
18 270 kW; Sulzer-Wärtsilä / six generators
connected to three elec. motors / 8890 kW /
3 screws / 18.75 kn / 112 pass. in 106 cabins /

5.11.1980 launched / 29.5.1981 delivered as icebreaker /
1992 refitted at Rickmers-Lloyd, Bremerhaven as
passenger ship for deployment outside the ice-breaking
season for expedition cruises / 24.10.1992 first transfer voyage Southampton—Cape Town / 1993 while
attempting the first circumnavigation of Greenland
trapped in 5 m thick ice on the west coast at 83°N.
Freed three days later by atomic icebreaker YAMAL /
1996–97 first circumnavigation of Antarctica for
tourists under charter by Hanseatic Tours / 1996
12 288 GT /

ms SOVETSKIY DAGESTAN (no photo)

IMO No. 8212544
Caspian Shipping Co., Baku
Brodogradiliste Uljanik, Pula; Yard No.: 358

11 450 GT / 3950 tdw / 154.46 m length oa /
17.51 (18.31) m beam / two 6-cyl. diesels geared to
2 screws; B&W Uljanik / 8700 kW / 17.25 kn /
84 pass. in cabins, 118 pass. unberthed / 72 cars,
65 trucks, 4 rail tracks with 414 m length /

21.2.1984 launched / 14.9.1984 delivered, then rail
ferry service Baku—Krasnovodsk—Astrakhan / 1994
renamed **DAGISTAN** / 20.6.2014 laid up /

AQUA HERCULES ex FINNHAWK (photo: Ivan Meshkov)

KAPITAN KHLEBNIKOV (photo: Nigel Kirby)

ms SOVETSKAYA GRUZIYA

IMO No. 8212568
Caspian Shipping Co., Baku
Brodogradiliste Uljanik, Pula; Yard No.: 360

11 450 GT / 3950 tdw / 154.31 m length oa /
17.51 (18.30) m beam / two 6-cyl. diesels geared to
2 screws; B&W Uljanik / 8700 kW / 17.25 kn /
84 pass. in cabins, 118 pass. unberthed / 72 cars,
4 rail tracks with 414 m length /

10.1984 launched / 4.1985 delivered, then rail ferry
service Baku—Krasnovodsk—Astrakhan / 1992
MERCURI-1, Mercuri Shipping Co., Limassol; after
conversion 86 pass. in 37 cabins, 24 drivers, then
service Kiel—Riga—Klaipeda / 7.1995 entered service
Karlshamn—Gdynia for Baltic Line / 1995 service
discontinued, home port Limassol, service Baku—
Krasnovodsk—Astrakhan / 1997 name transliterated
as **MERCURY-1** / 2000 home port Baku / 14.6.2015
laid up /

MERCURY-1 ex SOVETSKAYA GRUZIYA (photo: Askar Urazalin)

ms SOVETSKAYA KALMYKIYA
IMO No. 8212570
Caspian Shipping Co., Baku
Brodogradiliste Uljanik, Pula; Yard No.: 361

11 450 GT / 3950 tdw / 154.31 m length oa /
17.51 (18.30) m beam / two 6-cyl. diesels geared to
2 screws; B&W Uljanik / 8700 kW / 17.25 kn /
84 pass. in cabins, 118 pass. unberthed / 72 cars,
4 rail tracks with 414 m length /

2.1985 launched / 7.1985 delivered, then rail ferry
service Baku—Krasnovodsk—Astrakhan / 1992
renamed KALMYKIYA / 1994 renamed MERCURI 3 /
1995 renamed AKADEMIK M. TOPCHUBASHOV /

AKADEMIK M. TOPCHUBASHOV ex SOVETSKAYA KALMYKIYA (photo: Askar Urazalin)

ms SOVETSKAYA ARMENIYA (no photo)
IMO No. 8212582
Caspian Shipping Co., Baku
Brodogradiliste Uljanik, Pula; Yard No. 362

11 450 GT / 3985 tdw / 154,55 m lenght oa /
17,51 (18,30) m beam / two 6-Zyl.-diesels geared
to 2 screws; B&W Uljanik / 8700 kW / 17,25 kn /
84 pass. in cabins, 118 unberthed / 72 cars,
65 trucks, 4 rail tracks with 414 m length /

27.4.1985 launched / 31.8.1985 delivered, then rail
ferry service Baku—Krasnovodsk—Astrakhan / 1994
renamed AZERBAIJAN /

AKADEMIK HESEN ALIYEV ex SOVETSKAYA KIRGIZIYA (photo: Askar Urazalin)

ms SOVETSKAYA KIRGIZIYA
IMO No. 8212594
Caspian Shipping Co., Baku
Brodogradiliste Uljanik, Pula; Yard No.: 363

11 450 GT / 3950 tdw / 154.31 m length oa /
17.51 (18.30) m beam / two 6-cyl. diesels geared to
2 screws; B&W Uljanik / 8700 kW / 17.25 kn /
84 pass. in cabins, 118 pass. unberthed / 72 cars,
4 rail tracks with 414 m length /

3.1986 delivered, then rail ferry service Baku—
Krasnovodsk—Astrakhan / 1992 renamed KIRGIZTAN /
1995 renamed AKADEMIK HESEN ALIYEV /

NAKHCHYVAN ex SOVETSKIY NAKHICHEVAN (photo: Askar Urazalin)

ms SOVETSKIY NAKHICHEVAN
IMO No. 8225383
Caspian Shipping Co., Baku
Brodogradiliste Uljanik, Pula; Yard No.: 367

11 450 GT / 3950 tdw / 154.31 m length oa /
17.51 (18.30) m beam / two 6-cyl. diesels geared to
2 screws; B&W Uljanik / 8700 kW / 17.25 kn /
84 pass. in cabins, 118 pass. unberthed / 72 cars,
4 rail tracks with 414 m length /

22.3.1986 launched / 1986 delivered, then rail ferry
service Baku—Krasnovodsk—Astrakhan / 1994
renamed NAKHCHYVAN /

PROFESSOR GUL ex SOVETSKAYA BYELORUSSIYA (photo: Askar Urazalin)

ms SOVETSKAYA BYELORUSSIYA
IMO No. 8225371
Caspian Shipping Co., Baku
Brodogradiliste Uljanik, Pula; Yard No.: 366

11 450 GT / 3985 tdw / 154.31 m length oa /
17.51 (18.30) m beam / two 6-cyl. diesels geared to
2 screws; B&W Uljanik / 8700 kW / 17.25 kn /
84 pass. in cabins, 118 pass. unberthed / 72 cars,
4 rail tracks with 414 m length /

14.12.1985 launched / 5.1986 delivered, then rail
ferry service Baku—Krasnovodsk—Astrakhan / 1994
renamed BELORUS, then PROFESSOR GUL /

ms ÖRESUND

IMO No. 8420842
Statens Järnvägar, Helsingborg
Moss Rosenberg Verft, Moss; Yard No.: 204

16 925 GT / 6772 tdw / 186.52 m length oa /
23.11 m beam / four 6-cyl. diesels geared to
2 screws; MAN B&W / 13 200 kW / 15 kn /
12 pass. cabins / 50 wagons, 5 rail tracks with
650 m length /

19.3.1985 launched / 13.10.1986 delivered / 3.11.1986
rail ferry service Copenhagen—Helsingborg / 1.1.1992
to SweFerry, Helsingborg / 5.1997 home port Nassau /
2.7.2000 laid up in Middelfart / 2001 to SeaWind
Line, Stockholm / 7.12.2001–27.9.2002 conversion in
Landskrona and at Remontowa, Gdansk: 22 874 GT,
5143 tdw, 188.88 m length oa, 23.70 m beam,
17.5 kn, 240 pass. in 70 cabins, 124 pass. unberthed,
55 cars, 1150 lane metres, 650 m track length,
renamed **SKY WIND** / 10.10.2002–19.8.2007 service
Stockholm—Långnäs—Turku / 22.8.2007 **WOLIN**,
Unity Line, Nassau / 10.10.2007 entered service
Swinoujscie—Trelleborg /

WOLIN ex ÖRESUND (photo: Frank Lose)

SAILOR ex FINNSAILOR (photo: Frank Heine)

ms FINNSAILOR

IMO No. 8401444
Neste Oy, Naantali
Stocznia Gdanska, Gdansk; Yard No.: 489/01

19 991 GT / 8842 tdw / 157.61 m length oa /
25.30 m beam / two 12-cyl. diesels geared to
2 screws; Sulzer-Wärtsilä / 15 360 kW / 20.5 kn /
18 pass. in cabins / 2090 lane metres / crew 20

31.10.1986 launched / 21.10.1987 delivered as
cargo ferry under charter by Finncarriers / 29.10.1987
entered service Helsinki—Lübeck / 1.1996–17.4.1996
conversion at Turku Repair Yard: 20 783 GT, 119 pass. in
45 cabins, 1400 lane metres, 230 cars / 4.1996 entered
service Helsinki—Norrköping / 17.12.1996 entered
service Naantali—Kapellskär for FinnLink / 1.3.2000
entered service Malmö—Travemünde under charter by
Nordö-Link / 2001 to Finnlines, Helsinki / 10.1.2002
entered service Naantali—Kapellskär for Finnlink /

13.1.2004 entered service Malmö—Travemünde for
Nordö-Link / 22.2.2007 entered service Naantali—
Kapellskär for FinnLink / 14.3.–1.9.2011 service Travemünde—Malmö, at weekend Travemünde—Helsinki /
5.9.2011 entered service Kapellskär—Naantali /
13.11.2011 entered service Helsinki—Rostock /
11.1.2012 entered service Naantali—Kapellskär /
13.1.2013 home port Helsinki / 1.10.2013 also

service Kapellskär—Långnäs—Naantali / 3.11.2013
entered service Hanko—Paldiski under charter by
Navirail / 13.1.2014 again service Naantali—Kapellskär / 19.10.–9.11.2014 service Hanko—Paldisiki
under charter by Navirail / 11.2014–5.1.2015 service
Helsinki—Gdansk / 6.1.2014 service Hanko—Paldiski
under charter by Navirail / 2.2015 **SAILOR**, Navirail,
Tallinn, then service Paldiski—Hanko /

POSEIDON EXPRESS ex TRANSLUBECA (photo: George Koutsoukis)

ms TRANSLUBECA

IMO No. 8706040
Poseidon Schiffahrt, Lübeck
Stocznia Gdanska, Gdansk; Yard No.: B 498/01

24 727 GT / 11 500 tdw / 157.60 m length oa /
25.30 m beam / two 12-cyl. diesels geared to
2 screws; Sulzer-Wärtsilä / 14 400 kW / 20.3 kn /
84 pass. in 33 cabins / 2090 lane metres / crew 21

12.1.1990 launched / 1.12.1990 delivered /
14.1.1991 christened in Lübeck, maiden voyage in
service Lübeck—Helsinki / 7.11.1995 entered service
Lübeck—Turku / 2000 to Finnlines, Lübeck / 24.2.2001
entered service Kiel—St. Petersburg / 11.1.2003
entered service Lübeck—Sassnitz—St. Petersburg /
7.2010 service Travemünde—Turku / 24.11.2010
entered service Lübeck—Ventspils—Helsinki—St.
Petersburg / 10.2011 service Civitavecchia—Catania—
Valetta under charter by Grimaldi Ferries / 29.9.2011
service Civitavecchia—Catania—Valletta under charter
by Grimaldi Ferries / 12.6.2012–2.11.2013 service
Hanko—Paldiski under charter by Navirail / 11.2013
POSEIDON EXPRESS, Paradise Cruise & Ferry, Belize
City / 2014 service Novorossiysk—Trabzon—Poti /

ms NORD PAS-DE-CALAIS
IMO No. 8512152
Soc. Nationale des Chemins de Fer Français, Dunkirk
Chantiers du Nord et de la Méditerranée, Dunkirk;
Yard No.: 325

13 727 GT / 160.08 m length oa / 22.41 (23.02)
m beam / two 16-cyl. diesels geared to 2 screws;
Sulzer / 18 020 kW / 21.5 kn / 80 pass. in cabins /
1390 lane metres, 45 wagons / crew 35

15.4.1987 launched / 15.12.1987 delivered / 1.1988
maiden voyage in service Calais—Dover / 9.5.1988
entered service Dover—Dunkirk / 1994 to SNAT Sealink,
Dunkirk / 22.12.1995 entered service Calais—Dover /
7.1.1996 renamed **SEAFRANCE NORD-PAS-DE-
CALAIS** / 3.7.1996 laid up in Dunkirk / 29.11.1996
again service Calais—Dover / 15.11.2011 after
bankruptcy of owner laid up in Dover, later in Dunkirk /
11.6.2012 to Eurotransmanche, Dunkirk / 6.2012
renamed **NORD PAS-DE-CALAIS** / 28.11.2012–
29.6.2015 service Calais—Dover under charter by
My Ferry Link, then laid up in Dunkirk /

NORD PAS-DE-CALAIS ex NORD PAS-DE-CALAIS (photo: Frank Lose)

MANGALIA (photo: Olaf Kuhnke)

ms MANGALIA
IMO No. 8513663
Cia. de Navigatie Romline, Constanta
Intreprinderera Constr. Navale Constanta, Constan-
ta; Yard No.: 459

20 621 GT / 12 000 tdw / 184.90 m length oa /
26.00 m beam / two 8-cyl. diesels geared to
2 screws; MAN-Resita / 10 570 kW / 14 kn /
100 pass. / 10 rail tracks with 1600 m length /

3.1988 delivered, then rail ferry service Constanta—
Samsun / 2015 laid up in Constanta /

ms EFORIE (no photo)
IMO No. 8707549
Cia. de Navigatie Romline, Constanta
Intreprinderera Constr. Navale Constanta,
Constanta; Yard No.: 479

20 621 GT / 12 000 tdw / 184.90 m length oa /
26.00 m beam / two 8-cyl. diesels geared to
2 screws; MAN-Resita / 10 570 kW / 14 kn /
100 pass. / 10 rail tracks with 1600 m length /

1987 launched / 10.1991 delivered, then rail ferry service
Constanta—Batumi / 2015 laid up in Constanta /

JAN SNIADECKI (photo: Frank Heine)

ms JAN SNIADECKI
IMO No. 8604711
Polish Ocean Lines, Szczecin
Götaverken Arendal, Gothenburg; Yard No.: 952

14 417 GT / 5583 tdw / 155.19 m length oa /
21.60 m beam / four 6-cyl. diesels geared to
2 screws; Sulzer-Zgoda / 11 840 kW / 16 kn /
50 pass. in 30 cabins / 1175 lane metres, 5 rail
tracks with 615 m length /

21.2.1987 launched / 4.1988 delivered / 5.1988
service Swinoujscie—Ystad / 1996 to Euroafrica
Shipping Lines, Limassol /

ms OCEAN EAST
IMO NO. 9000912
Ocean Tokyu Ferry, Kitakyushu
Saiki Jukogyo, Saiki; Yard No.: 1013

11 523 GRT / 4036 tdw / 166.00 m length oa /
25.00 m beam / two 8-cyl. diesels geared to
2 screws; Pielstick-Diesel United / 21 200 kW /
21.5 kn / 112 pass. in 28 cabins, 350 pass.
unberthed / 75 cars, 1262 lane metres / crew 38

16.2.1991 launched / 30.5.1991 delivered / 10.6.1991
maiden voyage in service Tokyo—Tokushima—Kokura /
1995 service Tokyo—Tokushima—Shin Moji /

OCEAN EAST (photo: Hiroyuki Yoshimoto)

OCEAN WEST (photo: Hiroyuki Yoshimoto)

ms OCEAN WEST
IMO No. 9000900
Ocean Tokyu Ferry, Kitakyushu
Saiki Jukogyo, Saiki; Yard No.: 1015

11 522 GRT / 4036 tdw / 166.00 m length oa /
25.00 m beam / two 8-cyl. diesels geared to
2 screws; Pielstick-Diesel United / 21 200 kW /
21.5 kn / 112 pass. in 28 cabins, 350 pass.
unberthed / 75 cars, 1262 lane metres / crew 38

15.6.1991 launched / 9.1991 delivered / 22.9.1991
maiden voyage in service Tokyo—Tokushima—Kokura /
1995 service Tokyo—Tokushima—Shin Moji /

OCEAN SOUTH (photo: Osamu Taniguchi)

ms OCEAN SOUTH
IMO No. 9154074
Ocean Tokyu Ferry, Kitakyushu
Onomichi Zosen, Onomichi; Yard No.: 405

11 114 GT / 4810 tdw / 166.00 m length oa /
25.00 m beam / two 8-cyl. diesels geared to
2 screws; Pielstick-Diesel United / 21 080 kW /
21.5 kn / 50 pass. in 19 cabins, 98 pass.
unberthed / 75 cars, 1600 lane metres / crew 27

18.6.1996 launched / 28.9.1996 delivered, then
service Tokyo—Tokushima—Shin Moji /

OCEAN NORTH (photo: Frank Lose)

ms OCEAN NORTH
IMO No. 9154086
Ocean Tokyu Ferry, Kitakyushu
Onomichi Zosen, Onomichi; Yard No.: 406

11 114 GT / 4810 tdw / 166.00 m length oa /
25.00 m beam / two 8-cyl. diesels geared to
2 screws; Pielstick-Diesel United / 21 080 kW /
21.5 kn / 50 pass. in 19 cabins, 98 pass.
unberthed / 75 cars, 1600 lane metres / crew 27

20.8.1996 launched / 26.11.1996 delivered, then
service Tokyo—Tokushima—Shin Moji /

ms EUROPEAN SEAWAY

IMO No. 9007283
P&O European Ferries, Dover
Schichau Seebeckwerft, Bremerhaven; Yard No.:
1075

22 986 GT / 7550 tdw / 179.40 m length oa /
27.80 (28.28) m beam / four 8-cyl. diesels geared to
2 screws; Sulzer-Jugoturbina / 21 120 kW / 21 kn /
200 pass. in 81 cabins / 124 trucks,
1925 lane metres /

20.4.1991 launched / 2.10.1991 delivered / 7.10.1991
entered service Dover—Zeebrugge / 10.3.1998 to P&O
Stena Line, Dover / 1.12.2003 laid up in Falmouth /
10.6.2004 laid up in Birkenhead / 3.1.2005 entered
service Dover—Calais / 1.5.–10.2012 accommodation ship for workers on a wind farm under charter
by Centrica Renewable Energy on the east coast of
England / 22.10.2012 again service Dover—Calais /
4.4.2013 laid up in Tilbury / 1.9.2014 accommodation
ship in the North Sea under charter by Essent Wind
Nordsee Ost Planungs / 7.4.2015 laid up in Tilbury /
21.7.2015 entered service Dover—Calais /

EUROPEAN SEAWAY (photo: Frank Lose)

GALILEUSZ ex VIA TIRRENO (photo: Uwe Jakob)

ms VIA TIRRENO

IMO No. 9019078
Viamare di Navigazione, Palermo
van der Giessen-De Noord, Krimpen; Yard No.: 959

14 398 GT / 7324 tdw / 150.37 m length oa /
23.40 m beam / two 8-cyl. diesels geared to
2 screws; Sulzer-Grandi Motori / 11 520 kW /
19 kn / 50 pass. in 25 cabins / 1850 lane metres /
crew 18

11.7.1992 launched / 10.1992 delivered, then
service Termini Imerese—Voltri / 1997 to Tirrenia di
Navigazione / 1998 service Genoa—Termini Imerese /
2001 to Adriatica di Navigazione / 2005 to Tirrenia
di Navigazione / 3.2006 **GALILEUSZ**, Unity Line,
Limassol / 11.2006 delivered after conversion in
Szczecin: 15 848 GT, 6795 tdw, 120 pass. in 51
cabins, 1742 lane metres / 12.11.2006 entered
service Swinoujscie—Ystad / 5.2.2007 entered service
Swinoujscie—Trelleborg /

VIA ADRIATICO (photo: Nikolaos Saratzis)

ms VIA ADRIATICO

IMO No. 9019066
Viamare di Navigazione, Palermo
van der Giessen-De Noord, Krimpen; Yard No.: 958

14 398 GT / 7330 tdw / 150.43 m length oa /
23.40 m beam / two 8-cyl. diesels geared to
2 screws; Sulzer-Zgoda / 11 520 kW / 19 kn /
50 pass. in 25 cabins / 1850 lane metres / crew 18

18.6.1992 launched at Frisian Shipyard Welgelegen,
Harlingen, later completed at van der Giessen /
11.1992 delivered, then service Termini Imerese—
Voltri / 1997 to Tirrenia di Navigazione / 1998 service
Genoa—Termini Imerese / 2001 to Adriatica di
Navigazione / 2005 to Tirrenia di Navigazione / 2009
service Livorno—Cagliari /

ESPRESSO RAVENNA ex VIA IONIO (photo: Frank Lose)

1.1993 launched at Frisian Shipyard Welgelegen, Harlingen, under Yard No. 287, then completion at van der Giessen / 4.1993 delivered / 15.5.–8.1993 service Travemünde—Trelleborg under charter by TT-Line / 8.1993 cargo ferry service Voltri—Termini Imerese / 1994 **ESPRESSO RAVENNA**, Adriatica di Nav., Palermo, service Ravenna—Catania / 3.2015 service Ibiza—Denia under charter by Balearia / 22.8.–26.9.2015 service Algeciras—Tangier Med. under charter by Balearia / 30.9.2015 entered service Livorno—Cagliari /

ms VIA MEDITERRANEO
IMO No. 9031686
Viamare di Navigazione, Palermo
Fincantieri, Palermo; Yard No.: 5922

14 398 GT / 5535 tdw / 150.43 m length oa / 23.40 m beam / two 8-cyl. diesels geared to 2 screws; Sulzer-Grandi Motori / 11 520 kW / 19.1 kn / 50 pass. in 25 cabins / 1820 lane metres / crew 18

20.6.1993 delivered, then service Termini Imerese—Voltri / 1994 **ESPRESSO CATANIA**, Adriatica di Nav., Palermo, service Catania—Ravenna, also service Livorno—Cagliari /

ms VIA IONIO
IMO No. 9019080
Viamare di Navigazione, Palermo
van der Giessen-De Noord, Krimpen; Yard No.: 960

14 398 GT / 7300 tdw / 150.37 m length oa / 23.40 m beam / two 8-cyl. diesels geared to 2 screws; Sulzer-Zgoda / 11 520 kW / 19 kn / 50 pass. in 25 cabins / 1850 lane metres / crew 18

ESPRESSO CATANIA ex VIA MEDITERRANEO (photo: Uwe Jakob)

LEVANTE ex LAZIO (photo: Frank Heine)

ms NORBANK
IMO No. 9056583
North Sea Ferries, Rotterdam
van der Giessen-De Noord, Krimpen; Yard No.: 961

17 464 GT / 6791 tdw / 166.77 m length oa /
23.40 (23.90) m beam / two 9-cyl. and two 8-cyl.
diesels geared to 2 screws; Sulzer-Zgoda / 22.9 kn /
114 pass. in 57 cabins / 2040 lane metres /
crew 30

5.6.1993 launched / 29.10.1993 delivered / 31.10.1993
maiden voyage in service Rotterdam—Hull / 1.1.1997
to P&O North Sea Ferries, Rotterdam / 8.2001 entered
service Rotterdam—Felixstowe / 7.1.2002 entered
service Liverpool—Dublin for P&O Ferries /

ms LAZIO
IMO No. 9031698
"Tirrenia" di Navigazione, Palermo
Fincantieri, Palermo; Yard No.: 5923

14 398 GT / 5535 tdw / 150.37 m length oa /
23.40 m beam / two 8-cyl. diesels geared to
2 screws; Sulzer-Grandi Motori / 10 360 kW /
19.1 kn / 50 pass. in 25 cabins / 1820 lane metres /

6.11.1993 launched / 19.5.1994 delivered, then
service Palermo—Naples / 1995 home port Naples /
2000 service Livorno—Cagliari / 31.3.2012 laid up in
Crotone / 1.2013 to Levantina Trasporti / 29.1.2013
entered service Istanbul—Illichivsk under charter
by Stena Sea Lines / 6.2013 renamed **LEVANTE** /
12.7.2013 entered service Brindisi—Igoumenitsa
under charter by Harmonica Lines / 1.8.2013 laid up
in Crotone / 19.8.2013 entered service Algeciras—
Tangier Med. under charter by Balearia / 9.2013
service San Antonio—Barcelona under charter by
Balearia / 2.12.2014–3.2015 service Barcelona—
Mahón/Ibiza under charter by Balearia / 2.5.2015
laid up in Rijeka / 26.12.2015 entered service
Algeciras—Tangier /

PUGLIA (photo: Frank Lose)

NORBANK (photo: Gerolf Drebes)

ms PUGLIA
IMO No. 9031703
"Tirrenia" di Navigazione, Naples
Fincantieri, Palermo; Yard No.: 5924

14 398 GT / 5535 tdw / 150.43 m length oa /
23.40 m beam / two 8-cyl. diesels geared to
2 screws; Sulzer-Grandi Motori / 10 360 kW /
19.1 kn / 50 pass. in 25 cabins / 1820 lane metres /

5.1.1995 launched / 11.5.1995 delivered, then service
Naples—Palermo / 2000 service Livorno—Cagliari /
2.12.2014 entered service Palma de Mallorca—
Ibiza—Denia under charter by Balearia / 15.7.–
22.8.2015 service Algeciras—Tangier Med. under
charter by Balearia / 25.8.2015 laid up in Crotone /
9.-11.2015 service Piombino—Olbia under charter
by Moby Lines / 11.2015 entered service Livorno—
Cagliari /

ms NORBAY
IMO No. 9056595
North Sea Ferries, Hull
van der Giessen-De Noord, Krimpen; Yard No.: 962

17464 GT / 6722 tdw / 166.77 m length oa /
23.40 (23.90) m beam / two 9-cyl. and two
8-cyl. diesels geared to 2 screws; Sulzer-Zgoda /
24480 kW / 22.9 kn / 114 pass. in 57 cabins /
2040 lane metres / crew 30

13.11.1993 launched / 2.1994 delivered / 20.2.1994
maiden voyage in service Hull—Rotterdam / 1998
to P&O North Sea Ferries, Hull / 12.2001 home port
Hamilton / 7.1.2002 entered service Liverpool—Dublin
for P&O Ferries /

ms ULYSSE
IMO No. 9142459
Cotunav, Tunis
Schichau Seebeckwerft, Bremerhaven;
Yard No.: 1093

17907 GT / 5914 tdw / 161.50 m length oa /
25.80 m beam / four 6-cyl. diesels geared to
2 screws; Sulzer / 14000 kW / 20 kn / 100 pass.
in 50 cabins / 1950 lane metres / crew 43

1.2.1997 launched / 2.7.1997 delivered, then service
Tunis—Marseilles/Genoa/Livorno /

ms SALAMMBO 7
IMO No. 9142461
Cotunav, Tunis
SSW Fähr- u. Spezialschiffbau, Bremerhaven;
Yard No.: 1094

17907 GT / 5914 tdw / 161.50 m length oa /
25.80 m beam / four 6-cyl. diesels geared to 2
screws; Sulzer / 14000 kW / 20 kn / 100 pass. in
50 cabins / 1950 lane metres / crew 43

24.5.1997 launched / 29.9.1997 delivered and
christened, then service Tunis—Marseilles/Genoa/
Livorno / 12.2012 renamed **SALAMMBO** /

NORBAY (photo: Frank Lose)

ULYSSE (photo: Nikolaos Saratzis)

SALAMMBO ex SALAMMBO 7 (photo: Frank Lose)

REGAL STAR (photo: Krzysztof Brzoza)

SUPER FAST GALICIA ex ATALAYA DE ALCUDIA (photo: Gerolf Drebes)

ms REGAL STAR
IMO No. 9087116
MCL, Naples
Palumba, Naples ; Yard No.: 668

15 281 GT / 7045 tdw / 146.20 m length oa /
23.80 m beam / two 6-cyl. diesels; B&W /
8700 kW / 2 screws / 18 kn / 80 pass. in
40 cabins / 120 trucks, 1700 lane metres /

1993 launched at Severnaya Sudostroitelniy Zavod,
St. Petersburg, work discontinued / 12.1999 delivered
after completion at Palumbo, Naples / 2000 service
Savona—Catania / 2000 service Salerno—Palermo—
Valencia under charter by Grimaldi Ferries / 11.2003
to Tallink, Tallinn / 5.3.2004 entered service Paldiski—
Kapellskär /

ms ATALAYA DE ALCUDIA
IMO No. 9263370
Alcudia Maritimos, Santa Cruz de Tenerife
Hijos de J. Barreras, Vigo; Yard No.: 1612

16 686 GT / 7300 tdw / 159.70 m length oa /
23.70 m beam / two 12-cyl. diesels geared to
2 screws; Wärtsilä / 25 200 kW / 23.5 (25) kn /
120 pass. in 30 cabins / 225 cars, 1750 lane metres /
crew 20

4.12.2002 launched / 6.5.2003 delivered, then service
Palma de Mallorca—Barcelona / 5.2005 SUPER-FAST
GALICIA, Cia. Trasmediterranea, Santa Cruz de Tenerife /
7.2005 service Palma de Mallorca—Barcelona / 2008

service Barcelona—Valencia—Algeciras—Las Palmas
de Gran Canaria / 29.12.2008 laid up in Tarragona /
11.2010 service Algeciras—Tangier Med. / 2012 laid
up in Gibraltar, on 20.12.2013 in Algeciras / 1.2014
renamed SUPER FAST GALICIA, home port Valletta /
6.2014 service Port of Spain—Scarborough under
charter by Trinidad & Tobago Inter-Island Transportation /

ts 50 LET POBEDY
IMO No. 9152959
Rosatomflot, Murmansk
Baltiyskiy Zavod, St. Petersburg; Yard No.: 01705

23 439 GT / 3505 tdw / 159.63 m length oa /
28.00 (30.03) m beam / two nuclear reactors,
two steam turbines with 55 200 kW; Kirovskiy /
two generators connected to three elec. motors /
52 800 kW / 3 screws / 21 kn / 128 pass. in
67 cabins / crew 138

29.12.1993 launched, originally planned as URAL /
12.3.2007 delivered / 2.4.2007 commissioned as
icebreaker / 23.6.2008 first cruise to the North Pole /

50 LET POBEDY (photo: Kiselev d, CC BY-SA 3.0 - https://creativecommons.org/licenses/by-sa/3.0/deed.de)

STENA TRANSPORTER (photo: Frank Lose)

ms **STENA TRANSPORTER**
IMO No. 9469376
Stena Line, Hoek van Holland
Samsung Heavy Industries Co. Ltd., Geoje;
Yard No.: 1807

33 690 GT / 8423 tdw / 212.00 m length oa /
26.70 (31.62) m beam / two 9-cyl. diesels geared to
2 screws; MAN B&W / 21 600 kW / 22.2 (23.6) kn /
264 pass. in 130 cabins, 36 pass. unberthed /
4057 lane metres /

18.1.2011 delivered / 1.3.2011 maiden voyage in
service Hoek van Holland—Killingholme /

STENA TRANSIT (photo: Rob de Visser)

ms **STENA TRANSIT**
IMO No. 9469388
Stena Line, Hoek van Holland
Samsung Heavy Industries Co. Ltd., Geoje;
Yard No.: 1808

33 690 GT / 8423 tdw / 212.00 m length oa /
26.70 (31.62) m beam / two 9-cyl. diesels geared
to 2 screws; MAN B&W / 21 600 kW / 22.2 kn /
264 pass. in 130 cabins, 36 pass. unberthed /
4000 lane metres /

1.2011 floated out / 19.9.2011 delivered / 7.11.2011
maiden voyage in service Hoek van Holland—
Killingholme /

FERRY BIZAN (photo: Hiroyuki Yoshimoto)

ms **FERRY BIZAN**
Ocean Tokyu Ferry
Saiki H.I., Saiki; Yard No.: 715

13 000 GRT / 191.00 m length oa / 27.00 m beam /
252 pass. /

18.8.2015 launched / 12.2015 delivery / 3.1.2016
service Tokyo—Tokushima—Shin Moji planned /

The sister ship **FERRY SHIMANTO** and two further
sister ships are due for delivery 2016.

Appendix 2
Former passenger ships

– which today serve other purposes or have been laid up for many years unused and without any prospect of recommissioning. The vessels are listed in chronological sequence under their current name in the 2010 edition. Full details of the ship's life are given in an earlier issue. Only the events that have become known since 2010 are noted here.

HIKAWA MARU (photo: Hiroyuki Yoshimoto)

HIKAWA MARU, built in 1930
Still laid up in Yokohama /

QUEEN MARY (photo: Peter Knego)

QUEEN MARY, built in 1936 (IMO No. 5528793)
Still laid up in Long Beach /

UNITED STATES (photo: Jonathan Boonzaier)

UNITED STATES, built in 1952 (IMO No. 5373476)
Still laid up in Philadelphia /

SHANGHAI (also **SHANG HAI**), built in 1957 as
BAUDOUINVILLE (IMO No. 5066229)
1996 decommissioned, since then in Lloyd's Register without owner /

ROTTERDAM, built in 1959 (IMO No. 5301019)
15.2.2010 opened as hotel, conference center and museum ship in the Port of Rotterdam / 12.6.2013 to WestCord Hotels /

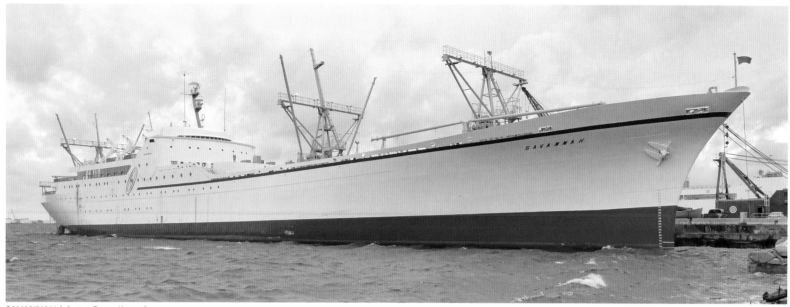

SAVANNAH (photo: Peter Knego)

SAVANNAH, built in 1962 (IMO No. 5314793)
8.5.2008 arrival under tow in Baltimore, where the ship is to remain until 2016 /

MING HUA, built in 1962 as **ANCERVILLE** (IMO No. 5015957)
2010 Sea World Plaza with the **MING HUA** redesigned for 60 billion yuan. Opening on board of the German "Löwenburg Brauerei and Restaurant", in addition to the existing hotel Minghua Cruise Inn /

LOGOS HOPE ex GUSTAV VASA (photo: Irvine Kinea)

ORIENT PRINCESS, built in 1967 as **YAO HUA** (IMO No. 6708109)
Still stationary tourist attraction and restaurant ship in Tianjin /

QUEEN ELIZABETH 2, built in 1969 (IMO No. 6725418)
Still laid up in Dubai /

LOGOS HOPE, built in 1973 as **GUSTAV VASA** (IMO No. 7302914)
Continued operation as mission ship / 7.2011 home port Valletta /

QUEEN ELIZABETH 2 (photo: Christian Eckardt)

OASIA ex VISTAFJORD (photo: Tony Davis)

SAGA RUBY, built in 1973 as **VISTAFJORD** (IMO No. 7214715)
20.2.2013 started on last world cruise with 44-day delay as a result of engine damage / 7.1.2014 end of last cruise for Saga Cruises in Southampton / 13.1.2014 arrival in Gibraltar for conversion work / 30.1.2014 **OASIA**, Millennium View Ltd. (FleetPro Ocean), Nassau / 2.2014 from Gibraltar via Penang to Sattahip, Thailand, there laid up. Conversion into floating hotel in Yangon, Myanmar planned /

BLUEFORT ex DIANA II AF SLITE (photo: Frank Heine)

NAGIA ex HAKATA (photo: Frank Heine)

ARV 1, built in 1979 as **DIANA II AF SLITE** (IMO No. 7816874)
1.2008 until end of 2008 conversion at Sembawang, Singapore into offshore Accommodation and Repair Vessel: 17 936 GT, 11 900 tdw, 523 pass. in cabins / 2011 home port Madeira / 12.2013 **BLUEFORT**, Highclare Ltd., Majuro /

PANAGIA AGIASOU, built in 1973 as **HAKATA** (IMO No. 7351848)
18.03.2013 towed to Aliaga for scrapping as **NAGIA**, on 25.3.2013 return to Piraeus roads, there laid up /

WIND AMBITION ex PRINSESSAN BIRGITTA (photo: Frank Heine)

CESME, built in 1974 as **PRINSESSAN BIRGITTA** (IMO No. 7347548)
20.5.2010 **WIND AMBITION**, C-Bed, London and conversion into accommodation ship, chartered in offshore sector /

REGINA BALTICA ex VIKING SONG (photo: Jochen Wegener)

REGINA BALTICA, built in 1980 as **VIKING SONG** (IMO No. 7827225)
27.5.2010 service Algeciras—Tangier / 15.6.—15.9.2010 service Almeria—Nador under charter by Acciona Trasmediterranea / 17.9.—10.2010 service Tvøroyri—Tórshavn under charter by Strandfaraskip Landsins / 10.2010 laid up in Tallinn / 9.6.—9.2011 service Almeria—Nador under charter by Acciona Trasmediterranea / 1.2012 offshore accommodation ship in the North Sea / 27.2.2015 to SweOffshore, Riga /

KAPITAN DRANITSYN, built in 1980 (IMO No. 7824405)
2012 last deployed for expedition cruises, continuing to operate as icebreaker /

AFRICA MERCY ex DRONNING INGRID (photo: Rob de Visser)

AFRICA MERCY, built in 1980 as **DRONNING INGRID** (IMO No. 7803188)
Continuing to operate as hospital ship /

C.S. WAVE MERCURY, built in 1982 as
MERCANDIAN PRESIDENT (IMO No. 8027808)
2010 **CS FUN AN**, SB Submarine Systems, Panama, continuing to operate as cable repair ship /

TANJUNG NUSANIVE, built in 1984 as **KAMBUNA** (IMO No. 8209688)
Continuing to operate as troop carrier for the Indonesian Navy /

TANJUNG FATAGAR, built in 1984 as **RINJANI** (IMO No. 8303252)
Continuing to operate as troop carrier for the Indonesian Navy /

HELIX PRODUCER I, built in 1986 as **KARL CARSTENS** (IMO No. 8420115)
Continuing to be deployed as Floating Production and Storage Offloading (FSPO) ship /

SOVETSKIY SOYUZ, built in 1989 (IMO No. 8838582)
2007 laid up in Murmansk, intended for scrapping / 2012 renovation started. Recommissioning without passenger transport planned for 2016 /

UTOPIA IV ex NEW AKATSUKI (photo: Vladimir Tonic)

ISKENDERUN (photo: Kai Ortel)

ISKENDERUN, built in 1991 (IMO No. 8417390)
Continued operation for Turkish Navy /

ms NEW AKATSUKI
IMO No. 9045895
A'Line Ferry, Naze
Hayashikane Dockyard, Nagasaki; Yard No.: 995

6412 GRT / 4322 tdw / 145.61 m length oa / 22.00 m beam / two 12-cyl. diesels geared to 2 screws; Pielstick-Diesel United / 11 900 kW / 21.50 (24.20) kn / 594 pass in cabins, 6 unberthed / 54 cars, 70 trucks / crew 28

5.4.1992 launched / 8.7.1992 delivered, then service Kobe—Naha / 9.2008 **AKATSUKI**, Palma Mangement, Panama, 14 250 GT / 10.2009 **UTOPIA IV**, Utopia Line, Panama, 36 Pass. / 2009 service Shimonoseki—Taicang /

YAMAL, built in 1992 (IMO No. 9077549)
2007 last deployed for North Pole cruises, continued operation as icebreaker /

YAMAL (photo: Pink floyd88 a, CC BY-SA 3.0 – https://creativecommons.org/licenses/by-sa/3.0/deed.de)

EUROFERRY MALTA ex LINDA (photo: Frank Heine)

EUROFERRY MALTA, built in 1995 as **LINDA** (IMO No. 9108556)
Continued deployment as RoRo cargo ship /

EUROCARGO NAPOLI ex NORSE MERSEY (photo: Manuel Hernandez Lafuente)

EUROCARGO NAPOLI, built in 1995 as **NORSE MERSEY** (IMO No. 9108568)
Continued deployment as RoRo cargo ship /

MONT VENTOUX ex LINDAROSA (photo: George Koutsoukis)

MONT VENTOUX, built in 1996 as **LINDAROSA** (IMO No. 9129586)
Continued deployment as RoRo cargo ship /

NORMAN BRIDGE, built in 1999 as **BRAVE MERCHANT** (IMO No. 9147306)
1.3.2010 renamed **NORMAN BRIDGE** / 18.3.–30.8.2010 service Boulogne—Dover
under charter by LD Lines / 8.9.2010 entered service St. Nazaire—Gijon / 22.5.2011
laid up in Falmouth / 12.2011 to Equinox Offshore Accommodation Limited /
1.2012 arrival in Singapore for conversion into Accommodation and Repair Vessel at
Sembawang Shipyard / 2012 renamed **ARV 3**, home port Madeira / 6.2013 renamed
AQUARIUS BRASIL / 2013 deployed off Brazilian coast under charter by Petrobras /

AQUARIUS BRASIL ex BRAVE MERCHANT (photo: Ian Shiffman)

Appendix 3
Passenger ships under construction

– in as far as they were not already presented in the main part as sister ship of an older unit. Only provisional reference values given.

TEXELSTROOM (photo: owner)

TEXELSTROOM, Texels Eigen Stoomboot Onderneming
IMO No. 9741918
Construcciones Navales del Norte, Sestao
16 400 GT / 1684 tdw / 135.40 m length oa / 27.90 m beam /
1750 pass. unberthed / 350 cars /
30.7.2015 launched / 2016 delivery planned, service Texel—Den Helder planned /

CARNIVAL VISTA (photo: Vladimir Tonic)

CARNIVAL VISTA, Carnival Cruise Line
IMO No. 9614141
Fincantieri, Monfalcone; Yard No.: 6242
133 500 GT / 321.50 m length oa / 3930 (4716) pass. in 1965 cabins /
crew 1450
25.6.2015 floated out / 4.2016 delivery planned /

KONINGSDAM (photo: owner)

KONINGSDAM, Holland America Line
IMO No. 9692557
Fincantieri, Marghera; Yard No.: 6241
99 500 GT / 285.00 m length oa / 2650 (3194) pass. in 1331 cabins / crew 1025
26.2.2015 floated out / 3.2016 delivery planned /

SEVEN SEAS EXPLORER, Regent Seven Seas Cruises
IMO No. 9703150
Fincantieri, Sestri Ponente; Yard No.: 6250
54 000 GT / 223.00 m length oa / 738 pass. in 369 cabins / crew 542
30.10.2015 floated out / 7.2016 delivery planned /

SEVEN SEAS EXPLORER (photo: owner)

281

GENTING DREAM (photo: owner)

GENTING DREAM, Dream Cruises
Meyer Werft, Papenburg; Yard No.: 711
151 000 GT / 324.00 m length oa / 3360 (4500) pass. in 1680 cabins /
crew 2000
10.2016 delivery planned /

SEABOURN ENCORE (photo: owner)

SEABOURN ENCORE, Seabourn Cruise Line
Fincantieri, Marghera; Yard No.: 6251
40 350 GT / 210.00 m length oa / 604 pass. in
302 cabins / crew 330
11.2016 delivery planned /

ORIENTAL PEARL 8 (photo: owner)

ORIENTAL PEARL 8, Dandong Ferry
Shandong Huanghai Shipbuilding
24 000 GT / 4700 tdw / 185.00 m length oa / 25.80 m beam / two diesels;
MAN / 21 600 kW / 1400 pass. / 1500 lane metres /
4.2016 delivery planned, for service Incheon—Dandong /

Newbuild, Dandong Ferry
Shandong Huanghai Shipbuilding
24 000 GT / 4700 tdw / 185.00 m length oa / 25.80 m beam / two diesels;
MAN / 21 600 kW / 1400 pass. / 1500 lane metres /
2016 delivery planned, for service Incheon—Dandong /

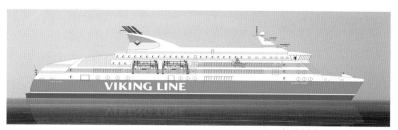

Newbuild (photo: Viking Line)

Newbuild
IMO No. 9430105
Factorías Vulcano Shipyard, Vigo
15 600 GT / 2300 tdw / 133.00 m length oa / 21.90 m beam / two 8-cyl. diesels;
Wärtsilä / 20 000 kW / 2 screws / 22 kn / 1500 pass. unberthed / 320 cars
2009 delivery as VIKING ADCC to Viking Line for service Mariehamn—Kapellskär
planned, cancelled after bankruptcy of builders IZAR Construcciones Navales,
Seville / 25.5.2013 launched / 6.2013 towed to Factorías Vulcano Shipyard, Vigo
for completion /

Newbuild, Algerie Ferries
Hijos de J. Barreras, Vigo
180.00 m length oa / 29.00 m beam / 2000 pass. / 700 cars /
2.2017 delivery planned, for service Algeria—Alicante/Marseilles /

Tallink newbuild (photo: owner)

Newbuild, Tallink
Meyer Turku, Turku
49 000 GT / 212.00 m length oa / 2800 pass. /
2017 delivery planned, for service Tallinn—Helsinki /

MSC MERAVIGLIA (photo: owner)

MSC MERAVIGLIA, MSC Cruises
STX France Cruise, St. Nazaire; Yard No.: E34
167 600 GT / 315.00 m length oa / 4500 (5700) pass. in 2250 cabins / crew 1536
5.2017 delivery planned /

WORLD DREAM, Dream Cruises
Meyer Werft, Papenburg; Yard No.: 712
151 000 GT / 324.00 m length oa / 3360 (4500) pass. in 1680 cabins / crew 2000
10.2017 delivery planned /

MSC SEASIDE (photo: owner)

MSC SEASIDE, MSC Cruises
Fincantieri, Monfalcone; Yard No.: 6256
154 000 GT / 323.00 m length oa / 4140 (5300) pass. in 2070 cabins / crew 1413
11.2017 delivery planned /

Newbuild, MOL Ferry
Japan Marine United
17 000 GRT / 199.70 m length oa / 27.20 m beam / 620 pass. / 113 cars /
2017 delivery planned for service Tomakomai—Oarai /

Newbuild, MOL Ferry
Japan Marine United
17 000 GRT / 199.70 m length oa / 27.20 m beam / 620 pass. / 113 cars /
2017 delivery planned for service Tomakomai—Oarai /

Newbuild, Rederi AB Gotland
Guangzhou Shipyard, Guangzhou; Yard No.: 14121001
200.00 m length oa / 1650 pass. / 1700 lane metres /
2017 delivery planned for service Visby—Nynäshamn/Oskarshamn /

Newbuild, Shidao Ferry Line
Huanghai Shipbuilding
20 000 GT / 196.00 m length oa / 28.60 m beam / 2500 lane metres /
2017 delivery planned, for service Shidao—Incheon /

Newbuild, Ferry Sunflower
Japan Marine United
13 500 GRT / 192.00 m length oa / 27.00 m beam / 709 pass. /
3.2018 delivery planned, for service Osaka—Shibushi /

Newbuild, Carnival Cruise Line
Fincantieri, Monfalcone
133 500 GT / 321.50 m length oa / 3930 (4716) pass. in 1965 cabins / crew 1450
Spring 2018 delivery planned /

SEABOURN OVATION, Seabourn Cruise Line
Fincantieri, Marghera
40 350 GT / 210.00 m length oa / 604 pass. in 302 cabins / crew 330
Spring 2018 delivery planned /

Newbuild, MSC Cruises
Fincantieri, Monfalcone; Yard No.: 6257
154 000 GT / 323.00 m length oa / 4140 (5300) pass. in 2070 cabins / crew 1413
5.2018 delivery planned /

Newbuild, Ferry Sunflower
Japan Marine United
13 500 GRT / 192.00 m length oa / 27.00 m beam / 709 pass. /
6.2018 delivery planned, for service Osaka—Shibushi /

Newbuild, Rederi AB Gotland
Guangzhou Shipyard, Guangzhou
200.00 m length oa / 1650 pass. / 1700 lane metres /
2018 delivery planned, for service Visby—Nynäshamn/Oskarshamn /

Newbuild, Celebrity Cruises
STX France Cruise, St. Nazaire
117 000 GT / 300.00 m length oa / 2900 pass. in cabins /
Autumn 2018 delivery planned /

Rederi AB Gotland newbuild (photo: owner)

Newbuild, Holland America Line
Fincantieri, Marghera
99 500 GT / 285.00 m length oa / 2650 (3194) pass. in 1331 cabins / crew 1025
Autumn 2018 delivery planned /

Crystal Cruises newbuild (photo: owner)

Newbuild, Crystal Cruises
Lloyd Werft, Bremerhaven
100 000 GT / 1000 pass. in cabins /
End of 2018 delivery planned /

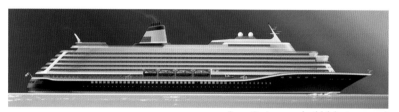
Saga Cruises newbuild (photo: owner)

Newbuild, Saga Cruises
Meyer Werft, Papenburg
55 900 GT / 234.00 m length oa / 540 cabins
Summer 2019 delivery planned /

Newbuild, AIDA Cruises
Meyer Werft, Papenburg
180 000 GT / > 2500 cabins /
2019 delivery planned /

Newbuild, Costa Asia
Fincantieri
135 500 GT / 323.00 m length oa / 4200 pass. in cabins /
2019 delivery planned, for Chinese market /

Costa Crociere newbuild (photo: owner)

Newbuild, Costa Crociere
Meyer Turku, Turku
183 200 GT / 337.00 m length oa / 5176 (6600) pass. in 2605 cabins / crew 1647
2019 delivery planned /

Newbuild, MSC Cruises
STX France Cruise, St. Nazaire; Yard No.: F34
167 600 GT / 315.00 m length oa / 4500 (5700) pass. in 2250 cabins / crew 1536
2019 delivery planned /

Newbuild, P&O Cruises Australia
Fincantieri
135 500 GT / 323.00 m length oa / 4200 pass. in cabins /
2019 delivery planned /

Newbuild, AIDA Cruises
Meyer Werft, Papenburg
180 000 GT / > 2500 cabins /
2020 delivery planned /

Newbuild, Costa Crociere
Meyer Turku, Turku
183 200 GT / 337.00 m length oa / 5176 (6600) pass. in 2605 cabins / crew 1647
2020 delivery planned /

Newbuild, Celebrity Cruises
STX France Cruise, St. Nazaire
117 000 GT / 300.00 m length oa / 2900 pass. in cabins /
2020 delivery planned /

Newbuild, Costa Asia
Fincantieri
135 500 GT / 323.00 m length oa / 4200 pass. in cabins /
2020 delivery planned, for Chinese market /

Newbuild, Virgin Cruises
Fincantieri
110 000 GT / 2860 pass. in 1430 cabins / crew 1150
2020 delivery planned /

Newbuild, Virgin Cruises
Fincantieri
110 000 GT / 2860 pass. in 1430 cabins / crew 1150
2021 delivery planned /

Newbuild, Virgin Cruises
Fincantieri
110 000 GT / 2860 pass. in 1430 cabins / crew 1150
2022 delivery planned /

Appendix 4
Passenger ships withdrawn since 2010

The ships are listed here alphabetically under their name given in the 2010 issue, which gives full details of their respective lives. Here only the events that have become known since then are recorded.

Shipbreaking at Aliaga, from left AL MANSOUR ex STENA NORDICA, BANASA ex METTE MOLS (later refloated and sold for further trade) and LISBOA ex DANAE (photo: Selim San)

AL MANSOUR, built in 1975 as
STENA NORDICA (IMO NO. 7360629)
3.2012 laid up in Algeciras after bankruptcy of shipping company / 20.8.2015 arrived for scrapping at Aliaga.

AMBASSADOR II, built in 1970 as
PRINS OBERON (IMO No. 7011515)
16.1.2011 arrived for scrapping at New Orleans.

ANCONA, built in 1966 as
SVEA (IMO No. 6608098)
30.9.2010 last voyage in service Ancona—Split / 16.12.2010 arrived for scrapping at Alang.

ANTHI MARINA, built in 1979 as
SPIRIT OF FREE ENTERPRISE
(IMO No. 7820473)
4.2012 home port Lome / 3.4.2012 arrived for scrapping at Aliaga.

ANTHI MARINA ex SPIRIT OF FREE ENTERPRISE (photo: Selim San)

AQUAMARINE, built in 1971 as **NORDIC PRINCE** (IMO No. 7027411)
12.2010 **OCEAN STAR PACIFIC**, Corporacion De Cruceros Nacionales, Panama. Conversion work in Willemstad / 11.4.2011 first cruise along the Mexican Riviera / 16.4.2011 engine room fire off Huatulco, towed to Salina Cruz and laid up, later to Mazatlan / 5.2012 to ALAS International Holdings / 7.2014 laid up in Guaymas / 8.2014 renamed **PACIFIC**, home port Basseterre / 13.10.2014 departure from Guaymas for scrapping / 12.12.2014 grounded off General Santos City, Philippines due to lack of fuel, towed free / 22.2.2015 arrived for scrapping at Alang.

ARIES (photo: Selim San)

ARIES, built in 1998 (IMO No. 9144275)
8.2011 home port Lome / 16.8.2011 arrived for scrapping at Aliaga.

AHURA ex ARAHURA (photo: Michael Pryce)

ARAHURA, built in 1983 (IMO No. 8201454)
29.7.2015 last voyage in service Picton—Wellington / 9.2015 renamed **AHURA**, home port Malakal Harbor / 3.11.2015 arrived for scrapping at Alang.

ATHENS, built in 1969 as **BRISBANE TRADER** (IMO No. 6909624)
22.4.2010 last voyage in service Durres—Bari / 5.2010 **WINNER 11**, home port Basseterre / 22.5.2010 arrived for scrapping at Alang.

ANTIC ex FAIRSKY (photo: Peter Knego)

ATLANTIC STAR, built in 1984 as **FAIRSKY** (IMO No. 8024026)
27.8.2010 some cruises from Lisbon as replacement for the defective PACIFIC DREAM, then laid up again in Marseilles / 12.2012 to STX France Cruise as part payment for the newbuild HARMONY OF THE SEAS of Royal Caribbean International / 3.2013 renamed **ANTIC**, home port Lome / 4.4.2013 arrived for scrapping at Aliaga.

AMET MAJESTY ex BORE STAR (photo: Marko Stampehl)

ARBERIA, built in 1975 as **BORE STAR** (IMO No. 7360198)
29.3.2011 **AMET MAJESTY**, Academy of Maritime Education & Training, Chennai / 2011 training and cruise ship for AMET University in Kanathus near Chennai / 9.6.2011 first cruise from Chennai / 17.5.2013 arrived for scrapping at Alang.

BAHAMAS CELEBRATION, built in 1981 as **PRINSESSE RAGNHILD** (IMO No. 7904891)
15.3.2010 first cruise Palm Beach—Freeport / 31.10.2014 grounded while departing Freeport, considerable water ingress. With tug support back to pier, there laid up / 1.2015 sold for scrap / 4.2015 **CELEBRATION**, Green Ocean Ship Management, Basseterre / 29.10.2015 arrived for scrapping at Alang.

ATLAS HAN ex TOR ANGLIA (photo: Selim San)

BAIA SARDINIA, built in 1966 as **TOR ANGLIA** (IMO No. 6600606)
5.6.2009 service Naples—Golfo Aranci/Palau/Cagliari / 23.8.2010 last voyage for DiMaiolines / 6.9.2010 arrival at Aliaga for scrapping, then as **ATLAS HAN** to Yazici Demir Celik Sanayi Ve Turizm Ticaret, towed to Iskenderun as accommodation ship for construction of a power station / 2015 scrapped at Iskenderun.

BENI SIDEL, built in 1982 as **CIUDAD DE SALAMANCA** (IMO No. 7909932)
5.2013 home port Lome / 14.5.2013 arrived for scrapping at Aliaga.

BERKANE, built in 1976 as **NAPOLEON** (IMO No. 7401215)
5.1.2012 arrested in Almeria / 18.2.2015 arrived for scrapping at Aliaga.

BILADI, built in 1980 as **LIBERTE** (IMO No. 7824912)
4.1.2012 arrested in Sète / 7.2013 home port Lome / 15.7.2013 arrived for scrapping at Aliaga.

MAESTRO ex RENAISSANCE (photo: Kaushal Trivedi copyright MidShip Century)

BLUE MONARCH, built in 1966 as **RENAISSANCE** (IMO No. 6604834)
3.2010 renamed **MAESTRO**, home port Freetown / 6.8.2010 arrived for scrapping at Alang.

BSP III, built in 1973 as FREE ENTERPRISE VII (IMO No. 7230616)
7.2014 laid up off Cilegon / 11.7.2015 capsized off Bojonegara after water ingress.

CAGAYAN BAY 1, built in1972 as **GOLDEN OKINAWA** (IMO No. 7210305)
2015 scrapped at Cebu.

CARIBBEAN EXPRESS, built in 1976 as **KRONPRINS HARALD** (IMO No. 7400778)
15.4.2010 service discontinued, laid up / 7.2010 home port Basseterre / 25.1.2011 arrived for scrapping at Alang.

CHANG XING DAO, built in 1982 as **TORRE DEL GRECO** (IMO No. 7820746)
2007 scrapped.

CLAUDIA M, built in 1969 as **FINNCARRIER** (IMO No. 6915881)
9.6.2012 entered service Livorno—Cagliari, also Livorno—Olbia under charter by Moby Lines / 5.12.2012 laid up in the Bay of Eleusis / 11.7.2014 arrived for scrapping at Aliaga.

CLODIA, built in 1980 (IMO No. 7717377)
1.11.2012 laid up in Olbia / 28.2.2013 renamed **CLODIAR**, home port Basseterre / 18.4.2013 arrived for scrapping at Alang.

CORA ex CUNARD ADVENTURER (photo: Kaushal Trivedi copyright MidShip Century)

CORAL, built in 1971 as **CUNARD ADVENTURER** (IMO No. 7046936)
2011 home port Valletta / 13.12.2013 **CORA**, Argo Systems fze, Basseterre / 31.1.2014 arrived for scrapping at Alang.

COSTA ALLEGRA, built in 1969 as **ANNI JOHNSON** (IMO No. 6916885)
27.2.2012 engine room fire in Indian Ocean, towed to Port Victoria / 25.3.2012 laid up in Savona / 5.5.2012 laid up in Genoa / 10.2012 **SANTA CRUISE**, Themis Maritime Ltd., Freetown / 26.10.2012 arrived for scrapping at Aliaga.

COSTA CONCORDIA (photo: Frank Lose)

COSTA CONCORDIA, built in 2006 (IMO No. 9320544)
13.1.2012 with 4229 persons on board en route from Civitavecchia to Savona collided at full speed with a rock off the island of Giglio as a result of negligent navigation by the master. 70 m long gash torn in hull, stranded off Giglio Porto and capsized. 32 persons killed / 17.9.2013 righted by Titan Salvage/Micoperi / 15.7.2014 refloated / 27.7.2014 arrived for scrapping at Genoa.

HARMONY I ex AXEL JOHNSON (photo: Peter Knego)

COSTA MARINA, built in 1969 as AXEL JOHNSON (IMO No. 6910544)
17.11.2011 end of last cruise for Costa in Savona / 21.11.2011 **HARMONY PRINCESS,** Harmony Cruises, Majuro / 13.1.2012 renamed **CLUB HARMONY** / 16.2.2012 first cruise from Busan / 2.2013 laid up in Mokpo, later in Gwangyang / 25.10.2014 arrived for scrapping at Alang as **HARMONY 1,** home port Basseterre.

DIPLOMAT, built in 1978 as **STENA TRADER** (IMO No. 7528661)
4.2010 service Santo Domingo—Mayaguez under charter by Marine Express / 3.2011 **PAVILION,** home port Basseterre / 12.8.2011 arrived for scrapping at Alang.

AMEN ex ISLAND VENTURE (photo: Peter Knego)

DISCOVERY, built in 1972 as **ISLAND VENTURE** (IMO No. 7108514)
2.2013 cruises under charter by Cruise & Maritime Voyages / 6.10.2014 end of last cruise in Avonmouth / 16.10.2014 **AMEN,** Liberty Resources Inc., Basseterre / 8.12.2014 arrived for scrapping at Alang.

DISCOVERY SUN, built in 1968 as **FREEPORT** (IMO No. 6815158)
7.9.2011 Discovery Cruise Line discontinued operation / 25.2.2012 arrived for scrapping at Chittagong.

OCEAN LIFE ex LEV TOLSTOY (photo: George Koutsoukis)

ACE II ex STENA JUTLANDICA (photo: Jürgen Saupe)

EASYCRUISE LIFE, built in 1981 as **LEV TOLSTOY** (IMO No. 7625809)
10.2009 Hellenic Seaways management, laid up in Drapetsona / 10.2010 renamed **OCEAN LIFE**, under charter by Blue Ocean Cruises in India / 15.11.2010 after water ingress as a result of defective ballast tank line laid up in Mormugao, following repair transferred to Greece and laid up in Ampelaki / 15.8.2014 arrived for scrapping at Aliaga.

EUROFERRYS ATLANTICA, built in 1973 as **STENA JUTLANDICA** (IMO No. 7218668)
8.9.2010 laid up in Motril / 22.12.2010 arrived for scrapping at Alang as **ACE II**, home port Basseterre.

EUROVOYAGER, built in 1978 as **PRINS ALBERT** (IMO No. 7613882)
30.6.–9.2010 service Al Hoceima—Almeria under charter by Comarit / 1.2011 service Algeciras—Tangier under charter by FRS / 12.12.2011 laid up in Messina / 27.4.2012 arrived for scrapping at Aliaga as **VOYAGER**, home port Lome.

ELIANA M, built in 1978 as **ESPRESSO VENETO** (IMO No. 7350985)
30.04.2012 arrived for scrapping at Aliaga.

DIAMOND ex TOR HOLLANDIA (photo: Selim San)

ENVOY, built in 1979 as **IBEX** (IMO No. 7716074)
27.4.–2.5.2010 service Travemünde—Liepaja under charter by Scandlines / 28.1.2011 **REYES B**, Boluda Lines, Madeira / 15.3.2011 entered service Seville— Las Palmas de Gran Canaria—Santa Cruz de Tenerife / 25.6.2011 laid up in Las Palmas de Gran Canaria / 12.9.2011 **ENVOY 1**, Boa Offshore, Panama, laid up / 9.1.2012 arrived for scrapping at Aliaga.

F. DIAMOND, built in 1967 as **TOR HOLLANDIA** (IMO No. 6704402)
11.9.2010 arrived for scrapping at Aliaga as **DIAMOND**, home port Kingstown.

KRITOS ex ISHIKARI (photo: George Koutsoukis)

RAIL TRADER 1 ex FINNFELLOW (photo: Selim San)

EROTOKRITOS T, built in 1974 as **ISHIKARI** (IMO No. 7394747)
28.8.2010 last voyage in service Brindisi—Igoumenitsa—Patras, then laid up in Perama / 12.2010 renamed **KRITOS**, home port Moroni / 11.1.2011 arrived for scrapping at Alang.

FELLOW, built in 1973 as **FINNFELLOW** (IMO No. 7315143)
20.4.2011 **NIKOLAY KONAREV**, Anship, Basseterre / 8.2012 service Mersin—Port Said / 3.3.2013 entered service Sevastopol—Zonguldak / 3.9.2013 arrived for scrapping at Aliaga as **RAIL TRADER 1**.

FILIPINA EXPRESS, built in 1973 as **FERRY AKASHIA** (IMO No. 7313858)
6.2011 renamed **PRINCESS**, home port Belize City / 28.9.2011 arrived for scrapping at Alang.

FUDI, built in 1979 as **STAFFETTA LIGURE** (IMO No. 7601994)
6.4.2011 capsized after malfunction of the ballast system during a shipyard overhaul in Tanjung Perak, Surabaya / 2012 scrapped at Surabaya.

ANI ex TRANSFINLANDIA (photo: Selim San)

FINLANDIA, built in 1981 as **TRANSFINLANDIA** (IMO No. 8002640)
20.12.2010 **SNAV CAMPANIA**, SNAV, Naples / 27.12.2010 entered service Naples—Palermo / 17.6.2012 entered service Genoa—Palermo under charter by Grandi Navi Veloci / 5.9.2012 arrived for scrapping at Aliaga as **ANI**, home port Freetown.

FLAMINIA, built in 1981 (IMO No. 7602132)
12.1.2011 last arrival in Bari, there laid up / 30.6.2011 laid up in Crotone / 10.2012 renamed **NEW YORK**, home port Basseterre / 26.6.2013 arrived for scrapping at Alang.

FOS 1, built in 1986 as **MIKHAIL SHOLOKHOV** (IMO No. 8325420)
2011 **PHOENIX**, Adalia Maritime Corp., Basseterre / 29.7.2011 arrived for scrapping at Alang.

FRONTIER, built in 1987 as **REPUBBLICA DI GENOVA** (IMO No. 8521206)
16.8.2010 arrived for scrapping at Alang as **FRONT**.

GEN. EDWIN D. PATRICK, built in 1945 as **ADMIRAL C.F. HUGHES**
5.2010 scrapped at Brownsville, Texas.

GENERAL JOHN POPE, built in 1943
2010 scrapped at Brownsville, Texas.

GEORG BÜCHNER, built in 1951 as **CHARLESVILLE** (IMO No. 5068863)
28.5.2013 towed from Rostock to Klaipeda for scrapping / 31.5.2013 sank off Polish coast after water ingress.

GEORG OTS, built in 1980 (IMO No. 7625835)
2010 service from Vladivostok to Sakhalin and Kamchatka / 18.1.2013 laid up / 8.2014 scrapped in China.

GIULIA D'ABUNDO, built in 1975 as **NILS DACKE** (IMO No. 7362110)
25.4.2010 arrived for scrapping at Alang as **ABUNDO**, home port Basseterre.

GOLDEN TRADE, built in 1988 as **AMERICANA** (IMO No. 8608119)
2.2010 arrived for scrapping at Jiangyin.

APOLLONIA ex GÖTALAND (photo: Selim San)

GÖTALAND, built in 1973 (IMO No. 7229514)
7.9.2010 to Ugtrans Terminal Co., Basseterre / 29.12.2010 renamed **APOLLONIA** / 19.6.2011 entered service Baltiysk—Sassnitz / 2.2012 home port Giurgiulesti / 6.2012 service Mersin—Port Said / 4.9.2012 laid up in Mersin / 28.12.2012 laid up in Sevastopol / 28.4.2013 arrived for scrapping at Aliaga.

HABIB, built in 1978 (IMO No. 7631236)
22.2.2012 laid up in Menzel Bourguiba / 31.7.2013 arrived for scrapping at Alang as **HABI**, Tanzanian flag.

HAI HUA, built in 1972 as **FABIOLAVILLE** (IMO No. 7204356)
2011 taken off the registers.

HSS DISCOVERY ex STENA DISCOVERY (photo: Selim San)

HSS DISCOVERY, built in 1997 as **STENA DISCOVERY** (IMO No. 9107590)
27.7.2015 arrived for scrapping at Aliaga, Tanzanian flag.

ILE DE BEAUTE, built in 1979 as **CYRNOS** (IMO No. 7715379)
2012 laid up in Bizerte / 4.7.2013 arrived for scrapping at Aliaga as **BEAU.**

ISABEL DEL MAR, built in 1988 as **NEW HARIMA** (IMO No. 8618140)
21.9.2014 arrived for scrapping at Aliaga.

WINNER 5 ex AUSONIA (photo: Peter Knego)

IVORY, built in 1957 as **AUSONIA** (IMO No. 5031078)
1.2010 renamed **WINNER 5**, home port Basseterre / 2.3.2010 arrived for scrapping at Alang.

JOSEPH AND CLARA SMALLWOOD, built in 1989 (IMO No. 8604797)
8.3.2011 last voyage in service Port aux Basques—North Sydney / 6.10.2011 arrived for scrapping at Alang as **SMALLWOOD**, home port Basseterre.

ADVENTURE ex KAZAKHSTAN (photo: Peter Knego)

ISLAND ADVENTURE, built in 1976 as **KAZAKHSTAN** (IMO No. 7359486)
5.2011 **ADVENTURE**, Exim Inc., Daressalam / 13.11.2011 arrived for scrapping at Alang.

KERINICI, built in 1983 (IMO No. 8209676)
2013 laid up in Tanjung Priok / 9.2014 **ARK**, Pacmar Shipping, Singapore. Conversion into accommodation ship planned / 8.12.2014 arrived for scrapping at Chittagong.

KC BRIDGE, built in 1980 as **OSUMI** (IMO No. 7908835)
31.5.2010 arrived for scrapping at Zangjiagang.

KILMORE, built in 1977 as **NORSKY** (IMO No. 7528582)
4.2010 home port Moroni / 3.5.2010 arrived for scrapping at Aliaga.

LISCO GLORIA ex GOLFO DEI CORALLI (photo: Marc Peper)

LISCO GLORIA, built in 2001 as
GOLFO DEI CORALLI (IMO No. 9212151)
9.10.2010 fire broke out in a trailer on the upper truck deck shortly after midnight off Fehmarn on a voyage from Kiel to Klaipeda. 204 pass. and 32 crew members taken to Kiel by Scandlines ferry DEUTSCHLAND / 21.10.2010 towed to Fayard, Odense / 3.1.2011 declared total loss / 18.2.2011 towed from Odense to Klaipeda for scrapping, arrived on 22.2.2011.

LISSOS ex FERRY HAMANASU (photo: Peter Knego)

LISSOS, built in 1972 as **FERRY HAMANASU** (IMO No. 7220269)
1.5.2011 arrived for scrapping at Alang.

MARINA, built in 1971 as **GREEN ACE** (IMO No. 7203467)
5.9.2011 arrived for scrapping at Aliaga.

SAR ex FERRY AKASHI (photo: Selim San)

MARRAKECH EXPRESS, built in 1972 as **FERRY AKASHI** (IMO No. 7236335)
5.2010 renamed **BNI NSAR** / 4.12.2011 laid up in Sète / 31.7.2014 arrived for scrapping at Aliaga as **SAR**, home port Lome.

MERDIF 1, built in 1973 as **ALBIREO** (IMO No. 7229980)
10.7.2010 arrived for scrapping at Alang.

MERDIF 2, built in 1972 as **ARKAS** (IMO No. 7213072)
1.2.2011 arrived for scrapping at Alang.

MIRAGE I, built in 1973 as **BOLERO** (IMO No. 7221433)
3.2012 home port Freetown / 19.3.2012 arrived for scrapping at Aliaga.

MOBY FANTASY, built in 1976 as **MANUEL SOTO** (IMO No. 7387706)
16.12.2013 arrived for scrapping at Aliaga.

MOGADOR, built in 1975 as **VIKING VALIANT** (IMO No. 7358298)
3.3.2010 arrived for scrapping at Alang as **MOGADO**, home port Freetown.

MONA LISA ex KUNGSHOLM (photo: owner)

MONA LISA, built in 1966 as **KUNGSHOLM** (IMO No. 6512354)
31.8.2010 end of last cruise for Lord Nelson Seereisen in Bremerhaven / 14.9.2010 laid up in Perama / 9.2010 to Daewoo Shipbuilding / 11.10.2010 from Perama via Suez Canal to Duqm, Oman, there converted into hotel ship / 12.2011 opened as hotel ship with marketing name "Veronica" / 3.10.2013 hotel operation discontinued, then laid up in Duqm / 19.11.2015 arrived for scrapping at Alang.

MONTE STELLO, built in 1979 (IMO No. 7807093)
26.1.2012 arrived for scrapping at Alang, home port Moroni.

MORNING SHINE, built in 1973 as **PEGASUS** (IMO No. 7302081)
7.5.2011 arrived for scrapping at Jiangyin.

NOMENTANA, built in 1980 (IMO No. 7602118)
29.7.2012 last voyage in service Civitavecchia—Cagliari / 31.7.2012 laid up in Trapani / 30.3.2013 arrived for scrapping at Alang as **NOMT**, home port Basseterre.

NORMANDY, built in 1982 as **PRINSESSAN BIRGITTA** (IMO No. 7901772)
25.11.2012 arrived for scrapping at Alang, planned conversion not realised.

OCEAN COUNTESS ex CUNARD COUNTESS (photo: George Koutsoukis)

OCEAN COUNTESS, built in 1975 as **CUNARD COUNTESS**
(IMO No. 7358561)
26.10.2012 laid up in Chalkida / 30.11.2013 burnt out during conversion work at Chalkis Shipyard / 10.3.2014 arrived for scrapping at Aliaga, home port Freetown.

OCEAN JEWEL OF ST. PETERSBURG, built in 1982 as **MIKHAIL SUSLOV**
(IMO No. 7625823)
2012 scrapped at Ciramar Shipyards, Santo Domingo.

OCEAN PEARL, built in 1970 as **SONG OF NORWAY** (IMO No. 7005190)
28.9.2011 after bankruptcy of charterer laid up in Gibraltar / 26.10.2011 laid up in Tilbury / 4.2012 to Asia Pacific Cruises / 6.2012 renamed **FORMOSA QUEEN**, home port Panama. Arrival in Guangzhou, start of renovation at Guangzhou Wenchong Shipyard / 26.10.2013 arrived for scrapping at Jiangmen.

OLA ESMERALDA ex BLACK PRINCE (photo: Cees Bustraan)

OLA ESMERALDA, built in 1966 as **BLACK PRINCE** (IMO No. 6613328)
2.2010 home port La Guaira / 27.10.2012 arrival in Santo Domingo, there laid up / 13.4.2013 home port Panama / 2013 scrapped at Santo Domingo.

OLEANDER, built in 1980 as **PRIDE OF FREE ENTERPRISE**
(IMO No. 7820497)
13.5.2010 last voyage in service Ostend—Ramsgate / 14.7.–9.2010 service Nador—Almeria under charter by Comarit / 12.2010–31.8.2011 service Algeciras—Ceuta under charter by Comarit, then laid up in Almeria / 5.2012–9.2012 service Almeria—Nador under charter by Ferrimaroc (Trasmediterranea), later also service Almeria—Ghazaouet / 5.2013 renamed **SHERBATSKIY**, then under charter by Acciona Trasmediterranea / 13.10.2015 last voyage in service Nador—Almeria / 11.12.2015 arrived for scrapping at Alang as **SHER**.

ONYX, built in 1966 as **FENNIA** (IMO No. 6600462)
4.2010 arrived at roads of Dubai / 4.2010 renamed **KAPTAIN BORIS** / 8.5.2010 arrived for scrapping at Gadani Beach.

OUJDA, built in 1975 as **VIKING VENTURER** (IMO No. 7358286)
4.4.2009 arrived for scrapping at Alang.

OUZOUD, built in 1974 as **PETER PAN** (IMO No. 7350088)
16.4.2010 arrived for scrapping at Alang as **WINNER 8**, home port Freetown.

ACIF ex SEA VENTURE (photo: Peter Knego)

PACIFIC, built in 1971 as **SEA VENTURE** (IMO No. 7018563)
10.2012 home port Lome / 7.2013 renamed **ACIF** / 7.8.2013 arrived for scrapping at Aliaga.

PACIFIC WINNER, built in 1987 as **REPUBBLICA DI PISA**
11.2009 **SEA ATEF**, Abou Merhi Lines, Valletta / 4.3.2010 arrived for scrapping at Chittagong.

PATRIOT STATE, built in 1964 as **SANTA MERCEDES** (IMO No. 5422409)
21.9.2011 arrived for scrapping at Brownsville, Texas.

PELLA, built in 1983 as **BIZAN MARU** (IMO No. 8319081)
3.11.2011 outbreak of fire on a voyage from Aqaba to Nuweiba 15 nm after departing Aqaba. One passenger killed, 1246 pass. rescued / 7.11.2011 ship capsized and sank.

LOPI ex EUROPEAN GATEWAY (photo: Peter Knego)

PENELOPE, built in 1975 as **EUROPEAN GATEWAY** (IMO No. 7400261)
23.8.2011 home port Limassol / 10.2011 service Libya—Tunisia under charter by
Marfamar / 29.11.2011 after end of charter laid up in Piraeus / 7.2013 arrived for
scrapping at Aliaga as **LOPI**, home port Lome.

PHILIPPINES ex AUGUSTUS (photo: Peter Knego)

PHILIPPINES, built in 1952 as **AUGUSTUS** (IMO No. 5030684)
11.10.2011 arrived for scrapping at Alang.

POLARIS, built in 1976 as **DANA FUTURA** (IMO No. 7358731)
5.9.2010 laid up in Igoumenitsa / 2.2011 renamed **LARISA**, home port Basseterre /
2.4.2011 arrived for scrapping at Alang.

DALMATIA ex POMERANIA (photo: Frank Heine)

POMERANIA, built in 1978 (IMO No. 7516761)
29.10.2010 last voyage in service Copenhagen—Swinoujscie / 2011 **DALMATIA**,
Blue Line Ferries, Panama / 4.4.2011 entered service Split—Ancona / 6.2014 home
port Limassol / 20.10.2014 arrived for scrapping at Alang.

OSTEND SPIRIT ex PRIDE OF CALAIS (photo: Selim San)

PRIDE OF CALAIS, built in 1987 (IMO No. 8517748)
20.10.2012 last voyage in service Calais—Dover / 31.1.2013 entered service
Ostend—Ramsgate under charter by TransEuropa Ferries, renamed **OSTEND SPIRIT**,
home port Ramsgate / 18.4.2013 laid up in Tilbury after end of charter / 10.11.2013
arrived for scrapping at Aliaga.

PRIDE ex PRIDE OF DOVER (photo: Selim San)

PRIDE OF DOVER, built in 1987 (IMO No. 8517736)
15.12.2010 last voyage in service Calais—Dover / 28.12.2012 arrived for scrapping at Aliaga as **PRIDE**, home port Freetown.

PRIDE OF TELEMARK, built in 1983 as **STENA JUTLANDICA** (IMO No. 7907257)
29.10.2010 laid up in Farsund / 19.10.2011 arrived for scrapping at Alang.

PRIMROSE, built in 1975 as **PRINCESSE MARIE-CHRISTINE** (IMO No. 7357567)
6.4.2010 last voyage in service Ramsgate—Ostend / 5.6.2010–3.2011 service Piombino—Portoferraio under charter by Blue Navy / 9.5.2011 arrived for scrapping at Alang as **ELEGANT I**, home port Basseterre.

LISBOA ex PORT MELBOURNE (photo: Luis Miguel Correia)

PRINCESS DANAE, built in 1955 as **PORT MELBOURNE** (IMO No. 5282483)
15.9.2012 arrested in Marseilles / 2.2013 to Portuscale Cruises, then laid up, later transferred to Lisbon / 5.2013 renamed **LISBOA**, home port Madeira, renovation work started in Lisbon / 3.2014 arrested in Lisbon / 24.7.2015 arrived for scrapping at Aliaga.

DAPHNE ex PORT SYDNEY (photo: Kaushal Trivedi copyright MidShip Century)

PRINCESS DAPHNE, built in 1955 as **PORT SYDNEY** (IMO No. 5282627)
29.4.2012 first cruise under charter by Ambiente Kreuzfahrten / 2.10.2012 arrested in Souda because of payment difficulties of the owner Classic International Cruises / 5.2014 renamed **DAPHNE**, home port Basseterre / 14.6.2014 arrived for scrapping at Alang.

PRINCESS OF PARADISE, built in 1974 as **HIRYU** (IMO No. 7377969)
1.12.2009 arrived for scrapping at Xinhui.

PRINCESS OF THE UNIVERSE, built in 1983 as **NEW YAMATO** (IMO No. 8217063)
16.8.2011 arrived for scrapping at Alang as **UNIVERSE**, home port Moroni.

RAHMAH, built in 1979 as **STAFFETTA MEDITERRANEA** (IMO No. 7811305)
29.4.2010 during conversion back into cargo ferry in Port Said a fire broke out, seriously damaging the ship / 26.4.2011 arrived for scrapping at Aliaga.

RAMADA AL SALEM HOTEL, built in 1958 as **SANTA PAULA** (IMO No. 5312745)
2002 scrapped in Kuwait.

REPUBBLICA DI AMALFI, built in 1989 (IMO No. 8521218)
10.2012 renamed **JAI BHOLE**, home port Basseterre / 7.11.2012 arrived for scrapping at Alang.

REPUBBLICA DI VENEZIA, built in 1987 (IMO No. 8511706)
15.7.2011 arrived for scrapping at Alang, as **VENEZIA**, home port Moroni.

RG I ex KAHLEBERG (photo: Ulrich Streich)

RG I, built in 1983 as **KAHLEBERG** (IMO No. 8306577)
30.12.2012 last voyage in service Umeå—Vaasa, later laid up in Vaasa / 19.2.2013 arrived for scrapping at Grenaa.

RODANTHI, built in 1974 as **VIRGO** (IMO No. 7353078)
2.2012 home port Lome / 14.2.2012 arrived for scrapping at Aliaga.

SAGA ROSE, built in 1965 as **SAGAFJORD** (IMO No. 6416043)
29.5.2010 arrived for scrapping at Jiangyin.

EASTERN LIGHT ex COTE D'AZUR (photo: Frank Lose)

ASPIRE ex ITALIA (photo: Kaushal Trivedi copyright MidShip Century)

SAPPHIRE, built in 1967 as **ITALIA** (IMO No. 6513994)
4.4.2012 renamed **ASPIRE**, home port Basseterre / 11.5.2012 arrived for scrapping at Alang.

SCOTIA PRINCE, built in 1972 as **STENA OLYMPICA** (IMO No. 7119836)
17.6.–10.2010 service Cesme—Ancona under charter by Marmara Lines / 13.6.2010 entered service Tuticorin—Colombo under charter by Flemingo Duty Free Shop Pvt. / 2.4.2012 arrived for scrapping at Chittagong as **PRINCE**, home port Moroni.

WESTERN LIGHT ex ARIADNE (photo: Peter Knego)

SEAFRANCE CEZANNE, built in 1980 as **ARIADNE** (IMO NO. 7229980)
7.2011 renamed **WESTERN LIGHT**, home port Belize City / 16.11.2011 arrived for scrapping at Alang.

SEAFRANCE RENOIR, built in 1981 as **COTE D'AZUR** (IMO No. 7920534)
7.2011 renamed **EASTERN LIGHT**, home port Belize City / 30.10.2011 arrived for scrapping at Alang.

SEATRADE, built in 1973 as **SVEALAND** (IMO No. 7301491)
2010 home port Limassol / 14.1.2012 arrived for scrapping at Alang as **SEA PROJECT**, home port Moroni.

SHEHRAZADE, built in 1975 as **BORGEN** (IMO No. 7358315)
9.9.2011 arrived for scrapping at Sachana, home port Funafuti.

SHUTTLE, built in 1987 as **OARAI MARU** (IMO No. 8613073)
5.2010 renamed **COLOSSUS**, home port Valletta / 6.2010 service Piraeus—Kos—Rhodes under charter by NEL Lines / 10.2010 service Corinth—Ancona under charter by NEL Lines / 17.11.2010 ran aground on a voyage from Corinth to Ancona off Lefka, ballast tanks torn open, fore ship badly damaged / 20.11.2010 towed free and to Patras for unloading cargo, then repaired in Perama / 4.1.2011 again service Corinth—Ancona / 8.2.2011 service Keratsini—Chios—Mytilene / 5.2011 service Keratsini—Kos—Rhodes / 16.1.2012 after end of charter laid up in Drapetsona / 2012 service Colombia—Trinidad & Tobago under charter by SC Line / 2013 laid up in Cape Town / 30.10.2013 arrived for scrapping at Mumbai.

SIREN, built in 1976 as **DANA GLORIA** (IMO No. 7358743)
30.3.2010 arrived for scrapping at Alang, home port Basseterre.

SNAV CAMPANIA, built in 1974 as **NORSTAR** (IMO No. 7360710)
1.11.2010 arrived for scrapping at Alang.

SNAV SICILIA, built in 1974 as **NORLAND** (IMO No. 7333822)
31.10.2010 arrived for scrapping at Alang.

STATE, built in 1950 as **PRESIDENT JACKSON** (IMO No. 7941904)
7.2007 broken up at Chesapeake, Virginia.

STATE OF MAINE, built in 1952 as **PRESIDENT HAYES**
11.2010 broken up at Brownsville, Texas.

ANNA MARINE ex BUFFALO (photo: Selim San)

STENA LEADER, built in 1975 as **BUFFALO** (IMO No. 7361582)
18.12.2010 last voyage in service Fleetwood—Larne, then laid up in Belfast / 6.2011
ANNA MARINE, Anship, Giurgiulesti / 26.4.2012 entered service Mersin—Port
Said / 9.2.2014 arrived for scrapping at Aliaga.

STENA PIONEER, built in 1975 as **BISON** (IMO No. 7361570)
24.12.2010 taken out of service, then laid up in Belfast / 6.2011 **ANT 1,** Anship,
Giurgiulesti / 9.2.2014 arrived for scrapping at Aliaga.

STENA SEAFARER, built in 1975 as **UNION MELBOURNE** (IMO No. 7361594)
24.12.2010 service discontinued, later laid up in Belfast / 6.2011 **ANT 2,** Anship,
Giurgiulesti / 2012 service Port Kavkaz—Zonguldak / 7.2.2014 arrived for
scrapping at Aliaga.

TRANSFER ex STENA RUNNER (photo: Frank Heine)

STENA TRANSFER, built in 1977 as **STENA RUNNER** (IMO No. 7528570)
5.9.2010 last voyage in service Harwich—Rotterdam, then laid up in Rotterdam /
22.10.2010 **TRANSFER,** Brax Shipholding, Riga / 2010 laid up in Gothenburg /
1.3.2011 arrived for scrapping at Alang.

STENA VOYAGER (photo: Micke Asklander)

STENA VOYAGER, built in 1996 (IMO No. 9080209)
20.11.2011 last voyage in service Stranraer—Belfast, then laid up in Belfast /
11.5.2013 arrived for scrapping at Landskrona.

SUBIC BAY 1, built in 1975 as **SAROMA** (IMO No. 7426033)
16.1.2015 during a voyage Butuan—Cebu grounded in Mactan Channel, then
towed to Cebu and scrapped.

SUPERFERRY 2, built in 1973 as **FERRY SUMIYOSHI** (IMO No. 7304663)
1.2011 to Negros Navigation Co., Cebu / 2012 **ST. THOMAS AQUINAS,** 2Go
Travel, Cebu / 16.8.2013 on a voyage from Agusan del Norte to Manila sank after
a collision with the cargo ship SULPICIO EXPRESS SIETE off Talisay City, only 750
of 831 persons on board rescued.

ST. GREGORY THE GREAT ex SUN FLOWER KOGANE (photo: Irvine Kinea)

ms **SUN FLOWER KOGANE**
IMO No. 9042726
Kansai Kisen Kaisha, Osaka
Kanasashi Co. Ltd., Toyohashi; Yard No.: 3280
9684 GRT / 3516 tdw / 150.87 m length oa / 25.00 m beam / two 14-cyl.
diesels geared to 2 screws; Sulzer-Hitachi / 18540 kW / 24.75 kn / 942 pass.
unberthed / 60 cars, 100 trucks /
10.3.1992 launched / 7.1992 delivered / 3.8.1992–1.2010 service Osaka—Beppu /
3.2010 **SUPERFERRY 20,** Aboitiz Transport System, Manila; 19468 GT / 1.2011
to Negros Navigation Co., Cebu / 5.2012 **ST. GREGORY THE GREAT,** 2GO Travel,
Cebu / 1.2015 renamed **GREGORY,** home port Moroni / 21.1.2015 arrived for
scrapping at Chittagong.

TAURUS, built in 1998 (IMO No. 9144287)
10.8.2011 arrived for scrapping at Aliaga, home port Freetown.

VENUS ex SOUTHWARD (photo: Peter Knego)

THE AEGEAN PEARL, built in 1971 as **SOUTHWARD** (IMO No. 7111078)
23.6.2010 **RIO**, Rio Cruises (Caspi Shipping), Valletta / 4.7.2010–19.6.2011 cruises
from Ashdod, then laid up there / 4.2012 to Venus Sailing Cruises, later to Chalkis
for conversion / 5.2012 renamed **VENUS**, cruises from Haifa / 15.8.2012 arrested
in Ashdod / 28.3.2013 arrived for scrapping at Aliaga, home port Lome.

EMERALD ex SANTA ROSA (photo: Kaushal Trivedi copyright MidShip Century)

THE EMERALD, built in 1958 as **SANTA ROSA** (IMO No. 5312824)
6.2012 renamed **EMERALD**, home port Basseterre / 2.8.2012 arrived for scrapping
at Alang.

THE OCEANIC, built in 1965 as **OCEANIC** (IMO No. 5260679)
4.5.2012 end of last cruise for Peace Boat in Yokohoma, then laid up in Kobe /
14.6.2012 arrived for scrapping at Zhoushan as **OCEANIC**, home port Funafuti.

TRANSLANDIA, built in 1976 as **TRANSGERMANIA** (IMO No. 7429229)
5.1.2013 last voyage in service Helsinki—Tallinn, then laid up in Tallinn / 12.3.2013
to Salem Al Makrani Cargo Co., Moroni / 4.2013 service Suez—Adabiya / 27.5.2014
arrived for scrapping at Alang.

CALY ex CANGURO VERDE (photo: Kaushal Trivedi copyright MidShip Century)

THE CALYPSO, built in 1967 as **CANGURO VERDE** (IMO No. 6715372)
3.2012 renamed **CALY**, home port Basseterre / 10.4.2013 arrived for scrapping
at Alang.

ADRIATICA QUEEN ex DANA REGINA (photo: Selim San)

VANA TALLINN, built in 1974 as **DANA REGINA** (IMO No. 7329522)
5.2011 to Albanian Ferries, Panama / 7.7.2011 renamed **ADRIATICA QUEEN** /
6.11.2011–29.7.2012 service Durres—Bari / 30.7.2012 laid up in Durres /
22.4.2014 arrived for scrapping at Aliaga, home port Lome.

ZOE, planned as **REGENT SKY** and never completed (IMO No. 7907685)
16.7.2011 arrival of unfinished ship for scrapping at Aliaga.

Register of Ships

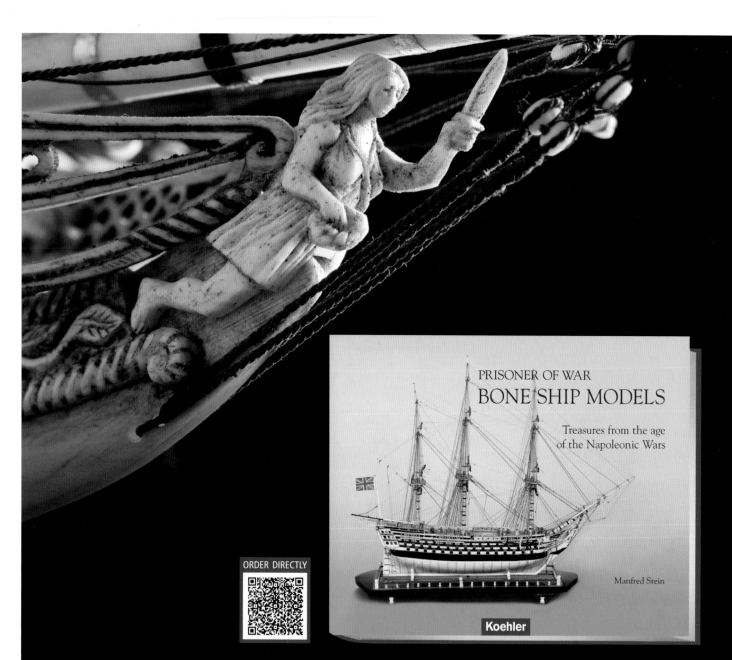

Manfred Stein

Prisoner of War – Bone Ship Models

Treasures from the age of the Napoleonic Wars

published in English

380 pages | 30 x 24 cm
numerous color illustrations I hardcover
ISBN 978-3-7822-1205-2

ORDER DIRECTLY

Prisoner of War – Bone Ship Models is a treasure chest about the historical origin of the bone ship. Its author Manfred Stein, an acknowledged expert in this field, collected numerous testimonies of these ship models. The result is one the most comprehensive indexes of bone ships which is published here for the first time. Stein refers about the historic events that paved the way for the filigree ship models of animal bones as they were manufactured in the early 19th century by French prisoners in the United Kingdom. This art was quickly refined and today we see an impressive range of bone ships in museums and collections all over the world.

The opulent work is illustrated in full color and shows in impressive pictures even the smallest details of these masterpieces of modeling.

koehler-books.de/shop